THE BEST
AUSTRALIAN
ESSAYS
2000

THE BEST
AUSTRALIAN
ESSAYS
2000

Edited by
PETER CRAVEN

Black Inc.

Published by Black Inc.
an imprint of Schwartz Publishing Pty Ltd
227 Collins Street
Melbourne Victoria 3000
Australia
61 3 9654 2000

National Library of Australia
Cataloguing-in-Publication entry:

Best Australian Essays
ISBN: 186 395 2500
Short stories, Australian - 20th century.
2. Australian essays - 20th century. I. Craven, Peter
A824.308

In memoriam
Helen Daniel 1946–2000

CONTENTS

Peter Craven
Introduction .... *xi*

Robyn Davidson
Self-Portrait with Imaginary Mother 1

David Malouf
The People's Judgment 11

Peter Ryan
The Twitterers' Defeat 15

Clive James
Party Town 19

Geoffrey Blainey
Globalisation: Unpacking the Suitcase 34

Hugh Stretton
Leaders 43

Don Watson
Garibaldi in an Armani Suit 67

Margo Kingston
Hansonism Then and Now 89

John Birmingham
S11 102

Paul Sheehan
The Parties are Over 112

Gideon Haigh
The Last Barbarian 121

Jack Waterford
Capital Letters 136

Cameron Forbes
Dubya and Good Ol' Al 146

John Clarke
Apology Made by John Howard on National TV 160

Raimond Gaita
Who Speaks, About What, To Whom, On Whose Behalf,
With What Right? 162

Robert Manne
What Justice O'Loughlin Could Not See 177

Guy Rundle
A Town Called Hackney Nation 187

Christina Thompson
Turton's Land Deeds 197

Helen Garner
The Feel of Steel 211

Fay Zwicky
Border Crossings 225

Edmund Campion
At the University of Sydney 239

Richard Hall
Reading Sydney: Three Ages, Three Winds 248

Peter Porter
John Forbes in Europe 260

Andrew Riemer
Dr Klemperer's Rage 272

Hilary McPhee
First Words 284

Kim Mahood
Dancing the Country 298

Sophie Cunningham
Buddhist Bootcamp 304

Drusilla Modjeska
Dots on the Landscape 312

Craig Sherborne
No Ordinary Neighbourhood 321

Catherine Ford
Surgery 330

Linda Jaivin
How Fengshui Changed My Life 340

John Carroll
Let's Reclaim the Game 353

Jack Hibberd
The Kingdom of the Imagination 361

Stephen Downes
How Australia Caught Gastro 372

Nicholas Shakespeare
Reflective Anglers 382

Inga Clendinnen
Penelope Fitzgerald 1916-2000 391

Ruth Park
VP Day 397

Ihab Hassan
How Australian is it? 405

Peter Conrad
Sydney, Not the Bush 418

Juliette Hughes
The Uses of Enchantment 433

Adrian Martin
The Offended Critic:
Film Reviewing & Social Commentary 438

Kevin Hart
Bitter Light 453

Pierre Ryckmans
A Portrait of Proteus 464

Notes on Contributors 499

Introduction

Peter Craven

People like essays these days, perhaps because quality journalism is thinner on the ground than it used to be or perhaps because it's produced in relative abundance for the niche market that appreciates this kind of thing. In any case, 'essay' is the word we use when something in a paper or magazine seems to have more than an ephemeral value or when something by an intellectual seems to communicate to more than a specialised audience.

There are classical precedents for the essay even if the ancients thought of their short to medium length attempts at describing the state of things as letters rather than essays and that notion is still in place at the dawn of the Christian era when St Paul writes his epistles. Interestingly enough, it's a few centuries later that Augustine, that great stylist and surveyor of his own interiority, first writes something resembling an essay in the modern sense.

From Paul to Augustine to Pascal may not be the straightest of lines but it's an unmistakeable genealogy. The essay gets going in something like its proto-modern form during the Renaissance with Montaigne and it's not hard to see those meditative plays of mind as standing midway between the sermon that provides a persuasive instantiation of Truth and the Shakespearean soliloquy which reserves its reverence for the dramatic representation of the individual consciousness. The essays of Montaigne influence the articulation of Hamlet's soliloquies but the full grandeur of the representation of a moody introspection which has a collective interest and a general moral application is arguably to be found in the sermons of someone like John Donne.

We are still reading the essay in order to enjoy the spectacle of the mind's self-portraiture, we still enjoy essays which are primarily investigations of the writer's sensibility in the way a lyric poem can be and we are also the heirs to that slightly later tradition (developed in tandem with the rise of journalism) of the essay, the shorter non-fiction form, as the natural form for telling a story that is true or marshalling an argument that wants to be true. Long before Dr Johnson writes his *Lives of the Poets*, with their combined mastery of narrative and analysis, the essay has established itself as a form in which a writer can also talk about things, in which he or she can report on the world.

The essay is not separate from the rise of modern journalism which is itself a product of early capitalism. Nor can we ignore the fact that the essay seems to get going not only at the point when the impulse towards articulate introspection is starting to separate itself from overtly religious expression but when the biggest kind of stories that can be imagined are taking the form of extended prose narratives which create imaginary structures but are humanly credible and have the appearance (though not the substance) of history. It's not for nothing that the essays of Montaigne are (like the soliloquies of Hamlet and the sermons of Donne) close in time to *Don Quixote*.

The essay which in one aspect represents the mind in the act of representing the quality of its own light and in another is the form that is used to depict and analyse the world is historically continuous with the rise of the novel. Both forms relate to the representation of subjectivity in an apparently objective world and both became literary commodities that absorbed the attention of a market that had been massively extended and unified by the way in which printing had enobled the dissemination of books and journals.

To varying degrees the pieces of writing collected in this year's *Best Essays* volume will reflect the different potentials of the essay form, bearing in mind that the term 'essay' is one of the loosest ones we have and in this series I have deliberately used it with maximum latitude to include any instance of non-fictional writing I like (as well as one or two where the lines of demarcation are impossible to draw).

It begins with Robyn Davidson's account of how a girl (her younger self) might deal with what happens to her mother. It's a staggering piece of writing, more powerful than most fiction and all the more deeply imagined because it is centrally concerned with the way the mind reconstitutes the torn horrors of experience and the sense of a person that might survive the brutalities of what happens.

That is followed by David Malouf's meditation on this country entering the year 2000, in the wake of rejecting the republic. The sophistication of Malouf's remarks about what a nation might mean have a maturity that we don't often encounter in the context of patriotic self-scrutiny.

The republic referendum is the subject of Peter Ryan's war dance in celebration of its defeat. One of the no doubt salutary bemusements of editing a collection like this is that you sometimes find that the best writing comes from people whose positions you disagree with. In 1999 I was struck by how little of what was written during the republican debate was of very high quality. A year down the track all I recall in support of the proposition is a lucid piece by my brother Greg Craven and a persuasive piece by Don Watson, not long before the vote, in which he prayed that a republic might deliver us from a tiresome nationalistic self-consciousness. Then, a month or two down the track, this old devil Ryan has the best tune. I admire Peter Ryan because he has to a very high degree the ability to allow the reader to imagine what it is like to hold an opinion that is different from his own. This is the novelist's gift and it is the rarest thing on earth for a writer of non-fiction to possess it with the degree of dramatic concentration that Ryan does. Of course it's possible to argue that the republic is one of those subjects that everyone in fact sees both sides of (however fiercely we deny it) but it was still refreshing to read this old digger getting such offensively Australian fun out of the defeat of widely espoused Left liberal piety.

In the course of his rant Ryan has occasion to rewrite one of Clive James's best-known comic poems. James himself can be read here on the opening and closing ceremonies of Sydney's Olympic Games. He is one of the world's most accomplished journalists and a famous funny man. What's notable about these two pieces is that his comic sense pervades everything in the writing (even when the wisecracking is in momentary abeyance) and what comes through the thin veil of irony is a sense of enthralment which would mean a lot less if the humour of the piece were not being used to displace fun into funniness. In any case I laughed aloud and even felt a twinge of fatuous patriotism at Clive James's 'Australianism' and his vain effort to disguise his own.

Geoffrey Blainey, like Peter Ryan and perhaps Clive James, belongs to the conservative side of the national temper but he has always combined this with a remarkable capacity to speak democratically, to tell the story of Australian (or any other) history as if it was the natural possession of the tribe. In this rationale for globalisation—of all things—the style of the master storyteller who is also a great historian is everywhere in evidence.

For Hugh Stretton, in contrast, the particular form that globalist economic policies took under that innovator Paul Keating is a legacy as cursed as any that fell on the House of Atreus. Stretton's frame of reference is, in fact, Shakespearean rather than Greek, but the remarkable thing about this essay is the way an original thinker can denounce a whole mode of thought that dominates both political parties while at the same time encompassing an Australian past that includes Nugget Coombes and one brave Aboriginal gentleman and look forward to the hopes of a future that might be dominated by a Natasha Stott-Despoja or a Noel Pearson. Nothing is more remarkable about this essay, in which one of the great old men of this nation's intellectual history decries the conceptual parameters of the economic world in which we live, than this capacity for hope.

For Don Watson, that most supple apologist for Paul Keating whose voice (for obvious reasons) blended with his own, history looks different and in this essay we have, again, the benefit of history essayed by someone who was a kind of practitioner and who certainly held the coat of one of the most stylish stone-throwers our political history has seen.

Margo Kingston is the journalist who came closest to a very different shadow on the political landscape, Pauline Hanson's. In her essay the most original of political journalists tries to sift the legacy of Hansonism and the way in which the bush may loom over whatever political future we have. The fascination of Kingston's work has nothing to do with style and everything to do with the intensity she brings to every aspect of politics, her refusal to be conned by the stereotyping of the media coverage of which she represents a radical but influential part.

John Birmingham is also, though more barricadingly and with more storm and fire, at war with the media images of an event like the S11 demonstration in Melbourne in which hapless demonstrators were trounced by police to the apparent satisfaction of Labor premier Steve Bracks, despite widespread accusations of 'undue force' from such radical quarters as the Law Institute. What I like about John Birmingham's writing is its passionate energy, the power of its anger and the smile on his face as he rides into battle. Such sweep and colour and such tumult of war is a gift contemporary Australian journalism scarcely deserves and for which it should be grateful.

Gratitude might not be the first word liberal-leaning people would use of Paul Sheehan, whose bestseller *Among the Barbarians* was seen in some quarters as providing a kind of intellectual rationalisation for the impulse that fed into Hansonism. Sheehan strikes me as a remarkable journalist because of his sense of drama, the seriousness with which he depicts a subject, the energy he brings to the delineation of opinion, his own and others. In the essay written for this volume (during the Olympic Games!) Sheehan brings the intensity of that 'barbarian' gaze to bear on the standardisation of current politics both in its journalistic representation and in the elimination of difference between the two major parties.

Paul Sheehan is one of the greatest masters of the newspaper profile I know. In Gideon Haigh's piece Sheehan himself becomes the subject. It is a slashing portrait, written with a fierce coldness but it shows at every point the hand of the man who could not only write a moving biography of the cricketer Jack Iverson but could write a company history, *One of a Kind*, which reads like classic non-fiction of unusual self-possession and panache. Even someone who is sympathetic to Sheehan's views on our Asian immigrants is likely to think that she knows the subject of this portrait better because of Haigh's delineation. And his portrait also has that paradoxical quality of upper level portraiture which means that although it may be seen as an overt hatchet job it leaves the reader with a sense of Sheehan as a powerful presence, beyond praise or blame.

Praise and blame are not the first qualities which one would associate with the political commentaries of Jack Waterford which have appeared in this series before. He is a dispassionate observer of a political process in which he finds much to deplore and the remarkable quality of his political commentary is not simply that it is so agnostic and unenthralled by the standard positions in Australian politics (finding things to respect in John Howard and things to regret about Aboriginal lobby groups) but that it constantly measures the realities of Australian politics against a sense of the proper polity which is untouched by cant or piety. People might benefit from reading Waterford decades hence when they want to know what Labor and Liberal politics had come to in Australia at the turn of a new millennium.

American politics is a different ballgame, a different theatre. Cameron Forbes in his portraits of the two presidential candidates of 2000 shows in his quiet way the kind of seasoned intelligence (amounting to wisdom) which a senior journalist can bring to the observation of a just slightly 'foreign' political climate, intimately known. His coverage of American politics, at a crucial time, was the outstanding example of everyday journalism I encountered this year. Sceptical and compassionate, beautifully written and controlled, with nothing showy about it, Forbes's dispatches from Washington were as good as anything of their kind published anywhere.

The comedy of John Clarke is uniquely Antipodean even if it is in a tradition of unemphatic humour that would communicate anywhere. His apology to the Aboriginals in which the actor John Howard, speaking with gravity and decorum, acknowledged the dignity of the white tradition and notwithstanding this the terrible nature of what was done was the greatest moment of political intervention this country has seen in years. The context in the TV show 'The Games' was the anxiety that Clarke and Gina Riley, the fools organising the future Olympics, feel, on opportunistic and PR grounds, that somebody called John Howard should say he is sorry to the blacks. The context is farcical and cynical but what happened on 'The Games' when the actor John Howard spoke with great poise and deliberation was at once magical and grave. There was no hint of parody in the speech which was precisely what so many people in this country would like to hear from our prime minister and the effect of this moment in a TV comedy was to make the political reality we inhabit, unreconciled to the blacks and proffering no apology, itself seem like a terrible parody. *The Games* apology is a short piece from another medium, it is written to be seen and heard, not read, but it is still an indispensable inclusion in a book of this kind. For many thousands of people it was much the greatest 'essay' of the year.

Raimond Gaita is also preoccupied with reconciliation in his essay in this book and he brings to its re-examination all the patient and passionate reasonableness that a philosopher with a sharp sense of justice can command. Robert Manne too, in his piece on the stolen generation court case, uses his formidable forensic skills (and a good deal more) to argue against the logic of the court's decision. This is an example of a naturally 'cool' writer writing out of moral heat and outrage. The combination is dramatic and forceful.

Guy Rundle is in his way as much a political writer as Robert Manne though his essay on Hackney in a densely imaginative quasi-fictionalised style is a testament to what a multicultural, even exotic, subject can yield in the way of depth and colour, Rundle unearths a vigorous part of Blair's Britain that fits nobody's preconceptions. It's to the credit of this formidable man of the Left that his writing has a complexity (and within that complexity a clarity) which will command anyone's attention.

Christina Thompson's piece about Maori New Zealand is in a category of its own. This is historical writing of some grandeur. It is perfectly pitched, deeply moving and so convincing in its narrative line that we feel reading it that we are witnessing the birth of a classic. This is writing which deserves the world's attention, not just the nation's. It is neither journalistic nor conventionally factional but in its cadence and its depth of feeling it is more imaginative than the writing of most good novelists.

The ability to convey feeling through the precise use of words and the ability to achieve an effect of moral gravity in the absence of fictional contrivance is everywhere evident in the astonishing piece included here by Helen Garner about her mother's Alzheimer's. It is one of those moments rare in fiction (and all but undreamt of in non-fiction) where you get an active, rather than theoretical sense of the moral value of literary effect. The same quality is there, more lightly but still discernibly, in the examples of Garner's column which are published in this book.

If Garner's writing has sometimes had the quality of the religious seeker, this aspect of life is highlighted in the rich agnostic essay here by Fay Zwicky in which a distinguished poet and critic indulges in a moment of meditative self-scrutiny in the dark wood of the journey, here apprehended by a sensibility that is the deep inheritor of Christian and Jewish traditions that interact and leave her wondering.

In the dark well of Zwicky's past there is her Anglican education at Merton Hall, the Melbourne girls' school. For the priest and poet Edmund Campion history takes the form of a sketch of a group of Catholics at Sydney University in the 1950s. Campion is one of those inimitable writers who finds grace in crispness, a world of suggestion in the plain elegance of prose.

The prose and something of the poetry of how Sydney has been represented is there in Richard Hall's rundown of the various voices which have shaped the story of a city's past, though few would better the sharpness and quietness of the chronicler's own retelling of the vocal history of Sydney. It's as a Sydney character that Peter Porter captures the voice of his fellow poet John Forbes and tries to see the man and his learning in the context of the poet's work. It's an essay which is both tentative and generous and it will remind many people both inside and outside the literary world of a great spirit gone. Andrew Riemer is another quintessentially Sydney figure though in his case that is always complicated by the ghosts of memory that flit (and are sometimes captured) from a Middle European childhood and the glow of memory that invests the doubly foreign country of the past. In the essay included here memory is the subject of Riemer's story and he tells it with the charm and skill of the formidable critic and beguiling writer he is.

In Hilary McPhee's piece it's the memory of first encountering a world elsewhere, going by slow boat to a northern hemisphere accompanied by the books and the imaginings shaped by books that structure a great publisher's account of her earlier self, ripe for a world Australia had led her to dream of. The dreams of a dancer, the expectations of an artist, are the burden of Kim Mahood's short essay which is glimmering and precise in its brevity, alive to the possibility of illumination and its frustration.

Illumination is certainly the hope in Sophie Cunningham's candid, heartfelt piece about a Buddhist camp. The writing is sometimes gritty, sometimes rueful, but luminous with a kind of hope that is beautifully rendered on the page. This is another example of a well-known publisher demonstrating grace as a writer.

And grace is one of the hallmarks of Drusilla Modjeska, the woman who allowed us to see—biographically and representationally, as a form of affective storytelling, how Cossington-Smith might have glimpsed her God in the sunlight that bathes a room. Here she begins with gumtrees (a complex icon in recent Australian cultural history) and manages to illuminate various works of art.

The world, of course, has more to it in some ways than spirits that move and souls that shape. In Craig Sherborne's essay it's the killing of children, brutality unto death, that gives the story its sweep and power as well as its sorrow and pity. This is writing in the most touchy and sensationalist area that modern journalism can arrive at and Sherborne presents it without prurience, with great moral power and tact so that a sense of loss, a hush at life desecrated and unavenged, sounds like a bell through his story's articulation. In some ways this is a companion piece, at least in ambit and technique, to the essay by Catherine Ford about surgeons and children in which a writer of fiction looks with great boldness and meticulous attention at the medical procedures which can *in extremis* sometimes save a child's life. This too is documentary writing of the highest order. It takes something like the form of the longer feature story and transfigures it out of recognition with no recourse save in shape and expertness of narration to the fabrications of fiction.

Another kind of feature story is casting its spell in Linda Jaivin's fengshui piece, one full of drollery and natty observation.

In John Carroll's jeremiad against the Docklands Stadium and what it represents in terms of the aggravated commercialisation of Australian Rules football we return to the form of the polemical essay though one which is punctuated by unexpected tenderness for the great Jack Dyer and highly appropriate (because contextually apt) reverence for the Homer of *The Iliad*. Polemic is one kind of alpha and omega for Jack Hibberd's denunciation of what he takes to be the effete derivativeness of so much of our theatre but he ensures that the persona of this piece (though continuous in his opinions with the notable dramatist Hibberd is) is also a marvellously curmudgeonly character, dramatic to his back teeth.

Football, theatre, food. Stephen Downes is one of those rare critical spirits who can fascinate with the flow of his sentences and the lucidity of his judgments even if you couldn't tell the difference between a great bouillabaisse and a can of Campbell's. He has a passionate seriousness about the apprehension of food that's entirely compatible with his lightness of touch as a stylist and they are both there in this erudite and diverting account of the history of Australian nosh.

In Nicholas Shakespeare's essay it is the romance and the reality of fishing as it exists for the player and as it is caught by a splendid writer like Robert Hughes that provides the context for a formidable piece of essay writing about things 'Australian' by someone overseas who spent some time in this country researching his monumental biography of Bruce Chatwin. And it's an overseas novelist Penelope Fitzgerald and her attempt at writing a historical novel that provides the occasion for a quiet sunlit piece by that notable historian and nothing if not stylish storyteller, Inga Clendinnen.

The stories Ruth Park has told in her day run the gamut of the Australian literature she has enriched for more than fifty years. Here she is represented by a marvellous account of the day World War Two ended in Sydney and by a beautifully shrewd and appreciative account of a novel.

Ihab Hassan, one of the heavyweight figures of postwar literary criticism, takes some examples of Australian literature as his subject and perhaps partly because of the freshness of perspective that comes from his North American vista puts much of our own literary criticism to shame. Peter Conrad, who as a Tasmanian is certainly homegrown, but has been schooled by his Oxford residence and his international audience, buys into the city versus the bush debate with the brilliance we associate with the author of *Modern Times, Modern Places*, finding a world of suggestion and arresting conjunctions between a proliferating abundance of apparently autonomous cultural objects.

No cultural object has so exercised the minds of readers, young and old, or book-buyers in the last year than Harry Potter and Juliette Hughes manages to talk about this endlessly traversed subject with a tenacity and a freshness that are at once engaging and tough. Another popular culture offering is Adrian Martin's essay in which a second encounter with Paul Verhoeven's *Showgirls* leads a distinguished film critic to rethink some of the basic tenets of his trade. If Martin sometimes sounds as if he is on the verge of discovering the wheel that is what gives this essay such a strange meditative quality because he dramatises the complex and simple processes by which he came to change his mind over certain critical principles with an absolutely disarming candour which stands— though it's not intended to—as an implicit critique of all kinds of theoretical suaveness, both traditional and postmodern.

Somehow at the end of this essay book we end up with the French and the second last brace of pieces by one of the most formidable students of French theory in the land, Kevin Hart, is in some ways a far cry from what we might expect from the poet-professor who is also a colleague of Derrida. Kevin Hart has always been a very able shirtsleeves literary critic of new books but in these pieces, the first about the thinker Cioran and the second about the fascist sympathiser Robert Brasillach he speaks out with great power and authority as a moralist. These are ethical essays that take account of charged historical contexts.

The long concluding piece by Pierre Ryckmans (Simon Leys) is about André Gide and it is a kind of anti-essay made up—artfully—of a number of discrete fragments that form part of a glossary to Gide, gestures towards a unity which is at any given moment partial and potentially in contradiction of some statement elsewhere. Ryckmans is a conservative thinker who might have been thought to have some affinity as a stylist with Gide himself. This essay is his reckoning with Gide and it is everywhere enriched and complicated by that kind of play of mind that gives this great sinologist such an affinity with his beloved Chesterton, though always with a disconcerting French accent.

This third *Best Essays* collection has benefitted from the help of many people, especially my fellow editors, of whom I would especially like to thank Kathy Bail, Morag Fraser, Luke Slattery, Jason Steger and Amanda Wilson. Philippa Hawker was, as she has been in previous years, more than indispensable.

Three weeks before this volume went to press Helen Daniel, the editor of *Australian Book Review* who had commissioned three of the pieces that appear in this book, died suddenly. Everyone in the Australian literary world is in her debt and this book is dedicated to her memory.

My friend Colin Oehring was a great source of strength during the preparation of this book. My greatest debt, as ever, is to Andrew Rutherford.

Self-Portrait with Imaginary Mother:
A Reluctant Memoir

Robyn Davidson

When I was eleven years old, my mother gave me a pair of gold sandals. These were for 'best', and not at all suitable for school. In all my life so far—that dreamy undifferentiated time of childhood—I had worn socks and sensible lace-ups to school. Other children were allowed to run around barefoot—there was cowshit between their toes, and their feet splayed out like thick t-bone steaks. But they were 'common' and the Davidsons were not.

What could it have been about that morning in particular, that gave me the courage to end my mother's dominion over me, to dress not only in the gold sandals but in a gathered green poplin skirt with rope petticoat, rather than the pleated tartan that was customary? Children mocking at first breasts perhaps. Or a boy sending love notes across the classroom. Loyalty to a future self conflicted with loyalty to my mother's realm. The old bindings had to be cut.

I am coming down the wrought-iron staircase inside our house. My mother is standing below me, more a force than a person. She is holding my blue lunch box; I am clutching my school port. We are arguing and I seem never to have fought with her before. I know that I will wear these clothes, these sandals. I have already won the battle inside my own will. I see now that such confidence could exist only because I felt sure of her love for me. I could make my bid for autonomy for the very reason that she has been a good mother—a mother who can contain the grief of this primal rejection, in order to give her child, again, life.

'Aren't you even going to kiss me goodbye?' she says. Not guilt or love or sadness must be allowed to weaken the momentum of victory. Without turning around, I flounce through the kitchen and out the front door. 'No, I won't.'

When I came home that afternoon, my mother was dead.

This could be the beginning of a memoir—a curtain drawn aside to reveal the whole landscape of life as it exists inside my mind and no one else's. But although I know the gold sandals were real, that I wore them on a particular day and this led to an altercation with my mother on the stairs, these facts exist as no more than an instant of sense perceptions filed in memory and encased as a kind of seed. The other details in the picture—the skirt, port, lunchbox; the duration in which the scene unfolds; the walk through the kitchen; the inference that I understood, at the time, the import of my actions—these have been furnished by imagination. If I continued with the story, it would unfurl out of that seed, that moment, and its relationship to what-really-happened would become increasingly obscure.

But factual truth is the least of my worries here. What I have written is inauthentic in a much more profound sense. The fight over the gold sandals had nothing to do with my mother's death, either in reality or in the depths of my own conscience. Or rather, it may have had something to do with it, perhaps even a lot to do with it, but not in the way I have intimated here. A *mea culpa* voiced through a little girl. An example of the temptations of sentiment, nostalgia, manipulativeness and self concern that make memoir, surely, the most difficult of literary forms.

I have been trying to write about my mother for over two years. Many beginnings have been produced, some of which reached as far as 30,000 words, others didn't struggle beyond ten pages.

I picture the false starts sometimes as fraying cattle pads, spreading out before me. (Cattle pads, for those who don't know, are grooves in the dust, made by cattle coming in to water at a bore tank. Some grooves are shallow and some deep. Theoretically, the shallow ones should converge into deeper ones, like tributaries into rivers, and those deeper ones converge until they become a single furrow. But of course it is not like that in reality. In reality, it is difficult to know which way these paths lead—in to the tank, or out to desolation). I am alone in the desert, wondering which cattle pad to follow, paralysed by the dread of choosing the wrong one. But I must choose soon, or perish where I stand.

Procrastination, impotence, doubt, fear, bewilderment, panic, cowardice.

Each beginning has been different in style from every other beginning. Some were completely fictionalised—a mother sitting in the buggy next to a father, driving up the dirt track to Stanley Park, the cattle station where I've decided I should be born. I have no idea whether my real mother ever sat in a buggy, or even if the memory of the Stanley Park buggy belongs to me or originated in someone else and was handed on. Perhaps I've entirely imagined a buggy, and planted it into the ground of memory. But the mother in my story was undeniably in that buggy, pregnant with me, and I felt closer to my imaginary mother than I can recall feeling to the real one.

Then there was that awkward attempt to write short 'meditations' each precipitated out of an object from the past. (One of which is sitting on my desk right now.) If I were to run out of real objects, imagination contained an infinite supply. My mother would emerge from these meditations as a whole piece of music is created from the individual strikes of a gamalan. It wasn't long before I admitted to myself that this was too contrived. Clever in a self-conscious *literary* way, but not true.

Another beginning described my surroundings at the time—a small room in India. Through the window I can see boulders and jungle. A langur sits on the verandah parapet, swinging its leg. The sounds of unfamiliar birds, and a far off truck grinding its way down the mountain, accent the silence. This sense of placement might, I reasoned, root the book, give it (and me), a feeling of safe territory from which to explore the past. But I wasn't actually in India when I wrote it, I was in Alice Springs. (I am now in London by the way, and there is no mnemonic object on my desk. I made it up.)

The most recent attempt, the one which causes me most embarrassment, was one in which I place myself at a London literary high table, and pull the scene to bits—its pretentions, its mediocrity, its envy, its insecurities. I, of course, am the alienated outsider, burdened by unwelcome insights and disappointments. I use this scene as a turning point, at which I, the author/narrator, realise that my life has run out of future, leaving nowhere left to explore but the past. I also use it to revile the whole industry of words—those who produce them and those who market them. While this distaste is real enough, I should not have taken it out on the imaginary people sitting at that dinner table. An author's job is not to judge her characters but to understand them. Which is the same as saying, to love them.

All of these beginnings could no doubt have gone on to become publishable books. But not THE book. Not the RIGHT book.

Every writer knows that the process of creation is something like drilling through surface rock in an effort to reach the lode-bearing stratum beneath. You work down through layers of banality and cliché until, with any luck, you see the gleam of something pure. Something simple and true. According to this metaphor, all my beginnings are tailings.

But why only tailings, after all this time? Not even a speck of gold? Why should I be so terrified of reaching the stratum, that the moment I think I might be anywhere near it, I shoot back up to the surface.

My mother hanged herself from the rafters of our garage, using the cord of our electrical kettle.

Where can I go with a sentence like that? How do I unfurl the story of her life, (a life rendered retrospectively tragic by that sentence), without descending into melodrama? Without seeming to beg for pity?

Most people assume that my problem is an emotional one. That if I could only get past the emotional block, I would have all the ingredients necessary for a successful contemporary memoir: exotic childhood, tragic event, mummy and daddy, boo-hoo, triumphant overcoming of wretched beginning, perpetrators exposed, victim (me, naturally), sanctified.

But my problem is not so much emotional, as it is technical. The right tone must be found to fit the material—restrained yet frank, personal yet transcending the merely personal, revealing yet reserved.

The tone will be established not just by what is divulged or withheld, but by how Robyn Davidson comes across on the page. What kind of character I make of myself.

My first book, *Tracks*, was an account of a journey I made, alone, across the Australian deserts. The person who made that journey—myself—became the central character in the book. This character/narrator/self did nothing factually different from what I did in reality. That is to say, the account contains no lies.

Yet it is deceiving. That Robyn Davidson may have a greater authenticity than the flux of contradictions, mental disappearances, worries, joys, memories and trivial self-talk that must have constituted my inner life at the time. Nevertheless, she is a fiction.

I feel I know this fictionalised self very well. In *Tracks* she is cocky and arrogant, but so full of youthful chutzpa that you forgive her. She emerges, ten years on, in *Desert Places*—a chronicle of two years I spent living with nomads in India—less appealing, but with more gravitas. Life has beaten the cockiness out of her, but what remains constant is her passion for truth, for getting behind her own, and others', acts.

I can see that she might be a difficult person to be around, but she has never been difficult to conjure. I have relied on her to fly to me, Ariel-like, from that other part of my consciousness where she dwells, and she has never failed me until now.

When I wrote *Tracks* I did not doubt that I had a right to speak. I did not know that what I was doing was extremely difficult. I was not aware of a vast audience out there in the dark. The fictionalising of myself was instinctive, guileless and completely candid. But I now know that writing is the most difficult thing on earth to do; that published words are powerful; that most of the print-noise these days is nothing but tailings and it is better to chuck in the shovel than add to that vast pile; that while one has a sacred responsibility to try to get at the truth, one has also to remember that truth is relative, and one person's version of it can bury another's.

In short, I cannot write innocently any more. My Ariel is chained to the wall of some psychic dungeon by a policing self-consciousness.

The belief that memoirists simply describe people who were (or are) already there, is as naive as the belief that we are transcribing events as they actually occurred. As if we need only pull back a curtain to reveal the scene as it was, the people as they were. Of course this is nonsense.

My sister's version of my mother's story is so different from mine that it is as if we emerged from different wombs. I would like to be able to leave my sister entirely out of my version. But whatever curtain I pull back, there she is, vast and unavoidable, centre stage, larger than my mother, larger than my father, and much, much larger than me. Even when I leave her completely out of the plot, her presence lurks behind the curtain. Up to now my sister has owned the copyright on my mother's story. Our story. If I tell it another way, if I presume even to have a story, she will be very upset. And I have always been intimidated by my sister's anger.

I don't feel anything when I think of my mother's death. I have imagined the act, what it required to do it, but I imagine it as one sees a scene in a film. It holds no special significance for me. I suppose by the time she killed herself I was already quite far away. In any case, when I touch the area around that day now, I can feel only callus.

The day opens for me at about 3.30pm. This must be the time, because I have just left the school grounds and am looking down the street towards our house. The port is in my right hand. We have only lived here for a year or two, having moved from the country. All of us, in our different ways, struggle against suburban life like trapped birds. I loathe the Moreton Bay beaches just a half mile from our house. The water is waveless and opaque and it contains jellyfish. There are mangrove swamps and moaning casuarina forests. The beaches are narrow and lonely. I hate swimming in the shark enclosure with the kids from school because my mother has bought me transparent Speedos, and you can see my bottom through them when they are wet.

Summer afternoon. Cotton frock. (No rope petticoat or gold sandals.) Right hand clasping handle of school port. I am standing still, looking down the street to our house, which is different from all the other houses. Our house is two-storey with 'patios'. Built by an Italian. My mother says it's vulgar. Inside the house, every room is filled with a thick dark misery, even though there is plenty of light pouring through the venetians. My mother, unable to get out of bed one day, told me God had come to her through the venetians and held her hand. Greg Hamilton, who passes me notes in school, reckons the house is unlucky.

It's as if I am on an escalator from which it is impossible to get off. Dread. I can feel it now. A swooning in the head, and the stomach revolving. Occasionally in my life I have wondered about the intensity of this dread. This wish to fall down where I stand, for some miracle to intervene and cancel the inevitability of that journey to our house. I have wondered if perhaps I already knew my mother was dead, if perhaps I had snuck home at lunchtime and found her dangling there. But there was no psychic foreseeing, no blocked memory to be tweezered out later by some crank shrink. The more appalling truth is that this was how I must have felt every day, when I looked down the street towards our house.

As I approach I see that there is a police car outside our house. My father is standing at the front of our house in his khakis. It appears someone has thrown a bucket of water over him. Next to him is our neighbour, Mrs Wallace. My father is trembling all over, and weeping. As I walk towards him he bends down to take me in his arms, something he has never done before. He says, 'Mummy's dead darling.' I reject him and allow myself to be held by the neighbour. I cry but only because this is expected. Later my mother's mother is leading me through the kitchen. Her bony hand is gripping mine but she doesn't seem all that aware of me. She shows me the electrical kettle and says something about my mother and the cord. I did not understand her because her voice was odd and high. I thought that my mother had tried to electrocute herself, and failed, so had to choose another method. I seem already to know that she has hanged herself, but I don't remember who told me. There are no details at that time. The garage rafters, the torn fingernails, my father giving her mouth to mouth resuscitation, these embellishments came years later, from my sister.

The next memory is being out on the golf-course behind the house with Mrs Wallace. She tries to say comforting things and I humour her. My dog, Goldie, is there. I feel I should be with someone else, not the neighbor. I still don't feel as I believe I should feel, I don't feel sad or grief-stricken, for example. But there is still that dread in my body. Not pain pain, but numb pain. Cold pain. It's not pain being done to you, it's pain that is you. The sort of pain that cannot be relieved.

Later, I am in the back of a taxi with my sister, who is eighteen. Or perhaps it's the police car. She looks as if someone has just slapped her in the face. She has taken control of things. I am to go and live with my father's twin sister on Tamborine Mountain. This is to save me from the worse fate of living with our grandmother in the pigeon box house she shares with Grandy. But I won't be able to take my dog.

Those are the seeds embedded from that day. I can go back to them, just as I went back to that memory of the gold sandals, crack them all open, and from each one I could fashion a deluge, an infinitude of memoirs.

But would they be true? Would they be fair? As dispassionately as I've tried to describe the residue of that day, the whole passage is still hopelessly skewed by the first person pronoun. Especially the bit about the dog. The dog was, indeed, destroyed, but the problem with including this fact is that it appears that I am asking the reader for special dispensation. I don't deny that to kill the pet of a child whose mother has just hanged herself is a strange thing to do. But the interesting thing about it is precisely that—that it is a strange thing to do. Not that it happened to ME. But if I leave out the dog, where does the leaving-out end? Whom do I erase from the scene of that day?

My sister, unlike my parents, is still alive. Her story is still unfolding. How can I assume the power of writing her into my version? And how could I be sure, while writing her lines, that I was doing my authorial duty to understand her and never judge her? To love her with the detachment necessary for saints and fictionalists?

What do we owe to the living? And what to the dead? What is the morality of memoir?

My mother died when she was forty-six. It never crossed my mind to write about her until I approached the same age. Then that forgotten, safely buried woman came back with, quite literally, a vengeance. It was as if she were begging me to release her from the prison of other peoples' stories. It was my duty to do so. There was no one else who could or would. I was her favourite. There had always been a pact between us. Now I must honour that pact and be her witness, her voice. She had been misrepresented, dishonoured, *murdered*.

My mother always overestimated my talents. The job she has given me is beyond them. I fail her as consistently as Hamlet fails his ghost.

How, I ask you—with her behind one shoulder and my sister behind the other, with all those readers sitting out there in front of me, their faces full of scepticism, or worse, the desire to see me fail, with that policeman on patrol down in the psychic dungeons—

how am I expected to come up with the truth when I know that no such thing exists? When I cannot even find a way past that imaginary woman dangling from the cord of our electrical kettle. Or that monolithic and terrifying imaginary sister. Or my imaginary self.

But what if I forget about them for a while, and imagine instead that most important character in any memoir—Time?

Were I to write again about the day of my mother's death, I might not mention the walk home from school, or the dog, or my poor father, or my sister. I might leave out entirely that impassable sentence—'my mother hanged herself...' I might try, instead, to focus on the kettle. It was one of those yellow, chunky kettles with a black, flip-up lid. Bakelite I should think. A fifties kettle. From that kettle, which sits on the laminex counter next to our new electric fry-pan, I might describe 1961 as it was in a kitchen in a suburb outside Brisbane. And from that year might unfurl previous years—Mooloolah siding on the North Coast line, where my sister rode her horse to school and sometimes let me double behind her, where my dad sheared sheep by hand while my sister and I stamped the wool in the wool press and the big green carpet snake stared down from the rafters above us, where I got stomach ache after stealing mad Valerie's peaches, where my mother and father flicked each other with tea towels in the kitchen and laughed til the tears ran, where the kids at school had cowshit between their toes, where I couldn't bear to see my sister teased, where I saw my father punishing the horse with his stock whip, where I was frightened of my sister's anger, where the Gripskie's bull chased Grandy and me up a tree. And before Mooloolah there was Stanley Park, the cattle station where I was born, and my mother's terror of snakes and loneliness, and the buggy by the barbed wire fence, and picking bluebells along the dirt track to the house, and sing-songs around the piano. And before that there was a war during which my mother and father fell in love, and before that war there was a depression, and before that there was another war, and my parents' worlds contained the seeds of these events, so that although the kettle is the only seed common to all of us, nevertheless coded in it are all these other memories that existed before I was born and that I have inherited.

The past is not sealed, not immutable, and it does not belong to any one. It is an impression left by the telling of stories. I want to invent a world for my mother in which she is free to speak for herself and for her time, to fictionalise her own life. It is what we all do, incessantly, in an effort to find a personal truth, to make sense of ourselves and of history, to keep the past open.

My mother is as close to me, and as hidden from me, as my own face...

The People's Judgment

David Malouf

Geoffrey Blainey's great phrase 'the tyranny of distance', when it was formulated nearly forty years ago, offered a powerful explanation of the problems of being Australian and of Australia's relationship to the world. It pointed to geography, seen in terms of position and distance, as a determinant of what we call history, that is, of our daily lives as they are lived through events and conditions.

The Australia Blainey was placing was nineteenth-century Australia, six weeks' sailing distance from Europe, in the age before international cables had made possible the wonder of instant communication and, of course, by the time he formulated it the conditions it described had already changed. Air transport had reduced travel time to a single day; satellite images were about to make every event on the globe instantaneously visible. And it was never quite true, even before technology changed forever our notions of distance and the globe. We live in feelings as well as in conditions and events. Distance is also measured by the heart. In those terms, Europe, Britain, were close, not far off. As for now and the century to come, the new communications systems mean that mere geography will never again determine our sense of where we stand.

In space as the net defines it—language space—El Paso Texas, Aberdeen and Longreach are equidistant from what can only be an imaginary centre: some forms of international business can be conducted as easily from Longreach as from Los Angeles. Once again the fact that our language is English has made us powerful well beyond our size. This is the new form of geography we live with and if it collapses the distance between hemispheres it also collapses the distance between, say, Longreach and Sydney. The space they exist in now belongs to mind, imagination and to the skills they demand to make them work, and this has meant a redefinition, a radical one, of what we do and who we are. No wonder that some of us need time to catch up.

Australians, and especially Australian men, have traditionally defined themselves by the sort of work they do. This is where their pride in themselves, their sense of worth and honour resides. That work had until recently been on the land. It depended on muscle, on hard physical labour and endurance.

The new economy is based on softer skills. The predominance now of service industries such as teaching and tourism means that we have had to redefine what we think of as real work and this is a psychological change as well as a change in 'conditions'. At this level, the level of feeling, it involves real pain, a strong sense, especially in the bush, that older Australian values, like the older skills, are no longer wanted and, for that reason, no longer respected; a sense of fracture, of alienation. And this has been intensified by the belief that those who manage our lives are driven by theories that take no account of how people actually live; that they have no ear, behind what sometimes appears as truculent opinion, for the pain, the anger, the frustration and foiled pride of individual lives. But people, in our system, always have the last word. Policies that take no account of feeling inevitably fail.

Take the attempt to convince Australians that they are really part of Asia. It failed because it was based on a 'fact' of geography that had no life in what people actually felt. Asia, of course, is a loose concept, but even when it was translated into something particular—India or Thailand or Vietnam—people still could not feel the tie, even those who had been to Phuket or Bali, were interested in zen or yoga, or had neighbours from one of these countries that they had been to school with; neighbourliness is about sharing things here. Neither did it touch us that we had strong trading links with these places. There was only one place in Asia that we felt close to: Timor. That closeness was based on events that went back half a century, but were still alive in our consciousness as real experience, and on a debt of gratitude and responsibility that we also feel, and for similar reasons, to the people of Papua

New Guinea, a bond of feeling based on shared suffering and sacrifice in which any difference of culture or skin colour is cancelled out by our common humanity. Bonds of this sort are not easily forgotten and not honourably shrugged off. They are the only ones that really move us. In this case, of course, there was a gap between what most Australians felt and what politicians thought was practically good for us, but in the end it was feelings that won out.

Then there is 'our link with Britain'. It upsets many among us that after 150 years of de-facto independence this link should still be so strong. A bond of emotion, of spirit, that for the vast majority of those who feel it has no hint of colonialism and in no way compromises their sense of themselves as wholly Australian, it has to do with family, identity in that sense, personal identity rather than their identity as Australians; it is no coincidence that so many Australians have a passionate interest in family trees and understandable that they might be curious about where their ancestors lived, for centuries in some cases, before they found themselves here. It is a link of language, too, and of culture in the sense of shared associations and understanding, of shared objects of affection, and a history of which we are a branch—a growth quite separate and of itself, but drawing its strength from an ancient root. We will know that this link has been broken when we hear an old hymn such as 'To be a Pilgrim', a folk song such as 'Waly Waly' or a ballad such as 'Comin' through the Rye' and are no longer moved, or when we no longer laugh spontaneously at old jokes from 'The Goon Show' or 'Fawlty Towers'. The fact is that the part of ourselves in which we live most deeply, most fully, goes further back than one or two generations and takes in more than we ourselves have known. To have no roots in time is to have no roots in place either.

We admire indigenous people for belonging deeply to time and drawing strength from it. We encourage non-English-speaking Australians to hang on to their language, accepting that in doing so they will also hang on to what is inextricably one with language, the culture it embodies: not just in song and story but in patterns of thought that are inherent in syntax and idiom. How odd that when it comes to those among us who are of British origin we feel they will only be fully Australian when they have cut themselves off from what we see in others as the nourishment of a complete life.

This, I suspect, had more influence on the recent referendum than we care to recognise; not because Australians are still colonial or have a weak sense of national identity or have not yet come of age, but because the case for the republic was put in terms that people had no strong feeling for, or which ran counter to what they actually felt. An Australian republic can only be argued for convincingly at the level of feeling—on what we feel towards the place and for one another. When it comes at last, some time in the next century, it had better be a true republic, one that is founded not on the loyalty of its citizens to their head of state, but on their loyalty to one another: on bonds, which already exist and which we already recognise, of reciprocal concern and care and affection. A republic based on loyalty only to a head of state is a monarchy in disguise, even when the monarch is elected and temporary. An elected monarch, as in too many republics one might name, can very easily become an autocrat.

Perhaps, after a century of theories and ideas and ideologies, some of them murderous, we might try listening at last to what people have to say; paying attention to what they have to tell us; accepting, too, and without resentment, that in being human they are imperfect, and that theories, even the most beautiful and idealistic, are for angels of the imagination, not real men and women. We might grant people the dignity of a life determined not by cold principle, but by what they will recognise as true to what they are.

The Twitterers' Defeat

Peter Ryan

Christmas Day in our house is always a great and happy occasion. This year, however, it will have to share its status as a joyous feast with another red-letter day: Saturday 6th November, the day Australians voted 'No' to a republic.

We had all endured several years of bullying by our 'betters', of relentless hammering by a monstrously one-sided media, the sneers of trendies, upstarts, expatriates, new arrivals and nation-swapping billionaires. Almost blinded and near-deafened by the screeching crescendo of 'Yes' propaganda that exploded over our heads on referendum morning, we Australians braved it to the polls, grasped our pencils in steady hands, and voted 'No'. (Spelt 'N-O'.)

A democracy going about its everyday business is rarely an edifying entity. Its main preoccupations seem to be the pokies, or the Melbourne Cup, a rather more interesting contest run a couple of days before the referendum. Democracy is inclined to take almost suicidally short views as (for example) running down its military forces so that an operation as tiny as Timor stretches them to capacity; or debauching its productive agricultural lands into saltpans. A democracy cannot be trusted to clean its teeth, wash its ears or keep its fingernails clean, let alone attend regularly to the requirements of its immortal soul.

Yet, every now and again, a democracy surprises us by proving that, underneath all that feckless untidiness, a mind and a heart are still somehow shrewdly at work. The referendum 'No' showed in particular that two democratic essentials remain strong and healthy: unsleeping suspicion of politicians, and a robust capacity to brush off the brainwashing of the media.

We ordinary Australian citizens have been so brow-beaten, hectored, lectured, cajoled and generally condescended to by impertinent republicans that we must now be allowed our little interlude of triumph. 'How are the mighty fallen,' says the Bible. A.E. Housman wrote of an earlier poll that he was glad it had turned out the way it did, chiefly, he said, 'because it will annoy the sort of person whom I do not like'. And readers will recall that modern Jubilate of Schadenfreude, Clive James's 'The book of my enemy has been remaindered/and I am pleased'. Elated by the referendum, I sought to follow him:

> The referendum of the twittering classes has been beaten hollow
> And I am ecstatic.
> A column of discarded prime ministers, bowing beneath the yoke
> Of public rejection
> Now understand their people regard them as a joke.
> Turncoat knights, still wearing their monarchic honours,
> Accept shy dreams of presidential office now as goners.

(Perhaps that is more than enough to demonstrate how much the better poet is Clive James.)

What high-piled dishes of sour grapes were being served up by the republicans on the Monday! What gnashings of teeth! What plaintive wails of 'We wuz robbed!' What unconvincing snarls of 'We will carry on the fight! We will keep on trying!' Who believes that? Isn't Kim Beazley carrying enough lead already in Labor's saddlebags? Does he need the extra weight of a republic on which workers—especially workers—have already spoken a firm and final 'No'? Apart from anything else, how would any government justify the cost—maybe $200 million of taxpayers' money on another referendum?

How emetic was the sight of Australia's two tallest has-beens, Gough and Malcolm, conspiring against the polity which at least had given both of them their opportunity of messing things up. 'Two constitutional vandals,' as Sir David Smith so neatly hit them off.

What effrontery of Whitlam, Fraser, Hawke and Keating to blame John Howard. Every one of these former prime ministers might, during his own term, have held his own referendum. Why didn't he?

Distasteful indeed was the performance of two ex-governors-general, of whom something better might have been expected. Sir Zelman Cowen and Sir Ninian Stephen had sworn a special oath of loyalty to the crown; no one could deny—or would even wish to deny—their honourable and effective tenure of their high appointments. But nobody knew better than they did that, for every real purpose, they were themselves Australia's head of state. No republicans were they, so long as they sat in state at Yarralumla. If later they had undergone a sincere change of view—for which we should think worse of no man—they should have, as politely as possible, renounced their titles and royal honours, and then become republicans. In fact, Sir Ninian, without excessive publicity, quite recently accepted from the Queen the additional high award of the Garter. Perhaps he recalled Lord Melbourne: 'I like the Garter. There's no damned merit about it.'

And to these two, add a cluster of judicial knights who seem in some doubt about which is the outside of their coats, yet who show no present disposition to revert to plain 'misters'. One hopes that the gongs of all of them hang heavy and uneasy round their necks, and that Sir Ninian's garter pinches him.*

Just sample the republican support cast and bit-players:

— Phillip Adams, whose referendum-day gallop in the *Australian* was so frenzied that the stewards might be wise to have him swabbed at his next start.

— Thomas Keneally, nimble-fingered author and founding chairman of the Australian Republican Movement, around which he bounced for years like a battery-driven garden gnome. On polling day he called us all a 'set of colonial ninnies', but by Monday he was more polite.

— Catholic Archbishop of Melbourne, George Pell (known in the diocese by some of his inferior clergy as Pell Pot). Deploring the power of external influences on Australia, this incautious prelate provoked the instant question from Bruce Ruxton—'Where do *your*

---

* Sir Ninian later denied that he was a republican.

orders come from?' (This, so far as I can recall, was the single note of humour in all those solemn convention days.)

Where did this republic come from? It had no grassroots, no genuine popular surge. It was a synthetic and divisive distraction invented by Paul Keating—a sort of prime minister's bright idea of the week. It was as real as his tax cuts ('L-A-W—LAW')—the ones we never saw. The expense of this foolish and futile project might well have been used by our defence forces, or by our hospitals. We saw the true quality of Mr Keating's patriotism in his appalling public statement, made even as our troops moved into East Timor. If this republic ever dares to raise its head again, inquire at once who its father was.

Consider the words of a wise Scot, George Buchanan (1506-82). This humanist scholar wrote much about government and kingship. He had (unlike the present generation of Australians) lived through dangerous and troubled times—wars abroad and squabbling factions at home. The first item in people's prayers was for a safe and stable government which simply worked well in practice. George Buchanan had no illusions about the personal qualities of royalty, especially as he had in turn been tutor to Mary Queen of Scots and to James VI of Scotland (James I of England). Buchanan wrote: 'A king is a thing which men have made for their own sakes, for quietness sake.'

For us today, Asia and the Pacific are no longer a 'quiet' place—on the contrary. Pressure to use or to occupy our so-called 'empty' lands increases. Our present phase of irresponsible global high-tech capitalism is producing unconscionable social harm—richer rich and poorer poor and many people out of work forever. The divisions are bitter, deep and growing between town and country.

Is this the time—just to soothe a parcel of ideologues and twitterers—is this the time to create bogus divisions about a constitution which, by common consent, is one of the fairest and most successful in the world?

Remember George Buchanan, and the deep and painful experience from which he wrote.

Party Town

Clive James

Just after lunch on Tuesday I left a London that was running out of petrol and on Wednesday evening I arrived in a Sydney that had everything, up to and including the Olympic Games. The contrast was stunning.

Prosperity, energy and sheer friendliness flooded the atmosphere even at the airport, where I was busted for drugs in the nicest possible way. In the customs hall a sniffer dog took an interest in one of my bags. Interest escalated into a passionate relationship. While the mutt was humping my hold-all, its handler, a dedicated but charming young lady, regretfully insisted that she had to frisk me.

Jetlag was joined by trepidation: what if some pharmacist for the Chinese swimming team had disguised himself as a baggage-handler at Bangkok and planted a gallon jug of human growth hormone in my spare underwear?

Barely had half my intimate garments been unloaded on the examination table before it transpired that the canine nark had been turned on by a box of chocolates I was bringing in for my mother. I should have guessed. Even when of German extraction, an Australian dog can only be a hedonist, and Sydney was out to prove that it can do hedonism better than any other city on earth or die trying.

If that sounds like a contradiction in terms then it fits Australia's collective state of mind as the Games get under way. Never in the world was there such a degree of national wellbeing plagued with so much insecurity, although it's a fair bet that most of the paranoia is generated by the press rather than the people.

For the media and the intelligentsia, two categories which in Australia share the one mind to an extent rare in the civilised world, there is a nagging, neverending doubt about whether Australia has yet taken its rightful place as a Mature Nation. Will the Sydney Olympics finally work the trick? Or will we screw the whole thing up?

Among ordinary people the same intensity of soul-searching is hard to detect. They just get on with enjoying the good life, on the sensible assumption that the rest of the world must be doing pretty well if it's got anything better than this.

A lot of the ordinary people were there among the milling foreign visitors as I arrived downtown in a cab driven by a Lebanese who had found the way with remarkably little trouble for someone who had immigrated the previous week. Squadrons of local roller-bladers in kangaroo-eared helmets zoomed politely through strolling swarms of guests joining one jam-packed pavement bar to another.

Australians from out of town were easily identifiable, especially if they were wrinklies. A wrinkly is anyone my age or even older. Wrinklies often still wear the Akubra hat of legend. There were wrinkly married couples in the full kit of Akubra, many-pocketed leisure suit and bulging backpack, except that the whole ensemble was coloured Olympic blue.

When there are wrinklies in the street at night, it means everybody is in the street at night. Ancient cries of 'No worries' echoed under the awnings, even as the fiendish music of the young blasted out of the bars.

A wrinkly myself and creased with it, I checked into the Wentworth. My usual drum is the Regent, but it was full of the International Olympic Committee, an outfit famous for living high on hot money. The Wentworth was packed out with a guest list that pays its own way and helps pay for the Games at the same time the executives of the giant electronics conglomerate, Panasonic.

The foyer was alive with Japanese executives in impeccably tailored suits, giving each other the cool nod that nowadays serves as shorthand for the formal bow. In my travelling kit of M&S black T-shirt stained with airline food, black jeans with Lycra content and 24-hour stubble, I felt lucky that my room hadn't been cancelled.

Born and raised in an era without air-conditioning, I opened my bedroom window to let in the warm Pacific night and crashed out to the sound of happy laughter coming up from the street in twenty languages, some of them spoken in countries where life is a lot less attractive. 'I know why they're laughing,' was my fading thought. 'They can't believe this is real.'

I woke to a late morning of perfect sunlight and ambled down to Circular Quay to take breakfast at Rossini's, my favourite snackeria on earth. For years it has been my custom to sit out in the sun here for a slow latte and cinnamon toast. The Bridge soars on the left, the Opera House ruffles its wings on the right, and the office workers pile off the ferries as I relax with the morning papers.

This time I had to queue up for a table. The whole of the Quay was one big multilingual *paseo* of quietly ecstatic world citizens. The newspapers, when I finally got a seat, revealed that they, too, had caught the mood. Their big question now was who would be chosen to run the last few yards of the torch relay and light the cauldron at the opening ceremony. Dawn Fraser? Don Bradman? Phar Lap?

On most mornings of the previous six months, their big question had been whether the Games would sink to destruction under a growing load of drug scandals, corruption and administrative incompetence, thereby further delaying Australia's pain-racked ascent to its rightful place among the world's mature nations. If experience had not taught me better I would have expected to arrive in a city with the same festive atmosphere as Sodom and Gomorrah on the morning after a wrathful God spat the dummy.

Certainly the press had not been deprived of grist to its mill. Two of Australia's members of the IOC had performed less than brilliantly. Both ex-athletes of distinction, they had fallen prey to the Olympic Movement's time-dishonoured habit of smoothing its way with fat from the pork barrel.

Phil Coles had copped some heavily discounted holidays during which his wife had adorned herself with jewellery of unexplained provenance. The depredation had amounted to only a few thousand Australian dollars—barely a small van-load of peanuts when you factor in the current exchange rate—but it had been enough to obliterate the kudos Phil had coming to him for doing more than anyone else to snare the Games for Sydney. Phil is a simple soul whose true stamping ground is the sand in front of the surf club, but perhaps he should have known better.

And Kevan Gosper, a more sophisticated spirit, should definitely have known better: when it was suggested that his little daughter might like to run the first leg of the torch relay in place of the Aussie Greek girl who had been scheduled for the task, he should have said no. On the other hand, his explanation: 'My fatherly pride simply clouded my judgement' should have been held sufficient. For the Australian press that had already called him a 'reptile', his tardy but remorseful *mea culpa* was merely a further sign of arrogance.

He went on to be inundated with the sort of abuse that Vyshinsky, during the Moscow show trials in 1938, used to unload on Trotskyite wreckers and other tools of imperialism who seemed to think that abject self-accusation could mitigate their perfidy.

The outfit running the Sydney Olympics is called SOCOG, pursuant to the standard Australian journalistic delusion that acronyms make prose easier to read. SOCOG's initial issue of tickets was a SNAFU, and it was assumed from then on that All FUp would be Situation Normal. The organisers have hence had to operate in a media climate by which everything they do right is their merest duty, while everything they do wrong is a calamity hindering Australia from taking its rightful place among mature nations.

There were also suggestions that Aboriginal leaders might, or even should, bring the whole thing to a halt with flaming spears, if an overdose of performance-enhancing drugs had not already propelled a majority of the world's athletes raving into Sydney harbour to drown bloodily among man-eating sharks trained on a diet of triathletes. No worries? Nothing but.

But at Rossini's I concluded that the press, at the eleventh hour, had caught up with the crowds around me. In both senses of the last word, 'She'll be right, sport' was the phrase that fitted. Hard-bitten journos had put off the burden of Australia's global destiny and begun to exult. Some of the exultation might be as debilitating as the previous angst.

Legitimate national pride is easily infected by nationalist fervour, especially when it comes to medal prospects. Australia has always punched a tonne above its weight in that department, but success can breed hubris. With feet longer than my legs and the facial profile of a racing yacht's keel turned on end, Ian Thorpe is a mighty swimmer, but the expectations heaped upon him could add up to a haversack full of lead.

Cathy Freeman has been hiding out all year from a double pressure: some of the Aboriginal activists didn't want her to run at all (conniving at the fake prestige of racist Australia, etc.) while many who wish her well imbue her inevitable victory with a mountain of symbolic significance (incarnating the multicultural unity of mature Australia, etc.).

There is much less press about her French rival Marie-Jose Perec, who is not only physically bigger but on several occasions, notably the Olympics in Atlanta, has run faster. If Cathy comes second, the press who have badgered her will bear a heavy responsibility, but you can bet that most of it will be transferred to her.

Still, you can't blame the media for being fascinated, and stuff about national prestige was nothing but true when it came to the torch relay, which had been a triumph, an example to the watching world, and huge fun.

The thing had fulminated its way all over Australia by now. It had been carried by celebrities, poets, artists, palsied kids who had to be carried themselves, and representatives of every known ethnic group including, bizarrely, Crown Prince Albert of Monaco. That night it was due to be carried past Circular Quay, where the crowds would be colossal. There was small chance of seeing anything at ground level.

Spotting the Paragon hotel, a classic two-storey sandstone edifice that was already old when I waddled past it as a tot on the great day my mother took me on the ferry to the zoo, I made my plans. That second storey was the secret.

That night I was in an upstairs room of the pub looking down into the tumultuous crowd. What I had failed to calculate was that part of the tumultuous crowd would be in the room with me. The joint was jumping with the young and beautiful. Jammed between two scintillating lovelies called Claire and Polly, each of whom had at least four boyfriends standing behind us, I had an upper-circle seat for the triumphal march from *Aida* revamped as a musical comedy.

The progress of the torch in our direction was visible in detail on a giant television screen hanging from the Cahill Expressway on the far side of the plaza. The screen relayed images from cameras all over the sky. Media helicopters thwacked overhead, weaving to avoid a giant dirigible marked G'DAY.

As they dodged the didge, they were getting pictures of heaven on earth. At the Opera House, Olivia Newton-John, radiant in jogging whites, passed the torch to the even lovelier Pat Rafter, his darling knees dimpling in the photo-flash. While the boyfriends blew satirical raspberries piercingly audible even through the uproar, Claire and Polly passed out screaming. They screamed 'Nice pants!' and 'Call it off, we've had enough!' Shouting was the only way to communicate basic information.

At that moment the Olympic rings lit up on the Bridge and fireworks erupted from the pylons at each end. One of the boyfriends, a pug-faced wag called Nugget, yelled, 'And we live here!' It was the right thing to yell.

The bunch around me were all in the professions: architecture, law, finance. They had all been at university together. When they were born, the Melbourne Olympics were already more than twenty years ago. This was their time, their city and, I had to admit, their country. Their combination of boundless energy, unbridled humour and fundamental gentleness would be the best guarantee for preserving the future that was already here.

As the torch went by, they assured me it was a fake and made sure I noted that down. They were referring to the hallowed tradition by which a hoax torch always precedes the real one.

It first happened when the torch went through Sydney on its way to Melbourne in 1956. The Lord Mayor of Sydney was presented with a flaming plum-pudding tin on a stick, fell for it, and launched into his official spiel. In the laughter that followed him for the rest of his life, his only consolation was that nobody did that to Hitler.

The big day dawned cool and cloudy. Out at Homebush Bay the Olympic stadia still looked good under a darker sky as the itinerant population roamed, schmoozed, kibitzed and rehearsed.

The great thing, for which the officials have received insufficient credit, is that it all got built in good time. The main stadium's 1500 eco-friendly dunnies have thrilled the nation. Earlier in the year I had flown in to host a black-tie fundraiser for the Australian Olympic team and had been massively impressed.

But did I really want to watch the opening ceremony from a box full of blasé journos sneaking sideways looks at the size of each other's modems? Or did I want to watch it in the city, surrounded by the best party on the planet?

It was no contest. The real story was in the streets. My Croatian cab-driver found the Harbour Bridge at only his second try. Watching the show on the giant screens in the city there must have been a million people. A lot of them were at Circular Quay and in Martin Place, my two choices of al fresco venue.

To get a view I had to play the wrinkly line for all it was worth. By a long mile it was the best show of its kind I have ever seen, perhaps the first great choreographic work of the new century. To know the whole world would see it brought tears of pride to my tiny eyes. It was a triumph for its impresario, Ric Birch.

In charge of the Australian contribution at Atlanta, he sent in a team of bike-riding inflatable kangaroos and earned an undeserved reputation for naffness with the Australian media, worried that he might have damaged our rating as an incipient mature nation.

But with this effort he proved himself the Diaghilev of the Southern Hemisphere. The aerial reef ballet staged in imaginary water was a miracle. My favourite bit was the fluttering swarm of jellyfish. The whole lyrical synthesis of the Aboriginal dreamtime and the modern age was an unrelenting wow.

At Circular Quay thousands of people were agog, as if an autistic Almighty had used human mouths endlessly to inscribe the letter O. The Tap Dogs extravaganza went down especially well in Martin Place, where the boys got exuberant. There being no more room on the ground, they started to climb anything vertical, including tall women.

One boy got all the way to the top of a flagpole. The cheers were deafening. He was part of the show. Everybody was. The pop anthems were uniformly dire, and Samaranch spoke English in a way that made you wonder if his Spanish is any better, but nothing could dent the show's integrity.

Asking Australia's Olympic women to share the final lap of the torch was the right thing at long last, because the women's vote lies at the heart of our democracy. All in all it was life that was celebrated, and not mere health. (In that respect, choosing the wheelchair-bound Betty Cuthbert to carry the torch into the stadium was a master-stroke.)

As for asking Cathy Freeman to light the cauldron, well, it might do as much to inspire her as to weigh her down, and anyway she is a brave girl who feels free to choose, so she must have chosen this.

But the best thing about the whole spectacle was that its precision wasn't military. When Nietzsche addressed the problem of whether there could be a work of art without an artist, the first thing he came up with was the human body, and the second was the officer corps of the Prussian army.

The idea caught on strong in Germany, where the Berlin Olympics in 1936 sealed the deadly conjunction between athletics and squad drill. (By no coincidence, the man in charge, Edgar Feuchtanger, turned up again as the commander of the 21st Panzer Division at Caen.)

Filmed by Leni Riefenstahl, the Nazi dream of beautiful bodies on the march had a long and sinister influence, but Sydney buried its last remains. At Birch's invitation I wrote the program note, so you must allow for a vested interest: but I guessed the show would be a bobby-dazzler and I was right.

What I didn't guess was that it would be so beautiful, a work of art. The sport will be hard-pressed to match it. In Martin Place there were a lot of broken beer bottles by the time I left, but as far as I could see nobody was getting hurt.

It was sad to think that an equivalent concentration of young people in Britain would have been hard to trust. I can remember when the Australians were the hoons, and the British behaved. The world has turned full circle: but when you think about it, the world does that all the time.

*

As the Games of the XXVIIth Olympiad ran out of events, the Olympic Village joined the party that had been raging all over Sydney since the torch arrived. Athletes with nothing left to do were whooping it up into the wee hours: a blast for them, but bad news for the marathon runners whose upcoming ordeal would be the prelude to the much-anticipated closing ceremony.

Pheidippides, the sole runner of the first marathon in history, back in the benighted era before endorsements, had been obliged to run the distance without benefit of sponsorship from a shoe manufacturer, but at least he got some kip the night before.

Press speculation was rife about how impresario Ric Birch could stage a finale that would top his overture, the opening ceremony that had stunned the world and given Australia confidence in its new position as a mature nation. Some of the other mature nations had already brought their teams home. When their empty chalets were entered to be cleaned, all too many of them turned out to be littered with syringes. Where the Bulgarians had been, the cleaners had to back out and wait for the army: there were needles in there like the floor of a pine forest after a tornado.

But the drug thing, like the bad weather, was by now a back number. Think-piece journalists raided the thesaurus to describe the sky: azure, cerulean, Arcadian, Poussinesque. This, surely, was Eden, and minus the serpent. The Germans and the Israelis remembered Munich, but if any terrorists were going to raise their balaclava-clad heads in Sydney, it was getting late. Either they hadn't come or they had gone native—dumped the AK-47s and gone into business selling Semtex to the female discus-throwers, who put it on their muesli.

When you considered that the Australian press, during the run-up to this Olympics, greeted their advent as if an invasion force of Martian troop-transports had entered the Earth's atmosphere, the papers had done pretty well. Their praise for Australia's champions might have bordered on the hagiographic, but the athletes of other nations got frequent mentions and the photo-spreads looked as if the United Nations had been reconstituted as a beauty contest. On television, Channel Seven at least did better than America's NBC, which was faced with the awful knowledge that it had paid more than a billion dollars for a ratings clunker.

Channel Seven had no problems with the time difference or the receptivity of its audience. Apart from its gift for the ill-chosen word, its only insoluble problem was with the events, which if they are to be covered fairly on screen must interrupt each other continually, thus guaranteeing that any given viewer, umpteen times a day, will be hauled away from something interesting to something soporific. By the final weekend the traffic in visual narcotics had thinned out, but there was still enough yawn-material available to ensure that anything gripping could be cut away from at the crucial moment.

Thrilling bike races through the crowded streets were interrupted by the thousandth transmission of the same commercial for Australian Mutual Provident, an organisation that is apparently dedicated to arranging for its subscribers a visit from their future selves, who will assure them that they were right to dream of that little house on the hill, because the time would come when they would magically be able to buy it, owing to the inspired assistance of Australian Mutual Provident. Watching transfixed, as a man will when he meets a funnelweb spider on his way to the woodpile, on several occasions I was visited by my own future self, who assured me that the time would come when the migraine induced by too many screenings of a transcendentally dumb commercial would melt away, after I had entered the headquarters of Australian Mutual Provident, tied up its executive in charge of advertising, and burnt the place down.

'The right to dream' was a media buzz-phrase throughout the Olympics, hanging around like a blow-fly at the barbie. Reserving to myself the right to dream of kicking the set in, I took solace in the thought of the imminent return to the bike race, but instead the screen was filled with a man in top hat riding a horse walking sideways, or six canoes with 12 men in them crossing the middle distance at a not-very-surprising rate. Channel Seven had a cable-TV subsidiary, but on that one you were likely to be confronted with a couple of small boxers in headgear the size of sofas hanging on to each other as if they had finally realised that a slow fox-trot felt better than getting hit.

Boxing has no place in the Olympics, not because it damages the brain—if you want to see a damaged brain, take a look at a Taiwanese judo competitor who thought he had devoted his life to an intricate Oriental art-form until a 200-kilogram Norwegian fell on him—but because you can get it better elsewhere. The same applies to tennis and football.

I would have said the same applied to basketball, in which America's Dream Team—a bunch of subluminary pros playing an exhibition tournament for charity—had been declared invincible. But by behaving as if their supremacy were beyond challenge, they made themselves so obnoxious that when the Lithuanians almost beat them the whole of Sydney went mad with joy around the giant TV screens.

In the whole of the Games I saw no event more riveting. In the velodrome there had been an event called the Madison in which about a dozen teams tangled in a flat-out dog-fight while the spectators, including myself, struggled for breath to yell with. When the British team crashed, I had to prise somebody's hands from my throat but found it easier after I realised they were mine. I had also developed an unexpected passion for the Australia's women's hockey team, the Hockeyroos. Men's hockey still strikes me as something a dweeb does to get out of playing rugby, but women's hockey is a different matter, or anyway it is when the Hockeyroos play it. They also attain a surprising level of pulchritude for women who could take your head off with a stick.

On top of all that, as the link-men say, there had been the last rounds of the men's platform diving. Every man in the final could do the inward three-and-a-half that Greg Louganis had astonished the world with only two Olympiads ago. With everyone diving to the same stratospheric standard, the medals were decided by the pointing of the toe, the shape of the haircut, the flaring of the nostrils. You have to see a dive like that go wrong before you can grasp what's involved. Not all that long ago a diver got killed doing the inward three-and-a-half. I watched the whole final as if Damocles beneath the sword were dancing like Fred Astaire. But not even that could touch the excitement of seeing Lithuania come within ten seconds of stuffing it to the Dream Team.

Despite what you may have heard, Australia's spirit of all-embracing Olympic tolerance does not exclude the world's only remaining superpower. But the Yanks are not always able to unpack the semantic content of a friendly heckle. It is a fallacy that Americans are without irony, but they do tend to take words at their face value; and it is misleading enough to do that with British English, while to do it with Australian English makes misapprehension a certainty.

Particularly when it comes to humour, Australian English is a richly ambiguous poetic phenomenon, which must be interpreted for tone. When T.S. Eliot said, 'We had the experience but missed the meaning,' he could have been speaking for American basketballers who switched Channel Seven on late at night and found themselves watching 'The Dream', the hit media experience of the Sydney Olympics. Hosted by two wits calling themselves Roy and H.G., 'The Dream' celebrated the Olympic ideal by inserting a pointed stick up its crazy date.

The Crazy Date was Roy and H.G.'s name for a certain legs-apart manoeuvre performed by gymnasts in the floor exercises and on the pommel-horse. The term depended for its evocative power on your being able to deduce, if you hailed from elsewhere, that a specific item of human anatomy was being referred to. You had to remember that the Australian scatological vocabulary is precisely visual.

Roy and H.G. did a short stretch on British television at one stage, but they are too fond of lingering improvisation to get going in a tight slot. (They would pounce on that statement: they are very rude.) The two-hour expanse of *The Dream* was ideal for them. They had space to do their thing, and so did their unofficial Olympic mascot, Fatso the Fat-Arsed Wombat. Fatso did his thing in the form of Olympic gold medals expelled majestically from his fundament as he wandered in graphic form across the bottom of the screen. Billie-Jean King, incidentally, was one American who got the point of 'The Dream' exactly. She came on the show to read the news, and looked more than ever the way she always did at Wimbledon—like the brightest girl at the ball.

Though the mass media had not been as triumphantly awful as the occasion might have invited, the truly heartening coverage was in the Australian ethnic press. If you were looking for the Mature Nation, there it was.

Admittedly the satellite digest edition of Bild had two screaming pages about how Germany's long-jump champion Heike Dreschler had seen off Marion Jones. The main piece was headlined *Der Sprung in die Unsterblichkeit*: the jump to immortality. It featured a Junoesque picture of Heike in mid-*Sprung*, looking like a wet dream by Arno Brecker. There was no mention that Heike began her career in the old East Germany, the Needle Park of the Warsaw Pact.

All this was pretty chauvinistic, not to say *volkisch*, but if you looked at Australia's home-grown German weekly *Die Woche in Australien* you got a different slant. They were telling two stories at once: one about the Fatherland, and one about Australia. Germany's obscure slalom canoeist Thomas Schmidt was congratulated for having propelled himself into the top rank (*Unbekannter Schmidt paddelt sich in die Elite*), but the main story was a hymn to Australia's heroes: Cathy, Thorpie *und so weiter.*

It was the same with all the other examples of the ethnic press I could lay my hands on. *El Espanol*, which caters for the Hispano-American community, lauded Milton Wynants of Uruguay for his silver in the cycling and was moved by the humility of *este excelente pedalista*. And *Edinenie* (*Unification*) praised Svetlana Korkhina for not letting her disaster in the vault stop her going on to win an individual gold medal. 'Not what the Russian Princess of Gymnastics had dreamed of, but all the same.'

CLIVE JAMES

The word for 'dream' is particularly beautiful in Russian, and so, of course, is Svetlana. There was a picture of her with her tongue sticking out, but she was doing it beautifully. The same paper, a few days before, had gone appropriately batso for Tatiana Grigorieva, now an Australian; but what impressed me was the connection with the homeland. This was the eternal Russia, the one that had been remorselessly assaulted for seventy long years by its own government: and now it was here.

They were all here, and in that lay the jest. As the other big Spanish-language paper *Extra Informativo* said in its front-page story headed (you guessed it) THE RIGHT TO DREAM, Australia is a country of the evolved world, *el mundo evolucionado*.

*

From the political viewpoint, all that stuff about Australia's delayed ascendancy to the status of a mature nation is an insult to the innocent dead. One of the oldest, most stable and productive democracies in existence, Australia was a mature nation when Russia, Italy, Germany, China and Japan were in the grip of madness. What happened to the Aborigines was no bush picnic, but their sufferings are further trivialised when Australia is portrayed as a racist country, as too many of Australia's subsidised intellectuals are fond of doing.

The question of Australia's institutional racism was settled at the Melbourne Olympics in 1956. The Olympic Village had limited accommodation and the citizens were invited to accept the visiting athletes into their houses. A full two-thirds of those who offered their hospitality asked for coloured guests, and the more coloured the better. After that, the White Australia policy had no chance of survival: and anyway, it had always been based on the fear that non-Caucasian immigrants, far from being inferior, might work too hard and do too well.

*

When the marathon finally got going on the last day, there they were again, working too hard and doing too well. In a light wind that made the harbour glitter like a tray of crushed ice, three men as black as Egypt's night were cheered to the echo through streets whose every shop window held more wealth than the annual crop yield of the countries they came from.

There was even a cheer for John Brown, the lone Brit who came fourth, although the television producer managed not to show him crossing the finishing line. Luckily the handling of the Olympics outstripped the coverage, just as it had outstripped all expectation.

My viewing point for the closing ceremony was down at Circular Quay. On the second floor of the Paragon, I found my chosen window seat already occupied by my young friends from the torch relay, Polly, Claire and Nugget the pug-faced wag. Polly and Claire were dressed to kill. As I complimented them on their shoes, Nugget poured a litre of lager on mine, probably by accident. Communication was by sign language. There were millions of people waiting for the showdown and quite a few of them were in the room with us. I could see the images on the giant screen but couldn't hear much, which was probably a mercy. In the winged words of Juan Antonio Samaranch, 'what I can say?' It got off to a bad start, with a vestal virgin routine scored by Vangelis that boded ill for Athens. The virgins wore Fortuny-style pleated gowns that stirred listlessly in the breeze, almost as if something were about to happen. Then one of the virgins slowly lifted a wreath. Nugget said they were the only virgins in Australia.

When the Aussies came on, things picked up, although the local pop music is more derivative than it thinks, especially when it has a statement to make. Sub-Springsteens and semi-Stones assured the Aborigines that salvation was at hand. No doubt Cathy Freeman was relieved to hear this. Arriving on the wings of a thong, Kylie Minogue turned the night around, although her Abba song Dancing Queen was a sop to the gays that they scarcely needed, because the Mardi Gras was in control out there like martial law. Some of the floats were quite good, but not the ones bearing Paul Hogan and Elle MacPherson. Hoges rode on an Akubra hat and Elle on a giant camera. Neither star had been given anything to do. At least Greg Norman hit a golf ball. In keeping with his nickname, Greg emerged from a great white shark. The relatives of two people who had been eaten by great white sharks off the coast of South Australia during the previous week were probably not watching.

I thought the Aboriginal ensemble Yothu Yindi was the best thing, but really it was no occasion for critical analysis. The maturity that Australia is right to be nervous about is cultural maturity, which can't be had by wishing, but only through achievement—through creativity in all walks of life. In that respect, the inspired contribution of the 45,000 white-hatted volunteer workers, many of them older than I am, was perhaps the most original feature of the whole jamboree. They were all charmingly helpful and some were outright funny. The visitors loved them. Small groups of Chinese would follow them around, confident that they were going somewhere interesting.

The Sydney Olympics, by synthesising what we already possessed, put us on our own map. We were already on everyone else's, as a destination, a refuge, an ideal and (whisper it) a dream. The opening ceremony brought Australia together. The closing ceremony might have tried to show a united world, but it would have mocked the very tragedies that have given Australia its unique life. Better to let your hair down and to camp it up.

The Olympics began with Cleopatra's arrival in Rome and they ended with Elizabeth Taylor's departure for the airport. Next day I did the same. I have done so many times, but never with such regret.

Globalisation: Unpacking the Suitcase

Geoffrey Blainey

The scale of globalisation is now remarkable, and to hundreds of millions of people in many nations, it is startling. Even to discuss globalisation is not easy. Some words, especially when at the height of their fashion, become like big suitcases packed with so many items that it is difficult to label the suitcase; and globalisation has become such a suitcase. Today the suitcase is too small, too heavy, for the task required of it.

Globalisation is seen as ultra-modern, as a trend unique to our time, but it is not new. The Roman and Chinese empires were forerunners of this trend though they did not cover the globe. The spread of Islam and Buddhism were versions of globalisation, and by 1800 much of the globe was being reached by Christian missionaries.

The nineteenth century experienced a phase of globalisation that was, in many ways, a herald of the present. That phase extended from about 1840 to 1914 and was marked by new forms of transport and a quickening flow of information. That world was quickly made smaller by the international telegraph, steam printing press, penny newspaper, long-distance railway and fast ocean-liner. By 1900, even before Marconi's invention of wireless telegraphy was effective, Australian and South American newspapers printed European news that was less than thirty hours old. At the same time, compulsory schooling and literacy were being introduced over vast areas of the world: the new desk in the new primary school was what the personal computer is today.

A revolution in global trade was also visible in global commerce by 1900. For the first time huge quantities of perishable foods were traded over vast distances; and some European shops sold New Zealand butter and Australian bacon. New technology, whether in the form of railways or telephones or battle cruisers, was quickly copied by rival nations. At the same time a vast flow of capital went from west Europe to most corners of the world. On the London stock exchange in 1900 many companies were active far away from their head office. Thus most of the big mining companies operating on the Golden Mile in Kalgoorlie sent their profits to their head office in London. Likewise large overseas-owned banks were more visible in Australia's capital cities than they are today.

A century ago, Australia was tied tightly into that expanding and dovetailed global economy. Australia's important export was wool, and nearly all of it was shipped to Europe where it was converted into blankets, overcoats, suits and guernseys and exported to many lands that formed a complicated web of trading links. Gold, the second largest export, was sent overseas where, in the era of the gold standard, the yellow metal had a global prestige such as no world commodity quite possesses today. Both the wool and gold were carried from the interior to the ports by a network of railways financed by long-term loans raised in the City of London which was the Wall Street of that era.

China and India, like Australia and New Zealand, were then part of that globalised economy. While many observers marvel at the recent opening of China to global influences, they forget that in some ways China was as much a wing of a global economy in 1900 as in the year 2000. While the new globalisation carries much that is new, it also carries much that is old.

Neither globalisation, nor some of the main arguments directed against it, are new. Thus one of the widely-voiced objections to the new globalising movement is that it breeds inequality, and that it transfers wealth from poor lands to rich lands. This argument was prominent during the street protests held in Seattle in 1999 and in Melbourne and Prague in 2000. Significantly a similar protest had been heard in the early 1900s. Then a vigorous debate centred on the question of whether globalisation, alias imperialism, actually resulted in a large transfer of wealth from colonial and low-wage lands to the rich and not-so-rich in Berlin, Brussels, London, Lisbon and Paris. Lenin, then living in exile from his native Russia, was one contributor to the massive literature generated by this debate. It was Hugh Stretton in his brilliant book *The Political Sciences* (London, 1969) who observed that the opponents of imperialism managed to enlist 'in a single crusade what had hitherto been scattered minorities—minorities which opposed inequality, poverty, colonialism, war, capitalism or the armaments industry.'

If capitalism invited attack in the early 1900s, it invites attack even more today. When globalisation is debated today, it is big business which arouses most of the fears. In 1900 the world had nothing to compare with the present Coca Cola, BP and scores of other mammoth global corporations. Today the huge multinational companies exercise power in nearly every nation. The success of these companies incites a widespread and understandable fear that national sovereignty is being jeopardised. They are seen as nations in their own right or as a species of floating nations lying almost beyond the reach of law makers in all but their homeland. Moreover, in a era when the ideology of democracy is more powerful and far-reaching than ever before, some of the biggest global corporations are seen as apathetic towards democratic practices. In their mode of organisation and sometimes in their secrecy, many of the big corporations resemble the socialist bureaucracies which they eschewed.

Globalism has admirers as well as opponents. To some it is seen as the harbinger of international peace. A century ago there was a confidence—widespread though not as strong as today's parallel confidence—that globalisation was helping to make peace the normal condition in 'the civilised world'. Many economies were becoming so tightly linked that astute observers thought that a long and major European war was highly unlikely. The war might quickly end, it was predicted, when one navy succeeded in cutting off the inflow of overseas grain, nitrates, copper and other foods and raw materials on which its blockaded rival hitherto relied.

Another version of this argument pointed to the inter-dependence of certain pairs of nations. Thus, Germany and Britain seemed to depend so intimately on each other in commerce, shared such strong cultural links, and even shared the same royal family, that a war between them, if ever it should come, was expected to be short. The forces fostering peace and internationalism seemed to be so vigorous that an optimistic and carefully argued article entitled 'Peace' appeared in the new edition of the *Encyclopaedia Britannica* published in 1911. It assumed that 'the reign of reason' would slowly supersede militarism, even perhaps in heavily armed France and heavily armed Germany. Those two nations, just three years later, defied this prediction. Sadly an article entitled 'Peace' was not to be found in the next edition of the same encyclopaedia.

The earlier and extraordinary globalisation—though less profound than we now experience—was not as permanent as had been predicted. It did not continue to produce the free and easy movement of money, ideas and people that had been expected. Nor did it reduce the independence of individual nations. Indeed in 1914 they asserted their independence with alarming results.

The first remarkable era of globalisation, and of relatively free trade, came to an end with the outbreak of the First World War. For the next one third of a century, at least until 1945, the forces working against globalisation were more powerful than those working for it. I am not predicting that the present period of globalisation will dramatically come to an end. But globalisation is to some degree an effect of peace. Therefore the return of serious tensions to the world could well retard globalising tendencies in the future as in the past. Today there is a tendency to see globalisation as a cause of international peace and therefore to think that peace is increasingly assured. One should be wary of putting too much faith in such an argument. Globalisation is usually more the effect than the cause of international peace.

The forces promoting globalisation today are probably more powerful than those which promoted it one century ago. Today's globalisation is aided by the dramatic shrinking of distance and the impact of a procession of brilliant technologies ranging from the jumbo jet to satellite, internet and global television. It is also aided by the fact that this is a period of relative peace between the major nations. Admittedly those who regularly view the television news would respond that this is not a very peaceful era. But our era is peaceful insofar as the big nations are at peace. Since the end of the Second World War two of the major nations have fought one another only once, and then only briefly. That was in the 1950s, during the brief phase of the Korean War when the United States and China fought on opposite sides.

Peace between the big nations promotes internationalism; it

promotes globalisation. If there had been a recent general war involving most of the great nations then globalisation would not have been rapid. If there had been prolonged tensions in the 1990s, if the Soviet Union and China had remained rigidly communist, then globalisation would have been slower and more cautious. Following the re-admission of the Soviet Union and China to the capitalist world in the 1990s, the United States has been more dominant than ever before. Sometimes, globalisation is simply another word for Americanisation, just as in the late 1800s the globalisation of culture, not least in sport, often wore the British colours.

While strong factors promote globalisation in the world, some factors are pushing in the other direction. Free trade is more victorious in speech-making than in actual trading behaviour. Many nations, while making glowing speeches about the virtues and morality of free trade and the need to lower the world's barriers, make little attempt to lower their own barriers. The EU and Japan are almost fortresses of agricultural protectionism. India and China, with a grand total of two billion people, are still strongholds of protection rather than free trade and laissez faire. Clever, camouflaged protectionism is practised by many governments.

True, the world has advanced a distance towards free trade in the last quarter century, but even that advance might not necessarily continue. A severe world recession would revive protectionism in many nations. Likewise an increase in international tensions would revive protectionism and stem the power of international corporations. In the Third World, hard-pressed governments will be tempted again to nationalise the assets of global corporations or to impose special taxes on them.

The future of globalisation could also be affected by a major change in intellectual fashions. In intellectual circles there are swings in fashion. Thus, in influential intellectual circles free trade is now as fashionable as high protectionism once was, while capitalism is more in favour than at perhaps any other time in the last 125 years. Socialism, however, in some form or other will probably revive. Young idealists will finds ways of explaining away the mistakes made by the Soviet Union in the 1920s or the East Germans in the 1970s. Basic ideas can usually be repackaged and resold. We forget that in the 1930s the system of capitalism was in disarray, and was associated with a massive unemployment not to be seen in the new Soviet Union. Though capitalism then was seen by many of its sympathisers as endangered or doomed, it was eventually repackaged. Just as capitalism shook itself and revived in prestige, the forces of the Left will probably regroup and revive. The long-term victory of global capitalism in its present form is not assured.

New technology at present promotes the creation of one global marketplace, promoting it in an astonishing way, but new technology can be two-faced. In some periods of history it favours national independence rather than inter-dependence. A brilliant new technology, and a revolution in ways of communicating, does not necessarily make for one world. It can bring remote continents closer together, but it does not always make their relations more peaceful. It can draw nations closer together but that does not necessarily make them see eye to eye. New technology can promote division rather than unity, and promote war rather than peace. Most international wars have been fought by nations that live side by side. To know one another is not necessarily to live in harmony.

The latest technology in communications has often been hailed as the prince of peace but often it can be the prince of war. The early printing presses spread the word but the word was capable of being either hostile or friendly. When the electric telegraph was born in the 1840s, it was at first hailed as a messenger of peace that would surely bring nations together. But along those copper-wires would come not only declarations of love but declarations of war.

New technology alters daily work, creates undreamed of wealth, and transforms long-distance transport. But it does not necessarily transform human nature and human relations. Those who view the satellite, internet and all the latest world-shaping inventions as sure guarantees that globalisation will make the world friendlier and more peaceful could someday be proved wrong.

Globalisation seems simple but is not. Extending far beyond the economic sphere, it is a complex and many-sided process. Various commentators who insist that they ardently oppose globalisation are also, perhaps unknowingly, the supporters of a different kind of globalisation. Some support the globalising effect of the dark-green movement while opposing the globalising effect of big business. Some who oppose American globalisation favour another form of globalisation: the influence of the United Nations covenants and committees. In the last fifteen years some of the intense debates in the federal parliament between Labor and Liberal were really disputes between exponents of rival versions of globalisation.

In Australia the process of globalisation does not proceed equally on all fronts. In some places it retreats, while in others it displays a mixture of advance and retreat. To take one simple example from the 1990s: the new laws on native title, which in themselves are largely a result of a global movement in favour of indigenous rights, repel the process of globalisation in large areas of Australia. They repel it insofar as they defend native lands against external commercial and cultural influences. Likewise, Australian laws on labour and immigration often retard globalisation. Members of a wide range of professions, extending from the theatre to medicine and journalism, fight globalisation within their own professions by trying to regulate the entry of foreigners.

In Australia at first sight the globalisation of culture seems as pervasive as the globalisation of the economy. The globalising tendency is so powerful in popular music and sport that Australia's cultural independence and identity are now said to be endangered. Australian songwriters and musical groups are at a special disadvantage—unless they stand at the very top of the pyramid of their profession. And yet even in the days when the brass band was king, most of the catchy tunes came from overseas. When hymn-singing was a popular art form, nearly all the hymns came from Europe. Even 'Waltzing Matilda'—the tune as distinct from the words—came from afar. A country with a small population will always be a cultural borrower and will sing imported tunes far more than local tunes. What has happened in Australian popular culture is that the American has challenged and partly replaced the European influence.

Spectator sport, aided by television, can besiege a local culture. The Olympic Games and the World Cup in soccer are outstanding international get-togethers, thrusting into the shade the world conferences on such important topics as trade and climate, and these global sports could well endanger those distinctive games that are a crucial part of a nation's culture. Sports that are played only in one nation—sports like Gaelic football in Ireland or Australian Rules football here—face a challenge from those international sports that reward their stars with fame and huge sums.

It is worth making a brief detour into Australian sport in order to glimpse the powerful and sometimes contradictory forces at work in the process of cultural globalisation. Back in 1950, when migrants were pouring into Australia, nearly all of them from nations where names such as Collingwood were unknown, the future of Australian football seemed uncertain. Soccer was expected to conquer the distinctive Australian football, but it hasn't. While international television has increased the magnetism of soccer in Australia, soccer is popular more as an imported television spectacle than as a live spectator sport. From the 1980s Australian football had no alternative but to respond to the competition of soccer by becoming a professional rather than a semi-amateur sport, thereby selling half of its body and soul to the television networks. Something important was lost but the game still flourishes; and it remains unmistakably Australian.

Even so, Australian football must be placed on the list of sporting species which are potentially endangered. I see little hope of it becoming a contagious international sport, except perhaps in Nauru, East Timor and Papua New Guinea. The distinctive product of a land where real estate was cheap, the game was and still is played on a huge arena. For that reason it can't be exported to those nations where real estate is expensive. Nonetheless it can take comfort from those North American games such as American football and ice-hockey which still flourish even though they are not international sports.

If attention were primarily concentrated on such endangered species as Australian football, the conclusion could easily be reached that globalisation was a growing menace to a sense of national identity as expressed in local sports and other cultural activities. That conclusion is premature. Globalism in sport has, overall, probably helped Australian nationalism and consciousness. For a long period Australians' sense of their own identity probably suffered because there were few rather than many global sporting contests. In essence for long there had been too few occasions in which Australians could shine by showing their prowess against other national teams. International sport is a relatively new institution, and even where it existed Australia was too isolated to take much part in it. Even the Olympic Games, reborn in Athens in 1896, was initially no more than a flea market attended by a tiny fraction of the world's best athletes. A hundred years ago an international football match was rare, and was little known in Australia. What could be called Australia's first really international test in Rugby Union was played in 1903—against New Zealand. Australia's only popular international sport around 1900 was Test cricket, but the arrival from overseas of a Test cricket team was a rare and long-awaited event. England's team sailed to Australia once in very four years. Cricket teams from India, the West Indies, NZ, Pakistan, and Sri Lanka did not arrive on their first tour until after the Second World War. South Africa was the only other Test cricket team to come to Australia, first arriving on tour in 1910-ll.

Australia was probably the first nation in the modern world to be obsessed by spectator sport; but victory in sport or displays of pluck in sport could not play a crucial role in shaping the consciousness of being an Australian until international contests became more frequent. In my view, globalisation—and especially the physical shrinking of the world by fast transport and by the swift communication of news—has accentuated the role of sport in heightening our national consciousness. The increase in global competition in a host of sports has multiplied Australia's opportunity to display itself on the international arena. In that context it has enhanced the sense of national identity.

As the world shrinks, many of the local and national loyalties seems to increase. It is almost as if globalisation carries its own antidote. It is almost as if nationalism is a response to a shrinking world.

In the next twenty-five years it is feasible that globalisation will continue but take a different form. At present it tends to work in favour of big business. But what happens if other global movements become more influential? If the dark-green movement grows in appeal, and if a resurgent Leftism wins power in several major nations, globalisation might become a different patchwork. The triumph of globalisation in its present mix is far from inevitable.

Meanwhile this heavily-loaded suitcase of a word is suffering under its own weight and complexity. The word 'globalisation' carries too many meanings. Such comprehensive phrases and words as industrial revolution and multiculturalism are difficult enough; but at least they each include the defining concepts of industry or culture which instantly limit the range of possible meanings. In contrast the word globalisation has almost no boundaries. It cannot be fitted into one suitcase. Perhaps the largest obstacle to discussing what globalisation means and will mean is the word itself.

This is an updated version of a speech delivered in Canberra on 8 August 2000 to a public luncheon hosted by the computer firm, Compaq Australia.

Leaders

Hugh Stretton

Three stories (about race and money, blood and money, and booze and gambling) introduce an Australian history of invention, betrayal and some promise of recovery.

Herbert was a short, skinny boy who grew up in West Australian country towns, attending the schools where his father taught. He went to Perth for his secondary schooling but came back to the country in 1922 as an apprentice teacher. That year he played football in a town team with an able Aboriginal captain. Aboriginal children were not doing as well as whites at their school work, but Herbert found that some brief one-to-one tuition could resolve their difficulties and level them up with the rest.

In Western Australia at that time indigenous people had no State or Commonwealth votes. Whatever the law said, its institutions did not give them much protection from white violence, exploitation or sexual misuse. They were officially regarded as racially inferior and likely to die out, but half-caste children had enough white blood to be worth rescuing, and an act of parliament allowed them to be removed by force to white-run orphanages whose whereabouts their parents were not allowed to know. Young Herbert nevertheless respected Aborigines and held more hope for them. But he was also clever, got a degree by part-time study, and switched from teaching to other work before long.

Late in the century another ex-teacher was researching how Commonwealth public servants had deprived Aboriginal

Australians of their right to vote. She came across a file of letters from Shadrach James to the Department of the Interior. He and his father had also been teachers. His father, an Indian, had moved to Australia as a young man. When he soon afterwards caught typhoid, Aboriginal people befriended him and treated him with traditional herbal medicine. He recovered, and worked in Aboriginal schools, where he taught some of the first leaders of Aboriginal political movements. He married the daughter of an Aboriginal woman and a white man. Their son Shadrach progressed much as white Herbert did a few years later (attended his father's school, qualified as a teacher, then taught for a time). Out of work in 1928 Shadrach moved with his young wife and children to a Victorian country town where he could earn his living in a fruit-processing co-operative. He was soon an elected official of his union, of the local government, and of the Aboriginal Progressive Association of Victoria. At intervals through the next seventeen years he wrote to the Commonwealth government to suggest practical things which it could do to improve the lives of indigenous people.

Public servants treated Shadrach James's letters and their author with contempt. Cursory notes dismissed him, first because he was unknown and then because he was known—'he's been writing to us for years'. They doubted his word, hinted that he had a police record, denied that he was a real Aborigine, and insisted that the Commonwealth leave Aboriginal issues to the States. Half a century later, reading through this miserable record of black intelligence insulted by white stupidity, the researcher grew increasingly angry and depressed until—with shock, disbelief, then tears of joy—she came to a memo dated 27 October 1945 which seemed to come from some different civilisation altogether. It was addressed to the head of the prime minister's department. For the first time in sixteen years it referred to James as Mr James. It recommended that the government adopt his intelligent proposals. A bureau of Aboriginal affairs might be established to do the work, but ministers should first consult Mr James about its design.

The memo was signed H. C. Coombs. Skinny little Herbert, nicknamed Nugget, now a Doctor of Philosophy in banking from the London School of Economics, wartime Director of Rationing and Director General of Postwar Reconstruction, had not forgotten his football captain or his black pupils. He was one of a number of able, educated men, imported to the public service during the war, who transformed it after the war. He did not think his nickname meant that he was worth his weight in gold; his country childhood taught him that a bullock team's nugget was the quiet, stocky beast that never stopped working and gave the team its strength. Seven prime ministers kept him in office for thirty-five years, valued his advice, and usually followed it. But it took twenty-two of those years after he read Shadrach James's letter, and a new generation of Aboriginal leaders, to create the white goodwill and the Commonwealth powers to begin doing what Mr James had recommended.

Through those years Nugget was more occupied with money than with race. He was one of Keynes's earliest disciples. Prime minister Chifley was another. Together they managed to make most of Australia's wartime banking controls permanent. Introducing the necessary legislation in 1945 the prime minister said:

> If, after the war, the trading banks' holdings of liquid reserves with the Commonwealth Bank were placed freely at their disposal they would be able by increasing their advances and purchases of securities to build up a secondary credit expansion of formidable dimensions...
> The Commonwealth Bank must be given authority to immobilise the liquid reserves of the trading banks to whatever extent may be desirable. No responsible government could afford to move forward into the postwar period without adequate means at its disposal to cope with inflationary and deflationary movements in the monetary and banking system.

The public bank could thus expand or contract the amount of private lending without destabilising the rate of interest or (therefore) the likely productivity of the credit. There were also national controls on the entry and exit of capital funds, on borrowing from foreign banks, and on foreign ownership of Australian banks and some other industries. Life insurers were given tax incentives to lend at low interest to government and for housing.

A conservative coalition soon replaced that Labor government. It retained a number of the wartime public service chiefs, with Coombs as head of the Commonwealth Bank then the Reserve Bank. Prime minister Menzies had promised the electors 'a bonfire' of the remaining wartime controls. Coombs persuaded him not to burn the bank controls, but he kept his promise about prices, rents, rationing and some other items. The bonfire coincided with the Korean War and a record world price for wool. The Australian economy responded with 21 percent inflation in a single year. Appropriate action stopped the inflation as promptly as it had started, and lessons were learned both from its sudden outbreak and from its quick end. The Liberal prime minister and the Country Party treasurer had grown up in country towns, then lived through the Great Depression. They distrusted bankers and had Coombs regulate them throughout the long life of their government. Helped by other wartime recruits to the public service a mostly-bipartisan strategy gave the country thirty years of steady growth, full employment, rising home ownership, declining inequality, restrained inflation, low real interest, balanced trade and payments, and negligible foreign debt. Thus the productive economy delivered better income and housing to more of its poorer households than most advanced economies did through those years. There was less for public welfare to do, and it was accordingly cheaper.

In the 1970s that strategy came to need repair or replacement. The economy was hit by stagflation—an unexpected combination of inflation and unemployment. That had a number of causes. The United States withdrew some critical support from the international financial system. Some international prices changed to Australia's disadvantage. Technical progress had farms and factories employing fewer people to make more and cheaper products, while rising incomes made labour-intensive human services relatively dearer. Demand shifted accordingly, making full employment harder to maintain.

A new generation of political and public service leaders had to respond to the new conditions. They were advised by a generation of Australian economists whose education had come under increasing American influence. Many of them thought that the continuing Keynes/Coombs policies were main causes of the stagflation. They set about dismantling them. Through the last quarter of the century they freed the financial system from effective government and cut the protection of Australian agriculture and industry. The banks responded with exactly the inflationary expansion of unproductive credit that Coombs had predicted. Without the lost controls, inflation had to be tamed instead by methods which halved the rates of investment and growth and quadrupled the numbers unemployed. Together the financial and trading freedoms ran the country into serious payments deficit and self-expanding foreign debt.

*

In 1968, before that rakes' progress began, Nugget had retired from the Reserve Bank. He spent the rest of his long life doing his best to help Australia's arts and its indigenous people. Those two good causes also got good service from a boy who was born a year before Nugget read Shadrach James's letter, and was elected to parliament a year after Nugget retired from the bank. Paul was the first child of Matt and Min Keating, working-class Irish Catholic Australians. Matt was a boiler-maker, working for wages when Paul was born, later a partner in a firm he helped to found. He was a tough, hard-working man with no respect for the intellectual classes. Min was a lively, sometimes fiery woman, and adored Paul. Friends see Paul as a combination of the two. Until he was twenty-two they lived in a twelve-square fibro house in a working-class bit of Bankstown. They were a solid family, faithful to what Paul's biographer calls 'the three traditional adages of Catholic childhood (go to mass, join the union, support Labor).'

Paul's sister Anne remembers him as 'a normal larrikin kid'. At his Catholic school he was in a clever class which sometimes gave its teachers trouble. He got by without distinguishing himself, and chose to leave school before he turned fifteen. He worked for local government, then for a Hong Kong trading company, then for the Electricity Commission, and managed a rock band in some of his spare time. He got some part-time secondary and technical education but didn't persist with it. He was a quick learner, but more from listening to people talk than from formal study.

Neither study nor his father's business really grabbed him. Politics did. He letter-boxed for the Labor Party at twelve and joined it at fifteen. He was president of what is now Young Labor at seventeen, a federal MP at twenty-six and a minister (the youngest in Labor's history) at thirty-one, in the last three weeks of Whitlam's government. He had become a friend and disciple of Jack Lang, the radical Labor premier sacked by the governor of New South Wales back in 1932. He admired and learned much from Rex Connor, the Whitlam minister who fought but failed to keep Australian oil and minerals in Australian ownership.

Early in 1983 a general election returned Labor to power. Its electoral platform promised 'the restoration and maintenance of full employment'. For that purpose:

> Labor believes that a dramatic change is required in the direction of economic policy, with new methods and programs... The achievement of our objectives therefore requires a national economic and social strategy. Such a strategy must involve an expanded interventionist role by government through the processes of economic planning and specific industry, manpower and regional policies.

Under Hayden as leader, that manifesto was the work of two able economists, shadow treasurer Ralph Willis and backbencher John Langmore. But in the weeks before the election, Keating and Hawke replaced Willis and Hayden. Starting dramatically in their first months in office the new pair led the government and the Labor Party to adopt most of the New Right program of deregulation, privatisation and small government (more of it than the Liberal/National government they replaced had yet adopted). Then for thirteen years (eight as treasurer and five as prime minister) Paul put into practice as much of that program as he could.

To many old Labor hands and young intellectuals that seemed the worst betrayal of the century. There had been others. In 1917 Labor prime minister Billy Hughes changed sides to lead a conservative government. Labor treasurer Joe Lyons did the same in 1932. In the 1950s 'split' some members left (or were driven out) to form the rival Democratic Labor Party.

Those departures at least left the Labor Party intact in opposition to battle for the causes it had always stood for. Scullin and Theodore led Labor back to power twelve years after Hughes's desertion. Curtin and Chifley did it nine years after Lyons' desertion. Whitlam did it seventeen years after the split. But since Hawke and Keating led the whole parliamentary party to change sides in 1983, the electors have had no chance to vote for any alternative to the Right strategy which both major parties now offer them.

How could Matt Keating's boy lead that betrayal of the party's history and aspirations? He was not its only leader or the sole cause of it. But such changes may be easiest to understand in the minds which made or believed in them, and we can try to understand this one in Paul Keating's experience of it.

He had been seven years in opposition as shadow minister for mines and energy. He learned about that industry as he learned most things, by going and seeing and asking and listening. He talked with other ranks as well as bosses, and boasted of having been down every mine in the country. He made friends with the industry's leaders by believing most of what they said and promising most of what they asked for, while expressing continuing respect for Connor and other Labor leaders whose policies he was quietly promising to reverse. A Shell executive admired how 'Paul Keating turned it all around without appearing disloyal.' A BHP executive thought that 'by the time [he] got into government in 1983 he understood mining and energy better than any politician. And the more he learned about the industry, the more he knew that Connor had been wrong.' While he continued to revere the past leaders and traditions of the party, his biographer reports that he was 'spreading the message that there was now a new generation of Labor politicians who had not grown up in the trade union movement and who were not bound by dogma. He was openly scathing about the party's Left wing, whose members he referred to as troglodytes with outdated attitudes.'

But for one 'not bound by dogma', the daddy of all dogmas was lying in wait. How much of the prevailing neoclassical economic theory Paul Keating knew before he became treasurer is not on record. What is on record is his opinion of its chief Australian exponent in 1979:

> No department in the Western world has had such a rein on economic policy, with a more compliant cabinet, than the treasury in this country has had for four years... it has doubled the unemployment level in Australia, has failed to contain inflation and has dragged ustralia deeper into recession.

After a few months as treasurer in 1983 he was a true believer in the department's dogma and most of its policies. Once again he had learned quickly by listening to the relevant experts. At the heart of what he learned was (in a crude summary) this.

Everyone is born with a mouth and a pair of hands (a need to consume, and a capacity to produce). As means of production some own land, physical capital, money to lend or invest; and all can learn skills and work.

Firms bid for those factors of production. Equitably, the people who contribute them are paid their market prices. In rent, dividends, interest or wages they each get what they contribute to the value of the final products. The firms compete to use those means of production most efficiently, inventively, productively, and compete to sell their products to consumers. Those which produce most efficiently and give the consumers the greatest value for their money are the ones which survive.

It follows that in dealing with business, government must often be cruel to be kind. Open the national economy to all comers. Enforce competitive principles within it. Let inefficient firms and industries fail, freeing their resources for more productive uses.

How could protected, over-burdened, over-taxed democracies restore those productive conditions? By three means: deregulate, privatise, and shrink government. Thus freed, the 'hidden hand' of market forces can arrange both the extremely complicated division of labour and the compelling incentives that an advanced economy needs. Capitalism can deliver its double miracle, reconciling individual freedom with disciplined efficiency, and private self-interest with mutual co-operation.

How could another Paul on the road to his Damascus (a quick learner passionate to get it right and do it right) resist such a brilliant resolution of the human dilemmas not just of economic scarcity, but also of conflict and co-operation, good and evil, self and other?

He did not have to abandon all his traditional commitments. In the market miracle there is still a role for government. It must provide defence, law and order, some public infrastructure and services. It may even intervene in the economy, in accord with old Labor values, to prevent monopoly or other market failures. And a productive economy is not all a society needs. A lot of its output needs to reach people who are outside the productive system, and perhaps also some losers from the competition within it. Families, charities and government all do some of that welfare work. It follows that you don't have to be hard-hearted to believe in the neoclassical imagination of untrammeled competitive efficiency. That high productivity can be accompanied by social policies anywhere from mean to generous. Now that communism is dead, Right and Left may well agree how to produce most wealth and income. But they can still fight elections about its distribution. And with transitional hardships in mind, they may also disagree about how quickly to drive the economy in the agreed new direction.

Paul certainly came to believe the essentials of the vision. Its logic and elegance helped. But at its heart is an act of pure imagination: how perfectly might an economic system work if government left it alone? There has never been such a system. But history and observation can support the dream if you want them to. All actual economies have lots of government. They all have lots of imperfections. Connect the two and what more proof do you need? It's at least worth a try.

Thus the rationalist or 'neoliberal' version of neoclassical economic theory seemed to promise optimum investment, employment, growth and wealth—and abundant means of compensating losers, if that were desired. It also promised least inflation.

Except for inflation, all the promises have been broken. A dozen good books have lately explained why, and done their best to measure the ill effects of doubled and trebled rates of real interest, diminished investment, continuing unemployment, rising insecurity, steeper inequality, unbalanced trade and payments, a dangerous increase of foreign debt, and a great switch of capital from new productive investment to incessant unproductive gambling on asset values and unstable rates of interest and exchange. It turns out that deregulation can reduce the efficient allocation and use of resources. In some circumstances, including twentieth century Australia's, free trade can kill more employment than it creates. It can increase the import bill faster than it increases export earnings. That can depress exchange rates and raise import prices as far as tariffs used to raise them. Privatisation can degrade some services and taxpayers can lose more than they gain by it. Small government can leave too few public servants, with too little skill or institutional memory, to do what a quick-changing, high-tech economy needs its public sector to do. This essay need not repeat that familiar history, or detail the flaws in the theory that guided it. Instead it tries to understand how it came to happen by imagining Paul Keating's experience of it.

He hated the ill effects but refused to surrender to them. As far as resources and tax restraint allowed he did his best to keep the government's social promises. He financed health minister Blewett's creation of the country's first satisfactory system of universal medical insurance. He financed better family and other allowances for a wider range of needs than before. He was a generous supporter of the arts. With his colleagues he did a lot of things, some kinder than others, to train and occupy people while they were unemployed, and to give special options and incentives to the young and the long-term unemployed.

Above all, specially as prime minister, he worked hard for indigenous people's land rights and other opportunities. He did that for the best of reasons, knowing it brought no net gain of votes. His radical Redfern speech in 1992 was a milestone on the road to reconciliation. He still speaks of that work as his best work, for which he most hopes to be remembered. The young Paul, passionate for good causes and doubly effective for them as statesman and street fighter, was there to the end.

One strong critic of the Right economic strategy went out of his way to praise Paul's personal commitment to his indigenous policies. Nugget Coombs in his nineties still spent time out of town with the indigenous people for whom he continued to work. In an article written not long before his death he praised the prime minister's response to the High Court's Mabo decision and went on to wonder about the enigma of the man: how could he have such vision and human sympathy but use such gutter language?

As the mistaken economic strategy blundered on, the other Paul became as deceptive and quarrelsome and unconvincing as the worst of his colleagues in defending the indefensible. But his friends' accounts of him suggest that even in that role he was more mistaken— or 'resolute in error'—than dishonest. His 1983 conversion to free trade and global integration endured. If the miracle was working imperfectly that could not be theory's fault or the market's fault: home and foreign governments, bemused by troglodytes, must still be hindering it.

Besides the pure attractions of the vision it offered more practical temptations. I can't know what part each of them played in moving Paul to act as he did. Readers can do their own guessing. But it is not hard to list the available temptations. Imagine that you believe in the new strategy and expect it to succeed. What additional attractions might it have for Labor contenders for power? How might you persuade people to tolerate its early hardships? When it fails to perform, how might you pretend that it still will? When it plainly won't, what might you do instead of pretending?

A first thought might be that if the Right strategy is likely to succeed, the Labor Party had better grab it and run with it before the enemy do.

For the Right faction of the party, the strategy had double political value. It got more support from business, the media and academic economists than Willis's and Langmore's official election platform could attract. And those respectable media, business and academic voices could help the Right faction to rubbish the Left faction as (according to the occasion) unworldly socialists, union racketeers or nostalgic troglodytes.

Some of the respectable voices were beginning to blame the unemployed or their welfare incomes for their unemployment and other unsatisfactory behavior. Labor ministers could call the criticism cruel and unfair, while dodging some of it themselves by doing moderately punitive things to train the unemployed and keep them hunting for the jobs the strategy was failing to create.

Paul's years as treasurer saw unemployment and its welfare costs increase by half or more. How might you defend policies which let that happen? You could explain that in the worldwide transition to a global market economy there are bound to be transitional stresses and costs. Cowards and sentimentalists may falter, and long to retreat to the cosseted, protected, unprogressive past. But a changing world allows no way back. Only market forces, finally freed of short-term, sectional, restrictive state intervention, can deliver the growth which can keep us up with the world leaders, and keep employment up with the rate of technological advance. But to prevail, that new vision requires some old-fashioned virtue: tough government, steady purpose, hard decisions, the long view. There must be no flinching even from The Recession We Had to Have. (Neal Blewett remembers himself, Don Watson and Anita Keating imploring Paul not to outdo that PR disaster with The Unemployment We Had to Have.)

All parties play silly rhetorical tricks. The cycle bottoms and begins to recover. Official unemployment descends from 11 percent to 9. Some reclassifications, disqualifications and dropouts get it down to 7 or 8. Growth recovers to 3 or 4 percent for nine continuous quarters! (Sounds a lot longer than two years.) The upward progress looks wonderfully steep on tall, narrow graphs whose vertical axes run only from 0 to 4 percent (growth) or from 12 to 6 (unemployment). If you're in office the great transformation is at last rewarding your stoic endurance of the transitional pain. If you're in opposition the government's incompetence is endangering a normal cyclical upturn with needless increases of insecurity, current account deficit and foreign debt.

Five and ten and fifteen years pass. The promised benefits of high investment, full employment and balanced payments continue to recede. The promises are harder to defend by serious argument. Two retreats from reason beckon. You can switch from repeating the arguments to characterising the arguers. Your lot are the bold, the innovators, the future-makers. The other lot are yesterday's men, troglodytes, stuck in the past. When even that wears thin, you can retreat to realism. Face it, social democracy is dead. Corporate America rules. Best comply, and glean what crumbs you can from the new masters.

Besides the PR conflicts there are three serious ones. Each springs from a contradiction at the heart of the Right strategy.

First, the continuing unemployment forces expensive dole and welfare spending, but you have promised not to increase taxes.

Second, technical progress keeps increasing the need for higher education and training. Many of the students and their parents can't pay for the extra education the economy needs them to have. If they don't get it our industries can't stay competitive. But you have promised not to increase taxes.

Third, research keeps adding to the expensive things doctors can do to improve people's health and prolong their lives. In half a century it has raised the amount that can usefully be spent on health services from about 3 percent to 10 or 12 percent of national income. But you have promised not to increase taxes.

Each process increases some costs which are best paid or can only be paid by government. And the three together dramatically increase the proportion of non-earning years in most people's lifetimes, and therefore the proportion of income they need to transfer from their earning years to their children's and their own non-earning years. Families make some of those transfers in cash and kind. But for many of them, public income transfers and superannuation schemes can be cheaper, safer and fairer than their private equivalents.

Hence the compound contradiction. On the one hand most people want the education and training that their career choices call for. They want as many years of life and health as medical advances can offer. They want a secure income in retirement, which they're likely to enjoy for much longer than their grandparents averaged. On the other hand their political, professional and business leaders keep urging them to vote for less taxation and smaller government, and the ruling theory defines those negatives as necessary conditions of economic growth and sustained employment.

Why don't you, as a politician, defy the theory and tax the citizens for the public services they plainly want to have? Here comes what seems at first sight to be the dumbest paradox of all. There are quite promising signs that solid majorities would welcome that strategy. They may vote 'No' if party pollsters simply ask them if they want higher taxes. But whenever they have been asked if they would pay a few more percentage points of tax to improve services to children, improve schools, keep technical and university education up to standard and open to competent students however poor their families, cut hospital waiting lists, improve the incomes and care available to old people, keep research and development up to US or European standards, keep banks and post offices open in country towns, and save Australia's soil and forests and river systems, 60 percent or more have always said 'Yes'. For twenty years majorities have been telling pollsters that they would pay higher taxes for good purposes. Why do their politicians fear they wouldn't, urge them not to, and accuse each other of plotting to tax them nevertheless? In five of the six elections which Hawke and Keating won they were offering slightly higher tax than their opponents were. Their successor's GST has been accepted much more calmly than either side expected.

It's a fair guess that the politicians privately fear what the influential rich might do to politicians who dared to tax them effectively. But their public excuse, endorsed by rich Right think-tanks, is that progressive personal taxation would drive foreign firms out of the country, deny Australian firms any serious executive talent by driving that out too, and ruin us all.

So if higher tax is unthinkable, how else can you, as politician, sustain the public infrastructure and finance the desirable increase of educational, medical and welfare services and superannuation, and the public contributions to private research and development?

You can make more users of the services pay for them directly or by private insurance. Where there's no profit for insurers, you can cap or cut the funding so that the people who manage the public services must degrade their quality as fast as they're compelled to expand the things they do or the numbers they serve. Where that might offend conscience or lose seats, you can finance unavoidable improvements by cutting less noticeable public investment and services. Where that also might lose seats, the best advice is to wake up, at last, to what you're missing. Think laterally. Shed your public-service blinkers and open your eyes to the wealth you have ready in your hands. Counting only the profitable services, State and Commonwealth governments began the 1990s with better than a hundred billlion dollars' worth of saleable public enterprises. Leading economists want you to privatise them for reasons of economy, efficiency and freedom. Whether or not you believe that stuff, the project pays big bikkies. So do it.

Using the capital proceeds for current spending would be improvident. But you can make it look holy if you use the cash to repay public debt, then spend the revenue which would otherwise have had to service the debt. (Other professions call it laundering the loot.) In the long run it's likely to lose money: you give up more revenue than you save in debt service, or there'd be no buyers for the services. And with or without laundering, all those options use capital instead of current revenue to finance current spending.

After the capital is spent comes the permanent loss of revenue. But that's five or ten years ahead: someone else's problem. (In 1994, when Mrs Thatcher's successors finished spending the capital proceeds of her privatisations, they had to legislate the biggest peacetime tax increase in Britain's history.) Meanwhile the sales may cut new private investment by diverting funds to buy the public enterprises. The new owners typically cut the numbers they employ and the pay and security of some of those who remain, especially the least skilled and lowest paid. Government has to pay the public welfare costs of that.

Among the casualties are also some of the most rewarding occupations. Keating's last and financially his worst privatisation was of the Commonwealth Serum Laboratories. That story of blood and money tells how far Matt Keating's boy had been driven by the ramifying effects of his private conversion and his great public mistake eleven years before. Two years after he did it he lost power to a government even further to the Right, and retired from parliament.

The First World War switched a lot of the Western world's output of pharmaceutical products to military uses. In 1916 the Commonwealth Serum Laboratories was founded (for a time under another name) to produce what Australia could no longer import. William Penfold, a very able young British bacteriologist, was head-hunted to direct it. It took over space and facilities at Royal Park where smallpox vaccine had been produced since 1881. It was soon producing tetanus toxin and serum, plague vaccine, diphtheria serum, tuberculin vaccine, and new vaccines in response to the influenza epidemic of 1918-19.

During the Second World War, Britain and America independently developed new means, called 'fractionation', of separating and storing components of blood for particular medical uses. CSL tried both methods, adopted the American one, and became Australia's main supplier of processed blood.

It is important not to buy blood as some countries do, from the people who give it. Donors who sell it include some, desperate for cash, who don't mind selling infected blood. Australian donors give it free to the Red Cross, who pass it to CSL, who process it and distribute it to doctors and hospitals. The Commonwealth pays the Red Cross to collect it and CSL to process it. In public hands the supply was unusually economical: it cost the Commonwealth about half its average price in other Western countries. But overall, with its other pharmaceutical business, CSL was a very profitable as well as a medically valuable enterprise. The government converted it into a saleable public company called CSL Ltd, over-rode its board and replaced its long-serving chief executive, and in 1994 privatised it. To get a good price for it they gave the company a national monopoly of the blood processing business, and a ten-year contract for its blood products at twice the price the Commonwealth was currently paying for them. The public would also insure CSL Ltd. against the effects of any contaminated blood.

The danger of contamination might increase with the completion of a new $200 million state-of-the-art fractionation plant capable of processing more than twice the supply of blood that Australia needed. CSL would make money by also processing other countries' blood. Strict rules, to be enforced by the Health Department, prohibited any mixing of the Australian and foreign blood. Among other things CSL was required to provide the department with plasma master files to allow each batch of foreign blood to be tracked to its source.

The shares fetched $2.30 in a public float. Six years later they were fluctuating between $26 and $30. What the government had described as a profitable deal for the taxpayers had brought them just under $300 million, and the private buyers about ten times as much: a capital gift of nearly $3 billion. The private regime had not brought any new capital to the business: the price they paid for their shares merely paid for the Commonwealth plant and other property which they took over, and no significant new capital was raised in the next six years. About 40 percent of the profits which drove the share price up through those years came, as far as outside investigators could estimate, from the national monopoly of the blood supply at twice its former cost of production.

CSL executives had generous share options. The *Australian Financial Review* named the managing director as the only manager of a privatised public company to make serious money out of such a float. By 2000 his salary exceeded half a million dollars and the value of his option shares, bought with an interest-free loan from the company, exceeded thirteen million.

In December 1999 the Commonwealth auditor-general issued a report on the government's management and regulation of the blood-processing business. Since privatisation the Commonwealth had paid CSL over $400 million without ever checking that the blood products had actually been received. When the company negotiated some millions of dollars worth of price changes, the Health Department did not seek any independent legal, accounting or industry advice. It accepted CSL's accounting advice on depreciation costs, unknowingly paid for them twice, then did nothing to get its money back. Public servants told the auditor-general that the Health Department had no corporate memory of the original contract. The people who had negotiated it had all moved on.

The blood as well as the money came under inexperienced supervision. Soon after the privatisation, Democrat senators wanted a senate committee to investigate past cases of blood contamination and current precautions against it. Government and opposition joined in defeating the proposal. One reason for that, the Democrat leader heard privately, was fear that a senate inquiry might affect the CSL share price.

In 1998 a public servant visiting the USA found that CSL had been importing and processing American plasma without telling the Health Department or showing it the required plasma master file. The Howard Coalition government took no action against the company, but amended the legislation to prohibit it from processing foreign-sourced blood without the express approval of the secretary of the Health Department. Six months later the department found that CSL was continuing to break the rule. Instead of acting to enforce the rule the secretary retrospectively approved the company's activities.

In one of the few independent accounts of this story Clive Hamilton, director of the Australia Institute, found it 'hard to avoid the conclusion that the regulator has been captured by CSL, and the objective of both is to avoid any obstacles getting in the way of CSL's commercial interests.'

As treasurer, Paul Keating had forced cuts in the number and tenure of Commonwealth public servants. As prime minister he presided over nearly all the sales of Commonwealth enterprises—only Telecom survived for his successor to sell. Through both periods the Commonwealth was also capping or cutting some of its revenue grants to the States. Those grants were vital for national as well as State concerns. There was no match between the States' large obligations and their limited constitutional rights to tax, which were further reduced in the 1990s by judicial decision. They were responsible for most of the country's roads and bridges and other public infrastructure. How could they meet the growing costs of their public hospitals and schools and technical education, and their many welfare services, for a population whose non-earning years in education and retirement continued to increase?

Desperate needs breed sickening remedies. Most of the States have acted to expand gambling, and their revenue from it. Their casinos attract high rollers from near and far who come for the fun or the money-laundering. For the poorest third or so of earners, hotels are now licensed to crowd their bars with electronic gaming machines. You can lose to those at ten times the rate you could lose at bingo. And unlike the capital proceeds of privatisation, the gambling revenue is reliably, seductively sustainable. As long as the legislators don't listen to the wowsers, the spoilsports, the moral police and joy-destroyers, this revenue can continue indefinitely for the hard-up state schools and hospitals and welfare services after the States' saleable assets are all gone and their proceeds spent.

The machines have addicted more than a hundred thousand of their couple of million players. Multiply the number of addicts by anything from two to ten for the harm their losses bring to kin and others. Like drug addicts, some finance their addiction by crime. Some are kept playing by free booze and credit right there in the bar. Those are criminal offences, but State police are short of money and numbers. State initiatives put the machines into the bars. Commonwealth financial policy drove the State politicians to do it. Nobody is as originally, creatively responsible for its unforgivable effects as are Paul Keating and the professors and treasury officers who implanted his market vision and supported his brave fidelity to it through thick and thin for thirteen years. Remember the human consequences as you understand Paul (rightly enough) as a Shakespearian victim of his formidable virtues as much as his vices.

All competent polls report that a majority of electors distrust the strategy of deregulating and privatising the Australian economy, but since 1983 neither side of parliament has offered any alternative to it. The strategy is 'inevitable and irreversible' only because our leaders make it so. National policies do need to respond to the global changes, and the best responses may well need to be inventive. But the bipartisan abdication of economic responsibility has prevailed for so long that for any inventive change of direction we probably need—which means that the major political parties need—new leaders.

Where might they come from? It's hard to know how many of the politicians who still vote obediently for the bankrupt strategy have private misgivings about it, or might be glad to replace it: party discipline is ruthless on both sides of the house. The few free to speak against the neoclassical faith are Democrats or independents. For a sample of those young enough to look further ahead than the next election or two, meet South Australians Nick Xenophon and Natasha Stott Despoja. Add a couple of activists who are not in parliament and not sure that they want to be: Jason Li in New South Wales, Noel Pearson in Queensland. If the ACTU continues to be led by women teachers, add one or two from the next generation.

Whether any of this group of six will turn up as national leaders in or out of parliament I can't know. They're merely here as samples of the available talent. But if you come across them one day as (say) chief justice, head of the industrial commission, minister for health and welfare, attorney-general, prime minister, and leader of the opposition, sleep easy, I'd say.

Nick Xenophon is Australian born of Greek and Greek Cypriot immigrants. He studied law at Adelaide University then started a practice which chiefly acts for plaintiffs, mostly workers, in cases of personal injury. In 1994 he became State president of the Australian Plaintiff Lawyers Association. In the same year the State government allowed licensed premises to instal gambling machines. Three years later it was pulling $160 million of tax from the machines, and South Australia had about 10,000 out-of-control addicts, many of them damaging other lives as well as their own.

Nick saw some of the worst effects at first hand, on some of his poorest, most vulnerable clients. In 1997 he resigned his position with the Plaintiff Lawyers Association to become founding convenor of the No Pokies Campaign Inc. Its aim was to improve the regulation of the hotel pokies immediately, and to rid the State of them altogether within five years. It exchanged strong support with the Adelaide Central Mission and other witnesses of the pokies' victims (ie. the publicans', the State treasurer's, Bob Hawke's, Paul Keating's and the taxpayers' victims.)

In the first year of the No Pokies Campaign there was a State election. For good publicity the campaign ran a team of candidates for the Legislative Council. When Xenophon was unexpectedly elected, his first words in private were, 'Oh shit (there go the next eight years.' His maiden speech explained that he was 'an Independent member, because the No Pokies Campaign is not a political party: it is a community association. I am acutely aware that an Independent has not sat in this Chamber in this century. For a number of years my philosophy in relation to joining a political party has been heavily influenced by the principles espoused by Marx—I am referring to Groucho and not Karl—who said "I refuse to belong to any club that would have me as a member."' More seriously, he suggested that the numbers voting for minor parties and Independents indicated 'the feeling in the community that the answers are not always found by looking to existing parties, structures and institutions.'

Neither party would legislate to ban the pokies or distance them from the booze. But for a while, in an evenly divided upper house, Nick could and did block the Liberal government's first attempt to sell the State's power supply, which the premier had promised the electors they would not do. Nick refused to trade one good principle for another. He accepted the government's claim that privatising the power could benefit the State's economy and people. But politicians who had won power by promising not to do something should not then do it without getting the citizens' consent to it by referendum. The government refused a referendum, so Nick blocked their bill. The press condemned him for frustrating the government's purposes and betraying his own. Why couldn't his precious conscience trade the power for the pokies, and thus do the South Australian people double service?

> The government says, and has opened the books as evidence, that without the sale taxes will rise... [But] Mr Xenophon, he of a score of advisers and little media games, need not worry. He has his bottom on the comfortable leather-upholstered Legislative Council benches for eight years... [He] could have extracted important changes to poker machine laws (to the liking of him and his supporters) from the government in return for supporting this legislation. He refused to do so. Holier than thou? Absolutely... The man has served neither his cause nor his State.
>
> The *Advertiser*, 9 December 1998

That sneering editorial twice implied that he was in parliament for his personal comfort and enrichment. Its 280 words could not spare three more—'without a referendum'—to report his actual reason for voting as he did. In the months that followed he learned more about the scheme and changed his mind about its economic merits. Five professors of economics, from the three South Australian universities and from widely different schools of thought, backed him strongly for financial reasons: the sale would not make the State and people richer, it would make them poorer. It has now passed parliament, and is doing so, since two other members crossed the house to vote for an amended version of it. Nick continues to educate and inspire public opposition to the pokies by other means.

Shirley Stott Despoja was a hard-working journalist and arts editor of the same newspaper. She worked shifts and had to be out a good deal, day and night, at arts events. And because she was a lone parent of her children Natasha and Luke, Natasha remembers that as a teenager 'I was Mum's date.' The three of them worked hard, lived frugally and liked each other. The house was full of reviewable art and writing. Natasha grew up loving books and music even more, she says, than chocolate. As a BA student she was immediately an activist against the Higher Education Contribution Scheme (HECS). (Thirteen years later, she has just initiated a Senate inquiry into Australia's higher education.) She distrusted the major parties, and worked for the Democrats for a couple of years before she joined them. She developed a strong interest in legislation and became the youngest woman ever elected to the Australian Senate. She was soon the Democrats' deputy leader there. She introduced an early bill about genetic privacy, and thinks hard about relations between government and biotechnology, among other issues. What most distinguishes her in her generation is simply her exceptional capacity: energy, brains, homework, fast, clear speech whatever the subject's complexity, and a serious intention to leave the world better than she found it. She lives unobtrusively in a city cottage in a quiet back street.

Bullying the unemployed to hunt for jobs that don't exist has its worst effects in indigenous communities. Some of those communities are graveyards of good intentions (black and white, local and national, communal and governmental). Others do better, but not so far with solutions that can simply be followed and succeed all over. One need is for candid exploration of what seem to be intractable troubles, though candid speech can sometimes make them worse. One candid debater is Noel Pearson, indigenous leader, lawyer and entrepreneur, who lately resigned from the chair of the Northern Land Council.

Noel bothers some people by seeming to commend incompatibles. 'There's no resolution to our social problems until we have, underlying our society, a real economy.' What sort of economy? 'Aborigines have been disempowered by misguided government programs. Indigenous families should be encouraged to educate and develop their own communities.' That sounds separatist. How does it fit with 'Until we restore economic relations of reciprocity like existed in the old days, our social relations will continue to be corrupted'? There are no proven solutions yet. As experiments fail, Noel writes them off and looks for better ones. That helps to explain the impression that he has incompatible commitments—they're successive rather than simultaneous approaches to profoundly difficult problems. He is currently negotiating with business leaders and the Queensland government for investment in enterprises that might be feasible in Cape York. His youth, fire, enterprise, candour about both sides' shortcomings, and (for opponents) language as startling as Keating's, promise powerful leadership and perhaps institutional invention.

Compare a gentler young non-white success. Jason Li's father came from Hong Kong to Sydney aged nineteen in 1959 as a student. He settled and stayed, and married another Hong Kong Chinese emigrant who reached Sydney via New Zealand. They quickly became Australian citizens. Renting, living frugally, working hard as he built a business and she took in ironing, they saved enough to put a deposit on a house and send Jason to Sydney Grammar School. 'In my heart,' Jason tells a Republican audience, deftly linking a personal and a political commitment and a touch of fun, 'they are beneath no family in the world, certainly not the British royal one.' There's serious literary and political talent in that sentence, if you think about it.

He got a first class degree in law then spent some years in Holland as associate to an Australian judge of the United Nations Balkan War Crimes Tribunal, learning more than enough about human capacities for evil. Hearing of Australia's Republican Convention he got elected to it and came home to an active role in it. Perhaps impressed by young Natasha's progress he ran but failed to get elected to the Senate. Travelled again, for an American MA in international humanitarian law, especially of genocide. Compared the US and Australia as immigrant societies with different racial strains and reconciliations. Came home again, and speaks widely and well, by invitation, on national and international themes.

He says that student life taught him to participate. 'I like to encourage people who haven't had a voice in the political process to have a say.' Participation 'forces you to realise that there are so many points of view out there that people feel as passionately about as you do about yours.' Meeting and talking between cultures can bring angry confrontations (as often in Noel Pearson's experience) or mutual understanding and solidarity (as more often in Jason Li's). Which effect might it have on their relations with each other? Rather than fight, they might agree that their Australian experience so far is of race and ethnic relations of very different kinds.

Jason's optimism rests on a difference between older and younger Australians. Those now in middle or later life deserve credit for a slow-built, hard-won multicultural success. Postwar immigrants brought up in different countries and cultures encountered each other as strangers. The Australian-born inherited varying degrees of racist feeling about European wops and wogs and slant-eyed Asians. But step by step they got to know each other, learned from each other, and developed a peaceful, multicultural society a good deal more interesting than the native-born had known before the postwar invasion.

Jason's central theme, which specially earns his place in this sample of talent, is that his generation of Australians have been born and brought up together within that peaceful multiculture. 'There's a lot of hope in Australian youth. They're people who have grown up with people of all different backgrounds. That to me is the new Australia. That's the Australia which I think can work together for a better future.'

The other characteristic which all four in this sample share is a strong will to lead rather than follow. Like it or dislike it, that Keating streak is as vital, for national purposes, as their other qualities.

*

What should our next leaders try for?

Except in its treatment of its Aboriginal people Australia has been a comparatively independent, inventive, egalitarian democracy.

We were early with religious equality, manhood suffrage, secret ballot, votes for women, the eight-hour day.

We developed an effective Labor Party and the world's first Labor governments.

We invented public institutions, sufficiently independent of government, to regulate wages and working conditions.

It has been to protect our wage levels and balance of payments and develop our productivity, rather more than to enrich our manufacturers, that we have protected some of our industries.

And for all but one of group of our people, we have achieved a peaceful and interesting multiculture.

But in face of the new global conflicts of the last twenty or thirty years we have so far been copy-cats rather than inventors. I believe that the Anglo-American economic theory which recommends a general weakening of economic government is wrong. All business needs government, some of it heavy and some light handed, much of it detailed to the needs of particular industries and markets. Without it the secret of capitalist efficiency—the harnessing of private interest to produce most efficiently the goods and services that the people most want—breaks down. Many of the new freedoms are actually damaging the efficiency they were meant to improve, as well as degrading valuable social bonds and qualities of life.

We should instead be using our resources and inventive capacities to develop for ourselves—and perhaps to show the world—some better uses of the new technology, better uses of affluence, and better responses to global conflicts of interest. But such adventures have to be well-led, technically competent, and democratically desired. It's the first two of those that most need repair.

Garibaldi in an Armani Suit

Don Watson

In 1993 a delegation came to Parliament House to show the prime minister and his advisers some new technology—*information* technology. It was the internet. They showed us as Stephenson might have shown the King his steam engine. One of them did front of house, demonstrating to all who passed how with this new device he could 'pull up' documents from the Library of Congress onto his screen. He 'pulled up' a letter from the Soviet archives— a letter from Lenin ordering the execution of some Kulaks. In recent years the letter has been frequently quoted as evidence that the architect of the Russian Revolution was a cruel sociopath, and Stalin less an aberration than his natural heir. Whether you accept this interpretation or not, it is a significant letter. The man who 'pulled up' the letter needed no convincing. As we read it on the screen and wondered how it had got there, he said—'I don't know who this Lenin guy was but he sure didn't like those Kulaks'. In our different ways we all bring a little bit of ignorance to history and add it to the pile. His might not have known who Lenin was, but he had grasped much better than us the part in history his machine was about to play.

I am going to talk about the Keating government, and Paul Keating in particular because I worked for him. I am not going to talk about everything that government did, or tell you everything I think or know about its leader. You need not fear that I am going to give you a history of the Keating government, or spend an hour of your time in praise or condemnation of it or him. I am going to talk about Keating and history and what this might tell us about history and modern politics. The anecdote is by way of setting Paul Keating prime minister in his time—which some people called the end of history.

As a subject of study and as a component of public general knowledge and debate, history has lost massive ground in the past twenty years or so. Both here and in the United States, the word 'crisis' is freely used to describe the pedagogical failure and the gathering wave of ignorance about history in the broad society. Australian history has been in particularly dramatic decline. This was the main reason for the Keating government's effort to re-instate the teaching of civics. Not that we thought civics would lead students back to the pleasures and possibilities of history. Ignorance of history is more than ignorance of significant facts. But it was a start, it might lead on to something with the States which are responsible for education. The Carr government, to its great credit, has gone further and pushed history back into schools and public life. In that sense at least, history is bound to judge the Carr government kindly.

Things are not so flash elsewhere, although six or seven years ago they were probably worse. Then it seemed Australia might be the first, if not the only, country to lend credibility to the claims of Francis Fukayama that with the collapse of the communist economies we were on the threshold of the end of history. Yet the experience of the Keating government tends to suggest the opposite (as one would expect—for everything in Fukayama's book there is something to contradict it): since 1992, when Keating first questioned a version of history which prevailed in some conservative circles, the subject has been at or near the centre of political debate. At times it rivalled the economy, which in the 80s Keating had made the indisputable 'main game'—even the 'sacred narrative', but that term won't do because it is a synonym for myth.

It should not occasion much surprise that history demonstrated such a capacity to stir the passions. Much more remarkable is its decline. History has contrived somehow to end up in its own dustbin. Yet history is nothing less than the whole human drama; it is pretty well anything we want it to be. To make it boring and irrelevant is a phenomenal achievement and one for which the history profession has to take a lot of the credit. But of course much else conspires to defeat history in the information age—a million other stories furiously compete, narrow vocationalism rules the roost, training is everything, economists who were once safely stowed in cupboards and spoke only at certain times of the year now run the debates, our imagination lies elsewhere—on the frontiers of a long technology-driven revolution such as this one, perhaps history was bound to be a straggler or something like the Drover's Wife.

There are good reasons why the young might pass the subject up. They do not want to inherit their identity—money yes, but not who they are. If they think history is boring it may be a sign that the Oedipal reflex is working. It is more worrying for history if our children reject it because they think it is unknowable. Their experience, and maybe their education, might tell them that meaning is elusive, subjective, ephemeral and ambiguous and pursuing it is a waste of time. Yet, while this attitude may cause concern among historians and give rise to furious denunciations of postmodernism, they can hardly think the problem is a new one. On the contrary, they have had to deal with it since their subject was first thought of.

Our despair need not prove fatal. It's like the Irishman and the anthropologist who asks him if he believes in fairies. He says— 'No! no! Of course not. But they're there.' They might deny history, but it's there. We know it will remain in the psyche, churning away even in those who think it's boring and irrelevant.

Perhaps historians need to recognise that what they do fills a sort of primal need. The need for stories is buried deep in our psychology; maybe in our DNA, like our desire for salt which a scientist I know says derives from our beginnings in the sea—it's a hedonic craving, which means it's nearly irresistible, even when we know it clogs our arteries and kills us.

History is a bit like that. It's a contradictory drive. On the one hand toward the lost past and our desire to preserve it in myth and memory. For these reasons we construct our sacred narratives. Also for these reasons, some of us feel a pang of gloom when we see an abandoned house, the image Freud associates with mourning. If melancholy and mourning are part of the human condition, so is history. And both of them can be as fatal as salt.

On the other hand there is the desire to make our own history— to pull down what is offensive to our modern eye, or no longer useful or profitable and to make our own mark. Like capitalism—to destroy so we can invent and renew. Like someone not wanting to look back, someone escaping from memory. There is Proust and there is progress. In the midst of one the other rears its head.

The paradox was alive in Paul Keating—the melancholy seemed to exist in proportion to the drive for change and renewal. He would re-design Australia on a drink coaster, launch brutal assaults on traditions, mock his opponents' attachments to the past—and every time he went to Cairns he'd groan and curse at what had been done to the architecture on the shoreline

He liked Neoclassical architecture and furniture because it was—remember—'eternally smart'. I suspect he liked Neoclassical economics for the same reason—for its simple lines. The Japanese beam, those buildings of Jefferson's in Washington—the things that will last forever, like the Labor Party, the Church of Rome and the message of Christ. I think the word 'eternal' is essential to understanding Paul Keating.

That may be why he never lacked resolve when it came to change. He was connected to tradition—Australian, Labor, Irish, Catholic, Sydney, family—and he knew the value of it but, as Paul Kelly once said, he was 'unburdened by the dead hand of the past'.

> Keating brought to caucus and machine politics the disciplined infallibility of his Catholicism. Dressed with the smart severity of a Jesuit, he slid along the parliamentary lobbies carrying ambition as an altar boy cradles his missal, reflexes sharpened to strike heretics.

Judging what was dispensable and what was for keeps was not such a hard question for Keating. He could go on changing and inventing and never fear the thread would break.

I am writing a book about the Keating government, or more accurately, Paul Keating's prime ministership, or even more accurately, Paul Keating and his prime ministership. I find the task produces these paradoxical responses. It is astonishing to me that the documents of just six years ago provoke the kind of feelings one associates with the sight of the metaphorical abandoned house. At the same time it often seems as if nothing separates us from those few years, that essentially the project is continuing, one is still having the arguments and one wants to win them as much as ever.

The task of doing Keating—even doing him slowly—is a hard one. I suspect it always has been.

Last year I read something that the US Civil War general and president, Ulysses S. Grant, said about beginning his memoirs. I've been quoting it ever since, particularly to audiences who are interested in writing. Grant said on his deathbed: 'a verb signifies to be, to do or to suffer—I signify all three'. As a verb is a doing word, so Grant was a doer and attracted to verbs. Victorians will conceive of him as a kind of prototype of Jeff. Some people are verbs and some are nouns. Grant was a verb. Bob Menzies was a noun. Bob Hawke was an adjective.

Ulysses S. Grant has become part of my campaign to persuade the government to declare a National Verb Retrieval Day, and a moratorium on the word 'enhance'. I want them to start with the public service and spread out into the corporations, the universities, schools and swimming clubs.

Grant also said that when he first put pen to paper—and this is the part which both inspires and haunts—'I did not know the first word I should make use of … I only knew what was in my mind, and I wished to express it clearly so that there could be no mistaking it.'

As he had just completed, in one year, the 275,000 words of his Civil War memoirs which John Keegan says is probably 'the most revelatory autobiography of high command to exist in any language', and Edmund Wilson ranked it with Julius Caesar's *Commentaries*; and as he commenced it only to restore his family's fortune which a friend of his son's had lost; and as he was diagnosed with terminal cancer just as he commenced—it would be a mean spirit who said the achievement was less than heroic.

His great strength as a general proved to be an equally phenomenal literary asset—his clarity of mind. Neither the mayhem of battle nor the clouds of memory could move it. As a general and a president and as one of the most famous men in the world, he understood the value of publicity and the perils of the press. But of the modern media and modern politics Grant knew nothing. Had he lived through that I wonder if he would have known what was in his mind.

As history students we were taught to never stray far from the evidence. We were taught how to assess the value of documents, even read between the lines; how to analyse them—and how to construct a convincing narrative. We learned that history is a very complex undertaking, much more complex than Grant's words suggest. But the most perfect mastery of the discipline, in any of its variations, is unlikely to save the historian who takes on modern politics.

What, for instance, do we make of a record which is written by journalists and politicians, mediated by television and radio? There is something always heroic about historians' assumptions—and those of journalists for that matter: three quarters of a century after Heisenberg established the uncertainty principle in physics, a century after Cézanne brought the same principle to painting landscapes, we march on as if reality can be described with an eye and an ear and a pen. In one of his columns in 1992 Gerard Henderson wrote that, while Paul Kelly's account of Australian politics in the 80s, *The End of Certainty*, was a tour de force of a kind, it suffered from being 'written in the hothouse, in-bred atmosphere of Parliament House' and was 'not history in the established sense', and 'by its very nature, it cannot hope to be definitive'. It's hard to argue with his case, but the question remains, who *could* write the definitive history? An historian in the established sense? I doubt it.

It is obvious that a government cannot succeed if the media is concertedly against it. It is said less often, but equally true that a government is half way to extinction if it blames the media for its misfortunes. This is all part of the exhausting, fiendish embrace of politics and the media: your most imaginative thoughts will be traduced, your noblest deeds scoffed at, your effort unrecognised; in fulfilment of their 'vision' requirement you will announce your intention to create a pretty little postmodern republic in the south seas, and to prove you are compassionate and wise you will offer to build a sophisticated safety net around the robust free market economy they asked for—and your policy speech will be headlined 'Pork barrel republic!'. But if you rail and shout you're gone. Take them with you when you pay the nation's respects to the martyrs of Hellfire Pass, and on the very railway where the thousands died they will shove a microphone under your nose and ask you about the latest current account figures. In the interests of regional stability and improving the current account figures you go and make friends with those on whom your predecessors made war, and the journalists will hound you about not going to a place in Vietnam where a dozen Aussies died and at dusk they'll sneak off into the jungle to get a picture of 'The graves Keating wouldn't visit!'.

But be seen to complain and they will skewer you, and your opponents will suddenly feel light-hearted and go around whistling and mocking, even if as little as a week ago they were privately crying foul themselves. Because they know the media will say that a political leader who turns on them is the leader of a government in decay, a leader who has grown arrogant and out of touch. And their office will divide in two—between those saying, 'Stop laughing, the pendulum could at any moment swing back through the wall and brain us', and those who say—'All the more reason to laugh and sing now.'

In a way the media is right: a government which blames them hasn't learned the lesson of Job—to grin and bear it. For the media may be likened unto God and bad weather—it may seem unreasonable and cruel, but a person looks a fool ranting at it, and gains nothing.

He looks twice the fool when, soon after, the pendulum does swing and he finds himself having to quickly affect an attitude of basking in the reflected glow of his opponents being barbecued. Not that anyone will really notice—that's the other thing about modern politics, the attention span is about 7.5 seconds, unjogged memory about 7.5 days and diminishing yearly. What political leaders have to keep telling themselves is that they will get unjust critical reviews and also unjust favourable ones—and in this at least they are no different to large groups of other people, including footballers, jockeys and novelists. They need to accommodate the notion that even when the media story is not the true story, it is the only story that matters, because nothing in politics is real unless the media says so—and one of the two major parties tags along with the idea.

They have to plough on—even in the knowledge that if their strategy is too plainly directed at massaging the media they will be accused of cynical manipulation and subverting policy to tawdry political purposes; and if their strategy ignores the media or offends it they will be charged either with being secretive and undemocratic, or worse, with political naivete and incompetence and being unfit to play the game. Ask John Hewson.

It is not just that meaning in politics is dependent on media interpretation. That has been the case for a very long time. It is also not new for the media to contain a range of human types from the near-depraved to the flawlessly principled and bright—which is a compass no wider than the community and the parliament can boast. What is new is the pervasiveness of the media. It is in everything. It's not the Fourth Estate but the range on which we all ride, the whole environment, and politicians must decide very quickly if they'll be a raptor or a rabbit. The politicians who survive and prosper must of necessity know the steps to the dance. While they may complain to journalists and editors on the telephone, they can't step away from it without stepping away from reality. It's a tar baby embrace.

The American commentator, Jonathan Schell, says that the people of the United States now see the politicians and journalists as a single class—a new leviathan of 'rich, famous and powerful who are divorced from the lives of ordinary people and indifferent to their concerns.' In Australia the trend might not be so advanced, but the same symptoms can be seen—in the last Victorian election, for example. Schell says it has expanded the gap which exists in any democracy between those who participate fully and those who only participate in elections. This gap used to be filled by political parties and civic bodies, including trade unions. All these are shrinking. And the widening gap is filled by a sense of powerlessness, disenchantment—and talkback radio shows which heighten these feelings and add to them demands and expectations which are often the antithesis of good policy.

Political parties now monitor and analyse the calls to talkback radio, as well as the opinion polls and focus groups. If in all other circumstances politicians are expected to be honest, on talkback the audience demands sycophancy and self-abasement. On the Laws program in 1995 a caller declared that in her part of the world women were having children for the sole purpose of claiming government benefits. Unable to persuade her that this was not a convincing reason to abolish the benefits, Keating finally exclaimed, 'What do people want?' It was a costly mistake that confirmed the perception of Keating as arrogant and out of touch, not to say wilful and undisciplined.

Meanwhile the temptation of flakiness grows stronger: governments construct policies in line with carefully monitored public expectations, which in office they must abandon or compromise. This meets another public expectation, that politicians are weak-brained and cannot be trusted. And the loathing grows. It is, as Schell says, a *folie a deux*.

The journalists clean up on both the swings and the roundabouts. For weeks in 1993 many of them urged the second Keating government to do the responsible policy thing and drop the tax cuts promised in One Nation. The government did the responsible thing and paid half, with half to follow. The media came blazing with self-righteous fury and labelled Keating a liar.

How an historian can be expected to read the diabolically difficult game of politics I don't know. I'm with that old deconstructionist, Lord Melbourne, who a century-and-a-half ago said—'I wish I was as sure of anything as Tom Macauley is of everything.' In addition to all the difficulties which have made practical people in the past say the historical enterprise is bunk, there are too many layers of motive and meaning to allow anyone who is not part of the game from knowing how it is played. Politicians and hard-nosed insiders of fabled acumen don't always read it well themselves. The Willis Letters are a case in point.

It won't stop people trying to find their way through of course. Postmodern commentators make sporadic forays that sometimes sound tantalisingly like the truth; but not the truth that matters. What is the use to a speech-writer to have the death of the author proclaimed? Psychoanalytic approaches are attempted and not without bringing enlightenment, but neither politicians nor the media will buy it as a significant factor in anything. Angry neo-conservatives and Left-liberals shout at the gates, sustained by the heat of their convictions but getting no nearer the light, for they don't know the 'reality' of things. They all get their moments and no one is going to make them pay for it.

Where does that leave the poor old empirical historians whose discipline holds them to account—or at least is meant to? It didn't matter much to the historian who wrote the entry on the republic in the *Oxford Companion to Australian History*. 'In the 1990s', he said, ' Paul Keating and his speech-writer, Don Watson, revived the patriotic republicanism of Henry Lawson, as if the only authentic Australians were those who wanted to separate from Britain.' So much for sticking to the evidence. There are times when you have to admit that Henry Ford was on to something. There are times when you think events can only be described by those who lived through them, by the likes of Ulysses S. Grant.

I don't know how modern political history can be written by anyone who has not actually lived inside the organism. As a hundred bad books attest, it is not a sufficient condition, but it is almost certainly a necessary one. It is not the whole story or the only one and it relies on uncertain memory and testimony of self-interested witnesses, but *The End of Certainty* is possibly as great a work of Australian history as anything to come from the academy in the last twenty-five years. It helps that Kelly is a formidable writer, but he couldn't have done it without having been there in the hothouse.

You can write credibly about football and art without having played at any of them. Politics is different. Modern politics is a game in which all day every day words are conceived, written, uttered and translated into instant images which are then written about again and translated into more images—and the context and motivation for each is different, and necessarily the meaning each time is different, though it may be disguised to sound or look the same, or even disguised to look different when it is really the same.

And the media—like a pack of dogs, or a herd of cows—come rattling up to Five Ways, saying. 'Which way? Which way? Where's the story? Which way?' And one says 'This way!' And they all follow. Except say Alan Ramsay or Laurie Oakes or Michelle Grattan who wander off down their own roads—and soon we hear the distant voices of the pack returning, saying—'What's Laurie doing? What's Ramsay's angle?' But never saying, of course, 'We went the wrong way'. The problem for constructing a convincing narrative for modern politics is that everyone—every politician and every journalist—is in the business of constructing and deconstructing convincing narratives daily. When you decide who won the news that night, or at the end of the week, what you're really measuring is whose story was best. Did your story survive? What is the history of this week? Of this morning?

What writer can accurately measure the difference, or say if what the media ran with was what the speaker intended, and if the doorstop was in any case a means of drawing attention away from something less palatable, or to steal the limelight from an Opposition statement later in the day—and who knows if more influential than anything said or reported was a curl in the politician's lip, an impression he gave of weariness or arrogance, or something else that did not register with the press or any poll or focus group. Why did hundreds of ecstatic schoolgirls mob Keating one day in the 1996 campaign? What had they seen that no one else had?

To state the bleeding obvious—the written record, the documents left for historians to study if they survive the shredder and the widespread indifference to posterity, will reveal what was said but not what was signified. They won't capture anything like the whole drama—which often resembled the advertisement in which a skier comes hurtling, yodelling out of the mountains and in a flurry of legs, arms and snow, crashes through the roof of a bar and with a smile asks the waiter for a beer. It never fails to make me think of Keating arriving at the Press Club or in the House for Question Time. But that's an ad—you don't see that on the news and current affairs shows, even if what you do see brings you not much closer to the truth of the matter.

And then there's the radio the next day. What they will make of his performance is another imponderable, and what the audience will make of the radio—you see one friend at the weekend and he tells you you're going well, you see another who listens to another station or watches *A Current Affair*, or her mother does, and she says your bloke's letting the Japanese cut down all the old growth forests for koala meat! He's a fiend! You ought to be ashamed! And you go back to work thinking what a great simplifier of things the Cold War was and Fukayama was right after all—the great issues must have been settled.

I don't know how in future the general histories will be written—from inside or outside. The major work on the 1996 election is Pamela Williams' *The Victory*. For want of much else most of the reviews treated it as the definitive work, the last word, and so, presumably, did the many people who bought and read it. In truth, much of it strikes me as excellent—but not the parts I know about. Williams makes damning personal remarks about Keating on the evidence of one, possibly two, not disinterested people. Labor's national secretary, Gary Gray, told Williams that Keating was mentally unstable. To say that his evidence was 'flimsy' and her use of it 'questionable' is to be more than generous. No self-respecting historian could countenance her method. But a self-respecting historian is unlikely to ever strike Williams from the record—though someone might one day make the point that Winston Churchill was lucky he didn't have Gary Gray around.

All this may not add up to the end of history, but it certainly doesn't seem set for a big win. Do we now say that there is no objective truth that can be known? Perhaps there never was, which is what Lord Melbourne seemed to be saying about Macauley 150 years ago?

Of course history has always been problematic. In any democratic society it is bound to be argued about. But it's fair to say I think that it has never worn so many disguises. Never have there been so many stories from which to choose.

We need a story, don't we? We need our own story. Read a child a familiar bedtime story—and change it. Put the fox up in the rafters and the hen circling on the floor. Make the first bowl of porridge just right, the second one too hot. The child will pick it up at once, and correct it for you, possibly angrily. This is the first flowering of political correctness. In its most basic form that is perhaps what history is. It's much the same with adults—and much the same with politics. Don't you dare change the story.

It was story-telling which made Paul Keating such an effective reformer in the 1980s. I don't mean sugar-coating, or even putting a spin on things—though there was plenty of that no doubt. I mean Keating made a drama out of the economy and he put the whole population in the theatre, even sometimes on the stage—he was centre stage of course. If you've got Fred Astaire in your cast you don't leave him shuffling aimlessly down the back. Sure, he was boasting when he said he had the markets in one pocket and the ACTU in the other, and the Governor of the Reserve Bank under his wing and this person doing these tricks, and someone else doing others—but it was more than a boast. It was an image of confluence and energy—or synergy if you like. Each Budget came as another act in the drama, characters were given roles, pulled off and reprimanded as object lessons if they didn't perform according to the text. He got the crowd barracking.

And he invented a language. He once said that he had spent years making words into 'hammers'. Sometimes these hammers were for beating people on the head. More often they were to make an indelible mark, so that the ideas would stick. That's how he educated the country in the necessity of economic reform.

He knew that he was replacing one story with another—the story of protection and regulation and reliance on commodities with the story which began when the dollar was floated and the financial markets were deregulated. The first story ended in the decline in the terms of trade, underdeveloped and antiquated manufacturing, increasingly futile and perilous attempts to ride on the sheep's back or on each new upswing in commodity prices. We all remember it—we could sing it in our sleep. This he liked to characterise as the Menzies story—with references to Qualcast mowers and Morphy Richards toasters. The second story was all about opening the place up, giving it a future, getting it up and running, lifting exports as a proportion of GDP from 14 percent in to 23 percent—you'll remember that story too.

This is what he was reminding the press gallery about on that night at the National Press Club when he compared himself to Placido Domingo and signalled the challenge to Bob Hawke. He was reminding them that he always gave value in the business of streaming the economics and politics together. That night he also reminded the press that they had been an essential part of it: '... I hope that we can continue between us, spinning the tale, the great tale of Australian economic change, and wrapping it up in interesting ways, with interesting phrases and interesting words.'

As treasurer, Paul Keating wrote history as he went. He told the press that they could attach themselves to John Hewson if they liked. But Hewson would never 'lift economics and politics to an art form'. By art form he meant story-telling, or something tantamount to history.

The Placido Domingo references and the implications for Hawke's leadership have obscured some significant larger elements in that off-the-cuff speech. He talked about more than economics; about lingering empire attitudes in Australia and South Africa, for instance. And how we Australians had too rarely run the place according to our own lights; how we'd never sat down and written a constitution 'which a couple of hundred years later could be as fresh as the day it was written'. 'We occupy a continent', he said, 'and we're one nation, and we're basically a European nation, changing now to adapt to the region.'

In those words can be glimpsed the kernel of the expanded story he told in the course of his Prime Ministership, the one which when it was thrown up against the 'sacred narrative' of the Menzies years caused grave offence—both real and feigned. No one wrote the Domingo speech for him—it was in his head. People who think Keating constructed his view of history to suit his political needs in 1992, should go back to that 1990 speech, and even further, to the 1970s when he assailed the Fraser government for continuing to think in colonial terms about the Asian countries. There is a consistent pattern to his thought.

Abraham Lincoln was unequivocal. 'As our case is new, so we must think anew and act anew', he said. Could this be a justification for re-writing history? Or a motto for good government which abandons the myths and pieties by which inaction—and political correctness—are justified? Lincoln knew his history and how to use it. How does he begin the Gettysberg Address? With history— 'four score and seven years ago...' It promises to be as platitudinous as any old Anzac Day address. In the great tradition of pious emptiness it pays familiar homage to the founding fathers of the republic—but then, in a silky shift of gears, it becomes revolutionary—the Gettysberg Address calls up history to demand a change.

And what did his opponents say about it—they said he was re-writing history. The *Chicago Times* said he had mis-stated the cause for which the soldiers at Gettysberg gave their lives and 'libel[ed] the statesmen who founded the government. They were men possessing too much self-respect to declare that negroes were their equal'. Lincoln, they said, had turned the words of the founding fathers into things they did not mean. How come no one now says that the Gettysberg Address is politically correct?

In Theodore Zeldin's *Intimate History of Humanity* he writes; 'To have a new version of the future, it is always necessary to have a new version of the past.' He is not advocating the application of the airbrush. He is saying that as much as we need the stories by which we know ourselves and secure ourselves in the cosmos, we also need to invent and renew ourselves. We need to balance the opposing forces.

For all his hard work in the 80s, when he got the prime ministership in 1991, Keating needed to renew himself and his government—the original title for the economic statement by which the government defined its attack on the recession was not One Nation but Renewing Australia. (One Nation seemed such a good name at the time.) But the recession had not only knocked the stuffing out of the economy, for the time being it had deprived the whole Labor reform program of legitimacy. As the author of that program, it had deprived Keating of legitimacy too. This was not what he had promised. It was a chapter from another book.

You can see the attempt to make the recession a legitimate part of the story in that remark about having to have it which haunted his whole prime ministership. Perhaps he should have said—*it is my melancholy duty to inform you that the world is going into recession and therefore Australia has also gone into recession*. How many in the population—or the press gallery—would have known he had borrowed it from Bob Menzies?

There were plenty who wanted him to apologise, to stand in the stocks of talkback radio and have those words thrown back at him—those words he had made into hammers. Jana Wendt conducted a show trial in his absence. But Keating had no bent for self-abasement. Instead he and the government came up with a statement which contained some carefully disguised old-fashioned Keynesian solutions, and equally old-fashioned messages of national strength and bonding and the realisation of dreams first dreamt 100 years ago. By 1992 the Keating government had a new story—and the polls showed it was back in the hunt.

Fukayama had just written *The End of History and the Last Man*. With the death of communism, he said, liberalism had achieved a Nietzchean final triumph. Ideology was dead—again. There was no longer any reason for any other isms at all: no elite for absolutism, no trade unions for socialism, no nations for nationalism. The end of history means the end of the political: ideologies, values and derring-do will be replaced by economics and technology and consumerism. Three years after One Nation, one year after Working Nation, in the same year as Creative Nation, the Japanese whiz, Kenichi Ohmae, published a big-selling book called *The End of the Nation State*. So what on earth was this specimen of a Last Man doing running around talking about republics and new flags and new senses of national purpose, and asserting some new national role in the region, and bringing forth grand new programs for the new Australia of his imagination, all trumpeting the word 'nation', and reviving civics for heaven's sake!? And what was he doing stirring up a hornet's nest about the wars, and biffing Britain and Bob Menzies? The Last Man, according to Fukayama, was meant to be a dismal creature—inhabitant of a liberal democracy when all are agreed on liberal democracy and have nothing to dispute but money and possessions. Without ideals, heroism or creative urges, the Last Man is Mediocre Man—or, if you like, a colourless nerd. Yet Keating was acting like some kind of Garibaldi in an Armani suit.

Political reality does tend to ignore intellectual fashion. The first and most pressing reality for Keating was to re-start the economy. The second was to puncture Fightback and its author, John Hewson. The third was to throw off the dark spectre—the recession. He discovered in the course of that first year that the second was his best answer to the third. One Nation was to deal with the first problem and give him the basis for an argument with the second.

But one other problem remained; namely, that even in the best of times economics is too barren a landscape for a prime minister to live in. Paul Keating needed something more human and more vivid—something half as rich as Menzies' tapestry of traditions, symbols, bogeys and signs of progress would do. And Providence being more wonderful than any other theory, it so happened that John Hewson knew nothing of such things and was only at home on economic turf. By softening economic policy at some of the edges—in car industry tariffs, for example—he led hard John Hewson into a policy billabong and, leaving him there, paddled furiously for the mainstream.

Before this, when all the debate, understandably, was about unemployment—and the Budget deficit, and the current account and the prospects for growth, and even as that word was mentioned, the threat of another inflationary boom and another recession—Keating inserted, of all things, some history. He decided that a new perspective on the future required a new perspective on the past.

To the economic commentators, and all those he had instructed in the reform story this was blasphemy. He'd jumped the monastery fence. John Hewson thought telling the Queen that Australia was going its own way showed a lack of respect. And then when Keating lambasted the Opposition for their sycophantic attachment to Britain, imperial honours, protected industries, sheep and Morphy Richards toasters—even after Britain deserted us for Europe, and failed to defend Singapore, and wouldn't give us back our troops—there was a terrible roar of protest which echoed all the way to London tabloids.

There had to be an explanation: it was because he was Irish; it was because he wanted a political diversion; it was because of Jack Lang; it was because he didn't have a proper education; it was because he was getting advice from some ning-nong with a dingo's degree in history.

It was the Singapore reference which offended most. In fact it is difficult to find a respectable history, including that by Winston Churchill, which does not fundamentally support Keating's interpretation. Gerard Henderson found Robert O'Neill to say it was not so. But Guy Wint and Peter Calvocoressi, Basil Liddell Hart, Paul Hasluck, E. M. Andrews, Coral Bell, David Horner, Hank Nelson and Bill Gammage say it more or less was. As for it being an Irish Catholic Labor version of history, it was pretty well identical to the version I got growing up in a Scottish Protestant rural conservative household. I've heard it said by people wearing RSL badges, at least after a beer or two has gone down.

Yet it was as if Keating had torn the sacred text, changed the words in the bedtime story—as if he had no right to speak on such subjects, as if he could not know. Anyway, what did history have to do with a prime minister? The RSL accused him of heresy, if not treason. Three years later the letters were still coming in. In 1995 I tracked down the author of an article in an RSL branch newsletter which claimed that Keating had said British soldiers were cowards who had run away at Singapore. He was having his lunch when I telephoned. I asked him where he got this idea. He said a friend had told him he thought he'd read it somewhere or heard it on the radio or something.

It was difficult for Keating not to talk about history. He couldn't advocate a republic or a new flag without talking about it. When the High Court put Mabo on his plate he was obliged to talk about it. He couldn't set things up for the Centenary of Federation without saying a word or two about history. And, although hardly anyone seemed to notice, his government coincided with the fiftieth anniversary of the last four years of World War Two. He hadn't chosen to make all the speeches of commemoration at all those war graves and over at the Memorial—he was obliged to.

He could have delivered more conventional speeches—there have been many wars in history and they have produced any amount of eloquent sentiments for a prime minister to choose from. And any amount of platitudes that doubtless once had meaning, but were now useful only in the way a door sausage is useful, and were about as stimulating. Keating believed he had a responsibility to invest the wars with contemporary meaning. He thought the sacrifice of Australians would cease to be understood if that link could not be made, if the word 'sacrifice' drifted towards cliché.

He went to Kokoda and, forewarning no one, fell to his knees and kissed the ground at the base of the monument. The press came running to his advisers asking who had put him up to this astonishing gesture. No one had. Later he talked to the children who had sung the national anthem and waved little Australian flags they had made at school. Keating patted one of them on the head. A sound boom picked up what he said. On the news that night we heard him say to the little boy—'don't worry son, we'll get you a new one of those.' The patriots shrieked. At Bomana cemetery he said that the soldiers who lay there had died 'not in defence of the old world, but the new world. Their world.' In headlines twice as big as the event the cry went up that Keating was discriminating between the fallen.

I would like to know if Geoffrey Blainey agrees with Theodore Zeldin. I think he must. Geoffrey Blainey has always understood the need to re-interpret the past and he has never shied away from the challenge. He is a master story-teller—a kind of Shennachie— who can tell an old story in words we in the present can understand and even feel. He can also change a story and get away with it. It was Blainey, after all, who offered a radical re-interpretation of Australia's European foundations; a new theory about distance as a prime influence on our development; a treatise on war which suggested among other things that the Japanese had had their reasons.

But Geoffrey Blainey came after Keating savagely. Blainey said Keating had 'done deep harm by altering the facts of history to support his political campaign'. He said Keating had appointed himself as the nation's 'wandering lecturer in history'. He said he had been 'impetuous' and 'silly' and he had 'blundered' in.

Other historians welcomed Keating's contribution, though Geoffrey Bolton was reported as saying that there was 'a worry when politicians interpret the past...'. It is not hard to see the dangers Bolton is pointing to—we don't want our politicians telling us what we should believe about the past. It is at least as dangerous, probably, as historians telling us what we should believe about the present. However there remains the difficulty (which Bolton of course recognises) of effecting some kind of constitutional lobotomy on our leaders. And it does create problems for speech-writers, so much of life being a dialogue with the past, so many electors wanting politicians in their speeches to recognise what has happened to them—it is the most powerful thing in a speech, this touching on people's experience. It pulls them into the country's story, it makes it a shared emotion. And often it has a useful humanising effect on the politician. We could go back to only talking about economics, but then some of us might go back to the British Isles.

Such nice considerations buttered no parsnips with Dame Leonie Kramer. On reading a transcript of an address Keating gave on Anzac Day 1992 in Port Moresby, she fulminated in the *Sydney Morning Herald* against his 'sentimental clichés' and 'rhetorical flourishes', and when he said that Anzac 'does not confer on us a duty to see that the world stands still', she said; 'Who in their right mind would suggest that the world stands still? The nature of existence is change...' And who in their right mind would argue with that, or feel the need to say it? Except I thought Lévi-Strauss had a point when he said that myths and legends had the capacity to make the world stand still, in a manner of speaking.

Kramer was particularly incensed by the passage in Keating's speech which contained the words '... Australia looks to America, free of any pangs as to our traditional links or kinship with the United Kingdom...' She responded fiercely: 'Why can we not acknowledge the common sense of turning to the US for help without discarding our origins, which in any case we share with the US?' Well, yes. But it does appear that Kramer thought the offending words were Keating's. They were, of course, famously Curtin's.

As Curtin is not in a position to defend himself, let me offer an answer on his behalf: he was not discarding our origins, but he knew he needed to acknowledge the past. He needed in a sense to bless it before passing on. But he also needed to stare it down for the power that it had. When you read about Curtin in those days it is very obvious that he knew just how momentous his actions were. That was one reason why it took so much out of him. Curtin was doing what we have a right to expect of political leaders but do not always get—a decision. Courage. Leadership.

If anyone wants another reason why he said he was turning to the US 'free of any pangs' about our spiritual ties to Britain—consider the possibility that there was some anger in it. And the possibility that this anger was shared by Menzies and by Casey, because assurances had been given in London. Menzies lamented to the high commissioner in London, Stanley Melbourne Bruce, that he was being urged to send Australian troops to the Middle East not only by Eden, but by 'old soldiers'. That is, by the past, by the legend of the First World War. Allan Martin quotes him in a letter to Bruce: 'If only a kindly Providence would remove from the active political scene here a few minds which are heavily indoctrinated by the "old soldiers"...point of view.' Menzies, Martin tells us, said that he had to remind his critics that 'this is not 1914...'

Perhaps the world does stand still, after all. Just as it moves under us sometimes.

The point is made not to dispute the value of the contribution Australian soldiers made in the Middle East or anywhere else. It's only to show that the most cultivated adults can be as prone to fury as any toddler when the words of a favourite story are changed.

When, as president of the United States, Lyndon Johnson became a tribune and battering ram for civil rights and the elimination of poverty, his old supporters were shocked—'Why, Lyndon why?', they cried. 'You never held these views before!' 'I wasn't President then', he replied. To be fair, it must have been a shock to hear Paul Keating weighing into history. This was the person who, Third Empire clocks apart, had done nothing but tear tradition down in the previous decade. That's if you count heavily protected industry, regulated financial markets, fixed exchange rates, declining terms of trade and centralised wage fixing as traditions.

Power does corrupt—sometimes it corrupts our perfect view of people. So Paul Keating wore a smart suit and believed that Neoclassical economics was the main game, and frequently talked about it as if it could only be played to the exclusion of everything else. Jack Lang wore a smart suit. Rex Connor believed economics was the main game. But Rex Connor believed we should buy back the farm. Keating didn't. And Jack Lang carried a Gladstone bag in which he kept in neat pockets—a shaving brush, a pencil, a tape measure, a diary and a KLG spark plug. I never saw Keating with such a thing—though he is a meticulous packer just the same.

There were commentators who felt that Keating's interest in history was too sudden to be anything other than political opportunism. There were some who felt that because he lacked a formal training in history he could not be right about it—so when he got his figures wrong at a doorstop interview in France or drifted into hyperbole or parody, they savaged him. Suddenly history became the knowable, verifiable, unarguable, immutable thing everyone who has ever practised the discipline, and everyone who has ever read it seriously, knows it cannot be.

This is a very small part of any history of the Keating government. For me the story has shifted in the past three years. In the aftermath of the 1996 election it was about how the election had been lost. I don't know the answer to that. I have read at least twenty good reasons and thought of a dozen or so myself. But I still don't know. The most satisfactory argument remains a line in *Middlemarch*: 'It always remains true that if we had been greater, circumstances would have been less strong against us.'

I have a feeling that politicians of the Keating mould are just now out of date. They are power politicians. It comes from the Catholic Church, the Labor Party and an uncluttered mind. Clausewitz, Henry Kissinger and Ulysses S. Grant are of the same mould. These days, however, the surveys show that people don't respect power in their leaders, but want to be 'empowered' themselves. They want respect.

Most writing about politics is about power—who won or lost, who is angling for a coup. It is always a better story than policy. It's addictive. It might not do a lot for sales if a book about Keating concerns itself too much with the policy effort—the effort to find an independent role in Asia before it was too late, finding some strategy to cope with the information revolution, dealing with the new social imperatives created by an efficient growth economy which seemed to shed jobs as fast it created them, globalisation, Mabo, the republic, the decline in regional Australia.

The evidence of four-and-a-quarter years in politics would fill half a dozen mechanics halls, and that's not counting the electronic stuff and how it looked and sounded. Or the stuff in memories. I don't know how an historian or any other commentator is meant to cope. Yet they try: not long after the 1996 election, I read a newspaper column by MacKenzie Wark in which he said that Don Russell and Don Watson were typical of their generation: good on ideas but with little concern for detail. With the greatest respect to MacKenzie Wark, I don't think he knows what details are.

Being a simple empiricist at heart I keep going back to the first meeting. It wasn't arrogance or pride I was presented with—but melancholy. Like a man with a sad fixation about what had been lost. It was there, on and off, all the way through. For an adviser or a speech-writer it could be worrying—but for an historian it was constant encouragement.

Hansonism Then and Now

Margo Kingston

In the two years since the annihilation of One Nation at the 1998 election campaign—despite attracting more than one million first preference votes—the effects of the Hanson phenomenon have intensified. I believe its impact on Australian politics and society will not be understood for at least ten years. But it is high time that we in the media think through what is happening in our society from the perspective of the forces unleashed by Hansonism, and respond better than we have to date in exploring and interpreting their impact.

In my view, the cargo cult of Pauline Hanson triggered the rusting-off of rural and regional Australians' voting traditions. Through Hanson, they saw the raw power of their vote, and have put it on the block for sale to the highest bidder, not only for cash but for reassurance that their experience and concept of being Australian is incorporated into our emerging national identity.

Five months after the federal election, the New South Wales election saw the National Party lose its safest seat, centred on Dubbo, to the independent, Labor-leaning Dubbo mayor. New South Wales now boasts three rural independents—all respected local identities, none of them rednecks. They represent three large, proud regional cities—Dubbo, Tamworth and Armidale. Their needs are being well catered for by the New South Wales Labor government, because if the rural independents hold their seats, Labor has a buffer against losing government. Meanwhile, New South Wales Labor has established 'Country Labor', with its own spokespeople and policies.

Who can forget the extraordinary climax of election day in Victoria—the home of small 'l' liberalism—in September 1999? Victorian regional and rural voters had given the thumbs down to Hanson. But then they did something no one who ruled or reported on Australia dreamed of: they put their traditional enemy, the Labor Party, into office. Victorian premier Steve Bracks worked hard for that result, but even he was shocked by the extent of his success. Jeff Kennett is still in shock, the Victorian National Party has split from the Coalition in opposition, and the rural seat of its former leader has fallen to Labor in a by-election.

On the federal level, the Victorian election loss has seen the Coalition fall over itself to cash up the bush. Daily press releases announce rural specific programs on everything from domestic violence to rural transaction centres. The Adelaide to Darwin railway is on the agenda, yet again. The Coalition and Labor believe that if they win over the bush (and the blue collar workers also attracted to Hansonism) they will win government, and any useful political analysis will filter all major political plays until the next election through that lens.

John Howard and Kim Beazley are still as one on the core issues of globalisation. Beazley differentiates himself only on Telstra, where he is playing to the bush's conviction that a privatised Telstra will mean fewer services. Howard's differentiation play is insidious, potentially disastrous for the nation, and means the trashing of the small 'l' liberal tradition of the party he leads. He is deliberately pushing the bush's socially conservative buttons, and has rolled-gold credibility with the bush on these matters because he too is unashamedly socially conservative.

Howard's downgrading of our commitment to United Nations human rights treaties feeds off the widespread feeling in the bush that one-world-government is the ruin of us all. It is intellectually dishonest and destructive of our established identity as a tolerant nation and a world leader on promoting international human rights standards. It works because Howard is blatantly appealing to prejudice and not doing his duty in informing the public of the facts. He is abusing country Australians, not helping them. And he knows it.

In reality, the civilising of the forces of economic globalisation—in which there is already a strong one-world regulation through groups such as the World Trade Organisation (strongly supported by Howard)—will only occur with the parallel development of world human rights standards. Human rights mean rights for country people too, such as the right to a decent education and accessible medical services. In addition, the fight for protection of the environment, child labour, and the wish of many countries to preserve unique economic/social traditions will only come through engagement with global economic forces, and again, this can only come through the mechanism of the United Nations.

Yet Howard does not chose intelligent, engaged debate. He does not respect the citizens he is appealing to, he exploits them. He chooses social populism, and refuses to argue his case on the merits to equally informed citizens. He has rejected rational debate and opted out of conversation with the informed, which in my view is the most dangerous game any political leader can play.

By the end of the 1998 election, I hoped that the 'two nations' of Australia would begin a conversation. I saw rural and regional Australians as a minority in their country, like many ethnic groups are. I thought what they were really demanding were 'special benefits' just like other minorities, and not 'equal rights for all Australians' as they claimed. I thought they deserved special treatment. But the opportunity for conversation and consensus was not taken. Instead, Hansonite social concerns have become central to Australian political debate.

When Labor leader Kim Beazley ended Labor's commitment to Aboriginal land rights by backing the Queensland Labor government's modification of the right to negotiate—for purely political reasons (that One Nations vote again)—and then ran dead on the United Nations human rights debate, I felt that the worm had turned. Now the 'politically correct' Australians—those who saw tolerance and acceptance of difference as central to Australia's identity—are the new oppressed minority. Neither major party represents us any more. We have been forced to the Democrats and the Greens. So much for engagement. Instead of talking and working together after the Hanson shock wave, the political establishment has just replaced the hegemony of one group with another.

I want to go back to the beginning.

In launching my book on Pauline Hanson's 1998 election campaign last year, Jana Wendt noted that the general havoc the Hanson phenomenon caused in the community was more than matched by the specific chaos she caused in the media.

> How to deal with her? Should she be laughed off the stage or was she a serious political force? Should she be reported in the same way that John Howard and the rest are, or was she a subversive who had to be flushed out of the works for fear that she might undermine a civilised polity? Back in 1996, many media outlets opted at first to ignore her in the fervent hope that she would implode or more conveniently just fade away. The others, who found her simply irresistible, felt the need to justify their fascination with her by crash-tackling Hanson at every turn. Few dared to authentically engage with her. Fewer still were prepared to write anything other than what their left liberal journalistic peers expected of them.

However, once we'd acted out our instincts on Hanson, we realised that our input only intensified her support; that the very fact that she was under attack by the media became an essential element in her appeal.

That shocking realisation triggered a rare self-consciousness in the media. In some media, news judgement was replaced with political judgment—would running a story help or hinder Hanson? If the editor judged it would help her, it was run small or not run at all; if it would hurt, it was featured, sometimes without the usual checking. This attitude, not only anti-democratic but also self-defeating (the public really aren't that dumb and we'd better get used to it) led to an extraordinary judgment by Brisbane's daily, the *Courier-Mail*, in the last week of the federal election campaign. An unprecedented attempt by One Nation to have police arrest the media was run in a single column on page eleven. While most media outlets believed the incident would help One Nation, itself a startling acknowledgement of the odour in which the media is held, the TV news led with it and the *Herald* and the *Age* ran the story on page one. Laurie Oakes, in accord with conventional wisdom, said in his report that the media had played into One Nations hands.

The *Courier-Mail*, after burying the story, then grotesquely ran a comment piece predicting that because of the media's behaviour One Nation would win six to eight Lower House seats. In other words, the paper openly admitted the importance of the story it buried, and chose to lecture the media on how it should have made a political judgment not to demand access to the costings document it was promised. As it happened the *Courier-Mail*'s judgment was wrong, and Hanson's support remained stable. But then, the media so often gets it wrong in picking public reaction, don't we? We've become specialists at it.

I don't want to single out the *Courier-Mail* for criticism here— my paper was as guilty as any other of being caught out on Hanson. When Hanson made her maiden speech in September 1996, I was chief of staff at the *Herald* Canberra bureau, and unsuccessfully argued that her speech should not be reported at all. I also had a personal policy of refusing to speak to Hanson's then adviser, John Pasquerelli, and not to write news stories about Hanson or her party. I even quietly cheered when watching violent protests at formation meetings of One Nation.

I was wrong. Most of us were wrong. The shock waves of the Hanson phenomenon had lessons not only for the political establishment but also the media. The media's roller-coaster ride with Pauline Hanson was a perfect starting point for our industry to engage in a most unusual exercise—self-reflection. It could, if we so chose, be used to focus the vague, cloudy certainty of all of us that the media isn't quite doing its job, that our readers, listeners and viewers aren't happy with what they're getting from us, and that we are losing relevance as a result.

Dick Morris, former spin-doctor to president Clinton, said in his book *The New Prince: Machiavelli for the 21st Century* that 'the media play the key role in bringing the private pains and needs of real people to public attention'. This role, along with its corollary— to scrutinise the powerful to ensure they are telling the people the truth—is the reason we have a privileged role in a democracy. The Hanson phenomenon exposed it as unfulfilled.

Why did the media and the politicians get such a shock at the appeal of Hanson's populism? And even after the bombshell she threw at us, why was the media again caught embarrassingly short at the recent Victorian election, when the country moved so strongly to Labor?

The incident that first pricked my conscience on this point was a letter from a listener to 'Late Night Live', Ms Susan Leembruggen. She was responding to my passionate advocacy of an independent Fairfax on the ABC program 'Late Night Live'.

My advocacy focused on the need for diversity of news and views, and for the freedom of some parts of the press from ownership by big businessmen with their own barrows to push. Ms Leembruggen attacked my argument on the basis that none in the press—independent or otherwise—were doing their real job anyway.

I quote from my book:

> You have lamented the so-called Pauline Hanson phenomenon, saying that Queenslanders are mostly good, tolerant people—amongst other such patronising comments. Both you and Phillip expressed your contempt and dismay over the consequent rising tide of social discontent—*inter alia* racism and its perceived concomitant, unemployment. On Monday night you spoke with passion and conviction about media ownership and the importance of maintaining the Fairfax newspaper as the last chance for some kind of impartial freedom of speech.

Yet what was the point of a free press, she asked, when the media had not addressed the real issues of the day—anxiety about unemployment and the disenfranchisement of large sectors of society through diminution of standards of living?

'This media neglect is a significant factor in the rise of Hansonism,' she wrote. 'Instead of academic arguments about Aussie tolerance and fair play' (remember 'tolerance' really means apathy, not acceptance) and the sense of abhorrence which goes with racism, you could more productively question the status quo in this country that gives rise to division and bigotry.'

In short, Hansonism was partly the media's fault for failing to act as the interface between the people and the powerful, and for turning our backs on the public to become just another part of a complacent establishment.

I was sufficiently disturbed to reply to Ms Leembruggen, and I wish I'd kept a copy so I could remember what rationalisation I used. But what finally pushed me into focusing on Hansonism was the Newspoll halfway through the 1998 Queensland election campaign, which showed that Maryborough, my hometown, could fall to One Nation. Had I really lost touch with my roots to such an extent that I could not understand, let alone empathise with, the mood of Maryborough? Studied avoidance of Hansonism became an obsession to work it out.

After a unique experience covering Pauline Hanson's campaign, my views on journalism and its future will never be the same. In the 1996 campaign, I was depressed at its studied stage management—it was an exclusive pantomime in which only the politicians and the media could play. On Hanson's campaign in 1998, the media became chasers and had to fight for its right to be present, as all the rules of etiquette and self-interest were thrown out the window, and the people—God forbid—took centre stage.

I describe in the book the media pressures and split second judgments—some wrong in retrospect—which resulted. A major reason I wrote the book was to describe what happened when the rules that have imprisoned us were disregarded, and thus hopefully open up debate on a possible 'third way' between all rules and no rules.

Coming out of the campaign, I was convinced that the health minister, Michael Wooldridge, was correct in his essay on the rise of Hansonism in the 1998 book *Two Nations* when he wrote:

> Why this malaise in the relationship between power and people? This is an Australia of two cultures, which have little in common and find it hard to understand or appreciate each others views and attitudes. The 'policy culture' sees 'the community culture' as uneducated, ignorant, backward and occasionally comic in its primitive beliefs. The community culture sees the policy culture as arrogant and divorced from reality. The policy culture often sees the community culture as a barrier to the better future it is trying to build, and views with suspicion and contempt political leaders who pander to the concerns of the backward mass. The community culture sees the policy culture as responsible for the mess were in, and sees political leaders as captives of the narrow elites, governing for the noisy few and ignoring the real people.

To the community culture, the quality media seems part of the elite, and is treated accordingly. Some elements of the tabloid media simply exploit fears and distrust and feed off them. It seems to me that the media groups which wish to serve their 'elite readership' should be striving to report and understand the community culture, because if the two cultures continue to drift apart, the elites will suffer in the end. That's the self-interested motive to examine our role and how we are fulfilling it. The idealistic motive is to help restore a coherence and common purpose among Australians, so the media deserves its place as an institution central to democracy.

Wooldridge's analysis seems to rely heavily on Canadian philosopher John Ralston Saul. His definition of 'the elite' in *The Doubters Companion* should, I believe, be required bedtime reading for all our elites, including the media, because in the end, it can only be the elites who are to blame for Hansonism. Ralston Saul wrote:

> Every society has an elite. No society has ever been without one. The thing elites most easily forget is that they make no sense as a group unless they have a healthy and productive relationship with the rest of the citizenry. Questions of nationalism, ideology, and the filling of pockets aside, the principal function of an elite is to serve the interests of the whole. They may prosper far more than the average citizen in the process. They may have all sorts of advantages. These perks won't matter so long as the greater interests are also served. From their point of view, this is not a bad bargain. So it really is curious just how easily they forget and set about serving only themselves, even if it means that they or the society will self-destruct.
>
> There is no reason to believe that large parts of any population wish to reject learning or those who are learned. People want the best for society and themselves. The extent to which a populace falls back on superstition or violence can be traced to the ignorance in which their elites have managed to keep them, the ill-treatment they have suffered and the despair into which a combination of ignorance and suffering have driven them.

As I said in the book:

> Now easy-going, 'egalitarian' Australia had its own unique brand of far right populism feeding off disgust with our elites. In our version we had a female leader and an

amateur at politics, which had made her both easier to pull apart and much harder, since Pauline's People, despite everything, admired her refusal to abide by the rules and her dogged insistence on coming back for more. Surely it was the duty of the elites to solve the causes of Hansonism, because Hanson was only the symptom, not the disease. After all the anger and pain of Hansonism, that was the lesson I felt I'd learned from her campaign. Pauline's People felt they no longer understood their society and what it was for, and many of them felt they were being told they no longer belonged to it. They couldn't make head or tail of the political discourse, and no one could explain it to them or even wanted to, let alone help them join the brave new world their elites insisted was inevitable.

So what could the media do to assist in restoring a real national conversation, and to heal the misunderstandings and resentments in our society? We all expect our politicians to adjust, but what about us?

Let's start with election campaigns. What on earth do we think we're doing thinking we've covered a campaign if we follow around the leaders and try and find a gaffe in their manipulative image making? That process not only locks out voters, it is more and more irrelevant to them.

Nicolas Rothwell's reports in the *Australian* during the 1998 campaign show the way ahead. He travelled the country talking to all sorts of people, and tried to distill themes and moods from those grassroots contacts. The standard gambit of going to an electorate for a day or two and reporting it is now drab and meaningless, and as formulaic, as most other election coverage. We really do have to connect with reality, and that takes time and effort.

I'd like to see the *Herald* send a reporter to two marginal seats— one in the city and one in the country—for the whole campaign. They would live there, get the daily direct mail, get to know the candidates and the electorate, and file daily reports. The reporters would thus be actually experiencing the campaign on the ground, and their position would also make them ideally placed to see what both parties actually saw as the main issues on the ground. Readers would get to know the main grassroots players quite intimately, as well as the lives of their voters. Reporters would also, like the voters, be on the outside looking in when the leaders' road shows visited, and be able to judge far more accurately their impact where it counts—on the ground.

Between elections, I'd like to see specialist reporters in the press gallery spend at least three months a year observing how their specialties play out on the ground. Immigration specialists could visit immigration centres for example, education reporters schools and universities, health reporters public and private hospitals. Now, we have a separation of abstract policy and the politics of it in Canberra, from the working realities covered by others, often without the big picture policy expertise. We need to connect policy and practice much more directly.

More radically, I think there's place for reporters to live for extended periods away from their middle-class lives. After the election, my editor gave me permission to live in Bourke for three months. The idea was to observe and report black-white relations and the difficulties and challenges of life in the country first-hand, I backed out of the plan when One Nation started a regular smear campaign against me on their website, for fear that I might be targeted for abuse, but I hope to try such an experiment sometime. One of the common complaints of political reporters, including myself, is that many grassroots groups can't give us a useable quote quickly, but seek time to discuss the matter between themselves. I am starting to think that instead of constantly demanding that real people meet our demands, it might be time for us to reach out and adjust to the way they operate.

There is also an urgent need for the media to make itself accountable. We spend so much time enforcing accountability on other establishment institutions; it is becoming increasingly untenable that our own house is in total disorder. Heaven forbid that the State regulate our behaviour, but really, surely we have an obligation to do so ourselves, if only to begin to restore our credibility with readers.

The *Herald* is now finalising a code of ethics, written by a committee of journalists, which will be published in the paper. The method of reader complaint is still under discussion, but I would like to see us appoint an ombudsman modelled on that position in the *Washington Post*, with regular columns from him or her responding to complaints and suggestions.

I also believe that the days when editors could refuse to report the media, its excesses, and the publics concerns with its behaviour on the basis that all this is just 'navel gazing' are nearing an end. The public is well aware that the media is not an impartial observer, but a major player. They want to know how the game works, and to critique it. To me, there is no excuse for the *Herald* not to have its version of 'Media Watch', and I am amazed that the *Australian*'s media magazine has not taken the plunge. I would like to see the *Herald* solicit readers' queries, and complaints about media behaviour, and reply to them in print. This step alone would help force us to examine ourselves, as well as help convince readers that we exist for them. If the public have faith in us, they will support us when our freedoms face erosion. If they don't, the State will find it much easier to constrain us.

At the press council, a complainant usually faces a newspaper executive with no knowledge of the story in dispute, who fudges and prevaricates in arrogant fashion. This only adds to the public perception that the media is a faceless octopus. I would like to see the reporter front instead, and engage with the reader. Having done this myself late last year, I found that the public members of the council had little or no idea of the pressures or constraints faced by a journalist, or the politicians' codes it is the political reporters job to deconstruct. Although the complainant lost his case, we shook hands at the end of it, and he was satisfied both that he had a fair hearing, and that the reporter was a human being who wanted to communicate with him.

In its review of my book, the *Courier-Mail* said it should not have been written. According to the paper, the book showed that I had lost 'objectivity', whatever that is, and had become 'too close' to my subject—as if the purpose of political journalism was not to get as close as the politician will allow. Is telling the truth about how journalism was practised on the campaign so frightening that it should be censored? Aren't Australians allowed to look each other in the eye any more?

There is much in my behavior in the campaign to be critiqued, and many journalists will profoundly disagree with my approach. But surely, if the book does create a debate on how journalism should be practised, that can only be a good thing. The time has come for journalists to abandon their raincoats of self-protection—

the myth of 'objectivity' for example—which serve only to stop debate in its tracks without engagement with the realities of journalism. Only if we are honest with ourselves and our readers can we adjust to the demands of the new millennium.

But has there been a real debate since the 1998 federal election? I believe that most mainstream media is still not listening, either to its chattering classes or its redneck readerships. Both groups now, on several fronts, have the same concerns, but the media is not seeing the significance of this, let alone reporting it.

There are two recent examples. This year, the Coalition and Labor did a cosy little deal to pass a law giving the prime minister the power to call out the troops to any State or Territory, without their request or even permission. No cause for such action was stated, so industrial disputes and civilian protests were included. Troops were given the right to search and seize, block off streets, and even shoot to kill.

The issue created not a ripple in the Canberra press gallery. My attention was drawn to the story when I began receiving emails from readers of my *Herald* online column setting out the proposed law and asking how this could possibly be true?

Herald reporter Toni O'Loughlin was interested, and began reporting the story. We were the only major newspaper to do so. Lo and behold, our readers were outraged, and the mail flooded in. John Laws asked Greens senator Bob Brown—who was running a sophisticated one-person campaign to amend the laws—onto his program for the first time. It was incredible, the John and Bob show. Laws even invited Brown back soon after, and publicly endorsed Brown's stand. Lo and behold, the sole One Nation senator, Len Harris, backed Brown all the way. The far Left and far Right were as one, and a whole lot of people in the middle agreed with them.

Grassroots feeling drove this story and deeply embarrassed the Labor Party, which was forced (partly due to union pressure) to reverse its public support for the bill and seek amendments.

The second example concerns the Melbourne protests outside the World Economic Forum. The unions were scared they would be implicated in violence and lose public support, but marched anyway. Peter Reith predicted union violence in the streets. There was none. What will the Hansonites make of this—the horrible unionists as core supporters of civilising economic globalisation?

Who will the Hansoiites relate to in this battle for the streets of Melbourne? My guess is the protesters.

Who organised these protests? Young people with all sorts of wild and woolly causes, operating outside the mainstream media. And what did the baby-boomer writers of the major papers do? Screamed cheap abuse at their successors, who have emulated the protest culture of the 1960s in a much less classist way. Sure, the only thing that unites the protesters is an emotional antipathy to the effects of economic globalisation. Just like the Hansonites. But that emotion is powerful, and is forcing the rich-list in world capital to listen, and to adjust. We must report this matter without malice or condension to remain relevant.

Two years on from Hanson's defeat, the media has got much better at reporting issues of importance to country people, but is still just as blind to some of the needs and concerns of its readers. The identity of our nation is being reshaped as we speak, and write. Our job is to understand and report these changes. Let's start doing it.

S11

John Birmingham

His lips were, dare I say it, unAustralian. They were lavishly, almost lasciviously pink, and seemed unnaturally full, as though injected with collagen in the minutes before going to air. His hair was blonde, and maybe thinning a little, but not ruinously so. Just enough, perhaps, to lend a little gravitas to an otherwise childish face. His eyes shone, but with a synthetic flicker. They were like lovingly polished marbles which threw off the blaze of the studio's high powered lighting. He seemed to pause before speaking, just long enough for a smirk—I was sure it was a smirk—to form on those curiously feminised lips.

'So much for nonviolence,' he read.

I actually gasped. I had been prepared for something special, this being Packer's network after all. But the arrogance, the contempt and the reflexive, unthinking stupidity compressed into that fleshy pink smirk and those four brief words were still literally breathtaking. The news reader was two or three pars into his lead story, the first morning of the S11 protest in Melbourne, before I recovered sufficiently to follow what he was saying.

Violence had flared, angry scenes had broken out, clashes had erupted between demonstrators and police. A sixteen-year-old code cutter could have hacked up a simple piece of software to generate the story from a database of network-approved phraseology. It might have been a little more challenging to load the computer-generated script with the appropriate subtext, a narrative of brave, beleaguered officers standing fast against a violent threat to civilised society. But it wasn't that subtle a subtext, so I'm guessing it could be done. And the news reader, with his eyes of glass and the heart of a tape recorder? Could he also be replaced by a cgi construct? A third or fourth generation Max Headroom to give protohuman expression to his ultimate owner's will to power. It would certainly be more efficient, more economically rational, and less harmful to the immortal souls of those currently forced by their lucrative contracts to utter such malicious bullshit as, 'So much for nonviolence.'

I doubt these thoughts bothered my pink-lipped friend though. He sailed on with a sort of spiteful cheeriness, throwing to vision of a flying wedge of police officers ploughing into a seething, screaming mass of protesters. The cops were attempting a rescue of WA premier Richard Court who had unwisely decided to emulate Bob Askin by 'driving over the bastards'. Unfortunately the bastards had surrounded his vehicle, cutting it off and subjecting the occupants to a sustained barrage of abuse and anti-mandatory-sentencing graffiti. One Aboriginal activist mounted the bonnet and danced a jig while informing Court he was under citizen's arrest for state crimes against indigenous people. The premier, he announced, now knew how the country's first inhabitants felt, being held to ransom for 200 years.

It was a wild scene, as baton charges always are, but it was unrepresentative. Most of the first day actually passed off without significant conflict, as the police struggled to counteract the fluid tactics of the blockaders. Mobile phones and message runners gathered reinforcements to any point where it seemed the blockade might fail. Horses were ineffectually deployed against picket lines, which had been trained to close up against them, leaving no gaps for the mounted police to break through. No central authority existed to organise the dozens of disparate groups which composed S11 and that lack of a command structure seemed to unhinge the police response. A number of megaphone-wielding enthusiasts from the International Socialists, the Democratic Socialist Party and its youth wing Resistance did try with varying success to marshal numbers into a couple of flash points, but many of the anarchically inclined protesters reacted as badly to their demands as they did to the cops'.

Despite the emphasis on conflict which dominated the mainstream news coverage, the reports of hundreds of eyewitnesses which quickly flooded onto the internet spoke of hours of inactivity, punctuated by shorts bursts of intense turbulence at isolated locations where forum delegates attempted to run the barrier. These moments provided the sound and fury on which television reporters insist if they are to have a story worthy of air time. They constituted only a fraction of the day's content however, with thousands of people protesting peacefully while trying to stay dry in the morning's downpour. Streakers against globalisation jogged past a swami-for-justice sitting on a bed of nails. Christians prayed, and true believers from One Nation railed against worldwide conspiracy as dreadlocked forest dwellers broke out the drums, rolled some joints and got jiggy with it.

The baton charge to rescue Court, in which one man lost seven teeth, provided much of the broadcast media action. The balance was down to one freelance guardian of the forum delegates' right to assembly—who sailed into a knot of picketers, windmilling his fists until taken to the ground with a bloody nose—and a group of three men tagged as neo-Nazis by some witnesses, and casino security by others. They attacked a thin line of protesters after a brief conversation with nearby police. One was alleged to have used a set of keys held inside his fist as a weapon.

The media, which had been indecently tumescent at the prospect of a week of Seattle-style street warfare just before the Olympics in Sydney, seemed unable to deconstruct their own imagery. Having composed a narrative in which foreign activists joined forces with domestic nutters to sabotage Australia's fifteen minutes of fame, many journalists and almost all commentators were incapable of understanding a simple premise. The vast majority of protesters were, in fact, nonviolent. Many had been trained in nonviolent dissent. Just as many had extensive experience of nonviolent protest. For all of their fearsome imagery, for all of the savage, howling mayhem of protest, the violence, when it came, was initiated by the agents of authority, not by the dissenting citizenry. Citizens do not launch baton charges or mounted attacks. They are the targets of baton charges and mounted attacks.

Allegations of protester villainy did surface, with the *Age* retailing instances of 'fish hooks being dangled from bridges to try to disable police; nuts and bolts being thrown at police; and ball bearings being thrown under police horses' hooves'. The Nine network also carried a story of unidentified anarchists invading an ambulance and assaulting the crew. At no time however, were any of these allegations proved. Indeed, no evidence in support of them was even advanced. No urine-soaked police uniforms were produced. No assaulted ambulance drivers were interviewed. No dangling fish hooks were ever photographed despite the presence of hundreds of still and video cameras. A horse which was supposed to have been stabbed turned out to have a grazed nose, according to police media (most likely sustained in a charge against a picket-line full of vegetarian animal rights activists).

This crucial disconnection between the world of real things and the world of fantastic narrative was to prove disastrous as the week progressed. With somewhere between one and two-thirds of conference delegates barred from the casino on the opening day, the rhetoric of press and electronic coverage shifted from a sort of pre-emptive *schadenfreude* to spluttering, belligerent outrage. Tabloid attack dogs and Victorian premier Bracks alike called on the police to bring down the hammer. The protesters were 'unAustralian' (even 'unVictorian') and therefore seemingly unentitled to the due regard of those authorised to use deadly force on behalf of the society they had so publicly betrayed and embarrassed. Bracks was reported to have said that the protesters deserved everything they got. Although he did not elaborate on whether these deserving victims of muscular law enforcement also included those hundreds of school students, previously characterised as innocent victims of a Resistance recruiting campaign, who were also in attendance. Apparently, in crossing over the Rubicon of civil disobedience, they too became unAustralians and thus unworthy of any previous concern for their wellbeing.

I suppose I should guard against a hint of outrage entering my tone. Weary resignation would be more appropriate. For what happened at S11 is an old, old story and I have both heard and written it many times before; in Queensland through the 1980s, at Aidex in Canberra at the turn of the decade, at any number of places in the last ten years—Coffs Harbour, Sydney, Parliament House, the waterfront. I have seen enough political violence to know that far from being unAustralian, it is in fact completely banal. And that rather than being the result of wild, antisocial renegades, it is almost inevitably an outcome of tactical decisions taken by the police commander on the scene, occasionally at the behest of political interests further up the food chain. I also know, down in my meat, that when the beast is unleashed the most dangerous place to be is not on a police line, but in front of one.

My first encounter with a police riot took place in 1989, at the University of Queensland. I was covering a series of demonstrations on that campus for *Rolling Stone* magazine and was lucky enough to be present when about thirty or forty cops stormed a sit-in. The students knew the raid was coming and had voted to carry on the occupation, but only with volunteers. Most wisely abandoned the building. About a dozen remained. Following the advice of the late Tasmanian war correspondent Neil Davis, that it is always safer to go in with the first wave, I charged in with the cops rather than waiting with the occupiers for them arrive. I wasn't all that surprised at the chaos within. The vicious fights between weedy, underfed college students and Bjelke-Petersen's praetorian guard were predictably one-sided. But I was totally blown out by the sight of one young, probationary constable who was so far gone in the moment, that when he could find nobody to punch, he launched himself at a wall-mounted telephone and ripped it right off its moorings before throwing it to the ground. Perhaps it was an unAustralian telephone.

After that I made the study of police officers during violent demonstrations something of an avocation. I travelled to the National Exhibition Centre in Canberra for the infamous Aidex Arms Fair riots, which I still regard as the most frightening police rampage I have ever personally witnessed. For three days I slept under a bush in a ditch by the side of the road while a medieval caravan of greenies, ferals, vegans and communists fed themselves into a threshing machine. I saw one cop shoot his entire wad, his eyes rolled back to whites, thin lips drawn back from his teeth in a canine grimace as he flayed into a knot of hippies with a riot baton. The nightstick was a blur, like a particularly impressive special effect, which conjured up flying clumps of scalp and gouts of blood wherever he cared to lay it. I saw another cop smashing the head of a female reporter from a community radio station into the side of a police wagon as yet another diverted metres out of his way to crack the kneecap of a woman who had broken through the line and was threatening to carry the demonstration a couple of metres closer to the arms manufacturers ensconced within the Exhibition Centre.

This too was another nonviolent demonstration. Like S11, Aidex was a largely unco-ordinated effort by dozens of different groups, most of them green rather than red. Decisions were mediated through a sort of mass fishbowling conference held at the start of each day, with the angry left of the ISO and DSP—or the Socialist Workers Party as I think they still were then—unable to swing the numbers behind a more confrontational approach. Nonviolence was a sort of mantra the majority of protesters invoked to protect themselves from some imagined karmic backlash. It's efficacy against a real world backlash was questionable at best. One of the saddest things I ever saw was a couple of hundred of these poor dumb bastards joining hands and dancing onto the road in front of the Centre, like children playing ring-a-ring-a-rosie. A baton charge broke them up in less than ten seconds, hundreds of blows falling on the exposed forearms of the enchanted circle people while the hard core Left, who had opted out of that particular doomed action, watched on with spastic rage.

I have never known the media, which is always prompt with reports of injury to individual police officers and fictional ambulance drivers, to fully detail the casualties on the receiving end of the baton attack. To wander through the camp outside Aidex each day was to bear witness to hundreds of broken ribs, fingers, wrists and jaws amongst an abundance of livid bruises, weeping wounds and black eyes. At S11, volunteer medical staff toted up a similar butcher's bill. One first aid co-ordinator posted to the indymedia website that on the first day at Crown they treated about 130 protester injuries, sending eleven to hospital by ambulance. On the second day, they tallied another 200, with thirty-one hospitalised, before he stopped counting. Most required stitches to the scalp and face, many from baton strikes to the fingers, kidney, liver and breasts (in the case of women). After being interviewed by a Melbourne newspaper the aid worker was upset to find his figures rounded down to about 'twenty hurt' on both days.

Fortunately the atomisation of reportage by the internet has meant that we are no longer hostage to the likes of Kerry Packer's pink-lipped vassal for accounts of such civil atrocities. Cheap digital recording equipment transformed hundreds of witnesses at Crown into reporters. Even those without access to camcorders could and did post extended personal narratives which invariably contradicted the mainstream media's initial reporting. (After a number of journalists were assaulted by the Victorian police their enthusiasm for Steve Bracks' enforcers was noticeably diminished. By late in the week some had even shifted their rhetorical ground enough to openly speculate on topics such as 'police brutality'. It's amazing how much the change from observer to participant can alter one's perspective on these matters.)

Dozen's of hotlinked websites now carry thousands of pages of first person narrative and video footage from S11. It would be a great pity if this archive were to be lost to future researchers as I believe it is an infinitely more accurate depiction of what happened there.

A.C., writing on the Melbourne indymedia site, captured some of the frustrating but reasonably peaceful tactics of the police. (The following extracts are reproduced verbatim):

> ...the day quietens down, but there is a sense of danger that is more palpable than Monday. A sound system is set up at King's Way on the overpass, which is teaming with people. This afternoon at King's Way, police engage in an exercise of psychological warfare designed to confuse, and tire the remaining crowd. Squads of police change formation, march from one entrance to another, put goggles on, remove goggles, display canisters of capsicum spray, put them away... the dog squad is brought out and lined up inside the compound. Unfortunately for the cops one of the dogs bites his trainer. Riot police march through a foot overpass back and forth from building to building. It works. The crowd expends its energy running from one entrance to another, is revved up by marshals, engages on one boring chant after the next—in other words reacts exactly as to be expected. It's easy to say this in hindsight, of course. At the time, how do you tell the difference between a formation of riot police designed to psyche you out, and a formation of riot police about to charge?

A young woman named Maya, in an article entitled 'How I was clubbed like some baby seal (or, thank god for the black bloc)', described her panic, and what she thought of as her own cowardice when she realised she was the weak link in a picket-line which would soon be targeted. (The 'black bloc' refers to groups of masked anarchists):

> ...then people were hugging me and telling me I wasn't weak, I was strong and asking if I wanted to go further

back or leave altogether. Nothing could have made me leave after that, but a little while later they attacked us and I couldn't hold the line. The truth is, even though I'm not very strong, I wasn't really holding on that tightly. I think I was panicking already. I was panicking. I started panicking the second they moved the Nimbin hippie bus.

…One of the cops hit me in the throat with his baton. I went strait down and thought I would be trampled by the police that were running past our former front line. The cop dragged me up by the neck (throat), which at least stopped me being trampled. I was screaming 'I can't breathe, I can't breathe, you're killing me, you're killing me.' Of course I can't identify him. A lot of the riot cops' masks were compleatly fogged up from their breath.

…After about 30 seconds or less, this cop picked me up and threw me backwards. I don't remember all of this. I know I ended up on the ground with a group of other (mostly) women from the blockade, and a group of at least four or five just went for us. If you could manage to get away, they would drag you back in. During this, one of the uniformed cops bit me. I have tooth marks in my arm. I don't know if this happaned to anyone else. The truth is, I'll never be able to get my head around any of this. At the time he was still yelling 'Get back! get back!' while he was holding on to me to prevent me getting away.

After the cop bit me I was really, really panicking. Either him or another cop picked me up and threw me at the police line. I wasn't really thinking straight at this point, but we could see that if you got too close to the line, they would just beat you and throw you back in. I was terrified of the cops, I was terrified of the horses, I felt like I was about to die. there was no way I could have gotten out of all that by myself.

Someone grabbed me. I don't know who. I think, (I think) he was with the black bloc. I'm pretty sure I saw a mask or balaclava. Maybe I just think that because I couldn't see his face very well.

But this black bloc guy grabbed me and dragged me through the line and no one touched us. I don't even remember how, but he got me out of the fighting. Maybe he saved me from a broken limb. Maybe he saved my life.

Then he left me with someone else and went back into the fighting.

> Thankyou thankyou thankyou thankyou. I hope
> I'm not overdoing it. I hope this is an appropriate forum
> to thank you a billion times and still feel it's not enough. I
> don't think anything is enough...

By the third day of the protest, some mainstream journalists, who realised they may have backed a loser on the opening day, began to log on to the independent sites to access this motherlode of alternative data. It is possible that the net's erosion of the old media cartel, organised around the twin poles of the Murdoch and Packer empires, influenced the eventual response of both the cartel and the State. Just as some of the media at last changed tack in the face of a terrible and sustained assault on a small group of dissenting citizens, so too was the political superstructure forced to adjust to a new reality. Steve Bracks began the week by claiming that the protesters deserved everything they got and finished it by inviting the heroes of the emergency services to a State-funded barbecue. But he was soon forced to withdraw the invitation after sections of his own party sided with the churches in condemning the actions of the police. Even the forum delegates began to get the message. Those who managed to attend the first day's much depleted sessions had to accept that theirs may not be the only story worth hearing.

It may be argued then that the violence at Crown had a positive, heuristic effect. Had the protests taken the form preferred by critics like Bracks, Court, and Bob Carr—that is had they been nothing more than a meaningless piece of irrelevant street theatre which had no discernible effect on the lives of the conference goers— they would have been contemptuously ignored. That is the subtext whenever a politician supports the 'right to protest' as long as it doesn't interfere with the legitimate concerns of others—I think 'people going about their business' is the preferred phrase. To label anyone who demurs from that line as unAustralian is an attempt to define them out of civil society. In the past this proved easier because of a commonality of interest between the owners of the means of communication and the State which protected their interests. (And because those threatening that arrangement were often so easily demonised anyway.) It may prove less so in future with the web providing the demons with their own means of mass communication.

The use of the term 'unAustralian' seemed to cause nearly as much anger online as the tactics of the police. More than one internet correspondent drew out the hypocrisy of political leaders trying to shame the demonstrators for violence which was actually the chosen strategy of the State itself. Australian history is debauched with violence; the institutionalised savagery of the convict era; the massacres of both black and white on the frontier in the nineteenth century; the slaughter at the Eureka Stockade; the anti-Chinese pogroms on the gold fields; the street wars of the Depression between fascist and communist private armies; the civil rights demonstrations in Queensland; the vicious attack by New South Wales police on Sydney's first gay Mardi Gras. These were all defining moments in Australian history, occasions when the nation's cultural narrative stopped and turned and lurched off in a new direction, driven by violent impetus towards light or dark, but always onwards, never back.

The Parties are Over

Paul Sheehan

The old political divides of Australia—between class, between left and right, between city and bush—have become so fluid as to be outdated, even banal. Compulsory voting is propping up an illusion. Behind the illusion, behind the surface opera of politics, the foundations of traditional Australian politics are rotting away. 'It's as unstable a situation as I've ever seen in Australian party politics,' says Bill Bowtell, a veteran of many political campaigns. Bowtell is a long-time reader of polling data and pulse-taker of the zeitgeist, and remains a lunch companion and confidante of Paul Keating.

'I believe the Australian political tradition is now at risk,' says Professor Ian Marsh, of the Australian School of Management. 'Twenty years ago, political party identification was very strong— about 90 percent. Now it's down to half that, about 46 percent. Our political structure is starting to look like the 1900-09 period, when we had much looser groupings and the great divide in politics was free trade versus protectionism... The whole point of the party system was to aggregate the various interest groups, but with the new pluralism in Australia we are seeing the disaggregating of interest groups.'

The great fault line in Australian politics is no longer between city and bush. It is much bigger than that. A gap is growing between the governors and the governed. A record number of votes were cast against the major parties at the 1998 federal election, a detachment masked by the compulsory preferential voting system which saw most of the votes eventually flow back to the big parties. But the major parties are no longer grassroots movements; they no longer reflect the mainstreams they purport to represent. Big-money donors have never been more important to their survival. In the past year, the Liberal Party has allowed a tobacco giant, Philip Morris, to sponsor its national convention and the Australian Labor Party is charging corporations $2,200 for 'unique access' to its politicians at the New South Wales State conference.

At the top of the political pyramid, John Howard has so far outdistanced two Labor legends, Paul Keating (who was prime minister for four years, two months and twenty days) and Joseph Benedict Chifley (four years, five months and seven days), and will soon outlast Andrew Fisher and Alfred Deakin. If he wins a third term, only Robert Menzies and Robert Hawke will be ahead of him. It sticks in the craw of many, many Australians that a man so devoid of charisma is being carved into the wall of Australian history. But what inspirational figure would go into politics today? What sort of man or woman would want to run the gauntlet of a news media so omnivorous, so self-referential, so casual in its violence?

At the bottom of the political pyramid a very different history is being written. John Howard's party is dying. Literally dying. More than 80 percent of Liberal Party members in New South Wales are over the age of fifty-five. Almost two-thirds of the membership is aged sixty-five or older. The ranks are not just ageing. Figures given to me from inside the party show that membership in the largest State branch, New South Wales, has dropped from 50,000 in 1975 to a rump of about 6,000 active members now. 'The energy seems to be draining away from our party,' says Joy Clayton, a Liberal stalwart and active branch member. 'We go to functions and the numbers are down. We have meetings and not much gets discussed. And we're getting a lot older.'

For years Joy Clayton has attended party meetings at the Rose Bay RSL with a dwindling band of regulars who mostly came to the party in the 1950s. They meet in a grey upstairs conference room.

> Years ago we used to have big meetings at the Royal Motor Yacht Club and we'd have 200 people. Now we're lucky to get thirty-five, even less in winter because some of the elderly find it too difficult to get there. It's disheartening

to see people disappearing one by one. Most of the members
are over sixty. The same people come to meetings year after
year, and we get no new blood... The last party conference
we had was a debacle. The few Young Liberals we have
spent all their time infighting. People don't want to belong
to political parties any more. Where is the camaraderie,
the social aspect of it all, the sense of nation-building?

These are big questions and the party does not know the answers.
'If we continue to preach to an ageing, ever-dwindling group, what
future do we have,' asks a former national president of the Young
Liberals, Jason Falinski (and one of the infighting Young Liberals
Joy Clayton was referring to). 'Every year we spend $1.2 million on
membership services while receiving only $400,000 in membership
fees. We have fewer members than we have ever had before, but
more branches than we have ever had... The Liberal Party in New
South Wales does not practise what it exhorts others to do. Some
branch structures exist for the sole purpose of supplying
delegateships to factional warlords.'

The Liberals have started paying people to man polling booths
at elections. They lost their one populist, Jeff Kennett, when he
crashed and burned in the 1999 Victorian election. They even lost
Kennett's seat, with a 10 percent swing, in a by-election after he
vacated politics. On 25 March 2000, the Liberal Party completed a
clean sweep of electoral debacles in Australia's three largest
population centres when Labor won 70 percent of the wards in the
Brisbane council elections, trouncing the Liberals by 55 percent to
35 percent in the primary vote across the socio-economic spectrum.
With five marginal seats held by the Coalition in the greater Brisbane
region, the Howard government could almost fall at the next
election because of Queensland alone.

'The Liberal Party no longer has traction in Australia's three
largest cities,' says Bill Bowtell. 'The whole small-l liberal wing of
the party is evaporating. Compare their power base today with the
1960s when the Liberals held most of the seats in Sydney and
Melbourne and Labor was scaled back to a working-class rump.'

Labor is not a working-class rump any more. It is not even working
class. The party has become what Arthur Calwell, its last blue collar
leader, feared it would become: *The time is coming when we will
either be a socialist party or we will finish up as a muddle-minded, middle-*

class, petit-bourgeois, status-seeking party. Labor has won big State election victories in New South Wales, Victoria and Queensland on the back of the Sauvignon Blanc socialists and is well-placed to complete a sweep of all the big political prizes in Australia by winning the next federal election.

But once again the surface is deceiving. The same big questions that hang over the Liberal Party are hanging over Labor. Why belong to a political party when all the action in politics has shifted to special interest groups? And how healthy is a party whose grassroots are withering? Labor's bastion, the union movement, now represents just 25 percent of the workforce. Only one in five employees in the private sector workforce belong to a union. The ALP has shrunk from being a mass political party to a political club.

Its top federal leaders—Kim Beazley, his deputy, Simon Crean, and the Left's factional chieftain, Martin Ferguson—are all the sons of former ALP politicians. They are among the large group—ten federal MPs—who are the children of former Labor politicians or union powerbrokers. This club looks after its own. Forty percent of the ALP's federal parliamentary party are former ministerial staffers. Fifty percent are former union officials while only four percent are former tradesmen. Labor's grassroots numbers are bogus, the result of years of large-scale, ritualised branch stacking. The secretary of the New South Wales ALP, Eric Roozendaal, has complained that big branches, like the federal seat of Fowler, supposedly have thousands of members but can't staff their polling booths.

'$5000 buys 300 members,' says Graham Hudson, a political science lecturer at Melbourne University. 'We have built a system of tinpot fiefdoms manipulated by second-rate people,' says John Button, the former Labor cabinet member and a famous cleanskin. Labor's ethnic strategy is also in tatters. The rampant use of ethnic branch-stacking has generated tremendous ill-will inside Labor's blue-collar constituency and trenchant criticism from party reformers such as John Button and Mark Latham. Andrew Theophanous, the former chairman of Labor's parliamentary committee on immigration, is facing twenty-seven charges of bribery resulting from an immigration scandal. A former Labor councillor, Phuong Ngo, once the leader of one of the ALP's largest branches, has just been tried, and survived a deadlocked jury, on charges of orchestrating Australia's first political assassination (the 1994 shooting of State Labor MP John Newman). Ngo is to be retried.

Labor's vulnerable underbelly, its elitism, has been mined by one of the federal government's hard men, Tony Abbott, the minister for employment services, who has lampooned the party over its 'hereditary peers' in safe parliamentary seats. 'The great democratic achievement of the Labor Party was to put the prime ministership within the grasp of wharf labourers and engine drivers. But if Ben Chifley were an engine driver today, he certainly wouldn't become a Labor Party MP because only full-time officials seem to have the capacity to work the numbers for pre-selection. There are only three current Labor MHRs who weren't union officials, political staffers or public sector employees before entering parliament and two of them were lawyers with union practices.'

'The fact that the current federal House of Representatives contains MPs who started their working lives as cane-cutters, itinerant meat workers and crocodile shooters, and these are all Coalition members, is a sad reflection on how Labor has become the new Establishment.' Abbott worries aloud that a political class is emerging, from both sides of politics: 'The biggest threat to Australia's political stability is not dissension over economic policy but the growth of identikit parties appealing to a narrow class of technocrats.'

While Labor and the Liberals have more in common than they would prefer to admit, there remains a very different major party, a true grassroots party, that until recently had as many active members as the Labor and Liberal parties combined—the National Party. 'If we don't have our membership fees we can't survive as a party, that's the difference between us and the Liberals and Labor,' says Helen Dickie, the party's federal president. Before 1982, when it was known as the National Country Party, it was not just a political force, but a social force. Country Party functions had a place in the social life of communities and a tribal claim on the allegiance of the majority of country people. In 1996 the Nationals had 110,000 financial members, compared with about 64,000 Liberals, 57,000 in the ALP, and a mere 6,000 for the Australian Democrats, according to *Australian Political Facts*, (1997).

But 1996 already belongs to the good old days. The entire Hanson phenomenon had not yet even begun until September that year, and it would rock the party to its foundation before it burned out three years later. But the pressures that created the Hanson phenomenon are still there. 'Our membership did decrease dramatically in the 1980s, but it's now on the increase,' says Dickie. The Nationals' grassroots strength began to drop during the 1980s as the rural economy contracted, and dropped again in the 1990s after the party returned to government as the junior partner in the Howard Coalition and ran into the Hanson uprising.

'The great shame of it all is that people don't trust any of the major parties any more,' says Independent MP, Tony Windsor, who increased his already huge majority in a former safe National Party region at last year's New South Wales election. 'People don't trust the process. They don't believe the promises.' Windsor is the bush politician—and former National Party member—who coined the term 'the sandstone curtain' to describe the indifference by the metropolitan coast toward the concerns of the regional hinterland. He tapped this sentiment to win 70 percent of the primary vote as an independent candidate for state parliament and is considering a tilt at the federal seat held by the deputy prime minister and Nationals' leader, John Anderson.

When I asked the Nationals and the Liberals for their party membership totals, neither would supply them—and this from a Coalition seeking greater transparency and accountability in the rest of society. 'We don't release our membership numbers but I can tell you they are holding steady,' said the Liberal Party's godfather and former federal president, Tony Staley. Holding steady? The Liberal Party has been losing members for twenty-five years.

As for the minor parties, they remain just that—minor. The Democrats may harvest an increased vote but it will be by default, or by protest rather than by inspiration. The effect of this stasis on the body politic could be that cynicism and disengagement become entrenched. 'You can cut the hostility towards politicians with a blunt knife; people hate politicians,' says former ALP senator and long-time Labor election strategist John Black. 'It's beyond party politics. It's mostly a question of who's in power.'

This is the most dangerous division of all, because it raises the spectre of a decline in the legitimacy of government and a weakening in civic cohesion. The process is compounded by a ferociously cynical and opinionated news media. Many accomplished people blanch at the prospect of public life because it now involves having to deal with the media's meat grinder. Nor do they want to confront the reality of branch-stacking, the tool favoured by political opportunists.

And Australia is no longer the society of social movements that it used to be.

Membership of religious congregations, charitable organisations, the Red Cross, are generally down. The national network of co-operative societies—grassroots capital formation—has been dismantled.

Australians have taken social cohesion for granted, warns Miriam Dixson, a historian and ALP member for more than forty years. She believes the issue of greatest concern to most Australians—cultural cohesion, social cement—has been buried in an avalanche of generalised negativity in the media and academia. She takes particular exception to the trashing and trivialising of what she terms Australia's 'Anglo-Celtic core culture'.

'If we are really serious about diversity, we must be equally serious about cohesion,' Dixson wrote in *The Imaginary Australian* (UNSW Press). '...[I]t is assumed that the institutional framework and the practices and rights embraced by the civic model will provide all the social cement we are likely to need in the years to come. This logic is frighteningly shallow.'

Frighteningly shallow, and insidiously destructive. But Australia has proved enormously tolerant and adaptive to change. Politics has had to change like everything else. Modern politics is now mostly about polling, and the level of polling is becoming highly sophisticated. The awesome (and costly) polling machine developed by former Liberal president Andrew Robb and current federal director Lynton Crosby is what got the Coalition over the line at the last federal election. And polling is another form of grassroots participation. It just bypasses the party system.

'Policy professionals demand a much higher level of analysis than they previously did or could,' says Jason Falinski. 'The development of information gathering tools, such as the internet, and analytical tools such as econometric modelling, which to most people looks like quantum physics, all mean that an average person is not likely to have the time, much less inclination, to develop policy that can be implemented by government... In the past, if you wanted to enjoy yourself or find out what was going on, you had to go out somewhere.

Now you can sit in front of the television or go on the internet. In 1975, the average time spent watching television was measured in minutes, 83 minutes a day. Now it is measured in hours—six hours per day according to some US studies.'

Television feeds the illusion of community political participation. 'Television makes people feel intimate, informed, busy, a kind of remote-control politics in which viewers *feel* engaged without the effort of actually *being* engaged,' says American communications scholar Roderick Hart.

The arrival of an active medium, the internet, which is increasingly displacing a passive medium, television, suggests that Australia's democratic tradition could be changed by a new form of participatory politics. This process has already been dubbed the Fifth Estate by American political strategist Dick Morris, who for years was a key adviser and pollster to president Bill Clinton. Morris has written a slim but interesting book, *Vote.com*, which argues the internet will do away with participatory democracy in favour of direct democracy.

> The Fifth Estate is a sort of committee of the whole, made up of citizens online... the triumph of people's politics over the power of intermediaries, particularly the power of the press and broadcast media, who make up the Fourth Estate. For the first time since the early nineteenth century, the United States is departing from the Madisonian model of representative government to return to Jefferson's radical concept of direct democracy.

Sounds like majoritarianism.

The emerging technologies already make possible new forms of community building, alliance formation, citizen participation, electoral feedback and even voting. And yes, they also enable new forms of branch-stacking, issue-hijacking, propaganda, hate speech and election fraud. But politics has always been both ugly and glorious.

The protest voters who mobilised behind Pauline Hanson and the demonstrators who massed outside the Crown Casino to blockade the World Economic Forum on the eve of the 2000 Olympics were very different people with overlapping political grievances. Both groups mobilised outside the conventional structures of politics and outside the conventional means of communication. Their greatest common cause was an instinctive fear of rising corporatism and globalisation. We now live in a world where we are told every day that job insecurity is progress. Corporate branding, marketing, positioning and public relations are seeping into every available seam of our daily lives. Spending on what is known as 'below the line advertising'—direct mail, market research, internet marketing, public relations and corporate communications—exploded from $4 billion a year to $14 billion a year in Australia during the 1990s. There is a name for all this: brainwashing.

A lot of people are increasingly restless and unwilling recipients of this relentless tide of corporate propaganda. Somewhere in the alchemy of our society we may be reaching the tipping point of a curdling, inchoate resentment at the massive disparities in income, not just within society, but within corporations.

We've already seen a rolling sequence of grassroots revolts against the prevailing political-corporate-media power structure: the unforseen tsunami that swept away Keating in 1996; the unforseen Hanson uprising of 1998; and the unforseen rout of the Republican referendum in 1999.

An axis of politicians without mass support, big corporations without public trust, and a plutocratic media living inside its own bubble has the smell of oligarchy. If that's the real fault-line emerging in Australian politics, it's going to be interesting to see how the Outsiders react.

The Last Barbarian

Gideon Haigh

Paul Sheehan's desk on level 27 of the John Fairfax headquarters at Darling Harbour is a small but well-positioned fortification overlooking the suite of editorial offices. From here, the *Sydney Morning Herald*'s resident dissident has an unencumbered view of the comings and goings at the seat of power; 'a bit like one of those Kremlin watchers,' says his colleague and friend Spiro Zavos, 'studying who's taking the salute at the May Day Parade.'

In but not quite of; the distance Sheehan preserves between himself and the apparatus of control is something he takes pride in. With proximity to power but not complicity, he can engage with journalism and deplore it simultaneously. He can write long stories for the front page, or hold loud telephone conversations with sympathisers dissociating himself from colleagues of whom he disapproves (like Aboriginal affairs writer, Deborah Jopson). He can discourse eloquently on politics, or despatch terse electronic messages, like one he sent David Marr after a dispute about the origins of the Hanson phenomenon: 'Get fucked.'

He can also savour the celebrity recently his, through last year's publication of *Among The Barbarians*: a wide-ranging critique of what he regards as the canards of the Keating years, from multiculturalism to the doctrinaire rewriting of Australian history. With 80,000 copies sold, it is the most successful Australian non-fiction title in almost twenty years.

Not that Sheehan's preening today. He's beat. He's forty-eight, looks older, suffers a painful back complaint called ankylosing spondylitis, and complains about the *Herald* turning him into a workhorse: 'If Mark Scott [deputy editor] or Peter Frey [news editor] give me the big eye, they know I'm a sucker. I used to run the newsdesk. I know the beast needs red meat every day. But I don't want to be a middle-aged news grunt.' Nonetheless, you sense he's looking forward to being interviewed. When he turns away, you notice that a label on the back of his chair reads: 'Barbarian'. When he turns back, he says: 'You just go for the jugular. Don't hold back.'

*

Not holding back is what *Barbarians* is all about. When he rejoined the *Herald* in January 1996 after a period abroad, Sheehan felt that too many journalists were: 'I was struck by the number and the ill-discipline of the ideological warriors in the media, and how partisan the news pages had become. And my God, I wasn't going to shut up about that.' When *Herald* artist Michael Fitzjames inquired about his intended brief, Sheehan replied simply: 'Thunder.' He scourged the gay lobby, roasted Paul Keating, hammered ethnic bureaucrats, and attracted the attention of Reed Australia's Jennifer Byrne. 'Heck!' she thought. 'This could sell a lot of books.' Sheehan signed to write *Barbarians* in November 1996, and delivered a manuscript in March 1998.

Between times, however, Reed had been engorged by Random House, and lost Byrne, the book's original champion; an inauspicious scenario for any potential author. Even Sheehan's mother didn't fancy *Barbarians*' chances; told the print run would be about 7,000, she worried: 'Wherever will we put them all?' So rather than leave promotion to Random, Sheehan took a DIY approach. Eschewing a formal launch, he spent the money on publicity postcards which he sent to everyone in his Rolodex. He rang old media cobbers—like 2UE's Alan Jones and 2BL's Richard Glover—seeking airtime. And when Sheehan guested on the former's programme at 8.20am on Friday, 22 May, he was literally hours away from one of Australian publishing's greatest success stories.

Jones raved: this 'absolutely magnificent' book, 'brilliantly researched' and 'brilliantly written' by a man 'highly educated with a brilliant mind', was a 'magnificent contribution to the proper and beneficial understanding of Australia'. Sheehan remained unconvinced of its commercial prospects; he actually bought a few copies himself that day. He needn't have: the entire first print run was gone within seventy-two hours.

The way Jones 'made' *Barbarians* has since become part of publishing folklore. Sheehan was duly full of gratitude when he was Jones' guest again three days later: 'It was all due to you... completely and utterly to do with the Alan Jones show'. In fact, this perception may sell the book slightly short. It sold in many places, like Queensland, where it received next to no publicity. And for her part, Callaghan believes 2UE's influence has been overstated: 'I've launched books on the Jones show before, and they've still sunk without trace.' The plain fact is that the very concept of the book was, for whatever reason, overpoweringly appealing to many people, including undoubtedly many who would seldom enter a bookshop.

Jones' encomiums were then echoed in virtually every organ of the metropolitan print media. Les Carlyon's review in the *Age* and *Herald* gushed: 'We need more journalists like Sheehan and fewer stooges'. Paddy McGuinness devoted his *Herald* column to the 'first-rate journalist' who had 'written the manual for the next five elections', Piers Akerman his *Telegraph* column to this 'stand-out' among the *Herald's* 'claque of black armband scribblers'.

The praise, moreover, continues unabated. *Adelaide Review* editor Christopher Pearson regards it as containing 'all sorts of wholesome, important and honest truths about Australia'. Publisher Michael Duffy, who described *Barbarians* in the *Australian* as 'brave, bold and brilliant', is awestruck at its success: 'Most Australian journalists would fear the social ostracism that would inevitabily follow such a book. Obviously for some reason, perhaps to do with his character, of which I know little, that didn't hold Paul back.'

*

Sheehan, though, has scarcely ever held back, even before *Barbarians*. Since joining the *Herald* in September 1975 as a cadet with a 'rickety' political science degree, his has been a restless, questing intellect in search of outlet. Erstwhile *Herald* contemporary Milton Cockburn notes: 'One thing that Paul saw extremely early is that it's the journalist who swims upstream who gets noticed.'

Sheehan had two spells in the US with the *Herald* during the Reagan years—first in New York, then in Washington—and proved one of the newspaper's most versatile and energetic correspondents. When there was a whisper in October 1986 that Malcolm Fraser had turned up *sans* trousers in a Memphis hotel, for instance, it was Sheehan who called forty people in a day and captured the former prime minister's grudging admission: 'I wish I'd never been to Memphis.'

So completely did the US get under Sheehan's skin, in fact, that he stayed there in 1989 rather than return to some cosy editorial sinecure. He moved to New York to live with his partner Susan Wyndham, then correspondent for the *Australian*, now a *Herald* deputy editor. He wrote a novel (unpublished), and tried cutting it as a freelancer, concentrating on his periodical of choice, *Atlantic Monthly*.

For Sheehan, who boasts not having voted since 1975, the non-aligned *Atlantic* represented the acme of journalism: 'It belonged to no party, it was contrarian only if the facts supported it, and it was rigorously researched.' The high standards of fact-checking, indeed, proved almost too rigorous. Sheehan could find time to write only one article in *Atlantic*: 'What Went Right', a consciously contrary celebration of airline deregulation in August 1993. Much the same applied at the *New Yorker*. Sheehan's frustration was immense: 'I had a relationship with the two publications that meant the most to me in the world, and realised I would go broke in writing for them.'

So where else to write the kind of journalism Sheehan admired: fact-rich, independent, 'going where the pack don't go'? One outlet was the 'Spectrum' section of his old paper, for which in May 1995 he published a lengthy essay entitled 'Four Stories The US Media Refuse To Tell.' In tone and content, it is highly anticipatory of *Barbarians*, especially the first stanza concerning interracial crime. In Sheehan's view, black Americans had for thirty years waged a 'Dirty War' of 'violent retribution against white America': in 1992, for instance, almost a million whites had been victims of black crime, and only 132,000 blacks had been white victims. He dismissed rationalisations: 'Apologists for black crime have always argued that such crime is largely economic, not racial; whites have the money while blacks have the poverty. This rationalisation is only partly true. Unfortunately the racist character of the Dirty War is obvious every day in a cascade of large and small animosities.'

In hindsight, Sheehan agrees that the phrase 'Dirty War' was somewhat provocative, but contends he was driven to it by the 'deafening silence, the deafening double standard'. He says: 'There was systematic, widespread violence by blacks in America against whites, and systematic, widspread silence about it... I just felt: "Why is it acceptable for this level of intraracial violence to be going on? Why isn't it is national outrage?"'

The reason, however, may not be quite so sinister. Statistically, because the white population of the US is seven times the size of the black population, crime occuring even in a random pattern will naturally feature many more white victims of blacks than vice versa. In fact, 80 percent of violent crime in the US is intraracial: a point Sheehan initially noted, then seemed to forget about. But don't take my word for it. Consider 'The Crisis of Public Order', an *Atlantic* cover story published two months later, in which Adam Walinsky covered the same issue: 'Most crimes, including 80 percent of violent crimes, are committed by persons of the same race as their victims. However the experiences of blacks and whites diverge in some respects... Blacks and whites are robbed equally—75 percent of the time—by strangers, but as these figures indicate, whites are far more likely to be robbed by strangers of a different race. This result occurs because there are many more white people and many more white victims.' Sometimes, perhaps, double standards are in the eye of the beholder.

*

The sense that double standards exist in Australia—that there are stories or views that journalists find inconvenient to report because of instinctive political affinities, that versions of history are suppressed by historians because of ideological sympathies, that politicians peddle certain policies because it suits their electoral purposes—provides *Barbarians* with much of its moral propulsion. Their existence is thus a fundamental question. And the answer seems to be: it depends on where you're standing.

Michael Duffy believes that tacit understandings discouraging dissenting thought *have* existed in the media, academia and politics: 'I think Paul's book was an answer to forces that were really there. It's quite amusing now that people who were on the Left and who supported Keating in his strident anti-Britishness are now saying: "Oh no, it wasn't as bad as that." Trying to find a strident multiculturalist is like trying to find a Nazi in Berlin in 1946. But they were there, and I don't think we should forget about them.' John Hirst of La Trobe University, whose 'Australia's Absurd History' published in *Quadrant* in March 1991 is probably the most cogent and reasoned critique of multiculturalism published, believes less in a conspiracy than in 'an overanxiety not to give offence to migrants' and that 'Australians should be allowed to be more self-confident about their history'.

But Henry Reynolds of James Cook University, whose histories of the dispossession of Australia's indigenous people have made him the avatar of what has been called 'black armband history', finds nothing unusual in what he's doing. Though Sheehan accuses him of indulging in the 'politics of embarassment' to shame his opponents, Reynolds denies he's out to embarass anyone: 'Although I write about Aboriginal stuff, I've also talked a lot about general Australian history, and thus have spent a lot of time discussing its successes. It *is* an exceptionally successful Western democracy. Yet, on that basis, some want to believe nothing but good about it, out of a juvenile desire for simple niceness, as though criticism might somehow bring the whole edifice down.'

Barbarians' sales might be read as corroborating the perception of double standards: there clearly *was* an undercurrent of dissatisfaction about the reporting of certain points of view that reflected itself in its popularity. But they might also be seen as invalidating it: the book received overwhelmingly favourable comment and prominence. The Sydney Institute's Gerard Henderson says: 'I don't think any author in Australia in the last ten years has received so many free kicks so soon. If I was into conspiracy theories, I'd've said there was a mate's club operating.' David Marr, Sheehan's colleague at the *Herald*, adds: 'What I can't understand is that notion of how badly done by he is. That book was showered with plaudits. The few dissenting voices were confined to obscure journals with academic audiences. If he'd published in the US, there'd've been critics on authoritative platforms ripping it to shreds. We are a far more gentle country, and *Barbarians* was treated very gently.'

Sheehan's own experience of what he regards as censorship is similarly ambiguous. It came in 1997 when he wrote a three-part series on Asian crime and welfare fraud for the *Herald*, which editor John Lyons declined to run. Sheehan recalls: 'He said: "I don't want some little Chinese kid beaten up in the schoolyard because of some thing in the *Herald*." I said: "Well, neither do I." So we got in there and we closed the door, and we had a bit of a rumble... I can't reconstruct the conversation but I can remember two lines of dialogue... I remember saying: "That's a pretty gutless stand." And he said to me: "Well maybe you want to work somewhere else." I said: "Now, wait a minute John, is this professional or personal?" He said: "It's professional." I said: "Well I want to go and fix the stories." He said: "It's just going to play into the hands of racists." I said: "I understand that. As if I didn't notice. I don't want to be the tool of racists".'

The stories, which in Sheehan's words were 'deep sixed', later became the basis of three chapters in *Barbarians*. Sheehan, nonetheless, felt aggrieved: 'After that rather tense little exchange in the editor's office, I thought: "I'm starting to bump up against some limits here".' But when this version of events was put to Lyons, now at the *Bulletin*, it was strongly disputed: 'I read it [the series] in disbelief. Allegations included "Asian immigrants" rorting Medicare, dealing in prescription drugs, obtaining multiple identity papers, saying that Australians are "dogs", stealing electricity, tax avoidance, "massive marriage scams", overstaying their visas, "pilfering on an enormous scale—every conceivable rort and deception is used to beat the system". It wasn't just the allegations that concerned me—the media run a lot of allegations about a lot of people. But these were unsubstantiated apart from a few nameless people. After a three-month investigation, Sheehan's supporting evidence for the Medicare racket was: "In King's Cross recently, two Asian men snatched a wallet... the only missing thing was the Medicare card". He accused an entire Vietnamese family of seven of rorting social welfare. He named the family, but did not seek comment from them. He based his demolition of this family... on the comments of an unnamed former Social Security officer...'

Lyons says that he asked Sheehan for objective documentary verification, from the Tax Office, the police or Medicare. None was forthcoming. 'Apart from a few books people had written saying Chinese immigrants were criminals,' Lyons says, 'he was not able to produce a single piece of documentation supporting his claims... In my view it was poorly-researched. No editor who cared about their paper's reputation would have published this stuff. Not one of the *Herald* editors I spoke to thought the piece was of a standard to be published.'

*

The foregoing argument is important to bear in mind when one examines *Barbarians* itself. The distinguishing characteristic of the reviews was their concentration on the book's symbolic importance: *Barbarians* represented to them an antidote to political cant, the politically correct preachings of journalists, and the ideologically motivated jeremiads of academics. Yet let us momentarily forget the ends, and consider the means.

Sheehan sticks by his book as a 'work of reportage'. Indeed, when I meet him, he throws down a very distinctive gauntlet. He's been reading my work, and has taken the time to peruse my last book. Or at least, knowing that I have some reservations about his sources and use of them, he's read the bibliography and counted its eighty interviews and 140 sources. He says: 'Well, I have to point out to Gideon that I have directly quoted 100 people in *my* book and have 130 sources.' He restates this in a sometimes belligerent twelve-page email to me after our talk, along with an attack on an academic I have spoken to about his work: 'I think these points raise a question: just how selective is your rigour?'

Welcome to another facet of Paul Sheehan: the itemiser. He's visited seventy-five countries. He's written 290 stories for the *Herald* since he returned. He watches birds and ticks them off in his field guide. He has a 'world-class ephemera collection', ranging from baseball scorecards and invitations, to crack vials and acupuncture needles.

The connection is irresistable: *Barbarians* sometimes reads like a 'world-class ephemera collection' of a book. Robert Manne of La Trobe University says: 'I found it quite a strange book. The collection of issues is a very odd assortment. It's a kind of miscellany of unconnected things linked by a polemical intent, to save a mythic Australia from the assaults of ne'er-do-wells and grumblers.' Even John Hirst, who some would regard as a natural fan, says: 'I was hopeful about it, but disappointed. I felt his heart was in the right place but I didn't think he was ever able to develop a coherent case. There's lots of issues taken up, but never really developed.'

Consider Chapter One, 'This Dog Bites': a sort of Australian panorama veering from eucalypts and sheepdog trials to traditional indigenous justice and 'a taste for wattleseed ice cream'. The effect, says *Eureka Street* editor Morag Fraser, is odd: 'What he seems to be trying to do is connect a string of symbolic, iconic and epiphanic moments to make a coherent whole. Some writers can do this very well, like George Orwell in 'Shooting An Elephant', because he does it with really telling observation, and control. But Sheehan just seems to write off the surge of adrenalin he experiences at seeing one of the narks trying to "put Australia down".'

Chapter Two, 'It Wasn't Luck', then attempts to rescue Australian history from perceived encroachments by historical relativists. Not, perhaps, a dishonourable idea. Yet in promoting his concept of 'Australian nativism', says leading historian Professor Stuart Macintyre, Sheehan 'pushes things in a very misleading way.' *Barbarians'* depiction of Federation as a popular nationalist movement, for instance, is 'difficult to sustain and quite ahistorical'. Then there's such assertions as 'Streeton, McCubbin and Roberts fed off the bush to create a distinctive Australian art' (their techniques were French), that 'Australian Rules football was a response to the popularity of soccer among British immigrants' (nobody played soccer here at the time), and that Australians rejected advice from British military authorities that their armed forces be formed to integrate with imperial defence forces (yes, but in 1914 that's exactly what happened). As for Sheehan's contention that 'numerous histories parrot a hatred of Australia', Macintyre says: 'Absolute nonsense.'

Chapter Four, 'Among the Barbarians', is perhaps the book's most contentious section. It revisits the idea Sheehan explored in 'The Dirty War', that of a fixation on white racism to the exclusion of other forms: in this case, the 'dynamic chauvinism' of the Chinese, with special attention on their 'self-interest and cynicism in Australia'. To be fair, Sheehan applauds Chinese cultural drive, which stands to be an Australian 'national asset', and the 'tough, durable, creative seam of Chinese history in Australia'. But you'd be forgiven for missing such qualifications amid generalisations like: 'China has shown itself a superpower with a chip on its shoulder and the Chinese have an enormously long cultural history of regarding non-Chinese as lesser beings.' Manne sees the chapter as characterised by 'exaggeration, slight hysteria and an amazing crudity of thought'. Gerard Henderson believes Sheehan got off lightly for it: 'What he's saying, in effect, is that first generation Chinese can't be democrats in a civil society. And I don't think people here understood quite how offensive that was.'

Sheehan points to his qualifying statement that ethnic Chinese in Australia embrace its 'new nationalism' with different degrees of ardour, and argues that the chapter quotes numerous sources: 'Geremie Barme, Sang Ye, there are twenty people here saying the same thing different ways.' In the email he sends me, he describes my 'hostility' as 'foppish'.

But what do the sources themselves think of their use? Barme of ANU, whose *In The Red: Chinese Contemporary Culture* is cited extensively, describes *Barbarians* as 'incredibly glib', its 'moments of clarity accompanied by huge waves of obfuscation'. Of material taken from his work, he says: 'It's not outrageously distorted, but it's completely decontextualised, to the point of meaninglessness'. Oral historian Sang Ye, whose *The Year The Dragon Came* is also heavily mined, says that he never minds being quoted, but 'would not ever use his [Sheehan's] style to 'cut' or 'edit' the voices of the people I interview.'

*

Sheehan's invocation of 'sources' raises the general issue of his use of academic literature and official statistics throughout *Barbarians*. At times, it's at least a little strange. He observes that journalists are inclined 'to skate over complexity, nuance, moral ambiguity and irresolution'. Yet, especially in trying to build a respectable intellectual argument against recent immigration policies, he often does exactly that.

One technique is to use only those parts of academic findings that support him. On page 123, Sheehan contends: 'The Australian public has not learned about the research of Harvard economists Larry Katz, Richard Freeman and George Borjas, who concluded that immigrants, for their first twenty to twenty-five years in a new country, are a net fiscal drain on society.' This is hyperbole: the Australian public, of course, *has* just learned about it in *Barbarians* (although the research escapes Sheehan's bibliography, because he's quoting from the *New Yorker*).

The Borjas team's findings, too, were complex. They found that unskilled migrants *did* tend to depress wages for the unskilled native-born, but concluded that immigration was less of a factor in American income inequality than technology, and probably no more important than the decline of unions and growth of trade. Borjas has also pointed out that the phenomenon of job competition may be economically beneficial: 'Lower earnings lead to higher profits for firms and lower prices for consumers.' And he believes, in any case, that economics shouldn't be the chief determinant in immigration policy: 'Should we not be concerned about our 'sentiments' and values and beliefs? Excuse me for being sentimental, but I believe all these things should matter.'

Then there's the method of advancing academic findings shorn of qualifications and assumptions. Sheehan quotes a 1996 study by demographer Charles Price to prove that, *contra* government statements, the Asian-Australian proportion of our population will near a fifth by 2025. What's unmentioned is that Price's *Immigration and Ethnicity* assumed annual average immigration of 98,500 including an Asian component of 49 percent. Yet total immigration intake fell from 99,139 in 1995-96 to 68,000 in 1997-98, and Price himself noted that all projections involve 'making some assumptions about what immigration trends will be like [and] this is difficult'. Asked about this, Sheehan says: 'I think I did say [in *Barbarians*]: "As a result of the changes in immigration, these numbers won't hold".' He didn't.

There's also selective reading of data. On page 130 comes the assertion: 'Are we importing criminals as some would have us believe? Yes. Check the prison statistics. Check the drug trade.' And Sheehan has a point: certain immigrant groups, notably the Vietnamese, *are* over-represented in prison statistics. Yet he might have also mentioned, given his orientation, that immigrants from all other parts of Asia are significantly under-represented in prison populations: according to Australian Bureau of Statistics data, considerably lower than per capita figures among the Australian-born. But this may have sat uneasily with the assertion: 'The Immigration Department, under political pressure from the multicultural industry, has allowed criminals and parasites into the country by the thousands.'

Finally, there's selective quotation. Developing his thesis on immigration by examining Australia's population-carrying capacity, Sheehan perpetrates a curious misquote of CSIRO scientist Doug Cocks. In his *Use With Care*, Cocks says: 'There are... good humanitarian and social arguments for allowing refugees and family reunion immigration into Australia and certainly such entry should be non-discriminatory as regards national or ethnic origin, race, sex or religion. What we should aim for here is to be the most generous country in the world on a population basis. This would only amount to a few tens of thousands of immigrants a year. Apart from that qualification, Australia must adopt a no-immigration policy. It is the one topic in this book on which I am prepared to take an unequivocal stand.' In *Barbarians*, the quote begins at: 'Australia must adopt....'

Sheehan agrees this was 'a mistake on my part' because he hadn't 'read it properly'. Later he writes to me pointing out—not a little proudly—that *Barbarians* later gets Cocks' suggestion of an optimum intake right: 0-50,000. Yet this is what makes it such a strange 'mistake', because *Barbarians* links it in the same paragraph to praise for the Howard government's new emphasis on skilled immigrants rather than refugees; an emphasis which Sheehan would know from his evidently full understanding of Cocks' argument that the scientist disagrees with.

Cocks isn't all that peeved, merely disappointed: 'I liked reading *Among the Barbarians*, although I agreed with Anne Henderson [who gave it one of the few hostile reviews in the *Australian's Review of Books*] that it was selectively done. Cleverly done but selectively done. I enjoyed talking to him [Sheehan], and I liked his values, but I'm not sure he was true to himself in the writing.'

*

Sheehan develops his thesis on Asian crime and welfare abuse in Chapters Eleven and Twelve, 'Strip Mining' and 'The Big Nowhere'. They contain some creditworthy reporting, and are written with genuine narrative verve. Yet in its segues from 'the new Asian crime operations' to 'Vietnamese gangs' to 'boatloads of illegal Chinese entrants' to 'four men from Hong Kong', it sometimes seems as if Sheehan wants to implicate every Asian in Australia in a web of malfeasance and deceit.

Sheehan is irked by this inference, pointing out that he never advocates cutting Asian immigration (quite true) and that pages 191-192 contain a lengthy qualification concerning immigrant crime which disputes assumptions that it is 'the product of a criminal mentality', and to the contrary 'has a number of logical antecedents'. These include geography (the Golden Triangle is in Asia), history (there have always been Chinese triads) and culture ('some immigrant groups simply have a different value system').

The *Eye*: 'So what you're saying is that it's not their fault that their criminals, that they've got good reasons to be criminals.'

Sheehan: 'You've made this accusation that I'm essentially tarring these whole groups as criminals, but I go to great lengths to say that whole groups aren't like this. What I'm saying is that where crime arises, it's a question of circumstance.'

It still seems a back-handed qualification. By similiar reasoning, you could regard Australia's foundation as a penal colony as a 'logical antecedent' for ours being a nation of criminals. Sheehan's attempt to stand up his anecdotal material statistically is then rather strained: his verification of widespread welfare fraud is the 'extreme disparity' that the Vietnamese-born comprise 0.8 percent of the population, but represent 1.8 percent of single-parent beneficiaries. He quotes Department of Social Security explanations for this discrepancy—that the proportion of Vietnamese women of child-bearing age, for instance, may be higher—but in the first edition says that this is essentially bureaucratese for: 'Vietnamese immigrants are expensive and will continue to be so for some time.'

As Michael Stutchbury remarked in a critique of *Barbarians* in the *Australian Financial Review*, however, Vietnamese-born account for 1.5 percent of women between twenty and forty-four: 'Sheehan's extreme disparity shrinks to not very much when the right numerator and denominator are used.' If it is the best statistical 'proof' available, others must have been pretty weak.

Sheehan: 'I was told by my sources that there was systematic rorting of the welfare system going on. I went to the statistics thinking maybe they don't bear this out. But the statistics said: 'Yes, there's much higher welfare dependency in these categories with the Vietnamese'.'

The *Eye*: 'For apparently good reasons.'

Sheehan: 'Some would be for good reasons. Some would be because of rorting.'

An unanswerable point, really, but not terribly meaningful. It's a peculiar *idée fixe*. Perhaps even an unpleasant one. 'That's what I find really disturbing,' says Anne Henderson. 'Why doesn't he take on the really powerful? Why does he pick on the most vulnerable members of the community? It's get-even stuff: the feeling that they've got more than they should have.'

*

Chapter Nineteen, 'Nomads', represents Sheehan's view of Aboriginal policy post-Wik and *Bringing Them Home*. He is open-minded about reparations to the indigenous population for past injustices. What he deplores is Aboriginal leaders who 'maintain a drumbeat of comments about "racists" and "rednecks".'

Henry Reynolds tends to agree that the word 'racist' is used too freely in public debate, but feels such criticism meretricious: 'They protest far too much about this. They should read some of the comments I receive. I've stacks of letters, ranging from the abusive and the nasty to the deranged. I'm called "traitor to the nation" and "nigger fucker". It's not nice, but it's also not particularly surprising.'

Sheehan's other beef is with the 'stolen generation' report: 'If you're going to make the grave accusation of genocide, then you'd better have all your ducks in a row'. Reynolds believes most of them are: 'The stolen generation was part of a quite systematic plan for demographic engineering, to assimilate the half-castes in the belief that the full-bloods would eventually die out. What I think critics ignore is that there is an enormous gulf between the 1930 and the 1950s: they are divided by the Holocaust, which completely discredits prior racial concepts. And it is hard, therefore, for them to understand just how racist the world was in the 1930s.'

In any case, believes Robert Manne, to simply jeer the HREOC is quite wrong-headed: 'The arguments are complex, but it's interesting to me that the use of the word 'genocide' causes such apoplexy. In the literature on genocide, one of the standard references concerning settler community treatment of an indigenous population is the Australian Aborigines. It seems to me that the likes of Christopher Pearson, Ron Brunton and Paul Sheehan would be better advised to discuss the idea rather than becoming mocking and derisive at its mention.'

Barbarians quotes with approval—if not outright endorsement—Brunton's critique of *Bringing Them Home,* which asserted *inter alia* that the HREOC glossed over cases of Aboriginal children removed from their families because they were 'at risk'. Sheehan tells me: 'I felt that what screams out of the report, and I wonder about its editing, is what sorts of environments were a lot of these people taken from? All the people mentioned in the reports were taken from their families, and they didn't want to be, and it was a defining tragedy in their lives. But I thought the report needed to go and look at the people who were 'at risk'... And I think that was a very large category.'

The *Eye*: 'What makes you think that?'

Sheehan: 'People have told me. Various people who work in the industry. I can't be more specific than that. But there's a sense that a lot of Aboriginal children are at risk today, and were at risk then. Even in 1999 there are lots of Aboriginal children who would probably be better off taken away from their drunken mothers.'

Transcribing this taped remark afforded me an interesting insight into both the power, and the responsibility, of journalists. I might have truncated the quote here, leaving Sheehan with this stupefyingly tactless generalisation. This would traduce him, however, for he qualified his remark somewhat in the next breath: 'I can't bring myself to make that intellectual step. I don't think you should break up families. But somehow the indigenous industry has to deal with it.' Not much of a rider, perhaps, but he said it.

This isn't a courtesy, however, that *Barbarians* itself extends very freely: purportedly composed of 'reportage', it reads and interprets selectively and partially to suit its author's purpose. As Morag Fraser says: 'The impression I get is of a ranging intelligence that stops very briefly on a number of sources, but only in order to arrive at conclusions not completely unpremeditated. It's very lively, but also superficial and misleading.'

Sheehan would claim this misses the point, that *Barbarians* is about restoring 'balance': 'One of the things I was doing was going to people I felt would balance the avalanche of contrary material who the media gave a free kick to all the time. I was self-consciously going to neglected sources at the risk of unbalancing the book.' Nonetheless, it might strike you as odd to accuse the media of misrepresentation, exaggeration and distortion, then produce a book composed of essentially the same things. It might also strike you as odd that Sheehan perceives such a climate of suppression here: one so well-travelled should know that, in certain countries, suppression of opinion exists that is altogether more pervasive and pernicious than anything that's ever existed in Australia. Perhaps it's the case that those who spend too long among 'barbarians' begin to acquire some of their habits.

Capital Letters

Jack Waterford

John Howard will be in London on 1 July playing the statesman, along with most of the State premiers and a large caravan of politicians, celebrating the 100th anniversary of the passage of the Australian Constitution through the British Parliament. At home, Kim Beazley will be playing the politician, maximising for Labor the antagonism flowing to John Howard from the chaos of the introduction of the Goods and Services Tax. The fate of each leader now depends on accountants and small business people, and the messages they give their customers.

Someone remarked recently that the last time the fate of a government turned so much on the actions of people in the finance sector was with Ben Chifley and bank employees in 1949. The bank johnnies couldn't even organise a decent defalcation these days, he added. Actually, that's not strictly true. For most of the past few decades, the fate of governments has rested on snap judgments made by operators on the international money market. On those judgments have hung movements in the Australian dollar, interest rates and our lines of international credit.

Those markets do not care very much about whether or not Australia has value-added taxes, though they put a great deal of store by whether the nation has a low tax regime. By which standards one might say that a holding budget put down by Peter Costello in early May—holding the fort until the GST regime and tax cuts were in place—achieved its end.

But it is voters who make the final decision, and whether they have been appeased is another matter altogether. The government had already stripped much of its natural surplus in tax cuts designed to soften the GST, but knows that rising interest rates have made many people feel already worse off. What discretionary money exists has been focused in rural and regional centres, but whether these feel that their concerns have been addressed is also doubtful. Government has treated the problem as primarily one of access to doctors. For much the same money, they might have widened their focus to rural health resources, particularly for older people, in a way that created work for nursing hostels and small hospitals in rural communities—thus doing something for community development. If there were an election in the next few months, the signs are that the Coalition would be down to about thirty seats in a 148-seat House of Representatives. John Howard must swing the present opinion of one in every twelve voters even to hold on.

His biggest problem is not that he has lost the confidence of ordinary voters, but that he has alienated the natural base he now needs most, small business. The GST is already a liability, and voters have not even experienced it yet. It is unpopular with the accountants—even as, no doubt, it is making them a fortune—but rather than wooing them, the government is abusing them. A lot of local opinion leaders in communities are bagging the GST. Whatever the Australian Competition and Consumer Commission and its zealous head, Alan Fels, do to monitor price movement, one can be pretty sure that most price changes over the coming few years will be blamed on the GST, and on compliance regimes. The unpopularity with many small business people is aggravated by the fact that many will now be paying a lot more income tax because it will be, for some, more difficult to feed themselves from the till.

Labor is taking a big gamble, because if things do settle down, it is going to look very naked. But if I were betting on an outcome for the next election, I would say that, at the moment, Labor must be very heavily favoured.

Howard is a very clever politician, one who fights best with his back to the wall. So he should not be discounted. He will fight with every dollar in his treasury, spending it not only directly on voters, but on public relations campaigns. A government which once prided itself on its economic rigour is now back into fairly conventional pump-priming and Keynesian economic policy. The tap is now back on. As with the last Fraser-Howard budget of 1982, the Howard-Costello budgets of 2000 and 2001 have shed most of their reforming zeal because Howard is in survival mode.

That he has not yet given up, however, can be shown by the stubbornness with which he still plays the game—against Labor, against his political enemies in his own party, and against the general political culture he hates so much, has worked so hard to dismantle, but which still mocks him about issues such as reconciliation. For John Howard, this is a continuing obsession. Much more than mere stubbornness, I think, it determines his attitude to things such as reconciliation and Australian history.

It is hard to see Howard as prime minister next time about, but dangerous to make too many guesses beyond that. The succession is far from certain and I cannot imagine him doing Peter Costello any favours. In any leadership succession, the moderates in his party do not have the numbers to get their own candidate up (if they had one), but they probably have the numbers to veto anyone they do not like. In that sense, the very wounded Michael Wooldridge may well be the king-maker. Right now, he might figure that he owes John Howard a lot.

*

In this winter parliamentary recess, one party steels itself for government eighteen months down the track. The other prepares itself to do what it must to stave off that defeat. Neither is a very lovely sight, and it remains to be seen whether either will be much more presentable after the party conferences and the outbreaks of internal brawling. Probably, however, it depends as much on substance as on $400 million of publicly funded Liberal Party public relations, or staged presentations of goodwill, harmony and slogans organised by ALP machine men.

Will these PR campaigns present us with politicians, of either side, who we can believe in? Or follow?

For me, the answer may well be 'no', if one recent test is any indication—the ALP would prefer to be led by a hard-nosed realist such as John Della Bosca, rather than a dreamer such as Barry Jones. Give me the dreamer any day. I am sure that Mr Della Bosca is a splendid person, but his rising to the top indicates that the political parties are out of touch with voters.

It is of no particular moment, in this context, that Mr Della Bosca comes from the NSW Right, the most powerful and ruthless machine in Australian politics. The machines and their machinations dominate both sides of politics.

The internal processes of both of the major political parties are, or have been, deeply corrupted in recent years. If people can advance up the greasy pole only by branch-stacking, manipulation and, often, outright fraud, how can we trust the products of the system? If politicians, even senior politicians, are deeply in the debt of other people, including those who have a chokehold over their pre-selections or advancement in the party, how can one be certain that they will make political decisions unaffected by their obligations to them?

Once the processes, though corrupt, were reasonably transparent—the appointment of power-brokers to cushy statutory jobs, the granting of public monies to public organisations which favoured the governing party. Up to a point one expects that: the purpose of politics is about exercising power and organised bodies in politics are about nothing if they are not about exercising power in a way which supports the interests that have motivated them in the first place. What is, however, increasingly obvious is the way in which many of those exercising power and influence behind the scenes are less concerned with theories of what is best for the nation, and more concerned with what serves the personal, and sometimes the financial, interests of tight cliques with little discernible body of principle. Some politicians seem above it, and some are. Others may have a distaste for the processes but have come to regard the business of getting pre-selected and elected, and keeping in with the power-brokers, as intrinsic to the game of politics. Kim Beazley, for example, is an ardent student and player in the disposition of numbers. So is John Howard. Both are too high up to have their fingers in the ballot boxes, but when scandal breaks, their first instinct, as often as not, is to calculate how it affects their own factions and positions. They will act, or push their own party to act, only when the smell is too intense, or when their failure to act becomes seen as a test of their leadership.

In this context, it is interesting to reflect again on the success of a new crop of independents of the ilk of Ted Mack (now retired from politics) or Peter Andren, the member for Calare. They have counterparts in most of the State parliaments. In most cases, they have been elected not because of some pressing local issue, or even because of a particularly woeful former local member, but because they have said they want to clean up the processes of government. Their calls for a more open executive and more independent and accountable institutions, and their assault on the perks and privileges of politicians, have attracted strong support.

Such idealists are often impractical, and they often think too much about the processes of government and too little about its outcomes. They often lack coherent ideas or policies about dealing with the full range of problems of government, and they lack the staff or the support bases which allow them to develop such expertise. At the same time, however, their clear idealism, and their articulations of notions of public good, make them particularly attractive politicians by comparison with those whose words cannot inspire and whose deeds do even less.

There are some who imagine that the ideal parliament would involve only independents, assessing each issue on its merits as it arose. That will never happen. Groups will always coalesce around common ideas or interests. Those who want better government would do better reforming the parties than establishing new ones or going off alone. Until the parties themselves focus on being organisations of ideas and ideals, open to public participation, accountable in their internal processes, and seen to prevent or punish those who corrupt its processes, they will find it more and more difficult to inspire and enthuse, more and more difficult to recruit the best and the brightest, and themselves less and less able to function with popular consent. For not a few voters, an amiable and eccentric Barry Jones, bubbling with ideas and enthusiasm, and almost unable to stop being decent, is a better symbol of a Labor Party than an apparatchik from the Labor machine.

*

Can John Howard make welfare work for him? On the face of it, it might seem that the best he can hope for is to neutralise the issue. He has been told often enough that he loses votes every time he campaigns on social issues, and picks them up again when the voters' minds are fixed on economic matters. He has been successfully cast as uninspired, mean-spirited and narrow-minded on almost any social issue, to the point where even his colleagues writhe at the prospect of his intervention.

That's not to say that some of his interventions have not been successful, at least in political terms. His work-for-the-dole scheme was cleverly targeted at pub-talkers who think that the unemployed are bludgers, and only later developed a rhetoric about mutual, or reciprocal, responsibility. Falling unemployment may owe more to an improving economy, but many will still give Howard's schemes some credit.

At the same time, he has disarmed many of the lobbies which might normally be expected to be highly critical. In some cases, the action has been ruthless—simply removing the government funding for advocacy services, with which governments have previously built rods for their own backs. If ever there was a case that government welfare money created its own dependencies, it has been demonstrated by the incapacity of many of these lobbies to sustain their efforts from their own resources, as they should have done long ago. Others have been compromised, not least the networks of church and community groups which are now so busy taking government funds to provide government services on contract that they scarcely have time to draw breath, let alone promote independent views.

It is easy enough to imagine that these policies come from a desire to punish those who are on welfare and those who have formed their political careers by speaking the language of entitlement. There is more than a little in that, given Howard's open resentment about the way in which the political culture of the 1970s to the 1990s was captured in this way. But seeing the development of such policies only in such terms is doing both Howard and his Coalition a serious disservice.

That Labor cannot find the language to attack him shows its own recognition that the older welfare philosophies are dead, and that the electorate is responding to new forms of government intervention. Labor, in fact, played a considerable role in developing some of the new ideology of welfare, from the time that it moved away from schemes of universal entitlement in the early 1980s, to the way it skilfully developed job-creation and regional policies in the mid 1990s.

It is clear that Labor wants such policies and recognises their political potency. At most, Labor promises more new model intervention or assistance than Howard is offering, or promises that the dividing lines will be set in marginally more compassionate ways. Only a few of the shadow ministry make anything but the most ritual bows to an older ideology, and their assistance is not usually regarded as welcome.

Howard, in short, has largely won the policy argument, as he has with the Goods and Services Tax, and the most that his rivals can do is nibble around the edges. They may well do so successfully—or be seen to have done so—because Howard has exhausted the patience of the electorate, but the next election is still Labor's to lose.

The cynic might wonder whether Howard would be prepared to gamble and take his welfare debate right into the centre of Labor uncertainty—Aboriginal affairs. He might well figure that he has nothing to lose, if only because Labor has kept its own flag waving by trading off Howard's missteps in the reconciliation and stolen children debate. Aboriginal affairs is the last great redoubt of old-fashioned welfarism, and the last area where some people appear genuinely to believe that more of the same might do the trick. There are plenty of others, not least Aboriginal people, who have the most profound doubts—doubts about the institutions, the policies and the programs, and about whether one can even identify targets which will, if achieved, make any material or social difference to Aboriginal people.

All along, Howard has been insisting that Aboriginal affairs is about health, education and jobs. He has rejected as empty symbolism talk of apologies and native title developments. He may well have made progress impossible by fundamentally misjudging the mood on the symbols and alienating the people whose assistance he needed. Yet the fact is that his government has been continuing to feed money into old welfarist policies from which, by any standards, the dividend is still meagre. Moreover, he has continued to work through the old mechanisms, focusing on communities rather than families, and on bureaucratic structures which measure inputs rather than results. Aboriginal affairs is wide open to genuine reform. The government could focus on transferring responsibility, 'empowerment', agreed target setting, getting kids into school and people into jobs, and making better and more accountable use of the resources of State and local government. Such reform would cause consternation in Labor ranks and suspicion among those who think that John Howard is incapable of entering Aboriginal affairs with good intentions. It would, of course, go down well in the pubs, but it might also make some difference.

*

Bob McMullan has taken up Labor's responsibility for Aboriginal affairs—a task one of his colleagues has likened to cleaning the toilets on the *Titanic*. One would have to look back to 1975 to find a minister as well fitted for the job. McMullan lacks close knowledge of Aboriginal politics and programs and has no background in the area. It might seem ironic to suggest that broad ignorance is a positive virtue, but the history of Labor's relations with Aborigines illustrates the point.

The truth is that Labor has been letting down Australians, particularly Aboriginal Australians, for a long time. Two decades ago, for example, Labor conceived the notion that all problems could be resolved by national uniform land rights legislation and that it could and would deliver this. In fact, the range of Aboriginal living conditions made that delivery highly unlikely. In any event, Labor had no policy or programs for the conversion of land into a base for Aboriginal economic development.

Architects of that policy, such as Susan Ryan, but particularly Clyde Holding, had established reputations for sympathy with Aboriginal affairs. When Labor came to power in 1983, almost every worthwhile program went on hold for several years while Holding struggled to get political consent to national land legislation. He failed, primarily because of Labor opposition in Western Australia and also because of prime minister Bob Hawke's unwillingness to use his political capital to push the issue.

There was an earlier model for Clyde Holding in Gordon Bryant, a decent man with a long background in the Aboriginal struggle, particularly as a result of his 1960s involvement with the Federal Council for the Advancement of Aborigines and Torres Strait Islanders. His relationships compromised him, as did his compassion when told of emergencies in communities whose poverty he knew at first hand.

Of Bryant's Labor successors, Les Johnson was most in the mould of Bob McMullan—he was calm, focused on getting order back into increasingly chaotic service delivery, and he kept a weather eye on public opinion. He developed relationships with Aboriginal political leaders based on respect and give-and-take, rather than on any repressive tolerances.

Ian Viner, the first Fraser Aboriginal affairs minister and, probably, the best, had no background in Aboriginal affairs. There was ample reason to be suspicious of him and of the Fraser government, not least its Country Party rump. At that stage, Malcolm Fraser wanted to have the Aboriginal issue neutralised and to have the portfolio deliver its share of the general government cost cuts he was promising. Viner, economically and socially conservative, but a lawyer, took the job as a brief, but progressively became a convert. But the detachment, and the high suspicion with which Aborigines treated Fraser (at least as great as the distrust between their successors and John Howard), meant that Viner made his own relationships, ones untrammelled by guilt or old histories. Most of Viner's Liberal successors, such as Fred Chaney and Peter Baume, went into the portfolio with backgrounds of identification with Aboriginal issues. But by the end of the Fraser era, there was not only a reasonable bipartisan approach on most Aboriginal issues (though one would never have guessed it from Labor propaganda) but some solid progress on the health and housing front, and some hopes in the education and employment field.

During Holding's period the bipartisan consensus began to collapse, primarily because Labor did not hesitate to use Aborigines as a stick with which to belt the Coalition. At the same time, Holding's incapacity to deliver was creating a critical Aboriginal constituency. The caravans parked around the offices of backbenchers such as Gerry Hand contained many who had fallen out with Holding (often for reasons to his credit). When Hand became minister, there was a new, but not necessarily more legitimate, ascendancy in Aboriginal affairs too.

After Holding and Hand, Bob Tickner, another minister with a long background in Aboriginal affairs, put all in the reconciliation basket. Had it been more than fine feelings, it would have been wonderful. But the vacuum within is nicely demonstrated by the fact that the most pressing issues of recent years—native title legislation and the question of saying sorry to the stolen generations—were not even issues at the time.

John Howard has insisted that real progress means work on the ground in material things—though his refusal to get the symbols right has made most of his work useless. Achievements, so far as they go, have come from David Kemp in education and Michael Wooldridge in health. The Labor style of opposition in this area—passion without policy or progress, from decent but marginalised Left spokesmen such as Daryl Melham—has meant that Howard has increasingly seen inaction and mean-mindedness as a workable strategy. Kim Beazley seems to respond by running for cover whenever Aboriginal issues surface.

Bob McMullan knows his Labor mythology and knows where Labor's instinctive sympathies lie in Aboriginal affairs. But as one whose focus has been economic, and who is unencumbered by much of the rhetoric which passes for policy, he might find it better to regard his ministerial vista as an Augean stables, rather than the sewerage system on a ship.

Dubya and Good Ol' Al
Cameron Forbes

George W. Bush II

The land is flat under the weight of a wide, wide sky. Mesquite holds down reddish sand. Occasionally, tumbleweed tumbles and cows wander but there is a dominant, steady, mesmeric movement, a relentless nodding of derricks. This is West Texas. This is oil country, love it or leave it country.

George W. Bush loves it. He spent his boyhood here, met his wife Laura here, found God here, became a teetotaler here and says he wants to be buried here. He left it as a failed oilman to make his fortune with a baseball diamond and then enter the family's first trade, politics. From the bastion of the Texas governorship he is challenging for United States presidency. By breeding, Bush is a member of the Eastern elite, but nurture has overridden nature. Inside—and sometimes bursting out—are a Texas swagger and an arrogant Texas smirk.

Next week Bush goes to Philadelphia for his coronation. How the Republicans want the White House back. They want to celebrate the end of the William Jefferson Clinton by crushing his chosen successor, Al Gore. They want revenge for eight years of Democratic presidential rule and who better to wield the sword than the son of George Herbert Bush, the man humiliated by Clinton when he slouched out of Arkansas in 1992. How they hate Clinton with his Southern good ol' boy charm, the way he touches upper arms and touches peoples' feelings, the way he can look people in the eye and show them he knows their happiness or pain.

Fact is, they have got themselves a Clinton. Bush is supremely at ease with himself and with people. Clinton was the son of small-town Arkansas, raised on the fringes of the middle class. His father, William Jefferson Blythe, died in a car accident while his mother Virginia was pregnant. Clinton took the name of Virginia's second husband, Roger, an alcoholic and, until the teenage Clinton confronted him, a wife-beater. He grew up in Hot Springs, headquarters of the biggest illegal gambling operation in the South. Hot Springs has been described as a 'vaporous city of ancient corruption mingling with purely American idealism'. But the town he was born in, flat and unprepossessing, had just the right name for a politician who feeds on schmaltzy symbolism. As he was reaching for his destiny at the 1992 Democratic convention, Clinton said at the end of his nomination speech: 'I still believe in a town called Hope.'

Midland doesn't have the same ring, but it's apt. George Walker Bush was born into a family of old Eastern money and old political connections. His grandfather was a senator, his father would be president and both were patrician. As a young family man, George Herbert Bush, a Connecticut Yankee, went south-west to make his own fortune from oil but when he left he soon shook off the Texas dust; George W. went aged fifteen to the preppy Andover boarding school then to Phillips Academy, studied (sort of) at Yale, his father's university, where he too became a member of the secret and prestigious Skull and Bones Society, and rounded off with a Harvard MBA. But he has remained rooted in Texas soil and there is a deal of truth in the way he defines the essential difference between himself and his father: 'He attended [the exclusive] Greenwich County Day and I went to San Jacinto High School in Midland.'

Actually, he only attended San Jacinto for a year, but Midland made him in the image of middle-class, conservative, small-town America, a safe, segregated America worshipping God and the entrepreneurial spirit but happy to take government subsidies, big on camaraderie but short on intellectualism. For Gore, who just cannot avoid looking like a tailor's dummy even in casual clothes and cowboy boots, the sight of Bush, loose and affable, must be teeth-grinding frustration. I have watched Bush shaking hands and chatting with surprised members of a convict work crew, sitting in a South Carolina diner as if he ate chicken there every night, mixing easily with blacks or Hispanics or unionists—positively Clintonesque. He charms women. The traditional gender gap in favour of Democratic contenders has disappeared. But, with him, there is never the frisson that occurs when Clinton, even post-Lewinsky, is in the presence of an attractive young woman. No one is going to say, as Southerners say of Clinton, that Bush is a hard dog to keep on the porch.

To reach Bush country, you fly into Midland-Odessa airport. If you leave the airport, cross the I20 and keep driving into the flatness and the oil derricks, when you look back you'll see the two towns equidistant on the horizon. Midland is the 'Tall City' with a modest silhouette of high glass towers that oil built. It was the home of the middle-class and those who liked to think themselves slightly above. Odessa, squatter, had some blue around the collar, some roughnecks and some riggers—and undoubtedly, more fun.

When George and Barbara Bush with two-year-old George arrived in 1948, they lived first in a small duplex Odessa apartment, sharing a bathroom with the mother-daughter prostitute team next door. After a year, they moved along the I20 to Midland, to a street of neat identical bungalows, but with a splash of individuality. Each house was painted a different colour—the Bush's was blue—and everyone called the street Easter Egg Row.

There's no Easter Egg Row now. Midland has grown on a diet of oil from around 20,000 in the 50s to about 100,000 now. The tall core is modern functionality and basically pedestrian-free. On the major roads that radiate out is the inevitable ugliness, chain restaurants, much Tex-Mex and clusters of cantinas. But the suburbs are the neat, tree-shaded, green-grassed American dream, with handy restaurants like the Garlic Press.

We drive along West Ohio Street to Bush's boyhood home. My guide is John Bizilo. He's eighty-one, spending his retirement bird-watching with his wife Ethelyne. He's now the most famous ex-teacher in Midland, indeed, in Texas. Make that America. The delightful couple is accustomed to journalists coming to visit. Ethelyne serves her macadamia-nut cookies and shows off her collection of Beanie Babies. In a note accompanying the field check list of the birds of Midland County she sent me, she said: 'Had I known that the Bush spanking was going to be such a "hot issue" I would have started a Guest Book. So sorry I didn't do that.'

For John Bizilo paddled the would-be president of the United States and leader of the free world: bend-over, whack, whack, whack paddled. Our tour had started at the Sam Houston elementary school, in room 13. This is where young fourth-grader George painted a beard and long sideburns on his face, disrupting Frances Childress's class. Frances led him (by the ear?) along this corridor to Principal Bizilo's office. 'My responsibility is to maintain discipline,' Bizilo tells the boy, taking up his paddle.

Decades later, Bizilo relives the event: 'He yelled bloody murder.' Bizilo stands up and rubs the seat of his pants, miming the young George. 'Hush up,' I said, 'or there's more where that came from.' He smiles a satisfied smile: turns out the Bizilos are among the few non-Republicans in Midland.

Bush was what Bizilo calls a real energy burner. He led the pack, played little league and did boy stuff. When the park behind the house flooded, he and his friends tormented the frogs. He learned easiness with his kind of people and an early if abstract lesson in race relations. Midland, white, church-going, was a place with an underbelly of racism and racist slurs were a common language. Once seven-year-old George used one in the Bush living room in front of his redoubtable mother Barbara. Michael Proctor, who lived across the road and was playing with George at the time, told the *New York Times* that Barbara Bush has grabbed her son by the ear and dragged him into the bathroom. She washed his mouth out with soap.

That same year, Bush's younger sister Robin, just short of four years old, died of leukemia. For the family, it was a searing loss, and it brought Bush closer to his mother as comforter. Recently a woman influential in Democratic politics said to me: 'George W. is his mother in pants.' She meant it as a compliment to Barbara, who is headstrong and quick-witted.

Midland, as seen through Bush's eyes, is a town of 'embedded values' and he regards his boyhood there as an idyll. There are other views. Larry L. King, son of Midland, author, actor and playwright, wrote in the 60s:

> Home is Midland, where what passes for skyscrapers rise
> off the bleached face of the vast and mismade plain. Where

the oillionaires and neanderthal Republicans with low, sloping foreheads and angry John Birchers (in full tremble over fluoridation of drinking water and impeaching Earl Warren) play and the skies are not cloudy all day…. Yeah, I remember Midland like some folks remember Mama. She was a hard old mother, this Midland…. I recall my halcyon years of sandstorms and talking in tongues at foot-stomping Baptist Youth Crusades for Christ and mowing rich folks' lawns under parboiling sun without being offered a snort of ice water.

When the Bush family left Midland, fifteen-year-old George entered a world of privilege. The *Washington Post* has neatly summed up his progress, or lack of it, through the 60s: 'As the war and youth culture rocked America, Bush partied, dated with gusto and flew jets part-time.' This last was a reference to his joining the National Guard, where he piloted an F102 fighter-interceptor, a move which has attracted criticism as a queue-jumping exercise to avoid Vietnam (though he did support the war).

The most notorious episode in this period occurred when Bush, a serious drinker, was twenty-six. He had taken his sixteen-year-old brother Marvin out and on return had run over the neighbour's garbage cans. Confronted by his father, he challenged him to come outside and settle the matter 'mano a mano'. It should have been a literally sobering experience. It was not, immediately. But not long after he worked as volunteer counsellor in a program for young blacks. By all accounts he was a great success in a practical demonstration that he hasn't a racist bone in his body.

Bush returned to Midland when he was thirty and began to put a life together. He married Midland girl and librarian Laura. He tapped into the cultural soil of family, friends, cookouts, tennis games and dinner at the country club. He followed his father into the business of drilling for oil in the surrounding desert.

Oil is a gamble, twice over. First there is the finding of it; second there is the world price of a barrel when you bring it to the surface, determined by forces far out of control of a wild-catter in Midland, Texas. George Herbert Bush won; George Walker Bush lost. Eddie Angelos is another winner. On the walls of his office are trophies: a fine mule deer head, stuffed ducks, photographs of Angelos and Ronald Reagan and of Angelos and Bush the elder signed effusively by the presidents. Angelos has served stints as chairman of the Texas Republican Party.

'Oil is a rollercoaster,' Angelos says. 'Boom or bust. Midland was about to die in January 1999, when oil was $10 a barrel. Now it's $30. The area has boomed several times: in the 50s, late 60s and early 80s. Most of the big companies have moved out. I think they've gone for good. But there's still a lot out there, in smaller traps. It's high risk, high return and demands a spirit of individuality.'

That morning Angelos had been out in the field at his latest well. At 12,000 foot he struck oil—only 5 feet from the spot indicated as a possibility by the seismic surveys. He spent a $1 million on the hole. 'What will be the return?' I asked. 'The bare minimum you want is three to one. This time it will be at least five to one. With my first well, thirty-five years ago, I got ten to one.' Angelos says Bush's father was a very successful wild-catter. 'George W. wasn't. He would say so himself. A hell of a lot of people went bust. He just didn't have the good fortune but I never heard any of his investors complain. They thought they got a good shake.'

Before he gave up, Bush had been bailed out twice. Commentors who are, if not political partisans, then personally anti-Bush, have been merciless, charging crony capitalism and trading on the family name. Molly Ivins, in *Shrub: The Short but Happy Political Life of George W. Bush*, wrote: 'The oil "bidness" was not good to George W. Bush's investors—who lost $2 million, unless they were speculating in political futures and cultivating connections.' But Bush would strike it rich. Using borrowed money, he took a $606,000 share of the Texas Rangers baseball club in 1989. The club prospered, helped by a most advantageous deal with the city of Arlington on the building of a new stadium. He sold out in 1998 for $15.4 million, a twenty-five to one return.

By this time he and his family were living in the colonnaded governor's mansion in Austin and it was not only his finances that had undergone a sweeping transformation. In the summer of 1985, Bush was still drinking like a good ol' boy, but he had been taking the Scriptures more seriously, reading the Bible from cover to cover more than once. The family had traveled from Midland to the family compound in exclusive Kennebunkport. There he had a conversation with evangelist Billy Graham.

'I met with Billy,' he would tell the *Washington Post*, 'but it's like a mustard seed. You know, he planted a seed in my heart and I began to change... I realised that alcohol was beginning to crowd out my energies and could crowd, eventually, my affections for other people... To put it in spiritual terms, I accepted Christ. What influenced me was the spirituality, sure, which led me to believe that if you change your heart you can change your behaviour.' On 28 July 1986, Bush changed his behaviour. After a night of partying with friends who had also reached the big Four-O, Bush woke with a hangover and decided never to touch alcohol again.

So now Bush has fortune, family and God. He has his own political record, having won an historic re-election as governor. He has, thanks to the rich and powerful, the greatest campaign war chest ever amassed in America. And, of course he has name recognition. His father had lost the 1992 presidential election with a derisory 38 percent of the vote, having been the target of a most insulting Clinton campaign slogan: 'It's the economy, stupid.' Now he is enjoying a resurgence of respect in Republican ranks.

But does George W. Bush have the right stuff to be President of the United States? Democrats claim that the Texas governorship is constitutionally the second weakest in the nation, take credit for progress and blame Bush for failings. They say he's a lightweight. Certainly he has maintained his Midland disdain for people he calls intellectual snobs and he is his father's son when it comes to being tangle-tongued.

Gore may cut Bush to pieces in the presidential debates, but Lanny Davis, a former special counsel to Bill Clinton and a supporter of Al Gore, has publicly warned Democrats not to underestimate him. 'This guy is very smart,' said Davis, who was a fraternity brother of Bush at Yale. 'The notion of lightness is totally missing the point. There are many smart people, intellectually smart as well as street smart, who don't have the energy or motivation at times to act smart, but that doesn't mean they're not smart.

'There are times when George coasted through Yale courses or through exams or seemed overly facetious. But don't mistake that for not being intellectually acute. My memory of George—and I've no reason to say nice things about him, because I hope he loses—is that he was an astute observer of people and had an incredible talent for getting along with people.'

Ah yes, a talent for getting along with people. That would be the Midland effect. Bush may not have found much oil in the surrounding desert, but he found himself in the Midland community—and a persona that is a powerful political weapon.

Al Gore

Among the small, jagged hills of middle Tennessee, pioneers scattered names that resonate with hardship and heartbreak: Difficult and Defeated. Then there is Nameless, surely a place where no farmer and no crop put down roots. And then there is Carthage. Carthage? The name has the ring of ancient glories, Phoenician sail dominating the Mediterranean and, finally, of a fate worse than Defeated: razed by the Romans and its lands sown with salt to make them barren.

Land-locked Carthage, Tennessee, is small—the population is still not much over 2,000—but proud, and proudly Southern. Since it was settled more than 200 years ago, Tennessee has been sending its sons into battle so enthusiastically that it became known as the Volunteer State. Carthage has played its part and carved its record of shed blood in stone. On the granite memorial outside the courthouse is the list of the sons of Carthage who died in the Revolution, the War of 1812, the 1846 Mexican War, the Civil War, World War One, World War Two, Korea and Vietnam. The toll in the Civil War was a terrible 136; in World War Two it was fifty-four.

Carthage is also a touch paranoid. It is the Smith County seat and the weekly newspaper, the *Carthage Courier*, proclaims on its masthead 'The Only Newspaper to give a Whoop about Smith County'. Relatively few tourists detour off Interstate 40 to visit. There are no liquor stores in Carthage, no movie theatres and no fine dining, though the Sonic Drive-in does a mean hot fudge sundae.

But come November, the world is going to notice Carthage. Yes sir.

Cross Main Street from the courthouse and walk along to Markham's Family Clothing Store. In pride of place, plumb in the customer's eye, is a commercial shrine to Al Gore. There are T-shirts, campaign buttons, bumper stickers, plates with his photograph, postcards of his farm and, on the counter, a neat arrangement of cobalt-blue coffee mugs, emblazoned 'Carthage—Home of Al Gore, 43rd President of the United States of America'.

Gore, Vice President of the United States and next week to be crowned Democratic candidate for the White House, calls Carthage home. Picture him as farm boy, mucking-out hog stalls, gee-hawing a mule team to plough a steep hillside, clearing heavy forest with a double-bladed axe: Al Gore, son of the soil, son of Carthage!

His enemies can't. They know myth-making when they see it. When Gore reminisced about his days in the hog pen, Republican National Committee Chairman Jim Nicholson retorted: 'You're shovelling a lot more of it right now than you ever did back then.' And the conservative *Weekly Standard* snorted 'How preposterous' at the vision of Gore down on the farm. 'Real farmers, even poor ones, have been hiring bulldozers to clear land since before Al Gore was born. No responsible farmer since the Dust Bowl days of the 1930s has ploughed a steep hillside.'

Gore, they insist, is the son of privileged, insider Washington. The place he really called home as a boy was Suite 809 of the Fairfax Hotel in the middle of prestigious Massachusetts Avenue's gracious Embassy Row. Bellhops, maids in white aprons and liveried doormen waited on him and when his father, Senator Albert Gore and mother Pauline left for a black-tie dinner, room service was his lot. When he left for school just up the avenue at exclusive St Alban's, he dodged through a lobby often full of the great and the powerful and the wheelers and dealers.

But indeed, work on the farm—some of it unnecessarily hard and hazardous—was part of the making of Al Gore. His presidential rival, George W. Bush wandered through boyhood and then much of his adulthood in Midland, Texas, a casual place set in far horizons. Bush was late to join the family political dynasty but came to it full of confidence, a hand-shaking, arm-squeezing, warm eye-contact easy mixer with people.

Gore was from his early years, a work in progress, carefully shaped first by Albert and Pauline Gore in the cause of political destiny and then by himself, as almost an intellectual exercise. His stiffness, inability to connect, and capacity to bore have become standing jokes. He unsuccessfully tries to fight fire with fire. 'Al Gore is so exciting that his Secret Service code name is Al Gore,' he says. The twins, Washington Gore and Southern Al, can change places in a single speech. With Washington Gore, each word stands alone, to a ponderous metronome beat. There is a deadening drone of facts and good intentions. But suddenly it's all twang. Southern Al is striding the stage, arms pumping. He is roaring: 'I want to fight for you.' And then the switch is turned off and Washington Gore walks away.

Bill Turque, the latest biographer, called his book *Inventing Al Gore*. The title catches the flavour of focus-group assessments. The worry about Bush is that he is a lightweight, affable enough but not intellectually equipped to lead the world's most powerful nation; the worry about Gore is that he reads the electoral wind and is willing to do almost anything to win political approval: change his dress (let's see you in those earth tones, Al) or pander to the Miami relatives of Cuban boat boy Elian Gonzales. There has certainly been a struggle in his life between principle and political ambition. With Bush, the impression is what you see is what you get; with Gore, the whole sometimes comes across as less than the sum of the parts.

Gore and Bush are frequently paired as sons of the elite. This is not accurate. Albert Gore did serve in the US Senate, the most self-important collection of legislators in the world, did dream of the presidency that Bush's father, George Herbert, would win. But Bush senior was born into a web of wealth and influence and chauffeured to his prep school; Gore senior was born into hardscrabble times and grew up in Possum Hollow, about twenty kilometres from Carthage.

A quaint name that, but Possum Hollow was not much different from Defeated or Difficult. There were close kin and mountain men and mountain music. Young Albert played thigh-slapping fiddle. But poverty limited life and Albert said later from his position of eminence: 'There was but one way to go from Possum Hollow—that was up and out. You couldn't get out except by going up and once you got out, you were pretty much far down that pole.' When he got out as the first of his Possum Hollow generation to go to college, he met Pauline LaFon, on her way up and out of poverty, serving coffee to pay back the loan she had taken out to study law.

So they continued up together. Albert would win a senate seat and they would buy 250 acres of beef cattle and tobacco land on the Carney Fork River, about ten minutes drive from Carthage. It was here they brought young Al from his Washington home in Suite 809 during his preppy school's holiday. Here he did hose out the hog pens, learn to square-bale hay and clear a forest patch with an axe. Here, despite the scepticism of the Weekly Standard and its worries about erosion, he did plough that slanted hillside.

There are different versions of that event and his parent's actions. David Maraniss and Ellen Nakashima, in their forthcoming biography, *The Prince of Tennessee: the Rise of Al Gore*, have Albert looking out the picture window to fifteen-year-old Al and the plough and mules on the hillside and saying, contentedly: 'I think a boy, to achieve anything he wants to achieve, which would include being president of the United States, oughta be able to run a hillside plough.' Turque, in *Inventing Al Gore*, has Pauline protesting at the risk. When Albert insisted, she said, sarcastically: 'Yes, a boy could never be president if he couldn't plough with that damned hillside plough.'

Away from Suite 809, Gore as a boy certainly saw more of the hard life than Bush did. For three or four weeks at a time in summer and once during a winter, he was left in the care of the Gore's tenant farmers, William and Alota Thompson. He shared a bed with Gordon 'Goat', in a drafty tenant house that had no indoor plumbing and only a small coal-burning stove for heat. (Perhaps the Gores could have invested money in better housing for the help.)

In his eulogy to his father, who died in 1998 at ninety, a long-defeated senator and a political figure of faded stature, Gore said that throughout his entire life in public service, he had never left his farm.

> He loved to raise Angus cattle. In the audience today are quite a few Angus breeders from around the country who were among his closest friends. It was his recreation. He always said 'I'd rather find a new black calf in the weeds than a golf ball in the grass.' Our farm was also an important school where he taught me every day. He must have told me a hundred times the importance of learning how to work.

The work ethic is indeed an admirable thing, but Albert Gore undoubtedly was aware also of the importance of roots and narrative in politics. The education of young Al continued in Suite 809, but here in the ways of Washington and the wide world at the dinner table. Pauline Gore told Maraniss and Nakashima: 'I selected guests for us. If it so happened there was a great guest who was a good conversationalist and the issue was proper for me and my son, I would see if I could wedge Al in.'

Central to an understanding of Gore is the way he has defined and been defined by two of the great issues of American life—the still unfinished business of race and the trauma of the Vietnam War.

When the family fled the miasma of Washington summers, Maraniss and Nakashima relate, Pauline Gore would hire a black youth from the Carthage neighbourhood, Abe Gainer, son of a laundry woman and several years older than Gore, to be a combination playmate and babysitter. Later Albert Gore took Gore to a mansion in Carthage he intended to buy, down into the basement and pointed up to old slave rings still embedded there. Gore was horrified. As a teenager in Washington he befriended Jerome Powell, who worked as a doorman at the Fairfax and was the lead singer in his own band. At Harvard, he requested a black roommate. He continued his search for the meaning of race as vice-president.

He interviewed experts on race, brought four easels into his office and classified the experts and their theories. He put alongside his summary of key questions, issues and goals. Then, after discussions with more experts, he hosted a series of three dinners at his residence which were supposed to promote debate among the guests and enlightenment for Al Gore. A divinity student for a time as a young man, and like Bush, a committed Christian, Gore came to a final, bleak assessment: racism is part of 'the evil that lies coiled in the human soul'.

Gore certainly has rapport with black Americans. His appearance at this year's conference of the National Association for the Advancement of Coloured People completely overshadowed George W. Bush's. His speech was interrupted by foot-stomping applause and 'amens' though he was in turn, overshadowed by Bill Clinton, who has the cadences of a gospel preacher.

This rigorous approach to race is the same one he took to the environment, which produced Earth in Balance, an impressive exercise in scientific and philosophical analysis and synthesis. But the issue of Vietnam only illuminates the paradox of Gore. Consider: Senator Albert Gore opposes the Vietnam War; Al Gore opposes the Vietnam War; but at a time when Bush and many others have found refuge in the National Guard, Gore, as befits someone from the Volunteer State, enlists and serves as a reporter.

Gore later talked of duty. But it was more complex than that. His father was paying a high political price for his opposition. This was Gore's later analysis of why he enlisted:

> The choice that had the most integrity for me personally was to go. And if I was going to look at my decision through the lens of politics and the morality of the war policy, then, ironically, because my father was a leading opponent of the war, my decision to go had integrity even within the

context of my personal opposition to the war.

Through the lens of politics, Gore thought his enlistment would help his father. And he was certainly told by Harvard professor Richard Neustadt, that if he went into politics himself, serving would give him legitimacy. As it happened, nothing could save Senator Albert Gore, whose stands on civil rights and on the war had alienated him from many in his Tennessee constituency. The father's defeat in 1970 was a bitter blow for the son, and a lesson in the perils of political risk-taking.

Gore made his own way into politics, first as a member of the House of Representatives for Tennessee, then senator, then for eight years, a heartbeat away from the presidency as vice president. John Nance, who was Franklin Delano Roosevelt's first vice president, once said, with eloquence, that the office 'ain't worth a pitcher of warm spit'. Gore has made more of it than most—perhaps any. He is claiming to have helped Clinton bring economic sunshine to America, which is allowable political exaggeration. He has been described as acting as 'the house moralist, the advocate for the option that would represent the unpopular, tough, but right thing to do'. He certainly needs to project this image in the campaign.

On election day, 7 November, Gore makes his bid for what he and his parents regard as his destiny. He may fail, of course. Bill Markham, friend, supporter and owner of Markham's Family Clothing Centre, has put a wry notice beside the presidential coffee mugs: 'Get yours early. No refunds if he loses the election.'

Gore was asked by an interviewer last year, as he was about to head down the primary campaign trail, where he would go after Washington. 'Home,' he said, 'to Tennessee. To my farm. I'd like to write. Fiction, non-fiction. That's what I'll do. That's where I'll go. To Carthage. Home.'

It's a statement to bring sneers from the Gore, son-of-Washington school. But Markham, pointing out Gore's string of congressional election victories in Tennessee, says: 'Well, sir, in Smith County we don't elect outsiders to Congress, and outsiders are pretty much anybody who don't live in Smith County.'

Gore's home is actually ten minutes drive from Carthage, an unprepossessing brick house, with two magnolia trees in front. It's set on eighty rolling acres, across the lazy Carney Fork from his parents' farm. The only nearby sign of life is at the Carney Fork convenience store a couple of hundred metres away, with its dank tank of minnows outside for bait and cholesterol-laden fast food spending the day inside.

And yes, it is a little difficult to imagine Gore here, but Donna Armistead of Carthage, his first girlfriend, describes him as having a great belly laugh, an impish sense of humour and 'a northern mind and a Southern heart'. Allowing for the romanticism of Southerners about themselves and their culture, this would be an appealing combination of warmth and intellect. Southern Al and Washington Gore working together just might take Al Gore to the White House.

Apology Made by John Howard on the 3rd of July on National TV

John Clarke

Good evening. My name is John Howard and I'm speaking to you from Sydney, Australia, host city of the year 2000 Olympic Games.

At this important time, and in an atmosphere of international goodwill and national pride, we here in Australia—all of us—would like to make a statement before all nations.

Australia, like many countries in the new world, is intensely proud of what it has achieved in the past 200 years. We are a vibrant and resourceful people. We share a freedom born in the abundance of nature, the richness of the earth, the bounty of the sea. We are the world's biggest island. We have the world's longest coastline. We have more animal species than any other country. Two thirds of the world's birds are native to Australia. We are one of the few countries on earth with our own sky. We are a fabric woven of many colours and it is this that gives us our strength.

However, these achievements have come at great cost. We have been here for 200 years but before that, there was a people living here. For 40,000 years they lived in a perfect balance with the land. There were many Aboriginal nations, just as there were many Indian nations in North America and across Canada, as there were many Maori tribes in New Zealand and Incan and Mayan peoples in South America. These indigenous Australians lived in areas as different from one another as Scotland is from Ethiopia. They lived in an area the size of Western Europe. They did not even have a common language. Yet they had their own laws, their own beliefs, their own ways of understanding.

We destroyed this world. We often did not mean to do it. Our forebears, fighting to establish themselves in what they saw as a harsh environment, were creating a national economy. But the Aboriginal world was decimated. A pattern of disease and dispossession was established. Alcohol was introduced. Social and racial differences were allowed to become fault-lines. Aboriginal families were broken up. Sadly, Aboriginal health and education are responsibilities we have still yet to address successfully.

I speak for all Australians in expressing a profound sorrow to the Aboriginal people. I am sorry. We are sorry. Let the world know and understand, that it is with this sorrow, that we as a nation will grow and seek a better, a fairer and a wiser future. Thank you.

Who Speaks, About What, To Whom, On Whose Behalf, With What Right?

Raimond Gaita

'We've given Ayers Rock back to the Aborigines!' Perhaps I remember those words so clearly because a friend spoke them to me over the telephone when I first went to England, surprised almost daily at the reforms of the Whitlam government and at the international interest they excited. Years later I reflected on the meaning of that 'we'. Had he said the same words to an English person, the meaning of it would have been different. Addressed to me, that 'we' wasn't so much a classification that included or excluded me: it was an invitation to be part of a community whose identity was partly formed by its relation to Australia and its past and by its preparedness to accept responsibilities for what had been done to the Aborigines—at that time (before we knew about the stolen children), the taking of their lands and desecration of their sacred places. Had I thought about it, that would partly have answered the question I did ask him, 'What does giving it back mean?' He couldn't say. In fact no one I asked could. No one was interested. Everyone was heartened by the generosity expressed in the gesture and enthusiastic in their hopes for a new era.

The enthusiasm was justified, as was much of the enthusiasm for multiculturalism and SBS, even though few people were then (or are now) clear about what multiculturalism means. Embattled politics being what it is in Australia, both the enthusiasm and the vagueness are an irritant to the Right which has, in my judgment, failed to see the wood for the trees on these matters.

Only five or six years before my friend told me about Ayers Rock, an incident occurred that I recount in *A Common Humanity* and that still shakes me. It happened in the late 60s at Melbourne University. I was a member of the Labor Club which was then a club of the radical Left. Like other members of the club, I was excited by the civil rights movements in the USA and by its more radical breakaway groups like the Black Panthers. One day a man came from Queensland to speak to the club. He told us that people were emigrating to Queensland from the southern states of the USA disillusioned with life there because of the progress made by the civil rights movement. Unable to tolerate the thought, let alone the fact, that blacks might vote and attend the same schools as whites, they thought Queensland might be more congenial to them. Or so we were told. We were also told that some of the immigrants went out on weekends in four-wheel drives to shoot Aborigines in much the same sprit as they shot kangaroos.

I'm now sure that the story wasn't true. At the time though, I gave it credence. Maybe. Maybe not, I thought, and the thirty or forty of my fellow students who attended thought the same, I believe. At any rate, no one said, 'This is unbelievable.' Yet I didn't—nor, I think did the other students—bother to find out whether or not it was true.

As I said, the memory of it still shakes me. How was it possible that idealistic young Australian students, sincerely anti-racists, should not care whether Aborigines were hunted for sport! What more damaging evidence could there be that we didn't care than the fact that we didn't even bother to find out whether it was so? I don't think one can answer those questions without recourse to the concept of racism. But whatever qualifications must be made to the claim that we were sincerely anti-racist students, the place to locate the racism that would explain (though not excuse) our astonishing omission is not, I think, deep in our hearts. It is in some of the institutions of Australian society that made Aborigines morally invisible to most Australians.

That wouldn't be possible now. But Aborigines are still only partially visible to the moral faculties of many (most?) Australians, even to many who are committed to reconciliation. Sorry Day is an example. It expresses a new aversion to racism that ensures there are not now examples like the one I just recalled. At the same time much of it is marked by a sentimentality that expresses the kind of goodwill that can quickly be eroded by the impatient belief that the Aborigines are asking for too much or showing excessive anger towards the government or (God forbid) to the white community more generally. Remember the tut-tutting when Noel Pearson was moved to call members of the Coalition racist scum. 'Mind your place. Don't rise above yourself.' If one denies that that was the tone, one can't, I think, deny that it wasn't far from it. Can one fully understand the evil the Aborigines have suffered and be so quickly stirred to indignation about what one takes to be their excesses? Can one really understand it and take most of them to be excesses?

*

Two years ago I gave a public lecture on genocide and the stolen generations at the Australian Catholic University campus in Ballarat. A small number of Kooris were in the audience. During the talk and afterwards during discussion they were sometimes irritable and impatient. Finally one spoke up. He was fed up, he said, with the many distinctions I had been making. Did I know what it felt like to be a victim of genocide? Did I not see that one can speak of such things only if one experienced them? Only Aborigines could speak with real understanding of the genocide committed against them. Did I even know any Aborigines? He finished, by wondering whether I was exploiting their suffering to make a name for myself, writing and lecturing about it.

Anyone who has spoken on platforms with Aborigines or to audiences where they are present will know his response is not unusual. People who are not Aborigines will know and perhaps be unnerved by the complex range of feeling—suspicion, pleasure, gratitude, hostility, warmth—Aborigines direct their way. Those feelings look inconsistent only if one presses them towards a resolution. But there is no need to do that. Those many conflicting responses appropriately mirror the situation of most Aborigines in contemporary Australia. They are true to it rather than a sign of a muddle.

I replied to the Koori that I spoke as a citizen—one whose conscience had belatedly been awakened, who wrote on matters of public concern and who believed he had something to say. Being a philosopher, much of what I speak and write about is of a conceptual kind. I have nothing to contribute to the historical argument. But it is not because I am a philosopher, I went on to say, that I believe the conceptual issues are the most pressing. Though we are far from having an adequate history, though *Bringing Them Home* makes no claim to being one and though its finding will surely be disputed, the broad picture is already clear. And the disputes about whether genocide had been committed against the children and their parents are not, for the most part, empirical or legal. They are philosophical and moral, enlivened by the question whether a criminal category whose paradigm is the Holocaust could apply to what was done to the children and their parents, even during the worst periods of the absorption programs.

I wasn't sure how he responded. He listened, at first with the same irritation as before, and then more attentively, but I'm sure that he wasn't convinced. I'm not even confident that he considered that I had given him something to think about. We came, he and I, from worlds that are too far apart to be bridged by a brief and irritable discussion after a public lecture.

To some my response to him may seen unnecessarily on the back foot. It's a matter for argument when one's shame and guilt make one too defensive. Argument about political correctness is in part about that and it is right that it should be. But there is, I believe, such a thing as the right to speak because of one's membership of a particular group, a right which is not merely a function of information or insight one may have come by in that way. 'Who are you to say this?' is not a question that can rightly be answered by, 'I'm curious about the matter and, like everybody, I have a right to say what I believe is true.' For the same reason, 'Who are you to put your nose in our troubles?', is not answered adequately by, 'I am a human being, concerned with right and wrong, justice and injustice.' Even bitter enemies in deadly conflict can (sometimes they do) respect one another, a form of respect that is almost always dependent on (though not entirely based on) contingencies that determine the depth of their involvement in the conflict that divides them.

A long tradition has disassociated depth from contingency, but our recent recovery of the important connections between depth of identity and rootedness, and authority and rootedness, has gone some way to correct that. While appeal to our humanity rather than to our local identities is rightly an ultimate moral appeal, by itself it seldom gives one the right to speak or the right to intervene, because it is often insufficient to command the kind of respect necessary for possession of that right.

If a Jew goes to Israel as a volunteer at time of war, a Palestinian may ask him scornfully why he is not prepared to live there, but he is unlikely to ask him why he is there. One can imagine a discussion between them in which both recognise that contingencies of birth and identity have generated moral necessities that have locked them in a conflict in which one may kill the other, but in which each may nonetheless respect the other. In some of his writings Amos Oz imagines just such discussions, emulating, I suspect, Albert Camus whose *Letters to a German Friend* were written while he was a member of the French Resistance. One might find the writings of both men a little portentous at times, but that should not get in the way of seeing the importance of what they are doing, of seeing the importance of such imaginary conversations as a means— perhaps an indispensable means—of helping those embroiled in conflict to judge the justice of their cause or its prosecution.

The question, 'Who has the right to speak, about what, to whom, on whose behalf?' inevitably comes up again and again. That it should sometimes come up uneasily, belligerently, neurotically, is hardly surprising given the situations that prompt it. It has not been asked often in Australia in connection with the Aborigines, but that is changing. It shows in a minor way in our embarrassment over not knowing what generic terms to use to describe those whom we murdered and whose lands and children we stole. Unsatisfactory though it is, 'Aborigine' strikes me as preferable most of the time to 'indigenous' and preferable almost all the time to 'first nations'. It is interesting that many Aborigines now use 'blackfella' and 'whitefella', but even if one ignores the fact that it is not only white Australians who must think about their attitudes to Aborigines, few who are not Aborigine have the authority to use those terms.

Impatience with fine distinctions can come from unlikely quarters. Last year I gave a lecture on genocide and the stolen generations to a group of lawyers in Sydney. I argued that there could be little doubt that during the period covered by *Bringing Them Home*, some Australian State governments enacted genocidal policies as they are defined by the 1948 United Nations Convention on the Prevention and Punishment of Genocide. I also argued that the United Nations' definition was inadequate, if only because it allowed *Bringing Them Home* to conclude, quite reasonably insofar as it was guided by the convention, that assimilation policies of the 70s and 80s were also 'arguably genocidal'. A more serious conception of genocide, I argued—one that is morally alive to the fact that Armenia, the Holocaust and Rwanda are our paradigms—can be applied to what sometimes happened to the stolen children and their parents. Our thoughts about this, I claimed, have been distorted by the understandable belief that genocide requires murder. That it needn't, becomes apparent to anyone who believes that the forcible sterilisation of a people for the purpose of their extinguishment as a people would constitute genocide. Accepting that there can be genocide without mass killing does not demean the Holocaust and it will enable us to understand better what it is about the Holocaust that we try to understand by bringing it under the concept of genocide.

During a discussion, a justice of the Supreme Court who had been listening attentively said something like this (I embellish a little so as to make the his point dramatically clear):

> I understand why you make these fine distinctions in search of an adequate label. I understand because I'm a lawyer and we lawyers are at home with this way of doing things. But don't you think that you must proceed differently if you are to convince those who are not already convinced of how long and how deeply the indigenous peoples of this land have suffered. To do that, you will have to move people—like Robert Manne does. Your discussion is too abstract, too dry.

I replied that the word genocide was not a label, that it denoted a concept we had reached for to characterise a relatively novel dimension of our political experience in an effort to bring that experience within the space of a common understanding. *Bringing Them Home* revealed inadvertently that genocide is a concept whose moral and logical structure is still unclear to us. Imagine, I suggested, that you are struggling in court with the evidence, with precedents and complex legal arguments, in an effort to determine whether the person before you is guilty of manslaughter or murder. Imagine now that someone says: 'Why get so bothered about a label? We've seen the blood, we've heard the lamentations and we've seen the tears. That's what matters, not this abstract argument.' Of course, I put the question to him rhetorically, but in fact many people asked something like it in the two great trials of Nazi criminals at Nuremberg and in Jerusalem when Eichmann was tried. 'We've seen the corpses piled high, we've heard the terrible stories telling how they suffered before they died. What does it matter whether you call the evil done to them mass murder or a crime against humanity?'

Although I was surprised that the question should have been put to me by a justice of the Supreme Court, I recognised it as a familiar and important one. The Koori in Ballarat was asking the same question. No matter that now stands before the Australian nation is so painfully a matter of the heart while at the same time so urgently in need of a cool and patient head, a head patiently open to the detailed and subtle examination of the concepts we need to understand ourselves and to have clear vision and realistic hopes. Amongst others, they are the concepts with which to explore what is at issue between those who require an apology from the prime minister and those who are content with what he is offering at present; those which enable us to judge which crimes are rightly called genocide and those with which to explore what is at issue in talk of self-determination.

I do not, however, want now to succumb to endorsing a sharp distinction between head and heart of a kind that I have been trying to undermine during most of my philosophical life. Understanding here, even of the distinctions that will delineate the structures of the concepts I just mentioned, is understanding in which head and heart must come together. Like all understanding, however, it must rise to the requirements of its subject matter, which sometimes looks very abstract indeed.

Much of what we need to think about is often discussed under the heading of collective responsibility. To understand the different ways indigenous and non-indigenous Australians can come together and the different ways we can't, we need to understand the ways we can call others and be called ourselves to lucid moral responsiveness to our past. If relations are even to be honest, let alone if they are to realise their human potential, we must acknowledge the different ways we should rise to those calls. One would have to be deaf not to hear that in the demands for an apology and more subtly in the ambivalent responses I described earlier.

Outside of academic circles, discussion of collective responsibility has been woeful because of conceptual illiteracy of an elementary kind—about the distinction between shame and guilt for example, or between apologies and expressions of regret. I am conscious that I now sound like a philosopher who believes he is in a position to tell people how to think. Some philosophers do assume that authority and I have often deplored it. Nonetheless we will need to think harder than we have done if we are to get beyond the sterile divisions between Left and Right that disfigure public discussion in this country. A right-wing intelligentsia—now grouped around *Quadrant* magazine—has considerable influence on the Coalition and, I suspect, beyond. (Apparently the prime minister has become an avid reader of *Quadrant* since Paddy McGuinness became its editor.) Not all of it members, by any means, are unmoved by the past and present suffering of the Aborigines. If their sympathies are somewhat dulled, it is sometimes because of the embattled nature of much of Australian public intellectual life, in which fine distinctions are treated with disdainful and sometimes explosive impatience. Often, it's not the suffering and injustice of the past the Right denies, it is the claim that we are collectively responsible for it; it's not attention to the wrongs done to the children but the idea that it could be genocide that angers them. (If it's genocide, Michael Duffy said, then Menzies and Hasluck share the same circle of hell with Hitler and Himmler). It's not greater participation by Aborigines in the life of the nation they are opposed to, it's the notion of Aboriginal self-determination that provokes their derision.

*

The friend who told me that we had given back Ayers Rock meant we gave back what we took from the Aborigines. Everyone would take him to have meant that and many would think he was right to mean it. Not everyone, of course, as is evident from some of the hostility to Paul Keating's Redfern speech. 'We took the traditional lands, committed the murders, took the children', Keating said, acknowledging the wrongs done to the Aborigines and also that their present miseries are not the result of a natural catastrophe, but largely the effects of those wrongs. He also accepted an obligation to relieve their suffering. That much the present government is prepared to admit and to do, although only intermittently and in ways that almost always muddy the waters. Keating's 'we'—we took the lands, committed the murders, took the children—implies, however, that the obligations he accepted derived from acknowledgement of (or perhaps was an expression of) exactly the kind of collective responsibility that John Howard and many of his ministers reject.

Collective responsibility needn't mean collective guilt, and more often than not it shouldn't because one can rationally feel guilty only for what one has done or failed to do. But it should be more than regret, more even than the 'deep, sincere and sorrowful regret' John Howard and John Herron say they feel. Regret implies little more than that one wishes that something hadn't happened. Compassionate Americans, Germans, Danes, Norwegians for example, could feel it about the crimes against the Aborigines. The saintly ones among them might also feel profound sorrow. Clearly, though, they cannot be asked to rise to the responsibilities implied in Paul Keating's 'we'.

Paul Kelly has wondered in one of his articles in the *Australian* whether there really is a significant difference between offering an apology and expressing sincere regret and sorrow, not only for the misery, but also for the injustices suffered by the Aborigines. The answer, as everyone instinctively knows, is that an apology in some way takes responsibility for those injustices. Howard knows that and with a degree of cunning trades on confusion about it, giving the impression that because he now professes profound and sincere regret, he has come a long way, while knowing all the while that the distance between his expression of regret and an apology is as huge as it ever was.

Keating's 'we' is not merely enumerative—not merely one that designates members of a group for purposes of classification. It's a 'we' of fellowship—the kind people mean when they suffer together or rejoice together, or the kind we mean when we speak of our mortality and intend to refer to more than the mere fact that all human beings die. The ancient Greeks expressed a fellowship of all human kind when, in accents of sorrow and pity, they referred to human beings as 'The Mortals'. Keating's 'we' is one of national fellowship—or if 'national' carries the wrong kinds of political implications, then a fellowship formed by love of country. Citizenship, of itself, falls short of it. An immigrant, recently naturalised, could not fully participate in that fellowship. As a citizen she could accept responsibility (through taxation and other burdens, for example) for alleviating the hardships and present injustices suffered by Aborigines. But she could not feel shame for past crimes and could not sensibly apologise for them. Lacking, so far, historically deep cultural and political ancestry in this country, she lacks the identity-forming relations to it that would make both shame and the desire to apologise appropriate.

Those who could honestly respond to Keating's 'we' divide into two groups. Both are attached to their country, are proud of it, and enjoy the celebration of its achievements. One group—the group to which the prime minister, senator Herron and Peter Reith (amongst others) belong—is proud of Australia, but indignantly rejects all suggestions that Australians should also be ashamed of the past treatment of Aborigines. Such calls to shame, they say, express 'black armband' responses to our history. Wishing to be proud without sometimes acknowledging that they should be ashamed, theirs is the corrupt love of country we call jingoism. The other group accepts that shame may be necessary for truthful moral response to the evil in our history—to the fact that is our history.

In order to be lucidly ashamed of Australia's treatment of the Aborigines, it is not necessary, as people who go on about black armbands appear to think, to descend into morbid self-abasement or always to walk around with head hung low, or to fear to criticise Aboriginal culture or institutions except with weasel words. Or perhaps they just pretend to think it to feed their rhetoric. But if the shame means anything, if it really is lucid, then it will be because one has become answerable to those who were wronged by one's political ancestors. And that, in turn, will mean something only if one is answerable to what they say in their own voice. It is essential, therefore, to nourish the conditions in which the Aborigines can find their voices and then to listen to them in a spirit of humbled attentiveness.

Howard and his ministers will not do that. That's why, from the moment they took office, they have stumbled from one insult to the Aborigines to another, genuinely oblivious, it would seem, to their gross insensitivity. Only a miracle could make Howard apologise with an open heart and a clear head. Rather than have a mean-spirited confused apology from him, one that demeans him, the indigenous and non-indigenous communities and the nation, it is best to wait for another government, or at least another prime minister.

Nor is that humbled, attentive acknowledgement of the wrong done consistent with a demand that seems now to be gaining favour, that the Aborigines should forgive if we apologise. Paul Kelly said in the *Australian* (5/4/2000) that we should stop talking about apology and talk instead of apology and forgiveness. To my ear he sounded a little fed up because demands for reconciliation seemed to him to be directed increasingly to one side only.

Forgiveness is, I suspect, not the right word to describe the kind of open-heartedness that many people hope from the Aborigines in return for a prime ministerial apology. For one thing, it is characteristically a response to guilt and most Australians are not guilty of things for which they are rightly ashamed. Reconciliation must reach out to those who are ashamed but not guilty as well as to those who are both. For another, it is doubtful whether political leaders or other representatives of political groupings can rightly forgive on behalf of those in their constituency (broadly construed) who were wronged. Could Jewish leaders forgive the Germans and their allies on behalf of the Jewish victims of Nazi genocide? I don't say the answer is obvious, but I'm surprised the question has not troubled Aboriginal leaders, the government and others who have assumed that forgiveness is the appropriate concept.

Be that as it may: because both sides speak of forgiveness, I will too. It will enable me to make my point even more strongly. The non-indigenous community may ask and hope for forgiveness, but it has no right to demand it. There will be no reconciliation unless the Aborigines forgive, but talk of reconciliation as a moral imperative has lulled some people into the lazy thought that if we are prepared to apologise, they should be prepared to forgive. Even if we knew that the Aborigines will deny us forgiveness, we have apologies and reparation to make, and we should make them unconditionally.

One hears too often nowadays the querulous tone I reluctantly believe I heard in Kelly's article, and much more of it is, I fear, latent in the body politic. When the prime ministerial apology comes as it will, if not from this prime minister then from a later one, then we may hear something like this. 'We've apologised. Settle down. Become good citizens, good Australians. Take your place in the multicultural life of the nation, as the Greeks, Italians and other foreigners have. True we owe you differently from them, and as part of practical reconciliation we will honour what we owe you in education and in health care. But stop this nonsense about treaties and self-determination.' After the apology, I fear that the humility that should attend the acknowledgement of wrong done will no longer inform the spirit with which the government, supported by the electorate, will seek to alleviate the material suffering of the Aborigines. The reason? Because, as I said earlier, most Australians have not fully comprehended the terrible evils done to them.

*

To come back to the Koori in Ballarat and to try again to capture some of the complexity of our exchange. At a point of tension in it—a point where he and I were both irritated with each other—I told him he couldn't have it both ways. He couldn't, I said, invoke—indeed exploit—the profound moral connotations of the concept of genocide and at the same time express impatience with the fine distinctions that are necessary if the concept's structure—and therefore its political, moral and legal ramifications—are to be made clear. And necessary too, I continued, if there was to be any chance of meeting the accusation that the application of the concept to what was done to the stolen children was stupid and indecent, an offence to the victims of real genocide and also to the stolen children insofar as it is assumed they are glad to profit from such a demeaning comparison.

In a generous review of *A Common Humanity* in the *Australian's Review of Books* (April 2000), Martin Krygier says that he wishes the issue of genocide had never been raised in the Australian context. He means I think, that he wishes it had never been raised in connection with the stolen children. The case for its application in other periods of Australian history is, I think, overwhelming and I doubt that Krygier would deny it. He goes on to say that it has, however, been raised in connection with the stolen children and in a way that now requires argument rather than sneers in response. He is right, of course, but I would put the point with a different emphasis. The reason it needs to be discussed seriously has not so much to do with the dialectics of discussion, with the fact that a case has been made and needs to be answered. It needs to be discussed because an element of our political experience seems to require it. If no one had ever raised the issue, we would have to raise it in order to understand ourselves in our history.

We are still a long way from serious discussion of it, I think. If we ever come to it, there will be much anger and pain. Some of it will be the anger and pain we are familiar with, only more so. But there will be a new dimension to it. As I said to the Koori in Ballarat, the concept of genocide is essentially a concept forged to make sense of an element of Western political experience. We are learning now that reflection on other experiences—notably those of some of the colonised peoples—will enable us to understand its structure better and thus to understand better even those aspects of the European experiences we were trying to capture with the concept, but whose significance was distorted by the horrific mass murder that seemed inseparable from its paradigms. But though reflection on the stolen children will help us to understand genocide, the stolen children themselves have nothing uniquely to contribute to our understanding of the concept. Not them nor Aborigines, nor even indigenous peoples more generally.

The Aborigines have told stories of the crimes they suffered that add up to genocide, and they (and others) will tell more. But the stories and the way they move us, are no substitute for the discursive elaboration of a concept whose essential grammar was set by European political theory in response to European experiences. To put the point another way. The genocidal aspect of the crimes committed against the stolen generations does not show in the suffering that the stories make real to us. It was not the genocidal aspect of the stories told in *Bringing Them Home* that made Kim Beazley and others weep when they first heard them. That is not because the stories that would reveal the genocidal aspect of what was done have yet to be told. At the level of story telling, at the level at which only stories can truly engage our sympathies, move us and make us weep, Aborigines may have much yet to tell. Perhaps those stories will teach us something new about the human condition. Perhaps you can't tell some of those stories unless you are an Aborigine. It may even be true that you can't fully understand them unless you are an Aborigine. But it is not true that the stories that only the Aborigines can tell, or the ones they can tell best, will make us see why the crimes against the stolen generations were sometimes genocide. The claim that the Aborigines have nothing uniquely to contribute to the discussion of genocide committed against them—I mean to the discussion of why it was genocide—

will offend many of them, as it did the Koori in my audience at Ballarat. It will also offend some whites.

Genocide is essentially a concept of Western political theory. So is the concept of self-determination, but in the latter case the efforts of first nations to be true to the experiences which make them call for self-determination may extend our understanding of political possibilities. The demand for land rights, for example, may merely be part of a demand for equal citizenship that acknowledges their history and the rights that should accrue because of it. But it may be part of a demand for forms of political association hitherto unforeseen.

We do not know—in principle do not know—the form of our future political relations, not at any rate if we remain open to the Aborigines' call for self-determination. The reason that we don't know is truly radical. It is not because there are a determinate number of options, but we do not know which we will choose or which will be forced on us. No amount of cogitating—not even if it is done by political theorists of genius—will by itself even map out the theoretical possibilities for us. Our ignorance will not be diminished by more facts and more brainpower. We do not yet know the possibilities, partly because it is not just a matter of discovering them, but of creating them. Or better: our conclusions will express what we discover in our living together, imaginatively but soberly responsive to what we can make of the truthful acknowledgement of the past and what it will make of us.

After the prime ministerial apology has been made, it will be a matter of urgency to struggle against the political inertia and the blandishments of a false realism that will undermine the conditions that would enable indigenous and non-indigenous Australians to explore together the radical possibilities in the ways they might live together in this land. Impatience with the vagueness of appeals to self-determination should gently be turned aside, for as I have tried to suggest, its vagueness is not itself the expression of intractable confusion. Unavoidably, talk of self-determination will do little more in the near future than gesture towards an outcome whose full conceptual character is in principle unforeseeable. In the meantime we should be careful in our use of the first person plural. We should not, for example, assume that the political fellowship in one political community that indigenous and non-indigenous Australians look forward to should be that of equal citizens in the Australian nation.

Australia, it must be admitted, is an unlikely place for experimentation in novel forms of political association. That happens successfully, one feels, only in places where there is a relatively sophisticated interest in the kind of conceptual issues that Australians appear to be impatient with. But there is in Australia a different kind of openness that may prove more important. It shows itself in the kind of decency that made multiculturalism such a success on the ground, despite Hanson and her followers and despite the misgiving of influential parts of the intelligentsia. And fortune can smile on anyone, as Aristotle was disposed to note when he contemplated the undeservingly lucky.

I will quote something I wrote in *A Common Humanity*, not because I think it is so marvellous, but because it makes just the point I now want to make in conclusion and I cannot think of how to put it better. I had been quoting Martin Buber on the nature of conversation. The basic difference between monologue and 'fully valid conversation', he said was 'the otherness, or more concretely, the moment of surprise'.

> His point is not merely that we must be open to hearing surprising things. We must be open to being surprised at the many ways we may justly and humanly relate to one another in a spirit of truthful dialogue. It is in conversation, rather than in advance of it, that we discover, never alone but always together, what it means really to listen and what tone may properly be taken. In conversation we discover the many things conversation can be. No one can say what will happen when we fully acknowledge the evil done to the indigenous peoples of this land and when they see and accept that we have acknowledged it. More importantly, no one can say what should happen.

What Justice O'Loughlin Could Not See

Robert Manne

In August Justice Maurice O'Loughlin delivered his judgment in the case brought against the Commonwealth government by two Northern Territory members of the stolen generations, Lorna Cubillo and Peter Gunner.

In a previous case, Kruger against the Commonwealth, the High Court decided that the Aboriginals Ordinance of 1918, under which 'half-caste' children in the Territory had been separated from their parents, was constitutionally valid. Counsel for Cubillo and Gunner, of course, accepted this. What they claimed, however, was that in separating these two children from their families and communities and in committing them to institutions, the Commonwealth had misused its lawful powers—had falsely imprisoned them, had breached its statutory and fiduciary duties and its duty of care.

Justice O'Loughlin comprehensively rejected all these claims. Although the legal reasoning was complex, from two simple propositions all else flowed.

According to his interpretation of the ordinance O'Loughlin found that the Commonwealth government was not 'vicariously liable' for the actions of its Directors of Native Affairs. Even more importantly, he believed the most critical section of the ordinance, concerning the 'care, custody and control' of the Aborigines, gave the director a plain right in law to act in any way he regarded as being in the best interests of the child.

O'Loughlin found that in the case of Lorna Cubillo, because of the death of key witnesses and the passage of time, no evidence existed, one way or the other, which could throw light on why the director, Frank Moy, had removed her from her family and placed her in the Retta Dixon Home. In the absence of this evidence he could not find against the director, let alone the Commonwealth.

In the case of Peter Gunner he found that good evidence existed which showed that the director, Harry Giese, had indeed formed an opinion about what was in the best interests of Peter before removing and detaining him and that, moreover, Peter had been taken to an institution at his mother's request.

Towards the opening of his judgment O'Loughlin quoted the words of a fellow judge who had warned about the 'unrealisable expectations' among those who sought legal remedy for great historic wrongs. By the end of his judgment what he meant was clear. In the cases he had heard the distance between what justice required and what the law could deliver was very wide indeed.

Let one small example illustrate the general point. In the course of the trial it was discovered that when Peter Gunner was sent to St Mary's Hostel his mother had been promised solemnly by a patrol officer that each Christmas her son would be allowed to come home for the holidays. For unexplained reasons this promise was never fulfilled. The failure to meet this promise—which severed Peter's connections with his community and culture in the critical years of his life—was a terrible wrong. Yet the simple fact of issuing this promise formed an important ingredient in O'Loughlin's conviction that Harry Giese had formed an opinion about what was in the best interests of this particular child and had, therefore, acted, in the case of Peter Gunner, according to the law.

In the Cubillo-Gunner decision, legal reasoning and moral meaning hardly touch. As a consequence the importance of the case is not found in the outcome of the judgment but somewhere entirely different—the court's findings about the facts.

For 107 days witnesses were called and argument heard about why Lorna Cubillo and Peter Gunner had been removed from their mothers and about what happened to them after they were institutionalised. Moreover, in preparation for this trial, both legal teams spent small fortunes sifting through government archives, searching for the documentary evidence that might throw light on the history of child removal in the Northern Territory. We are never likely to have a more probing investigation into the question of the stolen generations than we have had in the Cubillo-Gunner case.

What, then, did Justice O'Loughlin find? In 1947 Lorna Cubillo was an eight-year-old 'half-caste' who lived at an Aboriginal settlement, run by the Australian Inland Mission, at Phillip Creek. There is considerable uncertainty, which the court could not ultimately resolve, about Lorna's early years. What is clear, however, is that Lorna's natural father was a European, Horace Nelson, and her mother a 'full-blood' Aborigine. When Lorna was very young her mother died. In the Aboriginal way, her mother's sister, Maisie, raised her as her child.

The question of whether or not the 'half-caste' was an 'outcast' in the traditional Aboriginal world was pursued in this trial. According to the evidence he heard, O'Loughlin found it impossible to generalise. Nevertheless in the case of Lorna Cubillo it clearly was not so. Lorna, at Phillip Creek, was surrounded by a close extended family. Her 'full-blood' sister, Annie, gave evidence to the court, which O'Loughlin accepted, that at Phillip Creek the 'half-caste' children were all loved by their mothers and Aboriginal fathers 'like their own'.

The court established that on 23 July 1947, Amelia Shankelton, the woman who ran the Retta Dixon 'half-caste' Home in Darwin, and Les Penhall, a cadet patrol officer in the Northern Territory, arrived separately at Phillip Creek. On the following day sixteen 'half-caste' children, including Lorna Cubillo, were dressed in new uniforms, told they were going on a picnic and placed on a truck. The truck took off for Darwin. O'Loughlin concludes that it is almost certain that the removal of these children took place without their mother's consent. How could meaningful consent of all the mothers be obtained by an English-speaking missionary in a single day?

O'Loughlin accepts, on the evidence he heard, that, as the sixteen children departed, a terrible grief gripped the settlement and that, in the Aboriginal ritual of mourning, the women beat their heads with sticks until the blood flowed. He dismisses out of hand the shabby argument put by the Commonwealth that the suffering of the Aborigines at Phillip Creek went no deeper than the sadness of European parents at the departure of their children for a term of boarding school. Most importantly, after hearing days of evidence from Lorna Cubillo and from the psychiatrist who examined her, he is convinced that the eight-year-old girl did not recover, for the remainder of her life, from the shock of her sudden, inexplicable separation from her mother, family, community and world which took place on that day.

Two Aboriginal women and several of the former staff, called by the Commonwealth, spoke glowingly of life in the institution to which Lorna Cubillo was sent. O'Loughlin accepts the sincerity of what they have to say. But he also accepts that for Cubillo, and several other former inmates who testified on her side, the Retta Dixon Home was a place of dreary routine, overzealous and puritanical religiosity, where the speaking of Aboriginal languages was frowned upon, human warmth absent and corporal punishment severe.

In her testimony Cubillo recalled the terror she felt as a young girl when the missionaries told her that all the heathens, like the family she had lost, were condemned to perish in infernal flames. She remembered the pitiful time when some male members of her family visited her, and when she touched their hands through the fence and how she was reprimanded as a result. She remembered, too, her animal fear of a certain missionary—'the chief judge and whipper' as he was once called—who, on one occasion merely stared suggestively at her; who, on another, placed his hand high on her thigh; and who, on yet another, beat her so brutally with belt and buckle that her face was scarred and her nipple torn. This final incident was confirmed by much evidence brought before the court. The man who had flogged her told O'Loughlin that 'the rod of correction' was necessary to bring a child to God. He spoke these words with such an air of rectitude that it chilled the judge's blood.

Justice O'Loughlin is of the view that different Aboriginal children responded to their detention with a different intensity and in different ways. He brings down no general criticism about the manner in which Amelia Shankelton managed the Retta Dixon Home. Yet he has no doubt at all that Lorna Cubillo experienced detention at Retta Dixon as 'a time of loneliness, hardship and cruelty'.

Peter Gunner was born at Utopia Station some two years after Lorna Cubillo was detained. His mother was a 'full-blood' Aborigine, Topsy; his natural father a teenage European, with whom Topsy had a brief liaison, and after whom Peter was named. Great uncertainty surrounds the circumstances of his birth. The station owner's wife at Utopia, Dora McLeod, swore in an affidavit that, on the day after the birth of her baby, Topsy told her she had abandoned it in a rabbit burrow. The judge rejected this evidence. McLeod kept an extremely detailed daily diary. In this diary, concerning the supposed abandonment of Peter Gunner, there is not a word. Some uncertainty also surrounds Peter's relations with his mother in his early years. During the trial an old Aborigine from Utopia, Johnny Skinner, gave evidence that it was not Topsy, who took a tribal husband, but Peter's grandmother, who 'grew him up'.

No uncertainty, however, concerned the general wellbeing of Peter Gunner's Utopian years. He was surrounded by a large, extended family and was particularly close to an uncle, Motorcar Jimmy, with whom he roamed and hunted each day. No one suggested that as a 'half-caste' he was an outcast in Utopia. No one suggested he was physically neglected or in need of care. After listening to much evidence on this point O'Loughlin's conclusions were clear: 'Peter Gunner lived in a happy, healthy Aboriginal community and environment—a community into which he had been accepted and of which he was a part.' Everyone accepted that if Gunner had been left alone he would have passed through initiation into full Aboriginal manhood within the tribe.

He was not left alone. It was the responsibility of the patrol officers in the Northern Territory to file reports on the 'half-caste' children they encountered at the station camps. Peter was first seen when he was too young to be taken away. For several years no new sighting was made. A patrol officer, Harry Kitching, commented after a visit to Utopia in April, 1955, that as soon as he arrived the children and their mothers would simply disappear. O'Loughlin comments thus: 'Why would the mothers and children flee when a patrol officer appeared at their camp? There can be only one answer: the presence of a patrol officer was synonymous with the children being taken from their families.' And yet, as we shall see, the learned judge does not believe in the existence of a 'general policy' of 'half-caste' child removal. The mothers at Utopia apparently did not harbour similar doubts.

Eventually, in September 1955, Kitching located Peter. For reasons that cannot be known, Topsy now agreed that her son should be sent to St Mary's half-caste hostel at Alice Springs and to school. She was falsely promised that each year Peter would be sent home for holidays. Because of a change in the Ordinance, before

Peter could be lawfully committed to St Mary's, Topsy had to request that her son be declared a ward. As it turned out, the thumbprint she planted on the standard form was the most vital piece of evidence presented to the court.

Much court time was consumed by the presentation of evidence to prove that, at the time of Peter's admission, St Mary's was a poorly funded, incompetently staffed, comprehensively mal-administered, seriously unhygienic, 'stinking slum'. Much time, too, was taken in order to demonstrate that while detained at St Mary's, Peter Gunner was beaten regularly for his disobediences and was subject—as were several other Aboriginal lads—to serious sexual abuse. While O'Loughlin is not willing to make a generally adverse finding about Retta Dixon, he has no such inhibitions when it comes to St Mary's half-caste home.

After listening to days of evidence, Justice O'Loughlin was convinced that, like Lorna Cubillo, Peter Gunner had never recovered from the trauma of his separation from family and detention at St Mary's. Two psychiatrists who examined him thought he suffered from separation anxiety and chronic depression as a direct result. One said that he had never encountered so deeply defeated a man in his life. O'Loughlin, who had observed him closely in his courtroom, could not but agree.

In their pleadings, Lorna Cubillo and Peter Gunner agreed that they had been separated from their families not as a result of any assessment of their individual circumstances, but because of the existence in the Northern Territory of 'a general policy of removal and detention'. The Commonwealth denied this claim. As a consequence Justice O'Loughlin was obliged to assess a mountain of archival evidence about the policy and practice of Aboriginal child removal in the Territory over a period of fifty years. For once the cliché was true. History was on trial.

The most vital historical question O'Loughlin was obliged to determine was whether, as Cubillo and Gunner claimed, a general removal policy had ever existed. After weighing the evidence he decided that their counsel had failed to prove their case. Yet the more closely his judgment is examined the more questionable his reasoning on this point seems.

O'Loughlin, first, fails to distinguish clearly between the ideas of 'general' and 'blanket' policy. At one point he writes of a 'general or blanket policy', as if they are the same thing. At another he

quotes the evidence of a patrol officer, Creed Lovegrove, who denied
the existence of any 'blanket policy' for the removal of 'half-caste'
children. In fact counsel for Cubillo and Gunner had never claimed
there was a blanket policy for the removal of 'half-caste' children,
to which there could be no exceptions made. What they did claim
was that there existed, in regard to one category of 'half-caste'
children, those born of Aboriginal mothers and European fathers
living in the native camps, what might be called a general policy
thrust. This claim should not be controversial. In almost every
report of the Chief Protector of Aborigines during the inter-war
years, the policy of 'collecting' the 'half-caste' children from the
camps was outlined. In 1950, the Director of Native Affairs, Frank
Moy, wrote that 'it is the policy of this branch to remove the children
from their native mothers as soon after birth as is reasonably
possible'.

For fifty years the Northern Territory's Aboriginal administration
pursued a clear, general policy—to collect the 'half-caste' children
born of Aboriginal mothers and European fathers from the
settlements and camps. Because of his failure to distinguish clearly
in his mind between the ideas of general policy and blanket policy,
O'Loughlin, in his judgment, ends up by seeming to deny the
existence of a general removal policy, whose place in the
documentary record is as clear as day. When all the 'half-caste'
children and only the 'half-caste' children were removed from
Phillip Creek in 1947 was this not a precise example of a general
policy at work?

It is true that the fulfilment of the ambition of the removal policy
was more difficult than the policy makers might have wished. The
collection of the 'half-caste' children was reliant on the diligence
of the policemen and patrol officers, who covered vast territories,
and on the holding capacity of the extremely poorly funded
institutions to which the children were sent. Nevertheless, over
time, an impressive number of children were removed. When the
policy began it was estimated that in the Territory only two hundred
'half-caste' children had been born. In 1952 a count was made of
all the children who had been institutionalised in the past thirty
years. It arrived at a figure of 583. The failure to implement the
removal policy more comprehensively than this is no evidence, as
O'Loughlin seems to believe, that a general removal policy had
not been in place.

One of the fundamental historical and moral questions raised in the debate about the stolen generations is whether or not substantial numbers of the children taken from their families could be said to have been 'forcibly removed'. O'Loughlin pursued this question tenaciously. Yet, once again, his final judgment seems to me open to serious doubt.

After a careful assessment of the documentary evidence, O'Loughlin concludes that at no time before the mid-1950s did government policy require the consent of the Aboriginal mother before her child was removed. If consent was not required, and if, moreover, as everyone acknowledges, the Aboriginal administrators in the Territory were not obliged to justify their decision before a court of law, has it not already been demonstrated that these children were 'forcibly removed'?

For O'Loughlin, forcible removal occurs only in those cases where Aborigines resisted the removal of their children—where children had to be dragged from the arms of their mothers or where Aboriginal parents openly defied the policemen or patrol officers who came to take their children. In his judgment O'Loughlin records the mourning of the Phillip Creek Aborigines as their children were driven away. In his judgment he accepts that Aboriginal mothers routinely darkened their children's skins with charcoal or fled with them from the camps when the patrol officers arrived. Yet as only four or five properly documented instances of Aboriginal resistance to removal were brought in evidence before his court, he concludes that throughout the history of the Territory forcible removals of 'half-caste' children were, most likely, rather rare.

Even if one accepts O'Loughlin's narrow definition of forcible removal, I am almost certain he is wrong. What motive did the child removalists have to record the resistance of the Aborigines? What capacity did the Aborigines have to create a documentary record of their grief or resistance suitable for a court? Before the Second World War, Aboriginal children were removed by police who often rode into the camps. Were such removals not 'forcible'? Before his death the Acting Director of Native Affairs in the early 1950s, Reg McCaffery, was interviewed in Darwin. McCaffery was asked whether forcible removals had taken place during his administration. He answered thus: 'The children were taken off the breast forcibly... There were great scenes of gins screaming their lungs out. Great scenes.'

It is most likely that during the 1950s forcible removals became increasingly rare. And yet, although policy now required the patrol officers to remove the children only after a long-term campaign of persuasion had been pursued, there was no suggestion that in the end such persuasion would be allowed to fail. On one occasion Frank Moy expressed the new policy thus:

> If, at the first visit, the parents are loath to part with the child the matter is left until the next visit when another attempt is made and the process of 'educating' the parents is continued. Eventually... the child is willingly handed to the custody of the patrol officer.

Even the grammatical construction of this last sentence is strange. As forcible removal became less uncommon, irresistible persuasion took its place.

The most important historical conclusion of Justice O'Loughlin's judgment is that while the removal of 'half-caste' children may have been 'misguided' and 'paternalistic' it was certainly not based on racism or what he would call consideration of race. I am genuinely astonished at how he arrived at this view.

At its origins the motive of the removal policy was to 'rescue' 'part-European' children from the moral 'degradation' of the Aboriginal camp. The most basic assumptions of the policy—the belief that it was unconscionable to abandon part-European children to an Aboriginal life, and that it was necessary 'to elevate the half-caste to the standards of the white'—seem to me at least expressions of a racism of a disheartening and blatant kind.

Justice O'Loughlin clearly does not agree. At one point in his judgment he quotes the views of the Queensland Chief Protector, J.W. Bleakley. Bleakley thought that unless all the 'half-castes' were 'rescued' and sent to institutions to be educated, they were likely to pose a 'menace' to society and to breed more and more 'quadroons'. I see in this passage undisguised racial contempt. O'Loughlin sees in it the advocacy of a policy of 'care'.

Take another example. Dr Cecil Cook was the Chief Protector in the Northern Territory between 1927 and 1939. O'Loughlin acknowledges that Cook had strange views on eugenics and miscegenation. He is, however, incapable of accepting that Cook's drive to collect the 'half-castes' was driven by demographic nightmares of a helot class swamping white civilisation and by an ambitious, racial Darwinian program—to segregate the 'half-castes' from the 'full-bloods' and, through the encouragement of marriages between 'half-caste' girls and European males, to 'breed out the colour', to turn black into white.

In the inter-war period the Northern Territory policy of child removal expressed a desire to rescue 'half-castes' from their Aboriginality and, through a program of institutionalisation and education, to prepare the 'half-castes' for their biological absorption into European society. After the Second World War racial Darwinism might have been abandoned. The cultural rescue mission was, however, renewed. Justice O'Loughlin is right when he argues that those who separated the children from their mothers, families and communities thought they were acting 'in the best interests of the child'. What he does not see is how profoundly their conception of what was in the best interests of the 'half-caste' child was determined by racist assumptions of an unquestioned kind. I have no doubt that Justice O'Loughlin is a humane man, who was deeply moved by the pitiful stories he listened to in his court. And yet, like so many Australians of his generation, he just cannot see the racism of our past even when it is in front of his nose.

A Town Called Hackney Nation

Guy Rundle

The wedding in the town hall forecourt was a riot of colour. Local girl getting married and the guests had made a big effort, pulling out their most lavish wraps and fabrics for the occasion. Avoiding the alkies and junkies who made their home on the municipal benches, they mounted the stairs for the photo, pulling their draping hemlines over the wind-tossed crisp packets, kebab ends and smudges of shit—dog and human—in the forecourt. Backed by the grey Stalinist style council offices and the greyer sky, yellow patterns of sharks teeth bit into black and red lines, swirls of rococo mustard and turquoise hang off the shoulder and flowing to the ground. The women looked pretty good too.

There's a traditional African wedding here most Saturdays, but it's rare that the entire guest list will turn out in traditional garb as they did for this one. Usually it's a mixture, with a few brave souls going up against the English weather in Ghanian kente cloth and the rest in the sharp suits sold by the truckload in the dozen or so apparel shops cheek by jowl along the high street. Sometimes there's a wedding of white east-enders—Hackney is too far outside of the sound of Bow Bells to be proper cockney territory, but it's as east end as anywhere—and the suits are cheaper... And once I saw a black girl marrying a white bloke and the whole steps overflowed with three generations of eastenders, the old and the new, the wiry, dashiki and homburg, gold teeth and braidings.

Spend even half an hour in Hackney and you'd be convinced of the argument that Britain had become a multicultural society, a rainbow nation in which Anglo-Saxons are merely another minority, whether they liked it or not. You'd be wrong of course. Afro-Caribbean people—the term is interchangeable with 'Black'—number only around three percent of the UK population, and Indians and other Asians slightly more, and it is quite likely that in the entire swathe of land between London, Penzance and the south coast there are less of them than can be found in this one borough. Separated not only from the rest of Britain, but also from London—there is no tube service, so the area more or less falls off many people's mental map—it is a nation entire, a large sprawling area in the northern-most part of the east end, the name itself covering dozens of smaller areas of distinct flavour. From the vast council estates of Homerton, up to the markets and terraces of Dalston to the near Georgian quiet around Clapton Pond, there are places that are and aren't Hackney, crossing populations that interlace and interconnect while maintaining generations of continuity. In Dalston there are remnants of the old east end Jewish community, but the area is predominantly African and Caribbean who have taken over the running of the huge street markets that enswathe the area—hence the anomaly of a largely black area with a half dozen bagel shops. Down towards Hackney Central the area starts to be dominated by students, squatters, and artists—the borough of Hackney has the highest proportion of people on benefit and of those who listed 'artist' as their profession on the most recent census in western Europe—and West Africans, and then up to Clapton it's Jamaicans and second or third generation Irish. There are also sizeable Turkish and Vietnamese communities towards Bethnal Green. Cut off from the London sprawl for hundreds of years by marshes, the place has never surrendered its parochial feel. As Britain opened the doors to immigrants Hackney went from small town to global village, barely pausing for breath.

'You be craving him girl, you be craving him.' The girls at the bus-stop were taking the piss out of each other, about some boy, and the talk ranged across a whole empire, Caribbean strains until one suddenly switched into a creole 'tu n'a (sounds like) gabamallou???' my notes read. You be craaaaaving him. Then a woman they knew approached. Allo Mum, owww you doin, the vowels suddenly flat as a cap. So anthropologist 0—anthropologised 1. Again. In the terraced babel, the confluence of old empires, the endpoint of a diaspora, it is easy to believe that you have stumbled on authentic speech, that you have come to a place where people are really living in their language. Nor is it totally untrue. The West African creoles that circulate are partly from the Sierra Leonians, partly from the Ivory Coasters and others who come in via France courtesy of the EU, and they have circulated here for thirty or so years, against all odds. The rest of it is harder to pin down. Is the Caribbean schtick—craving, you be (the subjunctive returned via a long detour) craaaaving him—from local speech, or speech flavoured by US rap music? Is the sudden lurch into old east endese—allo (open your mouth as wide as possible and say the first vowel from halfway down your neck and you'll get the style of it) part of a multicultural repertoire, or is it a rip- off from 'EastEnders' and *Lock Stock and Two Smoking Barrels*? The success of Cockney chic has been such that even the Kensington yah! brigade are capable of coming out with 'yew doin moi (h)ead in, yew really are' (you are causing me some confusion), 'been vere, done vat, got va T-shirt' (i have already had that experience, thank you) at the drop of an aitch. Is it one, t'other or both? It's impossible to know. Yet there is nevertheless the pervasive sense that there is some sort of there here. Here is one place—Brixton is another, and Southall—where Afro-Caribbeans are in the majority and can create a community with less of a feeling of embattlement. That in turn creates a situation where one community carries on, while others drift through. Anyone who's white in Hackney is either a student-bohemian type, dirt poor or waiting for the Automobile Association van, whereas the black community encompasses a wide range of economic groups. The main street has its fair share of chain stores—Woolworths, Poundstretcher, Marks and Sparks— and a range of greasy spoons and cheap pokie dives, but there are also a range of upmarket clothes stores, hair and beauty salons, all of which specialise in the sort of clothes that, well, that only black people could get away with wearing: puffy shirts with gold chain hanging off the colour, straight cut pinstripe suits, fedoras for goddsake. The salons specialise in Afro-Caribbean hair, the styling of which requires special training. People hang out in them for hours, and on Friday night they stay open as late as the pubs, which isn't bloody hard. Down Graham Road on a ramshackle terrace of shops are the storefronts of the various organisations that have sprung up as the waves of immigrants from the former colonies arrived in the 60s and 70s: friendship and aid groups, a Rastafarian outfit, the Nation of Islam—whose bow-tied cadres can be seen selling 'The Final Call' outside the McDonald's on Saturday mornings, jostling for space with the (all-white) Socialist Workers Party table. There are the more obscure ones too—the Church of the Holy Tabernacle, whose members, on ceremonial occasions, wear velvet robes embroidered with gold leaf renderings of occult and religious symbols. Sweating profusely, they marched in full garb in the high summer Notting Hill carnival, hawking books featuring astrological diagrams of the Great Pyramid on the cover.

Yet such groups, both occult and political, remain on the fringes of contemporary black life, whose political organisation has become frayed since the high points of the 70s and 80s, when Hackney was the byword in resistance to the Thatcher government, with members of organisations such as the International Marxist Group sitting on the council. You can still see the remnants of that period in the names of the government buildings and streets: Nelson Mandela House, the CLR James Library, Maurice Bishop building, Sisulu Court, and so on. But the hard left were turfed out in the mid 90s by a right wing Labour group of astonishing incompetence, and now the place is so short of money that the schools go unheated and essential services unmaintained. Cascades of rubbish blow down Sisilu Street, because the borough cannot afford garbage collection more than once a week. As the new economy boom breaks over Britain, the place has gotten poorer rather than richer, but this sort of local underdevelopment hasn't propelled anyone to join the SWP.

Instead, the twin forces within black life are now Pentecostal Christianity and rap culture. Every Sunday you can hear the revivalist hymns pouring out from half a dozen churches, congregated in old garment factories and sports centres. Most are run as branches of US or Nigerian churches, who have sent missionaries to Britain, which they see as a godless land, whose own church has fallen prey to ecumenicism and perversion. Church-going for much of the black community retains the ritual lost by the white community at least a generation ago—whole families turned out, in Sunday best, on the bus. The Afro-Caribbean community newspapers—the *New Nation* and the *Voice*—both carry prominent religious sections that would be unsustainable in other publications. As with any charismatic tradition, much of the emphasis is on miracle healing, yet the claims of some of the African-originated churches are something else, the posters telling stories of regrown fingers, tumours extracted through the skin, and the like, a measure perhaps of the animist traces that remain in African Christianity.

The other focus of Afro-Caribbean life—rap—is no more than a hold-all term for a certain attitude, a mixture of American rap style, the old British ska/punk culture of the 70s and 80s and the Caribbean block party tradition, which was the root of the rave explosion of the mid-80s. It's a culture of substantial power and attractiveness, which is part of the reason for the dissipation of more conventional political organisation, for, in popular culture terms at least, black culture has achieved hegemony. The triumph of the DJ, club culture, the rave, drum 'n bass and the thousand variations in displacing the band, the pub and rock music as the focal cultural point, has been so total that one has to remind oneself that it was only in the late 70s that black culture managed to get any foothold in mainstream culture whatsoever. Now the entire culture has shifted to the point where that style—one which emphasises the carnivalesque, *jouissant*, desubjectivating aspect of popular culture rather than its authorial, textual nature has come to the fore. Of course, mainstream white rock music—or what clubbers refer to disdainfully as 'guitar' music—continues, but there is a pervasive sense that it does not command the heights of the culture. Once again, there is a great difference between London (and the other major cities such as Manchester and Liverpool) and the vast swathes of semi- suburban white Britain, where Phil Collins continues to rule unchallenged. Yet in places like Hackney black culture triumphs. This, despite the minimal mixing of white and black cultures. In a borough sixty percent black it is possible to walk into a pub on the main street and see not a single black face amongst the entire crowd. On the other hand, walk, as a white person into a Dalston club like the Orchid, and you will hear the wind shear as a hundred heads turn. There is no great hostility, merely curiosity and speculation. In fact a lot of black socialising occurs in places that look more like a Kingston shebeen than a bar. These are shopfronts with a few tables, a big freezer and a kitchen of sorts. They're halfway between a bar and a living room, a public space which hasn't yet been fully commodified. Up Downs Park Road, they alternate with Irish pubs, and you would no more walk into them than you would into someone's kitchen. Outside, the red BMWs cruise by, pumping out gangsta rap. Some of these guys are drug dealers (liberal to the last, I convinced myself for months that the three black-blue BMWs parked outside and the immaculate suits of the drivers, was evidence of the lucrative returns of the minicabbing trade) but most are people with good jobs who pay little or no rent on a council flat, and pour every spare cent into cars and clothes. And you walk on down the road, past the crowded shebeens, Lou Reed going round in your head. I wanna be black I wanna be black...

Well, part of the time. In Hackney the illusion is sustainable. Further out, the racist culture of the police force and the exclusionary nature of the establishment make it a lot tougher. Nor is the black community without internal problems, with more than a little intra-racial chauvinism between people of African and of Caribbean origin. The latter are accused by some of the former of having an excessive role in the high rates of single-teenage-motherhood (Hackney has the second highest rate of such in Western Europe. On some mornings the main street looks like a giant creche) and of perpetuating a 'mandingo' culture of fathering children by multiple women. Whether this has any basis in statistical fact I have no idea, but that it is an attitude abroad among the community, there is no doubt. Perhaps it is a melancholy measure of integration that people can feel relaxed enough within a community to hold ridiculous attitudes. One week soon after the Kosovo war, I heard one of the refugees—Kosovan, Serbian, gypsy, I dunno—who had managed to make it in, and gravitated, as you do, to Hackney, being berated for her fecklessness, workshyness and poor attitude. I turned round to see the woman—a twenty-year-old wrapped in riotously coloured traditional clothes and carrying the regulation swaddling baby—being laid into by a teenage black girl, half Scary Spice, half Alf Garnett. 'If she can beg for money she can get a job,' she was telling her friends. 'Vey come inna our country...'

Yet no matter how integrated peoples become, no one can ever—nor would one necessarily want to ever—dispel the ineffable strangeness of immigration, of diaspora. When a skeleton more than 9,000 years old was dug up in the Cheddar Gorge in South England recently, its DNA was tested against a randomly chosen local resident. They were found to have a match of sorts. Yet the bloke in the regulation old-Jamaican uniform of pinstripe suit jacket and trilby struggling against the wind down Mare Street is here because fifty years a ship named the *Windrush* docked with the first West Indian immigrants. Since for many years one of their main employers was the London buses, the communities developed around the depots—Hackney, Brixton *et al*. What a long, strange trip it is out of Africa to a frozen island off Europe that somehow got an empire. To what Naipaul called the enigma of arrival must be added that of persistance, of keeping on being here. Neither Jamaica nor Sierra Leone are the sort of places most people would want to return to these days, but what did it feel like for that first wave of immigrants to leave say, the Bahamas, and wind up in Wells Road, in a room above a chip shop, beside a railway bridge? In Hackney? They cannot have imagined that they would end up here. No one could, without immediately rioting. It was a round trip, a diaspora detour back to the islands, once sufficient savings had been made from the higher wages to be got here. Because surely no one could come from the Caribbean of all places to this septic isle and say to themselves with contentment 'This is it. I'll die here.'? Surely.

Who knows. But there is no going back now. Given enough time, you can get a liking for anything— kebabs and rain, egg and two and the 38 bus. And a fashion for retiring to Jamaica—where an English pension would make possible a life of prosperous ease— has been diminished somewhat by the fact that a few have been murdered for their money by gangs, and many have been shunned as foreigners. Home is what rusts on. Home is what sticks.

So they are here, and we are here, and the students are here, and the artists, and the poor and... the living cheek-by-jowl with the dead. In Ellingfort Road, squatters who had occupied a row of houses for more than ten years were given the whole street in recognition of the fact that they had restored them, built architect-designed infill housing, and created a working co-operative by pulling out the back fences and making a large vegetable garden. The street runs by London Fields, a pleasant enough park that once divided Hackney from London proper. Here they used to bury plague victims, now everyone picnics. One day there I saw the staff and regulars (insofar as there's a distinction) of my local—the Samuel Pepys, an all-hours bloodhouse that makes St Kilda's Esplanade Hotel look like the Royal Pump Room in Bath—gathered for an alfresco lunch—punks, crusties, thugs, dogs, grey white skin and silver studs, black T-shirts and torn fishnets—and imagined for a second that the dead had somehow melted upwards through the soil and come back to walk the earth. The past of the place is more present because it is so changed. The newsagent is full of pictorial histories of the area; sepia photos hang in the shops. They show the high street as it was at the turn of the century, before the Luftwaffe and the architects did their worst. Rows of glassed shops, bevelled windows, trams, men in wing collars and women in bustles, the genteel poverty of the Jewish East end, before prosperity came and they moved to Golders Green and points west.

Their masterpiece is the Hackney Empire, a huge old music hall theatre, built in 1901 at the height of ludicrous late-Victorian style. The main auditorium—three-stories high, festooned with balconies, boxes, and dress circles that come almost 270 degrees around, dripping with rococo decor—has played host to every major music hall turn of the century, from Max Miller to the alternative comedians of the 80s, from the Stones to Al Bowley. Closed for many years, it was reopened in the 80s and runs as a community theatre, with a mixture of local shows, and commercial one-offs, pantos and coach party matinees. Rarely sold out, you can slip in any night and take pot luck. It is one of the last places in the world where you can feel the old music hall experience. The genius of the Victorian theatre designers was to create auditoria which could either focus all attention on the stage—a sort of giant public television—or allow the audience to regard each other, everyone on display to everyone else. The walls are covered with tableaux of the institution from which it takes its name—red-coated soldiers struggling with lions on the African grasslands and whatnot. It's a huge *Boys Own* paper you can walk around, a giant camera obscura of the red bits on the map, a focus for its ruling subjects to feel part of that unimaginably far-flung expanse.

The irony that it is now maintained and patronised by the descendants of those whose labour was transmuted to its bricks and mortar was pretty obvious early on, but it was not until one night in the middle of the Writers Festival that it struck with full force. The ticket was sufficient to overcome the usual reservations about the celebrity culture of readings—Wole Soyinka, Chinua Achebe and Derek Walcott on the same bill. Both Soyinka and Achebe gave their own take on the ambiguous position of the postcolonial writer ('we knew that the British empire was the largest in the world' said Achebe, talking of his early years, 'and we were proud to have such powerful... owners') but the night belonged to Walcott, who read from Omeros, his reworking of Afro-Caribbean history through the medium of the Odyssey, its core scenes harking back to an African beach:

> ...As bulbs came on behind curtains, the shadows crossed
>
> me signing their black language. I felt transported,
> past shops smelling of cod to a place I had lost
> In the open book of the street, and could not find
>
> It was another country, whose excitable
> gestures I knew but could not connect with my mind
>
> ...Now in night's unsettling noises, what I heard
> enclosed my skin with an older darkness. I stood
> In a village whose fires flickered in my head
>
> with tongues of a speech I no longer understood
> but where my flesh did not need to be translated

In the belly of the empire, the diaspora is rehearsed and redeemed, despite the fact that it raises as many questions as it answers. For what is being returned, and to whom? Walcott, the tweed-jacketed American college professor, refracting a shared history through the medium of the founding narrative of the west, to an audience who would leave the theatre doyinn for a laaager an a curry. What could be returned to, and what would one be returning as? What returns to the exiled is a melancholia that is always on the point of being over, but can never be completed, because home is both there and not-there, the place you could only be going back to as it was, if you were not who you now are. In that space, a culture is made. And to pose the question as to whether that is sufficient compensation for all that is not is to make the mistake of thinking that things could be made otherwise.

Hackney is something special, but it is not the London I came to or for—the London of an Anglo-Australian childhood, of Tower Bridge and Tube maps, of Enid Blyton and the Beano. That London, insofar as it exists at all anymore, an interbellum idyll of a middle-class monoculture, has been driven to the redoubts of redbrick suburbs, Hampstead and Crouch End, Richmond and Muswell Hill. Knowing all one knows about what it was made of, one cannot mourn its passing... and so it stays on in me, here and not-here, there and not- there. It is a bus ride away but I was closer to it half a world distant, and now whole weeks go by that I never go in, a citizen of Hackney, a place more like Harlem than Hampstead. Nor would I want it otherwise, but to live in a land not only foreign but foreign to its idea of itself is strange, and you feel as if you tread light on the ground, across the garbage and the dead kebabs, thinking this is neither where I was nor where I aimed to be, but somewhere else entirely and in that, here, I am not alone.

On the evening of the wedding, waiting for the bus, I could hear the music from the reception, bubbling across the street. Rich, sweet African sounds, sixths and ninths, chords breaking up before they form. Somewhere here underneath the estates and the railway arches, the Tesco and the caffs are the pleasure gardens that Pepys mentions in his diary, forerunners of the Music Hall, where jaded Londoners would repair to strum lutes and canoodle in grottos. Long ploughed under, there is keen debate about where they actually were. Next to the depot, in the yard of St John-of-Hackney, you can sit on a sixteenth-century sarcophagus and wait for the 38 to Picadilly Circus, spread a newspaper or a McHappy meal from the McDonald's opposite. Whoever is buried there and why she deserved the honour is not recorded. The engravings say she was someone's wife and someone's mother but the elements have long since obscured all other details of her existence, down to her name.

Hackney, February 2000

Turton's Land Deeds

Christina Thompson

In the basement of the Lamont Library is a long, efficient-looking room marked Government Archives and Microforms. The first time I go there, on a Thursday, it is almost empty, just a few serious researchers, none of whom looks up when I come in. Outside the sidewalks are treacherous and the forecast is for more freezing rain. The library is inviting in an impersonal sort of way, all that beige furniture, the shadowless light, the metal filing cabinets with their cryptic labels: W1260, Y4750. There are cabinets on three sides of the room, each cabinet with many drawers, each drawer with many fiches, each fiche with many pages, each page with many words. It's like that nursery rhyme: kits, cats, sacks, wives, how many were going to St Ives? I have found in the catalogue something described as 'Turton's Land Deeds of the North Island', which I ask the attendant to fetch from the stacks. When it comes, all thirty sheets of it in a little paper pouch, he tells me the index is missing. 'Oh well,' I say cheerfully, 'I'll just start at the beginning.'

I begin by reading something called 'An Epitome of Official Documents relative to Native Affairs and Land Purchases in the North Island of New Zealand' compiled by H. Hanson Turton in 1883. There is a letter from James Busby, Esq., Resident at New Zealand, to the Hon. the Colonial Secretary of New South Wales, dated Bay of Islands, 16th June, 1837.

Sir,—

I have the honour to acknowledge the receipt of your
despatch of the 16th ultimo, which was delivered to me on
the 27th of the same month by Captain Hobson, of His
Majesty's ship 'Rattlesnake.'

War has broken out again between the tribes of the Bay of Islands,
the Nga Puhi and Pomare's people, the Ngati Manu of the southern
bay. This time it has something to do with a woman who was
murdered and eaten on being landed from a ship, and Busby writes
that he believes the man responsible to be the woman's former
husband. He describes the parties involved in the conflict as
'actuated by the most irritated and vindictive feelings' and says he
does not hope for a quick end to the hostilities. As a consequence
of the war, he adds, little or no land is under cultivation and 'It
may naturally be expected that the Natives will become reckless in
proportion to their want of the means of subsistence.'

Busby's purpose in writing is to ask that some paramount
authority be established over the people of New Zealand. He warns
that if some means are not found to stop their constant warring the
natives will annihilate themselves. The country, he writes, is being
depopulated. 'District after district has become void of its
inhabitants, and the population is even now but a remnant of what
it was in the memory of some European inhabitants.' So fast are the
people disappearing that it is a matter of debate as to the cause of
their decline. Some say that firearms have made their wars more
bloody, some that tobacco and grog have made them weak. Some
cite the spread of venereal and other diseases, the prostitution of
women and the murder of any half-caste children that they bear.

'The Natives,' writes Busby, 'are perfectly sensible of this decrease;
and when they contrast their own condition with that of the English
families, amongst whom the marriages have been prolific in a very
extraordinary degree of a most healthy progeny, they conclude
that the God of the English is removing the aboriginal inhabitants
to make room for them; and it appears to me that this impression
has produced amongst them a very general recklessness and
indifference to life.'

I turn off the microfiche reader and push back my chair. The
room feels suddenly close and airless, the light an unforgiving green.
Across the room a binder snaps, someone is getting ready to leave.

There is a hush in serious libraries made up of sounds, a cough, a rustle, the sigh of a pneumatic chair, in a thick, enveloping, general silence. It's like the fog in which researchers move, feeling their way through the blur of data, ships in port, tonnage, cargoes, cases of venereal disease. Only rarely does anything leap out, mostly it's a matter of accumulation, of evidence accruing like interest until it reaches a critical mass. But every once in a while a piece of the past comes flying through time at precisely the right angle and slices through the woolly wrappings of your mind. When this happens it feels as though you've been contacted by the dead.

I click on the microfiche reader again and feed in fiche after fiche, reading a paragraph here, a sentence there, making an occasional copy. I am stupidly unable to work the machine and the copies come out as negatives, rows of thin, scratchy, white letters on a page that is otherwise entirely black.

Busby's letter forms an explanatory preface to the text that follows: all thirty sheets of microfiche, all deeds to Maori land. The history of Maori land loss is a scandal, albeit a familiar one, a history of rapacious speculators, government seizures, confusion, dishonesty, naiveté. In the north, where European settlement started, land was sold by Maori chiefs on behalf of their tribes or *hapu* starting in 1814. The missionaries, Church Missionary Society and Wesleyans, were among the earliest buyers, acquiring tens of thousands of acres in the Hokianga, Bay of Islands and far north. Later there were traders, settlers, even Busby himself, who bought 50,000 acres between 1834 and 1840, a portion of which he intended to subdivide into urban blocks against the day when a government would be established.

At first the sales were piecemeal, but towards the end of the 1830s the acreage began to fly out of Maori hands, nearly ten million acres in the two years between 1837 and 1839. Fifty acres here for a double-barrelled fowling piece; a hundred there for a musket, a mirror, four blankets, some powder and a razor with a strop. Six hundred acres for eleven pounds cash, eleven blankets, ten shirts, six pairs of trousers, a gown, two pieces of print, a velvet waistcoat, three Manila hats, one pair of shoes, eight pairs of earrings, five combs, a musket, a double-barrelled gun, five fowling pieces, two bags of shot, three casks of powder, scissors, knives, razors, one hoe and a hundred and fifty pounds of tobacco, divided among eleven chiefly signatories to the deed. That makes one pound and one blanket each, plus a share of the other trade goods. Who got the velvet waistcoat, I wonder?

I think about how it feels to be descended from these Maoris. Surely it's an embarrassment and a hurt, all those deeds with one's own great-great-great-grandfather's signature. *How could they give it all away? How could they do that to us?* Oh, one can understand the allure at first of a pair of yellow breeches, a coat with braid, an axe, an auger. And, in the beginning, who could have known what the Pakeha had in mind? There weren't enough Pakehas in New Zealand in 1815, even 1820, to work the land they purchased, never mind occupy it in any meaningful way. But by 1837 this sort of explanation begins to make less sense. It is not so reasonable anymore to argue that Maoris do not understand what is happening, that they have no concept of private property, that the meaning of a deed is not clear. Nor can the mere novelty of manufactured goods, seductive as they may have been, account for this headlong rush to alienate their birthright.

What can have motivated them? Greed? Wilfulness? A conviction, all evidence to the contrary, that the Pakeha's presence was only a temporary thing? Or might it have been, as Busby contends, that everything Maoris did in those dark days betrayed a general recklessness and indifference to life? The words echo in my head like the tolling of a bell: *District after district has become void of its inhabitants, and the population is even now but a remnant of what it was in the memory of some European inhabitants.* At the beginning of the nineteenth century there were 200,000 Maoris in New Zealand. Fifty years later, when the first census was taken, there only 50,000 left. In the Bay of Islands, a heavily populated region, the collapse was particularly dramatic. Charles Darwin, who visited in 1835 on his way around the world in the *Beagle*, painted a melancholy picture of the place. 'Three whaling-ships were lying at anchor, and a canoe every now and then crossed from shore to shore; with these exceptions, an air of extreme quietness reigned over the whole district. Only a single canoe came alongside.'

It was clear to Darwin that the flora and fauna were under siege by foreign invaders. 'It is said,' he wrote, 'that the common Norway rat, in the short space of two years, annihilated in this northern end of the island the New Zealand species. In many places I noticed several sorts of weeds, which like the rats, I was forced to own as countrymen.' And it was no great leap from the fate of the rat to the fate of the Maori people. By mid-century the idea had become proverbial: 'As the white man's rat has driven away the native rat, so the European fly drives away our own, and the clover kills our fern, so will the Maoris disappear before the white man himself.' *Kei muri I te awe kapara he tangata ke, mana te ao, he ma*. 'Behind the tattooed face a stranger stands, he who owns the earth, and he is white.'

The library is now completely empty, even the attendant has disappeared. I pack up my notebooks and pencils and leave the fiches on the desk for someone to find. Outside, the promised sleet has started falling, glimmering like snow in the headlights but driving down like rain. It is five o'clock and dark already; the traffic in the square has slowed to a crawl. I turn up my collar, put down my head and dash through the darkness to my car. There's a parking ticket frozen to the windshield, but by my reckoning it's money well spent: $15 for six black pages and a sightline to the past.

When the first of my three sons was born I thought he should have a good name, a strong name, a name that would work in both our worlds. His father was a full-blooded Maori of the Ngati Rehia *hapu* of the Nga Puhi tribe. My family came to America from the British Isles in waves, starting in 1642. I thought our child should have a Maori name, but something pronounceable, something my American family wouldn't massacre or turn into a joke. For months I had been asking my husband about Maori names for boys, but he seemed unable to come up with a single suggestion.

'Well, there was a kid on my rugby team called Haircut.'

'Oh, come on. What about your uncles, your cousins? There must have been somebody you admired.' But there wasn't or he wouldn't, and so I pondered, but insecurely, not confident enough to choose a name in a language I didn't know. Several hours after the birth, we still had no idea.

'How about Manu?'

'No.'

'How about Kipa?'

'No.'

'How about Tame?'

'I never liked Tame. He was a liar and a thief... How about Maui?'

'Get off.'

At this point my brother walked through the door.

'It's Lincoln's birthday. How about Abraham?' And so we named him Aperahama, the Maori form of Abraham, a Hebrew name from the days of the evangelists, from the missionary period of New Zealand.

It turned out that there were several Aperahamas in the family already. Our son had an uncle Aperahama in Auckland and a cousin Aperahama in Perth. There was an Aperahama in his great-grandfather's generation, a mild, old man whom my husband remembered. He'd been famous in the little village of Mangonui for a tablesaw he built himself out of a diesel motor, a belt and a blade. It was a dangerous piece of equipment and everyone was always waiting for the day when it would take off one of his hands. He drove a Model A Ford with no brakes and played the violin. When he died, both hands intact, a son he'd had out of wedlock turned up at the funeral.

'How'd they know it was his son?' I asked my husband.

'Looked just like him,' he said.

There were lots of Aperahamas now, but there had been a time when it had not yet occurred to a Maori father to give his son this name. The first Aperahama in my husband's family was born about 1835, the youngest son of Tareha, a Ngati Rehia chief who had the strange fortune to be at the height of his powers when history brought white men to New Zealand. Tareha was a giant of a man and terrifying to see. He stood over six and a half feet tall and was so broad in the shoulders that there was not an armchair in the cabins of the visiting ships that would hold him. He had a mass of black curly hair and a great bushy black beard. On his face he wore the *moko* of a chief, an intricate tracery of blue-black lines carved into the surface of his skin. All the Pakehas in the Bay of Islands were afraid of him and were careful to keep out of his way. He was once accounted the greatest savage in New Zealand, wrote the Reverend John Butler in 1821. Only the other week he had killed and eaten three slaves at Waimate for stealing his sweet potatoes.

Tareha's *hapu*, Ngati Rehia, was part of the great Nga Puhi tribal confederation, whose members occupied the inland Bay of Islands in the eighteenth and early nineteenth centuries. Some decades before the arrival of Captain Cook, they had conquered the northern coastal area, occupying Rangihoua *pa* and the villages of Te Puna, Te Ti and Mangonui. The *pa*, a Ngati Rehia stronghold, was an impregnable fortress in Tareha's day, a mass of terraces, earthworks and palisades, where several hundred people might shelter from their enemies. Today it is a great barren, wedge-shaped ridge at the end of a long dirt road through some farmer's property.

To get to it you leave your car at the farmer's gate, climb over a stile and walk about a mile up hill and down, descending finally into the little valley through which the Oihi stream trickles down to Marsden Cross. From a distance you can see clearly that the earth has been worked, closer up the signs are more ambiguous. The ground is rough, tussocked with grass and the terraces are invisible on the golden hillside. You come upon them suddenly, climbing over a little rise and realising suddenly that you are standing on the flat. Here and there the suggestion of a footpath snakes along the hill. In some places you can see the outline of a *kumara* pit or a defensive trench. Nothing seems to grow there except grass; there is not a tree or bush anywhere on the hill. A line of scrub at the foot of the *pa* marks the stream bed. On the hillside opposite are rows of faint scarring that might have been *kumara* or potato plantations once upon a time.

On three sides a pyramid, the *pa* falls away on the fourth in a sheer vertical drop to the sea. From the top it commands a view of the entire Bay of Islands. It has unmistakably the air of a *tapu* or forbidden place, and the whistle of the wind across its summit is filled with spectral voices. It is not difficult to imagine the days when someone stood there and watched the sea for a churning school of *kahawai* or a fleet of enemy canoes.

At the beginning of the nineteenth century Rangihoua was commanded by Tareha's nephew Ruatara, a thoughtful and well-travelled man who had sailed on Pakeha whalers and seen much of the Pakeha world. In 1808 he met the Revered Samuel Marsden, the evangelical chaplain of New South Wales, who considered the Maoris ideally suited to Christian conversion. 'Their minds,' he wrote, 'appeared like a rich soil that had never been cultivated, and only wanted the proper means of improvement to render them fit to rank with civilised nations.' Six years later on Christmas Day, Marsden held the first Christian service in New Zealand at the foot of Rangihoua *pa*. Lifting up his voice, he sang the hundredth psalm—'Make a joyful noise unto the Lord, all ye lands'—and preached the glad tidings of the Gospel of Christ before a pulpit made the previous day from a section of a Maori canoe. The assembled Maoris stood up and sat down at a signal from their chief, but complained they could not understand a word of what was said. Ruatara told them not to worry for he would explain it to them by and by. Within a matter of months, however, he was dead of galloping consumption.

I tend to think of the name *Aperahama* as shorthand for everything that happened in these years. Like most Maoris of his generation, Tareha never converted to Christianity. His support for the missionaries, whom he saw as go-betweens and suppliers of European goods, was purely pragmatic. But as every year brought further transformations to the Bay—more ships, more buildings, more Pakehas—the opportunities to exploit them grew fewer. Tareha was among those caught with a foot in each world and all his actions have a sort of two-sidedness about them, a kind of shimmer or instability, so that it is difficult to know what to make of the things he did.

When in 1840 Busby circulated a petition among the northern chiefs ceding their sovereignty to the British crown, Tareha refused to sign and argued vehemently against co-operating with the British. He was in the minority and the Treaty of Waitangi was signed without him, inaugurating British colonial rule. At the same time, deed after deed for the sale of land in the 1830s and 40s bears Tareha's name. I have a black copy of one for 250 acres in the Mangonui District for which he received a great coat, an axe, an iron wedge, ten pounds of tobacco, some shot, a chisel, an auger, two frocks, a razor and a steel purse.

He was in late middle age when his last son was born, the one he named Aperahama. It is a name that signals the shift in political power, the end of one era and the beginning of the next. In one sense, it symbolises a loss of Maori *mana* or strength, and yet, it is a hopeful name, a survivor's name, one that speaks of endurance against the odds. Of all the Pakeha names, Abraham is the one that best expresses the aspirations of a Maori chief in a pre-Pakeha world—for land, influence, descendants and spiritual prestige. I can see Tareha sitting on the *marae*, with his back straight and his hands folded, listening to the missionary's words: *And the Lord brought Abraham out under the night sky and said to him, Look now toward heaven and tell the stars if thou be able to number them. And the Lord said to Abraham, So shall thy seed be. And I will make nations of thee, and kings shall come out of thee. And I will give unto thee, and to thy seed after thee, the land wherein thou art a stranger for an everlasting possession*. And later, when a son is born, Tareha looks around and sees that it is all slipping away. The things that they have always known are no longer to be taken for granted and in their place are new things, some of them wonderful like beaver hats, razors, gunpowder, frocks and augers, some of them horrible like the deep, hollow cough and the diarrhoea and the sores and rashes that none of the old people has ever known. And so he called him Aperahama in the hope that his sons would be as numerous as the stars and as strong as the Pakeha's bullocks, and that they would be leaders of men and that their enemies would live in fear of the thunder of their guns.

I guess I had something of the same in mind for my own son. But, you know, things don't always turn out the way you imagine. When my parents came to see him on the day he was born, they asked us what name we had chosen.

'Abraham,' I told them.

My father looked at me with a quizzical expression.

'Isn't that a Jewish name?'

*

The phone rings in the middle of the night. No one gets up to answer it and I come to consciousness just in time to hear the answering machine go on at the other end of the house. I know I should get up and intercept it—at this hour it cannot be good news. But I'm too tired and I let myself drift back towards sleep instead. My husband swings his legs out from under the covers and pulls on his pants. It's 3am and very cold. When he gets back to bed I am wide awake.

'Who was it?'

'Someone's died.'

'Who?'

'Nana Miri.'

It's my sister-in-law's voice on the tape. She is speaking to me, not my husband. She doesn't seem to realise it's the middle of the night—for her on the other side of the world it's dinnertime—and she thinks we are all out.

'I just wanted to call you to tell you that last night Nana Miri passed away. I knew you were specially fond of her and I thought you'd want to know. Well, I hope you're all fine back there. Bye.'

There's no point in calling back. It's too cold to sit up and she's not the one I have to talk to anyway. She'll only know the story third- or fourth-hand. I have to wait to talk to my husband's mother and I know we won't be able to reach her until after the weekend. There are so many deaths (or is it so many relations?) that my mother-in-law is at a funeral almost every week. All Saturday and Sunday she will be at the *marae*, talking, singing, sitting with the body, doing the business of death.

To my mother-in-law, her neighbour for over forty years, she was the Old Girl. My husband and his siblings called her Nana, though she was no blood relation of theirs. Other people of my in-laws' generation called her Auntie. For years I called her simply Miri, not realising how strange, even discourteous, that must have sounded. She forgave me because I didn't know any better and she never said a word.

She lived in Mangonui on the flat below the embankment, a stone's throw from the beach. When I met her she had been a widow for almost thirty years. Her children were grown up and gone away and she had one of her granddaughters to live with her. Like all the women of her generation she had had a great many children: ten, of whom five were still living. Of the five who died, she told me about two. One was a baby who died of dysentery while she was in the hospital miscarrying the next. No one told her until she came home, weak and empty-handed. The other was her youngest, a boy. There was a photo of him on the wall in her house, a slender, fuzzy-haired teenager with a shy smile, taken not long before he was killed in a car crash at the age of nineteen.

Nana Miri and my mother-in-law had known each other most of their lives. Their houses sat side by side on the flat, facing out to sea, identical timber boxes with flaking paint and a single sheet of corrugated iron for a roof. They each had a living room which doubled as a kitchen, two little bedrooms on one side and a dunny tacked on at the back. There was electricity and propane gas for cooking and no hot running water. There, however, any similarity between them ended.

Nana Miri was a small, energetic woman with strong features and a long plait of steel gray hair which she wore up in a bun. She had a taste for simplicity, clean lines and dark colours, and was always impeccably dressed. When she went out she wore a yellow flax hat with a black band and black trousers or a long black skirt with a dark jersey. She carried a flax kit, one of hers or one of Huia's, a plain one for shopping, a patterned one for church. In her house there were pictures on the walls and china in the cabinet. The carpet was swept, the dishes were put away. Behind the curtains that separated the bedrooms from the main room, the beds were made and the clothes were folded. The living room had a couch against one wall and a wood stove, a counter and a kitchen sink opposite. In the middle was a table where she served me tea with milk and sugar and biscuits on a plate. We took off our shoes at the door. It felt to me exactly the way my own grandmother's house might have felt, if I had had one.

Next door my mother-in-law's looked like it had just been hit by a tropical storm. A large woman with a big voice, she lived surrounded by the wreckage of her energy. All her children inherited from her this total disregard for order. There was not a single clear surface in the place; everything had a pile of something on it. There were piles of newspapers under the couch, piles of towels on the back of a chair. There were piles of clothing, piles of shoes, piles of papers. Some piles were a mixture: spanners, sandals and hairbrushes; fishhooks, lipsticks and bills. Part of the problem was that there were too many people in the household and not enough drawers. My mother-in-law also had ten children, all of whom had survived and had children of their own. A bigger part of the problem was that no one ever threw anything away. Her daughters tidied periodically, mainly by shoving more things under the furniture and pushing everything to the edges of the room. I tried once or twice to bring the chaos under control, but it was pointless. It was like trying to discipline entropy itself.

I used to escape to Nana Miri's and sit with her at her table, eating biscuits and drinking tea.

'I don't know how they stand it over there,' she would say, shaking her head. 'They're always yelling.'

'I know. Sometimes I think they're all mad.'

We were two of a kind, Nana Miri and I.

Strictly speaking, Nana Miri had no rights to the land on which she lived. She had been born in Te Hapua, about a hundred miles north, and orphaned at the age of three when both her parents died in the influenza pandemic of 1918. In Te Hapua, as in other isolated Maori communities, the sickness spread like fire through dry grass. The people coughed, grew chill, then burning, and

complained that their heads were being crushed between two stones.
They had sudden nose bleeds and when they coughed they brought
up a bloody, frothy phlegm. They were overcome with weakness
and lay down where they were with parched throats and aching
bones, alternatively shivering and throwing off the blankets laid
on to keep them warm. The ones that went blue died first, a thin
bloody trickle seeping from their nose and mouth. Others lingered,
fighting the pneumonia that followed hard on the heels of the
mate uruta, the death-cold.

The flu killed both the young and old, but many of its victims
were men and women in the prime of life. In Te Hapua it left
orphans by the score, and Nana Miri was sent to live with relatives
on the other side of Parengarenga Harbour. They say Parengarenga
means 'the place where the *renga* lily grows', but *rengarenga* also
means crushed, destroyed, beaten and scattered about, which is
how the people of Te Hapua felt at the end of 1918.

When she was seventeen years old she married Hemi Wakowski
and moved with him to Waipapakauri, where they worked digging
kauri gum. It was hard, back-breaking work, up to their knees in
the swamp for as many as eight hours at a time. But all her life
Nana Miri thought she must have been meant to live a long time,
since the flu hadn't taken her when it took everyone else. Hemi was
less lucky. Every year he grew more gaunt and hollow-chested and,
when he died of tuberculosis at the age of forty-six, he left Nana
Miri in a community to which she had ties neither by marriage nor
by birth.

It is rare, even now, to find someone in Mangonui who does not
have a tie to the *iwi*, the tribe, someone who, as they say, is not 'of
their bones'. The land on which Nana Miri lived belonged to my
father-in-law, Apirana, who gave it to her when she was widowed
and said it was hers to keep for as long as she liked. It was part of
a parcel of some 400 acres, all that was left of the thousands to
which the *hapu* of Ngati Rehia had once laid claim. Of these, the
most spectacular fifty acres at Rapanui Beach were leased to the
Pakeha for ninety-nine years. Another 200 were farmed by the
Mangonui Corporation, 100 were undeveloped bush and the last
fifty, on the inlet side of the peninsula, were occupied by the village
of Mangonui. There were arcane rules governing the placement of
houses and rights to this or that site, but Apirana had been the

sole survivor of five siblings and, as the son of the son of the son, back to Tareha himself, he had certain privileges.

Hemi and Miri Wakowski had come to Mangonui before the war, following Whareputara Rapana, Apostle of the prophet Ratana, a Maori farmer who, in that terrible year of 1918, had been visited by the Holy Ghost and told to unite the Maori people. In the year of the pandemic Wiremu 'Bill' Ratana was forty-five, a temperamental fellow with a taste for football, fast horses and drink. He caught the flu when it came to Wanganui and recovered, only to find that of the twenty-four members of his generation three remained: himself and two sisters. A week later he was sitting on the verandah of his house when a cloud rose from the surface of the sea and began to move towards him. Out of the cloud a voice spoke to him, saying, 'Fear not, I am the Holy Ghost. Cleanse yourself and your family as white as snow, as sinless as the wood-pigeon. Ratana, I appoint you as the Mouthpiece of God for the multitude of this land.' Later an angel appeared and repeated the message, telling Ratana that he was to turn the people from fear of roosters and owls and belief in ghosts and spirits hidden in sticks and relics of the dead. He was to preach the gospel, heal the sick and bring the people to Jehovah.

Out of the ashes rises the bird of hope. There had been others, Te Kooti Rikirangi, Te Whiti o Rongomai, who had gathered the people in time of darkness. And now, at the end of the Great War, in the wake of the pandemic, the air was full of 'thought-storms and semi-heathen superstitions'. The Apostles fanned out from Ratana's home with instructions to gather up the *morehu*, or remnant, and take them to the places where the Maori had been strong. Hemi and Miri Wakowski were among the thousands drawn to the Movement. They knew the Pakeha could not be trusted, they knew the past was a time of death. They looked to Ratana for a new beginning, for unity, independence, self-esteem. And that is how they came to Mangonui, an old place, a place with strength and *mana* from the old days, a place where they could make a new beginning.

'It was beautiful then,' Nana Miri told me, staring out the window over a cup of tea. 'Mangonui was just a camp. A mudflat on one side, a marsh on the other and a hill in-between. The old people came back from Waimate, no one had lived here for years, and we built our houses there where the oyster farm is now.'

And then as if she thought she might have given me the wrong impression, she looked at me sternly. 'It was hard, you know. Not like these days. We didn't have houses like this. We didn't have running water. But we had what we needed. *Kai moana, kumara*, chickens, a cow…

'You see those old trees?' she asked me, pointing through the window to a line of ancient peach trees and a scraggly lemon at the edge of the bush. 'We planted them. We planted fruit trees all over this place—plums, peaches, lemons, pears. Your father-in-law's mother's peaches were the best in Mangonui. Beautiful golden peaches in big glass jars. You ask your husband, he'll remember.'

Sometimes when I left Nana Miri's I'd go for a walk down the beach, past the *marae* and back up toward the main road. There was a turnoff to the right which led to the cemetery, a small, weedy plot with a loose wire fence and a creaky metal gate on crooked hinges. I liked to look at the old stones, especially the ones with the Ratana symbols, a five-pointed star balanced in the cup of a crescent moon, the image of the prophet and two whales, the twin square towers of the Ratana church, looking, I thought, vaguely Lutheran. I was never sure whether it was okay for me to be there, so I tried to make myself inconspicuous. The family who lived next door to the cemetery had a Rottweiler who guarded the place closely. He was chained, mercifully, to a house post, but whenever I came to look at the graves he leapt out the shadows, barking furiously and baring his teeth. No one from the house ever appeared, though I often thought I saw the curtains stir. I could imagine them inside, 'Nah, it's just Rawhiti's missus, you know, the Pakeha, in the cemetery again.'

The Feel of Steel

Helen Garner

The Baby Who Barked

First, the baby was born. Then everybody became ecstatic. When they brought her home two days later, the house overflowed with a new kind of air. People came in cars and on foot to adore her. Small crowds of visitors fell naturally into the configurations of religious paintings. The women pushed their faces in close, to smell skin. The men stood further back with their arms folded, smiling, talking quietly among themselves, but always with their bodies turned towards mother and child. The father's school friend struggled in, carrying, in a pot, the Greek tree that she was named after. It was found that one bottle can supply enough champagne for nine people to toast a baby.

She took the breast. Milk flowed. The father cooked and served. The nanna washed dishes and clothes. The granny got down on hands and knees and went at the kitchen lino. It was early in a Melbourne winter. The extended family hummed like a well-cranked top. The heartbroken old blue heeler slunk with impunity on to a forbidden rug, and rested her muzzle on her crossed front paws.

Two weeks passed in peaceable veneration. Everything about the baby was a perfect glory. Her hairline. Her orange poo. Her squashed right ear. Her long fingers. Her very small cough. 'Like a bark!' said someone fondly. One cough at a time, maybe once a day. 'Bark!' through stiffened pink lips. Then twice a day. Two at a time. Then three, then more.

And then one day when she coughed she didn't stop. Everyone rushed to the sofa. The mother held her folded forward like a tiny choking koala. Out, out, out went bark after bark after bark, and not a single breath came in. Her eyes screwed shut and disappeared. Her face went red, then royal purple, then greyish-blue. Before their eyes she shrank, intensified. At last she got to the bottom of it and a harsh thread of air sucked itself into her with a noise like a hammy actor dying. The man from along the street said, 'You take that kid to hospital.'

Whatever she had was very infectious. They put her in an isolation unit on the fifth floor, with her mother beside her on a fold-out couch; and every hour or so, for five days, the baby coughed and went blue and fought for breath. They even clapped a weeny little oxygen mask on to her. After each paroxysm, nasty pale sticky foam coated her lips and she sank into an exhausted sleep.

They pushed a tube down through her nose and sucked muck out of her. They got some blood out of her tiny sausage of an arm. The tests were 'inconclusive'. Whooping cough? Her parents weren't even sure how to pronounce it. Isn't it a disease of the olden days? Hasn't it been wiped out, like polio? It's coming back, said a nurse. I've seen this whole side of the thoracic ward—nothing but babies with whooping cough.

The baby coughed, the mother coughed, even the nanna coughed, but the father stayed healthy, which was just as well since attending mothers don't get fed: he was bringing in three meals a day. By the time the baby left hospital, she was three weeks old and a different, darker, more serious person. The nanna crept home and stayed in bed for a fortnight, choking and gasping, her tear ducts spouting water and the whole front of her torso in spasms.

And once they started telling people about it, they heard that whooping cough is indeed cropping up all over the place. The baby's uncle had it at fourteen. An academic in Newcastle at forty-two. Somebody's mother up in Woy Woy at eighty (she swore by Bonnington's Irish Moss). The baby's great-grandfather, from the Mallee, thought he felt it coming on, but claimed to have kept it at bay by frequent gargling with Listerine. One of the nanna's friends told her that she'd heard you can immunise a baby against whooping cough *with garlic*. Gradually it all started to seem a bit ordinary, a bit ridiculous, as if they had over-reacted.

But the fright was real. And the nanna had missed three weeks of the new life. She missed the baby and the baby's parents, and the work she'd been doing around their house, and the privilege of spending hours of each day holding her granddaughter in her arms, watching the waves of expression sweep and falter and resolve over her pure face.

Bottoms Up

So the baby's father will be running a Groovathon up at the snow? But of course the baby's mother can still go to the opening night of the Melbourne Film Festival! Of course the nanna will babysit!

Where else is the meaning, the joy of her life? And hey—didn't she bring up the baby's mother with her own bare hands, back in 70s Fitzroy when people slung their kids on the back of their pushbikes and zoomed away? Leave it to nanna! It'll be a breeze! The baby's mother can just express some milk, put on a wispy little dress and coat, pick up her friend and go!

The nanna arrives on the night with a journalist friend from Sydney, now an honorary auntie, in tow. Ah, look, the gorgeous little baby. How often does she have a feed? What? Which movie is opening the festival? It's not one of those bloody great four-hour extravaganzas, is it? You mean this will be the baby's very first bottle feed? Is that the milk? That tiny little packet? Shouldn't it be tipped into a bottle right now? What's that screech in the bathroom? Is that milk on the tiles behind the basin?

Brusque change of plan: the babysitters have to come along. Four women cram into the car with the baby and speed into the city. The baby starts to grizzle: the auntie furtively shoves a knuckle into her mouth. By Bourke Street, she's asleep.

In front of the cinema a limo has just pulled up at the roped-off red carpet. The onlookers include a tall, wolfish junkie in rags and beanie. His knees keep sagging and his eyelids sliding shut: only his curiosity about the stars in the limo is keeping him upright. The women push past him and rush up the stairs to the lobby, where they establish a beach-head against a wall. The baby sleeps in her capsule on the floor. Casting many a backward glance, the baby's mother and her friend disappear into the throng.

No public demeanour has so far been established for women in the position of the nanna and the honorary auntie. How the mighty are fallen! Critics who have kicked major butt in national publications, they now sit anonymous on the couch with their hands clasped in their laps, waiting anxiously to be useful. They console themselves by savaging in low tones the outfits of the passing festival-goers. The lobby clears fast. Now there's nobody out here, on the hectares of hideous carpet, but the sleeping baby and her two daggy bodyguards.

And the baby wakes up. She takes a look around the vast empty lobby, opens her mouth wide and begins to scream, her pink tongue as curved and rigid as a spoon. The auntie applies the knuckle. The nanna, suddenly amateur, dithers with the cold bottle.

Then out of the lollyshop and the bar pours a line of very young Village workers in name-tags. They head straight for the yelling baby, and stand around her in a respectful curve, leaning forward from the waist. The boy behind the espresso machine runs up with a metal jug of hot water. In a flurry of collective activity, her guardians warm the milk and get some into her. She gulps crossly, then spits out the teat. The nanna takes her wet nappy off and she lies there on her back, bare-bummed and cheerful, kicking her legs and staring. The staff contemplate her in silence.

'She's pretty cute,' says one of the boys. 'Whose is she?' 'I'm going to have kids,' says another boy, 'definitely.' 'If it wasn't for the pain,' says a girl, 'I'd have a hundred.' 'I have to finish my criminology degree first,' says a second girl. 'Are you going to tell her when she grows up,' says a third, 'that she once lay in the Village lobby with no pants on?'

Two hours later, when the cinema door bursts open and the baby's mother rushes out with arms extended, the nanna and the auntie estimate that maybe twenty minutes have passed. All the way up Bourke Street to the carpark at 11pm, the baby lies alert in her capsule, her eyes sparkling under the neon. The ragged junkie from the limo crowd is leaning against a rubbish bin outside a video arcade. He sees them coming and steps forward. 'C'n Oi've a look?'

The baby's mother is startled, but they pause. The junkie bends his basilisk stare into the capsule, feasts his eyes, then sighs, and with a tormented smile goes 'Aaaaaaaahh!'

The Feel of Steel

One day in the late 1950s, when I was fifteen or so and a bookish failure at sports, a Hungarian fencing coach turned up at our school. At his first demo lesson I was amazed to find that I could pick up the moves with ease.

The coach's name was Les Fadgyas. He'd fenced for Australia in the 1956 Melbourne Olympics. He was terribly impressive, but also funny, sweet and patient. We loved and respected him. When he met my mother, he clicked his heels and kissed her hand. Even in her dementia, now, she laughs with pleasure when reminded of that.

No doubt he wore an ordinary tracksuit, but in my memory, over these four decades, he has metamorphosed into a European nobleman—a hero in white jacket, mask and glove.

What Mr Fadgyas had at his disposal was a way of focusing and directing aggression: of making aggression and defence beautiful. The aggression in me, however, was deeply buried. I was quick and neat on my feet, but timid—not scared of getting hurt, but afraid to attack. Before competitions I was sleepless with fear. While one of my sisters made the state team, my fencing career involved a couple of inglorious competitive bouts and a slow fade-out. I left Geelong for university and never picked up a foil again.

Until last month. My sister faxed me as a tease a flyer she'd picked up in the Brunswick library: 'Fencing for Older Adults'. Something stirred. On the advertised day, I pulled on my runners and drove to the industrial back street of Brunswick where the Victorian Amateur Fencing Association (to which I must have once, incredibly, belonged) has its HQ, on the upper level of a huge warehouse.

I clanged up the fire escape and found a vast, bare, white space, daylit through the glass of a saw-tooth roof. The whole floor was a line of pistes, the raised fourteen-metre strips on which bouts are fought. There was nobody around. It had the stillness and the weird attractiveness of a place devoted to a formal discipline.

Four 'older adult' women turned up to the class. Judi and I had learnt before. Alice and Josie were complete beginners. The teacher, Ernie, was a small, chunky, friendly seventy-year-old with an English accent, in glasses and grey tracksuit. I was thinking wistfully of my Hungarian hero when Ernie seized a foil, raised both arms and fell with easy grace into the basic position. To see someone do that can take your breath away—the authority of it, the quiet readiness.

I've heard musicians and psychiatrists talk about muscle memory—how the body carries memories that the mind knows nothing of. Now for the the first time I understood it. When he gave out the masks and I pulled one on, the smell of cold wire shot up my nose, so familiar that I thought I was going to faint. When I took hold of a foil ('Pick it up lightly,' said Ernie, 'not with a battle-axe grip!'), it fitted my hand as if I'd laid it down only yesterday. When he called out '*En garde!*' my body dropped into the posture of its own accord. He showed us the salute: heels together, foil to the nose and down to the floor. We were hooked.

By the second lesson we'd learnt three moves. While Ernie and the others worked on the basics, Judi and I pulled on masks and breastplates, stepped on to the piste and crossed swords. I went for her. She blocked me. I went again. It was thrilling. Adrenalin streamed through me. I wanted to attack, to be attacked, to have to fight back. I remembered the lunges, the sliding clash of metal, how the sword hand rises as the foil-tip hits the target. It was glorious. We both burst out laughing. We only stopped because she didn't have a glove: I almost struck her hand and she flinched back. We lowered the blades. She pulled off her mask. Her eyes were bright, but I saw with a shock how gentle her face was, how feminine, under the cloud of hair.

The language of fencing is old French, beautiful and severe. Ernie used the phrase *le sentiment de fer*. The feel of steel. That's what I want. I want to learn to fight, but not in the ordinary wretched way of the worst of my personal life—desperate, ragged, emotional. I want to learn an ancient discipline, with formal control and purpose. I'm nearly fifty-eight. Will my body hold out? I hope it's not too late.

Not With a Bark, But a Whimper

The blue heeler at my daughter and son-in-law's place is sick. Last week she had a couple of what they think were strokes, where her legs slid out from under her and she lost control of her bowels and bladder. Since then, she's rallied somewhat, but my son-in-law is dark round the eyes and very quiet.

The old dog lies on her side on the floor, eyes open, breathing fast and shallow. They know she's probably dying, but the thing she dreads most in the world is going to the vet. If she can't cross over on her own, they're going to call a roving vet to bring the lethal hit to the house, rather than drag her against her will to her final moment.

Believing they'll have to make this call before the day is out, they drive her down to the banks of the Maribyrnong for a last outing. When they get home their faces are puffy. 'She couldn't walk,' says my daughter, 'but she lay on the grass and looked around and sniffed the air. We think she liked being there.'

That evening, the Western Bulldogs are playing the Brisbane Lions at the Gabba. I'm invited over to watch, but out of anxiety I don't make it till half-time. Two couches plus a row of kitchen chairs are packed with Bulldogs fans. They've eaten pasta and are drinking beer. On the floor at their feet the dog lies on a folded blanket, with her head on a clean white pillow.

They've laid alongside her her favourite toy, a metre-long stuffed caterpillar knitted in many colors. The dog's breathing hasn't changed: a steady panting. Her eyes are open. She doesn't seem to be in pain. She looks at me when I crouch down to greet her, but soon her gaze slides past me and out into the ether of dying.

The third quarter starts and soon the room is roaring and groaning. A fault in the TV distorts the players: they look stumpy and foreshortened, almost dwarfish. Things are going badly for the Bulldogs. The neighbourhood naturopath, a tall curly-headed woman, refuses to lose heart, but most of the men in the room have abandoned hope. Like wounded lovers they begin to console themselves with tart comments and fantasies of violence. 'He looks like a cassowary and that's the end of it.' 'He's in pain, which is good.'

'I want Libber to scratch someone. That's what I really, really want.' 'Oh, why doesn't he just give them the ball on a velvet cushion?' 'Come on! Hurt somebody!' 'Before the blood rule, you'd see blokes having to wipe blood out of their eyes before they took a free kick. The game's getting soft.' 'Look at all the behinds Brisbane have kicked!' 'There's eighteen behinds out there on the pitch.'

During the first quarter the naturopath has given the heeler a special herbal potion which, she says, can help the spirit of a dying creature to free itself and depart. From time to time someone will get down on the floor to sit by the dog, to stroke her head or squeeze some water into her mouth with an eye-dropper. She rouses herself to drink, then flops again.

At three-quarter time the pudding is served. The Lions are all over the Doggies. The vibe in the room drops steadily. 'My optimism is leaking away,' says the naturopath. The old dog suddenly tries to scramble to her feet. My son-in-law leaps up and helps her stagger out of the room into the front garden where she casts herself into a refreshing bed of violets. It's a cold night and the foliage is wet with dew.

Inside, the Doggies are getting a bath. There are long moments of despondent silence. People are collecting the plates when the final siren goes. I put on my coat and scarf. 'Say goodbye to Tess,' calls my son-in-law; under the Bulldogs beanie his face is strained. The heeler is lying in her chosen spot in the dark garden, head up, lungs labouring, neck hair bristling in its soft ruff. She dismisses me with a kind, mature look. Dying is hard work, and the way she's doing it accords with her character: fearless, sweet-tempered, uncomplaining. Along the street, hazard lights are flashing.

Is it the police, or just a taxi? The level crossing bells strike up their rhythmic clangor. I turn on my car radio: it's playing Beethoven's Fifth. Everything around me is seething with meaning, if I could only work out what it is.

'Meessing' in Action

A perfumed noon in spring, on day two of the World Economic Forum. I hear hoarse shouting from inside my suburban railway station as I stroll up the ramp. Three young blokes come brawling backwards off the platform and crash, yelling and cursing, into the wall of the boarded-up ticket office. I spot a bandanna, a thin white face, loose track pants. Oh, hell. Junkies. I've got a date in the city. Too late to take the tram. I put my ticket in the machine.

There are nine blokes, in a tight mass, further along the platform. No one else in sight. Should I bolt? It takes me three seconds to see that they are having way too much fun to be junkies. They're young, barely fifteen, ethnically various—Middle Eastern, Greek, Indian—and, except for one South-East Asian boy with an elegant haircut, who loops around the edges of the gang in a fastidious glide, they're all drunk. They are staggering and swaying about, buffeting and jostling and roaring.

My first urge is to move self-effacingly down to the other end of the platform. Then I think, Bugger them. Why should I? I pull *Who Weekly* out of my bag and take up a position in the sun, a couple of metres away from them.

They are *very* drunk. They are draping themselves on each other, falling about flamboyantly—and they are also, I realise, in love with each other, in the uninhibited bliss of youth. Right on cue, the white-faced boy in the bandanna yells in a shrill, excited voice, 'Let's go poofter-bashing, hey? Poofter-bashing?' The other boys, stumbling and grinning, ignore him. He shouts louder, 'First junkie I see today I'm gunna bash, roight?'

Out of the melee rises a lone voice of conscience. 'Hey gois? Gois? Have respect! There's a lady here! Have respect, man! Hey Meess! Meess?' He lurches up to me, a soft-faced boy with melting eyes and an incipient moustache. His eyebrows form an inverted V of earnestness. A cigarette burns between his amateurish fingers. 'Meess!' No one has called me Miss since 1972 at Fitzroy High.

'Scuse me, Meess. *I* can control my drunkenness. But if you don't like it, I'll shut them up. Those kids've drunk three bottles of Jim Beam.' The sober South-East Asian boy catches my eye, glances critically at his companions, then bares his teeth and draws a finger across his throat.

'How come you're all drunk at this early hour?' I ask primly. Whitey in the bandanna teeters past on an angle. So young, to look so mean! I can't hide a grin. His hard expression cracks into a smile of boyish sweetness. Blushing, he skulks away to the cyclone wire fence.

'Where *you* goeen', Meess?' asks my chivalrous friend, sprawling on the bench. 'To the ceety? We're goeen' to the, uhm, protest, you know? Down at the casino?'

'Watch out you don't get your heads kicked in,' I say.

He gives a daring shrug. 'Where *are* you goeen', Meess?'

'I'm taking my mum and dad out to lunch.'

His jaw drops. 'Your parents? They must be really old!'

'Sure, they're old—but not that old!'

'But *you* look old!'

'How old do you think I am?'

He broods on it. 'Seventy-two?'

My smile fades. I make a lowering gesture with my flat hand.

'Sixty?' hazards an Indian boy, sensing that his mate has dropped a clanger.

I lower my hand a fraction and wiggle it.

'Uhmmmm… fifty-three?'

'Fifty-seven,' I say.

They nod. My tactless chevalier gazes genially up at me. 'That's nice, Meess. You're takeen' your parents out. That's good.' The brawling breaks out again. Foul words fly. 'Have respect!' he shouts over his shoulder. 'We won't get violent,' he says to me, one hand out in a soothing gesture. 'I'm not scared of you,' I say. He looks confused.

The train pulls in. I head for the front carriage and they pour themselves into the last one, bellowing in a perfunctory and unconvincing manner, 'The workers! United! Will never be defeated!' I get out at Parliament and pause on the platform, wanting a last glimpse of them as they pass, but the windows show only calm, well-mannered passengers reading in rows. They must have got off at Central. Later I scan the TV footage for them, in vain. I liked them. I keep thinking of them, wondering if they got as far as the casino, or whether their fleeting attention was snagged en route by some other form of violence, or whatever it was they were looking for.

Our Mother's Flood

Our mother is eighty-one. She has a husband, a son and five daughters. In her youth she was modest, even shy—a sportswoman, small, slender and graceful, with beautiful legs and quick physical reflexes. I have to remind myself of this, because she's in a nursing home now, with shattered bones, chipped teeth, incontinence, and the alternating rage, euphoria and stupor of Alzheimer's disease.

Each of us has a different version, but we all agree, looking back, that it came on slowly, and that she was depressed for a long time.

I am ashamed to recall how harshly we witnessed the years of her decline. When she told the same anecdote over and over, in exactly the same words and with the same intonation, we would roll our eyes at each other behind her back, or joke about it on the phone afterwards. We were impatient with her growing fear of the physical world, her refusal to drive, her stubborn slowness, her resentful timidity, her inability to take pleasure in anything.

We thought it was just Mum growing old. We exchanged our brisk theories: she should get more exercise; she should drink less wine and eat more raw vegetables; she should see a psychiatrist; she should have more of a social life.

Then, wandering round the dark apartment one New Year's Eve, she fell. Dad woke and found her on the floor near the front door.

Her collar-bone was broken. She needed surgery. The morning after the operation, the orthopedic ward called: 'Come at once—we can't handle her.' *Our mother*, the most law-abiding person in the world, making trouble?

Dad and I rushed to her bedside, expecting to see a little old lady sitting up neatly in a nightie and a sling. Instead we found a raging virago, fully dressed, who took one look at us, muttered an insult, and stamped out the door. We ran after her. I corralled her in a visitors' lounge. There she stood, oblivious of her broken bone, blazing, exhilarated, in florid hallucination. She pointed in wonder at the swarms of insects that filled the room. She raved about a terrible flood which had washed people off their feet in the city and carried them away down the gutters. She cried out that she had seen a hundred Spanish galleons under full sail go sweeping down St Kilda Road.

Dad panicked: 'What the hell are you talking about? There are no insects! There's been no flood!' Her face went blank and her body jerked back, as if she'd been slapped. Some instinct whispered to me: *Don't fight it. Go with it.* Hiding my alarm, I said, 'A flood? Tell us more about the flood!' She relaxed, and let us lead her back to bed, talking all the while on strange nautical themes. She was on a ship. The captain had a moustache and smoked a pipe. 'When did you come on board?' she asked Dad. 'What's your cabin number?'

Shocked and moved, I sat with her that day and the next, while the anaesthetic left her system. As she dozed and raved, I realised that for the first time in my adult life I was thrilled by my mother's company. I could not get enough of her poetic flights of fancy. I held her hand, I stroked her hair, and she let me, this woman who had always been so reserved about touching or expressing affection. I opened my ironic intellectual's mouth and out of it came the incredible words 'I love you, Mum.' Sometimes I laughed at things she said, and so did she, gently, looking me right in the eye. Sometimes I would find tears running down my face. They were tears of joy, at the release of tenderness.

Once the violence of the anaesthetic had worn off, she went home to a sort of normality, but the break had damaged nerves in her right arm, and she could no longer knit, write or cook. Over the next year, in fits and starts, the illness crept over her. She and Dad had always travelled a lot—to Europe, to Western Australia, to the

Mallee to look at the crops, or just to the Healesville RACV for a weekend. But now her fragile equilibrium could not tolerate even a short trip away from home. In a hotel she would sink into sullen lethargy, or wander the passageways after midnight, or grow obsessed with looming disasters. She would come home disoriented. She lost her physical confidence. Instead of walking she shuffled.

Some of us floated the dreaded word Alzheimer's. Others, furious, rejected it outright. We began to squabble among ourselves. We didn't know where to go for help. Her female GP struck some of us as passive and uninterested, but our parents liked her and resisted pressure to change. We took Mum to a psycho-gerontologist who tested her short-term memory and found it almost obliterated. She was angry with him for confusing her with his silly questions.

She tried busily to invent little stories and excuses to cover her growing inability to cope with ordinary life. 'My husband usually does that!' she'd say brightly, when asked to fill out a form or write down her address, and someone would do it for her, at her dictation. We began to suspect that she could no longer read.

She fell again, broke a hip, needed to have it pinned. This time the orthopedic ward could not handle her mania at all. It was plain that she would not be coming home: that her care was too much for our father. Desperately the family searched for a nursing home. Our father inclined, in his distress, towards a hollowly luxurious up-market establishment in a remote suburb. We urged something further down the scale, more accessible, where even if there were smells she would have warm attention. Again we quarrelled.

At last we found a nursing home. Mum went straight there from the orthopedic ward. We called the Alzheimer's Association. They sent out a kind man who sat with us in Dad's living room, listened patiently and spoke carefully, managing to ignore the fact that the air in the room was zinging with tension.

When he'd gone we started to draw up a roster. 'She *must* have a daily visitor!' trumpeted one of us. Another, dull with misery, suggested that she wouldn't know whether we had come in or not: 'You're only doing this roster out of guilt. It's got nothing to do with what *she* needs.' '*I* go in there evvvvvv'ry single day,' said our father, over and over, till someone exploded: 'You're her *husband*! It's your *duty*! We've got *children*! We've got *jobs*!' People wept and raged. Each of us suffered a different version of the general horror, guilt and grief.

The whole dynamic of the family changed. With Mum no longer a presence, we split into shifting factions. Our relations with Dad, always complex, became strained and broke—then, as we organised ourselves round our adversity, they grew richer and more affectionate than they'd ever been.

The ability to visit Mum flickered unpredictably through our ranks. People checked up on each other. Resentments boiled over. Sometimes I'd go every other day; then for a fortnight, a month, I'd think of her hardly at all, and only distantly, as if she were already dead.

I still can't bear to picture her in her single room, with her hands clasped in her lap and her swollen feet placed side by side on the carpet, doing nothing, just sitting there staring dully into space. I'm afraid that this vision of her will drive me crazy. It paralyses me, until the guilt gets strong enough to force me back to her.

She has got used to being in the home, though she has no idea where she is, or why. Some carers are heroic in their gentleness and patience—with her, and with us. Others are offhand, even hostile. Possessions vanish. The management's ludicrous staffing policy leaves her, at times, neglected in the physical squalor of her condition.

Her moods are wildly erratic. Sometimes she knows me at once, smiles, and calls me by my childhood nickname. If Dad walks in, she'll switch gear, sob with relief, and pour out rambling paranoid tales about cleaners who leave bombs rolled up in the fresh towels, or men with guns who have already shot and killed her.

Next time she's one of two spoilt little princesses, or a station-owner's wife who has to cook for the shearers. For a whole week it was a matter of brooding urgency to get a train ticket to Geelong. There are days when she grumbles so relentlessly that the drone of her voice gets into my bones and drains all the joy out of everything. Then it's all I can do not to smother her with a pillow, or tip her out of the wheelchair into the lake and hold her head under with my boot. She is as unaware of my mutinous fury as if she were an empress on a throne. Her children confess these murder fantasies to each other, and double up in silent spasms of relief: without laughter it would all be completely unbearable.

With Dad she is often sulky and beetle-browed, taking out on him the suppressed anger of a long marriage. Faithfully he bears it. But then one day he'll bring her a salmon sandwich he's made at home, and she'll eat it with gusto and proclaim it 'the most delicious thing I've ever tasted.' We enter the nursing home with trepidation, never knowing what we're in for, whether we've got the emotional stamina to handle it one more time. Like her, we crash up and down, elated, disgusted, despairing, but somehow struggling on.

And there's something miraculous about the stories she comes out with—their emotional colour, their dream-like ingenuity. They are a game we can play. Imagination is the only hope we've got for communication with her.

She used to weep and rail at us when we'd get up to leave. A nurse said, 'Don't say goodbye. It only upsets her. By the time you get to the lift she's forgotten you've even been here. Sneak out. Believe me, it's kinder.' We were appalled by this suggestion. But one day, in the tense moment before parting, it occurred to me to say, 'I'm just going out the back, Mum, to hang out the washing.' Her agitation melted. She said pleasantly, 'Got enough pegs?'

Since that day, I imagine I'm building a house around her, where she and Dad can live together, in harmony, with all their children and grandchildren and great-grandchildren. It's a phantom house, of course. Cold facts have killed our longing for a material one. But it's wide and many-roomed, with a garden of leaves and blossoms, a swing, old sheds, a clothesline, a garage. When I walk out the door of her room, that's where I tell her I'm going: just out the back, or down to the shops to buy something to cook for our dinner. It works every time. But often I howl all the way up Punt Road.

Mum no longer cares for her once-beloved CDs, but she likes it when we sing. One day, wheeling her along the promenade beside the bay, my sister and I sang *The Carnival Is Over*. Mum looked round at us, and listened right to the end with unusual attention. Then she drew a deep sigh, and said, 'I love that song. Where do you *store* all the tears?'

Border Crossings

Fay Zwicky

I'm often asked, 'How did you become a writer?' a question not easily answered because there are so many mysterious factors involved: temperament, cultural background, historical circumstances, and many more. Although I was born into a Jewish family, my years spent at a Church of England school were equally if not more important to my emotional, intellectual, and moral development. Belonging, if tenuously, to one tradition and yet exposed to the freedoms of a country of transient allegiances, a country where you can re-invent yourself over and over again, where you can invent your community, your own mythology, I was ideally placed to become a story-teller. Whatever the influences determining the course of a life, the directions a writer's work takes will be affected by those cultural and ethical preoccupations and preconceptions with which one individual is saddled, whether present or absent from the stable of origin.

Just as some families destine their sons and daughters for the service of God in monasteries and convents, so my mother destined her children for the service of music. In our household, God was probably Mozart and Bach on good days, and Beethoven when days of wrath were upon us. Worship in the temple of Art is not marked by ethical or moral emphases but by rampant individualism, especially if you were born to run for the lives of Depression-reared parents.

When I was thirty-four years old, my father died and was buried at sea without the proper tribal obsequies: nobody to say Kaddish, the

Jewish prayer for the dead, for him, and nobody to throw a spadeful of soil on the coffin. I wasn't present when he died. It happened far away on a ship travelling the Tasman between New Zealand and Australia. At the time, I knew nothing about the Kaddish which is recited on every regular sabbath day in memory of deceased congregants as well as at the actual funeral service itself.

It is not, as I was to discover, a lament but rather a hymn of praise to God and a celebration of all creation. Although saying Kaddish seems at first acquaintance to be like the Christian ritual of praying for the souls of the dead to speed them through Purgatory, it's not quite the same thing. Purgatory isn't one of Judaism's anticipated torments and Gehenna isn't really the equivalent of hell. It was an actual place near Jerusalem where propitiatory sacrifices used to be made to Moloch, and today is where the ash-pits of the town's rubbish dumps stand. The notion of an after-life is less important in Judaic thinking than the memory of the dead retained and honoured by the living survivor.

At the time of my father's death, I knew well enough how to study books but I didn't know how to miss him. His death brought me up against my ignorance of just about everything: ignorance of parenting, ignorance about who, if anyone, one belongs to or wants to belong to, and where, if anywhere, one imagines oneself coming from.

So, against all the rules, I took it upon myself to make amends to him by writing my own 'Kaddish', a long elegy, trying to find a way into what his death meant through the rituals of a religious tradition of which I was an attenuated product, lacking both knowledge and allegiance. Instinct came first. Knowledge came later. Drawing upon traces of the re-discovered wisdom of a tradition, the poem is haunted by layers of ghostly presences, earlier generations of those whose lives went to make a family—with all that such a fallibly heroic enterprise entails. The act of writing the poem was a kind of half-conscious mission to speak up against our mutual obliteration.

When I began writing this poem nine years after my father's death, I didn't know that what the prayer can tell you about familial love, obligation, guilt, and grief is supposed to be spoken only by men. It was a non-Jewish critic who eventually enlightened me as to where authority about family and communal duty belong—invariably and unarguably with the male, the right to speak his sole province. So what about the man unlucky enough to have three daughters and no sons?

To find out more on the subject, I went back to the books and commentaries by various Jewish authorities, and found them, almost without exception, harsh and unyielding, the more so since my experience told me that women had deeper insights into and more sympathy with their fathers, especially those who grew up in an all-female household with a father absent for six years during World War Two. In fairness to the commentators, it should be said that the emphasis tended to fall on the potential for weakening tradition should the female be permitted to speak, rather than on women's inferiority. However, the traditional order of priorities has always rankled with me and continues to do so.

In writing my own 'Kaddish', I turned back half-consciously to very fundamental sources of nurture drawn upon in early childhood: fragments of ritual, nursery rhyme, Biblical lore, all tied in with memories of comfort, anger, shame, and loss. Fragmented memories and isolated images randomly recalled are of no significance in themselves—only the poet's search for meaning within a recognisable context can be of interest. And for this, the poet needs muscles, emotional, spiritual and psychic muscles that transcend the limits of the self. And muscles take time to develop, longer for some than for others.

So, growing up in a family without religious dogma, and the haziest connections with Jewish origins, it was really only the coming of World War Two and the gradual awakening to the fate of Jews in Europe that brought home something of what the religio-cultural meaning of 'being Jewish' was. The sense of being a stranger both to one's own and to one's adopted culture is a familiar theme in Anglo-Jewish writing. I never saw the state of estrangement from mainstream culture as something to be regretted, although I lacked the confidence when young to use its invaluable vantage points. Having one home to know the privileges of exile from is a necessity for a writer, as the work of James Joyce or Henry James can tell you. Having two is a luxury. Given the fact of that remote link with Judaism, it has always seemed surprising that what appeared to have so little substance in the sphere of language, belief, and way of life could have had so much impact on social identity, historical perspectives, and political attitudes.

My father and mother, like both my grandmothers, were born in Australia. Neither they nor I knew Hebrew or Yiddish. I attended the same Church of England school that my mother attended, and we both came top in what used to be called 'Divinity,' a subject later to be termed 'Religious Instruction', and eventually to disappear altogether from the curriculum. The first prayer I learned was the Lord's Prayer which my mother sat on the end of my bed and taught me the day before I started school—though she always denied this. I paid devout attention to the weekly chapel service presided over by the Rev. Townsend who, pinkly illumined by morning sunlight through a fine stained-glass window, radiated an aura of spirituality but who, in retrospect, was pretty thick-witted and had a middling reputation as a cricketer.

On leaving this school, I was presented with the complete works of Shakespeare on austerity rations rice paper. Stamped with the school crest in gold was the daunting motto: *Nisi Dominus Frustra* (without the Lord all is vain). The certificate gummed inside stated your name and the dates you attended school, in my case, 1941-50, the years that saw the bombing of Britain, the Holocaust and the war with Japan. When the school was evacuated to the country, I tasted freedom for the first time but it was not to last. Sent back to Melbourne to have a toe stitched back on after a typical act of disobedience, I was sent to another church school to get me out of the house, my omniscient mother having made up her mind the Japanese weren't coming after all.

Another motto, another school song. This time, *Vincit qui se vincit* (he conquers who conquers himself). Mottos always implied fruitless struggle whichever way you put the emphasis. Mine fell naturally on *frustra*, knowing full well the meaning of fruitless struggle where my mother was concerned, and, since her wrath was indistinguishable from God's, one didn't tangle willingly with such a parent. The second motto was equally discouraging. What was this self that must be conquered? And was the need to conquer anything what I cared about anyway? Conquest was for the strong of this world, and I was powerless, my outsider status confirmed by the lack of a uniform, a polysyllabic vocabulary, a prodigious piano repertoire and the mystery of Jewish birth.

Given this odd beginning, it's not surprising that it took a long time to find a voice for the buried self, or that I felt diffident about using a ritual when my father died to which I felt barely entitled by upbringing, but to which more atavistic sources compelled me. Back in the 70s I analysed this complex response in an essay entitled, 'Democratic Repression: the Ethnic Strain'. In this essay, I spoke of those authors who helped me find a voice at a time when it needed the sort of sanction the community I lived in didn't provide. These were Jewish-American novelists like Malamud, Saul Bellow and Philip Roth whose work, as I wrote, 'gave me a community I lacked in the Australian context... The concerns of Australian literature have always appeared essentially solitary, inward-turning, never outer-directed, the babble of speech masking a dumb void; a landscape without a recognisable human being in it.'

From the same essay, I went on to speak of problems encountered in writing the 'Kaddish' for my father:

> I would not have been capable of writing this in Australia ten years ago, so uncertain was I of my identification with the Jewish faith and the legitimacy of its existence in a bland Anglo-Saxon context. Nor would I have dared insert segments of phoneticised Aramaic for fear of revealing that exotic, interloping status of which I was ashamed and afraid... I felt the burden of those harsh, rasping syllables in the prayer for the dead as a personal penance... I could not reveal a long-kept secret, say prayers for the dead in my own tongue unless helped to find it.

A breakthrough came with the discovery of Alan Ginsberg's 'Kaddish' for his mother which I came upon seventeen years after it had been published. After reading this long, moving poem, I felt freer to finish my own, less vulnerable about exposing it to public scrutiny in what used to seem an uncomprehending environment. No Australian writer could do this for me, and I went on to describe growing up in this country as 'an exercise in repression'.

While waiting for this breakthrough, I took nourishment where it was available. This came from poetry, from words used precisely, magically and musically. I loved words, their sound, their weight, their capacity to open new worlds. I wanted to use them effectively for they seemed to be my first defence against powerlessness. The source of my first serious acquaintance with poetry came from the hymns we sang every morning at assembly, the words sometimes very fine and other times utterly banal. George Herbert and William

Blake rubbed shoulders with Edward Grubb and Percy Dearmer in our battered blue hymn books, but the combination of words and rousing music never failed to inspire a sense of well-being. We didn't always know exactly what we were singing about, but the music carried us along. For example, 'There is a green hill far away *without* a city wall.' If there was no wall, why was it necessary to mention the fact that it wasn't there? It took quite a few years before the real meaning sank in.

Another misunderstanding involved the word 'aweful' as in 'Let all your lamps be bright/ And trim the golden flame/ Gird up your loins as in his sight/ For aweful is his name.' Wasn't it meant to be a song of praise? Why did it seem to damn the Almighty? Just one more of those mysteries language set out to trap us in. Like those shame-making mispronunciations when required to read aloud in class, like 'misled' and 'awry', that one never heard uttered in everyday conversation.

The hymns I liked best were not about God directly but about nature. I obviously hadn't tapped these hymns' original sources in the Psalms which are full of imagery from the natural world. The one I liked best was a hymn ascribed to St Patrick and it was called, enigmatically, St Patrick's Breastplate:

> I bind unto myself today
> The virtues of the starlit heaven,
> The glorious sun's life-giving ray,
> The whiteness of the moon at even,
> The flashing of the lightning free,
> The whirling wind's tempestuous shocks,
> The stable earth, the deep salt sea,
> Around the old eternal rocks.

There was also a bit of plainsong, supposed to be by St Francis of Assisi, translated by Matthew Arnold, which had a wonderful line, the only one I can remember: 'Praisèd be my Lord God for our sister Water: who is very serviceable unto us and humble and precious and clean.' Brother Fire was 'mighty and strong' and the stars were set 'clear and lovely' in heaven which seemed cosmically reassuring in every way.

Coming from a home of some turbulence, I liked the bare simplicity and meditative stillness of the Sarum Primer of 1558. It seomed to offer a safe passage through a stormy world from

beginning to end, but I hadn't yet learned to question anything
about belief when I took its simple lines to heart:

> God be in my head,
>   And in my understanding;
> God be in my eyes,
>   And in my looking;
> God be in my mouth,
>   And in my speaking;
> God be in my heart,
>   And in my thinking;
> God be at mine end,
>   And at my departing.

The same need for peace in the awful upheavals of adolescence,
drew me to Miss Russell, my Quaker teacher who, sensing a troubled
child, took me to the Quaker meeting house on Sundays where I
encountered a productive silence for the first time in my life. It was
from teachers like Miss Russell with her gentle voice and soothing
kindness (she was extremely deaf) that I drew strength to help me
overcome my fear and self-consciousness. I will never forget her
intuitive tact in dealing with troubled young souls and I'm sure her
Quaker affiliation had much to do with her pacific and unintrusive
nature. It struck me as remarkable that, very late in her life, she
married the Jewish art master at Geelong Grammar, a refugee from
Hitler's Germany, and, although they didn't have long together,
I'm sure they were able to nourish each other.

It was Miss Russell who taught me that to reflect wasn't simply
an affair of the intellect and the will, but a gentler form of
receptiveness. Her wisdom instilled the notion of a conscience, a
social awareness of a wider morality that was never moralistic. Her
quiet voice spoke louder to me than all the fervent injunctions
addressed stridently at home, from pulpits of all denominations,
and sometimes in the classroom. Channelling my natural sympathy
for the poor and oppressed into creative paths, she gave me
translations of classical Chinese poetry to read, and encouraged
me to write and read poetry without feeling freakish.

There was no music in the Quaker meeting house, but the more
energetic side of my nature was to find satisfaction in the grand
martial rhythms of Mrs Julia Ward Howe's 'Battle Hymn of the
Republic' with its promise of vengeance on an Old Testamental

scale, the letting loose of destructive forces for mankind's betterment:

> Mine eyes have seen the glory of the coming of the Lord;
> He is trampling out the vintage where the grapes of wrath
> are stored;
> He hath loosed the fateful lightning of his terrible swift
> sword;
> His truth is marching on.

And this rousing revolutionary vision is followed by a graphic picture of soldiers huddling in encampments during the American Civil War that stirred my liberationist sympathies, and turned me eventually into a radical supporter of the oppressed and the enslaved:

> I have seen him in the watch fires of a hundred circling
> camps;
> They have builded him an altar in the evening dews and
> damps;
> I have read his righteous sentence by the dim and flaring
> lamps:
> His Day is marching on.

And, finally, at Easter, my need to share the pathos of the Crucifixion and identify with the rebel underdog found full and tearful outlets in sad hymns with solemn, funereal chorale music by J. S. Bach. As for example in:

> O sacred head sore wounded,
> Defiled and put to scorn,
> O kingly head surrounded
> With mocking crown of thorn.

The fate of the outsider who suffered multiple humiliations at the hands of the mainstream was uppermost in my garbled imagination, my sympathies always directed to the noble despised figure of the One who was Different in both life and literature. Mindful of my own early humiliations at the hands of the majority, I understood in my bones what it was like to feel and be thought stupid, the outsider with a lot on her mind and a weight on her heart like a guilty secret. So there were two kinds of education going on at home and at school. I took from each an enjoyment of and curiosity about the outside world which no amount of difficulty could quench, and for this I have to be grateful to the freedom to think that my parents and my education gave me, enabling me to cross borders without fear and to relish difference, to acquire the tools necessary in learning to discipline and shape the sprawl of raw temperamental protoplasm, and to avoid getting stuck in obsessional states of mind.

I've spoken so far about certain aspects of traditional rituals encountered prior to the development of consciousness, contacts charged with inescapable attitudes and values that have fed the poet's imagination. But what happens when these attitudes and values absorbed in childhood come under intellectual scrutiny? How does the writer deal with the question of belief?

As a child of the 1930s and 40s, I was brought up to be suspicious of abstractions, to be wary of easy consolations, to be sceptical of any ideology or theology purporting to offer solutions. Growing up in wartime, my generation was trained early to be alert to language's betrayals, obliged to bury the natural hunger of the young for miraculous revelation. Consequently, the religious impulse unmediated by reason has always made me uneasy. I'm pretty sure that my stroppy obsession with precision and accuracy in the use of language has at least part of its genesis in this growing up during the Second World War, a historical accident for which I've always been grateful. As Miroslav Holub the poet has said when comparing the beady-eyed attention we paid language with today's clichéd blur: 'Everything seemed so important, every image, every metaphor seemed to matter in a special way.'

Whether because one's senses are sharpened during childhood and times of crisis or because one's father suddenly disappeared for six crucial years, those early childhood years were the source of most potent memories. Across painstaking letters dispatched with poignant regularity from Borneo, Brunei, Moratai, Tarakan, Balikpapan was stamped the warning imprint, 'Careless Talk Costs Lives'. The impact of that cryptic message was to be felt far more deeply in my future work than I could possibly have realised at the time.

Back in our Australian provincial classrooms we studied examples of wartime propaganda, despising the rhetoric of nationalism and conceptually aerated adjectives like 'glorious', 'invincible', 'omnipotent', weighing up the approval, disapproval, and neutrality ratings of columns of synonyms: 'I am firm. You are obstinate. He is pig-headed.' While being alerted to the manipulative powers of language, I was manipulating myself into linguistic paralysis, scrupulous to the point of schizophrenic self-distrust. To this day, when confronted with an adjective implying judgment, I still mentally shift through those old gradations of approval to mild disapproval right across the spectrum to strong disapproval in order to reach a fair conclusion and to get as close to the truth of the matter as possible. Very ethical, very idealistic, but hard on the imaginative life and the notion of spontaneous utterance.

As undergraduates, we read existentialist philosophers, believed in free will, and took personal responsibility for our actions. The writers I most admired were European dissidents, starting with Nietzsche and Kierkegaard who displayed stoic courage, steely irony, an unsmiling moral strenuousness cut off from religious affiliation. Writers who came later like Malraux, Koestler, Camus, Sartre, Orwell represented freedom from prejudice and superstition. They emerged from the landscape of a war that took our fathers from home, writers inseparable from the apparatus of totalitarianism, the concentration camps, Nazism and Stalinism. Austere, tough, angry about social injustice, these were writers in whose work the notion of commitment to human solidarity was foremost, who raged against the dying of the light, and who, by testifying to the violence and futility of contemporary history, manage, in spite of everything, to keep faith and hope alive in the Western humanist legacy of art, literature, at least acknowledging if not accepting the legitimacy of Judeo-Christian religious tradition. The cranky moral earnestness of the Melbourne of my youth comprising a kind of stern Leftish didacticism coupled with the muscular Protestantism of my Church of England schooling slotted easily into the cultural and political upheavals that animated my literary heroes.

I'm not sure in what sense these early concerns of my world could be called 'religious'. Cultural and ethical maybe, but not necessarily spiritual, surely a necessary component of the religious sensibility. Passionate dissent is sometimes confused with religious inclination in this country, a kind of stroppy dissatisfaction with what this earth has to offer, and certainly my own writing seems to have depended for a long time on remaining adversarial, as if needing the skewed vantage point of isolation from which to maintain creative rage against injustice.

I suppose the notion of spirituality is a bit fraught for me because, as popularly understood, it implies a bloodless, ascetic rejection of the physical world, a disembodied religiosity that leave poetry and female experience out in the cold. So I'm sceptical of any system that divorces apprehension of the numinous from the life of the senses. It's not unusual for a writer keyed in early childhood to the rhetoric of prayer and chant to be capable of shifting easily between mundane recrimination and transcendence in later life. Emily Dickinson describes this duality of poetic understanding as the most natural way of being imaginable, especially in a poem called 'This world is not Conclusion':

> This world is not Conclusion.
> A species stands beyond—
> Invisible, as Music—
> But positive, as Sound—
> It beckons, and it baffles—
> Philosophy—don't know—
> And through a Riddle, at the last—
> Sagacity, must go—
> To guess it, puzzles scholars—
> To gain it, Men have borne
> Contempt of Generations
> And Crucifixion, shown—
> Faith slips—and laughs, and rallies—
> Blushes, if any see—
> Plucks at a twig of Evidence—
> And asks a Vane, the way—
> Much gesture from the Pulpit—
> Strong Hallelujahs roll—
> Narcotics cannot still the tooth
> That nibbles at the soul—

That tooth nibbling at the soul is known to all moralists and seekers of the Puritan persuasion, easily crossing denominational borders. Few poets have been able to dramatise the working of the mind scrutinising its motives so effectively. These most concrete metaphors illuminate the authenticity of her understanding of the meaning of faith far better than abstract instructions from pulpits.

Much of what has appealed to me in past brushes with religious experience has, in fact, been paradoxically removed from the physical world, its very bodylessness something of a relief from the burden of the flesh and its assorted mischiefs. I associate this relief with language—the mysteries of the language of prayer, the poetry of the Psalms and the Prophets, the differing narrative styles of the Old Testament and the Gospels, the formalities of ritual, the repetitive comfort of well-known liturgical structures absorbed unconsciously in childhood. To a child with an obedient, sensitive ear, the alternation of language levels from very simple everyday usage for the purpose of introspective meditation, through to the formal magniloquence of scriptural invocation celebrating major events in the ecclesiastical calendar, provided an invaluable training ground for the nurture and development of a poet.

I may be chronologically remote from my childhood and yet its simpler concerns are still very present. I feel very little different from the child who once took delight in the idea of Aaron's rod causing water to spring from the rock in the desert. Nor do I feel a whit less sympathetic to Job's dilemma than I did as an eleven year old deputed to write the Morality play for our primary school's enactment of a medieval fairground. True to a lifetime preoccupation with the question of undeserved suffering, I chose the nearest story I could find in the Bible to a tragic drama. Although the script of that early effort no longer exists, I remember the buzz I got from devising cheeky lines for the Devil's interview with God, and from working up a lather on Job's behalf.

Writing this play marked the beginning of my conscious opposition to the God of the Bible. I found myself much readier to invest Job with a tragic hero's resistance to and complaint about the disasters that befell him than I was in coming to terms with a God bent on testing Job's endurance with such monstrous indifference. I certainly wasn't able to accept the idea that the servant of God should suffer willingly in order that others may be improved. I couldn't come at it when I was eleven and I still find his submission troubling even though I'm less likely to say so with such defiance: too many things have happened since those days of heedless bravado.

At one point, you may remember Job says:

> Though he slay me, yet will I trust in Him;
> But I will argue my ways before Him.
> This also shall be my salvation,
> That a hypocrite cannot come before Him.

In these lines, it seemed to me that Job rose to inspirational heights, equally matched in his debate with God. But once God had spoken, Job gave away his swagger, his sublime defiance—

> Wherefore I now abhor my words, and repent,
> Seeing I am dust and ashes.

I have to admit I cheated on the original, refusing to have my hero abase himself in what seemed a craven way before God's harsh rebuke:

> Behold, I am of small account; what shall I answer Thee?
> I lay my hand upon my mouth.

I was ready in those days to back tragedy's capacity to glorify human resistance to necessity. Prometheus defied Zeus with all stops out—why should Job not be allowed the same spiritual flare before extinction? Because Job belongs to the submissive Hebrew tradition and Prometheus to the intellectual hubris of the Greek. Tragedy is only possible to a mind which is agnostic since there can be no compensating hereafter for a tragic hero. Less defiant today, I'm more likely to lay a hand over my mouth before putting the tragic foot in it. However, I began as an agnostic and an agnostic I remain, a stake in both the Hebrew and Greek traditions, too much of a Jew to be a Christian, too Christian to be much of a Jew.

Poetry has always seemed to me a source of hope, a means of speaking against any orthodoxy, be it religious, political, or social. It has offered a place for the dissenting imagination that hankers to encompass not only the truth of what is, what has been, but what might be or what might have been.

In the 1995 pages of my journal kept over many years, the following passage occurs:

> The Psalms have given me the most inspired comfort. But is it just a trick of language or do I actually take hold of something in the act of reading? Some sustaining force behind the words, the voice of the fallible human seeking redemption in a crazy act of faith in an unseen being. 'I am like a pelican of the wilderness; I am like an owl of the desert. I watch and am as a sparrow alone upon the house top.' The imagery is very poignant and feels right.

In the same engaging way, the poems of the seventeenth-century parson-poet of Bemerton, George Herbert, modest and radiantly illuminating about his inner conflict, have the familiar pull between the attractions of the world and the call to renounce it. Underneath it all, there is true belief in the One to whom he speaks as familiarly as to a mortal friend, his source of strength and survival. He's willing to go all the way with whatever God ordains whether he's 'cast down' or afforded help:

> I will complain, yet praise;
> I will bewail, approve;
> And all my sowre-sweet days
> I will lament and love.

That just about says it all: sour-sweet days. The state of exile is relative and it would appear that Herbert felt just as cut off in his village parish as I feel out of God's earshot on the remotest edge of this continent. We both received our sense of God from the stern, fallible beauty of the King James Version's resonant prose. It's an old infatuation, and even now I can't tell how much of its impact depended on the means of expression rather than what was actually being expressed.

There is an epigraph to a recent autobiographical memoir by the now-deceased young professor of philosophy at London University, Gillian Rose. The book is called *Love's Work*, and the epigraph is taken from an eighteenth-century Kabbalist called Staretz Silouan. It reads, 'Keep your mind in hell and despair not.' Taken together with Herbert's poem, I believe it offers a kind of answer to Job. I'm grateful to both of them. After all, keeping afloat, keeping one's spiritual stamina intact even in hell seems a not unreasonable aim for ageing agnostics.

At the University of Sydney

Edmund Campion

for Myfanwy

Half a century ago a young man took a tram from Enmore to Chippendale and enrolled in the Faculty of Arts at the University of Sydney. He was seventeen years old and, by today's norms, something of an oddity: he had never been in love, nor tasted alcohol, nor missed Sunday Mass, nor eaten meat on a Friday, nor read a book on the *Index Librorum Prohibitorum*. For that matter, the University of Sydney then was somewhat different from today's norm. It was the only university in New South Wales. In the whole university there were fewer than two dozen postgraduates pursuing PhDs, principally in the physical sciences. In the Faculty of Arts, the number of lecturers in the big departments, such as History, English or Philosophy, could be counted on the fingers of your hand. After World War Two, university enrolment, boosted by ex-service people, had soared; now they were dropping again to more comfortable proportions. On the campus there was plenty of space—car drivers, a rare species, could park outside the Great Hall, or wherever they pleased. Change, however, was on the way. A principal element of change was the Commonwealth scholarship which the Menzies government had recently introduced. Those scholarships begin the modern history of Australian universities, for they opened them up to society at large and pointed towards today's maxi universities. Previously, in all of New South Wales there had been only 400 free bursary places, and getting a tertiary education had been a restricted privilege. Now, however, the university would see a new population swelling its numbers and changing its ethos.

The new undergraduate from Enmore was part of this swelling population. His sister, already an arts student, in Orientation Week introduced him to the Newman Society, the Catholic society on campus. One of his first memories of the University of Sydney was a Newman hike one Sunday early in his first term. The young people he met there were similar to himself, products of Catholic schools. There, the religion they had absorbed with the air they breathed was disciplined, observant, dutiful, deferential to authority, fearful, guilty and sin-obsessed—the list is familiar from a lifetime's reading. Yes… but their religion was also celebratory, colourful, comforting, heart-stirring and sacramental: it saw the impress of the divine underneath and behind the whole created world. Their world, like G.M. Hopkins's, was indeed charged with the grandeur of God; it could indeed flame out… turn but a stone and start a wing. In class each day at school, nevertheless, religion had been chiefly a matter of 'apologetics', the school subject which trained them in debating skills to defend every corner of the Catholic package, from transubstantiation and the Trinity to the Renaissance papacy or the Inquisition. (When the Enmore undergraduate went into the army, for his national service, he found Protestant Christians amazed at the Catholics' ability, eagerness even, to get into arguments about the existence of God or the resurrection of Jesus.) In the schools Catholicism was taught as a set of intellectual propositions, rather than as a poem which invited and sustained heartstir.

So it was no surprise to find the Newman Society spending much of its energies in organising public talks on those aspects of the faith thought to be under challenge at the university: the infallibility of the pope, for example, or the sinfulness of abortion and contraception. Some intellectual champion, usually a priest, would be brought in to speak; a lecture hall would be booked for a lunch time; and society members would hand out dodgers at the university gates on the morning of the talk. At lunchtime the Newmans would be in the lecture hall to barrack for their champion and cheer as he rebutted questioners. It was like being at a prize fight—one at which you had fixed the referee. For behind the display of apologetics was a belief that we were the one true church, which had all the answers, if only you could lay your hand on the relevant papal encyclical.

A similar explanation might be found for the existence of a Catholic political machine at the university then. Tales of bubble-gum politics are not worth much space, although they may have had unintended consequences which make them notable. This story begins with a curate in a nearby parish who used to say Mass at the Catholic women's college, Sancta Sophia. Each week the girls would leave on his breakfast table a copy of the student newspaper, *Honi Soit*. The priest, who had had no contact with universities before this, was flabbergasted by what he read: it seemed to him blasphemous, atheistic, raunchy and possibly communistic. So he asked the Sancta undergraduates to recruit some male students and together they initiated a political machine housed within the secretive Santamaria political movement. By the time the seventeen-year-old turned up from Enmore, not only was *Honi Soit* edited by a Catholic, but there were so many Catholics on the Student Representative Council that at SRC Friday dinners an announcement was regularly made, 'There's either fish or chicken; but the fish is for the Catholics.' Overall, an acute observer might conclude that Catholics at the University of Sydney acted as if they were walking through unfriendly territory, which might be sown with land mines.

Yet there were unintended consequences of such political activism. More than they realised perhaps, those young Catholics had come from a small, tight, limited world. Everyone knows that the word 'ghetto' has a precise historical meaning; to use the word loosely can be a disservice to history. Nevertheless, one can say that the young Catholics of those years displayed a ghetto mentality, in that they mixed with their own, read their own, treasured their own and favoured their own; and that in time their political activism would erase the ghetto mentality, replacing it with an openness which gave them new friends, new thought patterns and new ranges of experience. It was as if previously they had spoken a foreign language; now they joined in the Australian conversation.

In any case, change was already in the air. On that first Newman hike, and at subsequent Newman picnics and socials, the seventeen-year-old had noticed an older arts student, a priest with an open smiling face, high intellectual forehead, athletic physique and an engaging, sympathetic manner. Later in the same year, at the annual Newman dinner, Cardinal Gilroy's auxiliary bishop, the historian Dr Eris O'Brien, would announce that this priest, Roger Irving

Pryke, was to be the first full-time chaplain to the Newman Society. (Typically, Gilroy, a mean man, did not provide any funding, as Father Pryke gradually realised—so fetes had to be organised.) The Newman Society had been a service organisation, providing daily rosary in a classroom, social events, those apologetical lectures and occasional weekend camps outside Sydney. Now, with Roger Pryke as chaplain, it became something else: a formational body. Put simply, it would explore new ways of being an Australian Catholic. A decade before the event, it would try out the themes and meanings which historians associate with the Second Vatican Council (1962-65). So that if you look at the University of Sydney in those days, you can discern, already dawning, the new light which was to break on the church in the Second Vatican Council.

> Bliss was it in that dawn to be alive
> But to be young was very heaven.

A single-sentence summation of Vatican II might say that it brought the church out of the Middle Ages and tried to find a place for it in modern times. A lengthier description of Vatican II would point to some of its outcomes: the Bible placed at the centre of Catholic liturgy, theology and spirituality; Catholic worship 'in a language understanded of the people' (to borrow a phrase from Anglicans); the love of God replacing the fear of God as the dynamic of moral choice; a morality of striving for justice and mercy rather than a morality of guilt; a recognition of the rights of conscience and religious freedom; acknowledging the brotherliness of other churches and the authenticity of other intellectual traditions; pluralism inside the church; the freeing of lay intelligence and the slow erosion of clerical control systems; and a laity who set their own agenda. These are observable outcomes of the Vatican II era; and there they are, at the University of Sydney, in the decade before the Vatican Council actually met.

The means Roger Pryke used to change the Newman Society from a service organisation into a formational community were not novel. They came from Joseph Cardijn's Jeunesse Ouvrière Chrétienne—the JOC, or Young Christian Worker movement in Belgium and France, also known as the Jocists. People of similar interests, such as those in the same faculty, met in a small group to become agents of change. Their meetings began with discussion of a Gospel passage which each member had already prepared and meditated. Thus, over time, their spirituality came to be biblically based as they encountered personally the Christ of the Gospels. Next, in the Cardijn Jocist pattern, group members came to grips with the real life of their milieu or environment... What was it like? What could it be like in, for instance, God's plan? And what could they do about it? It is difficult to convey the actuality of these enquiries into the milieu; for you can readily make them sound priggish or judgmental. In reality, these undergraduates were learning to take responsibility for their own lives, both as Christians and as university people. The groups leached out any latent proselytism or impulse to colonise the university; instead, they came to love the university and to want to serve it as intellectuals.

While this was going ahead, they were thinking seriously about Christian belief. Thus, in a paper on the Trinity, John T. Woodward reported:

> The emphasis of Sydney University Newman Society thought, in recent years, has been on three of the great doctrines of Christianity: the Incarnation, the Kingship of Christ and the Mystical Body. Our aim has been to form an apostolic ideology appropriate to the nature of the University and the nature of the Church.

So these lay people took responsibility for their lives as lay Christians. As Robert Vermeesch told a Newman camp, 'the layman is not simply the passive object of the clergy's ministry'. Behind Vermeesch's remark sat a recognition that lay people were not agents of a clerical mission or ministry; there was, rather, a lay vocation as genuine as any clerical vocation. This perception was sharpened by a remarkable English layman who turned up one day at a Newman meeting. John Kenelm Dormer was a member of one of those old English Catholic families you read about in Evelyn Waugh. Of independent means—his mother's father had founded Toohey's brewery in Sydney—he had led a restless life since serving as a captain in the war against Hitler. Somehow he had made contact with the English version of Cardijn's Jocist movement, to which he had responded enthusiastically. 'I knew,' he used to say, 'that if the church were true, something like this must exist.' In Sydney he became a great encourager of the new Catholics. It wasn't so much what John Dormer said that made a difference; rather, it was his capacity to listen and sympathise with them as they explored these novel relationships with church and university in night-long sessions in Sydney's companionable coffee shops.

This sense of a genuine lay vocation freed and energised a whole generation of Catholics, as they insisted that all were responsible for the mission of the church. Thus they anticipated the ecclesiology of Vatican II. They rejected a view of the church which promoted a churchmanship of the tiers: the directing/governing/owning level, the hierarchies; and the accepting/obeying/directed level, the laity. The bishops owned the church and only they, in concert with Roman authorities, would decide what was to be done. For a good example of such hierarchism see Cardinal Gilroy's pastoral letter for Advent 1959, in preparation for the Vatican Council. The cardinal gave a history of past church councils but seemed to have no idea why a council might be needed in the middle of the twentieth century. In this pastoral letter the only role for the laity was prayer. There was nothing about the laity reading, or discussing, or going to seminars, or contributing any ideas to the council's agenda. Such was not the role of the laity in his theology. About this time the cardinal told one of his seminarians that he expected that the council would be all over within a few weeks; after all, he said, the Roman Curia knew what was needed and they would simply tell the bishops what to do. By contrast to such hierarchism, the new-style Catholics saw their church not as a pyramid, but as a community of believers, a people, a family, a circle. We are all grown-up Christians here, they said.

The theologian who spoke most closely to the expectations of the Newman society Catholics was a French Dominican who is now largely forgotten, Yves Congar. From an early age, Congar had seen that the critical theological question for his time was the question of the church; and he dedicated his life to exploring that question, its history and its changing cultural forms, century by century. To him the word 'church' did not mean, as it often does in common speech, only the clergy; he gave it back its richer historical meaning, the people of God. Congar's *Lay People in the Church*, published in English in 1953, was seized on by his generation as the book which made sense of their own lives. It was a key text for that generation, the one, more than any other, which prepared them for what was to come. This note of the future was struck by

Pope John Paul II when he made Congar a cardinal a few months before his death, in 1995. Because his theology aimed at the future, said the citation, it needed courage to keep working at it. Here the Pope may have been thinking of the persecution Congar suffered. In 1954 the Vatican had forbidden him to teach, to lecture or to publish. He was sent into exile, first to the Dominican biblical school at Jerusalem (whose founder, M.J. Lagrange, had also been under a Vatican ban); then to Cambridge, where the local Dominican superior made life difficult for him. Well, it is an iron law of church history that those who would make a significant contribution must pay for it in blood.

This season of hope in the life of the church was also a time of change in Australian journalism. The year 1958 saw the appearance of Tom Fitzgerald's *Nation* and Donald Horne's *The Observer*, both of which were to have a profound effect on mainstream journalism. Both magazines were interested in religion, especially Catholicism, so that church historians neglect them at their peril. Donald Horne's recent book of memoirs, *Into the Open*, confirms what one had previously guessed at: that he thought Catholics had been left out of the national conversation and, through *The Observer*, he intended to include them in. He would draw his conversationalists, not from the hierarchies, but from the new university Catholics. On their part, finding it difficult to get a fair go in the diocesan papers or magazines run by religious orders, they had turned to these new journals to make their voices heard.

In all of this, Roger Pryke was not silent. Although other voices would be heard among Sydney Catholics, principally from Vincent Buckley's circle at Melbourne University (for a time the two Newman Societies were symbiotic), Father Pryke continued his central role as chaplain to the Newmans over this decade. A large part of his contribution was his leadership on worship. As a phenomenon of church life, the liturgical movement had spanned the twentieth century and Roger Pryke was a tireless activist. The core idea of the liturgical movement is that liturgy is neither a duty to be observed nor a private devotion; it is a public prayer offered together by the community of Christians. So Pryke set his altar in the middle of the circle and encouraged students to participate in dialogue Masses offered, not just by the priest, but by everyone. In time they would come to see that the prayer of all should use the language of all—in a memoir, one of Pryke's collaborators, Richard Connolly, records that the first person he heard arguing for an English-language Mass, at a sort of senior Newman discussion group, was another Pryke collaborator, James McAuley. English in the Mass was a signifier of a deeper shift in meaning; to the Mass as an authentic communal prayer.

I said above that one of the other outcomes of Vatican II was 'the love of God replacing the fear of God as the dynamic of moral choice; and a morality of striving for justice and mercy rather than a morality of guilt'. You will find no evidence for that sort of thing in the moral theology columns of the clergy's trade journal, the *Australasian Catholic Record*, until long after the council. But at the University of Sydney contemporary evidence of moral formation is hard to find, since much of it is necessarily done in private. Yet in the lives of Newman Society members, then and subsequently, guilt and fear are noticeably absent; and dedication to social justice as a religious imperative is a strong presence. One rare piece of evidence is an article by Roger Pryke, 'An Examination of Conscience for Students', in the *Newman Review* (February 1958). It is a description of the 'states of soul' (rather than 'sins') that might keep one from God. A quotation from the introduction conveys its flavour:

> Our focus should constantly be on Christ, while regularly examining our lives to see where we fail Him—but do not let us become spiritual introverts, picking away at our souls like religious woodpeckers. We centre on Christ, to know Him, love Him, serve and imitate Him.

Evidence of another kind can be found in contemporary Newman Society songbooks. Evanescent roneoed productions, these are a valuable historical archive for they open a window onto the mentality of the students who sang these songs. From this evidence a historian may conclude that, far from being fearful and guilt-ridden, these Newman songsters were joyful and happy Catholics—even if their sense of humour could prove too jocular for conservative clergyman. Young they might be, but their Catholicism was already grown-up.

Perhaps the aspect of this story a historian would find most significant is the way the Newman Society groups took on the central vocation of a university as traditionally conceived, namely the disinterested pursuit of truth. Again and again, in their published talks and articles, Roger Pryke and Newman Society leaders rejected any suggestion that they should be spin doctors for Catholic power structures, or proselytisers, or colonisers. Insistently they repeated that their call was to love the university and university values. So they came to acknowledge the brotherliness of other churches and the authenticity of other intellectual traditions. When Hugh Gough, the Anglican Archbishop of Sydney, made his celebrated attack on the university's philosophy department as an anti-Christian centre, he drew his firepower from a pamphlet emanating from the Aquinas Academy, a Thomist night school attached to St Patrick's Church in the city—it was noticeable how Newman Society leaders, including Pryke, defended the department's rights. Here was an ecumenism of the human mind and spirit wider than mere church ecumenism. It pointed the way towards today's Catholic pluralism.

Well, the seventeen-year-old lived through all this, and went elsewhere, and got a life (of a sort). And always in his heart he kept true to the motto of his first university, *Sidere mens eadem mutato*. Whatever his location, he kept faith with the poem of a grown-up Catholicism he had learned to love in the happiest years of his life.

Reading Sydney: Three Ages, Three Winds

Richard Hall

When the Scotsman John Pringle wrote of the three winds of Sydney in 1958 he was seeing them as a backdrop to a city, with seamless continuity, a place where most of the men in the city's centre wore blue serge suits, as they would have in John Kinsgmill's remembered Sydney of the 1930s. The 1950s were the last years of the Anglo-Celtic city, the coalition of English, Scots, and Irish that had rubbed along from the beginning, although not without tensions. The immigrants were coming, but they were still on the margins, put in their place by that patronising assimilationist tag 'New Australians'. In the early years of the decade writers of letters to the editor, the radio talkback callers of the time, worried that newspapers for the immigrant communities used their own languages: it was felt that this practice should rapidly die out. George Johnston in *Clean Straw for Nothing* has a revealing episode in which an old Sydney-sider can rebuke a newcomer for the offence of his accent. In those days the word *schnitzel* was a joke; spaghetti was something that came in cans with tomato sauce; Chinatown was a ghetto of a few mean streets. Some suburbs, certainly not all, had a token Chinese restaurant, the menus topped by sweet and sour pork, an unthreatening dish.

In 1954 when the Queen came, the crowds did line the streets and cheer. The State governor was a person of note, and the ABC sent a reporter out every Sunday to record the deep thoughts of that functionary as he moved from flower fête to RSL congress.

Archbishops and their coadjutors were taken note of. Vicars and ministers were men of substance in their suburbs, influential beyond their congregations, while priests of the Catholic Church could expect two-thirds of their faith at mass every Sunday. It was a stable world, or so it seemed.

But in 1958, the year Pringle's book *Australian Accent* came out, Sydney was on the cusp. The second age of the city was coming to a close. The first age, that of the colony, robust and pugnacious, ran from 1788 to the federation of 1901. The second age, an ordered Anglo-Celtic era, was very good at hiding away the unruly. It was a world of suburban respectability, and to be Australian was to be in the best of all worlds. Pangloss might have been the patron saint. But, as in occupied Europe during World War Two, there were resisters. Christina Stead and Jack Lindsay wrote about them, but it is significant that both had to flee.

Some would say the 1960s mark the end of that era, but then there are those people, like the not inconsiderable number who voted for One Nation in the late 1990s, who cannot accept that that era ever ended.

Pringle could see that change was coming but, shrewd observer though he was, he didn't know how far things would be changed. But then again some things have not changed. The best of his book is in his decription of the three winds of Sydney: the north-easterly, the soft, warm Pacific wind that brings the showers; the southerly buster, at any time of the year, sweeping in, jostled north by the front from the polar South, dumping the rain and dragging the temperature down. And then the westerlies of summer, dry, hot and nagging.

Both those who came to visit and those who stayed liked to exclaim at the extremes of the weather in Sydney. Bowes, a surgeon on one of the women's convict ships of the First Fleet, wrote in his diary of the events of 7 February 1788 when the female convicts were set ashore for the first time, provoking scenes of the utmost debauchery and riot, as the surgeon told it. He was the first but far from the last to deplore the morals of Sydney's inhabitants. But Bowes also recorded 'the most violent storm of thunder, lightning and rain that I have ever seen', which, although it killed five sheep and a pig struck by lightning, did nothing 'in the least respect' to damp down the debauchery. A few years later, in 1794, the painter Thomas Watling wrote of the westerly 'as a scorching wind so intolerable as to restrict respiration'. Charlotte Godley in 1851, while deploring the effect of the gold rush on servants' manners, took time to write of the menace of the brick-fielders, those southerly busters so-called because they came in over the brickfields on the fringe of the city and raised the most fearful dust. A few years later an English journalist, Frank Fowler, invoked the Apocalypse to deplore the westerlies as 'hot and murky as the breath of an oven, as though the Last Seal was opened and the breath of the Destroying Angel came forth'. Visiting writers again and again took note of the extremes of the climate, so irregular, compared to the order of the seasons at home.

Now in the concrete canyons of the Central Business District, the winds are lost, blocked and tamed. For office workers in a high-rise building near a window, the rolling grey clouds of a southerly front sweeping towards the city are safe theatre. But in the suburbs things can be different, very different. The flat plains of western Sydney can be still stifled by days of westerlies, which brush aside any of the north-easterly breezes that might have moved so far inland. The infamous hail storm of April 1999 played a trick of heading out to sea before veering back to shake the city by the scruff of the neck. Even the fastnesses of the high North Shore, proud of the high eucalypts or their English gardens, are clawed every few years by fierce southerlies that strip the boughs and bring down trees. For those who sail in small boats on the harbour, a southerly is an ambush to be feared. Sometimes even the usually benign north-easterly can force the yachts to run before the wind. A week of southerlies can throw up great waves that can rip away beaches. The winds with all their capacity for extremes are very much actors in the drama of the city. But for all that the people of Sydney have adapted to the extremes, just as the men and women convicts did that night in February 1788, and got on with their lives. Watling seems almost frightened of winds and landscape, but at the same time someone was tending the vines and citruses in the governor's garden.

Whereas many stayed, there were always some, even from the first days, who wanted to cut and run. The experiment of a penal colony at the end of the world was, as any scrutiny of the London press will show, regarded as an absurd act of folly. The officers of Admiral Malaspina's Spanish fleet who visited Sydney in 1793 noted the widespread opinion that the colony would be closed down. Governor Phillip had gone home by then. Although the colony had that formidable patron Sir Joseph Banks, it can be judged that if Phillip had brought back a negative picture, the pessimists might well have been proved right. We are in debt to Phillip not only for those first days but also for what he said when he went back to London. Even so the bureaucrats of Whitehall were not envisaging the dream of Empire, merely a self-supporting penal colony, with perhaps a few strategic advantages on side. The Blue Mountains loomed in the west, but it would be twenty-four years before a party crossed them. The Cumberland Plain and the fertile Hawkesbury River flats could support the colony.

By 1802 Henri Peron, one of the scientists on a French expedition under Captain Baudin, found a solidly established settlement grown to more than 3,500 people. Government was enlightened, industry and agriculture thriving, and there was even 'a sort of coffee-house'.

Others saw things differently. Three years previously, three missionaries driven from Tahiti by civil war and cannibalism found Sydney equally iniquitous: 'Adultery, fornication, theft, drunkeness, extortion, violence and uncleanness of every kind, the natural concommitants of Deism and infidelity.' This jaundiced view might have been influenced by the fate of a fourth colleague, who, while engaging in a spot of money-lending on the side, had tried to retrieve a debt from a sergeant. The sergeant killed him with an axe and was hanged the next day. But apart from that, the missionaries' horror should remind us that Fred Nile has not been the first to despair of Sydney's morals.

Despite the fine appearances praised by Peron, it was still a convict settlement, and held together by violence; executions and floggings were hardly worth a comment. The savages might be quelled by providential smallpox and the rifle, but the authorities could never be sure of the convicts. One threat was never very far from their minds: the prospect of a rising by the Irish convicts, augmented by prisoners from the failed 1798 rising. The Irish rebellion did come in 1804, botched in execution and bloodily put down by the New South Wales Corps, who killed nineteen in the only skirmish and hanged even more. The next rising, in 1808 by the Rum Corps against the governor, Captain Bligh, was more farcical than bloody, but it was an omen of Sydney's lasting mistrust of authority.

For the rest of that century the better classes and their newspaper leader-writers tended to pose the anguished question: what good could come of a colony so tainted by its origins? The querulousness was sharpened in the early decades by the competitiveness of the more successful emancipationists, ex-convicts, and, in later years, by a snobbish mistrust of colonial democracy. However, most of the locally born citizens of Sydney, the currency lads and lasses, were not much interested in the question. Dr Charles Darwin, coming in 1836, was one of the earliest travellers to put Sydney in the book he wrote about his tour, and he was much struck by the extreme rancour between the emancipationists and the free middle class. (By the way, Darwin seems to have been the first to see Sydney as a future city of suburbs.)

John Hood, who visited in 1838, in his book deplored the number of hotels, 'dens of iniquity'. There was one for every 140 souls, men, women and children. He then expressed surprise that the streets of Sydney were safe to walk at night.

Whereas some ex-convicts did very well and others lived humble lives within the law, there was a vigorous underworld of old lags. The diary of the police Inspector Nugent, whose beat covered the Rocks and the city up to Druitt, Park, and Macquarie streets, records 107 'disorderly houses'—that is, brothels—as well thieves' kitchens, gambling dens, and bent publicans galore. The transportation of convicts did end, but then the gold rush brought a new class of plebeian immigrant, dangerously inclined to democracy.

The idea of the convict taint gained some fresh impetus among newspaper leader-writers in the 1870s with the rise of the larrikin pushes of the Sydney slums. In 1881 a new periodical, the *Bulletin*, exploited the popular fear of that underside of society with its report of a day at the Clontarf picnic grounds. By an unintended irony the same Clontarf a decade before had been the scene of a riot by the more respectable members of society, who responded to an attempt on the life of Prince Alfred, one of Queen Victoria's sons, by attempting to lynch the assailant. But that was to look back, and in the early years of the 1880s the leader-writers returned to the larrikin threat again and again. Even a visiting actor, in memoirs published in New York, told Americans of this Australian horror. In 1885 a vicious Push rape of a girl at Mount Rennie led the city into a orgy of breast-beating sermons. The vengeance on the rapists seemed— to read the sermons and submissions of delegations—more important than the fate of the girl. The vengeance on four of the convicted, a shockingly bungled hanging, was the climax.

Politics in both Macquarie Street and the Sydney City Council was mostly petty and personal. On his visit to the colony in 1875 a rather priggish Havelock Ellis was, however, right when he characterised the Legislative Assembly as 'a body of businessmen, merchants, shop-keepers and the like'. Never far below the surface in politics was the tension between Catholics and Protestants. In 1871 a boxing match—illegal, as they all were—was tagged an Orange v. Green match.

Sydney was never without slums, but the snowballing growth of the city in the seond half of the nineteenth century meant that the old slums became worse and the new ones grew faster. There were only spasmodic qualms about health until the authorities were shaken by an outburst of bubonic plague in 1900. In the slums there were no pensions, for widows or the old; no unemployment benefits, only uncertain charity. The Chippendale slum streets walked by young H.M. Moran were a mile from the theatre where the visiting Melbourne artist Arthur Streeton would attend the At Home afternoon of Mrs Charrington, a leader of society who was rich enough to hire the theatre and an orchestra as her social stage. After expressing his pleasure at Mrs Charrington's generous hospitality, Streeton grumbled about the distractions of the Maritime Strike only a few streets away.

*

There are some historical events in Sydney better left in oblivion. With the anniversary of Federation coming, we can expect a bundle of recycled accounts of the dull, pompous charade played out in Centennial Park on January 1901 to institute the Commonwealth of Australia: the governor-general in uniform with his cocked hat, the soldiers and sailors, the parade of drays decked with the produce of industry and farm, the inevitable artillery salute—all the sedate theatre of the British Empire, which might have been played out in many cities: Montreal or Ottawa, Dublin or Belfast, Edinburgh or Dunedin. Nor are the staples of antipodean pride, 'first' events, like aeroplanes, trains, and so on, much worth revisiting. Not to say that a *first* cannot tell us a great deal about the city, like the first election day of 1843, with the mob versus the quality, and the backdrop of Orange v. Green sectarianism, the account of which survives in the 1931 centenary history of the *Sydney Morning Herald*.

Even the best of historians cannot quite achieve the immediacy of the contemporary voices. From them we can get a grasp of the city, a sense of place: physical geography, its people, their manners, their passions and contradictions.

The witnesses don't have to come from the great and the good. We are only able to read about the old Van Diemen's Land man who boasts of his depravity and then crawls as an informant to Inspector Nugent in the 1840s because the inspector left behind his running diary when he was summarily sacked. The diary turned up in the archives 150 years later. There is very little good writing about politics: forgotten brawls about personalities best stay forgotten. Alfred Deakin's razor-sharp portraits of Henry Parkes and George Reid, who really were giants, in his *The Story of Federation*, say as much about the Sydney society in which they flourished as it does about them. Perhaps it took a Melbourne man to write it. It is true that two of Sydney's twentieth-century politicians, Billy Hughes and Jack Lang, did leave memoirs, but they are rather too self-serving, too much concerned with themselves, or rather their fictions of themselves, rather than with the city.

Some witnesses have been hard to find. The royal marine, Watkin Tench's sensitive acount of first contacts with the Aborigines, rightly often anthologised, is generous and hopeful, but from that same year we can read a letter from one of the convicts, riddled with fear of and hostility towards the 'savages'. Then the smallpox came, and again in the 1830s, virtually wiping out the Sydney tribes. In 1845 Mahroot, the last male left of his tribe, gave evidence to a select committee of the Legislative Council. Its members spent a lot of time on theology, keen to ascertain the Aboriginal concepts of God and the Devil. When Mahroot, in the midst of their ramblings, burst out with: 'Devil devil is its all over small pox like', his questioners took no notice and continued striving to establish that the deaths of the tribes followed from drink and the men allowing their women to go with white men, the Aborigines lacking a grasp of the sacrament of matrimony. Someone was to blame, but it wasn't the councillors or Providence, which sent the smallpox.

In July 1890 the hubristic pride of the city and the colony of New South Wales was at its height (the discord of the Maritime Strike was a few months away). The press could celebrate with gross smugness an act of philanthrophy towards the surviving Aborigines by Quong Tart, the Chinese tea-shop proprietor and importer, who gave a banquet for the survivors of the Sydney tribes. A Presbyterian, Mason, reciter of Robbie Burns, and wearer of kilts, Quong Tart was generous with banquets; asylums, orphanages, hospitals, and ragged schools, all at one time or another benefited from his largesse. A remnant of sixty Aborigines had been expected at the Zoological Gardens, but only forty came, to sit down to a feast laid out on baize cloth on the ground, watched by spectators who had paid 1s 6d, proceeds to a new Christian mission. One of the men gave a speech of thanks; surprisingly, it was noted, in good English.

Witnesses to immigrant life were also hard to find. The prosperity of the city in the last two generations has been built on the sweat and shoulders of the immigrant workers, but they have been largely silent. There are some good poets, but little testimony of work or the way they lived. The migrant men and women were too busy, too tired: many of the first generation survived hostility or indifference by silence. Older Australian writers have passed them by, Patrick White's Himmelfarb in *Riders in the Chariot* being a rare exception. Rosa Capiello, an Italian, and George Papaellinas, of Greek parents, are brutally frank witnesses. She writes of female immigrant factory workers and their inner-city life in the mid-1960s. George Papaellinas creates the welder on the same car assembly line for thirty years, tired but unbowed.

Most writing about sport in Sydney has been ephemeral. There's nothing wrong with that; it's there to simply report. There has been nothing for Rugby League like the Englishman David Storey's *This Sporting Life*. Clive James's short, wry account of his life as a Rugby Union player, in his *Unreliable Memoirs*, says more about the game than a hundred match reports. In *The Homebush Boy*, his memoirs, Tom Kenneally's account of his 440-yard run glows with the passion of that high summer of schoolboy sport, the 1950s. Further back in 1843 the jolly reporter for the *Sydney Gazette* going along the Parramatta Road to see the Homebush Races went as much for the spectacle as for a wager and in a few hundred words freezes a portrait of colonial society.

Finding witnesses from the nineteenth century is in some ways easier than from the twentieth. There was a stream of English visitors, like Darwin, Trollope, Dilke, and Froude, who were good writers and who were concerned to find chapters for their round-the-world books. The shock of the novel geography stimulated them, and they praised the harbour in appropriately respectful, even fulsome, terms, but thought themselves obliged to make social observations; in particular, they nagged at the question of the society with the convict taint. In time the genre did run down. Marcus Clarke, writing from Melbourne, savaged Trollope for clichés.

The local press was vigorous. Journalists could write with originality and style, and were allowed to do so. A sports report could be a very polished piece of work, and even narrative reporting (for example, about the attempted assassination of the Duke of Edinburgh and about the Maritime Strike clash at Circular Quay) would give a striking portrait of what was happening. But from around 1900, the second age of the city, the press quickly lost that nineteenth-century gusto. The *Bulletin* fizzled out, but when two of the greatest writers of its heyday, J.F. Archibald and A.G. Stephens, moved out to establish *The Book-Fellow*, it turned out to be dull and stodgy. The metropolitan press reflected quickly the steep decline of the raffish side of Sydney in the years before World War One and the rise of suburban respectability. Politics had a lot to do with it. The non-Labor parties merged in response to the rising threat of the ALP and formed an alliance with the wowser Protestant churches, whose price was social control through a raft of anti-liquor, anti-gambling, and Sunday observance laws. These laws were unenforceable and turned many of the population, mostly working class, into offenders. From then on the laws fed and entrenched police corruption and created widespread public acceptance of corruption underneath the façade.

There were those who stood against the conventions, like the people in Jack Lindsay's memoirs and the characters in Christina Stead's novels, but significantly both those writers went into exile. The result is that for the twentieth century our sense of things relies more on literature and memoirs than on the press. Lennie Lower waging his endless war against the suburbs was rare exception.

> Chatswood is one of those places that is a stone's throw from some other place, and is mainly given over to the earnestly genteel. Here respectability stalks abroad adorned with starched linen and surrounded by mortgages.

Limited and insular as the society was, it was a good life, if you had a job. The King was his throne, and all was right with the world. The city ran on networks of understood codes on dress and manners. John Kingsmill delineates the vital hat and overcoat rules and the etiquette of a Bondi tram. They had their simple entertainments, such as Donald Horne's picture palaces, although never on Sunday. However, radio, which could be heard on Sunday, was the supreme popular entertainment, and Sumner Locke Elliott's virtuoso picture of 'the man with a thousand voices' freezes a long lost world in a frame.

The society that had ridden out a depression was shaken by the new war. There was no wild enthusiasm for war, as Elizabeth Harrower's image of the soldiers marching to the ships shows. The coming of the Yanks brutally challenged the stolid old mores. After six years of war and seemingly unending shortages, the mood of the city was nervy and bad-tempered, as Johnston's returning war correspondent and his wife found.

The literary visitors of this century were not up to the standards of those of the nineteenth century, with the exception of Pringle, but then while he went home after *Australian Accent*, the Scotchman did return to live in Sydney. Usually, however, the visits were shorter, and it showed. Jan Morris came twice, once in 1961 to criticise and then later to praise. Her two accounts form a Pauline contrast, but neither are up to the standard of her better writing.

In the wake of Pringle the pace of change has sometimes seemed giddying. The world of the two battling immigrants has gone. Christos worked as welder on a car assembly line; now there are no car assembly lines in Sydney and the Greeks are moving out of Marrickville to make way for the Vietnamese. Rosa Capiello wrote of Paddington and Surry Hills being working class. No more. Even the tight world of the Anglo-Saxon North Shore defined in Jessica Anderson's novels of manners has now to live with Chinese-Australian neighbours. Dorothy Hewett wrote of the rough slum world of Redfern in 1950, but now it is the place to buy.

It would be possible to fill the pages of a book with Sydney-Melbourne rivalries and differences, some of them real, but most of them constructions. Frank Fowler in the 1850s told his English readers that Sydney was staid compared to Melbourne, but others reversed that label quickly enough. Being born in Melbourne and having spent the first ten years of my life there, I always feel at ease; the streets of the city, the suburbs, the gardens, the beaches, and the railway routes, all have their resonances for me. Perhaps that is why I find myself so exasperated, or even angered, by those perennially boring beat-ups on Sydney v. Melbourne. On a football field, fine, but off the arena—get a life. So I steer away from all those banalities, though one exception that cannot be resisted, and which is certainly not banal, is Keith Murdoch's outburst of rage against Sydney in a letter in 1915 to Andrew Fisher, then still prime minister. It was the only time Keith Murdoch lived in Sydney and then only for a few months. A dour son of the manse, Murdoch found that Sydney, even its middle classes, was not serious enough about the war. 'I don't think the Sydney spirit would prevail in a war against the native tribes of Papua. It is a pity the aborigines were not Prussianised,' he wrote. Presumably what he means when he wishes the Aborigines had been Prussianised was that they would have repelled, even wiped out, those first settlers. Where, one wonders, would Keith Murdoch have wanted to set the boundary of Prussianisation—the Murray?

A warm corrective to the Sydney-Melbourne beat-ups is Glen Tomasetti's *My Sydney*, a story of a woman and her mother, remembering their lives in Sydney and Melbourne, which shows a harmony not only between the two women but also between the two cities. Both women offer their memories of places, of people, of sorrow and joy. In their minds, the cities are not trite, barracking rivals. A citizen can have an abiding affection for their Sydney with all its glories, its beauty, its commonplaces, its failures, its flaws, and its faults. There are always its surprises, too. To be lost on a summer day amid the towers of the city, then suddenly to look north up Phillip Street from the Bent Street corner and catch the shimmering waters of Sydney Cove, always the same Sydney Cove, is a sweet surprise.

But a city is more than the sum of its setting, its landscapes, its buildings. It lives in its people, their conflicts and contradictions, their crudeness and their subtleties, their achievements and their failures, their virtues and their vices. It lives in this past and their present. The visitors come and go, but the authentic voices of the city, in the end, come from its people.

There is an old Negro spiritual about paradise:

Twelve gates to the city,
Three gates to the east,
Three gates to the west,
Three gates to the north,
Three gates to the south.
Oh, what a beautiful city!

(Some sing 'Oh! What a wonderful city'.) Sydney does not have the twelve gates; it is not paradise; but despite everything that has been done to disfigure it, it is still a beautiful city, a wonderful city.

John Forbes in Europe

Peter Porter

Those who knew John Forbes are united in praising his extraordinarily wide knowledge of literature, history, world systems of thought and so on. He was the opposite of the 'know nothing' poet whose embrace of Modernism is due to an unwillingness to learn about the history and practice of his art, someone for whom the phrase '*ab ovo*' is an open sesame to easy writing. But this formidable knowledgeability was attuned to a fierce loyalty to Modernism and was never, as it is with many writers, myself included, an excuse to turn away from the regimen of experiment. To enter yet another sub-clause to this argument, Forbes, however, was not given to hagiography of modernist pioneers, with the exception of a tendency to overestimate Frank O'Hara. He was like a sophisticated early Christian—ready to be a martyr to his faith, but unwilling to suppress his scepticism in general or deny the relevance of history. One aspect of this which his many friends were obliged to accept was his frequently harsh opinion of their work—loyalty did not preclude severity of judgment or even out-and-out dismissal.

In such matters, John was very much a product of the prevailing Australian intellectual climate of his time. He was, though he may not have acknowledged it, in the broad stream of Australian knowingness, what I have called for my own convenience *The Saturday Morning Quiz Kids' Club*. 'Please Sir, I know the capital of Ecuador.' Whether this is part of that doubtful condition, 'The

Tyranny of Distance' or more probably a product of the fact-dominated educational systems ascendant throughout Australia, who can tell? But Forbes was in the line of—to name the more celebrated of its members—the club of Murray Sayle, Bob Ellis, Clive James, Bob Hughes, Barry Humphries and Germaine Greer. There is a 'Look at me' feeling in the work of these men and women, a sense of outraged resentment that justification does not come unsolicited to them as it appears to do to talented people brought up in Britain and the United States. But Australians have a special restlessness which has not been a force in America since Henry James's time—namely an obsession with the wider world, a determination to bring Australian sensibility to the judgment of older societies. That this should go hand in hand with nationalism and a dismissal of overseas standards is not a paradox—they are sides of the same coin. My proposal in this brief article is to locate John Forbes's developing talent as a poet not just in the Sydney and Melbourne he knew well, but in the Europe he visited surprisingly often and which he, unlike many of his fellow-countrymen, was prepared to observe in its contemporary reality, not just in its armorial state as culture out of books.

There is nowhere better to look at the Forbes picture of Europe than in his witty and Theophrastian poem 'Europe: A Guide for Ken Searle'. Forbes sets out to advise his artist friend on what he will find in the cradle of Western civilisation; he composes a series of emblems bringing national aspects of European culture into low relief. Satire is, I believe, a version of Pastoral in the Empsonian sense. It enables you to find a way of feeling superior to whatever feels superior to you, or what has simply ignored your significance. The technique goes back a long way—it's certainly in Shakespeare and in Goethe's version of Mephistopheles, as much as in those writers who are given the full trade description as satirists. To be *der Geist der stets verneint*, you have to know what you're reacting to and possess a natural aptitude for summing-up. 'Scotland is old-fashioned like a dowry/but unusual, like nice police. Mention/Ireland and you've already said enough.' How often I've wished that this last line had been followed by generations of Australian Irish! The Forbes knowingness has its confessional or perhaps skiting aspect:

> Consult my *By Trailbike*
> *And Hot Air Balloon Through Middle Europe*

for details of the Austrians & Czechs

but don't forget Bavaria's Oktoberfest
or that Rococo architecture was designed
to be passed out under, pissed…

This is followed by the justifying aside:

Besides, if you remove the art, Europe's
like the US, more or less a dead loss
…though
knocked out by what convinced me
'great art' without inverted commas is

(but not because of this) I hung around
with other Australians and hit the piss.

In the murky syntax of these last lines, the message is that no
matter how well-informed an intellectual Australian is, he or she
will always be faced with a duty to display the National Character
at its most democratic. Forbes, like many visitors to Europe since
the days of Ezra Pound, knows that Europeans are frequently
unworthy custodians of their own culture, but knows as well that
they live their day-to-day lives in the lands the great artists worked
in, and that, however well-informed we are, we don't. Modernism,
despite its ancestry in nineteenth-century France and Germany, is
in the gift of the new soceities, in America and Oceania. Thus the
call to 'make it new' will always be a duty for New World artists, and
especially ambiguous for those of them who feel the force and lure
of the Old World's precedents.

I'm not sure when John wrote 'Europe: A Guide', but know that
it was well after I got to know him. My understanding in general of
the dates of John's poems is inexact, chiefly because I was not in
Australia often enough to check his publications, which appeared
sporadically. I have acquired copies of most of them over the years,
but have never been able to map a convincing *catalogue raisonée* of
them: a properly edited *Collected Poems* will be welcome so that we
may read the poetry in some sort of order of its composition.

I remember vividly my first encounter with him, though even
here I am not sure of the date. It must have been soon after my first
wife's death—that is, subsequent to 1974. I had been reading at

the old Poetry Society headquarters in Earl's Court Square. God knows what the occasion was: Poetry Society meetings could seldom be described as 'occasions'. This rugged and loquacious young man came up to me in the basement bar and quickly said several reasonably rude things to me, implying that (1) I shouldn't think I mattered in Australia, and (2) England was rather a waste of time. Even then I found a sort of friendliness in John's aggression. But I don't want to sentimentalise him: he could be, and often was, a disturbing presence. At that time I must have represented many of the things he disliked about Australian expatriates. Later, he would concede that I had had good reasons to leave Australia when I did, and regarded me as an almost forgivable figure, someone who had had the ill luck to be born before Australian modernists saw the American *aurora borealis*. Until the bar closed we sparred in conversation and then he announced he had nowhere to stay for the night, and could I put him up? I did and didn't go to sleep until well into the night. He was a challenging conversationalist, but what I remember best about him was the range of his reading and the brilliant marginalia of his general knowledge. He would have been the ideal third person to have joined the famous introduction of Clive James and Les Murray to each other as freshmen at Sydney University where like two dogs sniffing they had calmed their suspicions by comparing notes on the World War Two Gromman Carrier-borne fighter plane. Forbes knew about weapons too though he didn't like them much. From that first occasion till his last visit to London in 1997, he slept a number of times in my flat in Cleveland Square. There was always something dangerous about having him to stay but also something almost apologetic and whimsical. My present wife, Christine, and I learned to keep the whisky away from him in later days—not to save our stock (I don't drink the stuff) but to save him. Being an alcohol addict myself, I am careful usually not to pontificate on people's fondness for booze, but at the time of John's final visit to England, it was plain that he was declining physically. His intellect appeared undamaged but he gave off a sense of emergency, of things closing in. I would not then have deduced any weakness of the heart but rather a sense of crisis in general. The question of his several addictions is not one I know much about. He has written in an honest and even jocular way of these himself, always avoiding being what Auden called 'a wet-leg', but he was almost helpless at keeping the effects from being visible to others.

One odd circumstance of that first overnight stay was John's willingness to bend the rules of hospitality in the interest of a greater force, curiosity. I found after he'd gone that he had rummaged through my papers while I slept and had left them disarrayed, which seemed to suggest he hadn't attempted to conceal what he'd done. I don't believe in *'De mortuis nil nisi bonum'* and hope that others will treat me similarly. So I report this not to reproach him retrospectively but rather to try to establish how other-worldly he could be—at least in the matter of social orthodoxy. I had no sense of deliberate iconoclasm in his behaviour: he was not like that shrewd exploiter of outrage, Dylan Thomas, who broke up the flat Norman Cameron lent him and stole shirts from one of his American hosts. I think this other-wordliness lay behind his way of handling money. He was not profligate in the way most of us are: it seemed more that he needed to let it slip through his fingers before it contaminated him.

As I wrote before, I'm not sure of the chronology of John's visits to Europe. Perhaps he had been in London a couple of times before he took me to lunch in Sydney by way of repaying my dining him in England. I've referred to this lunch in my tributary poem which follows, so I'll only sketch it lightly here. We went to his favourite Greek restaurant in an upstairs room overlooking Elizabeth Street and the end of Hyde Park. The food was not good but John's liking for it was based on the size of the helpings, which were enormous. I met him a short while after this at John and Lyn Tranter's house. I noticed for the first time how powerfully he was built: this was in his furniture removal period. I now think the impression I had of his hardihood was something of an illusion. I'm tempted to agree with Laurie Duggan that the sugar in the cough mixture can't have been helpful and may have underwritten his heart complaint.

Lost once more in chronological fog, I can only assume that John's poetry of this time reached me in the pages of his *Surfers' Paradise* magazine and various outlying publications. I was certainly familiar with 'Four Heads and How to Do Them' by the late 70s or early 80s. Somehow I don't seem to possess a copy of *Ode to Tropical Skiing*, which came out in 1976, but have read the poems it contains. I remember formulating the notion that John was in thrall to hedonism and often spoke of going dancing or surfing. It reminded me of my terrible childhood at boarding schools where the worst torture was school dances and compulsory enjoyment of girls' company. I thought he should try to enjoy his melancholy more, but Sydney is not a good place to be unhappy in. Later, in Melbourne, he let his erudite half-fatalism work through into his poems so that the cause of convictism-hedonism was subverted by the vistas of history. Peter Craven has written of John's reaction to a scholarly theological book which had been sent to *Scripsi*'s office: 'Bernard of Clairvaux was a complete shit.' This awareness of complete shittiness lies behind poems such as 'Holy Week', 'Europe Endless' and 'Ode to Karl Marx'.

My clearest memories of John in Europe come from later days, when he was writer-in-residence in Rome and finally when was at Loughborough University during the first quarter of 1997. But there are a few vignettes before that. I recall the serious and convinced cyclist who seemed to have travelled all over Britain by bike. He would suddenly appear on wheels with some adventure to relate, often an encounter with an almost forgotten poet or fugitive book. Once on cycling through Hampstead he'd spotted a book of poems by Kiedrych Rhys in a secondhand bookshop and bought it. I thought I was the only person in the world who had heard of Kiedrych Rhys. Needless to say, John knew his poetry already. Rees was an apocalyptic Welsh poet (not actually a member of the Apocalyptic School of the 40s—Treece, Hendry, Schimanski, W.S. Graham and others—but a permanently quarrelsome bard) whose reputation had sunk to near nothingness by the 80s. I'd come across him as an angry letter-writer in one of James Agate's *Ego* books, and had tracked down some of his poems in journals. Agate had fun at his expense, regarding him as characteristic of the preposterousness of modern poets. I remember one of Rhys's lines which earned Agate's particular scorn, 'Gleetcold shudders in the arms of whores.' Would I have remembered it if it had been truly bad? Possibly. John had a genius for delving into poets' work and finding rare gems. He once took me through John Manifold's work and proved to me that it was not all communist simplification, apart from two anthology pieces; though unfortunately this was after I'd made my ultra-orthodox selection from Manifold for *The Oxford Book of Modern Australian Verse*.

In between these glimpses of John in Britain and his period in Rome, we met up again at the ASAL Conference at Griffith University in Brisbane in 1990. Some of the most interesting conversations I had with him were conducted sitting on the open-air brick verandah of the Griffith Staff Club, where Michael Sharkey usually joined us. The university's architecture is of the brutalist persuasion but the straggly suburban bush has been left intact beside the unlovely buildings and this does much to make the site attractive. Sitting with our beers and sharing them with a flotilla of kookaburras who flew in from the trees was for me the highlight of the conference. The final dance with its Frank Moorhouse Trophy opened a further window on to John's determined pursuit of hedonism. He insisted on performing on the floor, which he didn't look as though he was enjoying. He was a little in thrall to a young researcher into contemporary Australian poetry named Erica Travers. I thought she wasn't giving him much in return for his co-operation on her thesis. But she had just got married, so her distancing is understandable. Soon after this I had dinner in Sydney with him and others, including Martin Johnston. John respected Martin greatly both for his erudition and his poetry. John assumed an unlikely role with Martin, the careful guide and minder. Johnston remained for him a touchstone in a world of precarious truthfulness.

John's tenure in the Trastavere flat which the Australia Council runs in Rome was not for the full six months. He came to Rome because the appointed incumbent wished to return to Australia. It is a city I know quite well—at least in its geography and visitable monuments—and I was able to share his views on Rome, though I never encountered him there. My elder daughter lived for three years in the Trastavere and while staying with her I could trace John's movements in the city. His great knowledge of literature, history, technology and film did not extend to painting, sculpture and music. But in Rome he broke his rules about culture-trawling and went to churches and galleries dutifully. Evidence of this is scattered through his last two collections of poems— 'Santa Sabina', 'San Carlino in Quattro Fontane', 'the Duca di Aosta' etc. He was the sort of Catholic who has a natural tolerance of the baroque, viewing it as a consequence of the counter-reformation. He fell in love while in Rome and put this baffled romance into poems. This was in line with his tendency to choose romances which had little hope of flourishing. Traces of his *idée fixe* (it did not amount to infatuation) are found in 'Troubadour', 'Satellite of Love', 'Humidity' and especially 'Love Poem', where the Gulf War rages on TV and provides the technically-minded poet with some further recognition of his unrequited passion. John's distant beloveds are not easily distinguishable in these poems, but then that pretty is much the case with all love poetry. His Rome poems are in the vein of 'Europe: A Guide'. He thought of the City of Caesars and Popes as begging to be upstaged, so he introduces a set of icons of his own, including The Ramones, Michael Cain and the Australian Sixth Division. One current obsession is sharply present in 'Europe Endless':

> 'it's true,' she said
> 'our rock music's shit
> but we invented sexual attraction
> didn't you know? in the 12th Century—
> I mean they had it before
> but not
> as a central, defining principle
> in the Subject's relation to the Other.'
> I looked across to her—
> > her fine-boned face
> > & deep serious eyes.
> > Thanks, I said
> Thanks a lot.

I've always thought that, broken heart or not, John's deepest affection in Rome was for the unreformed Communist Party of Italy, whose headquarters he often went to, and from where he came away with Agitprop posters. Not of course the larger post-Cold War party which adapted itself to share power with Prodi and the rest. A lost cause with an inflexible dogma always appealed to John.

His Melbourne years included work on *Scripsi* and I saw him a few times in the journal's Ormond College offices. Towards the end of *Scripsi*'s days, he made attempts to get overseas' residencies and I wrote recommendations for him at least three times. The one he favoured most and for which I thought he was particularly well-suited was a writer/artist attachment to Cork University. But Cork did not appoint him. He had several Australian posts of this sort in the 80s and 90s. In 1996 he applied for a one-term writer-in-residency at Loughborough University. Here I had a little influence since the former professor of English, John Lucas, was a friend of mine and I had been given an honorary degree by the university in 1988. Lucas was an admirer of John's poetry and had met him in Australia.

John duly arrived in late January 1997 and stayed the weekend before going on to Loughborough. It was clear to my wife and me that he was not in good shape. Loughborough was to disappoint him. The living quarters were spartan and campus life was desultory. The town itself is in the middle of the least-favoured landscape of the English Midlands. The university has a good tradition of English teaching though it is best known as the largest centre of physical education in the UK. I saw him quite often on his extended returns to London. He became a great fan of the Channel Four program *Eurotrash*. The mode of this send-up is to indulge in the worst possible taste in all matters, and to derogate seriousness and decorum. It also mocks the British, and the leering of presenter John Paul Gaultier (also a coutourier) with his 'Hello British chums' must have seemed to John to put Loughborough in its place. The program's sexual angles are notably trashy and appealed to John's sense of the grotesque.

At Loughborough and in direct reaction to it, John fell in love with Cambridge University, or at least its English school, or that part of it grouped around Jeremy Prynne. John Kinsella invited him to Cambridge and also arranged for him to take part in the Cambridge Poetry Festival at Easter. It was, to use a word beloved of academics, an epiphany. He described Cambridge as the last redoubt of the avant-garde. Among the Prynnites—not just the Master himself, whom I don't think he met, but Prynne's followers, mostly young dons or Ph.D. students—Forbes felt a sense of community which he had not had since early days in Sydney. There was a further attraction: both the girlfriends of these young and privileged academics, and female members of the circle in general, were the kind of woman created by God to be John's unattainable loves. One, who wrote intelligent but difficult poems, had, he said admiringly, 'a boyfriend in futures in the City'. And she was beautiful. He enjoyed the poetry festival and went to some parties and dances. I have a pamphlet he gave me titled *Sohelgel Eats a Bagel* by John James, a characteristic product of Cambridge poetry. James belongs to an earlier generation of Prynnites and the jokiness of his book is probably not as representative as I suggest above. But it resembles much of the poetry John was introduced to there. He

showed me an admired small book named *Hate's Clitoris*. I thought
it would have been more truly subversive if it had been *Kate's Clitoris*,
and anyway regular, tightly packed, ironic, rhyming quatrains
burdened with arcane syntax were pioneered years ago by T.S. Eliot
and Veronica Forest-Thompson. But then my view of the Cambridge
scene has always been that it is a species of 'dumbing-up':
philistinism by other means.

In April I read poems with John at Derby, home of Rolls-Royce
(*that German-owned company*, as John might have put it). This was
the only time we ever read poetry together. The audience would
not have have amounted to a quorum in a solitary confinement
cell, but the reading was enjoyable and I experienced that acute
sense of presence his work evokes—something I had only imagined
when reading it on the page.

Back in London he persuaded me to ring his friends Owen and
Cameron to press on them my opinion of Richard Wagner. I'm
afraid this was too equivocal for John. He wanted dismissal of the
Teutonic Overreacher. When he flew home in early June, he was
looking forward to returning to Cambridge before too long. He
was planning what became his ultimate book, *Damaged Glamour*.
The last time I spoke to him by phone we were both watching
Diana Princess of Wales's obsequies on TV. John rightly regarded
this as a piece of kitsch on much the same level as *Eurotrash*.

As we like to do with all poets whose work we enjoy, and despite
the sense we may have of the poet and the poetry being at odd
angles to each other, I have a list of Forbes works I especially enjoy.
But 'Speed: A Pastoral', 'Death: An Ode' and that wonderful prose-
poem 'A Dream' from *The Stunned Mullet*, the original search for
the Golden Bottle of Cough Mixture, are high points in Forbesiana
for me. I was even able to tell John one piece of Australiana when
The Stunned Mullet appeared. My father, a keen fisherman, informed
me that mullet cannot be caught on a line. They won't take bait.
They have to be netted, and sometimes before landing, if making
too much fuss, are killed by being hit on the head. Therefore, the
phrase. This may not be accurate but it allowed me to seem more
national than expatriate for a moment. When the whole Forbes
oeuvre is assembled, we shall see that it contains a harvest of fine
poems. It would appear that Australians are waking up to his quality
as a poet. Not too quickly, I hope: they need to do some work on
his poetry first. The recent TV documentary presented by Alan

Wearne showed dangerous signs of hagiography. I would be happier seeing the poet and his life passed over quickly, but the poems read and remembered. Looking through his verse and noticing its almost impeccable postmodern surface, I am, at the same time, reassured to observe ancient lineaments of pleasure and apprehension showing through.

When You Said Bessemer, Did You Mean Beckmesser?
In Memoriam John Forbes (1950-1998)

The winter sun's well-washed and the trees
are budless still; an expert voice discusses
the best recordings of *Don Giovanni*
on the radio.
                    There, that's scene-setting.
And the books of infamy are waiting
with ruled pages for our timid entries—
we've sorted through the hundred cards
of cricketers and Emperors; we've noticed that the bust
of Elagabulus looks so modern, like someone
in Scorsese, and our society is right on time
for end-of-century comparisons. Nuns and secretaries
use wrong secateurs—joking ends with weeping words,
the Cambridge nimbus like marsh lights—you see
the spastic towers of Ely Cathedral from your bike
and through your humid lids—awful flatness
in the Land of Faith, if that's what Medievalism was,
and duty boosting disproportion's angles.

So John you can truly tell us now,
from whatever viewpoint you adopt
out of a wealth of choice, how stupidly we fax
our lives to centuries, though it matters terribly
that even a poet should know how killing's done
in his own time. I picked the Nineteenth
out of all the centuries—it would have had
the wrong sort of Catholicism to interest you—
all in all you'd choose your own, I think—
it's nearly finished and it has such well-incised iniquities.
You were serious about your five decades
but I'm sure you didn't really like them much.
You'd laugh at altruism, but what do good boys do
on this warped earth but adopt the pose

of Mr Worldly Wiseman (and you didn't resent
the Protestant tang of English Literature)?—
remember, Americans are forced to be
solipsistic Puritans to make it always new.

We were friends, but not close ones—I liked
your verse more than you did mine, and that's a concord
to prefer. What comes back is so incongruous—
your buying me an enormous dish of beans like bullrushes
round a lake of lamb in that Greek Taverna
looking out on Hyde Park and Elizabeth Street;
your pride in your physique after coughing half the night
on whisky; your getting me to phone your Melbourne mates
to tell what I thought of Wagner,
your delight in J.P. Gaultier and *Eurotrash*.
And love, a topic I fight shy of. It was the best
impossibilist theorem, so you thought
and let the clever worldly girls be entertained by you
inside their academic cantonments. Theory (whatever
that might be) was a patois of Trouvère-Speak,
and Modernism a pinched Provence
still visitable by bike. Whatever filled the sky
with laser-lights, you would have known its name and number.

Late summer in Australia and you in earth,
Catholic interment. It is the present that is past,
our old enduring world comes back rehearsed.
I chose my title, a sentence no-one ever said,
to show however much at ease your century was
with smart technology, The Cultures are apart
by no more than a letter or two at any date
and clever devils filter through the Library air
seducing highbrows with nomenclature.
You're back unfurling a poem conjured by
the unreformed Communist Party of Italy
or endorsed with winter wings belonging to
some Delilah of the Groves of Academe.
You know that feelings have a way of getting lost
in Art's white-out, and that the opposite is true,
that loyalty to Poetry is its own reward,
hearning the 'School's Out' bell among the piled-up bikes.

London, April 1998

Dr Klemperer's Rage

Andrew Riemer

As it happens with most people, I am sure, I retain a few vivid memories of childhood which, far from diminishing, seem to grow in intensity as the years pass. Why the mind should select images of often trivial incidents for preservation, while others sink into oblivion, remains, I suppose, a mystery—perhaps one of life's most tantalising mysteries. I know this, nevertheless: that for all their brightness, and in spite of their almost tactile immediacy, those memory-images are frequently misleading, mendacious indeed, for in some instances they must represent experiences which memory itself could not have retained unaided. With such memories the distinctions between the individual and the community, for lack of a more precise term, begin to blur, so that what we remember is what we have heard.

The phenomenon is allegedly widespread in traditional societies. Among those of us who are inheritors of Europe's fundamental Cartesianism it is supposed to be extremely rare, if not non-existent indeed. So Thomas Mann, at the beginning of his cycle of novels about Joseph and his brothers, wrote of the well of time, of the deep enigma of life in biblical times when you could remember, as it were, your ancestors across centuries and millennia with the same immediacy as you remember what you had for dinner yesterday. There spoke a child of the Enlightenment. Yet Mann the artist, the visionary, knew that the true state of affairs is otherwise, that we too may remember that which we should not be capable of remembering.

My earliest memory must belong to that category. It is the last day of February, my first birthday. For weeks, apparently, a particularly virulent strain of influenza has been spreading throughout Europe, reaching Budapest at the time when my family was preparing to celebrate my birthday. A day or two earlier, my mother, who was even then a person filled with all manner of fears and alarms, issued an edict. If my father's relatives—his mother, my uncle, my aunt and her husband—wished to visit, they must come no further than the entrance hall. They could look at me through the glass door of the living room. Otherwise they would have to stay at home.

Inevitably, of course, that led to unpleasant scenes and arguments. My mother's people lived some 200 kilometres away near the Austrian border. So my father's family interpreted my mother's *ukase* as yet another confirmation of the provincial upstart's arrogance and hostility. The rift took months to heal. Despite all that, my Budapest relatives must have swallowed their pride, for I distinctly remember looking at them through the glass door as I was held, swaddled in layers of protective clothing, in my mother's arms. I remember my grandmother's smile, my uncle's customary air of bewilderment, the shape of my aunt's mouth, which always suggested a somewhat sour, cynical outlook on the world, and also the huge, menacing bulk of her husband, the manager of an abattoir for horses. What is more, I also remember—or believe I can remember—minor details of the *mise en scène*: the bevelled edge of the plate of glass, the shiny white paint of the surrounding woodwork, the light bouncing off the (for the time) ultramodern stainless steel door handle.

Yet it is absurd to imagine that I, individually, could have retained all that, especially as I have no other memory of the small flat where that incident took place—less than a year later, my parents moved to a house on the outskirts of the city which provided the site of my first continuous or perhaps independent set of memories. It is obvious to me that I possess that extraordinarily vivid image only because it formed a key episode in an often recounted family mythology, a mythology that became particularly meaningful and potent for my parents during their life in Australia, long after the other participants in that domestic drama had vanished, their fate unknown but only too easy to imagine.

So what I remember may be no more than what I had been told about since the time of my first memories. Yet for me it does not carry that implication: it is far too vivid and precise to be classed as mere folklore or anecdote. What is more, those incidental details strike me as accurate, though of course there is no way of checking on that. The block of flats where my parents lived from 1935 to 1938 still stands, having survived war and revolution, but it is protected nowadays by a high-tech security system no stranger could penetrate. So I assume that the memory or false memory represents a crossing-point of conscious, perhaps neurologically verifiable memories and that other memory which is lodged in the group, the family or the tribe. And it may also be that vividness and accuracy are preserved through the act of sustained telling and retelling, so bringing about the survival within the individual of images and sensations which lie beyond the boundaries of what science tells us we should be able to recall.

Consequently, that trivial incident in the entrance hall of a Budapest apartment in 1937 remains, for better or worse, one of the formative experiences of my life—though I cannot tell why, nor am I convinced that the memory would have been so filled with significance if war and persecution had not intervened. There is, besides, the outside chance that my parents, the only authorities on the subject, had made it all up. For it is true that all of us are prone to embellish memories, to make them more meaning-filled, more dramatic and spectacular perhaps, to such an extent that the line between shadow and substance is in danger of blurring, until it disappears entirely. Memories of that kind are capable of provoking disturbing moral quandaries. We are beguiled by the aptness of those possibly invented incidents and anecdotes; we persuade ourselves of their essential truth, yet we are disturbed (or should be, at least) by implications of something considerably less than truthful that seem always to hover around them. And we can spend a lifetime too, it sometimes happens, searching for some clue, some verification to assure us that what has lodged itself so firmly in our memory is not merely a figment of fantasy.

*

One of my memories of childhood is precisely of that nature. It comes from my eleventh year, the year after the end of the Second World War, when my parents were engaged in the tortuous business of obtaining permission to leave Europe and to settle in Australia. Many details of those years—the perils of war and of its aftermath—have vanished. One particularly vivid memory is as trivial in its way as that vignette of my first birthday party. It forms one of a cluster of memories which came to assume, after we settled in Australia, a deeply emblematic significance in the difficult, often painful task of adjustment to strange ways, to a perplexing language and to an environment so little resembling the familiar though sinister past.

In 1946, the last year we spent in Budapest, my parents took out subscriptions to the opera. The flamboyant Opera House, which had miraculously escaped the near-destruction of the city, had re-opened by the early autumn of the previous year, a mere six months or so after the end of the siege that began on Christmas Eve in 1944. The evenings we spent in that richly ornate theatre, witnessing high-romantic tales of passion, nobility, altruism and dastardly treachery, coalesced for me, an impressionable child, into shining images of an ideal life entirely different from the everyday life of privations and some danger we were leading in a ruined city, where we had recently endured terrible perils which we escaped, unlike most of our family, through good fortune and a small degree of prudence. For three or four hours on almost every Wednesday, the growing sense of apprehension about the new life we were planning to begin could be put aside. And so that fantasy-world, the resplendent cocoon of a gilt-and-scarlet theatre, remained for me the most potent and persistent memory of those strange months of preparation for departure, of waiting, of expectation and of some alarm too.

The specific memory that forms the centre of that cluster of images represented an event of considerable excitement for my father, who had been an avid opera-fancier since his teenage years. We discovered that Wagner's *Tannhäuser* was scheduled for performance in our subscription series. From the time of those teenage experiences, my father (like so many of Europe's secular and assimilated Jewry) had been a fervent Wagnerite. He had an inexhaustible passion for those long, bombastic pieces which, he well knew, provided one of the ideological platforms for the madness and evil that had brought us so much suffering and loss. Yet none of that seemed to have diminished his fervour. True, I remember him saying to my mother—who on the whole detested opera unless it had some good tunes and contained a ballet sequence or two—that *Tannhäuser* is not the best or most mature of Wagner. But at least we would see and hear some Wagner. And besides, he went on, the performance would be conducted by the famous Dr Otto Klemperer, the great musician who had recently returned to Europe from his American exile.

Even in those years, Klemperer—Dr Klemperer as he was always called—was a celebrity. Early in his career he had been one of Mahler's trusted assistants, second only in importance to Bruno Walter. Later, during the heady Weimar years, he led the avant-garde Kroll Opera in Berlin until the coming of the Nazis, when he had to flee from the city which had been, up to then, the centre of a remarkable cultural renaissance. And now he was back in Europe, and coming to Budapest what is more, to conduct Wagner.

There seemed to have been an unusual sense of anticipation in the theatre that evening—except, that is, among the rows of bemedalled Russian soldiers in the stalls, the upper echelons of the army occupying the city, who had obviously been commanded to turn out to confirm their (and the Soviet Union's) respect for culture. At most times they indicated the extent of their respect by what my parents and their friends regarded as uncivilised behaviour: talking, shuffling, yawning and disrupting the performances in all manner of ways. Dr Klemperer's evening promised to be no exception. As the houselights dimmed and as applause greeted the arrival of the conductor, the ructions from the stalls continued without interruption. Then the overture began with the horns sounding the pilgrims' hymn. But after a few bars the music stopped, with those squeaks and burps characteristic of an orchestra caught out by the realisation that the conductor has stopped beating time. A surprised silence, then a torrent of enraged abuse from the pit, in guttural German. And so, for once, silence fell on the auditorium and Wagner's longwinded and frequently tedious morality play began all over again, and crept to its conclusion over three endless acts. The great Dr Klemperer had conquered the all-powerful Red Army.

Or had he? In later years I came to have serious doubts about the accuracy of that memory. Had Klemperer really taken the dangerous step of abusing the audience, and the Russians in particular? That he demanded Teutonic discipline from his audiences was beyond doubt. When I was living in London in the early 1960s I attended concerts and opera performances conducted by the then world-famous and grievously incapacitated musician. Though his movements were severely restricted by ailments and mishaps of several kinds, his performances of Mahler, Beethoven and Bruckner, and the occasional snippet of Wagner too, revealed extraordinary authority, as did his ability to freeze into silence the least sign of inattention among the audience with a stern glance, a steady gaze at the offender.

In the London of those years, Klemperer's demands on his audiences became legendary, and they were accepted wholeheartedly by his many admirers. But the London of the time was not Budapest in 1946. In Budapest the Russians brooked no disrespect, no insult real or imagined from a defeated and humiliated people. What went for the foot-soldiers intoxicated with power on the streets of the city applied equally (so numerous anecdotes confirmed) to their superiors in bars, restaurants, nightclubs and brothels. In a world of absolute power, no one, not even a famous visiting conductor, would have remained immune from horrible retribution. Surely, I remember thinking in later years, someone must have warned Klemperer about the difficulties of performing in the theatre and cautioned him to be prudent.

So I began to entertain the suspicion that perhaps he hadn't told those Russians to behave themselves—even if the reprimand was delivered in an incomprehensible tongue. Perhaps, perhaps, I had merely wished for him to berate those people who caused us so much anxiety and fear at the time, people who committed far worse atrocities than being inattentive at the opera. In other words, the possibility occurred to me that that memory too had been contaminated by the desire to idealise, to make the remembered event more significant, more remarkable than it had been in pedestrian fact. But then I thought that I also remembered my parents referring occasionally to that outburst from the pit—at the time, for instance, when Klemperer came to Sydney a few years after we arrived, when they did not have enough money to spare for costly concert tickets. On the other hand, it also occurred to me that my memory of my mother and father remembering that performance of *Tannhäuser* might itself have been part of the process of embellishment to which such recollections are prone. There was no way of telling or finding out, at least until the early 1990s when, in the course of several visits to Budapest, I made the acquaintance of some elderly members of the administration of the Hungarian State Opera.

One of these people had no doubt that my memories were without substance. Klemperer, she pointed out, did not take up his appointment as musical director until 1947. Perhaps, she went on, I was thinking of some occasion between then and 1950, the year he resigned from the position. But no, I told her, that could not have been so, for we left Budapest in November 1946. Was it possible that Klemperer made guest appearances in 1946, when he might have been negotiating the contract for the post, I asked. The reply was noncommittal: possibly, possibly, it was hard to tell; the theatre's archives were in a parlous state after decades of neglect and indifference. But one thing was certain, my acquaintance added just as I was about to leave, even Dr Klemperer wouldn't have dared to reprimand the Russians in those years—for the sake of the company, of course, even if he himself felt safe from retribution. And I could be sure too that if he had done anything like that, he would not have been chosen as the company's director the following year.

So there it seemed to be, another instance of the treacherous nature of memory, a quicksand or more accurately perhaps like one of those whiteouts in snowstorms when all sense of direction vanishes. I cannot pretend that that impasse provoked an existential crisis. The whole business was, after all, entirely trivial. Neither the world nor my life would have become substantially altered had I been able to confirm that long-persisting memory by some documentary or other authoritative assurance. Yet the puzzle nagged at me from time to time, as it had done for many years. And that intermittent, sporadic nagging did much to strengthen the suspicion that some pattern, or even purpose perhaps, lies beneath the mind's apparently whimsical choices about what to hold on to and what to discard. That pattern or purpose cannot, I realised, be identified with any clarity. The closest approach possible is to say that the recollection of a short-lived fuss which may have broken out in an ornate, well-heated theatre in a near-destroyed city brought together complex strands of culture, history and sensibility. Certainly, as the years passed I came more and more to realise that my parents' seemingly quixotic decision to subscribe to the opera in 1946, when they were sloughing off both the remnants of their former lives and the horrors and perils of the previous few years, represented a deeply symbolic response to the confusions and paradoxes of our lives. For that reason, therefore, whether the illustrious Dr Klemperer had indeed berated those unruly Russians—who represented, we had come to understand by that time, a threat to our safety almost as dire as the Germans had done—carried a charge of significance far in excess of its apparent importance. And I, for my part, had to face the depressing possibility that the puzzle would never be resolved.

*

Not long ago I found myself in Budapest again. The purpose of the visit was banal: to write a travel piece for a newspaper on European cities in wintertime. The opera company was performing Wagner, I discovered—and the most taxing and demanding of his works, what is more, the four-part *Ring* cycle. Getting hold of tickets proved quite easy, so on four increasingly long evenings I sat in one of the stall seats where fifty-four years earlier members of the Russian occupying forces found it impossible to suppress their boredom when listening to Wagner.

This time the audience was respectful and enthusiastic, more enthusiastic, indeed, than the indifferent performances warranted. The reason for their enthusiasm was not hard to discover. During every interval I overheard patrons—mostly elderly—expressing delight that the cycle was being performed again, for only the third time, it seemed, since the outbreak of the Second World War. So perhaps the great days of the past, when musicians like Mahler were in charge of the company, would return at long last, I caught several people assuring themselves. In their minds at least, the return of *The Ring* had something to do with the death of socialism (as communism is always called in the former Soviet empire). And one evening, in the hubbub of the grand foyer, just as we were being summoned for the commencement of the next, interminable act, I overheard a very old gentleman making a comment about Dr Klemperer—though I found it impossible to make out precisely what he was saying.

A week later I was waiting to meet an acquaintance in Paris. We had agreed to meet outside one of the Métro stations on the boulevard Saint-Michel. I was early; the day was raw and damp.

When it started raining I took refuge inside a large bookshop. The wall next to the entrance was covered with an extensive display of compact discs. My eyes ran over the boxed sets of opera recordings. Amongst recently recorded performances I noticed a small section devoted to historic recordings. And in the midst of that, a plain, purple box with the legend:

OTTO KLEMPERER
The Rare Documents
RICHARD WAGNER
LOHENGRIN
Original Recording: Budapest, October 14, 1948

I bought the set, carried the talisman back to Sydney, and, at the first opportunity, slipped the first of the three discs into the player. As the laser beam engaged with the grooves the sound of not entirely well-tuned violins launched into the celebrated prelude, to the accompaniment of coughs, splutters, thumps and the incessant hiss of whatever recording technology was available in Hungary in 1948. The performance, as far as it was possible to tell, seemed not to have matched Dr Klemperer's demands or expectations. The principals were gutsy but unsteady; the chorus rough; the orchestra poorly co-ordinated. Yet despite those blemishes Klemperer's authority managed to shine through: a magnificent sense of structure and line, and above anything else an unmistakeably magisterial command of the score.

I found myself amused and bemused as Wagner's drawn-out and not a little absurd tale of the knight of the Grail whose name must remain secret unfolded. This was, in a way, my madeleine, unlocking the past, recalling once more that evening two years or so before this performance was recorded when Dr Klemperer may have roused on his unruly audience. On the later occasion, I came to realise, standards of behaviour seemed much improved. Perhaps by 1948 the Russians had given up demonstrating their respect for culture; or perhaps they had learnt to conform with Central European ways. Whatever the reason, the audience remained unobtrusive. There were, it is true, one or two outbursts of applause which interrupted the flow of Wagner's much-vaunted 'continuous melody', but they died down soon enough for the music to continue unimpeded. If anything, I felt slightly disappointed.

I played through the first two acts. The third act could wait, I decided. Yet a few days later I took the last of the discs out of its container to listen to the climax of the opera, where Lohengrin, the virtuous knight, having been forced to reveal his name, bids farewell to the people of Brabant and makes ready to board his swan-drawn boat to return to Monsalvat in distant Spain. At first the performance seemed indistinguishable from that of the earlier acts. Then came Lohengrin's farewell; that celebrated solo occupied track thirteen. As it began, I realised once again that the tenor singing the role was in much finer voice than the rest of his colleagues. There was impressive body and timbre to his voice, and even though the piece was performed in a clumsy Hungarian translation of Wagner's text, he alone seemed to have had the ability to infuse his words with dramatic as much as musical substance. The audience thought so too, obviously, for as his voice rang out with the final phrase, where Lohengrin names himself, a torrent of applause filled the auditorium.

Then everything seemed to fall apart. For a moment or two the music struggled mightily to ride the wave of clapping and cheering: the orchestra blazed away, the chorus screamed and screeched until the applause died and a high-pitched soprano voice launched into the next solo passage. The unfortunate singer did not get very far into her moment of glory. Obviously something appalling had taken place: the orchestra stopped playing, except for the first violins who persisted for a moment or two with their fussy passage work, unaware that the conductor had stopped beating time.

After that chaos, pandemonium. Bangs and clatter from the stage, or perhaps the pit. Incomprehensible muttering. Voices rising in anger. From the auditorium booing, jeers, whistles and the stamping of feet. More thumping and muttering and then, even more alarmingly, a minute or so of silence punctuated here and there by a suppressed giggle or two. Finally an outburst of febrile applause and, cutting through the noise, the clearly audible German words '*noch einmal*' ('once more'), obviously spoken by Klemperer himself. And so the performers made their way through the seven remaining minutes of Wagner's score, to be rewarded with far more subdued clapping.

So that small shiny disc, processed in Italy, manufactured in Korea and purchased in a Paris bookshop, seemed to contain confirmation of a kind of Dr Klemperer's disciplinary rage. In 1948, as much as in 1946 it would have appeared, he took his audiences to task for poor behaviour by stopping the performance, perhaps even by walking out of the pit—only to be coaxed back after an embarrassing interval. One did not, after all, interrupt Wagner's music with applause. To do so would indicate a remarkable lack of cultivation, and infringement of the most basic of civilised conventions. I felt elated: the fifty-four-year-old enigma seemed finally to have yielded its secret. Memory, I began to assure myself, may not be as misleading and treacherous as I had feared.

A few months later an additional titbit of confirmation arrived as unexpectedly as the discovery of those compact discs in Paris. An elderly lady wrote to me after reading a newspaper piece I had written about the unruly behaviour of audiences at concerts in Sydney. She remembered, she wrote, how all that shuffling, chatting, the beeping of wrist-watches and even mobile phones on rare occasions would not have been tolerated in the past. She recalled too the wonderful evening in Sydney—she was young at the time—when Otto Klemperer conducted Mahler. Did I know that he went as far as stopping the performance to tell the audience to be quiet?

And so I decided to write this essay about the strange ways of memory, about how trivial and inconsequential recollections may haunt us throughout a lifetime, only to find serendipitous confirmation when the sources of those memories seem entirely beyond recovery. All that was to lead to a resonant conclusion—or so I hoped to achieve—celebrating the mysteries of time, memory and chance.

I pushed the third act of *Lohengrin* into the player once more, whizzing through the first twelve tracks. Then the hero's narration began and, as before, the ecstatic applause broke out, followed by the mutters, the jeering, the silence, the renewed applause and those magical words '*noch einmal*' before the music took up once more. I listened to the track three or four times, my satisfaction growing with each repetition.

What happened next was shattering. Suddenly one word among those muttered imprecations caught by the microphone became comprehensible: the Hungarian word for 'boat'. A further playing of the track confirmed that all too painfully. What had happened at the Budapest Opera House on 14 October 1948, it became obvious, had nothing to do with Dr Klemperer's legendary bad temper.

A famous operatic myth tells of a celebrated tenor in the early years of the twentieth century, a star of the Vienna Opera, renowned for his powerful interpretation of the title role in *Lohengrin*, who had a most unfortunate drinking problem. One night, the myth recounts, he was so intoxicated that he missed his cue, failed to board his swan-drawn boat and was left stranded, so to speak, on the bank of the tinsel River Scheldt in Brabant. Making his way unsteadily to the footlights, he is said to have peered at the audience, and then asked: 'Ladies and gentlemen, does anyone know when the next swan leaves?'

Something not unlike that seems to have taken place on the stage of the Budapest Opera House on the night the broadcasting organisation had chosen to record Dr Klemperer's performance of *Lohengrin*. It was not, obviously, a question of an inebriated tenor. Rather, something must have gone disastrously wrong with the boat drawn by a cardboard swan: perhaps it got stuck, or collapsed under the weight of the singer, or suffered some other calamity. And through all the scurrying fuss, Dr Klemperer probably stood at the podium in the orchestra pit, his arms decorously folded perhaps, patiently waiting for the debris to be cleared or the mechanism to be unjammed, before lifting his baton once more and signalling with those two guttural words in German that the performance could continue.

First Words

Hilary McPhee

First came her stories like webs across the world. They crisscrossed
the Atlantic on steamers and the Rockies by train. They wended
their way down dirt tracks where the scrub met overhead. They
flew from Ben Lomond in the Tasmanian Highlands which we
could see from the verandah, to Welsh farmhouses of dark stone.
The air would shiver slightly each time she began.

*Once upon a time, when pigs were swine and monkeys chewed tobacco,
there was a little girl who lived at the foot of the mountains in the centre
of the universe at the bottom of the world...*

The storyteller was my grandmother and the child was me. We
came to her for stories. She had a way of seating herself when a
story was ripe for the telling, cushions at her back, hands folded in
her lap. Her house creaked in the night under the pine trees and
her stories invaded our dreams. I know now what a talented storyteller
she was. Then we took her utterly for granted.

These days I tell her stories, for they have become mine in the
telling, to my extended family, but they must compete with sound
bytes and flashbacks, videoclips and computer games. And I have
no doubt I fail to tell them as well as she did for I have the rapt
attention of small children only in very short bursts. My
grandmother could keep us by her side for hours.

An early memory is of her in a cane chair in the garden. There
is a heat wave and she is trading stories for buckets of water. Only
when she is soaked to the skin will she begin. *Once upon a time...*

On the farm, she travelled with the children in the back of the ute, she swathed in scarves in an old armchair and we under quilts, trembling with fear as she spun tales of murder and mayhem in the tall dark houses glimpsed from the road. But best of all were the stories at the end of the day when I'd creep into her bed, and my soft and powdery grandmother, her black hair in a long plait, and the lamp turned low, would start. *Once upon a time when pigs were swine…*

Her stories were vivid and shapely and we heard them again and again. Later I would catch something of their rhythms and word play in ballads and sagas, and know the power of her voice to enthrall and the feeling she had for the young imaginations drenched in her words.

She was born in 1894; a beloved only child in a family with a little money or the myth of money from her great-great-grandfather, a clergyman, who had invested during the early nineteenth century, surely somewhat dubiously, in Welsh coalmines. Family portraits survive and hang in a Tasmanian dining room.

There were stories of unfeeling trustees and money withheld and unsuitable marriages when good-looking rogues took advantage of well-to-do widows one of whom was my great-grandmother. She seems to have married an American twenty years her junior after my great-grandfather died. This young man—we were thrillingly told—went into the city of London every morning at ten *but never told his wife what he did there*. Perhaps she never asked. When it was discovered that he'd been through all her money, he returned to America, never to be seen again. Or so the story goes.

I know I should check the facts. There is evidence to be weighed, records to be searched, family members still alive who knew her differently. There will be shipping lists and parish records, deeds and wills lodged in three countries. The men I will find easily, labelled by their work and their bank balances, the buying and selling of land, and of houses kept by wives who were returned to at night. The women have left less of a mark but there are some family papers, recipes, photographs and I have a sampler in black cross-stitch done, my grandmother told me, by a child, my great-great-great-great grandmother, during the Napoleonic wars when children were forbidden to use coloured silks. Or so she said.

From packets of negatives she kept from before the First World War, I had developed photographs of a picnic by a lake, and there is the American husband, dangerously handsome and very young, in expensive-looking tweeds and brogues. My great-grandmother, his wife, is plain and dumpy and distinctly middle-aged. She looks fierce and unhappy, not at all the dashing figure of my imaginings. He is propped up on an elbow smiling calmly at the camera. Maybe for him it was all worth it—or maybe he has been maligned. Perhaps, somewhere in America, other pieces of the story that I have not heard have been planted in the heads of American children— swinging on porches, cookies and lemonade to hand—stories where my great-grandmother has become a wicked old English witch who made a fine young man's life a misery.

The historian at the back of my brain says I should discover what is true and what is false, make a properly considered account before it's too late. The rest of me, the part that was shaped by the sense of myself *at the centre of the universe at the bottom of the world* still sees, as if, through certain cloud formations and paddocks pale with tussocks, the shadows of other places she made my own.

I want to leave her and her stories be.

I have her autograph book full of poems and drawings and jokes in French, German and Italian, from 1907-8 which she spent in a Swiss finishing school learning European pronunciations for she wanted very much to be a singer. I recognise some of the names from her stories. Muriel Mamby, Katerina Gründlich, Aline Collière were the girls who hoisted themselves with my grandmother over the high stone wall to buy hot bread rolls from the baker and fill them with dark chocolate—girls who soon grew too fat for their corsets. I recognise the names of the two elderly *M'selles* who owned the school, who wore the same black dresses every day and who smelt of old hay. I know.

There was a great-great-great-great-great grandmother who was born during the French Revolution, a very old woman indeed by the time my grandmother's mother as a little girl was taken to visit her. She saw her wrinkled face and corkscrew curls against lacey pillows, for she was a vain old woman, and was shown, as a special treat, the wooden leg in the box under her bed. I know the sound a cotton reel makes when it rattles against a wooden leg. I know the lavender and starched smells of the linen closet where the giggling children hid and pulled on the thread to make the reel rattle and the old lady cry out for her maid: 'Bless me, Lizzie, there's a mouse in my leg.' The historian counts down the generations to see if this is possible—but whatever the facts of the matter, I know as if I were there.

I know what coal dust smells like from the coalhole in the pavement in a London street, the cry of the cats' meat man as he tossed lumps of meat every morning over the iron railings for the family's cats, the taste of roasted chestnuts bought from braziers in the snow on the way to church, and the heavy sounds of doors slamming and the shouts of guards on steam trains leaving country stations.

Then came the stories of endless wheatfields and sleeping for a week on the train to Vancouver. And the bush school at Kettering in southern Tasmania where the children from England hid their new shoes in the bushes and went barefoot like the others. The picnics on Bruny Island and Guy Fawkes Night in Syd's paddock with raspberry cordial and sausages grilled on burning stumps in the dark. And Hector, the dog who rode on the running board of the old Dodge car, and long summers under canvas and rockpools full of lobsters. Until the stories arrive at the family romance at the centre of my universe.

It had all begun, my grandmother said, on a cold winter's night on a railway station in Gippsland. Here, and I picture them in black and white like the films of the day, a young man stands, rain pouring off his hat, waiting for the train from Melbourne. He is, of course, tall dark and very handsome and he waits for a young woman he has only met a few days before. She will see him standing in the rain and fall in love with him on the spot, or so the story goes. I picture the pale faces of the man and the woman searching for each other so they can begin their lives together and become my parents. This is a story I wanted to be told again and again.

Where the young man, my father, came from was not part of the story. He arrived mysteriously, fully formed as it were, and stepped into the part that was awaiting him.

His family story amounted to less than a paragraph, the kind you could find in any Scottish guide book. The departure in small boats from Colonsay to Skye in the seventeenth century, the clearing of the glens in the 1840s to make way for sheep, and a large family shipped to Australia to start again. All that history—and only one glimpse survived that he gave me late in his life. In the kitchen of a farmhouse somewhere in north-central Victoria, a white-bearded old man sits at the head of the table speaking Gaelic. An old grace? Or a story from the glens perhaps? On either side of him are ranged many children and their parents. No one else is allowed to speak.

My father as a boy was given this image, for it does not have a story's shape, by his father. Where the farm was we did not know, nor who it was who sat at the head of the table. My father did not tell us and we did not think to ask. He was not a storyteller, my father, content it seemed to be a player in the tales of women.

The real stories, the ones with beginnings that made you listen, with narratives that wove in and out, the patterns and rhythms you never forgot, the real stories in our lives stretched back and forth through my mother's family. My mother and my grandmother exchanged letters every week across Bass Strait, their remarkably similar round and rapid handwriting shaping, embroidering the drama of everyday life, and, when suitable bits were read out at mealtimes, holding us all in thrall.

And then there were the books. My grandmother's little house was full of them. Bookshelves lined the main room with its bread oven in the hearth, and covered the top of the upright piano. Her bedroom was a mess; clothes on chairs, books everywhere, the windows open to the scent of cypress and grass.

She had some kind of standing order with the State Library which would send books to her each month in a wooden crate, and with Robertson and Mullens in Elizabeth Street, Melbourne who knew her tastes and would post her parcels of books on approval. Whenever I stayed with her, books would arrive at the post office counter in the general store or at the railway siding. The excitement of collecting them, unpacking and choosing what to read first infected us all. Then my grandmother and I would retire to our beds after lunch with the tin of Marie biscuits on the chest of drawers between us and read until dark.

It was inconceivable to be without a book. No train was boarded without buying something to read for the journey—the new Puffins for us, an *Argosy* or a *Lilliput* for her. She had every Penguin from no. 1 until they changed the covers in the mid 1960s when she wrote sternly to founder, Allen Lane, about the paperbacks looking too American, the dangers of dumbing down—or whatever for her was the equivalent.

Her reading was as real to her as life was. She would talk about the characters in a book and people she met, eccentric at best, certifiable at worst, the tragic farewell she'd watched at the bus stop, with the same intensity and curiosity. Later when she began long treks to the first film festivals, she'd return with the stories in her head as if she'd been inside the film. I first heard the story of

The Wages of Fear lying in bed in her little house with the wind howling through the pine trees. So vividly did my grandmother describe the journey down the mountain somewhere in Central America in the truck full of nitroglycerine which could explode at any moment that, when I saw the film years later, I recognised it scene by scene.

She lived inside books the same way. Dickens, Trollope, George Eliot, W.H. Ainsworth, Thackeray, Buchan, Shaw. They became prisms. Their characters were the people she knew; she described her own life in their terms. Her England, to which she never returned or even seemed to long for, was kept alive forever in her stories and nineteenth-century novels.

Not until I was in my twenties, having spent time in London and found myself to my surprise to be a passionate Australian fiercely critical of remnants of British imperialism and more attuned than I knew to the nuances of our provincial life, did I detect a note in her elderly voice at times of something very close to English condescension. I was dismayed, of course, and for a little while before she died, replayed self-righteously much of what she'd told me.

I didn't approve of the way she made funny stories in her long and sparkling weekly letters about the daily doings of the Tasmanian gentry and their rural labourers. Tasmania's convict history was of interest to her only in the lengths the locals went to to deny it, mercilessly mocked by her. The street of convict cottages that ran down to the river behind her house on my uncle's farm was simply there outside the window, part of the scenery. But the mummified cat she'd found in one of the garrets sat on her mantelpiece for years with silver paper eyes—and crept, of course, into her stories. Yet she was the first person to tell me about the Black Line and the shell middens the children found on the beach at Oyster Cove long after the people who'd left them had been removed to Flinders Island. Trugannini's skeleton on display in the Hobart Museum horrified her and she made us turn away.

I heard her adoration of gentlemen English cricketers as anachronistic and grating. Despite a long life of great freedom and eccentricity, she behaved always as if men were centre stage, and there to be cajoled and flattered. She, the most independent of women, widowed at thirty-six, deeply disliked modern feminism. She wrote sternly on my second marriage in the mid-70s that women could only be happy if they put men first.

Australian literature and theatre were irredeemably second rate for her. She attended local concerts and productions of plays in the absence of anything else but I cannot remember an Australian poem or novel she admired. This occurred to me at precisely the moment when I'd decided that they mattered to me a great deal.

*

Like thousands of other yearning young Australians in the mid-1960s, I couldn't wait to leave. Inconceivable to stay a week longer than necessary and even more inconceivable to plan to return. It was necessary to cast yourself adrift. You took only enough money to get across the seas to wherever you decided to stay. If you were a serious traveller, out of the clutches of parents and had avoided the concerns of many of your contemporaries who were starting to plan kitchen teas and choose bridesmaids, you went as soon as you could—and with no return ticket. The word was that you could earn a little money, when you needed to, by writing formal letters in English in Bombay, by selling your blood to an Athens blood bank, or by teaching Australian English to migrants waiting for boats in Brindisi or Piraeus.

Many who left in the 50s and 60s did not come back, or not until things were visibly improving after Whitlam was belatedly elected in 1972. Others stayed away, made names for themselves, some by keeping up a running commentary on the cultural and literary desert they had been forced to renounce. Others were celebrated when they did return, like George Johnston and Charmian Clift, who arrived home from Hydra to find their sex lives under the microscope and their literary reputations higher than they'd dreamed. Johnston's *My Brother Jack* had won the Miles Franklin in 1964 and had immediately been hailed as a candidate for the Great Australian Novel.

The Great Australian Novel was still waiting to be written in the 60s. Many of the critics and academics of the day told us so and young men in advertising agencies dreaming up copy for Holden cars and Slazenger tennis racquets joked that they would soon be off to Greece to write it. New novels were regularly reviewed in the newspapers in the light of whether they did or did not exhibit the kind of prose style and epic sweep that fulfilled the criteria for consideration as the Great Australian Novel. There was no suggestion that a woman might produce the goods. That went without saying. The themes of race and class in novels written by women between the wars had been replaced by what the critics liked to dismiss as the small palette, the domestic, the personal— not at all the stuff of a Big Novel which would put us on the map. If Australia could produce just one great book, one that was recognised by the international literary world, that made the reading lists of universities, one that would be translated throughout Europe, that would be permanently in stock in the best bookshops of London and New York, the country could relax.

'Going to Europe,' Shirley Hazzard wrote in *The Transit of Venus*

> was about as final as going to heaven. A mystical passage
> to another life, from which no one returned the same...
> There was nothing mythic at Sydney: momentous objects,
> beings and events all occurred abroad or in the elsewhere
> of books. Sydney could never take for granted, as did the
> very meanest town in Europe, that a poet might be born
> there or a great painter walk beneath its windows. The
> likelihood did not arise, they did not feel they deserved it.
> That was the measure of resentful obscurity: they could
> not imagine a person who might expose or exult it.

I left Australia in 1965 with a painter who was also a classical guitarist. We'd been married a few months before and spent much of the next five years pretending to other people that we weren't. He was going to Greece to paint. I was trying to write. We took with us two guitars, an Olivetti portable painted red, lots of notebooks and drawing materials and joined a ship from the British-India line which was taking Holden cars to Karachi and Kuwait and wheat to the railhead at Basrah. Peter was determined he would teach me to play Anon.'s lovely *Romance Antigua* on the long voyage around the coast of India and Pakistan and through the Persian Gulf to the Shatt-al-Arab where the Tigres and the Euphrates meet. And he did.

There were no other passengers but the two of us and the Captain's Scottish wife who lived in a British enclave in Bombay and who prided herself on walking ten miles each day around the deck of the small ship. We could hear her fast footfalls overhead as we lay on our bunk or worked at the twin polished wood writing tables. There was no air-conditioning or swimming pool and we spent more and more time in the deep salt-water bath drinking gin and reading books as we neared the equator. We had a steward all to ourselves, a rather grand Indian, who made it clear that we were a disappointment. We failed to play bridge in the salon at night where he opened the tiny bar, whether we were there or not, and had no guests to entertain on board in any of the ports.

The ship had a mahogany-panelled library containing a curious collection of 1950s British library fiction in glass-fronted cabinets— thrillers, romances, spy stories, travelogues—the kind of books that many Australian municipal libraries still received on standing orders. We were given a key and trusted to help ourselves. Dutifully we filled in the dark red ledger with the names and dates of the books we borrowed—and our comments for the next reader. The entries revealed the previous passengers as an idiosyncratic bunch. Some, like us, seemed merely to have taken a slow boat to Persia— eight weeks around India and the Persian Gulf which was cheaper than flying to Europe. I imagined them reading between bridge and naps and, like us, fighting the heat and boredom. '148° on deck at 5pm,' wrote one, 'but *The Snows of Kilamanjaro* and lots of G and Ts did the trick.'

Others, probably on their way between oil fields and jobs that were paying ten times the norm, were more demanding. '*Why no Atlas?*' was underlined furiously. 'Why no Kuwaiti dictionary?' Why indeed? The Kuwaitis by the time we got there were speaking formal English and French, the men driving Cadillacs, their wives wearing Parisienne clothes and lipstick beneath their *chardors*. We felt poor and shabby as indeed we were.

I read my way through the Dorothy L. Sayers, and the shelves of Christie, Ngaio Marsh, and Graham Greene, as soon as it became too hot for the Olivetti. Michael Innes was a find. His prewar *Hamlet Revenge!*, *The Journeying Boy* and *Lament for a Maker* were memorable in ways rare in thrillers. I didn't know then that Innes was the nom-de-plume for Professor J. I. M. Stewart who, as visiting Chair of English at the University of Adelaide, from Oxford and Queen's, Belfast had declared in 1940 that there was no Australian literature at all.

Geoffrey Dutton remembered attending the first lecture in Adelaide supported by the Commonwealth Literary Fund, given by Professor Stewart. 'I am most grateful to the C.L.F. for providing funds to give these lectures in Australian literature,' he began. 'Unfortunately they have neglected to provide any literature—I will lecture therefore on D.H. Lawrence's *Kangaroo*.'

The ship's library catered for idle reading in deck chairs in the shade, not for hard information about where the Arab world was heading and taking the rest of us. There was Kipling of course and a few romances of the Raj that I devoured looking for clues to the captain and his wife who spoke of India as if independence hadn't happened and of the Goan crew as if they were dim-witted children who preferred to sleep on deck beneath tarpaulins. As we steamed through the outbreak of hostilities between Pakistan and India so close we could see the flash of the gunfire, British flag flying, kedgeree on the breakfast menu, curries for lunch and roast beef and Yorkshire pudding at night, it was more like being in a *Boys' Own Album* than a serious encounter at sea.

*

We lived on the island of Ios in the Cyclades long enough to see all the seasons change, the tomato crop turned into dark red paste and sealed in pots and the salted fish hung in houses buttressed against the wind. The island was one of the furthest from Piraeus and had not yet made it into the guide books. There were no famous ruins or grand buildings just white windmills and little churches on every headland. There were no roads just endless steps up from the harbour and donkey tracks around the cliffs. There was a tiny square with weather-beaten tables where men sat drinking ouzo and playing cards, and a bearded priest in a high black hat who made his presence felt several times a day. There was no electricity or running water. But long after the *melteme* was freezing our fingers and toes and we'd run out of things to read around the little *petroleo* stove and the people we swapped books with had left, we stayed on playing at living the life of art on a Greek Island.

We had rented a room above the square. The villagers welcomed us and spent our rent money on refrigerators and television sets which sat in pride of place under doileys and framed photographs waiting for the day when the power supply would arrive. Every morning early Peter made his way through the ribaldry of the women to the village well with our pots and copper kettle, and I climbed the steps to the *yaoórti* maker who replaced yesterday's brown bowl with a fresh one full of yoghurt which had formed a creamy crust in the sun. We'd eat this on new bread and honey sitting on the wall of the balcony as the village woke up. Then at opposite ends of our long narrow room with its flagstones picked out in whitewash and its peeling blue door letting in a rim of hot light, we'd work until the early afternoons.

Re-reading now what I wrote then, I find stories full of the usual clunks and awkwardnesses of first real writings, problems which I dimly perceived but had no idea how to fix. There's a piece of a novel I remember starting in a white heat of what I mistook to be inspiration, of excitement as words poured forth, as if the torrent itself meant something. What I'd been reading shows. Koestler, Camus, Durrell, Huxley, there's even an attempt at an interrogation, Rubashov style. The voice I'm using is never mine or even, I am disconcerted now to discover, female. There are no echoes of the few contemporary women writers I'd found for myself. I was reading Muriel Spark, Doris Lessing, Margaret Drabble—but I'd gone to them for information about life, I think, rather than for the kind of sacred gravitas I had been taught to value above all.

The voice is a first person male, an 'I' recognisable now as if from a great distance. I watch him walk, slim-hipped, of course, through narrow streets in a town somewhere on the Mediterranean. He enters a cafe and orders a Pernod before he leaves with a young woman in espadrilles and a swinging skirt.

The 'I' is 'he' not me and not even someone I knew. He is inhabiting a place I had never been to, speaking in rhythms I do not recognise as mine. He is simply someone I have summoned to appear as Main Character in a fiction I am struggling to preside over in someone else's head.

*

The boat from Piraeus came once a week in winter and three times a week in summer bringing fresh fruit and a handful of visitors with paperback books in their rucksacks and bedrolls—books from Canada and California and Israel, in editions and imprints I'd never seen before. Here I first read authors who hadn't yet made it into the part of the world I'd come from.

In the long hot afternoons, after a sleep, we'd clamber down the terraced hillsides through olive trees and tomato bushes to the glittering sea. We'd read in the shade and bake ourselves on the rocks, then dive in and float with eyes wide open searching for embedded amphora and carved stones in the deep crevasses—for this, so the local stories went, was the land of Atlantis and of the goddess Isis.

Here I first read Ralph Ellison and Paul Bowles in old American paperbacks found in a secondhand bookshop in Haifa and left behind on the island by an Israeli boy called Harvey. A girl from Texas gave me Saul Bellow's *The Adventures of Augie March*, James Baldwin's *The Fire Next Time* and *The Group* by Mary McCarthy which would be banned in Australia that year. She wrote inside the covers in large loops 'Please return to Carole', but I never did. Sometimes parcels of paperbacks would arrive from my mother at the little post office in the field below the village which opened only on the days when the boat pulled out at five o'clock in the evening. Horne's *The Lucky Country* which had been published just after we left Australia and Patrick White's *Riders in the Chariot* came in the same parcel one day, both probably selected by my mother in the hope that I'd soon want to come home.

I first read *Riders in the Chariot* in the glare off the rocks on that beach in the Cyclades. It was a book that had grown out of White's sense of himself as an outcast 'first as a child with what strange kind of gift nobody quite knew; then a despised colonial boy in an English public school; finally an artist in horrified Australia' but it also came out of postwar Australia itself, a place full of prejudice and ignorance and moments of kindness and profundity.

> Then, as people will toss up the ball of friendship, into the last light, at the moment of departure, and it will hang there briefly, lovely and luminous to see, so did the Jew and Mrs Godbold. There hung the golden sphere. The laughter climbed up quickly, out of their exposed throats, and clashed together by consent; the light splintered against their teeth. How private, and mysterious, and beautiful it was, even the intruders suspected, and were deterred momentarily from hating.

Here were the big themes of the twentieth century reverberating in ways they only could, perhaps, in Australia, a place where there was a chance to make something from the damaged past. A half-caste Aboriginal painter, a mad visionary Australian spinster, an intellectual Jewish refugee from the evil of the Holocaust and a laundress who had heard Bach one winter evening in Ely Cathedral find themselves together in Sarsparilla, in the kind of limited world I knew about and was determined to leave behind.

But then the craving for experience, the impulse 'to know life' meant much more to me than facing the uncertainties and cruelties and possibilities of the place I came from. The imperative to escape ran deep.

*

Great grey London. We'd put London off for as long as the money lasted and there were still Peter's paintings to sell in Australia and I could catch the boat into Athens every month to the blood bank in the narrow back street where the drachmas I was paid covered the rent. London—the beginning and end of so many of the stories of my childhood, where I expected to feel at home. But of course I didn't. When I arrived burnt dark brown from the sun, in a handmade dress, with a bag stuffed with underdone stories and notes and a blue and white *flokarti* woven as a farewell present by Irene, our Ios landlady, I was foreign and knew it at once.

A week later Greece was a mirage. I'd walked into a job in the Publications Branch of the British Council in High Holburn where I catalogued onto cards British books I never saw for exhibitions in Nairobi and Johannesberg and on to Sydney. Peter was accepted by the Inner London Education Authority for a position teaching art to West Indian children in Brixton whose only playground was a huge wire cage on the school roof. We queued for and were miraculously selected to rent an ancient top floor studio flat in a building which backed onto the District and Circle lines at South Kensington but which fronted on to Thurloe Square opposite the Victoria and Albert Museum. We had a key to the garden and could watch the rich gently exercising old English sheepdogs and basset hounds in the evening and nannies guarding small children in the day. The studio had been built to house artists attached somehow to the V&A and I imagined art classes with models reclining against draped velvet bathed in the gentle northern light that poured in through the huge skylight. Lying in bed on the mezzanine we built, I could watch the clouds scudding overhead and once, in October, we saw the swallows wheel and head south.

Life, as it always does, intervened without me trying. London rapidly became no more than the city where I happened to live, where I went to the library and the pub each week and queued for the laundrette and cheap theatre tickets, where I caught the underground in the dark on winter mornings and walked home through Hyde Park from Marble Arch in summer. A few blocks away in Knightsbridge and Chelsea, swinging London was wearing mini skirts and Vidal Sassoon haircuts and sipping bad coffee out of Union Jack mugs and I too shopped at Biba in Kensington High Street and Habitat in the Kings Road, the Stones and the Beatles always in the air.

London was where my daughter was born. I spent the afternoons in the months before her birth and many afterwards, with her in a sling, walking the endless rooms of the Victoria and Albert Museum across the square. At first its enormous and eccentric collection of the 'world's applied art' seemed utterly random to me but slowly I began to make some kind of sense of the plastercasts and electrotypes of Baptistry Doors and Gothic portals, the roodscreens and tall stone crosses. Nativity terracottas and ivories and alabasters from medieval England and Italy flowed seamlessly into the vast collections of Islamic, Indian and Chinese art assembled with the unerring eye and confident aesthetic of English collectors of a certain class and era.

Of course I did not ponder the lack in the collection of applied Australian art. It went without saying that there wasn't any deemed suitable to be included. Not even a silver emu egg surrounded by filligreed Aborigines or a colonial governor's secretaire of Huon pine or a christening robe intricately embroidered for a squatter's child by their convict servant-girl. In the Cromwell Road next door, the Tasmanian devil and the platypus had made the grade in the Natural History Museum, and the three-and-a-half tonne Cranbourne meteor 'from Australia' drew crowds of schoolchildren.

I only half remember how the decision to return home after nearly three years away was taken, certainly it would have been lightly as those decisions seem to be. A craving for sunshine after a bad winter, certainly. An advertisement on the underground for cheap fares, quite likely. And, yes, a need to be part of the changes and the political unrest we were hearing about from friends, as if from the bottom of a well, and sometimes tucked away in the London papers about Australia's commitment of troops to support America's efforts in Vietnam.

But in any case I knew in my bones that it was inconceivable that my daughter, and in little more than a year, my son should grow up anywhere else.

Dancing the Country

Kim Mahood

I have a friend who walks and dances. This is what her art practice has become. A tiny Frenchwoman of forty-five, she recently walked more than 600 kilometres through the mountains of Spain, dancing passages of the country as she travelled. Just before visiting me in Australia she walked and danced the perimeter of an island in Japan. She says that when she dances a piece of country it knows her. This is not a New Age conceit. She has a robust French disdain for such sentimental notions. Her dancing is the nuanced and finely calibrated result of years of disciplined practice and study. Five years of training under a Japanese master of Butoh-inspired movement which minutely analyses the body's response to its environment, years of study of contemporary dance in France and the US. She has studied Tai Chi and the ritualised movements of autistic children. She is a highly-respected choreographer and teacher in her own right. Her body can become old or childlike, it can become many kinds of animal, it can be sublimely graceful, or limp and hapless as a dislocated puppet. It is a language infinitely beyond my capabilities to speak, but eerily accessible to watch. Wordless and profound, it speaks out of a visceral and neurological alignment with its subject.

I saw her dance the edge of a riverbed in Central Australia. The dry, hard, delicate country took hold of her body, teased and tested it, manipulated it, discarded it. It ran through her in tremors, lifted her and sent her crouching across the rocks like a small wounded animal. The dance had in it moments reminiscent of traditional Aboriginal dance, which she had never seen.

In France she lives like a nomad, her base a caravan she parks on the land of family or friends. On the long walks she carries a sleeping bag and an umbrella, a few changes of clothes and cooking utensils. Since childhood dancing for her has been survival. Driven by an equivalent need for emotional security and love, her life has been tempestuous, punctuated with unresolved love affairs. She dances them out of her system and moves on. She says the walking is changing her. In its slow rhythms she is finding a quiet inner companion, although she admits to succumbing still to the temptations of other forms of companionship, especially if she finds them walking beside her. When she is not walking she lives mostly in her car. She performs her dance as a gift, an ephemeral language which leaves no visible trace. But when she tells me that the country she has danced knows her, I believe it.

To walk and dance. She has invited me to travel with her through the part of France where she was born. I am curious to see how a European dances her birthplace. Here in Australia I have seen Aboriginal people dance their country, and white Australians formulating their own delicate and carefully observed steps towards a language for the country. I have another friend who is a visual artist. She walks the tracks and paddocks of the farming country where she grew up. The grid lines of roads and paddocks are intersected in her work by the curves of hillsides and creeks. The processes by which she makes the work mirror the processes which made the landscape. They begin with burning, a patterned pokerwork which underpins the structure of the painting. Textures are built and eroded, washed back and re-applied. These works are inhabited, they have a history. Much of what goes into their making is ultimately hidden. Layers are applied and erased, applied and concealed. The dance of making reflects the lived experience of walking, working, lifting, digging. Her body, like mine and all the others who have grown up on the land, carries in its bones the history of a way of life. We lack the grace, the subtlety of my friend the dancer. Our vertebrae grate, our movements are serviceable, economical. With the encroachment of middle age we negotiate the line between small, manageable discomforts and the kind of pain which will immobilise us and make work impossible. Artists, like farmers, are driven by imperatives which override physical discomfort. Our way of dancing with the country has a crippled, uncomfortable integrity.

The spinifex sandplains of the country which knows me are at least partly the result of millennia of firestick farming. Walking on it in bare feet leaves shallow prints, but boots break the surface and reveal a filtered layer of charcoal and ash. The country has a white history, but a short one. It began at the turn of the century with a surveyor, and resulted in a brief fiasco of gold fever. Later, with less hysteria but longer implications, it was extended by my family into the establishment of a cattle station. It is held now in an uneasy balance between cattle, gold and Aboriginal custodianship. My own passage through it pays homage to all these things. Although I carry my knowledge of the country in my head and my history with it in my bones and muscles, I carry too the maps that overlay it with a misleading sense of context. These maps don't offend me, since they continue in some way to be artefacts of the imagination. The leap needed to connect them to the country they describe requires an act of faith, an imaginative link which misleads again and again. And maps of Australia reflect a marvellous sense of Mark Twain's beautiful lies, with their hints of despair and bloodshed and confusion, along with lost histories and inscrutable ironies. Murderer's Bay, Lake Disappointment, position doubtful, Little Policeman Creek, the Twenty Mile. Twenty miles from where? one asks.

An English artist from Liverpool, now living in Belfast, came to the art school where I work. He is a climber, which seems to be a dangerous and eccentric occupation. His art practice involves, among other things, climbing gallery walls. He climbs the space of a gallery in the same way as he would traverse a rock face. It is rather nerve-wracking to watch. But the work I found most interesting was made by reproducing in sculptural form the mapped structure of a climb. An unclimbed rock face is an unacculturated space. Once a traverse has been achieved the climb has a particular structure, reproduced by every climber who follows. It becomes an invisible path across the rock. A clear space has been divided and activated. The objects are not especially pleasing to look at, and do not easily release their meaning, unless you know the story. I am ambivalent about them, although I find them conceptually interesting. To make concrete something as ephemeral as the dance of a body across a rock face disturbs my sense of the appropriate.

Maybe I am being unfair. To translate the object into movement, to relocate it into the place from which it has been extracted, opens up a curiously abstract space. Maybe one needs to be a climber to appreciate it fully.

One thing begins to emerge. Whether we dance the energy of a place or inscribe its history with the marks of burning, whether we walk country or climb it, artists follow independent trajectories which at times intersect uncomfortably with the societies they inhabit. And yet we are only doing what Aboriginal artists have been doing for a long time. They walk, dance and paint their country, map and link the sites that claim them, transcribe knowledge and stories into conceptual diagrams which carry multiple meanings. As their own society falls into deep crisis they give concrete form to its abstract language, and the work of some of the great artists acknowledges the shifts and changes occurring at the interface of culture. Great sums of money are paid, some of which finds its way to the people who make the paintings. But somehow the money makes no real difference. The old culture has a capacity to make money disappear in a way which affronts and horrifies white society. There is a peculiar and ironic intersection between the cultural renaissance of Aboriginal art and the climate of economic rationalism which has eroded contemporary society of many of its important values. The greater the gap between the compromised values of the West and the perceived integrity of traditional Aboriginal society, the more the latter is revered.

Which leaves us white artists in a strange limbo. Most of us lead relatively ordinary lives, holding down jobs, paying rent and mortgages, maintaining relationships with family and friends, making the space within all these necessities to do our work. Because the work is created out of a direct apprehension of lived experience, many of us operate within hermetic environments. The forms of visual language we create are not readily accessible to the broader public, but lack a context which makes their inaccessibility exotic and admirable. There was a time when the gap between art and society was not so great. But as our sense of the sacred hollows out, and the old forms no longer speak with any relevance to contemporary life, those of us who care deeply about these things (and of course I am not referring to artists alone) have to re-invent our own forms as best we can.

I used to think that a relatively affluent society was a good one for artists. There was enough largesse to skim a little from the surface, a neutral zone between affluence and poverty within which we were left alone to do what we needed to do. One could manage on the income of part-time jobs, sign on for social security through the long financial drought of the summer holidays from the tertiary institutions where many of us teach. There would be few artists, performers and writers of my generation who have not at some time subsidised their creative work with the dole. There were periodic convulsions among the tax-paying population about dole-bludgers, and we had to make a pretence of looking for proper jobs, but on the whole everyone co-existed peacefully enough.

Things have changed. There is a sense now of something punitive and hostile, which is most clearly manifested in attitudes like that of the current treasurer, exultant at having flushed out thousands of hitherto unregistered small businesses with the implementation of the GST. This fails to acknowledge that a large proportion of those so-called businesses are artists, actors, writers. There is something deeply disturbing in having to identify what we do as a business. When the dancer and the artist walk a piece of country, exploring its texture, attuning themselves to its language, they are not computing the economic profit or loss of their perceptions. And yet they are manifestly not hobbyists. Every life choice made since they were old enough to make choices has been driven by the necessity to pursue this intangible but deeply felt direction.

Most of the creative people I know have made accommodations with the society within which we live, made the smaller compromises in order not to make the big ones. But there is a force about now which is dangerously lacking in imagination. A sense that we are not to be allowed to get away with it, whatever it is. I am not sure that individual governments can be held responsible for this. It seems to me that in our over-civilised times something vicious and barbaric has got loose. To paraphrase the words of Yeat's great prescient poem, the rough beast has reached Bethlehem and got itself born.

There is a telling American euphemism to describe the poor—'fiscal underachievers'. It throws responsibility for their poverty directly back onto those who suffer it. It suggests that to fail to adjust to the supermarket mentality of our times is a moral flaw.

But when the beast begins to devour itself, which it will certainly do, we will need a language to drive it off. My friend who dances the country in order that it should know her, my friend who walks the paddocks of past and present, are listening to that language. No government measures, no social indifference, no moral prohibitions, no cool postmodern denial of meaning can displace the sense of being engaged in something real. The language to which they are giving a voice exists already. It is an old, rich, generous language, flexible and without boundaries, accessible to anyone who listens with care and attention. The only qualities required to hear it are imagination and humility.

Buddhist Bootcamp

Sophie Cunningham

A young *tulku,* or reincarnation, lived among us in the Tibetan monastery at Kopan, Nepal. His name was Cherok Lama, though I dubbed him Lama Sunglasses because he ran around in traditional robes and bright red sunglasses. While I struggle with the concept of reincarnation I can't deny that he was one of the most remarkable, self-contained and bright children I've ever met. Not so much a child as an adult in a tiny body. Only seven years old, he already spoke five languages fluently. Often he would command an audience of a dozen Westerners and monks as he told fairy stories such as 'Pinocchio' with the authority of a great speaker. Often with him was an even tinier monk, of three or so, who wore a Spiderman mask or green fluorescent sunnies. Before I began the thirty-day retreat I hadn't expected imperious baby monks who combined the ancient dignity of the East with a kind of Western cool.

The monastery is an hour or so out of Katmandu. It is surrounded by the mountains of the Katmandu valley, and, in a wider circle, by Himalayan peaks. November is a rare clear time and every morning and evening the peaks were bright and jagged, white snow turning pink with the rising or setting sun. Mt Everest was black, because on the Nepalese side it is too steep for snow. In the mornings the mist circled Kopan hill and blanketed the valley below, and at times it seemed as if we were floating above the clouds. As the sun rose higher the clouds would dissolve into wisps until Katmandu emerged below.

In Katmandu one fellow traveller had laughed when I told him where I was going. 'Buddhist Bootcamp' he called it. When I arrived I saw the timetable: morning bell rings at 5am, prostrations at 5.30am. A cup of tea (spiced, sweet and milky) at six, then an hour's meditation, then breakfast. This was followed by what I thought sounded nice—karma yoga—only to find that that meant cleaning the bathroom and toilet.

Teachings began at nine, and went for two-and-a-half-hours. We had a couple of hours off, followed by a discussion group and teachings from 3.30pm till five. More tea, more meditation followed by dinner and back to the temple for a relaxing visualisation and chant before bed.

Then there were the rules. We were to be silent from nine at night till after lunch the next day. In the last two weeks of the course we could only eat one meal a day. Men and women slept separately, even if they were a couple. No stealing, killing, lying, sexual conduct or taking of intoxicants. Not surprisingly there were long debates about caffeine—not an intoxicant apparently— and definitions of sexual conduct. Did flirting count?

I was there with about 250 foreigners; from Finland, Turkey, Jamaica, Taiwan, Spain, Singapore, Japan, America and elsewhere. The passionate Buddhists among us had heard about the course through friends, while others had simply stumbled across the monastery's website. We shared the space with a few hundred monks, largely Tibetan, aged from three to ancient. Their chanting and debating was a constant background noise, and a few younger ones were always playing football or just mucking around.

The monks speak of Kopan in a way that gives the monastery the timeless and elusive qualities of myth, though it was only founded in the early 70s. Lama Zopa and Lama Yeshe were boys in a refugee camp in Northern India after fleeing Tibet in 1959. As young men they went to Nepal. One day a blonde, statuesque Russian/Los Angelene hippie called Zina knocked on their door and announced: 'I want a guru.' Zina bought the land where the monastery now stands and asked her Californian friends to join her for teachings.

Thus began the course I attended. Zina became a nun, and in the early 80s died while meditating in a cave—she was found in meditation posture. The monastery's co-founder, Lama Yeshe, has also died and has been reincarnated as a young Spanish boy, Osel. He is the first reported Western reincarnation.

I was to hear many similar stories: a baby being recognised as a reincarnation after he toddled up to a cave and insisted he was the yogi who had meditated and died there. Great lamas dying while meditating, but not decomposing. Some had evaporated into what Tibetans call 'rainbow light'. One senior lama was thrown into prison by the Chinese. As they slammed the door behind them they said, 'Let's see where your Buddhism gets you now.' They went back a week later (he had not been fed) to find he had grown fatter; his wrists were straining against his manacles. To Tibetans, magic is as ordinary as the air people breathe. Such stories are not even magic. To quote our teacher, there is no limit to what the mind can do.

All the older lamas were refugees, forced out of Tibet by the Chinese in 1959 or soon after. No wonder, then, that in our course the Chinese were often invoked in teachings on the need to let go of anger. It was remarkable to be surrounded by a people who had been driven out of their land yet worked to cultivate compassion towards their oppressors.

Lama Zopa was taught English by Californians in the 70s. The results are bizarre. He lectured us in a mix of halting English and Hippie. Seated on his throne above us he would lean forward and say, 'I am thinking what I am telling you is important. I am thinking you should check it out.' Or he would combine pop culture with more traditional Buddhist homilies.

> We need to analyse attachment in clinging to life's comforts. From this attitude is not peace. Opposite of satisfaction. Like Elvis Presley I don't get no satisfaction. Sorry, made mistake. I mean those guys, Rolling Stones... [Everyone laughs.] Saw video of Elvis Presley's last song. The young people on ecstasy. Sorry, they were ecstatic. While he was singing, tears coming out. Even though he achieved everything, money, reputation, wealth. But no satisfaction in his heart. He sees his heart is empty.

All the classes and meditations were held in a small temple, and we sat cross-legged on cushions before the teacher. He sat in front of the lama's throne, which was crowned by a large portrait of the Dalai Lama. Behind his image was a beautiful golden, four-metre-high Buddha. The temple was ornate, with bright colours, traditional paintings and statues covered in gold leaf. Beauty is considered a sign of respect and devotion to Buddha.

The living quarters, sadly, weren't so lush. As I had booked late into the course, I scored the worst bedroom in the place—a dorm with fourteen women just outside the communal toilets. We slept on a mat on the floor, and at night the occasional mouse skipped across our hair. There was one shower—cold—between 100 or so people. This dorm we came to call the 'hell realms'.

The course fell into two halves, divided by a full moon and, for me, by a high fever. For the first two weeks our daily teachings were given by a German monk, Venerable Fedor, who had come to Kopan as a backpacker fifteen years before and decided to be ordained. He taught about guru devotion, karma, meditation techniques, compassion and emptiness.

Even when I found myself disbelieving, I still enjoyed the history, the stories and the immersion in another culture. I struggled with meditation but was excited by the possibilities it offered.

I was amazed at how easily many things slipped away. Coffee and alcohol, my bookends most days in Australia, were not missed for a moment. Sex? Frankly, it was a relief to be in a place where it wasn't on the agenda. (Lucky, really—my daily outfit was tracksuit pants, socks and thongs and a baggy T-shirt.)

But things weren't easy. As we inched towards the full moon, everyone grew increasingly feral. One woman had a psychotic episode and had to leave the course. We hit the centre of the teachings, which say that all life is suffering because it is temporary. Trying to explain this, Fedor talked of eating a pizza from Fire and Ice, a fabulous pizza parlour in Katmandu, and how the experience was tainted because, when the pizza was finished, one had to keep eating to retain the satisfaction. The class, drooling, struggled to see this as suffering.

Then there were hours of lectures on the hell realms—where you go if your karma is particularly bad. In one, you are crushed to death again and again by mountains that take on the shape of those you have mistreated. In another, my favourite, you hear the sounds of loved ones at the top of a tree. You climb the tree, are sliced up by the leaves as you climb, then, at the top, you realise your loved ones aren't there, so you climb down and are sliced up all over again.

The relentlessness of the classes began to get to me. My back was in agony from sitting cross-legged each day, and my meditations had gone from the profound to the profane: thinking about sex for half an hour, then falling asleep.

I started to argue with Fedor, quizzing him about Buddhism's stand on evolution, and the time frame for Buddha's next incarnation (ninety billion years). He patiently pointed out that traditional Buddhism still taught that the world was flat—suggesting, I suppose, that some patience on my part wouldn't go astray.

Things got even more heated when one man asked: 'Do Buddhist teachings say that all people murdered during the Holocaust had the karma to be murdered?' Fedor's answer was hardline: yes, people with that karma chose to be born Jewish in Germany at that time.

Nor did the definition of sexual misconduct leave much for gay or a lot of heterosexual couples, as it vetoed oral and anal sex. It was at that point that one American lawyer left the course. 'No head jobs? I'm out of here,' he muttered as he headed off to go elephant riding in Chitwan National Park.

Around this time quite a few people left the course. Many felt that parts of it had become too fundamentalist, puritanical and at times culturally specific. I became angry that my fantasy about Buddhism as a kind of all-embracing cure didn't seem to be true and I struggled to resolve the compassion of the Dalai Lama—a member of this particular tradition—with the harshness of some of the teachings. I was reluctantly impressed, though, that our teacher made no attempt to pretty it up for Western ears.

The day of the full moon, I got a high fever and for several days had to go to bed (more literally, to floor). My fever broke the day Lama Zopa arrived, and I started to shake off my general malaise. The monks painted beautiful symbols on the pavement with chalk and placed buckets of incense everywhere. More monks sat on top of the main temple blowing trumpets, and others chanted, deep and low.

A couple of hours before his arrival, monks put on traditional hats (they look like cocky crests) and waited in line. I dragged myself up to find hundreds of monks, Westerners and Tibetans holding incense and scarves with which to be blessed. The air was full of incense, and the sound of chanting was like a low rumble from below the earth. I felt like I'd been catapulted into another century.

Lama Zopa moved through the crowd, blessing everyone. A tiny man with an extraordinary presence. Nuns and monks had come from all over Nepal and the world to hear him. When he spoke he would cough and splutter and rock. Sometimes he would stop and meditate for ten minutes without speaking. At times he would appear to fall asleep—not surprising, perhaps, as he was reputed never to go to bed. He met with course members until three or even five in the morning.

There was a strange beauty to the way Lama Zopa used language which compensated for his linguistic eccentricities. Take this talk on compassion:

> From compassion one experiences tranquility, peace of mind, fulfilment. Better than a relationship. Brings happiness for many lifetimes. Ultimately your compassion becomes source of happiness to your family, to your nation, to all sentient beings. More important than emergency hospital. Think of the impact one person without compassion, say a torturer, can make. Then think of what you can do if you are compassionate.
>
> Stop killing is the minimum thing. Not even insects. Don't put your big feet on tiny fragile insect. [He slapped one hand down hard on the other.] Very important. Causes big change in you. Even our beautiful hands are meant for peace, not violence. Yet can become weapons. Destroy the world. [He made claws like a tiger and growled.]

One day I saw him crouched, chanting blessings over a praying mantis that had some legs missing. Another day he walked around the large prayer wheel that dominated the courtyard with a caged bird he was about to release. Easy as it was to laugh at such eccentricities, I also pondered on the absolute sincerity and love that lay behind these actions.

He had no sense of time and spoke till all hours, which was tough on those getting up at 4am as many people were. I took to missing the morning classes, going instead to Lama Zopa's classes in the afternoon and evening. This gave me the mornings free, so I found a partner in crime, an Irishman called Tom, and we took to sneaking down to Katmandu. On our first morning I found a Western cafe and ordered eggs Florentine, granola, fruit salad, fruit juice, coffee... Then we went shopping, and flirted while we did. Two weeks meditating on the nature of desire and attachment hadn't quite undone the habits of a lifetime.

The atmosphere lightened in the last week or so. On the last day we performed for the monks. We sang Christmas carols, did Irish jigs and a warrior dance. A group of hippies sang 'Imagine'. The baby monks roared with laughter. In lieu of TV, we would do.

And there was always the constant, fabulous mingling of cultures, from the lamas in sunglasses that greeted me on my first day, to this exchange which took place towards the end of the course. It began with Lama Zopa rocking on his throne, slapping his body, pulling at his nose and ears. Playing the clown. 'Who thinks they are [more] important than other people?' he announced, looking around the room. 'Maybe we feel we are the most important. What reason? What reason would that be?'

A seventy-year-old, deaf, Christian eco-warrior leapt up and yelled: 'Daniel, from Montana.'

Zopa: 'You? You think you are better than others?'

Daniel: 'Trout. I fish trout, so I suppose I think I am better than trout. I eat 'em.'

For the last three weeks Daniel had been trying to get permission from every nun, monk and lama he met to kill and eat trout. One of the nuns had told him he should imagine he was eating his mother as he ate the trout. Clearly this hadn't daunted his enthusiasm.

Zopa: 'Do you ever think what the fish likes? Must research what happens to the fish. Think how you would feel if you were hooked in the mouth.' He put his finger in his cheek and tugged on it.

Daniel: 'Trouts don't have so many nerve endings in their mouth.' Then he conceded: 'They probably wouldn't like it much.'

'I think the Montana fish will clap their fins,' Zopa said before clapping his hands in a trout-like fashion. 'Fish think he goes to course—now won't catch us. Maybe they make big party.'

When I got back to Australia people wanted to know whether I felt changed. I did. I loved the tea, and the chanting, and the company and the porridge for breakfast. I loved the mist curling up in the morning as we watched the sunrise. I loved Lama Zopa's teachings.

But people want to know about the hard core stuff. Did *anything* happen, they woudl insist? I suppose they meant levitation or something sexy and tantric. So, here is my moment, though it is as hard to hold on to as Daniel's writhing trout. One morning, wandering around the monastery on a walking meditation, the thought crossed my mind that I could be any of the people walking with me. For an instant, my insistent sense of individuality and difference slipped away, and I imagined the possibilities—the relief—of a life where the ego doesn't always demand to be at the centre.

While I didn't believe everything I heard, to be in a place where acceptance, not scepticism, was the order of the day gave me a lightness I didn't have before. And I won't let the fact that some Buddhists think the world is flat stop me from exploring a world in which magic is possible and the mind, with all its capacity for generosity and love, is considered limitless.

Dots on the Landscape

Drusilla Modjeska

It's the gum trees' country. They had it before we came. They'll have it again when we're gone.

Douglas Stewart

The nose of land that forms one side of Farm Cove, pushing into Sydney Harbour between the Opera House and Garden Island, was once covered in red forest gums: *Eucalyptus tereticornis*. There are red gums there still, but hardly a forest. The grass grows lushly inside the loops of road that run past the Art Gallery of NSW to Mrs Macquarie's Chair; wedding cars and tour buses snake their way to the end to photograph or be photographed. It's one of Sydney's premium sites. When Mrs Macquarie waited there for the ships that would bring news of England, Sydney Town's forest gums were already being cut down—you can see the devastation in early paintings—though from the vantage point of the Pinchgut prisoners out in the harbour on their island prison, there must have seemed a lot of trees between them and any hope of inland escape.

The gum tree. Our history began with an uneasy relationship to it. Our literature and art is full of it. It's almost a matter of legend that our first artists, struggling to find a form for the lugubrious trees that made them uneasy, hid their gawky branches under the shapes of European trees. Follow the art market of the twentieth century and see the shift from the money going to the painters who made gum trees look like gum trees to the moderns who caught the light to give the impression and feel of the trees.

In our novels, babies and wives and mates have been buried under eucalypts; women and girls have had their backs broken by falling branches; love affairs, adulteries and elopements have been conducted beneath the trees. When there were strikes by loggers and timber workers in our literary past, sympathy was rarely with the trees. The bush hero became a cliché of nationalist rhetoric until Patrick White wrote *The Tree of Man* and gave us the more difficult idea that our relationship with the trees might have more to do with poetry, even the sacred, than with our own identity.

In June last year a sculpture—if that's the word for it—entitled *Veil of Trees*, created by Janet Laurence and Jisuk Han, went up in the first of those grassy loops on the road down to Mrs Macquarie's Chair. A hundred red forest gums have been planted; among them glass panels rise, tall and thin, as elegant as trees. The glass is smoky in places, speckled with ash, traces of minerals and indigenous seeds. Lines of Australian poetry—and a few of prose—are engraved into the glass. Les Murray and Judith Wright are there, of course, as well as many others going right back to Henry Kendall and Charles Harpur. Some panels simply list the names of trees: *Eucalyptus argillacea, Eucalyptus intermedia, Eucalyptus cypellocarpa, Acacia cowleana, Casuarina glauca* ... 'It is your land of similes,' a quotation from James Macauley reads, 'the wattle/scatters its pollen on the doubting heart.'

This sculpture—'this passage of reflection where memory is gathered'—is very beautiful. It has a modest calm, a meditative quality that, like the trees, does nothing to vie for our attention. Janet Laurence and Fiona Foley's *Edge of the Trees*, in the forecourt of the Museum of Sydney, has a similar calm and in the middle of the city their poles are hard to miss. *Veil of Trees*, tucked on the edge of the city, doesn't seem to be getting the notice it deserves. People park along that road in a hurry to get to the gallery or are too busy lugging their picnics into the Botanical Gardens to notice glass panels growing among saplings.

Our art and literature might be full of gum trees, but day by day we hardly notice them. Is it that they are so much a part of us that we need something more dramatic to jog our attention? Or could it be that there is too much guilt for us to want to stand among the trees and reflect? For this sculpture—this work of art—seems to ask us to reconsider our relationship to the eucalypt and a past that is entangled with it.

The optimistic view would be to say that after 200 years in this country white Australians are finally understanding the value of the environment we have crashed into; there are signs of ecological consciousness all around us. The gloomy view would be to say that the ecological consciousness doesn't extend far if there's a conflict over profit or our comfort. We might argue over it, but we still fell the forests and pulp the trees.

Of all the fellings, perhaps the most contentious has been that of the river red gum (*Eucalyptus camaldulensis*). If the red forest gum is the most prolific of the eucalypts growing along the length of coastal eastern Australia, the river red gum is the essential tree of the arid south and centre. It is the river red gum that is the subject of *Karra*, an exhibition, curated by Vivonne Thwaites, which opened this month at Adelaide's Artspace as part of the arts festival.

Karra is the name given to *E. camaldulensis* by the Kaurna people of the Adelaide plains. It once grew all along the Torrens; it grew in the Adelaide Botanical Gardens, where there is still 'a remnant tree'; it grew in north Adelaide, where the smart shops are; it grew where the golf course is. It grows along rivers and taps into underground water systems so successfully that the early explorers travelling inland to the centre rejoiced to see it. It was so ubiquitous that we hacked away at it for years. Its hard water-resistant wood was felled for bridges and barges, fence posts and railway sleepers. There was so much of this mighty tree—it could grow to a more than thirty metres and last half a millennium—that we also felled it to burn in our grates and to fuel the engines that pumped the water out of the rivers.

Cut down, the river red gum could no longer play its part in the regulation of the water table. With water taken out of the rivers to irrigate shallow-rooted crops, with dams built and river banks eroded where trees once stood, the water table has changed; the land is growing salty, the water with it. The states along the Murray-Darling system, where the karra was once supreme, argue over how much more water can be pumped out, how many more trees cut. The New South Wales rice and cotton growers and their communities depend on the water. There's no federal law to stop logging on freehold land even as land management schemes hasten to replant. Some estimates say that 30 percent more trees are needed. Adelaide depends on water that reaches down to the far end of this great waterway. If it turns to salt, what happens to the city and its parks and gardens? You can't boil the salt out of the water as we did the bugs that got into Sydney's water supply.

Sydneysiders might be too busy to stand among young trees and reflect, but perhaps the citizens of Adelaide will be more inclined to visit an exhibition given to a single eucalypt. It might draw their attention to the river red gums that are still standing in their city, some of them 500 years old and marked with unobtrusive plaques.

'The new out of the old' is the theme for this year's Adelaide Festival. Passionate about the tree—its history and its redemptive potential—Thwaites approached photographer Agnes Love, sculptor and ceramicist Jo Crawford and printmaker Chris De Rosa with the idea for *Karra*, an exhibition in a performance space that 'would say what a poem or a song might say'. The artists spent a year researching and photographing the karra, collecting bark, visiting the sites where the tree still stands, tracing records, reading pioneer diaries and letters, looking at paintings, drawings and photos, learning its ecology. The result will be at Artspace in the Playhouse until 20 April: 'a repository for memory and history' and a prayer for the future.

'Over time,' Murray Bail writes, 'the River Red Gum has become barnacled with legends. This is only to be expected. By sheer numbers there's always a bulky Red Gum here or somewhere else in the wide world, muscling into the eye, as it were; and by following the course of rivers in our particular continent they don't merely imprint their fuzzy shape but actually worm their way greenly into the mind, giving some hope against the collective crow-croaking dryness. And if that's not enough the massive individual squatness of these trees, ancient, stained and warty, has a grandfatherly aspect; that is, a long life of incidents, seasons, stories.'

This quotation from *Eucalyptus* stands, with Les Murray's *The Gum Forest*, as a kind of prologue to *Karra*'s catalogue of four essays. Words are as much a part of this exhibition as images and paintings.

Botanist Martin O'Leary tells a story worthy of Bail, but it comes from a *Eucalyptus* published in 1895. Drawing nineteenth-century America's attention to the many benefits of the genus, the author, Abbot Kinney, reported a widespread Spanish belief that the eucalyptus had healing properties for conditions as diverse as typhoid, incontinence, gangrene and gonorrhoea.

In Cordova the young eucalypts were stripped of their leaves, and guards had to be posted to protect them.' In other Spanish towns, 'permits were issued for the picking of leaves, if evidence of medical need could be shown'. Kinney also reported that 'an Aboriginal man whose intestines were hanging out from a wound made a complete recovery with no inflammation after *E. camaldulensis* leaves were used as a dressing.

E. camaldulensis is a remarkable tree. O'Leary tells of its capacities to endure fire and flood, and to hollow out its limbs and even its trunk in order to take advantage of the droppings of the birds and animals that live in these convenient hollows. It is an adaptation in 'nutrient-poor environments', he says that 'at the very least takes about 110 years to begin'. 'No wonder the willows are weeping', goes a line from Nelson Varcoe's *Song for the River Red Gum* that is also part of the exhibition, 'they weep for those old gum trees'.

In the catalogue, linguist Rob Amery traces its history in language and Stephanie Radok its history in image and art. The Kaurna took the wood of the karra into their culture as containers, artefacts, weapons, canoes and music sticks, its richness spreading into their language and also into ours when the bark containers were named coolamon. Colonial artist H. J. Johnstone painted *River Red Gum* in 1880; Jimmy Kite, who accompanied ethnographers Baldwin Spencer and F. J. Gillen on an expedition through Central Australia in 1901-02, drew it. His Aranda name was Erliakiliakirra, 'the subdued'. Fred Williams painted the Murray and its trees in the early 70s; the large panels are on permanent display in the foyer of the Adelaide Festival Theatre. The Murray has also been the subject of Ian Abdulla's quirky silkscreens of the 80s. An etching by Chris De Rosa overlays an excerpt from a pioneer letter—Mary Thomas writing from Adelaide in 1839 to her brother in England—on a detail of a coolamon scar in the trunk of a river red gum. Work by all of them is reproduced in the catalogue. So are Gilbert R.M. Dashorst's precise and exquisite botanical paintings. But for me the greatest pleasure of this exhibition is Kathleen Petyarre's luscious *Dusk in Thorny Devil Lizard Country* (watercourses and rockholes), painted last year on Belgian linen. It is large and mysterious and powerful, a centrepiece among the detail, a focus for meditation, an invitation to a different way of mapping, and seeing, and feeling, the country.

Eric Rolls writes of the karra as if it were a living character, a grand and noble being. He invites us to consider the living it has given us—those bridges and wharves and fence posts—and he details the life it has given the creatures of the bush: the ducks and parrots and owls and possums and goannas that live in its hollow branches. Some of the river reds lived so long and were so huge that their hollowed centres could accommodate entire Aboriginal groups. There's one left as evidence in the Adelaide Botanical Gardens. When hollow branches were hauled out of the river, Murray cod that once ruled two kilometres of water from their fortress logs, lost their habitat and began to die. The river red gum is host to mammals, birds, fish, bees, fungus, grubs and parasites. It can feed and it can heal. On top of that, it helps regulate the water table. And we burn it for firewood. When Douglas Stewart says, 'It's the gum trees' country. They had it before we came./They'll have it when we're gone', I hope he's right. 'The most terrible invention of our industrial civilisation,' Gary Catalano said back in 1985, 'has not been the bomb but the idea that the self exists as something apart for earth.' He is quoted in the catalogue.

'We are ruined by the thing we kill,' Judith Wright says. Veronica Brady quotes her in a recent essay on Wright and the poetics of ecology. The point Brady and Wright both make is that we need to find a way of being in the world that allows truths and perspectives other than our civilised industrial ones, a mutuality with the environment. It's hard to find language for this, for our forms of writing are themselves touched by the kinds of separation—between self and other, self and earth—that Wright wishes to dissolve. Perhaps poetry, with its reliance on compression and image, can best do it.

> We with our quick dividing eyes
> measure, distinguish and are gone.
> The forest burns, the tree-frog dies,
> yet one is all and all are one.

That's Wright again. 'Often our imagination cannot fully absorb the truth of a city or of a land,' Simon Leys writes in his celebrated essay on Lawrence of Australia, 'unless a poet first invents it for us.'

When Stan Parker's grandson walks among the trees at the end of *The Tree of Man* down in the gully where there are still a few standing—a 'sculpture of trees'—it is poetry he feels growing in him. Even as a scraggy boy he understands that poetry is as much a part of 'the already scribbled trees' as it is of himself. And as the suburbs come lumbering down the road, stripping the bush before them, he knows that his inheritance is not this headlong rush into easy comforts but the story of the great gums and his grandfather's modest hut. 'So that in the end there were the trees,' is how the novel ends. 'The boy walking through them with his head drooping as he increased in stature. Putting out shoots of green thought. So that, in the end, there was no end.'

Forty-five years later, the frail hope that 'in the end there is no end' slips into a different register. One could almost plot the course of our history by the twists and turns of what our writers do with the eucalypt.

In *Eucalyptus*, Murray Bail, the least political of writers, avoids the pitfalls of ecology and politics by letting the genus *eucalyptus* become the subject—in both senses—of its own legends. We don't have to worry about anything as difficult as protesters sitting in the branches or salt rising through the paddocks. Perhaps, paradoxically, the success of his work, particularly overseas, has to do with the distancing effect of legend, while here in Australia it reminds us of how deep into our psyche and imagination the roots of the eucalypt have dug.

Eucalyptus is the novel that has introduced us to the poetry of the botanical names; suddenly they seem to be everywhere. Eric Rolls used them in *A Million Wild Acres* back in 1981, but not on the same scale and not as a kind of poetics. That book—dedicated to Douglas Stewart—was tethered in the present and in history, not myth (and was of course not fiction but passionately 'real') but somehow that tethering gave it, like *The Tree of Man*, its own mythic qualities. Because Rolls takes the question of ecology to the heart of his work, there is a profound concern—as there is in his catalogue essay for *Karra*—with the interconnectedness of everything, and in that respect it remains unsurpassed.

In *The Idea of Perfection*, Kate Grenville takes a different fictional tack, writing in the tradition of the Australian novel of politics and relationship that was once commonly set in the bush. By taking the fate of a rough-hewn timber bridge on the edge of a New South Wales country town, it is the awkwardness of connection—bridge rather than trees—that becomes the subject for contemplation. Viewed from below, the timbers of the bridge, 'wedged against each other into crude simple joints', were 'like two people holding hands'. The engineer has been sent to replace it with concrete; the quilt maker has been sent to help the townsfolk make use of their heritage. Outsiders both, their faltering progress towards connectedness is a kind of metaphor, or blueprint, for the urgent but imperfect possibilities between heritage and economics, bush and town, city and country.

One of the best pieces in Peter Craven's *The Best Australian Essays* (Bookman, 1999) was, I thought, Gillian Mears's 'Mono No Aware: The Slender Sadness'. Mears has lived for many years outside Grafton beside the Clarence River. At its headwaters is the Timbarra wetland plateau. A Brisbane-based company is mining for gold there, despite dodgy environmental reports, native title claims and a long campaign of protest that includes local landowners. To extract gold from ore, the diggings have to be irrigated with a solution of sodium cyanide. About two tonnes are used each day. Plastic sheeting is meant to prevent run-off as the gold is washed through the heap of ore. Cyanide eventually degrades when exposed to sunlight, but a spill into the creeks that feed the Clarence can have lasting toxic effects on everything that depends on the river. Which is why the plateau and its forest is also inhabited by the eco-camps.

Mears writes of journeying there to confront the complex interactions of the combatants, the moral cross-currents, the hypocrisies in every camp (and not only those we love to hate). And, of course, her own romanticism, squeamishness, prejudices, irritations and doubts. It's not hard to maintain the rage against mining company officials when you know what cyanide does, or against the QCs who respond to the plain complaint that this is our drinking water by saying: 'You'd better get negotiating because it's going ahead anyway.' Much harder to face are the ambivalences of the Aboriginal community and the stupid things the vulnerable ferals and protesters do.

'Nature lovers', says a sign put up by one exasperated landowner, 'please do not shit in or near the [fuckin'] creek!' He lets them stay, he tells Mears, because despite it all they are doing an 'amazing job'. But still the trees come down and the water is poisoned, and nobody much knows or cares, and would it be easier to stay on one's meditation mat? What can a writer do?

Well, she can write, and this compassionate, pliable essay is as good as it gets. In writing such as this, or in an exhibition such as

Karra, the distinction between art and politics is hard to maintain. Essay and exhibition, each comes out of thinking that resists the urge to pit one thing against another, ordering and classifying, as so much in our culture does. Reading them, my frail hope is that we are seeing a new poetics, 'shoots of green thought', emerging even out of the most contentious aspects of our relationship with our trees.

'A slender sadness,' Mears calls her essay. It's a long way from Marcus Clarke's early encounter with the 'weird melancholy' of the bush, but for each of them—separated by more than a century— something of the mysteriousness of the bush remains. While that's the case, perhaps Australia can still, just, be said to be 'the gum tree's country'.

> New trees step out of old: lemon and ochre
> splitting out of grey everywhere, in the gum forest

These lines from Les Murray's 'The gum forest', which reminds us how much we need our poets, are to be found both in the *Veil of Trees* and in *Karra*. As are these:

> Sky sifting, and always a hint of smoke in the light;
> you can never reach the heart of the gum forest.

No Ordinary Neighbourhood

Craig Sherborne

In the ghettos of the bush the children have children. At sixteen or seventeen they have their first; twenty years old is old. They become boy-dads with spindly goatees who wear check-flannel shirts and tracksuit pants; and girl-mums with lank hair and boab-shaped bodies in leggings. They quit school, don't have jobs and push prams to the local shops, strolling in the midday sun like it's an outing. They are the ones the middle-class call 'bogans'. Relationships break up, they make new ones, have another child. On it goes through their twenties. They create brittle step-homes, greenhouses for violence and child abuse, according to the experts. Sometimes they live in small, dying towns, caravan parks or low-rent homes with sagging verandahs and overgrown lawns. Sometimes they live in a place like Ashmont on the outskirts of Wagga Wagga, a brick-veneer queue of modern houses. It's a place where people have a protective layer against outsiders: eyes stare in challenge at a stranger's passing car, and mouths shut if a stranger asks too many questions. Particularly since 'it' happened. Backs are turned on non-locals with a sudden flick of rejection; lips twist to a hostile sneer.

The 'it' is the torture and murder of a seven-month-old baby named Jordan Anderson-Smith in Ashmont on 25 February. The infant's death was a slow one, his body was systematically smashed. So far no one has been charged with the crime and the case is drifting. The police have two 'persons of interest' on their books:

Jordan's mother, Louise Anderson—and her de-facto at the time, Chris Hoerler, twenty-three. Both say they didn't do it. In Ashmont, those protective layers have hardened. The police cannot penetrate the locals' code of silence, a resolve not to give up vital clues in the case. This was a brutal crime against a baby, a defenceless innocent. Surely there is somebody prepared to break the code for Jordan's sake?

'A lot of people are frightened,' says Kerrie Lewis, the detective heading the investigation. 'People are afraid of repurcussions.' But Lewis clams up when asked to explain exactly what she means by 'repurcussions'. She will not put a name to the fear, real or imagined, that the people of Ashmont are experiencing. She says answering the question could harm the prosecution's case should someone be charged over Jordan's death. Those few Ashmontians willing to provide an answer refuse to give their names, not even their Christian names.

'I live four streets from where the murder happened,' one woman says over her shoulder, changing her shopping to the other hand and hurrying off. 'It's had a huge effect.' This code of silence compounds the usual parochialism which usually permeates such communities: answering relatively tourist-like questions such as, 'What's the area like?' is an ordeal for some. The postmaster, a thin old man in grey uniform, shakes his cheeks and utters: 'I don't want to divulge what goes on around here.' Outside the Ashmont hotel, a teen father peeling back a lolly wrapper for his toddler avoids eye contact. He silently taps his finger on a line of graffiti on the wall. 'FUCK you, fuck me, fuck the world.' To the left of the angry scrawl, someone named Leonie declares heart-shaped love for Hoerler, dated 1996.

The local high school is Mount Austin. Its acting principal, Col Feather, a rumpled, weary figure in baggy jumper, refuses to discuss the area's teenage pregnancy problem—13.5 percent of all mothers who gave birth at the Wagga Base Hospital last year were under nineteen. That's double the New South Wales average. Feather presses his palms to the air and attempts a bit of bush-PR: 'We like to concentrate on the positive things.'

Wagga Wagga is a big, pretty town, population nearing 60,000. It has fine old stony homes with bull-nose fronts, knobbly vines and woody green gardens. There is a strip of shops it takes an hour to walk through. Ashmont is divided from the town centre by an industrial quarter—exhaust and windscreen repairers, wheel aligners, panel beaters, car dealers and barbeque suppliers, all in a row off the highway. Between the industrial estate and Ashmont's houses is a moat of grass—a treeless wasteland with a bike path. There are two sides to Ashmont: there is the better-off side where homes are owned, with shrubby, well-watered front yards. Late model cars decorate neat drives. Then there is the rest: the housing commission homes boxy, low-roofed, fenceless and without flowers; brown outdoor blinds are drawn even on cloudy days. Wagga Wagga lies in a productive farming region, but there are precious few jobs in town, especially for those at the bottom of the social heap. In Ashmont the main industry is unemployment; men poke about under the hoods of clapped-out Camiras and Falcon GLs parked three or four to a driveway. On front doorsteps kids giggle at their children just learning to walk. They smoke, chat across lawns, swig a lunchtime beer. This is the land of the idle poor, of break-and-enters and vandalism, of hanging around, being bored. This is the bleak, listless world into which Jordan Dean Leon Anderson-Smith was born.

His father, Cecil Smith was a seventeen-year-old schoolboy who paired off with Anderson at a party. Anderson was already heavily pregnant to another man and gave birth to a son, Brody, a week after the party. She was already the mother of a two-year-old boy named Jason whose father lived in Werribee in outer Melbourne, a friend of Brody's father. The relationship between Anderson and Smith started as a love-lust fling, but three months after their meeting it was still steaming along. Smith left home and moved a few blocks away to live with Anderson in a tiny house in Blakemore Avenue, a stone's throw from Ashmont's shopping centre. Taking on step-children must have been a big challenge at seventeen, but Smith says he was unfazed. He was used to kids, came from an eight sibling step-family, and besides, it was a way for him to stand on his own two feet, become independent, he thought. 'I think I moved in with Louise because I just wanted out of the house, something a bit different, a bit more freer,' says Smith. 'I wanted a bit more of a life of my own.' That life became little more than parties and sex. His interest in things outside began to wane. He dropped out of school, midway through Year 10—'Most of the kids in Ashmont leave in Year 10,' he shrugs. And he stopped concentrating on the one thing that could get him out of there—rugby league. Smith can play rugby league. He's burly, strong and a gifted user of a football. His cousin is St George-Illawarra halfback Wes Patten. Patten and Smith are close. Smith wanted to do what Patten did, make it into the NRL big time, but his life took a new course. Then Anderson became pregnant with his child, with Jordan. 'It was an accident really. A sort of accident, but young people love kids and want one of their own,' says Smith. 'You use condoms, and the girls use pills, but yeah it still happens, she gets pregnant.' But the affair was souring. 'We were fighting all the time. She never cleaned up, in the kitchen and stuff. She never cleaned up anything. I'd have to do it.' Seven months before Jordan was born, Smith moved back home.

Anderson and Smith kept in touch after Jordan was born. She would take the baby around to see her father. But both parents quickly moved on to other relationships. Smith became a parent again, with a new girlfriend, Tamara. Their daughter, Tahlia, was born a month after Jordan's birth. She was a sickly child, twelve weeks premature. Meanwhile, Anderson became involved with Hoerler, a squat, muscular Papua New Guinean, who had settled as a child in Young, north of Wagga Wagga. He moved in with Anderson at Blakemore Avenue.

Anderson and Hoerler hosted a party for six guests on the night of 24-25 February. The party ended sometime around midnight and the guests went home. A little after 3am a series of 000 calls for an ambulance were made from the house. Police will not confirm who made the calls. When ambulance officers arrived they found Jordan dead with Anderson trying to resuscitate him. They took over, but it was useless. Jordan was gone. Sudden Infant Death Syndrome, they thought. There was a small bruise on his left cheek, but nothing at first glance to suggest injury. Then, literally before the officers' eyes the bruising started to come out. When police looked in the baby's bedroom: they saw blood on the wall and in the bedding. Yet there was no blood on the baby. It made no sense. Anderson and Hoerler said that after the party they had gone to sleep on a mattress in the living room, with Jordan beside them. They told police they woke around 3am and found him dead.

Jordan's body was sent to the Institute of Forensic Medicine in Sydney for post-mortem examination. It took four days for a pathologist to analyse Jordan's injuries—there were so many. His face had swollen to a mask of purple bruising; his ribs were fractured; his liver ruptured. Some of the injuries were bizarre—Wagga Wagga coroner, Sev Hill, had seen nothing like them in thirty years of coronial work: 'The toes, it's as if they were clamped, as if put in a vice, or pair of pliers, crimped,' he says, pulling the pink ribbon from the files containing Jordan's records. He is sitting in his book-lined office in the town's courthouse. He studies the files in silence a moment, eyebrows arched in concentration over his spectacles. The arch collapses into a frown, a grimace. 'Yes,' he murmurs. 'That was one of the reasons why there was a delay in the (post-mortem) process, because they had to work out the injuries on the toes. The baby appears to have been tortured. It didn't happen in five minutes. It happened over a period of time. I would put it at an hour minimum.' Jordan must have been screaming at the top of his lungs, piercing the night silence. Neighbours must have heard something. Lewis finds this hard to stomach: 'When we went around and knocked on the doors, when we said to people, "You must have heard the baby crying," they said, "Some babies cry all the time. It's nothing unusual."'

The Department of Community Services removed Anderson's other two children from her care after that night. A written statement by DoCS for this story reads: 'Alternative care arrangements have been made for the other children in the family to ensure their safety and well-being.' DoCS will not comment on whether its staff had ever been aware of any child abuse in the Anderson-Hoerler home.

Coroner Hill thumbs to a remembered page in the files and gives a summary of its paragraphs: 'The baby had an immunisation needle on the 24th (the day before he died). It appeared to be a well cared-for baby. The doctor who gave the needle didn't notice anything amiss.' Hill turns to another page, a post-mortem document. 'The baby may have had some injuries prior to the injuries on the night because there seems to be some bruising on the scrotum which seems to be an older injury, but...' his voice trails off. He closes the files and ties the ribbon in a bow.

Three hundred and sixteen children were murdered in Australia between 1989 and 1999—8.6 percent of all homicides committed. According to a new report by Canberra's Institute of Criminology, 71.8 percent of the killers identified were male, most of them were the victim's parent, and 34.7 percent of them the step-parent. The last figure, however, is deceptive. The report's author, Jenny

Mouzos, explains: 'Statistically, children are in fact at much greater risk in a step-family than a biological family because there are fewer step-families in the population than there are biological ones.' The report moots a 'Darwinian view of child homicide' where step-parents are involved, a sort of genetic competing. It says people devote less time to children who are not theirs biologically, exposing them to potential neglect. It contends that step-parents are likely to be less patient and more aggressive towards the children.

Professor Ken Polk, a University of Melbourne criminologist and child homicide expert hones the profile—an archetypal killer emerges: 'These crimes are class crimes,' he says. 'Nearly always, the family units that are under exceptional economic stress, generally the two individuals are unemployed. They tend to have histories of drug use. They are young, very inexperienced individuals and parents, and the young male, the new de-facto, is totally unprepared for dealing with a situation where they are in competition with the child for the woman's attention…. If the individual has learned a repertory of violence then the violence gets played out.'

But haven't most of us known someone who would fit that mould? And they haven't gone bashing kids to death.

'I think what they [child abusers] see themselves doing is disciplining the child.'

Even to the point of torture?

'Yeah,' he drawls, unequivocal. 'They rarely see it as torture. They see it as discipline. Their interpretation is they are bringing the child into line.' Polk then loops back to where he started, the poverty trap argument: 'At the boundaries of mainstream society you are going to see more and more of these extreme kinds of responses [to poverty], of loss, alienation, lack of connectedness, anger, frustration, all this violence, then it replicates itself.'

Perhaps there's a sense something is missing from the explanation. Any reasonable person can accept that a theft-crime can be a poverty-crime, but it takes a long leap from there to infanticide. Brutality against children is our society's most enduring taboo, it repulses us morally; criminology's explanantion of why it happens seems like a lame excuse. We turn to our imaginations or religions for answers and find the word 'evil' to describe and understand the criminal.

Writer Helen Garner, felt the murder of toddler, Daniel Valerio was a case in point. The boy's step-father, Paul Aiton, was eventually convicted of the crime. Garner covered Aiton's trial for *Time Australia*, and wrote: 'I don't see how it is possible to contemplate Daniel's story without acknowledging the existence of evil; of something savage that persists in people despite all our enlightenment and our social engineering and our safety nets.' 'Evil' is a loaded term, we're used to associating it with tabloid sensationalism or pulpit theatricality. 'Savage' is much the same. But these words are all we have to express our horror. We speculate: at the core of the child killer, does a malign impulse exist that needs hateful, violent expression? An impulse criminologists haven't identified yet, put a proper name to?

No one will be charged with Jordan's murder; not from the current police investigation anyway, that's what coroner Hill predicts. The code of silence is holding. Police impetus is petering out. Initially there was a team of seventeen on the case; now there is only Lewis, with one or two officers available if she needs them. Then there was the Olympics factor—police officers from rural New South Wales, including Wagga Wagga, were commandeered to beef up Olympic Games' security in Sydney. Hill believes Jordan's case was shunted down the list of police priorities in the process. Speaking in the lead-up to the Games, Hill claimed: 'Police will have limited involvement until after the Olympics. I think that it's a sad thing to say.' Lewis backed his claim, to a point: 'It [the Olympics] has had some impact. Some.' But Wagga Police's crime manager, Grahame Winson rejected it. He admitted that thirty-eight officers from the area's 120-plus squad were assigned to the Olympics, but he claimed this hadn't hurt the investigation. Though he did offer this piece of doublespeak: 'We would like to have more [people on the case]. We have a full committment to it with limited resources.'

If no one is charged over the murder soon, Hill plans to stand the matter down for a hearing—everyone who has given evidence so far would be made to appear before him and tell what they know all over again, and be questioned. Not that he's confident the process will reveal the murderer. 'I think there will be an open finding once I've had the hearing, and then after that I would hope the police would post a reward.'

But hearings can turn up suprises. In the late 1980s Hill conducted a hearing into the murder of Sally Ann Jones, a teenager found floating in river shoals at Wagga Wagga. One of those appearing was a local mechanic named Kenneth Cannon. He claimed he discovered the body while going for a training run along the muddy banks of the river. His wife had given him an alibi. But at the hearing, his story suddenly didn't ring true to Hill, himself a keen jogger. 'He was wearing a pair of Dunlop K26s. If you are a serious runner you don't wear those. You get something better than that. And you don't run in mud.' Hill hassled the New South Wales commissioner to order DNA testing on Cannon. It was done. Cannon was convicted of the murder.

If there is music in Ashmont, a lightness of step, it's found in the pub on Friday night. In the lounge bar a one-man band strums his guitar. At smoky tables, hands clap in time and mouths sing along to the chorus of 'I Heard it Through the Grapevine'. In the public bar girlfriends sip on straws watching the boys play pool. The talk and swearing are loud and happy. Outside, it's a quiet evening with tall necks of smoke coming from the chimneys, and bats diving in silhouette through the air, their wings making a squelching sound; no work yet for police cruising the streets. Just some yelling and fighting, the usual kind of drunken thing. In the morning, the birds move in, skittering up through paperbarks, and then the kids who have kids start coming out, hunched behind strollers, scuffing their feet as if they've got the weight of the world on their shoulders.

A new family has moved into the house where Jordan was murdered; baby clothes are pegged on the line in the backyard where his clothes would have hung; a pram is parked near the front door where his pram would have been. The backyard is very small; the whole house appears pushed up tight against its neighbour. The neighbour is in her front garden. She has long gingery hair and wears a greying white T-shirt and short pants. The neighbour is Louise Anderson. 'The police say I can't say anything to anyone,' she insists, though this is news to them. Anderson untangles a hose and waters the few plants. Doesn't she find it difficult living so close to her old house? 'No.' Is she going to stay here? Stay in Wagga? 'I'm probably staying here. 'It's an alright town.' When she speaks she tilts her head back, then narrows one eye and purses her mouth, a look of timid defiance. According to one source in Wagga Wagga, Anderson is applying for a $50,000 victim's compensation payment through the NSW Victims' Compensation Scheme. Is that rumour true? 'Maybe,' she says, cocking her head the other way.

Smith reckons he's going to leave Ashmont. He has broken up with Tahlia's mother and plans to scrape some cash together and move to Shell Harbour with his new girlfriend, a twenty-two-year-old who lives in the block of flats next door to him. She has a three-year-old child to another man. He wants a fresh start, by the ocean, and hopes for a better chance at a job. He might even go to back to school and get his Year 12. And he wants to play rugby league, have another shot at the NRL. If it works out between him and his new girl, maybe they'll have a baby together, he says. But only after the relationship is established. At least that's the plan. In the meantime he's in counselling. He says: 'They've got me drawing pictures. When Jordan died, I'd dream I was down a hole, and my family was up top. At the start I stayed in my flat, and then I'd snap at people. And I was swearing at my mother, which I would never do because I have so much respect for her. I don't do none of that no more.'

By midday in Ashmont people move on to their steps to sit; cars get tinkered with; weekends or weekdays, the timetable is the same. Or they head into Wagga central, hang around, then go home. When they get home, some will find Lewis's calling card under the door. She has left one many times. On it will be a note for them to call her to talk about 'it'. But of course they won't . They'll tear up the card like always and throw it in the bin, determined to keep their nose out of such business, obey the local lore.

Surgery

Catherine Ford

In the Royal Children's Hospital cardiac unit very early on a calm September morning, a boy with blonde hair, a two-year-old with a heart problem, lies unconscious and on his back, prepared for theatre.

He might simply be asleep, except his head and shoulders, lowered slightly, tilt back in an unnatural arc. Thin tubes, secured tightly with flesh-coloured bandages, run from his mouth and nostrils to a monolithic humming machine lit up at one end of the table, and a catheter sprouts from his tiny penis, also bandaged.

Edging nearer I look at his legs splayed comfortably, his arms, the backs of his hands and their tiny depression where one day knuckles will show. His whole body is wonderfully white except for an oval bruise near a knee. I don't know him, although he is eerily like my own son, if a little slimmer and a year or so younger, and the thought of what this virginal child will endure this day brings on nervous tremors.

I am here today to observe an uncommon and very lengthy operation to reconstruct the boy's pulmonary arteries performed by the newly appointed director of the hospital's cardiac unit, Dr Christian Brizard, and his team.

Dr Brizard is a tall man with a long pale serious face who, when he's not wearing baggy green theatre pyjamas, favours pastel-coloured unmistakably French shirts, good jeans and dark-leather loafers. Dr Brizard and his wife and daughters and my family have been friends for some years, and I have always been curious about his work, which I think of as unimaginably difficult. Sometimes when our families come together over a meal, or meet in a park, Dr Brizard excuses himself and conducts conversations of the utmost gravity over a mobile phone about the care of a child patient and when he hangs up and returns to the group it's as if nothing particularly worrying has happened.

Like a number of surgeons I've known he seems preternaturally composed and, although he is just forty and youthful and good-humoured and perhaps because he is both French *and* a surgeon, he can also seem at times a touch disdainful. On the day of our interview, some days before this operation, he shows me two photographs hanging in his office, taken in 1922, of his grandfathers seated amongst a dozen or so other stern men in white caps and aprons. Pointing to them, he says to me, 'Looking very sad, no? A general tendency in the family.'

Another tendency then was medicine. Both grandfathers were, respectively, a physican and a general surgeon, at the Saint Louis and Salpetrière Hospitals in Paris in the early 1920s, one dying, he tells me, in middle-age of several heart attacks. His father was a physician who took him on hospital rounds and practised partly from a room in Dr Brizard's childhood home. He remembers being paraded in front of some of his father's patients who needed, he says, the reassurance of seeing their doctor's family.

He didn't know if he would become a doctor, but decided if he did it would be as a surgeon rather than a physician. He liked working with his hands and knew what the life of a physician was. 'A physician follows up the patient,' he said. 'It's a much more close relationship with the patient. A different set of mind. Being a surgeon, you're there when they're acutely ill, but you do not see them afterwards. This suits me better.'

Each year, he and his colleague, Dr Andrew Cochrane, perform some 650 operations between them, making them inordinately busy. Every working day is at least twelve hours long and often longer; every second weekend is spent on call. Although we are repeatedly interrupted by his beeper and then a trip upstairs to view a post-operative ultrasound of a patient's heart, Dr Brizard is generous in our conversation about his training and how he came to be here. He also wants, he says, to promote the unit's better-than-world-standard results, and the team who work with him, of which he is openly admiring. 'Every person in the chain is outstanding,' he tells me proudly. 'Outstanding anaesthetists, intensivists, cardiologists, very good nurses. All this makes the result. The surgeon is part of the process, not a minor part, but they're part of a team.'

Cardiac surgeons have to get their training on the side if they want to work in paediatrics, he explains, and must make a grab for the rare openings in exclusively paediatric practice that arise worldwide. The Royal Children's Hospital appointment was such an opportunity.

He spent 1990 here as a Fellow under the tutelage of Dr Roger Mee, a renowned New Zealand heart surgeon, because the Children's was 'the best unit in the world.' He returned to Paris as a consultant for six years, only to come back to Melbourne again in response to an offer to take up a permanent position here. He became the director of the unit earlier this year after the previous incumbent, an American, went home.

Paediatrics is coveted, he says, because it's more diverse than adult practice. The range of abnormalities is large, the physiology more complex, more technically and intellectually challenging. Although he sees no inherent hierarchy between paediatric and adult cardiac surgery, he's in no doubt about which one holds sway when it comes to economic terms, even when this goes against his own interests.

'It's as useful for the society to save the life of the father of four children, who is in his 50s, as it is to save the life of a neonate, and it's arguably more important to save the man's life. More people will suffer. When the neonate dies it is extremely sad, but perhaps the family will recover more quickly. *Comment on peut dire...*' He pauses, rooting around not for the English but, it seems, for his opinions on the forces which govern his job. 'Children's health has improved over the years and funding has dropped, in part, because of that, but adult surgery has always been better funded than children's, because of the value society has assigned to the adult over the child.'

He shrugs when I say he'd have trouble convincing new parents, even old ones, of these opinions. 'I believe every individual, every patient has to be treated as such,' he answers, 'and as best as we can offer.'

When I try to drag words from him on the emotional aspects of his work he becomes restless, or perhaps just bored with the questions. What of his personal feelings towards those in his care? What about children who die? What about the strains of accountability and contact with parents' fear? What, for instance, of the tension inside a person who saves lives by coming perilously close to ending them?

'Parents understand very well that their child doesn't have much choice. They have to go through that. We try our best to reassure the parents, but also give a realistic picture of the risk that that child is going to face. You have to build relations of confidence with the parents. But you cannot be emotionally involved, huh? Because then you lose your ability to take risks and the patient will not benefit from that.'

And working so close to death?

'When you operate on a patient you know there's a certain amount of risk... when something bad happens... that's part of our job,' he says. 'We lose patients. Patients under our care die. It is extremely sad. But when you have provided the best of yourself, well, that is it. And if you have a good relationship with the parents and you tell them what are the facts and what are the chances, then there is no reason why you shouldn't go home and sleep quietly.'

'You get accustomed to the responsibility and what cardiac surgery represents for the patients,' he continues. 'You know that you can mess an operation and that represents probably the death of the patient, but at the same time cardiac surgery is something that is extremely routine, and the routine is reassuring. There's a large part of the operation which is exactly similar to the previous one. You have to be very dedicated to the patient, but you have to be able to take some risks for them. If you're too afraid then you probably don't give them the chances and you do a lesser operation. You have to be confident with risk.'

And when a patient dies? 'When a child dies under my care and I have operated on the patient, I tell the parents. We make sure the parents are there because it's extremely important emotionally for the future of the parents, to be there. It's not the nicest part of our job, although it's really part of it. He leans forward in his chair and says with emphasis, 'But you know, it's rare.'

*

In the theatre, I'm greeted by Dr Robert Eyres, a highly experienced anaesthetist who was recently appointed director of anaesthesiology at the hospital. He's wearing the uniform green gear and battered white clogs on his feet and falling from under his theatre cap is hair that's longer than you'd expect. He has a slightly gruff, authoratitive air with something of the radical about him too, and amongst the people in the team I speak with this day, his skill and reputation seem practically legendary.

I mumble to him about the medical world being a rich place for writers, to which he quickly responds, 'We're very protective.' But as the day wears on he talks openly to me about his occupation and in particular, the surgical world, with the wit and intelligence of a good teacher.

Dr Eyres and I have in fact met before today, eight-and-a-half years ago, to be precise. He was the anaesthetist for an operation my first child, my daughter, needed at birth to repair a patent urachus; a condition, and therefore an operation, so rare the surgeon who performed it, the most experienced and apparently the best in his field, had neither seen it before nor, therefore, conducted the surgery needed. The operation took four-and-a-half hours and was happily a success. It was also an agonising experience neither I nor my husband, not to mention our daughter, would ever hope to have to endure again.

I remember Dr Eyres as if it were yesterday and how he spoke with us before our daughter was taken to theatre and how I pleaded with him in the corridor, forgetting dignity, to take extremely good care of our girl. I remind him of this now and he remembers the operation but not the importuning mother. 'The difference between your daughter and a child this age,' he says to me, perhaps trying to separate the experiences on my behalf, 'is a two-year-old has a pretty good idea that something's up.'

Nonetheless, standing next to Dr Eyres at the head of the operating table on which the vulnerable boy who resembles my son is laid out, dead to the world, I feel a wave of nervousness. 'Where are the exits?' I ask. His eyes crease above his mask. 'You're not going to need an exit. A chair maybe. Just give us a bit of notice,' he says, 'and try not to fall on any of the machinery.'

'And if I need to throw up?'

'You're not going to throw up! You'll just pass out. Even an anaesthetist in here,' he says with satisfaction, 'hit the ground with a bloody great thump last week.'

CATHERINE FORD

Having already seen to the initial job of putting the boy under, Dr Eyres wanders here and there, and I tag along, listening to his explanations, watching him direct a younger anaesthetist assisting on the case, a Dr John Roche, who is a Fellow from Oxford, here for a year. 'One of the reasons this unit has such a great reputation,' Dr Eyres tells me, 'is that it's consistently running close to 700 operations a year. That's three, on average, per day. Anything under that number and a team really isn't up to speed.'

For the anaesthetist in a procedure such as this, the transitions from waking to sleeping, going on to the by-pass machine and coming off, are the most critical, but in longer operations there are also periods of 'down-time' which require less vigilance. 'Some would argue that doing a dozen grommet operations in a morning,' Dr Roche tells me, 'is more difficult than a by-pass operation such as this, because you're always moving.'

They read the boy's information on one of two screens around the room. 'Most people who come in here want to throw something over them,' Dr Eyres says about the patient, 'keep them warm, but we need to lower his temperature to 33 degrees and keep it there. Ever seen 'ER'?' he adds. 'No? Me either. This kid's ten kilos,' he says, 'which is just perfect for me. The maths is easier.'

Dr Roche shakes his head, chuckles. 'Robert's great. Robert's a *character*.'

Both Eyres and Roche and a male nurse then arrange the boy, his limbs flopping heavily from side to side, onto his left, propping him there with the help of rolled up towels. This is really two operations in one, they explain; first they'll enter from his side, later he'll lie on his back for the second descent into the heart itself. Dr Roche runs his eyes and hands, as lightly as feathers, over every last centimetre of the boy's skin, checking air and drainage tubes, his temperature and pulse pads and drip. They must be perfectly, firmly, in place, he says, because the child will be hidden under sheets and everything about his progress, the crucial information, is relayed solely by these connections, which brings to mind other abstract and undoubtedly adrenalin-producing occupations: piloting an Airbus at night into Bhutan, say.

Dr Roche then places ten-centimetre-high perspex struts over each limb which, he explains, the surgeons will lean on as they operate. Theatre nurses, May and Violetta and Margaret, move in as he finishes, one washing the patient down thoroughly with a sterile solution, another counting and ordering dozens of instruments on trays—some delicate, some sickeningly functional-looking. A couple of nurses take a sheath of transparent adhesive material, like tough Glad Wrap, and stick it tightly across the boy's chest. Crisp green cover sheets are unpacked and arranged painstakingly over him. Little by little the child is reduced to a patch of white convex flesh with the dimensions, roughly, of a paperback book.

The young boy with ruffled hair and a latent personality is all but obliterated now. Only an act of imagination can restore him, which is of some help when one of Dr Brizard's assistants finally and without announcement steps forward, bends over the rectangle of skin and, with a scalpel pressed to one end, carefully, with a concentrated force, splits the rectangle lengthwise in two.

At this moment a transformation seems to occur in the atmosphere of the room, the focus over the table intensifies, the very air around us seems to zing with surges of energy. The surgeon, Dr Issam El-Rassi, a Fellow from Beirut, proceeds with prior instructions from Dr Brizard, who is still in his office, with Dr Sunil Kaushal, a Fellow from New Delhi, looking on. Dr El-Rassi takes no time at all, perhaps thirty minutes, to cut his way through the little flesh there is above the ribs, and then between the ribs themselves, to locate the collateral arteries Dr Brizard needs for the second stage of the procedure.

'The lung,' Dr El-Rassi says after a while, pointing, and I glimpse a dull red glistening form, inflating and deflating with mesmerising smoothness and regularity, its silhouette something like a young strawberry.

The two walls of flesh which descend from Dr El-Rassi's incision are centimetres deep and as densely massed yet porous-looking as the insides of a fine sea-sponge. The tissue is remarkably clean and almost entirely bloodless, but moist still and seeping and infinitely and minutely stippled, as with a fresh coat of paint on plaster. Dr Roche tells me the aesthetics of surgery is another reason why paediatrics is such a desirable place to be: 'There's no fat, and you get to work with tissue that's beautiful and healthy.'

The diathermy (an electric current issuing from an instrument like a ball-point pen with a wall connection), which seals the vessels in the path of the knife to prevent bleeding, gives off a disturbing meaty smell, but it also leaves behind a brilliantly clean incision, which, after more cutting, produces a cavity big enough to insert an orange into and one that is miraculously bloodless and ready for work.

Dr El-Rassi, hunched over under the lights, concentrates with an indomitable air. After some time, he calls me in closer and allows me to look down into the small shiny well he's exposed, and there, cradled at the bottom I see the heart. It takes my breath away. Unlike the lung it needs no introduction. I gaze at its slippery movement, its hypnotic happy bump-bumping, for perhaps a dozen seconds only, a dozen long seconds, with my own forgotten heart galloping loudly.

Before this operation I opened a volume of an old-fashioned children's encylopaedia stacked away in my daughter's bookshelves, turned to a chapter on the heart, and there among its many pages and diagrams I found an appealing and curious sentence which again came into my head: *The nervous government of the heart and its beating is very wonderful.*

Peering into Dr El-Rassi's well (and at this moment it did not seem to belong to anyone else), observing Dr Eyres' and Dr Roche's painstaking attention to the hidden boy, a deeper poignancy in the sentence manifests itself, and in the first of a handful of unforgettable moments during the day, I'm overcome by what I see.

*

When Dr Brizard works, he likes music playing, and around mid-morning when he enters the theatre he puts on a CD of African songs, then settles in over the excavation flanked by his assistants. He pokes and prods with instruments, conferring as he goes, occasionally muttering in French to Dr El-Rassi. Hours slip by. Every now and then one of the three surgeons stands up straight and bends his head and shoulders back, groaning.

Occasionally Dr Eyres asks Dr Roche to explain his methodology to him. 'How low will you allow them to go?' he asks Dr Roche, tipping his head toward Dr Brizard and his colleagues, as if they might be bullies or liars the Englishman should watch out for. 'You're about to go on by-pass,' Dr Eyres responds when Dr Roche explains his anaesthetic strategy. The younger man, in his inexperience, has taken more precaution than Dr Eyres thinks necessary. 'I wouldn't bother,' he tells him.

At one o'clock, four-and-a-half hours into the operation, I leave the theatre with Dr Roche to eat lunch in the staff lounge, and in the corridors of the hospital a mild disappointment steals over me. Perhaps the drama of the operating theatre, it occurs to me, is only notional after all. I eat in a great hurry, impatient with Dr Roche who is relaxing as he should be, eager to return to the theatre, to the seriousness there, the earnestness, the uncompromising focus at its bright centre.

During the afternoon Dr Eyres speaks about how the reputation of the unit has led to the most complicated cases being sent to it, not only from within Australia. 'We get all the difficult stuff,' he says. The team is so good and there is excellent communication between members 'when it's needed', he explains. Communication of that kind, he says, is something which only develops over a long time.

He idly tells me he once thought of moving to Italy to practise because he thought the world outside of work there was more to his taste, but he finally changed his mind. I ask him how much uncertainty there is in a job which for him seems like second nature. 'Something comes up at least once a week when I don't know what to do and have to nut it out on the spot,' he says, but in the hours I watch him he manages this case, supervises Dr Roche, consults with the surgeons, with nurses and perfusionists, deals with other cases over the phone and entertains me. He is sailing, a picture of easy control.

What about Dr Brizard, I ask him, how come he's so cool?

'Christian? Internalised!' he says. 'It's all internalised.'

When the afternoon draws to a close Dr Brizard and Dr El-Rassi and Dr Kaushal have completed the first part of the case and are well into the second. They have closed the boy up along the side of his rib-cage and moved into his chest from above, excising a patch of the pericardium—the membranous sac which covers the heart—creating from it, in a mind-numbing sewing exercise, a tube resembling macaroni, with which they'll repair the boy's defective connection between heart and lung.

'This is endless,' Dr Brizard finally declares, but in fact after the operation he tells me he likes the way heart surgery always has an end and you cannot rest until you get there. 'In just about everything else, I never finish what I start!' He also likes the exigencies of surgery, and the way no interruptions can be accommodated, 'Even,' he says, hopefully, 'if it's the president on the phone.'

I leave the theatre at 3.30 in the afternoon, seven hours after I arrived. I learn that night that the operation continued for another four hours, two of which were spent on a by-pass machine, and achieved what was hoped for; that the boy did well in intensive care and went home after only a week in the ward, where he continues to do well.

But at 3.30 I leave with such reluctance. I follow Dr Eyres and a nurse with a ginger goatie wearing a Mash hat wheeling another child from an adjacent theatre along a corridor toward intensive care, back into the orbit of his parents. They walk slowly without speaking, one steering, one pushing, and Dr Eyres controls the boy's oxygen by hand-pump as they roll along, and once again admiration gathers inside me.

How Fengshui Changed My Life

Linda Jaivin

What was a nice Sydney girl like me doing in a place like this? A dusty carport at the edge of a parking lot in Taipei on a stinking hot Sunday morning. Trying to make like cat's paws with my feet and snake heads with my hands. Taking the old Shanghainese teacher's bait time and again. Old Liu was seventy if he was a day, smooth-faced and pudgy in a singlet and baggy trousers. 'Hit me,' he'd challenge. I let loose with a hard left jab. My fist bounced off his plump tummy like it was a wall of rubber. 'Harder.' I slammed my best undercut into his stomach, the muscles of which balled up weirdly around my fist and twisted it until I was begging for mercy. 'I could break your wrist with my *qi*.' I believed him.

Qi is one of those things you learn to respect after you've been in China for a while. Life's vital essence, *qi* is what gets unblocked by acupuncture, what moves the calligrapher's brush, what you lose out of the top of your head on a cold day without a hat. It's energy and integrity as well. Its home is the *dantian*, the area about three inches below the navel.

Hou Dejian, one-time pop star, now full-time fengshui master and the subject of my next book, smiled and patted his *dantian* with alternating hands. Along with half a dozen other Chinese men, he paced a circle chalked into the ground with mincing steps, their toes gripping the ground through their sandals, their knees curved inward. Cat paws.

Old Liu applied one finger to my wrist. I went down like I'd just met Muhammad Ali fist first. I love Chinese kung-fu.

This particular branch of it, *bagua quan*, has a special connection with the *I Ching*, the ancient Book of Changes. The *I Ching* consists of sixty-four hexagrams, groupings of lines which are either broken (*yin*) or unbroken (*yang*). The Chinese have used the *I Ching* for nearly 3,000 years as a tool for divining the future. It's also the basis for fengshui. Fengshui, literally 'wind and water,' is the art of situating a tomb or house (or doors, windows and other objects within a house) in such a way as to maximise wealth, health and happiness. You'd think that between the two, everyone in China would be wealthy, healthy and happy—and they'd know what was coming around the corner. Trouble is, no one can interpret the *I Ching* with absolute certainty.

Hou was here to deepen his understanding of the *I Ching*. I was here to deepen my understanding of Hou. I'd known him for eighteen years, from the time he was one of the most popular singer-songwriters in the Chinese world. I knew him when he bizarrely and controversially defected from Taiwan to China in 1983, when he turned dissident on Tiananmen Square in 1989 and when he was kicked out of the mainland one year later. I knew him as he struggled to make sense out of his weird and dramatic history, and the weird and dramatic history of China itself, by reading and re-reading the *I Ching*, evolving his own system of fengshui as a result and eventually becoming a practising fengshui master. Now that I'd decided to write a book about him, however, I needed to get to know him all over again. That's why I was in Taipei, trailing him around, sharing his kung-fu lesson.

Old Liu sent me flying again. 'She's very strong,' he graciously informed the others.

The sweat was dripping off my forehead. I walked over to where Hou's friend had parked his car to chuck my hat inside. With a hand like a snake, I reached in the window to unlock the car door. This set off the alarm. The men stopped their circling to laugh. I was twice humbled, once by Chinese kung-fu, once by Western technology.

Although it was still the weekend, Hou had a fengshui consultation scheduled for that afternoon. Passing through the metal grille security door to his office, we placed our shoes in the cupboard and changed into red rubber flip-flops. Immediately, I found myself shuffling along in the slatternly, loose-hipped, slipper-dragging walk that to me, like oyster omelettes, betel nut stands and whole buildings covered in small tiles like public toilets, signifies Taiwan.

As Hou went to wash his face and change from shorts to trousers, I looked around the office. Half a dozen grey desks stood on one side of the central partition. There were a few computers, piles of newspapers and cartons of books Hou had written on the subject of fengshui, including separate 'how to' manuals for men and women. To the right of the entrance was an ornate red altar with flowers, joss, and a photo of Hou's father, who had died the year before. A beautiful Tibetan rug lay draped over a rack in front of Hou's own desk, making a semi-private space for him. The rug came from the Dalai Lama's own rug factory—a gift from the Dalai Lama's nephew, a mate of Hou's.

A corkboard on the wall was layered with clippings from the entertainment pages of the Taiwan papers, most featuring publicity shots of starlets or pop singers. Wavy red texta lines alongside vertical columns of characters in each story highlighted testimonials to the accuracy of Hou's fengshui readings. A singer moved her bed on his advice and she had a hit song! Someone else did the same and found the love of his life! I am trying to remain my usual, sceptical self, attributing much of this stuff to a combination of wishful thinking and serendipity, but I'm impressed.

A confident woman in her fifties, Ms Yang, arrived at the office with a paunchy, worried-looking man in his late forties in tow. She was a friend of Hou's, Mr Yu was a friend of hers. Mr Yu was the manager of a finance company. Hou called her 'elder sister Yang.' She called Hou, who was forty-three, 'Young Hou.' Hou called her friend Mr Yu and Mr Yu addressed Hou as 'Teacher Hou,' a sign of respect.

Mr Yu laid two maps on Hou's desk. One was of his home, the second a detailed blueprint of his office.

Sipping from bottles of flavoured mineral water accurately labelled in English 'Near Water,' we watched as Hou got to work. Mr Yu and Ms Yang leaned across the table, studying every mark that Hou made with his pen on Mr Yu's house plan.

'Yu's divorced,' Ms Yang offered helpfully. 'He wants to know if he'll meet someone new.'

'Not with the bed where it is,' Hou said, shaking his head sympathetically. 'Its position is bad for your career, too.'

Mr Yu, his pudgy face screwed up with concern, slowly rotated the blunt end of a toothpick in his ear as Hou showed him where he needed to shift his bed.

That done, Hou picked up the office blueprint. 'Okay,' he said in English. Turning to the whiteboard hanging behind his desk, he drew what looked like a tic-tac-toe board. In each of the outer squares, he scribbled a character: wind, mountain, water, sky, marsh, fire, thunder, earth. As he was about to explain the significance of these, the phone rang.

'South Africans? Australians? No problem.' He explained that some foreigners wanted a fengshui reading. Mr Yu and Ms Yang looked impressed. 'You can translate for them,' he said to me.

There was more bad news for Mr Yu: he needed to move the chairman of the board out of his big office with a view into a windowless back room where the computing centre was. The point was not the windows but the position of the office. Mr Yu's worry lines deepened on his face. The reception area was in the wrong place as well, Hou told him, illustrating the importance of the position of doors by launching into a riff on imperial history: the gates to the walled capital of Beijing all had different functions; ambassadors entered by one, victorious troops returning from battle by another and so on. Hou's face brightened as he spoke. Watching him, I realised that while Hou undoubtedly enjoyed helping people, as well as testing his theories in practical situations, the real joy in fengshui for him was in the history, the stories, the colour and light and art of it all, as well as the intellectual expeditions into the *I Ching*—not the repositioning of computer centres in company offices.

Mr Yu wiped his perspiring neck with a tissue and drank thirstily from his bottle of Near Water.

Chain-smoking Mild Sevens, Hou regaled his visitors with more fengshui anecdotes, about the late communist premier Zhou Enlai, about a businessman who grew fat because his desk was in the wrong place. Hou's eyes seemed to flicker a warning at Mr Yu's creeping paunch.

There was a commotion on the street below. I went to the small window, which I'd flung open earlier to drain the cloud of cigarette smoke, and peered down. A Christian marching band in white uniforms paraded noisily past under a Chinese banner reading: 'The King is the Light of the World.' I closed the window.

'The chairman of the board,' Mr Yu ventured with obvious discomfort, 'might not be very pleased to lose his office, and they'd have to shift all the computers, and when you move reception there's the question of all the phone lines...'

Hou smiled politely and rubbed his forearms with his palms. 'I can only tell you about the fengshui,' he said.

Mr Yu sighed. 'I'll move the chairman,' he said. 'I'll shift reception.'

Mr Yu's problems solved, or perhaps just beginning, Hou then turned to Ms Yang. Ms Yang was concerned about her daughter. Educated overseas, she was a television star who didn't have a steady boyfriend, didn't want to think about marriage, and worst of all, insisted on asking men out on dates when she wanted to see them. Hou studied the map of her home and concluded that her daughter's bed was in the wrong place. I reckoned it might be the right place, but bit my tongue.

I'd been talking to Hou about feminism ever since meeting him eighteen years earlier in Hong Kong, when he was a singer and I was a reporter. We'd always got along brilliantly despite our differences. He once told me that he thought of me as a mate, a kind of honorary male. I taught him the English phrase: 'I am a male chauvinist pig.'

Later, after Yang and Yu left to sort out their bed and desk issues, Hou asked me to draw a map of my flat in Sydney. I was a bit reluctant. My bed is heavy and I've got the biggest room, so I would be disinclined to take any advice that involved shifting. Although I wasn't entirely convinced of this fengshui business, it would feel a lot like tempting fate were I to get advice to move and then ignore it. Ignorance really was a kind of bliss. I told him that I could do a sketch of the flat, but I wouldn't have a clue which way was north.

'Why don't you call your flatmate? He could work it out.' Hou was keen.

'Okay, okay.' Borrowing Hou's phone, I left a message on the machine for my flatmate, Simon, asking him to draw up a map of the flat, include the points of the compass, and fax it to me.

The following morning, Hou picked me up in a cab and we went to a local television station to film his weekly segment for a popular Saturday night cable show devoted to superstitious practices of all

kinds. The self-mocking name of the show was 'Guihua lianpian'—
'Ghost Stories', a Chinese phrase normally signifying a pack of
lies. In the green room, we were joined by Tian Jiada, a teenage
singer with big eyes and a sweet, open face. He came with a small
entourage: an even younger fellow who introduced himself as Tian's
'student,' and a publicist in a sloppy joe, shorts and platform-
heeled silver running shoes. 'Tian Jiada,' someone whispered to
me, 'is a hot new "idol"!'

Tian gave Hou a copy of his new CD, passing it to him the
traditional way, with two hands and a slight bow. Hou asked Tian
to draw a map of his home and tell him where everyone slept. Tian
lived at home with his parents and sister. Hou had never met Tian
before. He knew nothing about him. 'Your father is a public servant,
head of a department, isn't he?' Tian looked stunned.

Someone from the station handed us bottles of Young Energy
Source mineral water. Hou returned to the matter of Tian's bed.
'You can't tell when a girl likes you, can you?'

Tian's round eyes grew rounder and his jaw dropped. 'This is
scary,' he whispered to me. Before it could get scarier, we were all
summoned to an altar that stood close to the studio entrance. It
was time to appease the god of television entertainment. In Taiwan,
this is not Kerry Packer. The presenters, guests, producers, camera
crew, assistants and I—everyone who was to enter the studio—
gathered round what appeared to me to be a fairly generic ceramic
deity. No satellite dish ears or box-eyes. The deity was surrounded
on the altar by pink plastic plates piled high with bananas,
watermelon, apples and star-fruit. Someone gave each of us a
handful of burning joss sticks and, led by Hou, we bowed to each
of the four directions, stabbed the joss into a large round incense
holder, and trooped onto the set.

Taiwan, for all its flash modernity, skyscrapers, coffee houses
and dance clubs, was at heart a superstitious old peasant with a
healthy regard for fortune-tellers and a ritual for every planting
and every harvest.

The set for this show looked like the lounge of a traditional
Taiwan house, down to the suggestion of bamboo outside the
darkened, latticed 'window.' The stage was covered with brocade-
edged tatami, and in the centre of the stage was a round hole, in
which stood a wooden table. A thin line of smoke drifted up from
a small incense burner in the centre of the table. The presenters

led Hou and Tian over to the hole in the tatami where the table was. They all sat down on the edge and dangled their legs. Organ pipes of varying length hung from bars at the back and side of the stage. There were twelve of them, numbered in texta with Roman numerals. This was a musical instrument of Hou's own invention, based on an interpretation of the *I Ching* and Chinese calendar systems. While producers and cameramen and sound engineers scurried back and forth, attaching microphones and testing angles, Hou asked me my birthday and birth year. He picked up a baton and struck one of the pipes. 'That,' he informed me, 'is your life note.' He then struck another. 'That's this year. They're in harmony. Things will go well for you.' I was relieved. I'm definitely more willing to believe the news when it's good.

Tian wasn't so lucky. His life note was out of tune with the year. His mouth made a big 'O.' Hou smiled reassuringly. He struck another, harmonising note. 'There.' Tian's features fell back into place. 'When you need to make a decision,' Hou instructed Tian, 'go to the piano and hit the note "so." Things will be okay.' Tian nodded, repeating 'so' under his breath.

Later, Hou told me that he would be putting out twelve CDs. People could buy the one appropriate for their birthday; each CD would have two tracks, 'Action' and 'Rest,' which would create harmonising sound environments. 'Do you think it will appeal to New Agers?' he asked. 'What do you think of the English name "Natural Vibrations"?'

'Perfect,' I replied.

During the show, Hou examined Tian's map again. 'You're sleeping in the daughter's place, not the son's. It means that you will be like a girl, obedient and domestic.'

'I do help a lot with the housework,' offered Tian.

'Ah,' Hou scolded, 'is that the business of the son or the daughter?'

I rolled my eyes.

Hou handed Tian a perspex disk the size of a saucer in which was sandwiched a photograph of a Taiwan coin. He invited Tian to spin it six times, thinking of a question he wanted to ask the *I Ching*. Heads (yang), tails (yin), tails, tails, tails, tails. 'What did you ask?' inquired Hou, marking down the hexagram on a small whiteboard.

'Will my new CD sell?'

'Hmm,' Hou replied. 'Maybe not immediately. Think long-term.'

Tian looked crestfallen. His bed was in the wrong place, his notes were out of tune and according to the *I Ching* he wasn't going to make the Top 10.

'You can't do anything about the weather,' Hou pronounced, 'but you can get an umbrella. Fengshui is your umbrella. It is also your compass and petrol station.'

After the break, Hou recorded another segment for the program. Standing in front of the camera, rocking back and forth like a rabbi at prayer, speaking fast, he gave the *I Ching* forecast for the coming week: 'For those of you born between 2 January and 2 February, Tuesday will be your lucky day. Don't sign any contracts on Thursday and careful playing mah-jong—don't place big bets.' I'd have thought that good advice any day of the week. 'For those born between 3 February and 5 March, Wednesday is your lucky day...' He worked his way through the calendar, the crew listening carefully for their own birthdays. It was a wrap.

Only Tuesday, but Hou was looking weary. His fengshui consultancy was a relatively new venture. 'I am prepared to work really hard for the next two years,' he'd told me earlier as we sipped cups of coffee while waiting for his first visitor of the day to arrive. 'Then, I hope that the business can start to run itself.'

The visitor, a Mr Chen from Taichung, a city in central Taiwan, detailed his theories on how the financial wellbeing of corporations and the career paths of politicians and pop stars are related to the pitch and sound of their names. He told us he communicates with spirits and can make flowers grow on vibrations alone.

'Good, good.' Hou nodded, his eyes slightly narrowed, a polite smile stretching his lips. He ran one palm up the opposite arm from wrist to elbow and back and then switched hands—a gesture I recognised as Hou's boredom tic. He asked Mr Chen what he based his theories on.

'I don't use reference books,' said Mr Chen, nodding earnestly. 'Some of my ideas come straight from the gods.'

Hou blinked. He explained that in working out his own system of 'natural vibrations,' he consulted over 400 books on the *I Ching*, including every classical source he could find. He read books on astronomy and calculus. He read about how an ancient sage cut bamboo into twelve lengths and buried them in the earth. Each vibrated in its turn and season, informing the farmers when to plant and when to harvest. Hou's own pipes, he told us, 'are based on a similar system that puts together music, time and the calendar.'

Once on the subject of his pipes, Hou perked up. The ancient Chinese, he said, used bamboo poles and shadows to measure the circumference of the world. 'Do you believe that?' he asked, then proceeded to draw diagrams that illustrated exactly how it worked. He spun the conversation onto the subject of cantilevered beams and Han Dynasty architectural achievements that no one in the 2,000 years since has been able to replicate. I sat back in my chair and smiled. I loved Hou's rants. You never knew where they'd end up. This one ended up deep in Taoist philosophy.

We all sipped at our tea and nodded silently for a while, three separate worlds of thought spinning around the same sun.

Then Mr Chen spoke. With an air of having saved his best bit for last, he revealed that he'd worked out an idea for a song that Hou should write: 'Because it contains every hexagram of the *I Ching*,' he said, eyes shining, 'it will contain the universe. It will be a pop song that will last forever.'

Hou smiled wanly. He asked me what I enjoy the most.

I said the feeling of being creative, of writing something that I like. He asked Mr Chen. Mr Chen said 'entering the meditative state.'

'How about you?' I asked Hou.

'I love it when I have nothing to do, no demands on me at all, no worries, nothing. Lying on my bed and watching the curtain flutter in the breeze. When I lived in New Zealand, I made fires in the fireplace and then watched them for hours. Like a cat.'

Mr Chen listened, a dubious expression on his face. 'The Buddha's light casts no shadow,' he said after a while.

Hou rubbed his arms again and opened another pack of Mild Sevens. I went to the window to let in some air.

On Wednesday, Hou took a call from a woman who had been scammed out of half a million Taiwan dollars—some AUD$21,000. Should she get gangsters to beat up the men who conned her? She wanted him to consult the *I Ching* for her. 'Act rationally,' he advised her. 'Under no circumstances hire gangsters. Pay your debts slowly. Sleep in a protective position.' He then discussed different ways she might handle the situation.

'I hate taking money from people like that,' he told me afterwards. 'They're all people with problems. And sometimes their problems are very serious.'

'Do people without problems come to you as well?'

'Yes. But it's these people who really need help. Sometimes I can't take their money. It doesn't feel right.'

'But this is how you're earning your living.'

'That's right.' Hou sighed.

On Friday evening, the Taiwan equivalent of the Grammies were being held, and Hou had been invited onto an entertainment news show the night before to predict the winners. It was a long time since he was part of the pop scene, and he didn't know who most of the nominees were. Yanmei, his wife, briefed him before we left. She cautioned him not to be too exact or insistent with his answers: the winners would be announced the following night.

Yanmei was in her late twenties but looked sixteen and had a youthful exuberance that was very appealing. She possessed a solid, practical streak that perfectly balanced Hou's airy-fairy approach to life. She worked for the company, called 'Heirs, Inc' after one of Hou's most famous songs, 'Heirs of the Dragon.' She was a lot less inclined than Hou to give out freebies.

Cameras rolling, the female presenter spun Hou's giant coin and the male one slapped it down on the table. Spin, slap. Yang. Spin, slap. Yin. And so on for six tries. Hou drew the resulting hexagram, which, he explained, signified running into a waterfall while climbing a mountain. 'Which of the nominees in this category has overcome quite a few obstacles, and come at his career from a side path?' he asked. They thought about it a second and named one. And so they went through all the categories, spin, slap, spin, slap, spin, slap. The list was drawn.

On Friday evening, Hou took me to see a 'spirit calligrapher' whom he considered extremely good. He had visited Dr Li several times before and thought I'd find it an interesting experience. In the tiny foyer of Dr Li's flat, we paid 1,000 Taiwan dollars each—$42—and signed our names in a book. The flat was full of scrolls. They hung over every available space on the wall and protruded from plastic tubs. Some forty people milled about, mostly women aged from their early twenties up through infinity. There was an air of excitement as the middle-aged Dr Li entered.

After chatting a while, he moved to stand before an altar placed above a large table. We followed. After bowing to the gods, and offering them plates of fruit, he appeared to enter a trance. His eyes didn't roll into his head or anything; he just went inward in a way we could all feel. Everyone went very quiet. He consulted the list of names of everyone who'd come that evening and selected a brush from a rack on a long table set with brushes, saucers of ink and sheets of paper. He dipped the brush into water, mixed it with ink and painted like, I suppose, a man possessed, with utter concentration and at an almost manic speed. He'd look at a name on the list, and then paint an image such as bamboo, flowers, or landscapes in a traditional but naive style. Then he calligraphed a string of roman letters in black—the 'spirit writing' that would unlock the secrets of the picture—and wrote the person's name onto the painting as well.

His wife, a moon-faced woman with a lacquered hairdo, washed, dried and replaced the brushes as he discarded them. Other helpers removed the paintings as they were done, taking them to the drying racks and replacing them with fresh sheets of paper. When the paintings were dry enough to be handled, another group of helpers took them over, looking up the equivalent sounds to the spirit writing in dictionaries of classical Japanese, producing several different possible 'translations' into Chinese characters.

When it was all over, Li smiled and informed one of his visitors that whatever she was thinking about was useless.

A small whisper of amazement went through the room. It was one of those mysteries-of-the-Orient moments.

Now through with his trance, the amiable Dr Li sat down at his desk. Everyone pulled up small red plastic stools and gathered round. He called out a name. A woman in her thirties brought her stool forward. Her painting was of two bamboos crossed by a third. 'So,' he said, 'what do you want to know?'

'Should I go to America with my daughter?' she asked. 'We'd like her to go to school there.'

Dr Li shook his head. 'Only if you want to risk your husband having an affair while you're gone.'

The woman looked faint. She nodded weakly as he pointed out how the third bamboo crossed over and separated the other two. Her daughter would kiss that American education goodbye. I felt sad for her and wondered, not for the first time, at the strength of apparently well-educated people's beliefs in this sort of thing.

He held up a picture of a snail. 'Jia Peilin.'

'That's me,' I squeaked. Jia Peilin is my Chinese name. The words on the painting were *mangong chuxi*, or slow labour produces results, though the word for results is also a word for play or movie.

'A novel of hers is being made into a film,' Hou informed the interested crowd.

Dr Li pointed out all the grass under the snail. 'You are well nourished.' I certainly had been eating well all week—Yanmei had seen to that. 'You are also a "chosen person".' He pondered the implications of this. 'That could mean you are one of the Goddess of Mercy's little helpers on earth.'

'Or,' Hou offered, 'just Jewish—the chosen people. She's Jewish.'

Dr Li nodded enthusiastically. 'Yes, maybe both.'

He informed me that things were going well for me but I really ought to have a husband.

Yeah yeah. Tell it to Bridget Jones. Politely, I murmured something about looking into that when I got back to Australia.

Hou's painting was of a basket full of fish, carried on a pole. The basket was loosely woven and some of the fish were falling out. Dr Li advised him to cut down on all the expense-account wining and dining, to hire a mature assistant, and plan his business affairs more wisely and thoroughly. He was losing too many fish. I thought that Yanmei, with her sharp business sense, would probably agree.

When Dr Li finished all the readings, the tension in the room eased. It turned into a kind of party when the assistants passed around sliced bananas, pears and yellow watermelon from the altar.

When we got home, Yanmei excitedly related how nearly every one of the predictions Hou had made for the music awards had come true.

'How do you like that?' Hou grinned.

On Saturday, Hou taught a master class in fengshui to about half a dozen students, including a beautician, a businessman and a lawyer. The students' kit included one of Hou's books on fengshui reading, a photocopied *I Ching* kit and a compass. He wore coloured braces, a tan polo shirt and black trousers; when he stood sideways to write on the chalkboard his round little tummy protruded over his stick legs like a beachball on chopsticks. His lecture ranged from Babylonian astronomy to physics, the dangers of living too near to radio transmitter towers, and Confucian injunctions against incest. He then demonstrated what they all had to do with fengshui. We learned not to build L-shaped houses, and the basic principles for determining the correct place for your bed within the home. He mentioned that he'd worked out a southern-hemisphere variation. Like the rest of the class, I was swept away in the flow of Hou's words, only occasionally wondering at his logic.

Then, the fax machine pinged and trilled. Hou stopped talking and we all looked over at it. My flatmate Simon had finally gotten around to sending through the map of our flat.

'How's that for timing?' I joked.

'Good, good. Really good,' Hou answered. He made a few quick calculations and showed the map to the class. My bed was fine. Ideal. Health, wealth and happiness was mine. Phew.

The position of Simon's bed, on the other hand, was potentially disastrous for his career, health and love life. It ought to be, hmm, where our bathroom was. But all was not lost on the fengshui front: Hou declared that if Simon kept the bathroom clean, airy and bright, everything would be fine. If he didn't, in addition to jobs and relationships mucking up, he'd get respiratory problems and people would talk about him behind his back. It occurred to me to get this in writing.

I flew back to Sydney the following day and showed Simon the diagnosis. He bought a mop, air freshener and cleaning supplies and within two days the bathroom was clean, airy and bright, and remained ever so.

I love fengshui. I believe in fengshui. Fengshui changed my life.

Let's Reclaim the Game

John Carroll

My apprehensions were first roused at the 1993 Grand Final. It was one of those sunny afternoons in late September in which the air has a special early spring quality—that fresh spirit-lifting tang and lustre. The Melbourne Cricket Ground was packed, yet the atmosphere once the game started was strangely flat. This was not, moreover, because the game quickly turned into a rout, Essendon crushing Carlton.

It was because half the crowd—at least—had no deep personal involvement. They were there because of corporate block booking—executives, clients, and guests having a pleasant afternoon out attending a major event. It was no longer 90,000 fans on the edges of their seats, their stomachs churning with worry, on the instant finding themselves screaming with exhilaration, then dropping their heads, covering their eyes, unable to look.

Standing-room was no longer packed with nervous shuffling, pale, jubilant, tortured fanatics present at a day they would remember for the rest of their lives, they who would decades later recount to their grandchildren, their eyes misting over: 'I was there in 1993, I was close by on the half-forward flank when Michael Long got the ball, stopped, glanced towards three hovering Carlton players, they mesmerised, before he sauntered off, casually weaving past them to thread a goal.'

If the custodians of the game could sacrifice the atmosphere of the greatest day of their year to the balance sheet, where would they not be prepared to go? Did they not realise that the goose they cared for depended in its capacity to lay on its own morale? The people loved their game because of some strange magical property in the whole—in everything that went with it, from daggy beanies to exhilarated identification with a godlike passage of play.

Perhaps 'charisma' is a better word. A sensitive intangible essence, it is vulnerable to a mere whiff of chill air, or pollution, enough for many to turn their backs sadly, and never return.

This is not to question that adaptation to the times was necessary. The conflicts here exemplify the ambivalent pressures of globalisation. Continuing vitality has depended on changes that cater to television, going national, reducing the violence on field. Two years ago the Australian Football League could pride itself on record crowds, the success of the Sydney Swans, potentially that of the Brisbane Lions and ever-new levels of funding. But the age-old message that the art of custodian requires a deft balance of change and the preservation of tradition has been rammed home in 2000— with plunging attendances, and across the nation, growing insecurity in financially marginal clubs, and the failure of the new 'state-of-the-art' stadium at Docklands.

Colonial Stadium it was named, after a financial and insurance conglomerate. 'What's in a name?' Shakespeare might ask. Nothing, the AFL would reply, apart from sponsorship dollars. Yet, once upon a time the people titled their grounds—Windy Hill, Punt Road, Victoria Park. All those are now gone. Of the old that remain Princess Park has been metamorphosed into Optus Oval, and Geelong's Kardinia Park into Shell Stadium.

Colonial is symbolic of what has gone wrong. Its conception was radical—in terms of the traditions of Aussie Rules. It assumed as the way of the future the American model of the multi-purpose entertainment venue. This had worked in Melbourne with Crown Casino, locals flocking to a building they liked from the outset—a minority to gamble.

But football was not virgin terrain. To innovate required taking on the vernacular—local tradition, that is, with its eccentric and untidy customs, its deep, established ways of going about things. That vernacular had accepted heaps of change in the last decade— and especially the loss of the freedom around lunchtime on Saturday to make a spontaneous decision to go along to the footy, knowing from habit that there would be quick and easy access at the local ground. We can now but surmise about a growing collective unease at the levels of disruption to the game.

Then came full-blown Corporatism. Colonial had a roof which would be closed whenever weather threatened, thus banishing wind, rain and mud—bowing to the logic of convenience and comfort. It geared itself to advance ticketing, by means of credit cards, thus excluding a majority of the less well-off fans. The reality in the early days was tens of thousands stuck in queues outside the state-of-the-art stadium listening to the first quarter via the tiny roar of the handful inside, before many gave up and went home.

Corporatism in its self-cocooned, congratulatory pride forgot basics, such as turf will not grow without sunlight, which means that at Melbourne's latitude and with encompassing high stands the surface will need a miracle to ever last—in practice that means waiting for the invention of a new hybrid supergrass. By the mid-point of Colonial's first season its grass had indeed not turned to mud, but to sand. Fortunately the unthinkable is not thinkable—replacing the surface with Astroturf—for Aussie Rules is evidently too fast for American plastic. Jokes also abounded about no lines of sight, seats that only existed on the tickets, abandoned coaches' boxes, commentators blinded by reflecting glass, and acoustics that split ears even when the ground is half full and the roof open.

The big money is now in television. Aggregate ratings will be higher if games are spread over more days, and at different hours. In 2000 one round might stretch from Thursday till Monday, and on a single day from noon till midnight. Hence the demise of the Saturday afternoon match—who cares about the fans! The TV camera can project virtual ads to cover the paddocks of vacant seats; it can simulate the roar of the non-existent crowd. The players, now paid such extravagant sums—eighteen year olds in their first year, $75,000—are entertainers professional enough to perform on cue in an empty stadium. And why not? International soccer has gone this way, and look how successful it is!

Why not—because this game is singular, and it is ours. It resists a world in which a global slick of uniformity—the aesthetics and dramatics of the airport lounge—is taking over. It is thick with that rare blend of experience and memory, of smells and sounds that make people feel they belong, that this is home and I like it. Its quality is there in the wild, nasal flamboyance of a Jack Dyer or Rex Hunt commentary—comic, absurd, brilliantly inventive while oozing local cadence and slang, yet at times grave with nostalgia. It is there at the 'G'—where else—in the contrast between the members, their stands and the rest—an amused play of derisive distinction which is full of affection. Needless to say, the stands at Docklands are standardised, tidied up—that is, all the same.

Never has Australian English found a greater exponent than Jack 'Captain Blood' Dyer. His radio commentaries surfed along on a waywardness of metaphor and syntax. My own nostalgia for home during a five-year period as a student in England was never as acute as once when a fellow expatriate played a Dyer Grand Final tape—my team was not playing. I recall sitting in awe listening to two-minute sentences, metaphor piled on metaphor, clause on clause, the subject always 'he', the dramatic intensity building up relentlessly following 'he' and his exploits, until the climax was finally revealed—the identity of the player. No doubt the goal was already long kicked.

The resonance was that of the Homeric battlefield, transplanted three millennia and ten thousand miles. I played the tape in Cambridge to George Steiner, whose literary criticism is well known for its focus on language and translation. He was spellbound by the evocative incantatory flair and originality of the English.

And legend has it that Captain Blood, once captain of the mighty Tigers, was the man who shed more blood, and evicted more teeth into the hallowed turf than any other ruck-rover come centre-half-back in the history of the game. Huge and splendid, a modern Achilles, godlike, he was capable of turning a match by his own ferocity of will. Years later, on radio, the most striking thing about him was the richness of his reminiscences, his praise for the greats of old, and the warmth and care with which he talked to eager young boys about their heroes. To me, Jack Dyer was one of the nation's great educators.

It is knowledge of such a time, not long ago, one still seeping into the present, exemplified by men like Captain Blood, that anchors the loyalty of the fans. Immersed in love of the traditions of their game, they are outraged about some of what is happening now.

Now we are witnessing yet another example of the new corporate indifference to the people. Any sense of public responsibility, of being a servant of the vast ramshackle collective that is the game, is shrugged off. In this case, the defence goes, the players want more money, so do the clubs, so why should the custodians say no?

The clubs are themselves struggling to resist the same pressures. Last year Geelong persuaded one of its greatest players of the recent era, Gary Hocking, to change his name for a week so that he could officially enter the team list and the *Footy Record* as 'Whiskas'—an advertising gimmick funded by the tinned cat food company. The effect on the player and the team is hard to gauge. It might be shrugged off as a lark, Hocking secure enough in his identity to take this as a bit of fun. Or it might sow the seeds of unconscious doubt about how a club that lays one of its senior players open to such ridicule can be taken seriously. The power of the football ethos is deeply tied to some elusive, indefinable code of honour, which means that a club has to move very carefully when the dignity of its players is at issue.

The Kangaroos, one of the dominant teams of the 90s—until recently North Melbourne—are near broke and half-uprooted. Given a pitifully low supporter base, they have unsuccessfully tested alternative home pastures in Sydney. The Kangaroos' management is understandably desperate. Late in the 2000 season the team played one match in orange jumpers, not the regular blue and white. They were sponsored by the Orange telephone company. The team looked absurd, and played as if it felt absurd—played without pride. From that point the Kangaroo season collapsed, a couple of weeks later being thrashed in the first final by a record margin of twenty goals. By the end of the finals their most reliable player of the year, Peter Bell, announced he was leaving for Fremantle. It goes without saying that without funds a club cannot survive, but at what price honour?

Narrow rationalist thinking is accompanied by the temptation of the successful to presume that, because what they have done has prospered, whatever else they plan will work. The classical wisdom of our culture warned about the Midas touch. Do the AFL Commissioners ever descend from their plush 5-star glass boxes? Do they assume they can just throw up a new stadium, computer-simulate flavour, atmosphere, evocative sound? Do they take it for granted that they can do better than their predecessors?

Our local example of how to get it right, the MCG, has evolved over many decades into a sporting venue people love. Just to arrive there after a time away, pass through the turnstiles and on into the gloomy concrete intestines, breathe in the characteristic odour of dankness, meat pie and keg beer, then climb any set of stairs, is to find oneself strangely and joyfully at home. Something incontrovertibly real possesses this open circular cathedral, the way light floods into it, the immaculately mown green expanse below—and in spite of the felt presence of the ghosts of sporting greatness. The evolution of this human creation of right order has depended on an unfathomable mix of some good design, slow painstaking change drawing upon generations of experience, and luck. The MCG has its own spirit. How do you plan that?

The new corporate arrogance was exemplified by Channel Seven management, headed by principal shareholder, Kerry Stokes—who lives in Sydney. It suspended one of its football commentators for criticising the playing surface at Docklands, in which it has a major investment stake. At the time the turf was so bad that a solitary gust of wind, like some celestial golfer, could rip out huge divots. The journalist had merely referred to one flank as 'death valley'. Other commentators, on radio station 3AW, quick to express concern about the censorship of fair comment, may have saved his job.

The fate of the particular journalist is of less significance here than the general effect of this flexing of editorial muscle by an ownership feeling a twitch in the hip-pocket nerve. All Channel Seven commentators will have had doubt cast over future comment critical of any enterprise in which their owner has a financial stake. They are only human. They have been robbed of that certain innocence necessary to their professionalism. From now on self-censorship is inevitable, and the more potent in that much of the time it will be unwitting.

So the Marxist caricature of the rapacious entrepreneur, with no vision beyond his own ego and his own belly, threatens finally to become reality in the West. The times are proving that the noble domain of sport is not immune.

It would be wrong just to blame the executives. What about the rest of us, we whose duty it is to do the checking? This is the period in which the intellectual Left, with a major real role for the first time since the 1930s, went missing. The ALP's younger Turks became indistinguishable in their beliefs from a John Hewson— or, for that matter, the key AFL power-broker, Graeme Samuel. Concurrently, their university counterparts enveloped themselves in impenetrable postmodernist abstraction. Just at the moment that Marx was ditched by his intellectual heirs his powerful analytical polemic gained renewed bite. Take the famous passage from *The*

Communist Manifesto:

> The bourgeoisie... has left remaining no other nexus
> between man and man than naked self-interest, than callous
> 'cash payment'. It has drowned the most heavenly ecstasies
> of religious fervour, of chivalrous enthusiasm, of philistine
> sentimentalism, in the icy water of egotistical calculation.

But Aussie Rules is owned by the people. Steeped in the vernacular, as can be heard every game day on talkback radio, it needs to be reclaimed from the AFL. The first positive sign, a big one, was the universal condemnation of Colonial Stadium. Polarisation spread. Handled badly and it could turn into all-out cultural war, with the rival armies based respectively at the people's ground, the MCG, and at AFL/Channel Seven's Colonial. So far that has not happened.

Australia is in part a federalist culture. Each club has its own ways and style, its own reservoir of fortitude. There are variations from State to State, suburb to suburb and between social classes. These differences are there to be proclaimed. One suggestion put to me by a friend is a boycott of AFL merchandising—almost every item bearing the official AFL logo is manufactured overseas, out of cheap, drab synthetics. The fans should return to knitting their own scarves and beanies, from Australian wool, which is receptive to dying in the rich original colours. Orange would be precluded. Such a simple, visible act could serve as a rallying badge of tribal assertion.

Australian Rules football is one arena in which the people can take on rampant corporatism and win. Increasing unease about 'globalisation' was expressed in September this year by mass three-day demonstrations outside the World Economic Forum in Melbourne. Those demonstrations were gravely weakened in their impact by lack of concrete focus, by the absence of specific issues clear-cut in their human costs. In the case of football no fan needs to be a gifted social scientist to chart with some plausibility, and in colourful detail, the gains and the losses that have followed from rapid economic change. Moreover, the vitality of this arena is illustrated by the fact that there is no need for government to step in, to check the excesses of globalisation.

By the end of the 2000 season there were signs of the AFL backing down. Next year's fixture, for example, will return to a more traditional format. Any cautious optimism, however, needs to be restricted to the city. In the bush, declining population and resources are killing local leagues.

In the booming metropolis the weight of public opinion could command an influential media—notably newspaper and radio—and forge its discontent into a two-pronged weapon. There was the financial leverage of losses at Docklands, the power of the bottom line. There was, perhaps even more persuasively, the power of social shaming. A major attraction for many of the entrepreneurs and executives who become presidents of football clubs is the status they receive. On the instant they become well known and respected public figures. Very few among their number were ever star players so for them, in terms of glory, this is as good as it has been, and as good as it is going to get. The last thing they want to attract is the stigma of ruining the game.

In Australia today there is no more visible, concrete example than the AFL of the workings of globalisation, of its potential for both progress and ruin, and of the way citizens can play a role in determining the direction it will take. It might just happen that the people, with continuing vigilance, succeed in reclaiming their game.

The Kingdom of the Imagination

Jack Hibberd

'I thought he [Jack Hibberd] had passed away.'

Daniel Keene
24 August 1999 3LO, Jon Faine

Kandinsky said towards the conclusion of his life that if you live long enough you can be famous three times and dead three times. I have been famous once and dead once.

It appears that the last is the wish of some of my theatrical comrades—at least dead, silent, or silenced, as an artist and thinker. Soon after the above in his interview with the highly reticent Jon Faine, Daniel Keene asserted that I had proposed a moratorium on funding for the performing arts because I had 'stopped writing plays'. The clear implications here are that my proposal had been motivated by vengefulness, bitterness, and vanity.

I recently returned home from five weeks overseas to digest controversy and hate mail. The prime cause of the frenzy had been my submission early in the year to the Nugent Enquiry, a submission greeted without an echo—except for a bureaucratic receipt: number 1. Later in the year my proposal, titled 'A Grand Denial', attracted publication in *Overland* (number 155), and thus public appreciation.

The submission argues that the bulk of funded theatre as it is practised in Australia today exists as a child of the nineteenth century, and the games that he plays are stylistically and existentially anachronistic. Even the mammoth Shakespeare finds it impossible to elude entirely the prevailing modes of Edwardian naturalism, psychological melodrama, and pantomimic camp romps.

The ineluctably central and principal argued theme of the submission is that events, individuals and organisations have conspired to deny Australian audiences the rich fruits of twentieth-century theatrical Modernism, the greatest epoch of stage inventiveness since the English and Spanish renaissances, and the most diverse ever in stage history.

This has left us with deprived, untutored and ignorant audiences. Serious readers of fiction are free to, and do, enjoy the plenitudes of Proust, Joyce, Musil, Faulkner, Marquez etc. Theatre-lovers are dependent on what is served up to them by our taste-framers, at government expense.

I should add, that by Modernism I mean the ensuing movements and individuals, their theories and practices: Symbolism, Alfred Jarry, Expressionism, Dada, Surrealism, Pirandello, Brecht, the Theatre of the Absurd, Artaud, Dario Fo, the Polish avant-garde, and a few others.

Theatre once occupied, illuminated and reshaped the very dream and nightmare centres of social, spiritual existence. It increasingly languishes on the periphery (despite having homes in the middle of cities), because much of it is Deadly (Peter Brook's term) and impertinent.

My proposal for a five-year funding moratorium, *and the putting-aside of 80 percent of projected monies* (my emphasis), was designed to revitalise the theatre from the bottom up, constructively; to relocate it at the heart of living; to make it cheaper (actor-intensive, design-lean) and to compel it to be expressive of inner modern experiences, and finally to remove it from the gormless backyards of literal representation and restore it to the kingdom of the imagination.

Incredibly, the core argument of 'A Grand Denial' has been fastidiously ignored, silenced, by commentators, especially by those who have bothered to read the document. Instead, they have latched on to the superficial, the literal, or have become personal, attributing to me most mean and begrudging motives.

Around the time 'A Grand Denial' was published I made an appearance on ABC TV 'Arts', once again tackling the neglect of Modernism and the need for a moratorium on funding to swab the decks. This really riled the deckhands and passengers.

Raymond Gill (the *Age*, 16/8) gets off to a crackling start in his response by brandishing the portmanteau platitude 'baby-boomers'. He seems to think that the whole of the generation born in the later 40s and early 50s were culturally, politically, homogeneous, when in fact they were quite divided.

I, for example, supported the wrong side of the Vietnam War until reasonably late. At the Pram Factory I had many hectic disputes with feminists—not so much over the furthering of female emancipation: I forcibly argued that their theatre had to be as good as their politics, a principle never attained.

The political idealism (eventually dominant), the broad intellectual curiosities, and the informed nationalism of the 1970s have certainly evolved into individualism, materialist careerism and slavish Americanisation across the 90s. This irrefutably entails a decline.

I am not a victim of nostalgic disgruntlement and intolerant ageing, as suggested by Gill (again indulging in automatic platitude). Since these do not motivate me, they have nothing to do with my hard-eyed analysis of our theatre today. This facile tactic more importantly directed attention away, inciting a younger generation to scowl at a fuddy-duddy baby-boomer impervious to the inevitabilities of progress.

Further on, in relation to TV 'Arts', Gill states 'Maybe it was selective editing, but Hibberd gave the impression that nothing of worth had been done since his *heyday*.' (my emphasis, *pace* Keene).

In the ABC interview I made very guarded remarks about the Australian Performing Group, asserting that they at least made some attempt to come to grips with Modernism.

In truth the APG only partly grappled with some of Modernism's sinewy innovations, and were significant, memorable, for the creation of a uniquely expressive Australian physical and comic style, which was native and only slantingly related to Modernism The two must not be confused.

I did not give the impression that nothing of worth has been produced since my 'heyday'. This once again imputes that my motives are spiteful and conceited. I would not promote such an impression because I would be claiming that the twenty plays I have written since 1977 (*pace* Daniel Keene) are worthless.

To the contrary, some of the plays I have composed during the 1990s are superior to the best of my first period, and variously blend and bend many of Modernism's strands. Gill is not only mean-spirited but irrational—surely as a professional arts editor he knows I am still writing plays and having them produced. Or does he too wish me moribund and mute?

Geoffrey Milne (*Eureka Street*, vol. 9/no. 8) proves comparatively fair and generous, sidestepping *ad hominem*, degrading imputations. Nevertheless, the title of the article—'Australian Theatre in Crisis' (again)—and Milne's declaration that Australian theatre is always in crisis—belittles the case mounted in 'A Grand Denial'.

If the Australian theatre is always in crisis, then its potentates have not in the past seemed terribly aware of it, and now hardly seem aware (except in the trite economic sense), and assuredly do not act upon any rare constitutional awareness. This crisis is the most grave and profound because it is *existential*.

Again, remarkably (because like Gill he has read 'A Grand Denial'), Milne ignores the central argument concerning Modernism and its blanket repudiation and burial in Australian theatre. He does not produce any sonorous evidence that drowns out, silences, my case.

The 'new directors', from John Bell to Neil Armfield, from Bruce Myles to Ariette Taylor, have not engaged, practised, and pushed forward Modernism—chiefly because they have not bothered with such an enterprise.

Nor have other artists quoted, such as Andrew Bovell, Timothy Daly, Daniel Keene, and Raimondo Cortese. To these could be added Katherine Thompson, Elizabeth Coleman and Matt Cameron. These playwrights either work the lodes of psychological melodrama or the maze-like tunnels of Postmodernism.

Postmodernism, it should be pointed out, has little to do with Modernism, being a chronological term, depicting that which followed Modernism, intellectually and creatively, in time. It is not an evolution out of, or even an imaginitive reaction against, Modernism. The preoccupation with relativity, patterns and games of Postmodernism render it a troubled and troublesome aesthetic for the theatre. Drama in a crucial sense axles on ritualised and meaning-charged games of life and death. Postmodernism's theatre entails games about games: a formula for emptiness.

The very few exceptions that prove the rule about the dearth and death of Modernism are Kosky's *The Dybbuk* (Artaud), Michael Kantor's *Excavations* (Brecht, Beckett), and Justus Neumann's *The Last Days of Mankind* (Georg Grosz, Expressionism).

Gill talks of the breakthroughs made by me, 'David Williamson, Sue Ingleton, John Romeril, and others'. How my good friend Sue Ingleton, a gifted stand-up comedienne and seasonal actor, earns inclusion as an innovator is quite beyond me. It suggests the arts editor has a palsied grip on our recent theatre history and its significant forces.

The breakthroughs made in the 1970s largely entailed collectively bold treatments of Australian language, social mores, and history, with enhanced comic and physical expressiveness. Much of this last quality has disappeared from our mainstages today, where the Theatre of Arthritis and Eloquent Heads looms once again.

With respect to Modernism, I was then affected by Pinter and Beckett; John Romeril was inspired by Brecht and Off-Off Broadway. Williamson, comprehensively untouched by Modernism, merely extended (and still does), less turgidly, the habits of Arthur Miller's psychological melodramas.

Wesley Enoch, in a friendly response to 'A Grand Denial', yet again does not accost my spinal argument, and indeed dismisses it with an astonishing utterance: 'As we are reminded over and over again we can never go back to a past which really didn't exist anyway.'

I am urging the incorporation of vital ingredients of the past, not replicating literally the past. Why bother with Shakespeare? Why bother doing *Box the Pony* and Enoch's *Stolen* in a few decades time? Why bother reading the exemplary works of history, records of and testaments to their epochs, histories that ethically keep alive the tragedies of the Holocaust and the decimation of Aborigines?

Here is Enoch once more: 'It amazes me that history is never seen as that thing happening now.' Is Wesley a hierophant of the cults of Instantaneity and Amnesia, sister ideologies to Postmodernism? Those who are ignorant of the past are doomed to repeat it; and those who deny the past are ignorant. The director of *Stolen* is not ignorant.

And yes, theatre is 'designed to be in constant flux'. Its essential character entails dynamic ephemerality (which creates urgency and impact). But elevate and rarefy that ephemerality through a cult of instantaneity, but hack it out of living thinking time through a cult of amnesia, then you court huge perils: lack of urgency and impact.

I would have few misgivings about including Aboriginal theatre in my moratorium on funding—in contrast to Katharine Brisbane ('The

Arts and the Pre-emptive Buckle', the *Weekend Australian*, 30/10) who would have these artists as the exception. Over the last decade or so they have created a need for a non-nineteenth-century style of theatre that authentically crosses demarcations of colour, class and age. Recent national successes would suggest that, in a temporarily fundless climate, they could survive and thrive, thus providing an artistic *model* for our antiquarian and semi-parasitic white theatre.

Wesley worries about who will pay the interest on government capital loans which enabled the erection of theatres and art centres. That could readily come out, annually, of the 20 percent of projected monies *not* put aside. I am not advocating demolition. Besides, many of these complex edifices could harbour attractive, lucrative cinemas—orthodox and IMAX—while new theatre companies could be allowed to emerge organically out of communities elsewhere, communities which might discover civic pride and a depth in their pockets as they do in Germany.

Unconnected to all of this, I would have no misgivings about including opera in my funding proposal. Opera hogs a huge hoard of the Australia Council budget for comparatively few people, among them stalwarts of the Nugent Enquiry. Grand Opera (which I love) is a nineteenth-century phenomenon par excellence, and now Capitalism's badge of Conspicuous Consumption. If the well-heeled crave opera, they can pay $500 or more a soft seat.

While on the subject of money, we have Raymond Gill approaching his end sensationally. He says I suggest 'starving those who make theatre of all funding for five years'. Why should they starve? Those theatre artists who can create a new theatre that the public really needs, that sings to them, for which they are prepared to pay—these artists will not starve. Only the artistically impertinent, their sycophants and parasites, networkers and their sanctimonious congregations of arts bureaucrats, will starve.

More importantly, Gill fails, conspicuously, to mention my putting-aside of projected monies for possible future use. Had he done so, it would have diminished the impact, and lessened my perfidy. At the end of five years there could be a funding bonanza. And five years is not a long time, even in the life of an arts editor. With this travesty of omission, Gill has lifted kerbside journalism to new heights.

Here is Raymond's end: 'This from the writer who in 1996 received a (*sic*) Australia Council $80,000 two-year fellowship.'

Thump. For asperity of spirit and anti-intellectual steam this takes the cake.

Is an Australia Council grant meant to buy your silence? Is criticism of the state of Australian theatre an act of gross ungenerosity and sedition?

Why does Gill adopt this censorious and spite-engendering stance? It could be well argued, and more to the professional point, that my proposals in 'A Grand Denial' constituted an act of courage.

You don't need to be an Einstein to work out that such proposals would render me extremely unpopular with funding organisations, theatre companies, arts agenda-setters, the whole of the dominant profession. This would make it much more difficult for me to secure assistance, and new productions of my plays. Does Gill really think that I did not forsee this?

I am the least paranoid of creatures, yet have recently observed resentments and blanketings issuing from the generation beneath me (that of Gill, Keane, Faine, the authors of hate mail etc.).

Towards the end of last year's Performing Arts Market in Adelaide (conducted at festival time) a lunch was held for the participants. Douglas Horton (Chamber Made Opera) joined my table and quickly asked what I was doing there. I told him I had a production of *A Stretch of the Imagination* on the go. 'Oh,' he said, with vinegar in his voice, 'you've dusted that off have you?'

At that same market a person (belonging to the same generation), whose name I shall not divulge for diplomatic reasons, spent time, I was informed from three different sources, poisoning the minds of visitors against the 'text-based' *Stretch*—texts (can you believe it?) were deemed unfashionable. Whatever, we found it almost impossible to attract international festival directors near the show.

Jon Faine knows that I am very much alive and still writing. Nonetheless he chose not to refute Keene, and allowed falsehood unimpeded dissemination across the airwaves.

In an ironic coda to all of this, we had Gill, the master-blanketer, asserting (the *Age*, 13/10), with breath-arresting self-satisfaction, that debates in the arts are 'usually initiated and conducted by arts journalists'.

He persists: 'No wonder we seize upon any utterance by Barry Kosky—at least he expresses an opinion.' At the risk of sounding gratuitous, 'A Grand Denial' is chock-a-block with argument and evidence, opinion if you like. It seems to depend on where one is lodged in the arts fashion parade for an opinion to be taken seriously.

'At a time when the Nugent Enquiry is assessing the future of these companies you'd think at least one of them would seize hold of every avenue available to argue their point of view. For a creative industry, those who work in it can be remarkably timid.'

What reward honesty and courage? On the evidence with respect to myself, Raymond Gill and some other arts commentators could not conduct a one-man band let alone a debate.

These commentators might owe more respect to Katharine Brisbane. Arguing from a different angle (*Weekend Australian*, 30/10), she too proposes a moratorium on funding. So far this has been greeted with silence.

A woeful paradox ooccupies our antiquarian theatre: in relation to Australian writing it is obsessed with the new, the recent, the novel, the young. A phenomenon I call neophilia. This is despite (or because of) the theatre being largely controlled by that generation born in the second half of the 50s and the 60s—the generation following the 'baby-boomers'.

We have a monomaniacal and half-critical cultivation of young playwrights, new plays, first plays (a first play from an older writer can be prized). But what kind of intellectual and artistic milieu are these fresh talents enjoying? I couldn't imagine a more dreadful one. These writers have little hope, here, of seeing the masterworks of the century done in super-modern styles.

Neophilia as well entails a cult of the instantaneous, a fetish for the present, flirtations with the masturbations of Postmodernism. Hand in hand with these goes a disregard for the past, for tradition, immediate and remote, locally and internationally. Inside this lurks a gerontophobia, or 'ageism'.

Tradition is not some stuffy artefact that occludes the dynamic dash of progress. It should be a living intellectual organism, a kind of laboratory whose experiments and proofs should continually be put to the test in the present. Without this process, we are in danger of whelping a generation of deluded ignoramuses, who will continue to belch out naive naturalism, camp romps, and fatuous Postmodern maze-plays.

Our neophilia partly belongs to global phenomena, to new technology, the so-called electronic and cybernetic age, and new sensations of time and space. In the theatre its local force derives from a conviction by those at the helm that we are small and possess no past achievements, that we must therefore pin all our hopes on youth (in every sense), and pine for a callow genius who will engender the Great Australian Play (GAP), and enfranchise us globally.

If our theatre is rather like the fool of Lucretius, who, in wishing to go forward, executed backward leaps, what of the other arts and their compartments? Are they marked by a similar backwardness, immaturity and insecurity?

Certainly the arts are highly compartmentalised in Australia. If one has made a name in one art form, there is a robust, even bullying, tendency to compel that artist to remain pigeon-holed. It is a rare artist that is welcomed in another compartment. Louis Nowra is probably the great exception—but then he has not yet turned his hand to poetry: a delight in store for him. The poets, in my experience, are the most ferally territorial. They seem to hunt in packs, like wolves. They are notoriously divided, however, and are capable of (at the highest levels) taking out, maiming or rusticating a perceived rival. Paradoxically, they are the most drenched in Modernism of all our arts, and adopt strong aesthetic positions.

Music and dance have embraced the twentieth century, whereas the cinema and the novel languish in the literal aesthetics of the last. The fictional forays into Modernism, by the likes of Gerald Murnane, David Brooks, Tom Flood, do not hold up, being solipsistic, hermetic, overconvuluted, and unerringly humourless.

Our cinema is backward, and rigidly conservative in its adherence to the tenets of Naturalism: 'the fourth wall' (ignoring the presence of the audience) is as Berlin-like as in the theatre. Never have I known a group of artists who so puritanically, so authoritatively, define what is art and what is not, what is cinematic and what is not. I cannot imagine composers, choreographers, even poets, behaving in this narrow fashion. Australian cinema has not been touched by Fellini, Antonioni, Resnais, Godard, Lynch etc. The perils of compartmentalisation are greater here. If you write in a non-naturalistic style, and come from the theatre, screenplays are promptly deemed non-cinematic and, with crackshot literalism, theatrical.

Perhaps an Australian novelist or filmmaker will argue for a moratorium on funding in their respective zones? I doubt it. Besides, there is a mortal crisis in the theatre; the novel and cinema are merely anaemic, in need of blasts of blood.

Should nothing much, or the simply negligible, occur in the theatre across a fundless five years, then there is no broad social and deep existential need for drama and comedy. If theatre artists, unencumbered by obsolete impedimenta, cannot create a fresh art that galvanises, disturbs, astonishes, jolts, their immediate paying communities, it is dead like the dodo.

Are the blanketings, the acrimony and treachery, which I have been compelled to entertain, part of larger forces in our society? Katharine Brisbane does not think so, feeling that among us 'at bottom there remain received values of egalitarianism, loyalty to community, and suspicion of personal ambition'.

The recent Victorian election results would seem to endorse these convictions. Yet other unlovely traits still prevail in the collective Australian psyche. Bullying, for example, is much commented upon by outside observers, and would appear to derive ultimately from our military foundation, pioneering white supremecism, land and gold avarice.

Then there is envy, which some speculate derives from an uncanny grasp of our continuing inferiority and mediocrity. It might be of use here to paraphrase Manning Clark: never underestimate the depth and ubiquity of envy in the Australian character.

Now another human trait, always lurking, appears of late to have emerged into the open: treachery. We have had the treachery of SOCOG towards ordinary Australians, the treachery of other Australians towards the Melbourne Olympic bid. We have increasing treachery within the media. Blithe and brazen lying, a breed of treachery, by public figures is now considered de rigueur. Promises now routinely come as hollow as the the Grand Canyon.

We have had the treacheries of corporate Australia to the national estate, to consumers, and to workers. There has been the treachery of Labor governments to the socially disadvantaged, of Liberal governments in plundering the sovereign estates of the people, and the great late treachery of economic rationalism, a religious mask for fanatical avarice. Is there looming a treachery of generations?

For many, mainly the powerless and penurious, the last fifteen years have not been an edifying spectacle. Is a culture that rolls over so readily, owing to thinness and lack of deep purchase, a culture that is rapidly losing distinctiveness in a blandifying wash of globalisation and brute capitalism, a popular culture that thrives on imitation, equipped for the authentic independence of a republic?

Or will the symbolic imports of a republic stimulate us to self-examinations, to new and distinctive ingenuities, to nurture bold indigenous decencies? In the event of a directly elected republican leader, will Australia have the capacity to throw up a human of the stature of a Mary Robinson or a Vaclav Havel, a visionary and ethical paragon capable of rising above the economic slagheaps and providing intellectual, spiritual and creative leadership? I sincerely hope so.

How Australia Caught Gastro

Stephen Downes

Chop and three veg? Except at Christmas, I never noticed the third. In our house there was chop—or chops, usually two—mashed potatoes and boiled peas. Or chop, boiled potatoes and boiled beans. Or roast lamb, roasted potatoes and—sometimes—roasted pumpkin. Two vegies and only two, you see? An onion was occasionally boiled with the spuds. Boiled cabbage and cauliflower were also served.

Sausages were fried or baked at least once a week—terrible, salty, thin, slack and farinaceous phalluses. Steak of any sort was rare, eaten perhaps a handful of times a year. Beef was 'corned', preserved in brine, and boiled. It arrived under a glutinous white sauce of flour and milk thickened with cornflour and tasting of salt and pepper. Fish was only ever salted cod. Only. We didn't eat flake and chips on Fridays like those bloody Micks. Sold in large fillets from shallow paling boxes, the cod was much more appetising— bright-orange. It came from New Zealand, so people said. And it was orange because that was the way fish were. Books showed enigmatically, though, that fish weren't necessarily orange. The resulting conundrum dinned in my brain—and no doubt those of many other bright children of the 50s. Orange cod was the fish we ate, said our mothers. So we ate it. Poached lightly, it tasted of salt and its texture was lightly gelatinous. Its flesh flaked off in shining shallow parabolas, though, the best thing about it. Playing idly with food was a legitimate pursuit back then. Food had other purposes because its primary one—the enjoyment of eating it—was incidental. It always is when food is bad.

Chicken was a delicacy, roasted and consumed perhaps once a year. It was held in similar awe to Christmas turkey. No other poultry ever made it to our table. I remember eating tripe only once. Bits of stomach glided like miniature stingrays in another white sauce. (These sauces were similar in construction, you might recall, to homemade glue.) The ox's gut, as my father delighted in calling it, was slimy and tasteless, and made me retch. But we had baked kidneys a few times. Bought by accident attached to proper food—chops—they were cooked because they were there and nothing was wasted. They teased the senses. I found the whiff exquisite, as powerful as argument, capable of altering your views. Suddenly, a shrivelled kidney had parted the curtains around an unknown domain. I peered through, entirely mystified but enthralled. Later, I nodded knowingly as Mr Leopold Bloom ate 'with relish the inner organs of beasts…'

Because we were Methodists, the Sunday roast was on Friday night. Traditional in other Australian households, the day of rest's celebratory leg of lamb was mythic for many Australian Protestants. (Sunday was reserved for hardship in worsted suits. Two attendances at church, one at Sunday school and visiting infirm, if not dying, relatives swallowed entirely a day cherished by non-Protestants.) The dripping—fat—from the roast was collected in a special canister and used for Sunday lunch to fry cold potatoes from Friday's roast. Cold slices of meat were carved from the leg to accompany them. If we wanted a snack after school we ate salted and peppered dripping, which had a lovely khaki sheen, spread on a slice of bread.

Very, very rarely our mother tentatively and sullenly cooked something fancy. Formally schooled in housekeeping, she had nevertheless been brought up to believe that cooking to give pleasure was faintly sordid, a mild form of prostitution. She sweated and scowled as she prepared—biennially, if we were lucky—Cornish pasties. Notwithstanding her fear of what we might call gastronomy—although it was a word she never knew—there was something secret and atavistic about her culinary endeavour. Cooking for pleasure was anathema to her religion and better judgment, but she herself was convinced her hands worked ancient magic into these pillows of skirt steak and two types of turnip. Despite all, she was proud to celebrate a ritual handed down from ancestors of whom she was unquestioningly proud. The Irish of my father's side has fouled my efforts at Cornish pasties. Forces of fancy fight the correct outcome. I can do a perfect *beurre blanc* or *sauce Périgord*. But I cannot properly conjure a Cornish pastie.

I was brought up privileged. Smug, postwar, upper-middle-class Methodist. Many Australians ate worse, but most ate similarly. Yet, believe it or not, in recent years we have founded a great gastronomic culture on this Jurassic culinary age. In about a quarter of a century we have developed the world's best restaurants. We have democratised fine eating out, which, for entrenched cultural reasons, is an impossibility either side of the Atlantic. Drawing from multifarious resources, our chefs have created a distinctive culinary style. We have learned to grow and cook a vast range of fine raw produce in paddocks and at home. Galvanised by commercial cooking, Australians have taken to frying in woks, crushing garlic and fresh herbs in mortars and grilling octopus.

The restaurants have led. The best of them serve dishes as refined as their counterparts in the world's much-better-known eating cities. Moreover, they are priced reasonably enough for all of us—with a slight effort—to afford.

One of the biggest social changes in Australia over the past half-century, this gastro-Gestalt has taken us completely unawares. We blink, astonished. Generally, its importance—the amplitude of the achievement—has gone unnoticed. Even food and restaurant commentators underrate it, claiming we have appropriated other cuisines, been adaptive, not all that creative. The contrary is the case; as far as cooking goes we have done something new. We really should celebrate it. We don't really know precisely how or why this came about, but to deny or belittle Australia's culinary revolution demeans a social triumph worthy of the universal recognition it is getting. As Californian chef Jeremiah Tower said in the *New York Times* in 1998: 'These days London and San Francisco are gastronomic suburbs of Sydney. Australia is the epicenter.' *Times*' critic R.W. Apple Jr, who quoted Tower, described meals in Melbourne and Sydney as 'almost an unbroken series of culinary exclamation marks'.

Perhaps we are not yet in an explaining mode, still gathering breath. No one, at any rate, has analysed why our grub has become a gorgeous butterfly. Let me have a stab at it here.

Immediate reasons for our gastronomic awakening are readily recited. Migration is the first named, and there is early evidence of its contribution: Chinese cafes have been around since goldrush days; much later the Massoni family's Florentino was, in the words of Leon, son of founder Rinaldo, an attempt to bring a 'touch of Tuscany' to 1930s Melbourne. Postwar migrants are seen to have been the most influential, especially Italians, who are said to have taught us the food exotica we have come to love. I doubt it. Their legacy is in a myriad poor restaurants, mainly in Carlton and especially in Lygon Street. Apart from a handful of Italian restaurant families—Triaca, Massoni and Codognotto the leaders—and a few professional chefs such as Silvana Palmira, who have taught us what quality cooking meant, Mediterranean migrants have had little effect on our gastronomic broadening.

Yet the Australian creed of giving things a go meant we were eager to learn. Even if the culinary zenith in 1950s Australia was a perfect pavlova, newspaper and magazines regularly published recipes and expert food commentaries. For William Heinemann Ltd to put between covers in 1955 *Continental Cookery in Australia*, a handsome hardback of 174 pages by one Maria Kozslik Donovan, was unlikely to have been a gamble. Hungarian by birth, Mrs Donovan travelled widely, married a Melbourne University law professor and wrote a syndicated newspaper column called Epicure's Corner. (Her acknowledgments suggest that the column appeared in both the *Age* and the *Sun*.) She hoped her book would be a 'good, down-to-earth companion to the Australian housewife', she wrote in the introduction. About 135 recipes follow, including for bouillabaisse, haricot bean soup, *pilau de volaille a l'orientale*, 'The Fondue', liver sautéed with claret, pot roast *à l'Esterhazy*, cassoulet and linzer torte. She opines in her recipe for 'mock *pâté de foie gras*' that what 'few people realise is that foie gras paste can be made at home at a fraction of the cost of the tinned variety'. Was she joking or was she joking about the world's most exquisite food!? She did take arms over cornflour, though, which should be 'banned altogether from our kitchens'. While the only spaghetti most Australians ate was bought as soft short worms in cans, Mrs Donovan was dangerously in the know. She was the kind of woman who would apprise us of the 'niceties' to be observed when eating spaghetti. 'First... [it] should never be broken into pieces.' With perseverance anyone could eat noodles like those 'devilishly clever' Italians 'twisted around the fork in the proper way'. Paradoxically, though (and in the same breath), she found it snobbish for non-

Italians to eat spaghetti properly—'not unlike Westerners who like to show off in Chinese cafes by juggling chop-sticks'. Yes, we did have a way to go. Get there, though, we did.

Migrants en masse were not the answer. They had mostly come from peasant poverty, and country folk, despite the myths and the clever marketing of regional recipes, eat neither diversely nor well. If people cannot afford a range of ingredients they will cook a restricted repertoire of simple dishes. They are stuck in a gastro-rut. Most postwar migrants had neither the skills nor the money even to cook well at home. Moreover, within a generation many had swung over to eating poorly the Australian way. Migrants tend to change habits to adapt to a foreign culture and not vice versa.

That Australians travelled much more from about the mid-60s on is also cited as an important factor in our gastronomic reform. In *One Continuous Picnic*, a detailed history of important aspects of Australian eating, Michael Symons cites figures for Australian residents taking overseas trips. From the 1950s to the 1960s they doubled. Ten years later, the numbers had grown six times—in 1972 Australian residents left 500,000 times for OS. Four years later there were a million departures, and these days, of course, a multitude of Australians have travelled, often widely. The culinary discoveries made on these voyages almost certainly stirred demands for better food back home.

Putting a brake on the natural improvement of our restaurants were restrictive liquor laws. 'Ending the 1916 emergency wartime measure of closing hotels at 6.00pm proved to be a long and arduous mission for reformers in Victoria', writes Alleyn Best in *The History of the Liquor Trades Union* in Victoria. Tasmania dropped the regulation in 1937 and New South Wales in 1954. A Victorian referendum early in 1956 on ten o'clock closing was seen as a chance to 'internationalise... drinking laws in time for the... Olympic Games'. The temperance alliance, which had had a long history of obstructing liquor-law progress, rallied again, and the referendum was soundly beaten. Only six of Victoria's sixty-six electorates voted for later closing.

Initially adopting the Anglo-Saxon tradition of restricting alcohol access, Australia battled temperance movements and brewery cartels—an unholy alliance of partners with very different vested interests—over decades to liberate alcohol enjoyment. The power of Victorian killjoys was awesome, and among the most potent were Methodists. The Rev. H. Palmer Phillips, a former director of the church's Social Service Department, declared in 1959 that hostility to the 'evils of liquor excesses and gambling [had been]... abundantly justified'. Postulating why, his argument was simple. 'If the churches do not act, there is virtually no opposition.' In its general rules, the Methodist Church required its members 'to accept the standard of personal abstinence and to use their influence to discourage the use and manufacture of alcoholic beverages'. While it encouraged them to attend cake-icing demonstrations, an illustrated talk on leather or a craft competition in which a potato and carrot were 'transformed... into an animal'—all 1950s activities of Ivanhoe Methodist Church—Methodists were required to fight mightily against the demon drink. I believe they eventually recognised that razor wire had been strung around their minds; their church and its anti-alcohol rhetoric declined sharply from the early 1960s.

The Phillips Royal Commission heard all views in 1964, at any rate, and on 1 February 1966 the first relatively liberal licensing laws were introduced in Australia's most restrictive State. Pubs could open until 10pm—even 11.30pm if alcohol was sold 'with substantial refreshments'. Restaurants could serve liquor until 11.30pm, and a new permit allowed restaurateurs to let patrons bring their own liquor. Virtually a right in other States if not inscribed in law, 'bringing your own' in Victoria catalysed massive interest in eating out as a pastime. Only fourteen BYO permits were granted in 1966; ten years later 391 new permits were awarded.

In their entirety, though, Victorian liquor laws remained voluminous, complex and often petty, and in 1988 a new Act honed them to become Australia's most liberal. Brian Kearney, CEO of the Liquor Licensing Commission reported in 1998 that the new laws had resulted in a 'dramatic expansion' in the number and diversity of styles of licensed premises, the emergence of casual drinking and eating, new gastro-precincts, improved quality and a 'cafe society'. All this, added Kearney, against a backdrop of less alcohol consumption. Further freedoms were gained with a new Act two years ago that reduced the number of licence types and simplified the process of getting or changing a licence.

Australian liquor-law reform happened as inevitably as Topsy's growth. Happily for us, it has since the 1950s resulted in more, rather than less, access to alcohol. Liquor liberation in itself, however, cannot explain the incredible improvement in our restaurants' quality or diversity. Greater access to alcohol simply gives more opportunity to experience good food in the way in which it has been traditionally enjoyed. Better foodstuffs and improved cooking are not axiomatic because a rough Rutherglen red is on the table.

More potent forces have acted. Indeed, a model existed for what happened in Australia for a decade from the early 1970s, the years of our culinary birth and infancy. Gastronomic revolution had occurred before—only once, and unsurprisingly in the home of the modern restaurant, France. Moreover, it happened as a consequence of the political revolution.

By the time of Louis XV, France had boasted several centuries of culinary brilliance. By the mid-eighteenth century gastronomic refinement had reached its peak, according to Jean-Paul Aron, who detailed the development of French public consumption in *The Art of Eating in France*. This supreme indulgence, however, was reserved for nobility, a privilege of high birth. For thirty years before the revolution, most peasants and citizens lived in varying degrees of hardship and poverty. In his landmark history on late-eighteenth-century France, *L'Ancien Régime*, H. A. Taine says: 'Life to a man of the lower class, to an artisan or workman subsisting on the labour of his own hands is evidently precarious; he obtains simply enough to keep him from starvation and he does not always get that.' It is not uncommon for peasants to live 'only on buckwheat' and drink only water. Vineyard workers beg for bread. Workers sell what belongings they own yet some still die of cold. In remote parts of France peasants cut green crops and dry them in ovens 'because they are too hungry to wait'.

Then came revolution, brought on by poor economic management, repressive feudal laws, high bread prices, a rotten harvest of 1788 and an irascible if not starving population that had simply had enough and weren't going to take any more. The nobility decamped, and their chefs had no choice but to take their skills where they could be marketed—into the streets. As an anonymous chronicler quoted by Aron says: 'When the revolution came, changing the laws of our cuisine and dispersing, abroad and elsewhere, those superb artist-chefs who had hitherto worked exclusively for the great noblemen, one saw gastronomy descend into the Third Estate and even into the petite bourgeoisie.' (Upper and lower-middle classes, shock horror!)

In the second half of 1789, Robert, who worked for the Prince de Condé, opened a restaurant called Méot with a brigade of colleagues from the Condé palace. There was Beauvilliers, running before the revolution but brought to glory because of it. There was Boeuf à la Mode and the Cadran Bleu. Somehow, money was found to pay for meals at the new public eating houses despite its scarcity and rapid devaluation. Fine foodstuffs, too, were rare but obtained.

In heady post-revolutionary days restaurants were in fact just what the practical and fatalistic French needed. Terror reigned, the plummeting blade accelerating in its rails. But what Aron calls the 'masters of the hour' patronised restaurants to eat, drink and be merry for tomorrow... No one predicted tomorrow. Legislators, speculators, nouveaux riches, members of political clubs, lobbyists from the provinces, exploiters, wide-boys, snake-oil salesmen and profiteers all met to eat in the new restaurants. (Sound familiar?) Fateful decisions were made at table, and those who used to practise luxury trades such as goldsmithing and haberdashery became caterers, restaurateurs and bar-owners. In his two-volume history, *France 1848-1945*, Theodore Zeldin observes that while there were fewer than fifty restaurants in Paris in 1789 there were almost three thousand by 1820.

Zeldin identifies culinary professionals and commentators as the catalysts of gastronomic development. The most famous gastronomic writer, Jean Anthelme Brillat-Savarin, and his book *Physiologie du Goût* (Physiology of Taste) were important, says Zeldin, because they provided a 'justification of concern about food'. A magistrate and politician, Brillat-Savarin lived through the revolution and knew the mover-shakers of his time. But, for him, eating was the supreme pleasure, and he felt it should be more widely enjoyed. He even devised a series of dishes that were tests for the true gourmand. A force for gastronomy alive, he has become even more of an icon dead—his book came out in the last year of his life.

Of earlier importance was Grimod de La Reynière, who wrote an annual *Almanach des Gourmands* between 1803 and 1812. He couldn't believe that so many French were interested in what he referred to as his 'publishing bagatelle'. But his commentary was an important foundation for food appreciation in France. A barrister, Grimod set up a tasting jury to which cooks sent their dishes for 'legitimising'. Not critical enough, the jury was soon wound up, Grimod having been accused of partiality.

Zeldin posits that four types of people created French cuisine following the Revolution: professional (male) cooks, restaurateurs, gourmands and (female) cooks in middle-class homes. And even if the parallel with Australia's experience isn't absolutely precise, I believe four types of people have created Australian cuisine: professional cooks, restaurateurs, gourmands (or quasi-gourmands) and the middle class. A *sine qua non* of gastro-development is discretionary expenditure—money in people's pockets. It was crucial following the French Revolution and equally important in Australia.

Encouraged by the Whitlam Labor government (1972-75), Australian wages soared from 1970. Measured quaintly by the Australian Bureau of Statistics in those days as 'average weekly earnings per employed male unit', they rose 9.6 percent in 1970 and 11.3 percent the year after. Settling back to 9 percent in 1972, the 'equal-pay' Arbitration Commission judgement resulted in a 15.3 percent increase in 1973 and a sensational 27.9 percent in 1974. I returned to Australia late that year and felt the kind of euphoria about social change that might have had a parallel with feelings among the French middle-classes in France's post-revolutionary period. Strong growth in Australian earnings—above 9.9 percent—continued in all but one of the years 1975-80. Interest rates and other inflationary factors need to be considered, certainly, but there is no doubt that in a vital decade for Australian restaurants consumers had money in their pockets.

And they spent much of it on dining. Eating places proliferated. Restaurant liquor licences increased from ninety-four in Victoria in 1967 to 266 nine years later and BYOs were booming. By 1977, the *Age*, for one newspaper, was keen to publish much more on food and drink. Yet very few Australian restaurants of the period were original, innovative or important. In Melbourne especially, we were the victims of allegedly authentic French BYOs, which were easy critical targets for someone like me, who had been living among the French bourgeoisie and had witnessed what they called the 'correctness' of their food. The Australian restaurants that did sow the seed of our endemic cuisine—Tony's Bon Goût and, later, Le Café Nouveau in Sydney, and Neddy's in Adelaide—were creating astonishing offerings, bearing in mind what most of us knew about food and ate at home. (At Neddy's in the late 1970s Cheong Liew was serving sharks' lips and sea cucumber with a chilli sauce.) Restrictive liquor laws no longer hobbled gastronomic adventuring, and the most wowserish elements of Australia, especially the noisy Methodist Church, were defunct. (Methodism disappeared altogether in 1977 with an amalgamation of faiths to form the Uniting Church. Whereas in 1976 Methodism claimed 7.3 percent of the Australian population, by 1981 the Uniting Church could muster only 4.9 percent.)

In short, we had the money to spend on food, and the best of the print media were not only encouraging us to do it but spreading the word about adventurous and original chefs, their dishes and the ingredients they were using. What happened next—in the 1980s and 1990s—is an exciting tale too long to detail here.

Certain may argue that the recent infatuation with eating-out was a worldwide phenomenon spurred on by economic booms. That might be true, but the result in Australia is unique, attracts world notice. Moreover, only Australia among Western nations has truly democratised public dining: you pay a fortune in London, Paris, New York and Los Angeles to eat restaurant food approaching the quality, refinement and originality of its counterparts in Australia's best places. And why may all Australians eat well in restaurants? I believe it is because we have been suspicious of traditional social stratification on which the eating-out experience in other Western democracies depends. Importantly, chefs and restaurateurs have been prepared to chance their arms with new and original dishes and eating-out concepts; they are well aware that the great Australian tradition of giving things a go nurtures innovation. No gastronomic yoke harnesses us to the notion that white beans and only white beans shall accompany roast lamb, for example. It's a priceless trait when a chef is keen to try out sharks' lips and sea cucumbers on his customers.

Reflective Anglers

Nicholas Shakespeare

I didn't fall in love with fishing until I was thirty. One September afternoon in Scotland, a friend rigged up some rods and took me to a sluice gate near Golspie. Fish are kind to learners. On my third cast I hooked a salmon. The tug on the line had the firmness of a handshake and was a reminder of the hand in my favourite childhood legend, rising from the riverbed to catch a sword. The passing of Arthur was the first thing I read to cause me to burst into tears. When it's my turn to be taken, I'd prefer to go like Arthur Ransome's friend Mr Fearn, found dead from heart failure on the banks of the Esk, a fresh-killed salmon at his side.

That five-pound handshake at the sluice gate welcomed me to a world I had previously wandered through with my eyes half-closed. I began at last to understand my friend, who I'd known for seventeen years but had not fathomed until the moment of my own induction. When he plopped his line into the unknown he was trading in mystery, or what psychologists might call a water-based religion. For him, I realised, the world was cast afresh each day he fished; each cast a prayer.

'There is no going back in the matter of sensation,' wrote another fisherman, Ernest Hemingway. Initially, I piggybacked off my work as a journalist and fished in Iceland, Patagonia, Canada. Nowadays, it's not the work that determines where I fish but the fish. Last week, I caught my first 'trophy' on Lake Snyder near the Arctic Circle. There was a boil on the virgin water as the pike surged after the lure, darkening to a bluish green the instant before it struck. I thought at first it was a 'lunch fish', but in a reverse of the normal angling story the pike grew in the net until, by the time my Dene guide held it up, it had expanded to forty-seven inches. 'Jesus, people go their whole lives without catching a fish like this.' He stroked it back in the water, and gradually the dorsal fins straightened and the pike glided off, shaking its head as if it had been at the dentist.

The effect of sharing the company of this creature, if only for a few seconds, was to make the energy drain from my body and my limbs shake. I felt italicised, privileged, connected. I felt like shouting, as Thomas McGuane shouts after landing an eighteen-pound trout: 'I'm a human!'

I've also fished in Australia and it was here that I received the email asking me to review these books. I must say I hesitated. I'm a pupil of the Robert Hughes school, indicated by his subtitle: *Reflections of a Mediocre Fisherman*. I still feel myself to be a novice, pre-linguistic, overly conscious perhaps of the gap between language and experience, between the fish and the word. I also agree with Craig Nova: 'Maybe it is not a good idea to think too much, or to try to make sense out of things. Maybe the wise thing is just to come up here to fish for brook trout.' And so I took a rod to the rivermouth near where I live on Tasmania's East Coast. The Swan River opposite Coles Bay is one of the most beautiful places I know. Whatever my anxieties, they soon dissolve in the water. I'm surrounded by hungry pelicans and seagulls and the only people I meet on the sand are fishermen with their small sons. (Last year, one of them asked: 'Shakespeare? Any relation to the reel-maker?'). Anyway, I was hoping to catch a bream for dinner and had reached the trance-like state that comes from staring into water when my line went taut. I jerked back, but the hook remained snagged. I thought I had caught on a submerged log and was preparing to snap the nylon (four pound breaking strain) when, without warning, the line moved parallel to the beach, towards the sea. Minutes later, I reeled in my first shark: three foot long, an agile, twisting sliver of grey-blue. I had not seen an equivalent hue on land. I was looking at a new colour. Next day I emailed back: Yes, I'd love to do the review.

Purists will open the bellies of their catch to study what the fish has fed on and so choose a suitable lure. Because I let him go, I never found out what my shark had eaten, but it is odd what treasures you do find in a fish. One seventeenth-century pike was found 'to have an infant child in its stomach', while on Midsummer Day, 1626 a sizeable cod was caught off the Lincolnshire coast and taken to the Cambridge fish market where a canvas sack was located inside it, covered in grassy-smelling slime, and containing three treatises bound together. 'This Booke was then and there beheld by many with admiration.' In the same spirit I finished reading these three fishing memoirs. The authors are fine writers who present themselves in their brightest lights, in their spawning colours. Each is very distinct from the other, but each, in his individual way, helped me to understand why I enjoy this activity so much.

'To read a fishing book is the next best thing to fishing,' wrote Arthur Ransome, my favourite author on the subject. (Asked what were his politics, Ransome once replied: 'Fishing.' He also said that the only creative act of which he felt proud was the invention of the elver fly.) Ransome was aware, of course, that the fisherman who writes has a tremendous advantage: he is speaking to a converted audience who largely forgive his tangles. However clumsily he unravels his story, he cannot fail to interest at least a percentage of his readers. It's not like writing a novel. And yet many fine books— an astonishing number—have been written by novelists, biographers and critics who just happen to fish.

'The similarities between the angler's work and the writer's need not be laboured, but they exist,' writes Hughes. The angler has to know how to read: the water, where the fish live, how the fly will present itself across a stream rippling with maybe ten different currents. He selects a fly from his fly-book and his method of casting his line has this in common with a line of prose: it cannot hide his character—although, paradoxically, everything condenses towards trying to suppress it.

To have any chance of catching a fish so alarmable as the trout you have to blend in with your surrounds, take on their pace. You have to be what normally you are not. A large, impatient, noisy critic like Hughes has to distil himself into a still, small silent shadow, while gregarious souls such as McGuane and Nova must find contentment on their own, studying the habits of their prey until they are indistinguishable from the fish. (A friend of Isaak Walton was struck by how closely he resembled a pike. His face was 'hard angular, and of no expression. It seems to have been "subdued

to what it worked in", to have become native to the watery element.')
Fishing and writing demand, as it were, the same sort of deliverance
of self that Flaubert applauds in his letters: 'One must by an effort
of imagination transfer oneself into one's characters and not draw
them to oneself.' And yet fishing has an extra dimension that is
akin to reading: it concentrates the mind, while at the same time
liberates it. It is much less about catching a fish than releasing the
fisherman. Hughes is well acquainted with this ecstatic freedom.
'Fishing enabled me to be alone; to dream, yet with the senses on
full alert.'

Hughes's dreamtime lies within the reach of anyone able to bait a
hook and it is what many of us, really, are fishing for—a settled but
excited state of mind in a place of outstanding beauty (or, in Nova's
phrase, 'a sense of what may be possible after all'). Hughes, referring
to the mystical connection that can result from such a combination,
calls it a 'feeling of oceanic peace and oneness with the universe'.
This, as he knows, is close to the language of organised religion. He
is not alone in appreciating why Christianity should have adopted
the iconography of his favourite pastime, a fish sketched in the dust
a coded emblem of one's faith. McGuane again: 'The motto of every
serious angler is "Nearer my God to Thee".'

Does any other sport appeal so shamelessly to the Bible? Anglers
like to remind us that Seth, the son of Adam, was a fisherman, as
were four of the apostles who were mending their nets when Jesus
offered to make them 'fishers of men'. The Bible is just the
beginning. All three writers ransack world literature to justify the
moral superiority of their hobby. 'As the shark rose out of the water,'
recalls Hughes, 'I would be frozen by a delicious terror that, I
would learn from Edmund Burke a decade later, is the root of the
sublime.' When selecting a fly, McGuane invokes Camus's belief
that the only serious question is whether or not to commit suicide:
'This,' he says, 'is rather like the nymph question.' Nova cites
Camus, Emerson and Ford Madox Ford, whose image of a woman's
eye—'the grey blue colour of the rubble on the bottom of a stream'—
makes the author realise the lack of beauty in his early books and
his determination to do something about it. By and large, the
references are familiar and poached from two authors in particular:
David Profumo and Graham Swift, editors of that superb fishing
anthology, *The Magic Wheel*. In vain did I comb these memoirs for
the fisherman's story I like best, about a Chinese sage who sat all

his life by a river, dangling a straightened hook in the water, catching nothing. Word of his peculiar habit spread through the empire until it reached the ears of the emperor himself who one day made a detour to the river. 'Pardon me,' he asked the sage. 'What on earth are you fishing for?' The old man turned to the emperor: 'You.' Which, I suppose, explains the motto of the Flyfishers Club, now moved to a yellow attic above the Savile. *Piscator non solum piscatur*: there is more to fishing than catching fish.

Anton Chekhov, Sergei Aksakov, Charles Kingsley, Ransome, John Buchan, George Orwell, Ernest Hemingway, William Faulkner: these writers have all written about fishing. At the head of the river, and surviving repeated moves to push him in, sits the biographer Walton. Max Hastings called Walton 'a pompous old ass', but Hughes and McGuane devote worshipful chapters to him. His *The Compleat Angler* appeared in the mayfly season of 1643 at the price of eighteen pence and in it Walton employed one pleasure to celebrate another: 'in writing of it I have made myself a recreation of a recreation.' It has become, extraordinarily, the most reprinted book in the English language after the Bible and *The Pilgrim's Progress*.

Walton was sixty when he published *The Compleat Angler, or The Contemplative Man's Recreation*. As Lord Grey wrote in *Fly Fishing*: 'The time must come to all of us who live long when memory is more than prospect.' Hughes, McGuane and Nova are writers not far from their sixtieth year. They've logged the years, filled their creels. Like Walton, they are taking stock, casting a reflective line over their life and twin passion. Like Walton, they have absolutely no doubt about the restorative powers of fishing: 'Peace and a secure mind / Which all men seek, we only find.'

Nova's full title is *Brook Trout and the Writing Life: The Intermingling of Fishing and Writing in a Novelist's Life*. It is the only horrid thing in his book. This small volume covers a lot of ground and time. I enjoyed it so much that I read it twice. The temperature of Nova's prose is like fishing itself: he recreates the experience, catches our attention, makes us hungry for what he wants to tell us. As a guide to angling the book is negligible, rather as Bruce Chatwin's *In Patagonia* might strike a tourist to that region. But as a mapping of Nova's personal journey, it left me wondering if he will write anything so good again. He catches his first brook trout after his father dies and because of a woman he meets at a party in New York, a blonde girl with a red sweater and spunky smile. She can make the call of a loon and has a house in the country with a stream. There she gives him a bamboo trout rod. Not long afterwards he hears a little watery snap! and feels the ominous tug, 'sudden, serious, with all the purpose that millions of years of evolution can bring to one small act'. That tug, for Nova, has 'the urgency of a promise being kept'. He finds himself holding in his palm a creature (*Salvinelinus fontinalis*) created from the softest leather imaginable, its silver sides spotted dark brown, like old wood which has been 'handled and waxed and rubbed into darkness—that of a dining room table, say, made before the revolution and used steadily'. He is hooked.

McGuane rightly observes of the brook trout: 'Some of the most appalling arias in angling literature are directed at this lovely creature, who was with us before the Ice Age.' Nova is an exception. His growing love of trout fishing is played out against his career as husband and writer. He falls in love with the blonde, marries, and has two daughters whom he teaches to fish. Throughout this period he labours as an impoverished novelist: 'There is no silence like the silence that comes from a publisher when things are going badly.' Nova's days on the water become the constant, weaving together—and making sense of—the critical events in his life. 'The moment of illumination has often come here, with a trout taking a fly out of the boundary between its world and mine.' Fishing sharpens his memory and perception, allows him to see connections that might otherwise have drifted by unnoticed (the odour of the water, for instance, like the smell of his newborn child). And the more he observes the fish, the weather, the river, the more does he learn things which unconsciously feed into his own life and work. If a problem crops up, his wife orders him to her Fish Cabin: 'We always seem to see things a little more clearly after you come back from the river.'

Nova's deadpan voice is reminiscent of another trouter, Richard Ford's sportswriter, but he is a more seductive everyman even than Frank Bascombe. With his money running out, his hands sweating, he is taught by the arrival of his daughter to write about the one subject he has avoided: 'love for another human being with all its attendant imperatives and disasters.' He is also forced to undergo a chilling lesson in hatred. One day an anonymous letter threatens murder unless he pays a ransom. The letter instructs him to wear waders when he makes the drop-off. The waders are 'to walk though the blood in your house if you betray me'. Abruptly, Nova has crossed the boundary. He has become the prey.

How does Nova survive this horrifying ordeal? By fishing, naturally. 'There is something else to these endeavours, something more profound and difficult to describe than just catching fish, something that has to do not only with being alive, but with the impulse towards persisting in the face of difficulty.' This, he suggests, is the brook trout's glittering gift. It rises with it from the deep, finning between the seen and the unseen until it bursts through the surface. You can call it a refusal to despair.

Montana novelist McGuane is not so philosophical, although he has enjoyed a wider beat. These thirty-three essays are more a series of narrative reflections. They meander river-like—and sometimes aimless as driftsmoke—through his forty-five years as a fisherman who has covered much of the globe's water, always, he says, with the same feeling of 'excited anticipation'. Raised two miles from the Canadian border, the son of Irish Catholics, McGuane believed, when young, in angels 'silvery and rapid' and one foot high. He found them in the rivers of Russia, the lakes of Canada, in the sea off Key West. 'Early on, I decided fishing would be my way of looking at the world. First it taught me how to look at rivers. Lately it has been teaching me how to look at people, myself included.'

McGuane, a modest world-record holder (a fifteen-pound mutton snapper, caught on a fly), is an excellent example of the way fishing can compel you into so intense a discrimination of your surrounds that you become part of them. It isn't, he says, simply a matter of decoding the position of the sun or the speed of the water or the shape of a glinting shadow, but of transferring yourself into the imagination of a sleepy but susceptible trout, tarpon, tuna, whatever. He is, in fact, a lot more fish-centric than either Nova or Hughes. Family life makes him moody as a sea trout. Not until page 179 do we learn that McGuane has a wife. She accuses him of being 'a salmon-steelhead whore', which is hardly surprising. As his daughter says: 'All my dad cares about is the f-word.' And they have a point. Everything reminds McGuane of fish. 'It is a fact that we are made almost entirely of river water.' On his travels he cheerfully determines to break the water barrier. 'I try to tie flies that will make me... take further steps towards actually becoming a fish myself.'

McGuane's passion is helpless and infectious, but his prose is not without its windknots. Like his hero Walton, he can disappear into the quaint and picturesque, into phrases such as 'the vaunted river fish of yore'. There are passages marred by inconsequentiality, by sentimentality, by cliché (Victoria's Empress hotel 'exactly the place to sport an RAF moustache'). Sometimes you have to re-read him in order to catch his original meaning. Here and there an essay smacks of a travel article he may have written to cover his fare to remoter fishing grounds. And the further he steps from his native riverbank, the less precise grows his memory, the splashier his irony ('fun-loving Oliver Cromwell'), the more callow his remarks about other fishermen—competitors, bankers and time-sharers who have made his favourite rivers anything but silent. When his eyes stray from the fly that ordinarily constitutes his universe, he is a fish out of water and his poetry suffers. In Argentina, 'stratospherically high overhead Andean condors with their twelve-foot wingspreads trained their mystical telemetry on the ancient plain'. McGuane's sky may teem with condors, but in the Andes these gigantic birds are as rare as the most elusive tarpon.

If McGuane tends to see fish as characters in a novel, and Nova as emissaries of luck, Hughes views them, not surprisingly, as works of art. His striped bass leaps from a Bridget Riley canvas, 'its silver-flanked body tinged with topaz bronze and striated by horizontal black lines', while bluefin blood, he assures us, 'will dry as hard as crimson acrylic'. Of the three, Hughes is the least interior, the one most reluctant to release his fish, but he is also, strangely enough, the author most physically present in his surrounds. To read him catch a yellowfin tuna off Montauk is practically to be in his boat. He sits you in troll position, hands you some expensive kit (from 'Urban Angler in New York') and grips your rod as the reel screams and the line tears away. Afterwards, he guts and fillets the fish and gobbles it down for breakfast.

A Jerk on One End is a marvellous illustration of why, when they fish, men again become little children. Hughes's first sexual memories are associated with fish, as a pre-pubescent getting hot and flushed over certain salmon spawning sections of Henry Williamson's *Salar the Salmon* ('In Australia in 1950 there were no sex manuals'). And fishing leads to his first visual image of a semi-naked woman—a blonde on a Rain-beau reel pictured fly-fishing with a leaping trout at the end of her tense line. 'I could not hear the word nymph uttered without thinking of her.'

Hughes is incapable of writing a dull or a slack line and there are at least two passages I would commend to a future anthologist: an imaginary account of what it would feel like to be caught by a fish, and the scene in which his purist father belts him for deploying a live grasshopper: 'People who use live bait on trout are not fit to fish. They are thugs.' But more than a good writer, Hughes is a serious one. He wants to save the world. A robust conservationist, like every true angler, he converts his passion into a Swiftean polemic. He has harsh words for the pursuit of big-game records. He lashes out at chemical pollution and the deep-sea nets each year responsible for twenty-seven million tonnes of waste fish. And he argues our need, daily more pressing, to understand our part in a chain of being whose integrity we violate at our own peril. 'Angling at its best,' he believes, 'is a means to that understanding.'

His understanding begins with his first tug and his discovery that there is something unmistakable about catching a fish. If ever there was a 'moment of truth', this is it. The fish either escapes, leaving you holding a straightened rod (is there anything more dead?). Or the fish does not escape. For Hughes, as for McGuane and Nova, even the smallest brook trout lifted flashing from the water stands as a true image, a true sentence, the scrap, as it were, of a greater truth. A muscle of light and agitated life that connects the angler to the universe. 'In looking for one fish,' says McGuane, 'you find another—and maybe in the end you find it all.'

For these three anglers, each fish is a link to a different world, each handshake affirmation of membership to an aquatic confederacy. It is why, in the end, the most magical part of fishing— for each of them—is not about catching the fish. It is about letting the fish go. One of the high points of Hughes's fishing career takes place in the dawn off Long Island. He stands at the bowsprit, poised to fling his spear into the vitals of a giant bluefin tuna. 'And then I caught its eye, that huge eye with its hypnotic black centre, evolved to capture every last photon in the deep sea. God, it occurred to me, was looking at me through that fish.' It is a terrific Arthurian moment when he flunks it. Paralysed like Sir Bedevere, he watches the hand descend empty into the deep. But he hasn't flunked it, not at all. 'I will never forget the sight of that bluefin, in the splendour of its unreflective life, or how it slid out of sight with the merest quiver of its body, cleanly accelerating through the blue, gone forever.'

Penelope Fitzgerald 1916-2000

Inga Clendinnen

Penelope Fitzgerald began writing in 1975, when she was sixty. She went on to produce three engaging biographies, the last and best being a composite study of her father, who became editor of *Punch* when Penelope was sixteen, and his three very different brothers; one an Anglican priest, one a Roman Catholic polemicist, and one a classical scholar and cryptographer. This complicated family subject, with its tensions, its subdued treacheries, its perverse rapprochements, precisely suited her talents. (Always a benign goddess, she played her own small domestic role masked.) At sixty-one she wrote a detective novel prompted by the Tutankhamun exhibition in London. Catholic Uncle Ronnie had written detective stories to make short clerical ends meet. Penelope wrote hers to divert her husband as he lay dying.

There followed four great novels drawn from the experiences of her own modest life, rendered marvellously comic in the telling. The Knox brothers' lives and writings had been full of public clamour, charged with public import. Hers have the quiet of the home cave. Fitzgerald was the laureate of family, of the arbitrariness and the incorrigibility of human affections: the preferences we feel, on no clear grounds or on no grounds at all, which prove ineradicable through time. There may have been villains in her books in the eyes of other characters, or even in their own, but she never thought them villains. Her tranquil affections did not waver.

Then, having drawn enough from her own life, came three historical novels, and then a fourth, *The Blue Flower*, which brilliantly joined history and family. In a year of heavyweight American contenders—de Lillo, Roth—this delicate, old-fashioned novel took out the American National Book Critics fiction award, to loud incredulity. In that novel Fitzgerald also decisively subverts an argument I had been fussing over, off and on, for years. Henry James has insisted that good historical novels could be written only about events occurring within the previous fifty years: beyond that, he said, the novelist was condemned to the gruesomely false and the merely picturesque. Here he is putting down an unfortunate woman foolish enough to send him a copy of her novel, *The Tory Lover*. On 5 October 1901 he replies, after some preliminary cozening ('charming touch, tact and taste... a fellow craftsman... a woman of genius and courage...') thus. The italics and the capitals are, of course, his:

> The 'historical novel' is, for me, condemned, even in cases of labour as delicate as yours, to a fatal *cheapness*, for the simple reason that the difficulty of the job is inordinate and that a mere *escamotage*, in the interest of ease, and of the abysmal public *naïveté* becomes inevitable. You may multiply the little facts that can be got from pictures and documents, relics and prints, as much as you like—*the* real thing is almost impossible to do, and in its essence the whole effect is as nought: I mean the invention, the representation of the old CONSCIOUSNESS, the soul, the sense, the horizon, the vision of individuals in whose minds half the things that make ours, that make the modern world, were non-existent. You have to *think* with your modern apparatus a man, a woman—or rather fifty— whose own thinking was intensely otherwise conditioned, you have to simplify back by an amazing *tour de force*—and even then it's all humbug...

Then, with the knife well-planted, comes the characteristic backward step, innocent hands upraised: 'I speak in general, I needn't keep insisting, and I speak grossly, summarily, by rude and provisional signs, in order to suggest my sentiments at all.' [Henry James to Sarah Orne Jewett, 5 October 1901, *Henry James: Letters*, edited by Leon Edel, The Belnap Press, Cambridge, Mass., 1984, Vol. iv, pp. 208-9.]

'Rude and provisional' perhaps, but this is well thought and said better. There are famous exceptions to the Jamesian rule: for example, J. G. Farrell's *The Siege of Krishnapur* is a tour de force firmly set in the days of the Indian Mutiny. But perhaps imperial powers change more slowly? Perhaps they don't change at all? For nearly every other case the fifty-year rule seemed a good rule of thumb. (David Malouf's magical *An Imaginary Life* only masquerades as 'historical'.) And then Fitzgerald wrote *The Blue Flower*, and I was confounded. This is indubitably a great novel; it is set at the close of the eighteenth century; and it stars the youthful German poet-philosopher Fritz von Hardenburgh before he became 'Novalis'. German Romanticism, at once so florid and so prissy, is about as far from modern sensibility as you can get.

From its first page we know we are entering the country of the past: as we enter the courtyard of a mansion along with two young men, 'great dingy snowfalls' of soiled linen come cascading from the upper windows and balconies, because this is the day of the One Great Wash of the Year. Fitzgerald's nearest literary relative is Turgenev, in the irony of the glance, the tenderness for the unheroic and the domestic—and in the lovely gratuitous detail which warms a scene into life: here the children's undergarments 'fluttered through the blue air, as though the children themselves had taken to flight.'

Another country. Nonetheless, we instantly recognise the people scurrying about gathering up the linen and the two mildly abashed young men entering the courtyard as people. Two large, complicated, talkative families are the centre of the action, which would give a merely competent writer all manner of difficulties. Fitzgerald sketches them so distinctively that we effortlessly recognise each family's ethos, and each individual's exclamations. They are endearingly translucent to us because she has none of our fashionable anxieties regarding the otherness of others: she flits in and out of her characters' heads; we hear the words they speak, we are told what is in their heads as they speak, and we wonder how people manage to communicate even as well as they do. She makes her most prescient observer-commentator a small boy gifted with perfect insubordination. With him we watch the complex little dances of shifting alliances and understandings within the elastic embrace of family love. Fitzgerald understands the imperishable allure of domesticity as few writers do. And, as with Turgenev, there is no notion of life being confined to the novel: we have the sense of it constantly spilling over, extending far beyond the edge of the page.

The core narrative is a love story. A budding philosopher is bowled over by a merry, loud, ill-educated girl who is at ease with herself, charmed by life, and quite unprepared to pay him the deference to which his doting family has accustomed him. She holds to cheerfully simple opinions which shock him: ('to decide she does not believe in the life to come. What insolence. What enormity'). He discovers her to be at once intractable, and irresistible.

These people are people, but they are not as we are: 'Novalis', the philosopher-poet recognised rather ruefully by his attractively chaotic family as a genius, addresses his playful thirteen-year-old love as 'My Philosophy', he discourses at formidable length on the latest salt-extracting methods, he ought to be an idealistic bore—and we do not find him ridiculous. Or no more ridiculous than do the people who cherish him, and who lovingly, patiently listen to him. There is a plain commonsensical person in each of these households, a Penelope, and they are crucial: they give us a quiet corner to sit while the arguments and the high-falutin' talk swirl around us. Meanwhile, physical settings are evoked with grace and magical economy. An older man and his young companion are on an expedition, conversing amiably as they go. It is November, 1794. Listen:

> As they plodded on together, drops of moisture gathered and slowly fell from their hat-brims, the ends of their noses and the hairy tips of the horses' ears which the animals turned backwards as a kind of protest against the weather. Earth and air were often indistinguishable in the autumn mist, and morning seemed to pass into afternoon without a discernible mid-day. By three o'clock the lamps were already lit in the windows.

The evocation of time and place is not the least exotic, and it is utterly embracing, utterly persuasive: we think: 'Of course. That is how it must have been.' The 'picturesque historical details'—the village abortionist called 'the Angel Maker', the horse not yet 'roughshod' slipping on ice—slide into the action with such lovely nonchalance it is impossible to do anything but nod: this is simply the way things were. And I am drunk with envy and admiration, because this is how historians ought to write—if they dared. The novel's epigraph is a notation from Novalis himself: 'Novels arise out of the shortcomings of history.'

The 'shortcomings of history' are multiple, and, after reading this novel, rather too painful to count. Above all, historians cannot hear chatter. Daily talk is lost to us. With Fitzgerald we eavesdrop on family exchanges (the poet's beloved Sophie assessed by his younger brother, himself later to be smitten: 'Empty as a new jug, Fritz'), we laugh, and as we laugh we realise that these are authentic human voices we are hearing, the idioms different but the sentiments familiar; that these families are not posed for the page but fondly, furiously feuding in the ways large and loving families do. There is a great deal of love in this marvellous book, and even more of that rare commodity, intelligent affection. (There is no sex at all. Presumably Fitzgerald believes most people knew and know how to manage that on their own.) Novalis is a dreamer, possibly a genius, but he is also a chronic innocent, a social fool. His insubordinate young brother, equally intelligent, is very much smarter and more cynical: a radically different kind of thinker in the making.

Fitzgerald is a connoisseur of the idiosyncrasies of love, but there are no *longeurs*: she moves her characters briskly through the narrative, a briskness aided by the brevity of the chapters which are as crisp as cinematic 'takes'. We watch an exchange, we know both parties better, the story moves forward a notch—and the sense of the relentless forward movement of time is at once disturbing, and entirely natural, because we know, as the protagonists do not, that time is running out as the pages to come thin under our anxious fingers. We wonder what shape this story will have. What will finally happen? Only in novels, never in history, is contingency at last overcome.

And then, in an elegant manoeuvre which reminds me irresistibly of an expert skier making a casual, eye-dazzling turn, Fitzgerald shifts her weight, adjusts her balance—and we are skimming in a quite different direction. Novalis is no longer the hero. Laughing, shrieking Sophie, the 'empty jug' we have come, rather guiltily, to cherish precisely because of her blessed exuberance, is stricken with tuberculosis. Subjected to a series of terrible operations, she suffers them with the resolution and moral grace the moonstruck Fritz had always tried, in the face of all of the evidence, to ascribe to her. (Here Fitzgerald draws on Fanny d'Ably's exquisitely horrible account to her sister of her own mastectomy, performed in 1811.)

Sophie dies two days after her fifteenth birthday. She is Sophie to the last. She does not lose her laughter. But she has become our Sophie now: we weep for her, and resent it when a note tells us that her Fritz marries before the year is out. But that is how life was lived, had to be lived at the turn into the nineteenth century. Nearly every one of the children we meet in these pages will die before their thirtieth year. It is that familiarity with death—with its prospect, and its reality—which makes this novel truly historical. These people's lives are shaped by exigencies different from ours. Curiously, and despite the dread, their world seems more open than ours. They hope more than we do. Some of them are ready to seek the blue flower of unique destiny, while others strive to guard the seekers against death.

Now Penelope Fitzgerald herself is dead, and for some of us darkness will be mixed with the colours of the world for a season. She was eighty-three years old, she was a realist, perhaps she didn't mind her dying. But I mind. Every one of her books was different, and every one of them seemed to speak directly to me, for my private pleasure and enlightenment. I have been saving one of her novels, the Russian one, *In the Beginning of Spring*, unread, like a hoarded Christmas chocolate tweaked occasionally for the premonitionary joy of hearing the red-gold cellophane creak. It was a reliable something to look forward to. Now? I suppose I'll still read it. But not yet. It would make me too sad, knowing that she, a quiet presence living in another country, has quit our shared world.

VP Day

Ruth Park

And what kind of day was it, that Wednesday? Blue, beaming, unexpectedly warm. We had spent so many August days chilled to the bone because of the long coal strike and the absence of gas. I had even set a chimney alight when trying to heat our small baby's bottle on a fire kindled in a disused grate.

But here it was, 15 August 1945, the feast of the Assumption, a holy day of obligation. Mass at St Fiacre's, Leichhardt, was almost over when a boy entered the sanctuary and whispered in the officiant's ear. Immediately the priest turned to face us, saying quietly, 'Thanks be to God, the war is ended.'

The response was an extraordinary silence. We were struck dumb. All those years, all those deaths, all those tales of frightfulness and despair—over? A chance to see once again some of the sons and husbands and brothers longed-for, anguished over, whisked away years before in a war that wasn't ours until Japan entered the conflict? As a nation ours was so small, barely seven million population, and yet it had been bled of youth. In the previous five days there had been rumours of peace, even some premature small roughhouse celebrations, but we hadn't really believed it. But now... suddenly someone sobbed, someone laughed, everyone rushed for the door, forgetting to genuflect, forgetting everything.

I tore down Catherine Street towards Parramatta Road, but had not gone a hundred metres before the air was simply split asunder with unimaginable noise. It was the rare, rare sound of a city yelling its head off with joy and relief. Surely this astonishing, truly organic bellow was heard only two or three times in the twentieth century? One could barely distinguish individual sounds—steam train whistles with their lanyards tied down, factory hooters, tram bells, motor horns, air raid sirens, and underlying all in huge basso harmony the deafening growl from Allied ships moored in the harbour. In Parramatta Road people were already doing knees-up in the roadway; all traffic had stopped; shopkeepers were beating hell out of their tin garbage cans; a pub owner let loose 300 metres of bunting from his upper windows and then hastily hauled it in again. Alas for thrift—every fifth flag was Japanese. The publican had saved the bunting from 1918 when Japan was a World War One ally.

The time was 9.30am.

Thus began VP Day. Prime minister Ben Chifley had planned to announce victory in the Pacific at 11am, but common human exuberance beat him. Tasmanian operators of banned ham radios got the news first and sped it around the country. Chifley made his speech at 9.30. He did not tell us to behave ourselves as three State governors did, but we knew that was what he meant.

No one mentioned Japan that day. Though 18,000 Australian POWs were still held in frightful slave labour camps in Malaya, Burma and Japan, the prevalent spirit of VP's vast crowds was euphoria, not revenge. We did not yet know even the critical historical events of our joyful morning. Here they are.

9.00am, Sydney time: British prime minister Attlee and US president Truman announced surrender.

9.15am: US admiral Nimitz ordered ceasefire in the Pacific.

11.15am: The Japanese high command ordered to give ceasefire order in same region.

11.55am: The Japanese cabinet resigned and war minister general Anami committed hara kari 'to atone for failure to accomplish his duties'. Even so the Japanese people, who had endured saturation conventional bombardment for over a year, the horrific Hiroshima bomb on 6 August and its Nagasaki twin on 8 August, the day Russia also declared war on Japan—these resolute people still would not believe in the surrender until their emperor spoke to them of bearing the unbearable.

By this time, a million people were dancing, singing, hugging and shouting for joy in the central business district of Sydney. My husband and I, having by great good luck obtained a babysitter, were embroiled in an almighty squash inside a tram going townwards but terminally marooned somewhere near Annandale. We had known all traffic was to stop on the fringes of the city; all bridges were closed; all traffic halted. Still we thought we could walk. An hour later, having been disengaged from innumerable other, but amazingly good-tempered bodies, we walked. Parramatta Road and George Street were slowly moving rivers of people—British sailors, nursing sisters, American soldiers, walking Australian wounded, and thousands and thousands of shabby, scruffy looking Sydney civilians. We were all shabby after five years of war; rationing had done its work. Martin Place was where we were all going, to the cenotaph.

The earsplitting mechanical hullabaloo had ceased but the city rang with amplified music, 'Rule Britannia', 'Brown Slouch Hat', 'Waltzing Matilda' and Bing Crosby. Rickety platforms had been hastily erected, and from these the great radio stars of the day led community singing, relayed advice from the city's authorities, and altogether did a great job of keeping order. John Dunne of 2SM, Jack Davey in the Domain, 'Mo' in Kings Cross, Alwyn Kurts of 2UW in Hyde Park—their distinctive or genial voices gave a warmly familiar air to an extraordinary event. The thousand police on duty, reinforced by specials and both US MPs and Australian provosts, stood around looking benevolent. (Our military police bore the old army title, pronounced provo, or in most cases 'dirty big provo'.) They had little or nothing to do, for the hotels had been shut since nine that morning, and the atmosphere of cheerful friendliness was unmarred by hooliganism or disruption. True, I was one merrymaker 'spoken to', asked for my identity card by a young policeman, all because a group of new friends and I were dancing down Pitt Street with tin garbage can lids tied to our feet. He suspected these lids were stolen, he said. We said no, we'd brought them with us in a tram, an excuse he generously accepted.

The things one remembers: gracious Martin Place a metre deep in torn-up paper—a perfect snowstorm of hated official forms—manpower, rationing, priorities—mutilated ledgers, phone books, records. Kids having snowfights with this paper. A lone street sweeper climbing on the roof of a castaway taxi and doing the hokey-pokey with his broom. On the steps of the GPO a soldier dressed in nothing but a digger hat and a loincloth, bearing a placard: 'Gandhi. Me want to fight on.' A little further along was a professional fire-eater who filled his mouth with kerosene and sprayed it out on a lighted match.

'Bloke on fire! Put him out!'

Down went the fire-eater under an onslaught of sand from the GPO's fire buckets.

Enormous conga lines formed, coming from nowhere and going anywhere. One moving down George Street met a Chinese dragon which refused to move, partly exploding in a fusillade of fireworks. The dragon, shaken, turned into York Street to recover and became entangled with a huge cheesecloth worm created by the girls from the rag factories. Meanwhile, the conga line swept on and met another coming the opposite way. Both struggled onwards, whirling confusedly about each other like mating snakes, until dozens of dancers fell exhausted and had to be revived in the Archibald Fountain.

In the afternoon the Archibald Fountain became the centre for exhausted stragglers. They desisted from shouting and dancing and did quiet things, such as participating in kissing marathons. Winner: British sailor at two minutes, fifteen seconds and near suffocation. American serviceman mistakenly kissed Australian who had swapped clothes with his girl, an AWAS. Threatened mayhem.

Aussie: 'I look all right, don't I? What are you going crook about?'

Chess players placidly played on under the spring-foliaged trees. But people who had long yearned to climb the florid fountain statuary now did so. Diana wore an AIF slouch hat and Apollo a green jungle shirt. A young soldier crept out to the end of the god's outstretched arm and clung there, a drenched koala. A mounted policeman halted his stately progress on a white horse with a V for Victory painted in red on its forehead, and gravely watched.

Crowds, young and old, civilian and service, began to wander back across Hyde Park from St Mary's. Eighty thousand people visited the cathedral that day. Ninety-five thousand attended St Andrew's Anglican cathedral. Packed thanksgiving services were held in every city and suburban church. The great day was not all fun and games.

As the westering sunlight left Martin Place, searchlight crews manipulated beams from each end of the plaza in a monster V for

Victory. I recall the pale blue of the beams and the huge auras of heat around the bodies of the units. At this time also neon lights appeared magically in the dusk, most blinking or gap-toothed, many sputtering into hissing death. What a marvel for the children! So many of the blackout kids had never been told that once there were lights in the sky. The crowd roared as defective signs once more advertised items vanished for years: Navy Tobacco, Mazawattee Tea, Tangee (lipstick).

The flag on top of the Bridge's arch was illuminated, a tiny island of light in the growing darkness. It said it all.

A Bold Novel

Nadia Wheatley, long admired for versatiliy and technical skill, is also a seriously serious writer. Bold, too. In her new novel *Vigil* she does not hesitate to use an in-your-face text when needed, and an almost tender obliquity, again when necessary. How well she depicts the uneasy, Weimar-like atmosphere of our present world, almost devoid of ethical values, enlightenment, disinterested love, or human respect. Has the wooden horse already entered the city? Nathan doesn't know but he suspects.

Nathan is the protagonist, whom we first discover at a funeral. Not just any funeral, and Nathan is not just any young fellow. He is the last of a trio entangled in a long, exasperating and almost inexplicable friendship. Now the other two are dead, senselessly and without dignity, as so many of the young ones are.

The ten-year friendship of Nathan, Tim and Dean is neither unusual nor noteworthy. Beginning accidentally, it continued in an often cranky, intermittent way. There seems to be no affection involved; in fact, Tim irritates the hell out of both the others. He trots around with a book and chess set, speaks posh, and finds nothing uncool in being known as the petted treasure of an anxious mother. Dean, Nathan says, is someone no one wants for a mate. Though it is not stated, maybe he is grubby and smelly, and has no proper money for lunches or anything else. His father is in prison, and his goodhearted, sloppy mother has a surfeit of kids and no ability to manage on welfare. Dean falls asleep in the daytime because he has been awake all night looking after a yelling baby while Mum has a night out. At eleven he is virtually the father of the family. Dean is a skilled shoplifter—how else would he get the things he longs for so he can keep up with the other kids?

All three boys appear to lead completely unmonitored lives; the disarray of their immediate adult world leaves no time for responsible parenting. The parents, often single for one reason or another, seem to look upon their children more or less as people that happen to be bobbing around in the same sea of troubles as themselves. But not to worry. You can always laugh or have another drink.

Never think, however, that this is a dreary underclass story. It is exciting, comic, suspenseful and often adventurous to the point of wildness. It is also emphatically another book about teenland, many of which seem to the adult reader to be excursions to a literary theme park. 'On your left you may observe rapture, mutiny and infatuation; don't on any account miss the miseries,' says the guide. But we know already about the inevitable calm of maturity, or, in a truly trendy book, the even more deceptive calm of suicide.

Wheatley isn't writing about that largely artificial construct called a teenager, but about a youthful human being—one of those who go about disguised as a boy. And what a superbly realised boy he is. Nathan is as combative as they come, fearful and fearless about everything, fanatically loyal and loving, though he doesn't know it, bleeds easily and tells no one. One knows he will never be completely healed of the wound caused by the loss of Tim and Dean. Tormented by guilt, he feels that he should have been there. He thinks of the three prongs of an electric plug. Take one away and you get no power. A clue to his pain is apparent in the several majestic extracts from John Donne's sermons—no man is an island and so forth. Nathan's bewildered consciousness of guilt, his horror lest his influence, his very presence in the Gang of Three, in some way set his friends on the road to folly and death—these emotions are his subconscious acceptance of Donne's terrifying statement.

'I never did anything to stop them,' he says. It is true that aside from his own misdemeanours, he accepted stolen goods from Dean, encouraged Tim in his awkward attempts to shoplift, regarded apathetically the petty or more serious larceny, both adult and juvenile, which seems a significant part of the culture of this no-hoper town. But children and adolescents normally feel that way. Don't interfere. And don't let anyone, especially those in authority, interfere with you. Still Nathan suffers.

Parents will read this novel with interest and maybe a sense of identification. Girl readers will discover a great deal about boys.

But will boys read it? This is an era of disturbing illiteracy among young people, particularly males. Can one think of another historical period when undergraduates were offered remedial reading assistance? By illiteracy I mean not simply the inability to read and write one's own language, but an inability to follow text, to understand how sentences relate to each other, to have a vocabulary that exceeds what you might call a cerebral subsistence level.

How do I know? Because of thousands of letters from students. Children's writers (all, probably) have a more wide-ranging and particularised contact with children than other professionals in the literary business. Their letters seem unmonitored by teachers, and are frank to the point of calumny. A surprising number find reading anything at all burdensome as well as boring. They often kindheartedly point out 'it's not just your book'.

Of course I am generalising, which is unfair. But how else can one tackle this question? Some Year 12 students have the intelligence of a person in his twenties. But Year 12 students have also produced the following comments: 'I skip all the conversation and description and stuff like that'; 'I only like books with blood and guts in them and yours hasn't'; 'I don't like reading about why people do things, and what they think and that'; 'Why don't you put in more go go, like TV has?'.

In short, what in the literary world is regarded as good writing, such as a capably sustained storyline, well-developed characters and skilled dialogue, many young male readers dismiss as junk. They leap from peak to peak of action with little or no interest in the valleys. They are the offspring of the huge movement away from the enjoyment of words to the passive pleasure of visuals.

If they become restive when trying to read a simple narrative, what will they make of the high-tech style Wheatley has chosen for her *Vigil* text? Brilliant and careful it is, and justly conveys the quantum jumps, dreamlike memories, disordered ideas and emotions expressed in Nathan's agitated musings. But is this style appropriate for the projected readership?

The writer employs first person, second person, sometimes third in straightforward narrative; present tense, past, a hinted future. Few of these short bites are consecutive; many links are fragile or even, because of time switches, mysterious. Read in one sitting,

Vigil might knock even an adult out of his socks. But if the book is read, as we mostly do, whenever we have leisure to do so, there's an uncertainty about which character was with us last time, and an uneasy feeling of being lost in time.

How Australian is it?

Ihab Hassan

for Don Anderson, Gay Bilson, Bernard Smith

The question is probably all wrong.

How can an American—well, an Egyptian-born American, if hyphenate we must—pronounce on Australia? I came to the Antipodes late in life, drawn to the Pacific, that great wink of eternity, Melville called it, drawn to horizons more than to origins. I made friends and became in Australia a wintry celebrant.

That's personal. Geopolitically—and I believe the political is also personal—questions of national identity threaten to consume us in their rings of fire. Imaginary communities? In each, the instinct to belong is primal, like earth, like water or fire. The mass soul, Elias Canetti said, 'foams like a huge, wild, full-blooded, warm animal in all of us, very deep, far deeper than the maternal'. Kin, clan, co-operative behavior, E. O. Wilson would concur, are governed by 'epigenetic rules'.

Still, I resist the atavism of identity politics, the dark lure of the cave. Am I, then, the one to ask: 'How Australian is it?' Perhaps the question can be goaded with reflection into a wider light. Les Murray, writing nearly a quarter of a century ago about reservations, preserves, ghettos, all those enclaves of exclusion we know about, declared: 'What I am after is spiritual change that would make them unnecessary.' It is also what I'm after, in this brief and blatantly selective essay: distant convergences, broader sight.

*

But slowly now. Australia does have a distinctive locus and history, to which myth clings. The sense of place, coast or outback, seems ineluctable, even in a modern novel like Christina Stead's *For Love Alone*, set mostly abroad. In a prologue titled 'Sea People,' Stead acknowledges the 'inversions' of the Antipodes, then makes the case for 'the many thousand miles of seaboard' her ancestors hug, shrinking from the interior, a 'Sahara, the salt-crusted bed of a prehistoric sea'. And so, people of that 'sea-world, a great Ithaca,' are always asked abroad, 'Men of what nation put you down—for I am sure you did not get here on foot?'

For Love Alone appeared in 1945; the year augured the postwar era. Yet mythic Australia—true always in its ghostly, affective way—continues to haunt writers, even those who try to exorcise it with postmodern ironies. Classics like Henry Lawson's 'The Drover's Wife' still seem unappeased, echoing in Russell Drysdale's painting and Murray Bail's story, both by that name. (More of them later.) And Lawson's flawed, little masterpiece, 'The Bush Undertaker,' can't leave myth alone. Its closing sentence, compulsively superfluous, reads: 'And the sun sank again on the grand Australian bush—the nurse and tutor of eccentric minds, the home of the weird.' Did it need to be said after what we had read?

Perhaps it did. Inga Clendinnen takes up this story again in her Boyer Lectures for 1999, *True Stories*. Its grisliness and parsimony, she feels, make Sam Beckett seem 'anodyne.' Really, anodyne? (Even in refined minds, it seems, cultural identity can assume superiority, not simply difference.) No matter. Myth lives on like an amputated limb, an imaginary wound. Nibbling baklava or sipping latte, nowadays, we suddenly experience the ache, or think we should experience it, till something else makes sense of our lives.

In America, driving SUV's to the supermarket, we pretend that four things shaped our history: Puritanism, Slavery, 'Indians' (genocide, that is), and the West. (Hiroshima, Vietnam, and Bill Gates came too late.) And in Australia? The Bush, Aborigines, Transportation, Gallipoli? How many New Australians would agree? No accidental tourist, an amateur (loving) visitor rather, I whisper to myself: the Bush and its Aborigines, yes, and Australian English too. But I would not dare say this out loud, only in print.

*

The bush first, the bush again, because I find it easier to access, though I claim no kinship to Leichhardt, Burke, or Wills. The bush oppresses, or simply presses on, much nineteenth and early twentieth century Australian writing, and lowers in foreign works like Lawrence's *Kangaroo*. Surprisingly, I have said, it persists in more recent fiction, re-imagined through earlier imaginings, through *Voss*, *A Fringe of Leaves*, and *The Twyborn Affair*, down to media kitsch, down to *Crocodile Dundee*.

A few instances. In Thomas Keneally's *Bring Larks and Heroes*, Australia is still that 'obdurate land', that 'grotesque land', 'evil' to its afflicted settlers 'because it was weird'. In that desolation, people unite 'to ward off oblivion'. (American Puritans spoke in the same accents two centuries earlier.) Thus the bush, no less than colonialism or the carceral system, disfigures both victim and victimiser—all the way back 'home' to England or Ireland. It is as if the wildness of it all could creep westward across the Indian ocean to taint Europe, as it crept eastward across the North Atlantic even after 1776.

In David Malouf's *The Conversations at Curlow Creek*, however, the land appears as 'an infinity of cold and light'; it raises 'the ceiling of the world by pushing up the very roof of your skull'; it demands legend—Adair becomes O'Dare—and delivers marvels to bored or brutalised minds. Ever on the prowl for the imaginary, Malouf also sees the bush as a kind of excess, abandon, vertigo, like opera, reaching for that impossibly high angelic or demonic note, an excess that civilisation must repress, that colonialism must choke. This much Captain Adair understands about himself, and about his operatic parents still alive within him. But opera gives joyous form to the irrational—back to Nietzsche and *The Birth of Tragedy*—as colonialism never can. And so the bush remains formless, the true secret and irrepressible domain of our condition, just like that wild patch of land, somewhere in Brisbane, which bulldozers threaten to turn into a shopping mall in Malouf's recent story, 'Jacko's Reach'.

My point is that the bush is Australian, indeed, but that it alters with the times. It mutates in the artistic twilight zone. It can become an aspect of myth, opera, sexuality, colonialism, the uncanny, or the human condition. How Australian is that?

*

And Aborigines? That is a topic I can neither evade nor satisfy, a knot of violence no foreigner can hope to cut, let alone untangle. (Piety here will not serve: like all moralising, it is but the shadow of virtue, unearned rectitude.) Still, I took heart from Patrick White's deep tact in portraying Aborigines. And I learned from Bernard Smith's *The Spectre of Trugannini*, his 1980 Boyer Lectures, that veracity demands nuance. Smith's premise is that a culture needs to 'put down firm ethical roots in the place from which it grows.' A culture cannot live off the universals of another, though it may challenge or modify them. Hence Smith's 'Antipodean Manifesto,' which avoids essentials—how Australian is this or that—in favour of dialogical, historical arguments, subject to the ambiguities, more, the outright paradoxes, of history.

In that paradoxical sense, may not Bennelong, or any 'Jacky Jacky' for that matter, remind us, painfully, parodically, that hybridity is our destiny? Does not a native 'clown' mime the desperation of living in multiple, divided worlds? The question is prickly, not because it hints political incorrectness but because suffering in Aboriginal mimicry overwhelms laughter. Yet mimicry, in the conflict and evolution of cultures, may point a way beyond assimilation, through and beyond pain. Mimicry assumes a certain empathy; empathy both acknowledges and effaces difference.

Can Aboriginal suffering offer itself to any restitution or better, any future widening of life? Clendinnen remarks: 'But there remains a scar on the face of the country, a birthstain of injustice and exclusion directed at the people who could so easily provide the core of our sense of ourselves as a nation, but who remain on the fringe of the land they once possessed.' An ennobling, perhaps enabling, idea. But how many Australians, again, believe it, outside academe? And what can the statement practically mean? That collective guilt and right recall can create a decent society? That the revived debates about reconciliation, the stolen generation, and a prime ministerial apology can serve as foundational moral acts, guiding future policies toward all minorities, not only Aborigines?

Possibly. Memory, however, has seldom stanched ethnic or racial violence. Walter Benjamin, much quoted if seldom understood, thought that no document of civilisation is free of barbarism—or, as someone forthrightly put it, civilisation rests on the shambles. This is less cynicism than unillusioned historical clarity: we should learn what history never seems to teach us.

As a boy in Egypt, I read James Fenimore Cooper's *Deerslayer* and *The Last of the Mohicans*, and moved freely, fancifully, in their wooded worlds. That may have been a form of historical fecklessness. But to say this is not to say I believe that the genocide of Native Americans can provide the core experience of my citizenship in the United States.

Many decades later, I read with dread and admiration— admiration also in its older sense, wonder—Sam Watson's *The Kadaitcha Sung*. I felt the power and passion of the book, its brutal truth, its craft in an alien tongue. I marveled, too, at the sheer supernatural energy in the novel. But drawn as I am to spiritual things—again, more of this later—I found its allegorical magic alien: I could never make sense of my world with what the Kadaitcha sing.

The indigenous claim to social justice and shared humanity are unassailable. But we need also to recognise that if intellectuals have an iron obligation to speak the truth to power, as Edward Said says, they must also speak it, in whispers or in thunder, to themselves. That may be harder in our impacted, hybrid moment, rife with ideological mendacity, internet terrorism, media hype, nationalist frenzy, *fatwa* justice.

*

So how Australian can anything remain in this geopolitical climate? I have ventured: the bush and its Aborigines, setting aside Australian English, a daunting topic, crying for sustained treatment by a native Australian—if you doubt me, browse Les Murray's *Fredy Neptune* or *The Penguin Book of Australian Slang*. Yet even bush and Aborigine may be more distinctive on a literal than on a subliminal level, there where symbols hum and meanings buzz, and change brushes by like a bat in flight. Put otherwise, all life is translation, as the poet James Merrill said, and we are all lost in it. Lost and metamorphosed, I think. But that still leaves the titular question unanswered, precisely because in subliminal Australia values shift, languages slide—the pundits of theory call it 'semiosis unending'.

The matter is neither theoretical nor abstract. Consider America, for an instant; an instant may be all we have in technoculture. According to a US census, persons speaking Spanish at home increased, between 1980 and 1990, by 50.1 percent; Arabic, by 57.4 percent; Chinese, by 97.9 percent; Vietnamese by 149.5 percent; Hindi and Urdu, by 155.1 percent; Mon-Khmer, by 676.3 percent. (Many of these new immigrants are smart, talkative, educated; some of them will return home.) Though statistics can lie, the 'ethics of impermanence', which Bharati Mukherjee applies to the new Americans, seems to have become a demographic law. Who thinks, who dares now to ask, 'how American is it?'

Is change any less flagrant in Australia? No doubt, Australians themselves live their own changes while others merely pretend to perceive it. Still, cultures are famously invisible to themselves. And the brute numbers are there: so many tourists, students, immigrants, trading partners from east Asia alone, so many military and economic concerns touching the Pacific rim. So much public and private anxiety about Australia's identity, role, destiny in the world. The Anglo-Celtic heritage, of course, remains vital—it's claptrap to say otherwise. But like all strong cultures, that heritage knows how to adapt, adopt, absorb, and sometimes refuse what comes its way. It knows how to translate or refigure whatever migrates.

Translation in cultures or languages, however, is never a cinch. It brings confusion, error. It brings worse: baneful conflicts imported from other times and other places. (Watch what you say to a cabbie, in Melbourne or Sydney, about Lebanon, Bosnia, or Kashmir.) And yet translation works, seems to work better in Australia than in America, though neither will be loved universally for whatever it does. And if translation works, does it not make sense, after all, to ask 'how Australian is it'?

Though I find cultural nationalism self-indulgent, and the cultural strut as tedious as the cultural cringe, I do feel, when I visit Australia, a zest and vibrancy that suggests an Athenian moment. Is it the 'lucky country' all over again? Has it finally overcome the 'tyranny of distance'? What is this rich efflorescence in all the arts? And yes, how Australian is it?

*

I know: I keep asking the question only to duck it. Is there any other way? Perhaps it's what the query itself demands. At least, that is what contemporary Australian writers—the best of them, the most inward with their culture and craft—seem to do. Of course, it would be tempting to isolate tropes and strains in classic Australian writing, recalling Manning Clark's 'Tradition in Australian Literature' (1949). But I prefer to let contemporary artists speak. They rework their own tradition, and in so doing answer, as much as it needs answer, the pesky question. But they will not speak with one voice.

I return to that emblematic story, Lawson's 'The Drover's Wife' (1894). It will not escape our stereotypes about grit, self-reliance in the bush, its mean pleasures and prodigal solitudes. That's what survival takes. But the story also limns a mother's love, facing down evil, all those black, slithering snakes in a stringy-bark shack. What is it all about? Try answering that and you come nearer to answering the question about 'Australianness' before it dissolves into the *mysterium tremendum et fascinans*.

Now re-view Russell Drysdale's painting, 'The Drover's Wife' (1945), which many Australians will have seen, seen in reproduction, at least. No children, no snakes here; bare, spindly trees; a wagon, a horse, an ant-like man in the far distance; hard, blue sky above the red earth. The rest is the woman, hulking in the foreground, with her suitcase and shadow. As in Lawson's story, the sense of bleak, of clumsy, endurance comes through; the big feet press firmly on the ground. One wonders how a woman could stand so full in such a spare, ungiving space—where did the fat on her body, her legs, come from? But the real difference between story and painting is loss: the eyes in the small face, half-hidden by the sadly tilted hat, the eyes have a thousand-yard stare. Right over the viewer's head. Do they express bewilderment, resignation, old hope, terminal loss? Where is the woman going with her suitcase, her back to the puny man? Right out of the frame? And what else, of Australia, is going out with her? Myself, I think this lumbering woman, with small head and shaggy dress, stands up front, at once curvaceous and columnar, saying: I am here, I may be Australia, take it or leave it. But is that what the picture really says?

Questions again. It's what Murray Bail proffers us in his story, 'The Drover's Wife' (1975). Bail: sly, knowing, ironic, secretive, acutely intelligent, gruffly urbane, always sere. That's a distance from Lawson. Watch him go at Lawson, and how Australian it is, through Drysdale. (No need here to invoke postmodern reflexivity or intertextuality.) In Bail's story, a dentist speaks: that's Hazel there, my former wife—why do they say she's a drover's wife? Bail, ever the trickster, is at it from the start: 'There has perhaps been a mistake—but of no great importance—made in the denomination of this picture' (reproduced on the cover of Bail's book). A 'mistake made'? By whom? 'Perhaps'? 'Of no importance'? And where did Drysdale find Hazel to pose? Come off it now, Bail.

This is not the place for a fussy *explication de texte*. The point is that Bail's smart narrative takes up an icon of Australian culture, wraps it in ambiguities, casts upon it a hundred lights and shadows—and ends by reaffirming it somehow. The trick is in Bail's flickering realism, a style of enigmatic banality, which undermines the world of common appearances without quite erasing it. That person there in the picture is Hazel, a real person, the dentist avers. (Real just in what sense?) And she does—or does she?—elope with a drover. But why does she elope at all? Because she feels 'in her element in the bush,' and the silence of the drover 'woos' her? Because, unlike her husband, she likes snow on Ghost Gums; she enjoys chopping wood; she kills snakes. She is 'Australian' all right, 'the silly girl.' In brief, the stereotypes somersault back on their feet; reality wavers, but only for a moment; and even those bushflies, absent in Drysdale's picture, make their way back into the story. This is 'a serious omission,' the dentist grumbles, deadpan. 'It is altering the truth for the sake of a pretty picture or "composition".' Is Bail kidding us, or what? Not entirely. The tacit pain in the tale, the husband's loss and wife's loneliness, put reality back into place. Beyond all ironies, the Drover's Wife lives.

Is that Australian? Australian enough so that, though the mystique may mutate in history or flicker in language, it won't dissolve. Thus in Bail's recent, magic romance, *Eucalyptus*, the author feels obliged to say on the first page:

> But *desertorum* (to begin with) is only one of several hundred eucalypts; there is no precise number. And anyway the very word, desert-or-um, harks back to a stale version of the national landscape and from there in a more or less straight line onto the national character, all those linings of the soul and the larynx, which have their origins in the bush, so it is said, the poetic virtues (can you believe it?) of being belted about by droughts, bushfires, smelly sheep and so on; and let's not forget the isolation, the exhausted shapeless women, the crude language, the always wide horizon, and the flies.
>
> It is these circumstances which have been responsible

> for all those extremely dry (dun-coloured—can we say that?)
> hard-luck stories which have been told around fires and
> on the page. All that was once upon a time, interesting for
> a while, but largely irrelevant here.

Again, really, 'largely irrelevant here'? So what is the passage doing at the commencement of this Calvino-like, yet very Australian, fairy tale called after the eucalypt? Repudiating the stereotypes by perpetuating the archetypes, no doubt, unsettling the scene. And, of course, making a space for Bail.

This can be hazardous. In Bail's earlier novel, *Homesickness*, for instance, the attempt to 'flicker' Australian reality largely fails. Bail, however, is crucially right: scratch any so-called distinctive culture, and what do you see? Our common condition, the museum of personal obsessions and human conceits. Thus, thirteen Aussies on a world tour begin—gradually, zanily—to see themselves in an entirely empty museum, let's say in Russia:

> ...they followed remaining squashed together before
> disintegrating: shoulder-blades, ear, pelvis, heart,
> movement, elbow, nose, eyes, air, rib cage, bladder,
> cigarette, trees, thorax, shoes, penis, shadow, postcards,
> memory, mountain.

So, how Australian are these body parts? (The passage I quote is no more cryptic or elliptic than any other in the novel.) Still, Bail manages to insinuate whimsical little essays, micro-parodies, and allegories of Oz throughout the novel: bits on gum trees, racial laws, Australian speech, Drysdale's 'The Drover's Wife' (again!), corrugated iron structures (Australia's answer to the Ionic column), explorers of the outback, Ayers Rock (like the nose of a man in Derbyshire, 'it rose out of the red skin and stubble with monolithic force'), boomerangs and kangaroos, the great Australian emptiness ('a country... of nothing really', a character mumbles).

These riffs are sometimes comically brilliant, sometimes merely bizarre. But Bail has a larger ambition than to inflict arcane jokes on bemused readers. He seems to say: look at Australians abroad, look for the odd detail, and you might perceive Australia anew. A right good novelistic notion. Only, *Homesickness* failed to renew my perceptions of the Antipodes. What it does renew, despite assorted infelicities—taxonomic fugues, tremolos of erudition—is our insight into postmodern tourism; and by guiding us through some phantasmic museums of the world—the museum of the leg, of marriage, of gravity, and, yes, of corrugated iron—the novel glimpses the interior museum of us all.

But all this is not to say that in an age of both global tourism and cybertravel, none of us have or need a home. Surely, that's one abstraction we have already seen horrifically blooded.

*

So, finally, how Australian is it? The question may be all wrong. For one thing, what is the 'it' in the question? Beer, barbie, beach, language, literature? Hardly the latter: where is Peter Carey, Elizabeth Jolley... ? For another, who am I to pronounce... but I have already entered that disclaimer.

What I have attempted here is to chase the question into some awareness of itself. In this, my covert example may have been Walter Abish's novel, *How German Is It?*, which appeared in 1980 before its author had ever visited Germany. An American of Jewish extraction, a consummate artist, Abish recreated 'Germany' by questioning our sense of it. So does the visionary company of Australian writers—note their surging presence in the *New York Times Book Review*—recreate 'Australia' in ingenious ways.

Consider a signal example: Gerald Murnane's *The Plains*. This lean, hypnotic allegory enjoys a crepuscular existence, perpetually out of print. Yet the novel lives on, still original in its apprehension of Australian life, or rather, of hermetic reality. Of course, we may choose to catch in it hints of Kafka, Borges, or Coover. Allusive as it may be, though, the work remains seamless, perfectly singular.

In allegory, interpretation is a formal, if necessary, clumsiness. Set, apparently, in the immense plains at the heart of the Antipodes, a country contrasted with '"Outer Australia"... the sterile margins of the continent', *The Plains* probes the enigmas of identity, homeland, natural environment, ultimately, of mind and all its representations. The narrator—no one here has a proper name—offers himself to the latifundian masters of the plains, philosopher kings one and all, as a filmmaker. His avowed purpose: to capture the gnostic mystery of their land. But, of course, this lucid madman, no madder than any of us, dissolves into his languages, into his arts. Can we wonder that, at the very end, he admits in a typical moment of metaphysical melancholy:

> I would always ask my patron at last to record the moment
> when I lifted my own camera to my face and stood with my
> eye pressed against the lens and my finger poised as if to
> expose to the film in its dark chamber the darkness that
> was the only visible sign of whatever I saw beyond myself.

This eerie, terminal image of human endeavour, however, should not obscure the relevance of *The Plains* to our topic. Though the work moves in 'shadowy areas that no one properly occupies', though it dwells in a virtual, heraldic, imaginary space where time is a 'pathless plain', though it seeks the occult at the heart of ordinary things, it also challenges our worldly ideas of belongingness, of self and place. Thus one great landowner states: 'I've spent my life trying to see my own place as the end of a journey I never made.' A writer of the plains argues 'that each man in his heart is a traveller in a boundless landscape'. And an extremist denies outright the existence of Australia, maintaining that it is a 'legal fiction', superfluous to the 'real, that is spiritual, geography' of the world.

The Plains does not make our query, 'How Australian is it?', nugatory; it radically alters the terms of discourse about it. Who, after letting this noetic quest seep through consciousness, can rise to wave a flag? But then, flag-wavers under every flag have seldom been readers of avant-garde fiction. And other readers? How many will bother to ponder the intricacies or inconsistencies—say, about the patron's daughter—of Murnane's veiled narrative? How many will simply note its (mock) masculinist ethos, its insouciance of plot, its abstract and elusive style, before putting the book away?

*

Gerald Murnane and Murray Bail may adhere to the Uncanny School of Australian Fiction. They also stand high among original writers of our era. This is not to deny that other writers, like Kate Grenville, can render Australian characters dazzlingly, without turning the continent into a gnostic dream. But what did Patrick White mean—it was just a jacket blurb—calling *Lilian's Story* 'an Australian myth' transformed into a 'fiction of universal appeal'? What myth, particularly Australian? Certainly not that of the Terrible Father or the Fat Lady, both universal as they come. Perhaps the myth of freedom, unfettered existence, marked by historic rebelliousness, distaste for authority and genteel pretensions, an egalitarianism sparked less by resentment than, in Lilian's case, by an immense appetite for life. As she puts it with typical zest and insight: 'I fill myself now, and look with pity on those hollow men in their suits, those hollow women in their classic navy and white. They have not made themselves up from their presents and their pasts, but have let others do it for them—while I, large and plain, frightening to them and sometimes to myself, have taken the past and the present into myself.' But the wonder and untamed energy of Lilian surely revert to fictions from Rabelais to Marquez, Grass, Bellow—or else they are entirely her own.

*

I suspect the question, 'How Australian is it?', lives precariously in the imaginary space between the concreteness of culture and the universality of the human condition. Without conclusion, then, let me close with a key text that inhabits that space: David Malouf's *A Spirit of Play*. (Australian epics like *The Great World*, even fables like *Remembering Babylon*, are unmanageable here.) Speaking as a Boyer Lecturer for 1998, the pre-eminent novelist perceives, questions, and reinvents Australia, all at the same time, in terms open to our common understanding.

For Malouf, Australia at the start of the third millennium is a 'raft' on which people have scrambled, 'a new float of lives in busy interaction.' It is also an ancient continent to which Europeans brought, as a kind of gift to the land, a way of seeing it, not simply in itself but also as 'it fitted into the rest of the world.' (Call it colonialism if you wish, but it has been more than that.) And so, if Aborigines are a land-dreaming people, latecomers share a sea-dreaming. This makes for a 'complex fate'—the phrase is Henry James's about Americans—multiple allegiances to different worlds, multiple tensions between cultures and environments, which Australians need not scramble to unify. Or, as Malouf puts it: 'Our answer on every occasion when we are offered the false choice between this and that should be, "Thank you, I'll take both."' Thus 'identity' becomes a confident way of being in the world, rather than some anxious definition, provided mostly by others. No cringe or scratchiness necessary, a level gaze at the world.

A Spirit of Play ends with a plea for Falstaff, for the festive, motley, carnival aspect of existence, say gay Mardi Gras in Sydney, a civic occasion of tolerance and laughter, mockery and release, death too (AIDS), which must stalk every feast. 'Finding a place for Falstaff,' Malouf concludes, 'acting imaginatively in the spirit of lightness he represents, is the way to wholeness; and wholeness, haleness, as the roots of our language tell us, is health.'

Health, yes, but also death, I insist, death and rebirth, both warp and woof, the loom of being. And this means spirit. Can any carnival sing out, beyond camp, folly, misrule, without the music of spirit? Can any culture, really? Identities created by an assured way of being in the world flow toward ultimate mysteries, sometimes called sacred, beyond the horizons of their assurance. And they can do so without benefit of dogma—church, mosque, temple, shrine—because spirit finally empties itself out of its own forms.

It may be wise to recall, from time to time if not in every sublunary hour, recall even in robustly secular societies, that identities dissolve where human beings attain their fullest destiny. Home is not where one is pushed into the light, but where one gathers it into oneself to become light.

Sydney, Not the Bush

Peter Conrad

In 1930 the photographer E. O. Hoppé came to Australia, where he spent ten months taking pictures for a volume entitled *The Fifth Continent*. Though he conscientiously documented the bush, and lined up the so-called 'wild men' to compose a 'dusky background' for his images, he expected more of Australia than eroding plains, mozzy-ridden jungles and lunar deserts. 'The spiritual home of the white races,' he declared, 'is naturally in the cities built up by their vigour and vision.' Had Australians constructed that white, shining, spiritual citadel?

Hoppé was not sure. He considered urbane Melbourne virtually Bostonian, but in Canberra he thought that the government buildings and the lamp-posts looked as if they still had price-tags on them. In Sydney, the prodigality of nature blinded him, mercifully perhaps, to the defects of culture. The city was synonymous with its harbour, which is actually a negation of the city, a dazzling emptiness at its centre; and around the foreshore, Hoppé saw only verdure, not signs of vigorous, visionary human effort. He called Taronga 'the happiest zoo in the world', because 'its boundaries come right to the ocean-edge and make a natural home for water-loving denizens of the animal world', while across the harbour lay the Botanic Gardens, 'Mecca of typists in lunch-hour'. The typists, like those water-loving denizens, could be considered fauna, nibbling their sandwiches among the flora. The gardens for them were Mecca, a place of pagan worship. Where, however, was the spiritual home of the white races?

At the time, the question was fair enough, and in a way it still is, though of course we tactfully rephrase it. Australians live and work in cities, but our 'spiritual home' is still the bush, or what lies beyond it in that unpopulated and once unimaginable terrain which used to be called the Never Never. Australia derives its idiosyncratic character and its collective myths from this landscape. Some kind of god, certainly not the Christian one, made the country. Man was left to make the towns, which he did, to begin with, half-heartedly. I still remember with a shudder my first trip to Canberra in 1965. I went there to be interviewed for a National Undergraduate Scholarship, and one evening set out to walk from the ANU campus to that tantalising location called Civic. Blitzed by blow-flies, misled by country lanes, I never got there—though if I had, all I would have found was some optimistic plastery arcades.

I turned the scholarship down, and went to university in Hobart instead. That at least, I remember thinking, was a city, with tram-lines, milk bars, musty thrift shops and houses containing staircases. Of course if I looked more carefully, I had to admit that here too the civic pretence soon faded out. Our city skulked in the foothills of a bad-tempered, intimidating mountain, and slid into a harbour much emptier and less sunnily scintillating than Sydney's. Intermittently frequented by boats which took our apples off to be eaten in England or by a flotilla of rowdy yachts which, having set off from Sydney, made a teasingly brief visit for a few days after Christmas. Was this a city, or only a town? Did cities perhaps exist only in the congested northern hemisphere?

Canberra, apologetically adopting the bush as camouflage, seemed then to be the most modest of capitals, despite a ceremonious town plan devised by an American architect who never visited Australia, and a water spout which pays disoriented homage to Lake Geneva. The city's inventors worried about what to call it. Naming a place, like christening a child, evokes sainted precedents and sets a wishful agenda for the future; it is an act of appropriation, but also a magical charm. Australians are hard-bitten, laconic ironists, reluctant to make grand statements or to hold tickets on themselves. (If you ask an American how he or she is, you will probably be told 'I'm great!'. If you ask me how I am, the best you'll ever get is 'Not too bad', even if I happen to be feeling great.) So it was never likely that the Australian capital would be called something trumphal, like Centropolis, or assigned some imported literary deity as its godfather: among the rejected suggestions for a name was Shakespeare. Reviewing the discarded names, I have come up with a personal favourite, which is Sydmeladperbrisho—a compound, as nonsensical as supercalifragilisticexpialidocious, of all the state capitals, which positively trips of the tongue. Its separate syllables could also have been jumbled up and recombined, depending on your own allegiances and your sense of priority. Why not Hosydmeladperbris, or Brisadmerlperhosyd?

I once spent many stalled hours pondering the paradox of the Australian city while travelling between Sydney and London in a Qantas 747 which happened to be called City of Townsville. Here was a town which translated itself into a ville and then promoted itself to city status, now painted across the side of a machine which soaringly contradicted the civic aim of laying foundations, tethering yourself to a spot on earth. My pleasure in the conceit did not outlast my discovery that Townsville got its name from its founder Robert Towns, an English seaman, although it wasn't until 1866, two years after Towns' initative, that the settlement qualified as a municipality.

Even so, Towns was right to think ahead. Before you can build a city, you must imagine one. On a mound of vision in Montefiore Park, the sickly green copper figure of the surveyor-general Colonel Light imagines Adelaide. A scroll droops pen from his hand. His left leg is anchored—as his rapt, springing pose requires if he's not to fall off—by the trunk of a beheaded tree: advance warning that culture will require the brutal clearance of nature. But even after you have enticed people to live there, your work of fabrication is not done. A city is a small world walled with echoes and allusions, stocked with precedents and predecessors.It saves you from being alone, because it embeds you in a shared past. The streets are paved with quotations, like the bronze plaques of Writers' Walk on Circular Quay.

A city requires memories and corpses, which take a while to accumulate. The visionaries are not the founders or planners like Light, whose gaze is in the direction of the non-existent place. That role devolves on artists, the writers and painters who look at what does exist and construct the city, mapping its by-ways and filling its vacant lots with stories. The man-made objective setting remains the same, but everyone who passes through subjectivises it in a peculiar and personal way. Take the case of the Domain in Sydney. A free-thinker like Norman Lindsay could not cross it without scoffing at 'Sydney's self-appointed evangelists, afflicted with megalomania'. But the depressed insurance man in Donald Crick's novel *Martin Place* hears the noise of the stump orators differently: 'From the Domain rose the noise of dissent, like echoes of his own discord.' Cities encourage and license such simultaneities.

A decade before Hoppé, D. H. Lawrence spent a season in Australia. His novel *Kangaroo* attributed his own first impressions of Sydney to the hero Somers. How, he asks as he surveys the straggling, improvised bungalows, do you *make* a new country? In England, where the landscape was barbered and parcelled up and domestically annexed aeons ago, no one remembers. In America, the arduous business of making the country is abbreviated by a profiteering impatience, and a brisk contempt for the land itself. The Manhattan grid was geometrically laid out to the top of the island long before anyone went to live in that wilderness of numbered blocks to the north. American cities are still made, or serially re-made, overnight. I went to Houston for the first time in the late 1980s, just after the end of the oil boom. I remember the drive in from the airport through a scruffy desert, with tumbleweed careening across the highways and roadside sheds selling guns or liquor or the services of lap dancers. Then, out of this nowhere, a vertical illusion suddenly sprouted: a line-up of postmodern pinnacles, including a Dutch guild hall which had grown to a tremendous height after guzzling steroids. The young black woman who was driving the cab glanced in the rear-vision mirror and noticed my jaw drop open at the shock of it. 'Don't worry, honey,' she said. 'Dey's all empty.' The oil boom which conjured up those towers was over, and the instantaneous mushroom clump of a city was already as obsolete as Venice.

Australian cities grew more gradually, and never got speculatively ahead of themselves like Houston. Kangaroo, the demagogue in Lawrence's novel, understands the contribution writers must make to the civic, civilising project and tries to recruit Somers: 'Australia,' he says, 'is waiting for her Homer—or her Theocritus.' The self-qualification in his phrase is perceptive, because the founding of a literature requires you to get the genres in the proper order. First comes Theocritus, the pastoral poet. 'Some description of landscape is necessary,' as Murray Bail puts it in *Eucalyptus*. To start with, you need poets for whom culture is a branch of rural cultivation, a species of husbandry: Spenser with his later ego Colin Clout, who is a shepherd, or Milton in *Lycidas* seeking pastures new; Patrick White jackerooing in the Snowy Mountains, then self-sentenced to 'rustication' (as he put it) at Dogwoods where he bred schnauzers, or Les Murray reflectively supporting his bulk on a fence at Bunyah. After this, you can advance to Homer, and plan the creation of an epic. Pastoral cultivates the land. But the concern of epic is the city. The land is always the same, governed by seasonal cycles. The city, however, is perpetually being created and destroyed by its human imaginers. Carthage falls and so does Troy, while Rome is founded; Brecht curses the arrogant towers of Manhattan and predicts that they will one day be dust.

Australian literature acquired its epic not long ago—though the self-deprecating national sense of humour twisted it into a mock-epic. The setting is cinema conveniently called The Epic in Manly, a suburb whose name, equally conveniently, pays homosocial tribute to the epic cult of virility. In *Holden's Performance*, Murray Bail's hero gets a job at the cinema, where one of his chores is to clean up a puddle of vomit expressed by a drunken cricketer on the foyer carpet. The orange and russet mess forms itself into the map of Australia, 'a work of art, containing its own spontaneity and moral force'. The drunken poet is topographically meticulous, since he even manages a couple of supplementary heaves to fill in Tasmania, with a blobby overspill for the Bass Strait Islands. Flies authenticate the design by settling on the Northern Territory. Holden Shadbolt preserves this action painting under a glass dome borrowed from the confectionary counter, while the sight rouses his demagogic employer Screech to a proud tirade. It reminds him of the theatre's name: EPIC, he explains, abbreviates the slogan 'Even Patriotism is Colourful'. Bail's joke is brilliant, and not so very far-fetched. I wonder if he knew that, when the radical novelist Upton Sinclair unsuccessfully campaigned in 1934 for the governorship of California, he called his party EPIC? The acronym, in Sinclair's case, stood for 'End Poverty in California'.

Despite this loud, liquid rallying city, the Australian tendency is to stray back from epic to pastoral. Cemented suburbs like the one in which I grew up can't do without their nature strips, and even Sydney has its Agricultural Show, when the country—riding high on the sheep's back—returns to town. I was staying at the Wentworth Hotel in Sydney last November, and one night did a jet-lagged double-take as the lift doors opened on the bar and I stepped out onto bales of hay, as if I had staggered into the stables. The room had been pastoralised, I discovered, in preparation for the Melbourne Cup next day. Oswald Spengler described the modern city as a 'daemonic desert of stone', and the painter Francis Picabia or the architect Le Corbusier saw Manhattan as a cubist sculpture. Australian cities do not fit these arid and abstract definitions. Ada Cambridge in 1891 pointed to the view from Dawes Point, above the piers to the west of where the harbour bridge is now anchored, as an instructive example of 'how the charms of nature and the utilities of modern civilisation may blend'. To clear the Australian land counts as vandalism, not progress. In Brent of Bin Bin's *Back to Bool Bool*, a character who has just got off from the migrant boat at Circular Quay complains about the deforestation of Hyde Park during excavations for the railway tunnel to Bondi Junction. Where are 'the great Port Jackson and Moreton Bay figs with their marvellous roots, that made Sydney different?' The city's character, for him, derives from vegetation not architecture, and the settlement's initial name of Botany Bay is a 'certificate of original glory'. Displaying that certificate, every Australian city makes room for its Botanical Garden. In Perth, half of King's Park is still an unedited, unmolested excerpt from the bush, and even neoclassical Adelaide has those bewildering dessicated squares of sun-burned grass where the Greeks and Romans would have installed a paved agora or a forum.

'The Mitchells', in Les Murray's account of a Wordsworthian communion between countrymen who have not been defensively individualised by urban life, ends with a sudden, startling challenge to the alienated, un-neighbourly city: 'sometimes the scene is an avenue'. I love this poem, but I wonder whether that cosy avenue might not be a cul-de-sac in Melbourne—or should I say in Erinsborough?—called Ramsay Street. Our literature mistrusts urbanity. The talk in *Illywhacker*, as Peter Carey says, is 'a celebration of towns as plain (and plainer than) Geelong'. Rather than the condensation and verticality of the city, Murray celebrates sprawl, which is a suburban disfigurement, while Carey praises plainness or flatness, a topography which looks the way a drawl sounds—the 'uneventful horizons' stared at by vacant-eyed cockies in the Western District of Victoria, or 'flat-featureless landscapes where it is the lot of sheep and their gaolers to spend their lives'.

If you focus on the taciturn, low-brow vista beyond the suburbs, the city in the foreground comes to seem chimerical, even fraudulent. Hal Porter once likened Hobart, which starts on a waterfront and arduously climbs a mountain, to 'such upstairs/downstairs Old World cities as Naples and Genoa'. Of course the comparison was too good to be true, because it depended on an undemocratic spatial hierarchy. Porter therefore withdrew the compliment by going on to call Hobart a 'minified' version of hilly San Francisco—'without', he added, 'the tang, glamour, ebullience, and uproar'. How can you have a city without such vices? Gwen Harwood, writing to Thomas Riddell from her family home on Grimes Street during 1943, did her witty best to incriminate or begrime Brisbane: she gave her address as Crimes Street SW1 or Grime Street, and renamed the suburb of Auchenfower, Urbs Beata. Adelaide in *Holden's Performance*, 'a small city and flat', dwindles to a luminous mirage when they tear up the tramlines. The metal grid organised space and the inflexible schedule made sense of time. When these are removed, there is only a blinding blankness left. In *Illywhacker*, Carey shows how easily Sydney can be unbuilt. All it takes is an experimental act of hooliganism. Scrape away at the granite veneer of the Bank of New Zealand in Martin Place and you'll discover brick beneath; even the ersatz granite is only terracotta tiles. Augustus, the epic hero saluted by Virgil in *The Aeneid*, was said to have found Rome brick and left it marble. Carey finds Sydney granite, but leaves it wattle and daub.

The bush at least is idiosyncratic, authentic, and so is its wildlife (which is why one of the names proposed for Canberra was Marsupalia). Australian cities, built so belatedly, could only seem like imitations of prototypes in other places. Sydney is always being uprooted or displaced by metaphors which seek to build bridges to the multiple elsewheres it allegedly resembles. Christopher Koch in *The Doubleman* calls King's Cross 'a southern hemisphere Montmartre'. Peter Corris in *The Empty Beach* remarks that the palm trees on the Parade at Bondi 'would go better in Singapore', while the blocks of flats are a hopeful exercise in 'Hollywood Morocco', almost plausible in the right light. Koch convinces himself that an

Elizabeth Bay boarding-house is 'Sydney's version of a Venetian *palazzo*'. The analogy with Venice has always been alluring. 'All it wants is a gondola!' says Madge about the harbour in Arthur H. Adams's *The Australian*, published in 1920. A poster with an aerial view of the moonlit city by Douglas Annand, designed for Australia's 150th anniversary in 1938, is called *Venetian Night: Sydney Harbour*. The analogy doesn't really work, because Venice lacks the balance between nature and culture which characterises the Australian city. Venice is all culture, with no nature at all except for occasional rooftop gardens and wet streets.

When the harbour bridge opened in 1932, an article in a commemorative book published by *Art in Australia* tried twinning Sydney with another maritime city, arguing that its destiny was to become 'a New York in miniature with skyscrapers exceeding 150 feet'. North Sydney and Mosman had the dubious honour of impersonating 'a second Brooklyn': Brooklyn, as they say in those parts, should be so lucky. David Williamson in *Emerald City* settles for comparing Sydney with Oz, the illusory destination at the end of the yellow brick road. At least that's more appetising than another metaphor which I came across in a brochure about Melbourne, produced by the Australia Publicity Council in the late 1950s to attract overseas investment. A photospread on the coalfields of Gippsland was accompanied by an earnest testimonial, which vouches that 'Visiting industrialists have seen the Latrobe Valley of the future as "the Ruhr of Victoria"'. May that particular future never come!

This pining habit of metaphor, which conditions the way we see our cities, is one of the strange, sophisticated idiosyncracies of the Australian literary imagination. James McAuley referred in 'Terra Australia' to our 'land of similes'. (His metaphor, incidentally, was made metaphorical by a misprint or by simple inattention when the expatriate novelist Colin MacInnes cited the phrase in his 1967 guide to Australia and New Zealand, published by *Life* magazine. MacInnes quoted the phrase as 'your land of smiles'. Unfortunately the land of smiles, in Franz Lehar's Viennese operetta, happens to be China; McAuley's poem, splendidly muddled by MacInnes, thereby becomes a 'gentle affirmation', reflected in what he calls the 'fine smiling eyes' of the orientally inscrutable McAuley himself.) Our metaphors empower us to contradict reality, as Shelley does when he tells the skylark 'Bird thou never wert'. Tasmania's official metaphor is that of the heart. Hal Porter, however, preferred to liken the island's shape to a 'much-kicked bucket', as if expressing a wish that Tasmania itself might kick the bucket. I'm not sure that my already complex feelings about my native state will soon recover from hearing Sir Les Patterson liken the bushy female pudenda of his Lesettes to the map of thickly forested Tasmania.

Trained on Sydney, the metaphoric eye sees the city as a body— an organism, not the product of human ingenuity and engineering; nature as yet undeformed by culture. Whenever Somers in Lawrence's *Kangaroo* is asked how he likes Sydney, he replies with diplomatic obliquity, 'The harbour, I think, is wonderful.' Its wonders are corporeal. He first glimpses 'the famous harbour spreading out its many arms and legs', and later—coining a genuinely Homeric epithet—refers to 'the many-lobed harbour'. Even more deftly erotic, he sees the 'hidden and half-hidden lobes intruding among the low, dark-brown cliffs'. For Ada Cambridge's heroine in *A Marked Man*, the inner port is deliciously closed off by 'two little grassy tongues of land'. Kenneth Slessor proposed a more uninhibited reading of the scene in 1950. The water now fondles the foreshore like an exploratory male seducer: the city is shaped by 'the fingers of the Harbour, *groping* [my italics] across the piers and jetties, clutching deeply into the hills'. Slessor described the harbour waters 'dyed with a whole paint-box's armoury of colour'. Mixed metaphors prove as intoxicating as mixed drinks: colours, for the enthusiastic Slessor, are armaments. The cocktail goes on to get frothier. 'The water is like silk, like pewter, like a leopard's skin, and occasionally merely like water…'—just for a change! 'Sometimes,' Slessor continues, 'it dances with flakes of fire, sometimes it is blank and anonymous with fog, sometimes it shouts as joyously as a mirror'. Wait a minute: how can a mirror shout? I'm reminded of the use Narcissus found for water. The city of similes is a looking-glass world.

Metaphorical last waves like the one in Peter Weir's film are always threatening Sydney with dissolution. Lawrence's metaphors inundate the city. The ferries, he says, allow the citizens to 'slip like fishes' between the two shores. Vivian Smith described the city as 'a room for undersea', an arcaded Atlantis, and when Shadbolt in *Holden's Performance* takes the bus into town from Manly he feels the water lapping at the jetties, curtailing streets, reclaiming domain:

'Water everywhere,'he notes, like the thirsty ancient mariner. At least Bail, a proud modernist, sees all this water as a technological aid, not just a natural amenity. Sydney, he points out, is 'water-cooled like the majority of four-stroke car engines'. He adds the customary metaphors, noting that San Francisco and Venice are—if you permit me to commute between similes—in the same boat.

A metaphor is a vehicle, literally a transporter, a device which makes metamorphosis possible. In 1970, David Malouf's volume of Horace acts as transport, projecting him through space and time. He reads the book thirty miles outside Sydney (which 'glitters invisible/ in its holocaust of air'), but is equidistant from Rome, 'two thousand years from here'. A metaphor works like a harbour cruise: once embarked, you can elide the sight of the squat, ragged, suburban foreshore. A trip on the water enabled Sydney's early novelists to describe the city while keeping it invisible, as it still is in Malouf's poem. The characters in Louise Mack's *The World is Round* go up to the North Sydney Suspension Bridge for a moonlight picnic. Once they reach the middle harbour, Mack announces 'The city was out of sight now.' The Lane Cove ferry performs the same service for the heroine of Louis Stone's *Betty Wayside*: 'the noise and stir of the city were left behind'. Seen from Cremorne in Adams's *The Australians*, 'the jagged city sky-line' is 'blurred and liquefied by the heavy heat-haze'. At last the case-hardened eye of Peter Corris disenchants the distant view. If he validates the illusion you peer at from the other side of the harbour, it's merely to underline real estate values: in *The Dying Trade*, 'Mosman looks nice from across the harbour and just as good up close'. Corris's detective, of course, lives in Glebe, without so much as a harbour glimpse.

Novelists before Corris compose the setting pictorially, like those photographers who greased their lenses or shot through euphemising veils: these impressionistic tactics allowed Jack Cato to present a landscape in the Tasmanian Midlands as an illustration to Gray's *Elegy*. Adams saw the warships at Fort Denison as 'faint washes of liquid grey laid on the warmer haze by a delicate water colourist', and Christina Stead in *Seven Poor Men of Sydney* assumes that the estuary and its untouched hills 'sprang from the artist's brain and straightaway came into life and breath upon canvas'.

Even while they are blurring the view and translating culture back into nature, like the ferries in *Kangaroo* which turn Sydneysiders into fish, these metaphors admit that nature is altered, perhaps perfected or perhaps replaced, by culture. The advent of the bridge announced that there was more to the harbour than lobes and fishes. Hoppé, who photographed it just before the completion of the span, liked its closure of the vista, which blocked off the mazy meandering infinitude of water. The *Art in Australia* souvenir edition acclaimed the bridge as the 'acme of precision', and was glad that its construction had stamped out the 'dissolute streets and crazy buildings' of The Rocks. Another telling metaphor, especially given the abiding concern to dissolve Sydney, to merge it with the harbour: the streets are now seen as dissolute because of their unmodern, picturesque crookedness, not because of the rough pubs situated in them.

'The bridge is certainly the simplest answer', as John Philip remarks in a beguiling poem about the Manly Ferry. It was the answer to many questions more complex than that of the quickest route to Manly. All at once it modernised Sydney, and belatedly sponsored a modern refraction of the city. Grace Cossington Smith painted the curvature of the span, still with a gap in the middle, as an essay in cubic and volumetric forms, and a 1932 linocut by Ailsa Lee Brown, *Moths Around the Quay*, looked down on it futuristically, from the viewpoint of a pilot high above: the quay is a vortex of agitated shipping, whipped up by the plane's propeller. The bridge, like metaphor, is a transporter; from the first, it had more to do than carry traffic. That's why it's a grander thing than its drab, dwarfish English prototype in Newcastle: the difference lies in the ways it has been looked at, and the almost supernatural jobs it has been called on to perform. Eleanor Dark in *Waterway*, published in 1938, regards the bridge with 'wilful mysticism'. The hero of her novel likens the span to a 'ghostly arc', or—when the sun rises, ridging the sky with flame—to a rainbow. Rather than grey steel, it displays the shimmering polychrome sign of a covenant, which might perhaps harmonise the conflict-ridden, accident-prone society of the novel, a harbinger of 'ultimate good'.

Hart Crane saw in the fraught, tense suspension of the Brooklyn Bridge with its vibrant cables a new mode of heroism, loftily absorbing the stress of contemporary existence. The bridge gave Sydney its share in this modern technological epic. Our Homer was an engineer, or a whole team of them. Robert Emerson Curtis published fourteen lithographs about the building of the bridge in 1933. Those gods in machines who rule the classical world have been usurped by god-like machines, which deify the men who operate them. Curtis's captions strive to invent an appropriate Homeric diction, ennobling the workers with capital letters: 'From his lordly seat in the clouds, the Driver of the Creeper Crane is the High Master, the Weaver of Steel'. Curtis's metaphors sanctify the bridge—he entitles the shadowy nave under the pylon 'Cathedral'— but they also acknowledge that the city, as Spengler said, is a demonic invention, the profane collective fantasy of men. He likens the twisted cables, not yet braided, to 'Medusa's locks'. More startlingly, a reporter from the *Sydney Morning Herald* in 1928 watched the riveters lobbing incandescent clumps of steel from hand to hand, and called them 'playful Satans'. You wouldn't find such a knowing literary allusion in a newspaper today. Pandemonium, the demonic parliament erected by the devils in *Paradise Lost*, took slightly less effort than the bridge, and 'rose like an exhalation'.

Yet in Australia we don't allow ourselves to believe in our own myths. Even Robert Emerson Curtis, for all his determination to make the bridge Herculean, can't stop himself registering an ironic quirk of its Ocker physiognomy which Whitman or Crane, the acolytes of the Brooklyn Bridge, would never have noticed. He illustrates the iron case of the cable anchorage, and calls it 'one of four immense "warts" on the buttock of the Bridge'. He sees it, quite literally, warts and all. The opening ceremonies also comfortably slid back, in accordance with Australian priorities, from epic to pastoral, from Homer to Theocritus. Ours is a country in which a poet like Les Murray can refer to 'us primary producers, us farmers and authors'. The Historical Pageant which trundled across this monument to structural engineering included a series of floats representing the triumph of primary industries. An allegorical Australia had her golden chariot drawn by six merinos, 'classic specimens of milking cows, milk cans, separators and so forth' were mounted on the Dairy Float, and Bacchus boozily presided over the Show in Centennial Park. *Art in Australia* therefore commissioned an article from the president of the R.A.S., whose task was to explain what the show 'Means to the Nation'. The enterprise, Sir Samuel Hordern argued, was of 'constructive National value as an essential stimulant to breeding and culture'. The culture he meant had nothing to do with the writing of books or even the building of bridges. Culture, at least when not being used as a dirty word, was still an abbreviation of agriculture.

Hart Crane's Brooklyn Bridge is both harp and altar. Unlike messianic Americans, we domesticate our bridge rather than sanctifying it: its fond nickname is the coat-hanger, just as the new and crassly marmoreal apartment building on Bennelong Point has come to be known, less fondly, as the toaster. The Sydney Opera House has not been so easy to make affectionate, belittling, metaphorical jokes about—and that's its importance, both as an iconic completion of the urban vista, finally ensuring that the city is not upstaged by the harbour, and as the symbol of a new Australia which consists of more than trees, sheep and flies. When the architect Harry Seidler first saw Utzon's design, he sent him a cable acclaiming it as 'pure poetry'. What Mallarmé called 'la poésie pure', that earliest announcment of linguistic modernity, was dispensed from having to mean anything in particular. Its words were no more than signs, and they could signify anything at all. Like the purified language of Mallarmé, the Opera House offers an education in abstractness. You can imagine what Whitman or Crane would have made of it—Whitman who listened to outdoor performances of opera at Castle Garden just off Wall Street, and Crane who likened the cables of the Brooklyn Bridge to the lyre of Orpheus. As always, we Australians dread sublimity, so Clive James has jocularly called the Opera House a portable typewriter stuffed with oyster shells. His metaphors, I suspect, are a bit formulaic: he also said that a body-builder looks like a condom stuffed with walnuts. But the zany surreal object he imagines is an apt enough tribute, because the Opera House is less a building than a metaphorical facility—another transporter, ready to metamorphose into a seagull or a yacht, anxious to take flight or set sail. Opera, cramped onto its exiguous stage, is itself a metaphor for something unuseful and perhaps supernatural. Hence Jan Morris, in one of her recent descriptions of Sydney, squeezes all the harbour and the rowdy city too into the space beneath those ceramic sails. 'Few cities on earth,' she said in 1992, 'can offer so operatic an approach'; Sydney itself—'born for show, with a façade of brilliance, and a gift for exhibitionism'—is the opera. I relish the fact that, in the concert which opened the Opera House in 1973, Birgit Nilsson sang the final scene from Wagner's *Götterdämmerung*, in which Brunnhilde ignites a funeral pyre and burns down the hall. Inside the opera house, it could be admitted that cities are perpetual ruins, monuments to a restive human creativity which relies on destruction and never attains completion.

Of course the Opera House did not resolve Australia's pitched battle between nature and culture. Les Murray in his poem 'Sydney and the Bush' declares that there can be 'no common ground' between them, and happily imagines fashionable suburbs floating 'at night, far out to sea', like the litter of Malibu beach-houses decanted into the ocean by mudslides on the other side of the Pacific. My own sympathies are with Corris's inner-city private eye Cliff Hardy, who in *The Black Prince* goes on an uncomfortable excursion to the Daintree rainforest in north Queensland. He camps out, eats damper, and sums up his feelings with an alliterative grimace: 'I was notorious for preferring pavements to paddocks, beaches to the bush'. I have made my own small contribution to the campaign by maligning Mount Wellington. The description of the mountain in my book about Tasmania was actually an oblique portrait of my father, who resembled it: mountains, as Edmund Burke said, exemplify the fear excited by sublimity. I have never been forgiven for my impiety. A while ago, on Margaret Throsby's radio program, I grumbled again about the bad temper of that extinct volcano and its oppressive profile. When I got to Hobart a few days later, the owner of the bookshop in which I was reading told me that a local beldame had popped in to complain about me. 'Did you hear him on Margaret Throsby,' she asked, 'criticising the mountain?' I felt like the dandified Mr Amarinth in Robert Hichens's novel about the aesthetes of the 1890s, *The Green Carnation*. Mr Amarinth allegedly 'said something scandalous about the North Pole' and 'ruined the reputation of more than one eminently respectable ocean which had previously been received everywhere'; he covers 'Nature with confusion by his open attacks on her'.

Mount Wellington will outlive me, I know. But meanwhile, isn't it culture's project to quarrel with nature? Let us by all means, as Bail recommends in *Eucalyptus*, name and number the trees. Having done so, we can ignore them. The creation of a literature is more like architecture than forestry. Trees, Bail concedes, should recede into 'part of the scenery, in front of which all cultures go through their motions'.

Others have triumphed over nature more spectacularly than I did when I aimed my paper darts at the impervious flank of Mount

Wellington. As the Sydney drag queens prepare to go bush in *The Adventures of Priscilla, Queen of the Desert*, Terence Stamp wonders why Guy Pearce is packing so much otiose glitter. 'Ever since I was a lad,' Pearce earnestly explains, 'I've had a dream—to travel to the centre of Australia and climb King's Canyon as a queen, in a full-length Gaultier sequin, heels and a tiara.' 'Great,' sneers Stamp, 'that's just what this country needs—a cock in a frock on a rock.' And so it is, and this is just what the country gets when those three ambisexual human art-works clamber through the scrub and teeter like spangled skyscrapers on the edge of the canyon, swaying (as the tallest skyscrapers do) in the wind. I can't imagine Les Murray approving of this, and I wonder whether Hoppé would have recognised the drag queens were establishing a 'spiritual home' in the outback. But it's a signal moment in our history, which moved me almost to tears—well, almost—when I saw the film for the first time a few weeks ago.

Actually those sacred monsters don't need to leave Sydney: a prototype or predecessor beams across the harbour from Milson's Point. I am thinking of the florid human sun whose gaping mouth is the gateway to Luna Park. Her tiara is made of fizzing electric bulbs, and the pylons between which she is squeezed mimic the pinnacles of the Chrysler Building, the jazziest of New York skyscrapers. Aptly, she has established herself on the ground vacated by the engineering workshops of the bridge builders. Her eyes wide with excitement, she dazzles the Opera House with her portcullis of cosmetic dentistry. Long before the Mardi Gras made Sydney (as David Malouf has claimed) a carnal, carnivalesque place, this ignited female face symbolised its seductive allure, offering slippery dips, peep shows, barrels of fun, and an invitation to the giggle palace. Of course the city is a spiritual home, though not exclusively for Hoppé's 'white races'. But it is also an erogenous zone, concentrating all the pleasures frowned on in country towns. Whether you give the credit to Priscilla's passengers or to the art deco sorceress on Milson's Point, the outcome is the same. In Australia, nature has at long last been triumphantly topped by high-heeled, tiara'd culture.

The Uses of Enchantment

Juliette Hughes

Even now, every so often you come across someone who hasn't heard of the Harry Potter books. They've probably just come out of a coma, or perhaps they've been yachting solo around the equator for a twelve-month. Or perhaps they are just not readers. Harry Potter frenzy has subsided to a lively simmer in the months following the extraordinary scenes that accompanied the launch of *Harry Potter and the Goblet of Fire*, the fourth book in the series, but is set to bubble up again next year when the film is released. In the meantime the backlash has been gathering force. There had to be one; some critics are suspicious of joy and distrust delight.

In the weeks leading up to *Goblet of Fire*'s July release, there was some tutting from commentators on Bloomsbury's nefariousness. Their sins were venial, and consisted of being mysterious about the title and refusing to give out review copies to leak the plot before the embargo date. All we were told was that Harry would be experiencing the first twinges of adolescence, that the book was to be twice as long as, and more dark and complex than the previous one (each book in the series has been longer and more complex than its predecessors, reflecting the protagonist's own growth in years and understanding) and that a friend would die. There was resentment, but Bloomsbury could hardly be blamed for hyping its salvation.

For a long time Joanne Rowling had been given a dream run in the media as the underdog who had made good. The legends abounded: how, like the Brontës, she had had to hide the fact that she was female. (She did it behind initials as did the brilliant American writer S.E. Hinton, author of *The Outsiders* and *That Was Then, This Is Now*.) Rowling even had to borrow the 'K' from her grandmother's name, as the publishers felt that not only would boys not buy the book if it were obviously written by a woman, but that a double initial would look more convincing. It is also part of legend that the first book was written while she was very poor, supporting a small baby on her own. She says that she did, as the stories have it, write for a couple of hours at a time in cafes, using the light and warmth to get away from her drab, chilly flat in the Edinburgh gloom. One article I read recently waxed rather expansively on that snippet, having Rowling scribbling her story on paper napkins. And now that the backlash from such glorification has started, the inaccuracies in commentary do not stop with Rowling's life story; the books are now frequently criticised for having a male protagonist, for being monocultural and for being escapist and unrealistic.

All these criticisms seem to me to be fatuous or just wrong-headed: Harry is a genuine creation, as full of life and interest as any character who has become real to author and reader. The creature of Rowling's imagination happens to be male: why don't those discontented by this write their own books, with female protagonists? And Harry's friend Hermione (a whole generation is going to grow up able to spell and pronounce that name) is such a strong and attractive character that it's merely silly to complain that the book title isn't *Hermione Potter*. In a recent interview in the *Times*, Rowling said that Hermione was based on herself, and that she hated to make characters to order:

> What irritates me is that I am constantly, increasingly, being asked, 'Can we have a strong female character, please?' Like they are ordering a side order of chips. I am thinking, 'Isn't Hermione strong enough for you?' She is the most brilliant of the three and they need her. Harry needs her badly.
>
> But my hero is a boy and at the age he has been girls simply do not figure that much. Increasingly, they do. But, at eleven, I think it would be extremely contrived to throw in a couple of feisty, gorgeous, brilliant-at-maths and great-at-fixing-cars girls.

As an Australian commentator who praised the book faintly before deploring its lack of black characters had perhaps forgotten Angelina Johnson, a senior student and excellent Quidditch player, cause of some rivalry among Harry and his friends as they cast around for partners in the school ball. (Harry and his best friend Ron end up double dating with twins Parvati and Padma Patil, although Harry has heart-burnings about the girl he really wants to go with, Cho Chang.) In other words, Hogwarts, the wizards' boarding school, has about the same admixture of cultures as any average British school, and Rowling's inclusion of foreign-sounding names never looks clunky or token.

As for the books being considered shallow or escapist, to read any one of them, particularly the last two, is to be exposed to a mind of refreshing, often humorous honesty, that creates a world very like the 'real world' that some librarians seem to want to rub children's noses in but that also happens to contain enchantment, both of the wizarding and of the joyous kind. Rowling's witty takes on government bureaucracy, media, education and class are politically very literate and genially sceptical. And her moral centre (unlike Roald Dahl's, with whom she is often compared) is firm: the evil characters in her books are mainly characterised by racism, cruelty and lust for dominance. Her creation of Rita Skeeter, the tabloid journalist, will immunise millions of young minds against the kind of lying rubbish that gets written in magazines and newspapers about the unfortunate famous.

And Tolkien wrote half a century ago in his lecture 'On Fairy Stories' that escape was not such a bad thing after all—if you are a prisoner of war it is the right thing to do. He went on to argue for the acceptance of mythic reality, the deep dreaming that underpins our being. The Gradgrinds were around then too, demanding their brand of dreary faux-realism as the standard fodder for young minds.

The problem with it all seems to me to come down to the traditional librarians' hatred of books that people actually want to read. Rowling's books are this generation's Narnia, its Faraway Tree, almost its Middle Earth. There was a void and she has begun to fill it. But the 2000 Carnegie Medal (awarded by the British Library Association), in what was for the reading public around the world the year of Harry Potter, was awarded to Aidan Chambers' latest, *Postcards From No-Man's Land*, a book 'for fourteen-year-olds and over' with a seventeen-year-old protagonist, that deals with adultery, euthanasia and sexual confusion. *Harry Potter and the Goblet of Fire* was not even commended. It was a fairly hefty rebuff, not only to Rowling, but to the millions of people who had bought the book and pronounced it good. The Carnegie judging panel of thirteen librarians said of *Postcards* that it was 'the kind of book that gives you hope for the future of literature for children and young people, the kind of book we all wished we had been able to read in adolescence.' For me, that seemed less of a comment on the Chambers book than a snipe at the Potter phenomenon.

When there is such a serious rift in judgment between such a body as the Library Association and the reading public, it gives cause for wondering exactly how that body perceives itself. Not to have awarded Rowling the medal may have been understandable since the third Potter book won it the previous year. But to exclude *Goblet of Fire* from any form of commendation whatsoever argues that the Library Association is at best somewhat out of touch with what young people really want to read, and with what might actually get them—bored and overstimulated as they are with television's nightly dose of sleaze, violence and greed—to learn the joy that can be had when you are so deeply involved in a book that you literally cannot put it down.

Snippet: In the early 80s, when I lived in an inner suburb of Melbourne that has since become too expensive for me to move back to, I suddenly had a yen to re-read some of the old favourites of my youth, so I went to the local municipal library, ensconced in late Victorian stone beside the town hall. I searched for *Anne of Green Gables* or any other L. M. Montgomery books; there were a few in the catalogue but they were not on the shelves. Thinking that they must be lent out, I went to the librarian's desk to reserve them. I was asked to wait. After about fifteen minutes a fresh-faced young woman arrived, not to take down my details, but to ask me why I wanted the books.

'I just want to read them again,' I said.

She replied something to the general effect that, seeing I was a mature thirtyish sort of woman, she'd get them for me from their closed storage, whence they had been banished along with the Susan Coolidge *Katy* books. I was too surprised to reply, and she went on to say that such books were no longer kept on the open shelves because they were very bad for young girls who might feel they had to become housewives or some such thing if they read them. I asked if *she*'d read them. She suddenly looked cagey and said yes, but she'd been younger and had been very bored by them. I told her that L. M. Montgomery books had lots of heroines who were writers, not housewives at all. She looked at me pityingly and went away to extract me my filth from the forbidden stack. Montgomery had joined Enid Blyton and Richmal Crompton on the Librarians' *Index Librorum Prohibitorum*.

A few years later the *Anne of Green Gables* film came out and the resulting demand for Montgomery books has made its substantial contribution to keeping librarians in work and bookshops in business. The Harry Potter books have kept them even busier. I bought my copy from the little local shop. They couldn't afford to discount it to $19.99 as had KMart and Target, but loyal customers gave them a welcome mid-year boost that would probably cushion them from the GST and get them through till the Christmas rush.

The Offended Critic:
Film Reviewing and Social Commentary

Adrian Martin

> *Hate, we mustn't forget, is a thoroughly moralised feeling.*
>
> William H. Gass

On the Greek island of Hydra, there is only one movie theatre—and at the time of year I happened to be there, that theatre does not open for business. For an obsessive movie watcher like myself, only a television set can provide any solace. And on one particular night, there was only a single film screening on the slightly fuzzy, hotel room set, an American movie with Greek subtitles. It was *Showgirls*, directed by Paul Verhoeven and written by Joe Eszterhas, released worldwide in 1995.

On the film's initial release, I wrote a long, very negative review and delivered it over the airwaves of Radio National. As is so often the case with reviewers and critics, I managed my bad vibes by channelling them back at the movie—how often have you read that a film is 'confused', when it is plainly the critic who is experiencing the confusion? I argued, essentially, that *Showgirls* was a really, really bad film. I actually felt a little uncomfortable doing this, because every other reviewer in the world seemed to be arguing exactly the same thing—Verhoeven's expensive, splashy melodrama was almost universally damned, appearing on innumerable 'worst of the year' lists (it didn't do much business at the box office, either). So I in fact went to *Showgirls* in 1995 hoping to salvage it from the pack of middle-of-the-road reviewers—and I failed in my mission.

Instead, I became something very particular: The Offended Critic, declaring my high-minded offence for the world to hear. I was offended not so much by the film's sensational, supposedly titillating qualities (I could have done with more of those), but rather, what I construed as the film's hypocrisy, its hidden conservatism, its double standards. Here is just a little from my *Showgirls* review:

> I don't think I have ever seen a film which proposes such an absolutely dualistic distinction between evil corruption on the one hand and moral decency on the other. On the bad side of that equation, the film racks up lesbianism, perversion, monetary greed, showbiz celebrity, deceit, careerist backstabbing, even a stray night of casual sex. On the good side, there's love, friendship, independence and a fierce commitment to one's art. All the bad things the film calls 'whoring'. All the good things the film calls knowing yourself, loving yourself, sticking to your good moral principles. When big-budget American films start denouncing decadent-capitalist 'whoring', you know you're in a high bullshit zone.

Three and a half years later, on front of a TV set in Greece, I remembered this review and wondered, all of a sudden, what the hell I had been going on about back then. *Showgirls* no longer struck me as an offensive movie; the grounds for my moral-political indignation had just about vanished. What I once found grinding, heavy-handed, preachy and insidious, I now found funny, light-hearted, energetic and exuberant.

Showgirls is a clever, playful, intricate film in ways that I simply could not, would not see (or enjoy) in 1995. As such, it now joins the army of gaudy, trashy, multi-levelled popular films that I love and have publicly celebrated and championed down the years. When I reviewed *Showgirls* in 1995, I thought I had pretty much got it in a nutshell, seen through its tricks, its seductions, its sleight of hand, its pernicious ideology. In 1999, on the island of Hydra, I learnt the lesson that *Showgirls* knew more than I did.

The type of rush to judgment that I initially performed on *Showgirls* is something I believe none of us are entirely immune from. Taking offence, making a show of it, is a peculiarly self-theatrical, melodramatic, histrionic gesture in the annals of criticism. It is an attractive gesture—attractive to a reading or listening audience, as well as flattering to the one who performs it—because it appears so proud, firm, strong, certain. In fact, the best image of this theatre of offence is probably Elizabeth Berkley, the star of *Showgirls*, swinging around sassily, throwing out a line or giving the finger, before she strides grandly and proudly (as she so often does) out of any situation that has started to bug her, some tawdry business that she has suddenly and magically 'seen through' for all its sleazy, corrupt ills.

*

Today, we read and hear many political, ideological judgments about the social worth—or danger—of films. Reviews and op-ed commentaries determine, in ringing tones, whether a movie is sexist, misogynist, homophobic—or progressive, promoting fluid sexual identities; whether it's regressive and repressive, or on the other hand liberating; whether it bolsters conservative nuclear family values, or subverts them; whether it's militaristic, or pacifistic; whether it reinforces stereotypes and caricatures of races and nations, or expands them; whether it massages and perpetuates an exclusively bourgeois view of experience, or critiques it; whether it shows us, in a salutary fashion, the materialist, soulless emptiness of the modern world, or indulges, wallows in that emptiness.

This is film criticism as social commentary—a mutation that especially occurs whenever a particular film becomes more than just another film, but a case, an event, a media phenomenon (as with *Lolita* [1997], *Life is Beautiful* [1997], *Happiness* [1998], *Saving Private Ryan* [1998], *American Beauty* [1999] or *Romance* [1999]). Such commentary always involves a definite, shorthand judgment on the politics, the civic morality, or (more abstractly) the underlying ideology expressed by a movie. Make no mistake, social commentary of this sort has become almost as popular a mode of tagging and rating movies in the public media sphere as old-fashioned remarks on the actors, story or special effects.

What happens when such social, ideological commentary becomes damning—nay, offended? My overwhelming impression is that film criticism or cultural commentary which exhibits offence is, in almost every case, weak and unsatisfying. It comes to appear so particularly as we begin to move away from the first flash of white heat in the public debate over a movie.

Offended critics, and declarations of offence, are everywhere these days, even in the least likely places. Opponents of the new *Lolita* seem to believe that simply by virtue of showing the story of Humbert and Lolita on screen, the film amounts to a condoning and encouragment of paedophilia, and a worsening of exploitative social attitudes towards children. Likewise, *American Beauty* seems to some to present a simple, amoral apologia for men in mid-life crisis who lust for teenage girls.

The *Herald Sun* in Melbourne fired a small campaign against the local production *Redball* (1999), accusing the film of irresponsibly implying that all members of the Victorian Police Force are corrupt, perverted, excessively coercive, on the take— and what's worse, it was partly funded by a Victorian government subsidy! (This is the old, familiar 'abuse of the taxpayers' money' line of public offence).

Roberto Benigni's *Life is Beautiful* raises the hackles of those for whom the Holocaust can never be approached via the genre of sentimental comedy—using apparently sophisticated ethical-aesthetical reasoning, they propose that such monumental terror must only ever be depicted obliquely, indirectly, humbly (as Primo Levi does in literature, Claude Lanzmann in film or Serge Daney in critical writing).

Whenever characters die in films—for instance, when the lesbian played by Kathy Bates dies in the political satire *Primary Colors* (1998)— this is instantly condemned around the traps as a wilful ideological act on the film's part: a violent, dismissive, exclusionary gesture of 'killing off the dyke' (or the black, or the Arab, or the woman).

And a final example: a review in a Melbourne suburban newspaper by Deb Verhoeven of the sci-fi blockbuster *The Matrix* (1999) complained that it is 'socially conventional'—a rather telling phrase which means, in the context of the review, that there are no really key roles for women or blacks in the film; or at any rate, no roles for women or blacks that are taken by Keanu Reeves.

Surely something is going nutty when every individual character in a film—of a particular gender, sexual orientation, colour, nationality or age—is taken as a representative of their entire class? This holds movies to an extremely restrictive 'politics of representation', implicitly or explicitly demanding that they must always deliver 'positive images' of the group in question, and mirror progressive social dynamics in their plots. No wonder so many commentators were perplexed by *Romance*—Verhoeven labelled this, too, 'quite a conservative film'—which is as much about women's sexual alienation, debasement and shame as it is as about liberation, autonomy and self-discovery.

This sorry situation reminds me of a bad John Sayles film, where plot and characters seem to have been arrived at through a cerebral, schematic process resembling, more than anything, an Equal Opportunity arbitration hearing. When Offended Critics come out with their most sweeping, generalising, totalising claims, I instinctively resist their political gesture, because, at the very least, something of the common, everyday reality of what it is to watch films has been ruthlessly evacuated: for example, the artifice, the superficiality, the abstraction, the formulaic qualities of many (maybe most) popular genre films, where generic goodies and baddies are of course going to be cornily cast from some handy 'social deviant' stereotype-pool.

All these 'profitless interpretations' (in Stanley Cavell's phrase) are enough to make one decry the baleful effects of 'political correctness' in arts criticism—even as, by 2000, we well and truly know the term to be impossibly loaded and/or tritely meaningless.

*

It is not all that hard to work up a case against such angry and pointed social commentary upon movies. This case usually comes from cinema scholars or critics who, quite simply, get sick of hearing films being discussed by people—especially those star newspaper columnists called upon to comment authoritatively on everything occuring in society—who sometimes seem to know so little about the medium and its history, but nonetheless pronounce so confidently on the latest movie event.

In fact, I would propose that one of the principal impulses driving the discipline of cinema studies over the past thirty years has derived from a feverish attack on sociology and sociological method—or at least, an attack on a caricature of what sociology is and does, when it presumes to talk film. Like all caricatures, this version of sociology is a bit of a straw man. But, again like all caricatures, it also carries a grain of truth.

Nothing sends a certain kind of cinema scholar into paroxyms of rage and annoyance faster than what is known as 'window on the world' commentary. This term refers to how a film can be taken as an immediate, mirror reflection of people, places, events, problems in the real world; a window opening up on certain topical, problematic issues; or a trigger for public discussion.

Window on the world talk is often referred to, dismissively, as a realist approach to film. Of course, this so-called realism is a relative stance: no one actually, naively believes that fiction films are simply documentary reflections of reality (and even the documentary mode itself is under intense suspicion these days). But such commentary moves quickly to the conceptual point where the link between depictions on screen and phenomena in the world—the link, in short, between cinema and reality—can be proposed, observed and adjudicated upon.

Responses to this state of affairs from aggrieved film aesthetes, cinema scholars and pop culture connoisseurs, are many and varied, but they all share a fundamental reflex. Film is not reality, they cry, not a reflection, not a mirror; instead, it's a text, a mediation, a fabrication, a fiction or a fantasy. Films cannot be abstracted or dissolved into the public coinage of real-life issues, social tendencies, historical events, documentary glimpses of behaviours and lifestyles (so the argument goes); they have their own materiality, their own language, their own codes, conventions and history—and, not least, their own internal, animating agendas.

In a provocative address to secondary media teachers in Hong Kong a few years back, the expatriate Australian cinema scholar Sam Rohdie counselled against using movies as mere triggers to discuss topical events like homelessness, apartheid or environmentalism. 'Because films provoke fantasies and desires, they may also provoke our secrets, our immoralities, what we like but are forbidden to have. Social issues in films are often alibis for what really interest us'. Taking Spielberg's *Jurassic Park* (1993) as an example, he remarks: 'To discuss the themes in the film would not particularly illuminate the mechanisms of film.'

Another striking, local instance of this opposition to social or sociological commentary on a controversial movie event can be found in the issue of *Metro* magazine containing a dossier on the New Zealand film *Once Were Warriors* (1994). Geoff Mayer contends that 'most New Zealanders... mainly considered the film within a "realist" framework which was seemingly dependent on the film's ability, or inability, to capture the "truth" and "reality" of Maori life in South Auckland'—with special emphasis on issues of domestic violence and masculinity. Mayer concludes by suggesting that: '*Once Were Warriors* is a film that deserves to be seen for many reasons although it should not be confused with reality—nor should any film.'

Sylvia Lawson, a keen media watcher, eloquently summarised the frustration of many critical practitioners when she plaintively protested: 'It simply isn't possible to talk sensibly about a film anywhere without discussing the sounds and images it's made of.' She was referring specifically to the debates around Dennis O'Rourke's documentary-cum-personal-essay film *The Good Woman of Bangkok* (1991), helpfully collected in the Power Institute anthology *The Filmmaker and The Prostitute*. In those debates, the film itself, any index of its materiality, seemed sometimes lost in the heated exchanges that it prompted about Australian men exploiting Asian women. In the rush to praise or condemn the film's depiction of this situation, too many filmic and extra-filmic levels were collapsed, condensed, short-circuited.

Inevitably, the tendency of these counter-sociological moves is to stress the autonomy of film vis-a-vis whatever 'real issue' is being floated. The various schools and methods of criticism devoted to 'close reading' make their primary appeal to 'the text itself', rather than to broad social issues. A barrage of theories and devices get this more apparently sophisticated, cinema-oriented discussion going. Genre is stressed, for instance—*Saving Private Ryan* is considered as a venerable combat film, activating certain conventions and traditions, rather than a you-are-there record of what taking a bullet into one's flesh is really like (the realist fix of many commentators on the film, and indeed the basis of Spielberg's own hype for it).

Often what a film is nominally about—the Vietnam war, street gangs, religious debates—is breezily dismissed as almost irrelevant, a mere pretext or handy, disguised metaphor for what the critic thinks the movie is really, deeply, often unconsciously about in its 'imaginary': usually, something related to sex, gender or the institution of the nuclear family. Not so long ago, every third film was diagnosed as being really, secretly about the dirty machinations of the Oedipus complex, as it plays out between men (fathers, father-figures, sons, son-figures) in a patriarchal system under threat—and, as a matter of fact, I think the neo-Nazi moral-panic movie *American History X* (1998) would serve rather well as the latest example of this particular displacement of social anxiety. In many ways, this is the newer-fangled, neo-Freudian version of a previous generation's appeal to the eternal, Jungian verities of a 'collective unconscious' underlying every cultural expression.

A more literary tradition in cinema studies stresses artistic intentionality, aesthetic point-of-view, the precise mood and tone of a drama or comedy—in other words, just how (according to the critic's reading) we as viewers are being asked to consider, regard, reflect upon what we are seeing. The latest *Lolita*, for instance, offers itself up easily to such salvation-by-criticism. It may not be a particularly high, complex or subtle artistic achievement, but it definitely has a dramatic, aesthetic point of view. It is clearly not asking us to love, identify with or emulate Humbert's perverse longings, but to see them as deluded, arrested, pathetic, maudlin. A similar sort of perspective clearly mitigates the 'amoral' goings-on in *American Beauty*.

Such anti-realist, sometimes anti-content arguments have been taken to their furthest extreme in discussions of screen violence. Critics who have regard—love, even—for violent cinema in its diverse forms, who want to defend it against the moral panics that regularly surround it, have developed a multi-layered, action-packed response to those who decry everything from *Taxi Driver* (1976) to *Terminator 2* (1991) as dehumanising, desensitising cultural influences. Tarantino says it, anti-censorship spokespersons all over the world say it: screen violence is not real violence, and should never be confused with it. Movie violence is fun, spectacle, make-believe; it's dramatic metaphor, or a necessary catharsis akin to that provided by Jacobean theatre; it's generic, pure sensation, pure fantasy. It has its own changing history, its codes, its precise aesthetic uses.

By now, however, I fear that these arguments—the recourse to genre, 'the imaginary', artistic subtlety or pure fantasy—launched variously by film critics, cultural students and pop-trash-genre buffs, have themselves become too pat and simplistic, a way of stopping debate dead rather than elaborating it. They constitute less a reasoned defence than a sign of anxious defensivness, or what Paul Willemen calls a 'neurotic knot', within public discourse.

*

How to untie that knot? Personally, I am inclined to see another, more intriguing meaning hidden in Mayer's warning that *Once Were Warriors* should not be 'confused with reality'. Let's not think of confusing film with reality as a naive act, or a simple error. Let's think of it as a fully dynamic, projective, complex process—and also something that is intermittent, not constant for the whole of every film. There are moments (we all know them) when we do feel extremely close to what we witness on screen, when we are 'taking it very personally', as the saying goes—taking it personally as flattery, or insult, or seduction, or assault.

At such moments, films touch precisely the part of us that really wants to see, or not to see, some image of ourselves up there, some constructed mental picture we have of our lifestyle, our behaviour, our world, our politics, our community. At such moments (whether the rational, theoretical, aesthete part of us likes it or not) we really do *want* films to be mirrors—or at least, we want that film to behave like a mirror should behave, as it did for Snow White's wicked stepmother. This has nothing to do with so-called realism, but everything to do with the public politics of film criticism, including its displays of offence.

There is an intensity, an irrationality, a potential hysteria in this everyday process of confusing film with reality—naturally, since it touches and sets in motion every one of our intimate, psychic, conscious and unconscious mechanisms of defensiveness, vanity, desire, longing and aspiration. I'm not just referring to intense emotions related to our personal experiences of love or beauty or ageing—I'm talking about our political passions too, the identifications and investments that are just as much bound up in and affected by the wiles, strategies, doubts and terrors of our baser selves. Willemen was right to suggest (in his book *Looks and Frictions*) that it's useless taking psychoanalysis on board as a theory of pleasure, desire, satisfaction, liberation from repression (Rohdie's formulation: 'I think the cinema is essentially about fantasy, hence about pleasure and desire')—unless you're also willing to take it on board as, equally and crucially, a theory of mechanisms of resistance and transference, with all the complex, unconscious confusions, sublimations and denials these processes entail.

Often, our mirror-relations to movies turn us into viewers who entertain extremely split, dissociated relations with the form and content of a film. We can find ourselves admiring or defending a movie's style while decrying its supposed message—but then we are stuck with the niggling problem of cleanly, clearly separating the 'how' from the 'what' of cinema, when we know this to be, ultimately, impossible. In films as much as in daily life, the 'manner' of whatever we encounter fully determines its effect upon us.

These common complexities of the film-viewing experience were brought home to me in 1999 when I participated in a radio debate on Todd Solondz's 'American independent' film *Happiness*. I thought I'd kicked off with a good point on air by suggesting that people (such as Robert Manne) who like the film and champion it (in however disturbed or queasy a way) take it as precisely a mirror reflection, a snapshot of what the Western world (or at least American society) is really like today, with its pervasive alienation, humiliation, perversity and misery. Yes, I was once again trotting out the old 'critique of realism', the aesthete's stand against simplistic, one-to-one-correspondence social commentary.

Later in the discussion, I produced one of my favourite quotes from the annals of critical literature: the filmmaker and teacher Jean-Pierre Gorin's late 70s comment that each of Rainer Werner Fassbinder's screen characters was 'a flat encephalogram. Each line, each life is drawn straight and shallow, and it doesn't take very long before it falls in on itself'. Gorin added: 'Fassbinder's problem is that once he's constructed his first few visuals, he's said it all. He has nothing in reserve but all the obviously depressing moves.' To me, in the light of Gorin's remarks, Solondz rated as a neo-Fassbinder.

Off air, Graham Little, another participant in the discussion, politely pointed out to me that, given my comments, wasn't I being a trifle realist after all, despite my protestations to the contrary? And he was right: if I say that I don't like *Happiness* because it shows people who are drawn shallow and can't move anywhere except down, and if I publicly prefer movies where characters express more life, craziness and resistance, that's because, fundamentally, I have in my head and heart this image of the world that I want to see on screen—because that's either how I think the world really works, or because that's how I wish it would work. And I think many of our most intense love-or-hate reactions to films come down to something like this. Maybe Barbra Streisand was right, after all, when she asserted in *The Mirror Has Two Faces* (1996) that 'academic opinions are purely subjective'.

*

The projective process helps to explain why offence is such a prevalent stance in acts of criticism. However, I don't think it entirely excuses all crimes against reason committed by Offended Critics in our present climate, and nor do I think it validates just any old social commentary. The anti-realist critique has helped us a little, but has generated its own problems: ultimately, the knight's move to sever film from reality is as disturbing and dissatisfying as the sociologist's tendency to mistake film for reality.

In a way, many of today's critics and cinephiles have managed to inadvertently retrace the same backward step made by François Truffaut over forty years ago, when he withdrew from believing (as a critic) that 'every good film must express simultaneously an idea of the world and an idea of cinema', and adopted the simpler faith (as a director) that films need only 'vibrate' with the joy or agony of 'making cinema'—a creed that profoundly informed the French New Wave and all the subsequent postmodern movie movements launched in its youthful image.

How to break this impasse? Clearly, an effort has to be made to get those old sparring partners form and content back together into some kind of marriage, however progressively arranged. Plus something a little larger and grander than form meeting content—that 'idea of cinema' recombined with an 'idea of the world', however multiple those ideas are going to be. And with all that, a sense of the knotty, life-and-death, psychic drama underlying any evaluation of film, no matter how seemingly objective.

Rather than dissociating form and content, cinema-idea and world-idea, I suggest we consider the category of *sensibility*—the sensibility of a film or artwork, which is always individual to a particular aesthetic object, although it invariably incorporates a myriad of impulses, conventions and traditions that bring along the baggage of their own histories.

When you react to a movie, you react to the whole thing, its entire gestalt of form and content—and you react as fully you, body and mind, emotions and personal history combined. Everything that fits under the category of formal elements in a film, all the things sometimes wrongly considered as on top of or beneath the plot—the colours, the rhythms, the feel of the sound and its ambience, the choice of music, the particular, characteristic way in which people are filmed and gestures and incidents conveyed, the shapes of the narrative structure—trigger in us intense reactions of taste and distaste, tied to all those complex mechanisms of desire and defensiveness. This intensity is completely personal, and completely cultural, all at once; it's completely whimsical, and completely historical.

Rather than reducing a film to a series of paltry tokens—characters, stereotypes, plot moves, 'messages'—that are then ground through a grey mill of political adjudication, one can argue, politically, *from* sensibility and *about* sensibility. And one doesn't have to fall back into that slightly elitist, literary trap of always stressing the subtle artistic intention, the dramatic irony, the suggestive mood or the camouflaged, authorial point-of-view. Sensibility takes in all that, but it's also, equally attuned to the immediate, surface, moment-to-moment level of sensation in a work, that 'erotics of art' to which Susan Sontag advised us to attend on a level 'beyond interpretation'. Sometimes, our gut reaction to a film—that overwhelming sense that something in it is intensely true, or irredeemably phony—is in fact a quite reasonable place from which to start (so long as it is not deployed as either an absolute or a show-stopper), since it arises from the whole personal and political formation I'm calling a sensibility.

How can a category like sensibility help us navigate that split between film-as-a-world and the real world? In fact, sensibility has everything to do with reality—with the reality, especially, of cultural expressions, of styles and idioms that embody attitudes, values, ways of life. I'm sticking with my distaste for *Happiness*, for instance—not any longer because I want to attack supposedly dim-witted realists, but because I've realised that I really do detest the sensibility of that film, its mixture of nerdy superiority, casual cruelty and flip, nihilistic humour. And I detest, right inside that, how Solondz's lazy, uninspired way with narrative, and his absolutely inert, schematic approach to film style, reinforce, authorise even, the facile bleakness of his vision. I don't think Solondz sees the world as it really is, and I don't think I see the world as it really is either—but I do think there should be occasion to collide and debate these various speculative visions.

Life is Beautiful presents an equally intriguing *cause célèbre*. I don't believe a persuasive case can be argued against this film from the *a priori* position that a comedy about the Holocaust—maybe even any coventional, representational film about the Holocaust—is an ontological impossibility, or a cultural travesty. The history of popular film, and popular culture more generally, shows us that any form whatsoever—absurdist comedy, exploitative horror, pulp-trash fiction, tasteless parody—can be (and probably will be) applied to the events of our collective, real-life history; and that all sorts of unlikely insights may well be generated from these sometimes bizarre mix-and-match experiments. *Life is Beautiful* expressed little for me personally—so desperately determined was it to keep the star and the kid in the foreground the whole time, even in the camps— but I wouldn't move to rhetorically 'disallow' the film, as some especially offended viewers have done.

A similar outcry happened amidst the negative, offended reactions to Spielberg's *Schindler's List* (1993): how can anyone turn the Holocaust into a big budget, spectacular, voyeuristic Hollywood movie, and centre it on some saintly, individual saviour-hero? Well, that's too much offended moralism up front, too many defensively loaded assumptions, before we even get into the movie. I was more persuaded by Camille Nevers, a game critic in *Cahiers du Cinéma*— contributing to a dossier titled '*Schindler's List*: Is it Beyond Discussion?'—when she implied that it's good to have Hollywood movies about the Holocaust, good to have spectaculars and thrillers like *Schindler's List*, because the film creates a heightened, expressionistic 'fictionalised fear' in which 'suspense is an *apprehension* of death, a phantasm of death'. According to this account, Hitchcockian suspense techniques can offer an artistically true and valid intimation of dread (both personal and historical), thus helping us to appreciate the enormity and significance of that real-life terror. It is because of encountering Nevers' wild speculation that I now persist in considering an episode of 'The X-Files', about the discovery of alien corpses in a discarded experimental lab, as being pop culture's greatest and most haunting contribution to this century's intellectual and artistic reflection on the Holocaust.

*

The American art critic Dave Hickey offers a rich account of what it means to relate to cultural works fully, simultaneously as form and content, sensibility and ideology. A superb chapter in his *Air Guitar: Essays on Art and Democracy* recounts the tale of how, as a schoolboy in the 1950s, he was interviewed by a sociological researcher out to prove, at all costs, the pernicious ideological effects of cartoons (Donald Duck, Tom and Jerry) on children; and how utterly betrayed Hickey felt, as a child, by this experience at the hands of institutionalised authority. He speaks back for both the adult he is and the child he was by arguing that cartoons worked on two levels for the kids who enjoyed them:

> ...the intimidated, abused, and betrayed children at Santa Monica Elementary, at the dawn of the nineteen fifties, without benefit of Lacan or Lukács, managed to stumble upon an axiom of representation that continues to elude graduate students in Cultural Studies; to wit, that there is a vast and usually dialectical difference between that which we wish to *see* and that which we wish to see *represented*—that the responses elicited by representations are absolutely contingent upon their status as representations—and upon our knowledge of the difference between actuality and representation.

Hickey's short, profound book *The Invisible Dragon: Four Essays on Beauty* touches at many points on our current regime of critical offence. Hickey detests the way in which our art institutions—not just the big public galleries, but the whole government-subsidised culture of small, alternative artspaces—have managed to sanitise art and its effects, to bureaucratise it, turn it into an art that is first and last 'good for you', wholesome, educative and edifying. And this code of aesthetic and cultural good is always tied to what Hickey sarcastically calls the 'higher politics of expression'—a 'puritanical canon of visual appeal espoused by the therapeutic institution'. His thoughts find an echo in the film criticism of Willemen, who celebrates that radical cinema which is 'contradictory, never pure, innocent or simply politically correct or incorrect'.

Hickey describes how, when the art institution goes into bat to defend supposedly scandalous or transgressive artworks, it effectively lessens their impact and meaning, by severing form from content, style from sensibility. He takes the example of Robert Mapplethorpe's privately circulated pornographic tableaux (known as *The X Portfolio*), which were reclassified by the institutions as art proper—as works that involve a safe critical distance, an encompassing moral point of view, a considered discourse upon society and its trends—the moment they actually managed to transgress or scandalise anyone outside the back room, artworld cloister that had previously sheltered them. But, Hickey writes, 'it was the *celebration*, and not the marginality, that made these images dangerous'—and 'it was exactly their beauty that had lit the charge'.

The beauty of these extremely explicit, pornographic images was persuasive, Hickey argues, and thus celebratory. And what they celebrated, unambiguously, was their own content. These tableaux invited you in to look in awe, to worship, perhaps ultimately to emulate, to join the celebration, or at least seriously ponder it as a living possibility. They were not meant—to use the worst cliché of current arts criticism—to 'disturb', or provide some cute frisson as regards the perverse, the abject or the supposed 'dark side' of human nature (as horror films are also often said to do). And nor could they possibly be construed (I hope) as ponderous reflections on our society's lack of morality or spirituality (which is how some commentators chose to take such a proudly, fiercely amoral contemporary work as Cronenberg's *Crash* [1997]). Mapplethorpe's images gave us something to see, and something to see represented, and challenged us to embrace both in one.

Hickey suggests that, once subject to the baroquely sado-masochistic call of Mapplethorpe's imagery, 'we have to trust someone, give ourselves up somehow to one position or the other'—even if only in our imaginations. Such a response might help to get us past that frozen, defensive moment of offence which casts everything in black and white, into moral dualities of good and evil, progressive and reactionary. Many cultural works, if we're honest about their effect on us, put us into contradictory positions, and make us feel acutely ambivalent—even *Showgirls* does this.

Confusing films with reality, in the positive sense, should be a sticky business, a sometimes embarrassing encounter. For it's only when we let ourselves be moved—truly moved in an unsettling rather than reassuring way—that our sensibilities can ever possibly change, adapt and grow. And when it comes to our precious, precarious ground as individuals—or as citizens—our sensibilities are just about everything we've got.

Bitter Light

Kevin Hart

A couple of years ago I was standing in my favourite Paris bookshop, Companie, with a very thick book in either hand and a puzzled look on my face. I had just picked up the new Gallimard edition of Emile Cioran's *Oeuvres* in my left hand when I saw the even more recent Gallimard edition of his *Cahiers, 1957-1972* which I grabbed with my right hand. As though being punished for greed, I could open neither volume, although I could see from the back covers that I could afford both. After a moment, though, I put both books down and walked away. I certainly wanted to have Cioran's books in French, and I was very curious to read his notebooks, but something in me rebelled against reading him in such weighty tomes. Cioran is such a gloomy writer that the thought of completing the first hundred pages of a book and finding hundreds more still to go is hardly enticing. Besides, a virtuoso of the fragment like Cioran should be read in slim collections with lots of white space around each explosion of thought. I would do better to look for the original thin books in those secondhand bookshops a little further down the Rue des Ecoles.

Several months after I got back from Paris the whole of Melbourne was brimming with Christmas. Waiting for a tram, I saw that the young man beside me was completely absorbed reading a paperback. I looked closely; it was Cioran's first work, *On the Heights of Despair.* The next day, walking down Lygon Street, I stopped to chat with a former student sitting outside a cafe. His friend put down her book, Cioran's *All Gall is Divided*. Later, a friend dropped round: he was reading the same title. Over the next week I checked several local bookshops. Each had a healthy stack of new paperbacks by Cioran, though by the following week the stacks had become very thin indeed. When Christmas came, the first present I unwrapped was a slim book: Cioran's *The Trouble with Being Born*. I opened it at random: 'I was alone in that cemetery overlooking the village when a pregnant woman came in. I left at once, in order not to look at this corpse-bearer at close range...' It was going to be a troubled Christmas.

Who is Cioran? What does he write? And why are people reading him right now? The first question seems the easiest to answer, although it might turn out to be the most difficult. Cioran was born in Rasinari, Romania, in 1911, and his father was an Orthodox priest. He moved to Paris when he was twenty-six, by which time he had already written four books in Romanian: the first, *On the Heights of Despair*, was the creature of an insomnia that haunted him throughout his adult life, while the last, *Tears and Saints*, set the tone for the fierce railing against Christianity that marks his life's work. 'Religion', he wrote, 'is a smile masking cosmic nonsense, one last waft of perfume drifting over nothingness'. Reading that, one might picture Cioran as an elegant wit, a belated habitué of eighteenth-century salons. There's some truth in that picture, yet we get closer to our man when hearing him say, 'In vain do we try to cast off saints. They leave God behind them the way the bee leaves its sting' or, with less flourish and more feeling, 'We cry in God'.

Before he left Bucharist, Cioran had toyed with writing a dissertation on tears, and the last book he published in Romania suggests the thesis he may have proposed: 'Tears did not enter this world through the saints; but without them we would have never known that we cry because we long for a lost paradise.' We must look to the saints, he says, if we are to find the source of the 'bitter light' that comes to us through tears. He gazed intently at the saints, especially the female mystics, admiring them for their 'voluptuousness of suffering'. Yet it was music rather than the saints that best captured for Cioran the colours of losing paradise. If this makes him seem like an aesthete, again there is some truth in that. 'I dream of a world in which one might die for a comma', he wrote, and like an aesthete he tended to scowl at all political parties, entrusting himself to an indomitable scepticism from which he did not exclude the blandishments of art. Literature, he pointed out, lives on a 'cancer of the word'.

Once he arrived in France he lived in cheap hotels and ate in university cafeterias until, in 1949, he could afford an apartment. Thereafter he eked out a life in Paris, becoming known as an acute and wayward moralist, and—according to St-Jean Perse—the greatest French stylist since Paul Valéry. In saying that, Perse was not playing the diplomat but simply telling the truth; and if we agree that brevity is the epitome of style, he was surely right. Cioran died in 1995, having outlived the existentialists whose works seem prolix and pallid when placed beside his, and having anticipated the postmodern prizing of the fragment. Properly understood, however, he is neither an existentialist nor a postmodernist. He founded no 'ism' and had no disciples.

Yet Cioran has never been so popular, especially with young adults. Some associate him with Nietzsche, but he was never comfortable with the mythology surrounding Zarathustra and, in the end, rejected the philosopher's ideas as well. The German sage spoke of nihilism as the 'uncanniest of guests', and found its meaning in the judgment that the highest values devaluate themselves. We ask 'Why?' and can find no answer. More sceptical than Nietzsche, Cioran does not believe that history tells the story of how philosophical idealism degenerates. The abyss has always been there; and the truth comes into sharp focus, he thinks, only in Vedanta. 'Since nothing has real substance, and life is a twirl in the void, its beginning and its end are meaningless.' Cioran never argues, he states; his words never explain, they explode. He may draw energy from the *Maximes* of La Rouchefoucauld, but his fragments are neither as neatly balanced as the Duc's nor as scrupulously impersonal in tone. Labour though he did to sew himself into the straightjacket of French prose, Cioran never felt comfortable in the land of Descartes; it was a culture stripped of vitality. Someone in him wanted to have lived in Czarist Russia or to have been a Spanish noble. Reflecting on his style, he exclaimed, 'To have foundered somewhere between the epigram and the sigh!'

What is it in Cioran that attracts people these days? Perhaps it is the sense of homelessness that his writing evokes so powerfully. An exile most of his life, Cioran affirmed the state of displacement as the most conducive to the life of an intellectual. He may be right, although to us the word 'intellectual' is covered in rust. The world has changed immeasurably since Cioran wrote, yet with each move closer to complete globalisation everyone loses more sense of home. Whether we like it or not, whether we travel or stay put, we are all destined to live in America. Today, we do not leave home, it is home that leaves us.

Or perhaps it is Cioran the sceptic who captivates his readers. 'Scepticism is the rapture of impasse', he says, which pitches things too high for most of us. We may not believe in our politicians or our priests, yet I doubt that even the coolest of sceptics finds the experience of not believing in anything particularly pleasant. It was Flaubert who said, 'I am a mystic and I believe in nothing', but it was Cioran who called it 'the adage of our age, of an age infinitely intense, and without substance'. That age no longer exists, if indeed it ever did. Our difficulty is otherwise: we want to believe but can find nothing credible. Like Cioran, 'We cry in God' but, unlike him, we long to find a meaning in life. As churches increasingly become social work centres, we seek comfort in spirituality, often forgetting that the true spiritual life is both close to home and very exacting. Cioran would laugh at what we seek and what we find.

It is life, not death, that is 'the Great Unknown', Cioran tells us; and we make life tolerable, he adds, by mystifying it. Cioran was always quick to expose mystification, and all too slow to admit mystery. The wise person knows how to distinguish the two, and in recognising the truth of that statement we realise that although Cioran was often brilliant he was never wise. What we mistake for wisdom in his fragments is a voice that speaks to us with authority. It is not the impersonal voice of a moralist from the age of reason, someone who analyses society with the skill of a forensic surgeon, but the very personal voice of a man who uses a scalpel on himself. Seen rightly, the two thick books I held so awkwardly that day in Paris comprise a long autobiography, endlessly interrupted and endlessly self-lacerating.

All autobiographies are suspect, and this one is no different. I did not know it at the time, but not long before I had arrived in Paris a damaging article on the 'young Cioran' had appeared in *Le Débat*. The author, Alexandra Laignel-Lavastine, had shown that the Romanian Cioran was not always sceptical about politics. He had passionately identified with fascist plans to revive Romania in the 1930s, and had returned to Bucharist at the end of 1940 where he played, at best, an equivocal political role. Democracy must be liquidated, he had argued before leaving for Paris. He had seen at first hand what was occuring in Germany while visiting Berlin and Munich from 1933 to 1935. In the interests of a virile nation to come, decadence must be countered; and, as Cioran coolly points out, the Jews have no interest in this. Their stake is 'Judeo-Romanian Capitalism'. His was not the worst sort of anti-semitism around, apologists will say, but horror is always horror. In 1937 he published a book, not yet translated into English, called *Romania's Transfiguration* which indicates his cultural politics. Yet in later life he said nothing about his early journalism, except perhaps obliquely in an unsatisfactory essay on the Jews in 1956 which even one of his greatest admirers, Susan Sontag, admitted that it displayed 'a startling moral insensitivity'. Now more than ever we will read Cioran in a 'bitter light'.

A couple of weeks ago, I was talking with a friend who was visiting Australia from Paris. While we were driving south of Adelaide I said I was writing a review of Cioran. He told me that, somewhere on the Rue des Ecoles, he had bought a secondhand paperback German edition of Nietzsche which, it turned out, had belonged to Cioran. Then he said how he had read the article on the young Cioran in *Le Débat*, and found that he could not live with those books in his apartment. I understood my friend's feelings entirely. Some things have moral stains that cannot be eradicated or ignored.

I do not know if those stains spread through all of Cioran's works, whether there are whole books that escape them or whether everything he wrote is marked by them. I do not know. Before I could begin to tell I would have to read him very closely, looking minutely at the relation of text and context. Did Cioran confess in some way? Did he repent? Should we judge his later works by his early ones? Like my friend in Paris, I have no answers. What I know is that, when I see volumes by Cioran in local bookshops, I walk past them. Many years ago, when I learned the full facts about Heidegger's involvement with the Nazis, I felt something similar. The case against Cioran is different from that levelled against Heidegger; yet even though the aphorist means far less to me than the philosopher, I find my reactions are as raw with regard to Cioran as they once were with Heidegger. We live in a society overly eager to expose human frailty, a society which tends to trivialise evil. Yet writing about the young Cioran is a different matter. It is awareness considered as responsibility, not just perception.

*

'When are words as noxious as actions?' This is the central question that Alice Kaplan poses with regard to Robert Brasillach (in *The Collaborator: The Trial and Execution of Robert Brasillach*), and it is the right question to ask. If she does not fully answer it in this fine account of the most famous trial of a French collaborator with the Nazis, it is because the issues raised by Brasillach's case are, as she says, 'profound and irresolvable'. The central question quickly frays into others. Should a journalist be executed for writing columns that help the enemy? Should he be excused because he also wrote drama, fiction and poetry? Or does his gift make him more liable to blame than others? In an attempt to stop the fraying, we can tie the questions together: What is the responsibility of a writer with regard to the nation? Immediately, though, the fraying begins again, for we must also ask what the nation's responsibility is with respect to its writers. Was France right to make an example of Brasillach, to let him become the symbol of all that went wrong under Vichy?

Robert Brasillach was thirty-five when, on 6 February 1945, he was executed by a French firing squad. Only eighteen days before, the Court of Justice of the Seine had found him guilty of 'intelligence with the enemy'. In the interval between trial and execution, a petition for his pardon signed by fifty-nine writers and intellectuals was delivered to Charles de Gaulle. It was pointed out to the general that the condemned man had neither killed nor profited during the war, and that his case resembled that of Henri Béraud who had been pardoned several weeks earlier. Yet no pardon for Brasillach was given. The general alluded to his decision only once, in his war memoirs, telling us that 'in literature as in everything, talent confers responsibility'. Many would have agreed with de Gaulle's phrasing of the matter, Jean-Paul Sartre and Simone de Beauvoir included, and we can do no better than inquire what Brasillach's talent was, what sort of responsibility he had, and how the two should have been linked.

A student at the prestigious Ecole Normale Supérieure in Paris, Brasillach had as good a start in French cultural life as could be given. He chose to be a writer and never ceased writing: his *Oeuvres complètes* run to twelve volumes. That Brasillach could be charming and sentimental is readily apparent from his fiction, though neither quality recommends it nowadays. That he could be incisive and scathing is evident from his criticism; along with his autobiographical writing, it is the most durable of all his work. (His *L'Histoire du cinéma*, written with his brother-in-law Maurice Bardèche, remains an important study.) And that he could be cruel and vulgar is plain from his political columns. While still a student, Brasillach gravitated to the politics of Action Française: a mixture of Catholicism, nationalism, royalism and anti-semitism that was repeatedly condemned by the Vatican. By 1931, when he was twenty-one, he was literary editor of the movement's newspaper, *Action Française*, pages that were avidly read by people of the Left as well as the Right. Over the coming years, though, he shifted his allegiance, increasingly identifying himself with *Je Suis Partout*, the French weekly paper of international fascism.

In 1937 Brasillach became editor in chief of *Je Suis Partout*. Compared with others on the staff, most notably Pierre Antoine Cousteau and Lucien Rebatet, his was sometimes a voice of moderation. The weak Vichy government could be tolerated, he thought, so long as it actively went about realising an authentic French national socialism. During the occupation of Paris, the paper was unflaggingly pro-Nazi; and until 1943, when Brasillach resigned as editor, its name and his were synonymous. As Brasillach's lawyer pointed out in the trial, *Je Suis Partout* was not without culture. André Bellesort, the secretary of the Académie Française, had written literary criticism for it, and the playwright Jean Anouilh had also contributed. Yet judge and jury would have known that the paper regularly published the names and addresses of Jews who were contravening Vichy's anti-semitic laws by making livings under assumed names. This is denunciation of the innocent. It is evil. Yet it does not approach the sheer cruelty of Brasillach telling his readers that, 'We must separate from the Jews *en bloc* and not keep any little ones.' That was written in September 1942, the year when Vichy sent thousands of Jewish children to Auschwitz: 2,464 teenagers, 2,557 between six and twelve, and 1,032 under six.

Did Brasillach know that Pierre Laval, the Vichy prime minister, was deporting these children in order to fill the quota set by the Nazis? The question can cloud the central issue. To write such things is morally objectionable in any context. To write them in such a charged political situation is to be a party to horror, regardless of what course or form it takes. For who knows if the Gestapo decided to act in certain cases only because of what was published in *Je Suis Partout*? As de Beauvoir put it, 'There are words as murderous as gas chambers.' Not only must Brasillach take responsibility for the denunciations that regularly occurred in his paper but also he must be seen as a seducer of the young. That was a line run by Marcel Reboul, Brasillach's prosecutor, and since Brasillach had repeatedly told the court that he took full responsibility for his actions—as a French anti-semite, not as a collaborator—it was likely to have been taken seriously by the jury.

Brasillach steadily maintained that he was a French nationalist, a Vichy patriot, and not a Nazi traitor. He argued that his anti-semitism was thoroughly French. There are many shocking things in and about Brasillach's trial, and one of the most striking to our eyes is how small a role anti-semitism played in his indictment and prosecution. Under the occupation, 76,000 Jews, mostly refugees, were deported from France, and it is estimated that 65,000 of these did not return alive. That was Vichy's action, not France's, was the Gaullist line. Yet suffering and death cannot be swept out of history or national consciousness by an appeal to the abiding legality of the Republic. It was not until 1995 that Jacques Chirac accepted responsibility on behalf of France for those deportations. Indeed, the Republic and Vichy were never mutually exclusive, certainly not with respect to the Jews. To be sure, the liberation courts which tried collaborators like Brasillach had been reformed before going about their business. Yet they were in no position to distinguish themselves from Vichy in all ways. Judges who had sentenced resistance fighters to death were relieved of their duties before the purge, while those who had applied Vichy's anti-semitic laws were not thereby dismissed.

Thinking of France's relations with Germany during the occupation, Brasillach once mused, 'We will have lived together.' Of course the French had to share everyday life with Germans, and had to keep pondering when the necessity of dealing with foreign soldiers or even Vichy law became passive collaboration. In his eloquent memoir of occupations in the two world wars, *French and Germans, Germans and French*, Richard Cobb lets us glimpse how Parisians were thinking over the course of the war. In 1939, the Berlitz school in Paris had 2,470 students learning English and only 939 taking German; in 1941, a year into the occupation, we have only 625 learning English and 7,920 taking German. Cobb concludes that this is a 'vote of confidence in the future of collaboration and of the belief in a long occupation'. A more charitable inference would replace that 'and' with an 'or'; but here, as everywhere in collaboration, the lines are not always clear and distinct. 'Collaboration' could mean different things in 1940-41, when people indulgently thought of Vichy as the 'floating republic', and in 1942-43 when deprivation and suffering were rife.

The image of Frenchmen having 'slept with Germany' was precisely what de Gaulle wished to wipe out of history when he declared Vichy to have been illegal. And only because Vichy was deemed illegal could Brasillach be tried before Laval and Marshal Pétain were themselves brought to court. Yet Brasillach's prosecutor did not forget the image of 'horizontal collaboration'. Reboul's speech dwells on the image, casting Brasillach as a homosexual who not only enjoyed being buggered by Germany but also took pleasure in seeing France raped. What the jurors—all four were male—made of this we do not know, though doubtless Reboul was confident that his metaphor would help his case. I suspect it did: Brasillach was rumoured to be homosexual, and merely to play on that suspicion would have turned the jury against him. Besides, as Kaplan says, the image 'targeted a nation of men who had felt defeated and powerless for four years'.

To play on a jury's fear of homosexual acts, real or allegorical, can only strike us as disreputable. Fifty-five years ago no one questioned it, and it worked like a charm. Is there anything a laywer will not do to win a case? Brasillach's lawyer, Jacques Isorni, would have said yes. That he played rhetorical games of his own is clear from his defence, but they were more artistic and less successful than Reboul's. He was high minded. As the novelist Roger Grenier observed, 'Brasillach's lawyer wanted a beautiful trial'. After reading Kaplan's narrative of the trial, which includes useful sketches of the four jurors, one is left with the uneasy feeling that Isorni lost the case in part because he conducted too much of the defence on the high ground of literature. A jury of four working men from the suburbs was not to be swayed by appeals to the inestimable value of poems that Brasillach would write if spared. Nor were they likely to agree that this was 'a trial of opinion', as Isorni urged. They knew that denunciation was a deed.

Had Brasillach been an extreme right-wing ideologue who had confined himself to writing fiction and literary criticism during the war he may not have been executed. He may not even have been brought to trial. That he called in *Je Suis Partout* for the death of communists as well as government ministers who had served the Popular Front, and that his paper published denunciations of individual Jews, brought him to the attention of the liberation courts. In the short trial—it lasted a mere six hours—it was not conclusively proven that Brasillach's publications had led to particular deaths. Yet it was plain that he had wanted Frenchmen to be murdered and that this would have been welcomed by Germany. He was found guilty of treason, and rightly so.

That said, Isorni was correct to maintain that his client had been singled out, and was facing punishment for misdeeds that others had committed who had not been brought to trial. Of particular interest is the claim that Brasillach was not the only person to wish to see the defeated Popular Front punished. But is Isorni on solid ground when he says, 'there was nothing unusual about his severity except in its literary form'? To put things in this way is to suggest that words have criminal effects only when they are memorable. It is to slide over the fact that they were published in a newspaper, and not to take into account the power of newsprint in forming public opinion. We get onto firmer ground when we think about the journalistic context of Brasillach's remarks, not their literary form. But that thought only takes us so far. Charles Maurras was jailed for less than a year after calling for the death of Léon Blum, the leader of the Popular Front, in *Action Française*. That was in 1936-37, though, when France was not at war.

Brasillach gave himself up, was tried and executed, when Paris was free but France was still at war. His more extreme colleagues at *Je Suis Partout* were in Germany at the time. When returned to France two years later, Cousteau and Rebatet were tried, condemned to death, then pardoned. Their sentences were commuted to forced labour, and eventually they were granted amnesty. Maurras, the mentor of all the younger fascists, was condemned to life in prison then released so that he could be treated at a clinic. In his final year he produced a collection of poems, *La Balance intérieure*. Louis-Ferdinand Céline, a greater writer than Brasillach but one whose anti-semitic works certainly helped the Nazi cause, also sought refuge in Germany before being detained in Denmark. In 1949 he was condemned *in absentia* to one year in prison and was fined. Wounded as a French solider in the First World War, he was able to be granted amnesty. De Gaulle even commuted Pétain's death sentence to life imprisonment. Guilty as he was, Brasillach did not receive justice. Why not? Because he was condemned not as a human being but as a symbol.

In all likelihood de Gaulle believed that one exemplary execution would suffice. It would indicate his power, and serve as a tonic to those still fighting for France. Perhaps it did those things. But no one can kill a symbol. For the extreme Right, Brasillach went to death as a martyr for fascism, and he remains more potent in death than in life. At first his memory was kept alive by his brother-in-law, Bardèche, who helped to open the despicable field of Holocaust denial. Then the task of maintaining Brasillach as a myth of the far Right passed to Jean-Marie Le Pen, for whom the blood of a dead fascist writer is a pure as that of a dead resistence fighter. To identify the two is mendacious, to invoke purity as the basis of comparison is odious: no blood is pure. At the end of the twentieth century Robert Brasillach is represented by the extreme Right as a man whose innocent death testifies to a higher order. He is being promoted by neo-fascists as a Christian martyr, and it is gravely offensive.

A Portrait of Proteus

Pierre Ryckmans

*To tell the truth, I don't know what I think of him. He is never the same
for long. He never gets engaged in anything, yet nothing is more
engaging than his permanent evasions. You cannot judge him, for you
haven't known him long enough. His very self is in a constant process of
undoing and remaking. You think you have pinned him down, but he is
Proteus: he adopts the shape of whatever he happens to love. And you
cannot understand him unless you love him.*

André Gide, *Les Faux-monnayeurs*

*Gide is one of the few writers who really nauseates me, so I am
naturally not an authority on him.*

Flannery O'Connor, *The Habit of Being*

The starting point of this (rather whimsical) little glossary of the
Gidean enigma was provided to me by Alan Sheridan's work, *André
Gide: a Life in the Present*. Sheridan's massive opus (700 pages) is a
model of meticulous scholarship. To appreciate the biographer's
achievement, one should consider how daunting was his task. Gide
was a compulsive diarist; besides writing some sixty books (essays,
fiction, theatre, travelogues, criticism, poetry, literary translations),
he kept for more than fifty years a journal that fills thousands of
pages. Members of his own small circle of close friends were equally
addicted to graphomania. First of all, Maria Van Rysselberghe—
nicknamed La Petite Dame—The Tiny Lady—who knew him for
half a century and was his most intimate companion (or should we

say accomplice?) during the last thirty years of his life (inasmuch as any sort of intimate companionship could be achieved with such a slippery eel) kept an accurate and vivid record of his daily utterances and deeds, together with perceptive portraits of his literary friends and transcripts of their conversations (four volumes—nearly 2,000 pages—crammed with information). Gide's best friends were also writers: Roger Martin du Gard, Jean Schlumberger, Pierre Herbart. After his death, they all wrote memoirs of the Gide they knew.

Thus, the first and main problem of Gide's biographer was not how to gather information but how not to drown in it. Sheridan succeeded in bringing this literary flood under control and in organising it into a lucid synthesis. Yet, just as the damming of a big river cannot be achieved without inflicting some damage to its wildlife, the discipline that Sheridan had to impose upon his rich material was perhaps not entirely compatible with the lush ambiguities and contradictions of his subject. Now, in contrast with whatever certainties the reader may feel able to derive from Sheridan's authoritative study, my only purpose is to warn him against the temptation to draw conclusions—for Gide must always present an irreducible elusiveness: he was truly the great master of intellectual escape—the Houdini of modern literature.

Anti-semitism

In 1914—he was then a middle-aged, well-established writer—after a lunch with his old friend and former schoolmate Léon Blum, Gide noted in his diary how he respected Blum's intelligence and culture, but resented his Jewishness. He expounded at some length on this theme:

> There is no need to enlarge here on Jewish defects; the point is: the qualities of the Jewish race are not French qualities. Even when Frenchmen are less intelligent, less resilient, less worthy in every respect than the Jews, the fact remains that only they themselves can express what they have to say. The Jewish contribution to our literature... does not so much enrich us, as constitute an interruption in the slow effort of our race to express itself, and this represents a severe, an intolerable distortion of its meaning.

After World War Two, at the end of his life, he was still casually making disparaging remarks on the Jewish character, in front of his secretary Béatrix Beck, a young widow whose dead husband was Jewish.

Yet would it make any sense to call Gide an anti-semite? With equal reason, he might also be called a Stalinist Bolshevist, an anti-Stalinist and anti-communist, a Christian, an anti-Christian, a defeatist advocate of collaboration with Hitler, a sympathiser with the Resistance, a libertarian, an authoritarian, a rebel, a conformist, a demagogue, an elitist, an educator, a corrupter of youth, a preacher, a débauché, a moralist, a destroyer of morality.

Literature was the overwhelming concern of Gide—it was the very purpose of his life; besides this—as he himself proclaimed—'only paederasty and Christianity' could absorb his interest and fire his passion. On all other matters—which were of basic indifference to him—he had no strong opinions, his views were vague, contradictory, ill-informed, tentative, inconsistent, malleable, banal, vacillating, conventional. Herbart—who was his closest confidant and constant companion during the last twenty years of his life—observed that he usually thought in clichés that could have come straight from Flaubert's *Dictionnaire des Idées reçues*; having quoted another of Gide's offensively stupid remarks ('I suffered yesterday: all the interlocutors I had to chat with were Jews'), Herbart added this flat comment: 'This means precisely nothing: he "thinks" by proxy.'

I do not know to what extent such an innocent explanation will satsify most readers—but Blum himself would certainly have endorsed it, for even though he was hurt when he eventually read the passages of the *Journal* quoted above, his affection for Gide remained undiminished until his death.

In conclusion: it would be very easy to compile a damning record of first-hand evidence on Gide's anti-Semitism; in all probability, it would also be misleading. This example may serve as a handy methodological caution before perusing my little ABC.

Biographical outline
Gide was born in 1869. Though he died in the middle of the twentieth century, he remains in many fundamental respects a nineteenth-century writer.

He was an only child; his father was a scholar (a professor of Roman law)—a frail and refined man who died too early to leave any deep impression on his son; André was not yet eleven at the time of his father's death. His mother, possessive and authoritarian, came from a wealthy family of business people in Normandy; she gave her son a stern Protestant education. From a very early age, Gide experienced an acute conflict between the severe demands of his mother's religiosity and the no-less tyrannical needs of his precocious sensuality.

But it was not until a visit to Algeria in 1895 that he discovered—under the personal tutelage of Oscar Wilde—the exclusive orientation of his own sexuality. That same year, his formidable mother died, and 'having lost her, he replaced her at once with the person who most resembled her': within two weeks, he announced his engagement to his first cousin Madeleine (niece of his mother), who had been his beloved soulmate since early childhood. Their marriage was never consummated, Gide having assumed from the beginning that only 'loose women' can have any interest in the activities of the flesh. And, in turn, when forty-three years later Madeleine died, Gide once again felt the same sense of 'love, anguish and freedom' he had experienced on the death of his mother, and he noted 'how subtly, almost mystically' his mother had merged into his wife.

Gide's daughter, Catherine, was born in 1923. Her mother was Elisabeth Van Rysselberghe (1890-1980), the daughter of the Tiny Lady. Elisabeth, who was briefly Rupert Brooke's lover, bitterly regretted not having been able to give birth to the poet's child. In 1920, she thought that Marc Allégret—then Gide's teenage lover—had got her pregnant, Gide was ecstatic; he said to his old lady-friend, the prospective grandmother, 'Ah, *chère amie*, we are making possible a new humanity! That child is bound to be beautiful!' Once again, however, Elisabeth's hope did not come to fruition. Gide had always thought that she deserved to have a child; a few years earlier, during a train journey, he had slipped a note to her: 'I shall never love any woman, except one [thinking of his wife, Madeleine] and my true desire is only for young boys. But I cannot bear to see you without children, nor do I wish to remain childless myself.' Eventually, in 1922, on a secluded beach by the Mediterranean, he rediscovered with her 'all the liberty that fosters amorous dispositions'. Catherine was born the next year.

Gide followed the growth of the child with sporadic interest; he observed her with an eye that was, by turns, now fatherly, now entomological. Elisabeth eventually married Herbart, her junior by fifteen years (but the age difference was of no real significance, Gide reassured the future mother-in-law, because, after all, Herbart was more interested in his own sex), and Catherine came to live with her mother and Herbart when she was not pursuing her education in Swiss boarding schools. Occasionally she spent brief holidays with Gide who, one day, informed her that he was her real father. The girl was thirteen at the time and the psychological impact of this revelation had a complex effect on her.

Catherine is rarely mentioned in Gide's Journal. In 1942 (his daughter was nineteen), he noted: 'Catherine might have been able to attach me to life, but she is interested only in herself, and that doesn't interest me.' Sheridan comments pointedly: 'In other words, the daughter was behaving like the father, and the father didn't like it.'

With the total freedom that his inherited wealth (as well as the considerable fortune of his wife) gave him, Gide devoted most of his very long life to literature. He employed his time reading and writing—writing mostly about what he had read—and travelling. At the same time, religion continued to claim his soul and paederasty his body. The conflict reached a climax in 1916 when, through the pressing—and sometimes clumsy—interventions of his Catholic friends (Paul Claudel, especially), Gide came close to converting. But eventually he resisted the religious temptation and opted resolutely for the pursuit of a sexual obsession which was to assume manic proportions with the passing of the years.

From his earliest work, *Les Cahiers d'André Walter* (published in a private edition, paid for by his mother, in 1891), Gide's literary activity never slowed. His most seminal work, the book that established him as the guru of rebellion against the bourgeois order, as the *maître à penser* for at least three successive generations of young men, is *Les Nourritures terrestres* (1901). Martin du Gard wondered if one could not apply to it what Sainte-Beuve once said of 'those useful books which last only for a limited time, since the readers who benefit from them wear them down'. The problem is also that these sorts of books usually generate mediocre imitations and eventually we cannot avoid reading them through the prism of their vulgar caricatures. Today, alas, *Les Nourritures terrestres* reminds us of nothing so much as the kitsch of Khalil Gibran.

The quality of Gide's short fiction is displayed in *La porte étroite* (1909) and shines to perfection in *La Symphonie pastorale* (1919). Both novellas benefit from the inner tension of his religious inquietude, still unresolved at the time; in the latter work, in particular, the spiritual ambiguity is handled with diabolic cleverness and, in spite of its stilted dialogues and cold stylistic mannerisms, the book remains deeply affecting and comes close to being a masterpiece. In his more ambitious and longer fiction, *Les Caves du Vatican* (1914) and *Les Faux-monnayeurs* (1925), he betrays the sorry fact that he is not really a novelist: he is short of breath and has little imagination. These books were hugely successful in their time, but have not aged well. Mauriac was probably right when he observed that, half a century later, Gide's novels had already become mummified, whereas—in paradoxical contrast—those of Anatole France (so cruelly derided by the surrealist generation) still retained an astonishing freshness.

In 1924, he published *Corydon*, a defence of homosexuality. His argumentation is clumsy and his sincerity more limited than it may appear at first, but it took considerable courage to come out at that time, in such a public fashion.

He twice commented forcefully on public affairs—even though his notorious lack of a sense of reality ill-prepared him for this sort of activity. After a lengthy journey into black Africa (French Congo and Chad, 1925-26), he wrote an eloquent denunciation of the colonial exploitation of the native populations. Then, during the 30s, he foolishly became a fellow-traveller of Stalinist communism. His performance as 'useful idiot' was short-lived, however—a brief visit to the Soviet Union opened his eyes. It did not require exceptional percipience to appreciate the plain evidence that was under his nose, but it certainly took exceptional courage to spell it out publicly. On his return to Paris, he immediately wrote a truthful and scathing account of his political disenchantment. Against all expectations, natural justice rewarded his audacity: *Retour de l'URSS* (1936) was prodigiously successful—this iconoclastic little book was reprinted eight times in ten months and sold nearly 150,000 copies; by the end of 1937, it had been translated into fourteen languages. None of Gide's other works was such an immediate success.

Almost until his death (in 1951), Gide continued to write, polish and edit his *Journal*—probably his most important work. But apart from his own publications, his role in and influence on the French literary scene were also asserted through the *Nouvelle Revue Française*, which he had established in 1909 with a few friends. (When the Nazis occupied France, Otto Abetz who was in charge of German cultural policy observed: 'There are three powers in France: communism, the big banks and the *Nouvelle Revue Française*.')

Gide was awarded the Nobel Prize for Literature in 1947. The official statement of the Nobel committee was typically vague, but Gide wrote a clear reply:

> If I have represented anything it is, I believe, the spirit of free inquiry, independence, insubordination even, protest against what the heart and reason refuse to approve. I firmly believe that the spirit of inquiry lies at the origin of our culture. It is this spirit that the so-called totalitarian regimes, of left and right, are trying to crush and gag... What matters here is the protection of that spirit that is 'the salt of the earth' and which can still save the world... the struggle of culture against barbarism.

Character

Gide had a genius for friendship. Those who were in close and constant contact with him all loved him. If we except the sad onset of senility in his last years—which, in the end, generated some strain in the harmony of his small 'family' circle—for most of his life his presence seems to have brought abiding stimulation and delight to his entourage. 'Good nature is the most selfish of all virtues', Hazlitt once observed, and it was certainly Gide's colossal self-centredness that enabled him to be generally benign to everyone. His selfishness was quite absolute—on this score, those who knew him best and had most affection for him had no illusions. He was also tolerant and easy-going: his unflappably pleasant disposition was built upon a bedrock of indifference to whatever did not have direct bearing on his own person. His aptitude for happiness was irrepressible and disarming. As he confided to the Tiny Lady: 'It is incredible how difficult I find it *not* to be happy!'

Gide enlivened all he touched; routine and stagnation were banned from his life. He was in a state of permanent 'availability', of vibrant expectation towards what the next moment would bring. He never really settled down anywhere: 'What I need is constant change, I dislike all habits.' He was unable to settle in any place for long, either in body or in mind. He spent more time in hotel rooms and in friends' houses than in his own apartment. In a sense, his entire existence was just one long holiday, his leisure was unlimited, his freedom boundless and his money plentiful. He had no family responsibilities, no professional obligations. At any time, on the spur of a fancy, he could travel to exotic places; then, on his return, he would rest in the splendid country mansions of various acquaintances, where he enjoyed the condition of a guest of honour—and of a shameless parasite. Most of his initiatives were taken on the prompting of a sudden inspiration, all his moves were dictated by mood and whim.

Yet, to a superficial observer, these appearances of carefree and luxurious bohemianism could be misleading.

As Herbart perceptively remarked, gratuitousness was utterly foreign to Gide (which is ironical, considering that he had coined in his fiction the notion of *l'acte gratuit*): with him 'impressions, readings, things and people are being sorted out and assessed in the light of a single criterion: their usefulness'.

In this respect, it is significant to note in his diaries the recurrence of expressions such as 'profit' and 'benefit'; whenever he records encounters with new books or visitors, instead of saying 'this book is beautiful' or 'this person is charming', he often writes: 'I greatly benefited from reading...', 'I derived much profit from the conversation of...' Similar phrases crop up dozens of times in the *Journal*.

What redeemed his monstrous self-absorption and made his company so pleasant and rewarding for his intimates was his restless and ravenous appetite for discovery, his polymorphous curiosity. Béatrix Beck recalls how exhilarating it was to work as his secretary; at the time, she wrote to her sister: 'Gide has become my only interest—which means that, from now on, I am interested in everything.' Gide used to end his letters with the courtesy phrase *attentivement vôtre*—but, for him, this was not an empty formula; he was indeed paying attention to his interlocutor, whoever he might be—and here the distinctive quality of the Gidean dialogue is to be found. Furthermore, his attention was not directed only at people, it seems to have extended to all creatures.

The Tiny Lady recorded a typical scene: 'At lunch time, in the midst of an exciting conversation, he abruptly stops, and examines a fly that has a tiny parasite on one leg. In these matters, nothing escapes his eye.' Or again, when he went to visit Hermann Hesse at home, in Switzerland—Hesse had just been awarded the Nobel Prize for Literature, and Gide was to receive it the following year—during this first meeting between the two grand old men of letters (they had already been corresponding for some time), most of Gide's time and attention were lavished on a cat which had just had kittens. Thus the interview passed agreeably for both of them. Hesse was fascinated by Gide and Gide was fascinated by Hesse's cat.

Gide's indecisiveness and hesitations, his ditherings, vacillations and contradictions were legendary among his friends. With him, no decision was stable or final; sometimes, in the same breath, he managed to opt simultaneously for one course of action—and for its exact opposite. It was impossible to predict what, in the end, his choice would turn out to be and it was wiser not even to ask. He thrived on ambiguity, he relished muddles. He displayed this attitude in all matters—big and small: whether he should seek reconciliation with God and whether he should have coffee after lunch.

Living at his side, the Tiny Lady was in a privileged position to observe on a daily basis his mental pirouettes and somersaults and, as she herself was bold and decisive by temperament, she recorded these constant acrobatics with a mixture of amusement, amazement and exasperation. One day, as Gide was once again deliciously writhing on the hot coals of one of his religious crises, she snapped back: 'If it is your wish to go to God—go! but don't fret: *soyez net.*' Alas, for Gide, to be driven into a corner was unspeakable agony; he always avoided the straight line, as he once said: 'A direct path merely takes you to your destination.'

Corydon

'If I had listened to other people, I would never have written any of my books,' Gide once observed. It was particularly true of *Corydon*: his close friends were all aghast when he expressed the intention of taking a public stand in defence of homosexuality. They strongly advised against such a project, believing that it would provide ammunition to his enemies, undermine his moral authority and destroy his reputation. But it was as if their apprehension worked only to spur him on his reckless course (he often confessed that recklessness appealed to him.) To Martin du Gard, who implored him to be prudent and not to rush things, he replied: 'I cannot wait any longer… I must follow this inner necessity… I need, I NEED to dissipate this fog of lies in which I have been hiding since my youth, since my childhood… I can no longer breathe in it…' Martin believed that his wish to 'come out' partly reflected a tendency inherited from his Protestant education: the need for self-justification (which remained with him all his life) and perhaps too an unconscious Puritan desire for martyrdom, for atonement. His wife Madeleine, whose eye could penetrate his soul, made the same observation when she tried to warn him against publication: 'I fear it is a sort of thirst for martyrdom—if I dare apply this word to such a bad cause—that pushes you to do this.' And to Schlumberger, who thought that Corydon would bring discredit on his moral authority, he replied:

> You fear that I might lose my credibility on all other issues, but should I not in fact maintain it by acquiring a new freedom? We were not born simply to repeat what has already been said, but to put into words what no one before us has expressed. Don't you see that, in the end, my credibility will become much greater? Once a man has no more need to compromise, how much stronger he becomes! Misunderstandings suffocate me… I want to silence all those who accuse me of being a mere dilettante, I want to show them the real 'me'.

Gide eventually published, and not only was he not damned but, in the end, he was rewarded with a Nobel prize. Gide's argument—developed at a length that borders on the ludicrous—is that homosexuality, far from being against nature (as its traditional critics used to insist) is, in fact, to be found in nature. Here, his many examples, drawn from the natural sciences, seem to miss the real issue. Of course, there may well be scientifically observed instances of homosexual cows, and homosexual whales, and homosexual ladybirds: after all, isn't nature the greatest freak show under heaven? Earthquakes and plagues, two-headed sheep and five-legged pigs: whatever is, is in nature (with the exception of a few productions of the human soul, such as Chartres Cathedral, the music of Bach, the calligraphy of Mi Fu, and so on). Exhaustive catalogues of natural phenomena prove nothing either way.

Furthermore, not only would it be quite feasible to demonstrate that, in given circumstances, for various species of creatures, homosexuality may indeed be 'natural', but one could even argue (at least this was the view of Dr Johnson*) that, on the contrary, it is the state of permanent, monogamous union between a man and a woman that actually goes 'against nature'—since it is, in fact, a crowning achievement of culture (a fact acknowledged by all the great world religions, which share the considered opinion that in normal circumstances such a state cannot be attained without some form of supernatural assistance.) The point is: the issue that should be of primary concern for us is not what naked bipeds can come up with in their original state of nature but how human beings, clad with culture, are more likely to achieve the fullness of their humanity.

A second problem of *Corydon* is that it is almost exclusively an apologia for paederasty, but in this respect it is also essentially fraudulent, for Gide's frenzied sexual activities—especially the monomania of his old age—were not paederastic *à la mode antique* but flatly and sordidly paedophiliac—very much like the sex tours that, today, bring planeloads of wealthy Western tourists to the child brothels of South-East Asia. Now, homosexuals are usually keen to draw a line at this point: they insist—not without reason— that their sexual orientation implies no more inclination towards paedophilia than is the case for heterosexuals. If they expect, however, to find in Gide an advocate for their cause, they would be well-advised to reconsider the moral (or at least tactical) wisdom of choosing such a champion.

Devil

In 1920, as Gide was working on his autobiographical narrative *Si le grain ne meurt*, he explained to Martin du Gard:

> Strange to say, my dear: if only I could borrow
> Christian terminology, if I dared to introduce the

---

*Boswell: *Life of Johnson* (entry of 31 March 1772): 'A question started whether the state of marriage was natural to man. JOHNSON: Sir, it is so far from being natural for a man and a woman to live in a state of marriage, that we find all the motives which they have for remaining in that connection, and the restraints which civilised society imposes to prevent separation, are hardly sufficient to keep them together.'

character of Satan into my narrative, at once everything
would become miraculously clear, easy to tell, easy to
understand... Things always happened to me as if the Devil
existed, as if he was constantly intervening in my life.

At that time, he had already adopted a certain tongue-in-cheek
approach to this subject, which earlier on had pressed hauntingly
upon his mind. Since early childhood, his devout Protestant
education had familiarised him with the Holy Scriptures; more
especially, well into middle age, he remained a profound reader of
the Gospels, from which he eventually derived a distinct awareness
of the presence of the Evil One. He remarked to Schlumberger:

It is strange to see the sort of reserve which inhibits
Catholics, and Protestants even more, when they speak of
the Devil. They simply conjure him away; they grant him
only a negative form of existence... And yet, in the Gospels,
the reality is totally different: the Devil has a fiercely
personal existence, he is even more sharply characterised
than God.

He went on to comment on the theme of 'enslavement to the
Devil': 'The Devil forces his slaves to recruit new subjects for him—
hence the need to pervert, to find accomplices.'

In 1916, an intense religious crisis brought him very close to a
conversion to Catholicism; it is reflected at great length in his
Journal, well summarised by Sheridan: 'Gide returns obsessively to
talk of God and the devil, sin and guilt, with scarcely veiled
references to masturbation and his attempts to resist it.' (Note that
he was forty-eight at the time.)

Throughout this period, Gide certainly addresses God as a
believing (and doubting) Christian would:

Lord! You know that I have given up wanting to be in the
right in the eyes of anyone. What does it matter if it is to
escape submission to sin that I submit to the Church? I
submit! Ah! Untie the bonds that still hold me back. Deliver
me from the terrible weight of this body. Ah! Let me live a
little! Let me breathe! Snatch me from evil. Let me not
stifle.

Eventually Gide pulled out of this crisis and broke away from the Catholic friends (such as Claudel) who had been trying—with more zeal than tact—to drag him into the Church. Yet the religious issue never really left his mind—to the perplexity of the Tiny Lady, for whom this lingering preoccupation was utterly incomprehensible—and he could truthfully state once again: 'In the end, only two things have ever interested me passionately: paederasty and Christianity.'

At the end of his life, his anti-Catholicism became nasty and obsessive; in 1947, Schlumberger, who admired Gide and was no altar boy himself, was shocked by the narrow-minded hostility that coloured Gide's comments on the Church: 'I am upset by the stupid anti-clericalism that reigns in his house.'

In traditional Catholic circles, it was widely—though not universally—believed that Gide was possessed by the devil. Once, during a family dinner, Claudel declared, as he was holding a *crêpe flambée* on his fork: 'This is how André Gide is going to burn in hell!' A witness of the incident reported it to Gide, who was hugely amused. Frequently confronted with this prognosis of eternal damnation, he repeated what La Fontaine had replied in his own time to similar curses: 'I sincerely believe that the damned in hell eventually feel like fish in the water.'

When Gide died, he was buried next to his wife, in the village of her country estate. The ceremony was simple and attended only by relatives, close friends and some villagers. Gide's nephew, who was a local notable, thought it proper to invite a Protestant pastor to say a few words. The pastor simply read a short passage from Gide's *Numquid et tu*, written forty years earlier, at the height of his religious crisis: 'Lord, I come to you like a child; like the child you want me to become... I renounce everything that made me proud and which, in your presence, would make me ashamed. I listen and submit my heart to you.'

Immediately after the ceremony, Martin du Gard and Schlumberger protested loudly against this religious intrusion, which they thought a betrayal of Gide's intentions, a denial of his clearly stated beliefs, a violation of his final wishes. They were right, of course. And yet the intervention of the hapless pastor, however indiscreet, was poignant: after all, these were once Gide's own true words and they were also words of truth. Hell is not 'truth seen too late' (as Hobbes said); on the contrary, it is truth seen too soon, and knowingly rejected.

Dialogue

'Outside my capacity for sympathy (which constitutes all my intelligence), it seems that I have no existence at all, and my moral persona is nothing but a number of possibilities, which, in turn, are called Menalque, Alissa, Lafcadio.' Gide wrote this to a friend: he knew himself well.

His instinctive urge to sympathise was the reflection of a deeper need: the need to please. He had been aware of this since his youth: at the age of twenty-four, he noted in his *Journal*: 'My perpetual question (it is a morbid obsession) is: am I lovable?' And fifty-five years later, at the end of his career, he concluded in that same *Journal*: 'My extraordinary, my insatiable need to love and be loved: I believe this is what has dominated my life and driven me to write.'

'He always tried to charm people, and in large part he succeeded,' Béatrix Beck observed. The Tiny Lady often had to warn him against this excessive eagerness to make himself congenial; for instance, after he had managed finally to establish pleasant relations with a person who had previously been hostile, she advised him: 'Be careful, don't spoil it. As the situation has become fine and easy now, don't exaggerate, as you often do; you get carried away by some sentimental impulse of yours, and you tend to say things that are true only for a moment—and this is a sure recipe for creating horrific disappointments later on.'

Gide was aware of the problem himself: 'I am all too inclined to espouse other people's points of view.' Even in friendly exchanges, he would instinctively recoil, from contradiction, and ensure smoothness at any cost. Here is a typical little episode from his *Journal:*

> Valéry asks me: 'Do you know anything more boring than
> *The Iliad*?' I repress a spontaneous impulse to protest,
> but I find it more companionable to reply: 'Yes, *La Chanson
> de Roland*.' He approves.

Thus agreement had been secured—but at the price of suppressing his own deeply held views on the matter, for we know how much he actually loved Homer: in the very same *Journal*, he had clearly noted not long before: 'I re-read with delight the last six books of *The Iliad*.'

Similar occurrences are frequent; for instance, the Tiny Lady records (in 1937) that, in a conversation with the German scholar

E. R. Curtius, Gide echoing his good friend's view, expressed his 'great admiration' for Thomas Mann's *Joseph and His Brothers*. Yet, from the *Journal*, we learn that, two years later, he was still plodding through that very same book 'with increasing boredom.'

He admitted that, 'Rather than confronting opposition, I prefer to adopt the opinion of the other party.' Sometimes he would rally so quickly to his interlocutor's views that it made the latter worry; Schlumberger recorded his uneasy feelings at the outcome of a discussion: 'I am rather scared when I see him abandoning his position with so little resistance.' In fact Gide himself was troubled by his own instinctive reaction: 'I often feel as if I were a horrible hypocrite; I have such an acute need for sympathy, I virtually *melt* into the other person. With complete sincerity, I adopt other people's opinions and so give them a misleading impression of agreement. I would inevitably disappoint my own side—if I had one.'

He suffered from being unable to say 'No'. He wanted to break with his Catholic friends, but felt hopelessly entangled in the nets of their kind concern. When the Tiny Lady reproached him for his lack of resolution, he finally let his frustration explode over her: 'You must understand that I am full of weakness, I have no resistance to others, no resistance to any expression of sympathy. These people deprive me of all my resources, they rob me of my arguments, they prevent me from saying what I wish to say. I am bold and free only when I am in front of a sheet of blank paper.'

The written word was the last refuge of his sincerity: 'I put all my integrity into my writing, whereas when I deal with people, my only desire is that everything should go smoothly; probably it is simply that I want to please, and this is obviously a form of coquetry.'

The desire to please, the constant fear that he might disappoint other people's expectations made him nervous: 'I smoke too much, out of nervousness; there are so few people with whom I can be completely natural! I am too tense, and I smoke to give myself some poise, to overcome my agitation.' He was simple and unpretentious, but also very awkward. Yet dialogue remained for him the essence of human life; he conquered his interlocutors not only with his unassuming manners but, more importantly, by being an attentive listener.

Whenever he had drafted a new piece of writing, or if he had made some mistake, he amazed his friends by the meekness and humility with which he would accept their criticism, however sharp and bruising. But, on every occasion, his critics would rapidly discover that, if he had yielded to their attacks and agreed with their suggestions, it was in order to mend the flaws in his original position which, in the end, he would resubmit in a form that was now impregnable.

His receptiveness and malleability were thus deceptive—and he was the first to acknowledge the fact: 'By using sympathy, anyone can easily manipulate me. In the past, I warned Claudel: beware, I am made of rubber. I agree with everything, as much as possible, and I would go to the very edge of insincerity—yet make no mistake: once alone, I revert to my original shape.'

The paradox is that, on the deepest level, he was absolutely blind to the point of view of others, and radically unable to see the glaring evidence that had been in front of him all his life. The most tragic example of this incredible insensitivity is the way he treated his wife, Madeleine: he finally succeeded in alienating— irreparably—the trust of the only person he truly loved.

Herbart

Gide's enemies spread many calumnies about him during his life; these should naturally be ignored—and anyway, they pale in comparison with the truths that his friends published after his death. The most penetrating psychological portrait of Gide was written by Pierre Herbart: *A la recherche d'André Gide* (1952). Herbart (1904-74) was the husband of the mother of Gide's daughter (a diagram of the relationships within the Gidean 'family' would rival in its complexity the lines of descent within the chimpanzee cage at the zoo).

In Herbart's view, Gide's deepest compulsion was to charm people and to win their sympathy; his obsessive fear was of disappointing their expectations; he was, therefore, totally dependent upon the others—his self-esteem was conditional on their approval. With this attitude, according to Herbart, he betrayed his lack of 'virility' and his absence of 'morality'. Needless to say, neither term should be understood in the narrow sense: Herbart himself was bisexual and, in his younger years, had led with cool shamelessness the life of a gigolo—unorthodox sexual practices and unconventional moral behaviour could not really shock him. But what flabbergasted him, however, was the crass lack of common decency with which Gide could, for instance, have the cheek to complain that his long-suffering and saintly wife would not co-operate in procuring local little boys to alleviate his sexual needs during his stays on their country estate.

According to Herbart, Gide is 'emasculated': one cannot trust his word, nor his loyalty, nor his discretion. He is amoral, not by a bold choice, or as a challenge—but simply and literally because he is missing that particular sense. He can experience physical or aesthetic repulsion but rarely intellectual, and never moral, repulsion: his ignorance of morality is innate and invincible—he does not have the faintest awareness of what morality might mean.

Gide's inner world is characterised by an extreme spiritual poverty: the whole realm of human passion was always a closed book to him. He has no great genius, no imagination, no original ideas. With him, style is everything: he picks up clichés and 'Gidefies' them—giving them a form that is unique.

His strength resides in his tireless curiosity, his absolute freedom, his uncompromising pursuit of excellence. But he is utterly devoid of the tragic sense of life; he has no experience of pathos. Hence the weird feeling which often affects sensitive readers when they delve into his works—and on this point, Herbart quotes a passage from Julien Green, Gide's junior by thirty years, and a friend who shared both his Protestant upbringing and his sexual orientation:

> A short while ago, in a bookshop, I was browsing a reprint of Gide's *Journal*. I have never read it in its entirety, but this time, reading a few pages convinced me, once again, that I shall never be able to persevere with it to the end. Why? I don't really know. Its style is exquisite, and every page is full to the brim with great intellectual riches; but at the same time as the book yields all that it can give, it also freezes the heart, and as one reads on, one feels left with less faith, with less hope, and (I say this with regret) with less love.

Literature

Literature was the very meaning of Gide's life—its ultimate goal. He loved literature with a devotion that was admirable and touching. Reading was as essential to him as breathing: it was both a vital need and a constant joy. Often it was also a convivial celebration, a fervour he shared with those whom he loved most: when he was with his wife in their Normandy estate, or with his friends in Paris, entire evenings were spent reading aloud to each other.

Gide was a deliberate, slow and omnivorous reader. He was never without a book in his hand, or in his pocket, or at his bedside. He read in order to write; he drew all his writing out of himself, as one draws water from a well, and only an uninterrupted stream of reading could ensure that the well would not run dry.

In his approach to literature, besides the solid foundations which traditional French schooling provided to all the children of the bourgeoisie, he had nothing but his own voracious curiosity. His enjoyment of literature was never warped by the sterile games that academics play professionally—he never attended a university. He belonged (as his biographer Alan Sheridan accurately observes) to the vanishing breed of 'common readers'. At the conclusion of a symposium on his beloved Montaigne, Gide's characteristic contribution was simply to suggest with gentle irony that Montaigne would probably not have understood a word of what had just been said about him.

He was a good Latinist: from his adolescence until his death, Virgil's *Aeneid* was his constant reading. He had a loving familiarity with the French classics: Montaigne first and foremost, but also Pascal, Racine, Molière, La Fontaine, Bossuet, La Bruyère, Voltaire, Stendhal, Balzac, Flaubert. On Hugo, he was ambivalent: 'Sometimes execrable, always prodigious.' He ignored Dumas.

What set him apart, however, was his openness to foreign literatures, which was exceptional for his time and his milieu. He knew some German, a little Italian, and worked hard on his English. His command of foreign languages always remained shaky ('Honestly, as regards foreign languages, I am a hopeless case') but his hunger for learning and for discovery were impressive. He set himself to read Goethe (one of his greatest cultural heroes) in the original, and he devoted years of strenuous work to Shakespeare, painstakingly translating *Hamlet* into French.

Strangely enough, however, he eventually became quite disenchanted with the play: '*Hamlet* lacks artistry. I wish an Englishman could explain to me in what respect it is admirable. Reading it, I never feel that I am in front of something beautiful, which I would want to transmit to others. It is muddled and amphigoric.' Actually, on the subject of Shakespeare, his evolution—

from admiration to aversion—very much duplicated that of Voltaire, and he ended up with some curious pronouncements:

> I deny that there are any human lessons to be derived from his plays; his most sublime lines are in fact utterly banal, his psychology is conventional. Generally speaking, theatrical works always give me this impression, with the sole exception of Racine.

And again: 'The English are irritating with their habit of always praising Shakespeare without reservation.' He found *As You Like It* 'completely devoid of charm'. Immediately after World War Two, he had the chance to watch *Richard III*, staged in Paris by the Old Vic: he confessed he could not understand a single word. At the very end of his life, he saw Laurence Olivier's *King Lear*; Maria Van Rysselberghe, the Tiny Lady, reported: 'Gide was utterly disappointed by the play; he thinks it is one of Shakespeare's weakest works, without any psychological interest, quite boring in fact.'

He also expressed some other puzzling value judgments; for instance, he found Samuel Butler's *Erewhon* quite superior to Swift's *Gulliver's Travels*; and he could not understand the popularity of the latter.

He loved Browning's poetry. George Eliot's *Middlemarch* provoked his enthusiasm; as to Jane Austen, he found her novels extraordinarily well crafted, but with 'a somewhat low alcohol content'. Henry James was a disappointment: 'a mere socialite' (*un auteur de salon*); 'his characters live only in their heads, they have nothing below the shoulders'. He was bored by *The Ambassadors* and could not finish it: 'His manner reminds me of Proust, but, unlike Proust, it is dreary, and worst of all, it lacks effectiveness.' He read most of Thomas Hardy's novels: *The Mayor of Casterbridge* was his favourite. Joyce's *Ulysses* was 'needlessly long; after all it will remain only as a sort of monster'.

Claudel led him to discover Conrad's novels, the reading of which gave him a desire to meet the author. He visited Conrad several times in England and developed a deep affection for him. Gide loved *Lord Jim*—'One of the most beautiful books I have ever read, and also one of the saddest; and yet utterly soul-stirring'—and he translated *Typhoon*. This translation was made with loving care, yet the result is odd: the style is pure Gide, with all his syntactical mannerisms, and it is riddled not exactly with blunders (Gide was too conscientious and circumspect for that), but with omissions and inaccuracies that constantly betray his uncertain grasp of the original.

After Conrad's death, Gide wrote a short but warm essay in his memory, concluding: 'No one ever led such a wild existence: and afterwards, no one was ever able, like him, to submit life to such a patient, deliberate and sophisticated transmutation into art.' Still, for all the praise and friendship that he lavished on Conrad, one wonders to what extent he understood either the man or the artist. He was bored by *Nostromo* and abandoned it; nor could he finish *The Secret Agent*. His lack of interest in these two prophetic works suggests an incomprehension that ran deeper than his inability to appreciate Conrad; it makes one doubt if he really understood the twentieth century. In later years, he even revised his earlier admiration and sadly came to the conclusion that, 'as regards Conrad, I cannot rank the writer as highly as I used to; yet, as I loved the man very much, it pains me to acknowledge this'.

Russian literature occupied an important place in his reading—Dostoevsky above all, and also Chekhov. He disliked Tolstoy. It is always interesting to explore the dislikes of an artist—sometimes they define him more sharply than his predilections would:

> I keep reading *War and Peace*, and the further I go, the more I dislike it. Of course, Tolstoy's direct observation of life is prodigious. In contrast, whenever Dostoevsky reports a conversation, one always feels that no one, anywhere, ever spoke in such a manner—whereas with Tolstoy, one's reaction is always to say: How true! But Tolstoy's dialogue, however lifelike, is nearly always devoid of interest. It is full of absurd platitudes...For me, everything in Tolstoy is uncongenial, rightdown to the even light that bathes with the same indifference a Napoleonic battle and Natasha's needlework.

Writers are often tempted to be mean to each other: rivalries, backstabbing, jealousy are all too common among them. Gide's little circle, however, was remarkably free from these poisonous practices. In the end, Gide himself was able to extend this artistic generosity even to his intimate enemy. When Claudel's masterpiece

Le Soulier de satin was first put on stage, Gide—not without glee—pronounced it a disaster. But later on, the Tiny Lady recalled how he came to the dinner table with a copy of Claudel's play in his hand: 'God knows how much I normally dislike this sort of stuff, but I just opened the book at random and came upon this passage—it is truly, absolutely admirable!' For him, the Tiny Lady concluded, the literary excellence of a work always swept away all other considerations: 'How I love to see this aspect of his character; it reminds me of what Flaubert said: "Aesthetics is but a superior form of justice."'

All his life he regretted having once—briefly, but glaringly—failed to uphold this 'superior form of justice', when he overlooked Proust's manuscript of the first part of *A la recherche du temps perdu*. Although he personally took the blame for this error—and never forgave himself—it seems in fact that the decision not to accept Proust's masterpiece was taken by Jean Schlumberger (who remained largely unrepentant). Eventually Gide made up for his earlier blunder by writing (in 1921) a sensitive and generous essay on Proust. His private comments about Proust, as recorded over the years by the Tiny Lady, do nevertheless reflect curious contradictions—enthusiasm alternating with irritation.

He paid considerable attention to younger writers. For instance, he felt genuine affection for Malraux; he admired his ebullient intelligence and his passion for heroic activism, but rightly saw that he was not a good writer. From the start, he recognised the exceptional brilliance of Sartre, whom he befriended—though he was disappointed (with good reason) by Sartre's later novels. He extolled the merits of Simenon ('perhaps our greatest novelist') at a time when the literati still affected to despise this all-too-successful and prolific thriller writer. More importantly, he discovered the poet Henri Michaux; he sought out both men personally and extended his friendship to them. Today, with the benefit of hindsight, one may feel that he overestimated the achievement of Simenon (in whom he appreciated all the things that he himself most cruelly lacked: a creative imagination, a sense of reality, experience of life); and though he detected a deep originality in Michaux, he never really took the full measure of his genius. Nevertheless, in both cases he displayed qualities of perception and generosity that were truly admirable.

Gide believed that his great contemporaries Valéry (his old friend) and Claudel (his intimate enemy), and he himself would eventually be recognised by posterity as having been on the same side—not simply because they belonged to the same era but, more profoundly, because 'they had all shared the more or less secret influence of Mallarmé'. In fact, the literary affinities between the members of 'the team' are quite questionable, but what is certainly worth pondering is Gide's acknowledgement of Mallarmé's influence, which, in his own case at least, was deep and long-lasting. (Actually, instead of subtitling his biography of Gide *A Life in the Present*, Sheridan could have called it, more appropriately, *The Last Writer of the Nineteenth Century*.)

In Gide's case, the Mallarmean inheritance found its expression in the absolute primacy he gave to form and style over all other concerns. On this point, Gide's literary aesthetics never wavered: as early as 1910, in an essay on Baudelaire, he said, 'In art, where expression alone matters, ideas appear young for only a day... Today, if Baudelaire still lives on, it is thanks to his formal perfection. No artist ever relied upon anything else to achieve lasting fame.'

During his final illness, he hardly cared to communicate anymore; still, he persisted, even on his deathbed, in correcting syntactic and grammatical improprieties in what was being said to him. The Tiny Lady observed: 'He does not make allowance anymore for the slightest linguistic lapses, as if his entire capacity for attention was now exclusively focused on that single issue.'

Gide had invested all his resources in his style; he trusted that it alone would ensure his immortality. We are not yet in a position to assess whether this wager will ultimately pay off. Predictably enough, Claudel took a dim view of the matter: 'Gide deludes himself that he is simple, whereas he is merely flat; and he thinks he is classic, whereas he is bleak—as bleak as the moonlight over a beggars' jailhouse.'

Madeleine

Two different images of Gide's wife have emerged: recent accounts have portrayed her as a gloomy and narrow-minded bigot who was a hindrance to her husband's human development; but it is interesting to note that none of those who expressed this view ever had the chance to meet Madeleine Gide; whereas those who actually knew her—and especially Gide's closest friends—have provided very different testimony. Shortly after Gide's death, Schlumberger was moved to write an entire book (characteristically titled *Madeleine et André Gide*: the very sequence in which the two names are printed restores a hierarchy more in conformity with natural justice) to vindicate Madeleine's memory. And even the Tiny Lady (who would have had reasons to feel uneasy, if not hostile, towards her) was deeply impressed by her personality; three years before Madeleine's death, she noted: 'Even though she is self-effacing, she cannot remain inconspicuous; there is a superior quality of sensitivity that radiates from her entire person.' She never doubted Gide's sincerity when he claimed that Madeleine was the only person he had ever really loved, and she clearly analysed what her death meant for him—a disintegration of his own life: 'He has been hit in the most vulnerable part of his heart. The principal character in the play of his life is no more. He has lost his counterpart, the fixed measure with which he confronted his actions, his true tenderness, his great fidelity; in his inner dialogue, the other voice has fallen silent.' Her comments echoed Gide's confession: 'Since she is no more, I am merely pretending I am still alive, but I have lost interest in all things, myself included; I have no appetite, no taste, no curiosity, no desire; I am in a disenchanted world, and my only hope is to leave it soon.'

Madeleine's intelligence matched her sensitivity; she was deeply cultivated and had sound literary judgment— for instance, though she admired Gide's works, her admiration was never blind: whereas Gide greatly valued his own poetry, she told him with frank accuracy that it was embarrassingly mediocre. She wrote well: her letters and fragments of diaries (quoted at length by Schlumberger) are impressive, both for the natural elegance of their style and for the lucidity of her psychological perceptions.

Gide's personal predicament sprang from the radical separation of love and sensual desire: for him, these two emotions were mutually exclusive—he could not desire whom he loved, he could not love whom he desired. Madeleine must have confusedly sensed this from the beginning (after all, in his *Cahiers d'André Walter*, Gide had clearly confessed: 'I do not desire you. Your body embarrasses me, and carnal possession appalls me.') She originally rejected his offers of marriage, and yielded only at long last, under pressure from his unrelenting entreaties. She had suffered a psychological trauma in her childhood: she had witnessed the infidelity of her mother and, as a consequence, sex inspired in her instinctive fear and revulsion; thus, the perspective of pursuing with her cousin André that pure union of souls that had enchanted their adolescent years could appear genuinely attractive to her.

Gide, on his side, had started his conjugal life in a state of ignorance; later on, he brought to it his inexhaustible resources of self-deception: after twenty-five years of marriage, he earnestly expounded to Martin du Gard his theory that homosexuals made the best husbands:

> The love I have for my wife is like no other; and I believe that only a homosexual can give a creature that total love, divested of all physical desire, of all turmoil of the flesh: an integral love, in all its limitless purity. When I compared my marriage to the wretched, discordant marriages of those around me, I thought myself privileged: I thought I had built the very temple of love.

It was only after Madeleine's death that he eventually woke up—to some extent—to how grim her fate had been:

> I am now astonished at the aberration that led me to believe that the more ethereal my love, the more worthy it was of her; and in my naivete, I never asked whether she would be content with so disembodied a love. So, the fact that my carnal desires were directed towards other objects hardly concerned me. I even arrived at the comfortable conviction that things were better thus. Desires, I thought, were peculiar to men; I found it reassuring to believe that women—apart from 'loose women', of course—did not have similar desires... What I am afraid she could not understand was that it was precisely the spiritual power of my love that inhibited any carnal desire. For I was able, elsewhere, to prove that I was not incapable of making love to a woman, providing nothing intellectual or emotional came into it... It was only later that I began to realise how cruelly I must have hurt the woman for whom I was ready to give my life... In fact, I could only develop as an individual by hurting her.

When she embarked on marriage, Madeleine was innocent, but not blind. Her intuition made her rapidly aware of the peculiar nature of Gide's sexual compulsions. According to Gide himself, the revelation was made complete for her during their honeymoon in North Africa. In the midst of a railway journey, she witnessed his furtive and frantic attempts at caressing some half-naked young boys who were on the train, and that same night, she told him, not with reproach, but in sorrow and anxiety: 'You looked like a criminal, or a madman.'

A pattern of separate lives progressively developed between husband and wife. Their intimacy was maintained through the constant flow of loving letters which Gide kept writing to her while they were apart—which was most of the time. Gide pursued his life of freedom with his friends in Paris and abroad; Madeleine withdrew alone to Cuverville, their country estate in Normandy. Gide came for occasional visits; they would again share their old enjoyment of literature and, as in the past, they would spend their evenings reading aloud to each other their favourite authors. Madeleine's only request was that Gide, during the time he was in the country, should refrain from preying upon neighbouring children, so as to avoid any scandal ('Do it elsewhere if you must, but not in Cuverville. Here at least, spare me this shame.') Gide promised, but found this constraint unbearable; he often complained in his diary of the 'suffocating' atmosphere of Cuverville, and 'the bad sexual hygiene' from which he had to suffer there; he thought that this repression of his sensual impulses severely hindered the inspiration for his literary work. Often, he would furtively break the rules—or advance the date of his departure, and escape back to Paris.

It was then that the only tragedy that touched his entire life occurred. He fell in love with a sixteen-year-old adolescent, Marc Allégret. Marc's father was a Protestant pastor who, in his missionary zeal to evangelise French Africa, neglected to look after his own family—or rather, worse than neglecting it, whenever he was away and busily engaged in converting the heathen, the pious fool could think of nothing better than to entrust the care of his five sons to Gide, an old friend of the family, who diligently undertook to debauch as many of them as he could lay his hands on. (I am not competent to adjudicate on the vexed issue of priestly celibacy; I only feel that one major objection that can be made to married clergy is that it is too cruel and unfair to their children.)

With Marc Allégret, Gide experienced for the first time—at the age of forty-nine!—the ecstasy and the agony of being totally in love with another human being; he discovered passion, he discovered jealousy; desire merged with love—it had never happened to him before. And even, many years later, after the great fires of passion had burned themselves out, the relation with Allégret retained a sort of warm glow that was to last till Gide's death. Marc was not a homosexual—Gide actually seduced him with the promise to procure him his first mistress ('Uncle André' delivered the goods: he introduced Marc to the daughter of the Tiny Lady, Elisabeth); he turned into a very active womaniser and eventually made his career (financed at first by Gide himself) in filmmaking. His works turned out to be rather facile and shallow; but later on, he was followed on the same path by his younger brother, Yves Allégret, whose films have better stood the test of time.

In 1918, Gide decided—against Madeleine's most earnest entreaties—(she had guessed the entire situation, and her personal distress was compounded by her realisation that Gide was leading the adolescent astray, while betraying the naive trust of the father) to take Marc with him on a long visit to England. On his return, however, his life changed forever—though he did not realise it at first. It was only a little later, when one day he asked Madeleine to lend him the collection of his old letters, just to check some information, that she told him that these letters—his very best writing, their common treasure—existed no more: she had burned them all during his recent absence. Gide was so stunned by the news, he thought he would die. As he was to recall later: 'Those letters were the most precious achievement of my life, the best of me! Suddenly there was nothing! I had been stripped of everything! Ah, I can imagine what a father might feel on arriving home and being told by his wife: Our child is dead, I have killed him!' Madeleine said: 'If I were a Catholic, I'd enter a convent... I was suffering too much... I had to do something... I re-read all those letters beforehand. They were the most precious thing I had'. In the memoir he published after his wife's death, Gide returned to this episode:

> For a whole week, I wept; I wept from morning till evening... I wept without stopping, without trying to say anything to her other than my tears, and always waiting for a word, a gesture from her... But she continued to busy herself with petty household chores, as if nothing had

happened, passing to and fro, indifferent to my presence, as if she did not even notice that I was there. I hoped that the constancy of my pain would triumph over that apparent insensitivity, but no; and she no doubt hoped that my despair would bring me back to God, for she admitted no other outcome… And the more I cried, the more we became mutually estranged; I felt this bitterly; and soon it was no longer my lost letters that I was crying about, but about us, about her, about our love. I felt that I had lost her. Everything was crumbling within myself: past, present—our very future.

Madeleine knew of Gide's paedophilia; it scared her, it hurt her—but it had not affected her feelings for him: after all, an intelligent and virtuous woman may continue to love her husband, even after she discovers that he is an alcoholic, or a kleptomaniac, or a drug-addict. With his passion for Marc Allégret, however, Gide had betrayed her—he had killed their love.

Eventually, the couple's old way of life resumed its former course—at least in its outward appearances. Yet Madeleine renounced all her earlier enjoyment of culture and literature, devoting herself entirely to numbing household chores and to charitable work among the local poor. She came close to converting to Catholicism; but finally did not make the move, as she probaby feared that her husband might misinterpret this as an attempt to break further away from him.

The very heart of their union had died. Martin du Gard who was their guest for some days left this description:

> Their behaviour with one another is odd; it is a sort of caring politeness, a mixture of spontaneity and formality; an eager exchange of courtesies—there is tenderness in the way they look at each other and chat together, and at the same time, at the very bottom of it all, there is an impenetrable cold—something like the low temperatures of the deep; it is not the conjugal intimacy that is missing here, but even the simple sort of familiarity one would find between two friends, or even between two people travelling together. Their mutual love is obvious, but it is sublimated, devoid of communion. It is the love of two strangers who are never really sure they understand each other, nor really know each other, and who, deep in their

secret hearts, do not have the slightest communication.

A few weeks after Madeleine's death (in 1938), Gide visited Martin who wrote in his diary:

> [He told me that] this was the first real grief of his life. He spoke to me about her, at great length, of their past together, ancient and recent. It is with me, he said, that he feels the freest to confide, and I believe this to be true... But I was amazed to observe that his sorrow is not mixed with any sense of guilt. Not the slightest expression of remorse. In fact, he does not feel at fault at all, nor in the least responsible for her sacrificed existence. He merely thinks: I was like that; she was like that; and so, great suffering for both of us—it could not have been otherwise.

Proteus

In Homer's *Odyssey* (IV, 351), Proteus is a minor god who possesses vast knowledge and is able to adopt diverse forms in order to elude questions. The only way to force him to answer is to pin him down firmly until he resumes his original shape. Gide often referred to the figure of Proteus, not without a degree of self-identification; one characteristic example is found in his draft for a preface to his play *Saul*: 'Because of his multifaced inconsistency, Proteus is, among all the gods, the one who has least existence. Before he chooses, an individual is more rich; after he chooses, he is more strong.'

Reality

In a long passage of his *Journal*, Gide made an intriguing observation: 'What is lacking in me, I think, is a certain sense of reality.' And he gave various illustrations of this—for instance, the difficulty he had in recognising people: 'It is not that I lack attention or interest... but even though I am extremely sensitive to the outside world, I can never fully believe in its reality... The real world always remains somewhat fantastic for me... I have no feeling of its reality.'

The material circumstances of his life certainly contributed to his abiding sense of unreality. In 1935, under the influence of his short-lived and sentimental conversion to Marxism, he had a sudden illumination and realised for the first time—at the age of sixty-seven—that he never knew what it meant to have to work for a living. He noted in his *Journal*: 'I experience today—earnestly, acutely—this inferiority: I have never had to earn my own bread.' But this belated discovery does not seem to have occupied his mind for very long: he made no further mention of it.

His attitude towards money could provide another example of his uncertain perception of the practical world: his stinginess was notorious—there are countless anecdotes that document his odd obsession with frugality—but there is equally abundant evidence of his extravagant generosity. In the end, was he profligate or miserly? The mass of contradictory information on this subject suggests one conclusion: he simply had no concept of money—for him, money had no reality.

It is not rare for creative artists to have only a limited grasp of the trivialities of practical life; often, this very infirmity is the price they pay in order to concentrate on their art. Yet such a disposition is hardly conducive to shrewd political judgment, and scarcely qualifies aloof poets or inspired writers to pronounce with authority on all the important issues of the day.

Gide allowed himself, with reckless naivete, to be abominably deceived and manipulated by the criminal impostors of politics. I have already mentioned his inept and notorious flirtation with Stalinism during the 1930s; at least he was eventually able to redeem his foolishness with a courageous gesture: the publication of his *Return from the USSR*. His other great political test took place at the time of the Nazi invasion of France. This time—luckily for him—the vigilant concern of his close friends ensured that his performance remained strictly private, but from their personal records it is evident that his dismal vacillations gave them ample cause to worry.

After the meeting between Pétain and Hitler that paved the way for French collaboration with the Nazis, the Tiny Lady was flabbergasted by Gide's attitude: 'It is strange that, on this issue, his reactions remain weak and uncertain. He instinctively inclines towards this sort of view: "Anyway, since we have lost, why resist?"'

In November 1940, Gide told her that he had 'read with tremendous interest a page by Renan: "World government, should it ever take place, would probably best suit the German spirit"— and he went on: 'Naturally I wholeheartedly wish for a British victory—I cannot do otherwise—and yet, at times, I cannot help thinking that this may not be the best way out of the predicament which the world is now facing. Who knows? We are perhaps not being fair to Hitler when we refuse to believe that his ultimate dream could be world harmony.'

In 1941, the indecisiveness, the volatility and confusion of his political opinions caused Martin du Gard increasing concern: 'Our old friend is less and less capable of steering his own boat. I have the feeling that he has lost his compass and allows the stronger winds to determine his course. There is some amount of senile childishness in his attitude.'

In the end, his salvation came by pure accident: in 1942, he went to North Africa on a visit, but because of military developments, remained stranded on the other side of the Mediterranean for the remainder of the war—safely out of political trouble. He made only one feeble attempt at commenting on current affairs, in an article published after the liberation of Paris; it did not have any impact, but Schlumberger read it with consternation: 'It is full of worn-out clichés and reflects the naivete of a man completely out of touch with the current of ideas. He even has one lamentable phrase about "mighty and glorious Russia", as if he were doing his best to forget his *Return from the USSR*.'

In 1950, 'the senile childishness' that Martin du Gard had already detected ten years earlier grew to disturbing proportions; one day, for instance, he agreed on the telephone to sign a manifesto—without knowing what the issue was (it was about the admission of communist China into the UN). He cried out to his friends: 'I understand absolutely nothing, I have no idea what the question was!' The Tiny Lady concluded with despair: 'This small anecdote is typical of his behaviour: ever more vague, inexcusable, changing, illogical; he was already like that about the small things of life; what would you expect him to do now faced with the fate of Europe!'

His friends loved him dearly; nevertheless, when he finally died, they breathed a sigh of relief: 'He was less and less able to control his own actions; we were living in constant fear of what the next day would bring. His model death (scrupulously prepared for, but helped by a set of favourable circumstances) provided a majestic cover-up for everything. It came not a minute too soon!'

Sexuality

Gide repeatedly confessed his puzzlement: 'I shall die without having understood anything—or so little—of the physiology of my own body.' Or again: 'I grow old without any hope of ever knowing my own body.' One day, he explained to Martin du Gard with detached objectivity the physiological details of his sexuality. In his own opinion, his condition was abnormal: 'a physiological paradox... a pathological case.'

Yet, on another occasion, he also confided to Martin du Gard his indignation and sorrow at often being accused of corrupting the young: 'How unfair! How could it be perverse to initiate young people into sensual pleasure?' And he explained at great length that his role was always, first and foremost, that of a patient educator: 'Nothing, during the troubled years of adolescence, can replace the beneficial influence of a liaison—sensual, intellectual and moral—with an older guide, worthy of trust and love.' This is the theme he had developed in *Corydon*, but it had limited relevance to his own practices, for, in fact, what he called his 'adventures' usually took place with children, street kids, bellboys, little Arab beggars and diverse defenceless destitutes, furtively and sordidly, in conditions that certainly left neither time nor space for any form of enlightened communication.

The Tiny Lady observed:

> One could not emphasise enough how odd his temperament is. His sensuality is so deep, so demanding, so tyrannical, ruling an entire part of his life—and yet it reaches its fulfilment so easily, so lightly, so quickly... It is bizarre to the point of defying belief. Seeing how devious he can be in order to attain the object of his desire, people naturally misjudge him, and they assume that he must be depraved to the same extent. On the other hand, one can easily imagine what sort of fallacious pretexts he has to invent in order to justify his insinuating and hypocritical manoeuvres, when one considers how incredibly harmless are the actual activities in which they eventuate. It seems to me that these peculiar sexual inclinations are an important key for understanding Gide.

Eventually, the way in which he became a slave to his mania distressed even the friends who had originally shared his inclinations. Schlumberger concluded: 'During his life, Gide's concern was to win respect for homosexuals; yet, because of his particular obsessions, in the end he succeeded only in bringing discredit to their cause.'

Still, any person who happens to believe in the Christian faith that was originally Gide's would be unqualified to censure his infirmities; for the fact is that we all belong to a fallen species; to whatever degree, innocence escapes us; one way or the other, we are all cripples. In Gide's case, the contrast—so extreme and tragic—between, on the one hand, the splendour of his intelligence and culture, the nobility of a mind open to all humanistic endeavours, and on the other the grotesque and gruesome tyranny of his obsessions, is heart-breaking and should inspire compassion.

Yet, how is compassion to be proffered when its very need is being strenuously denied? For, after all, the real problem did not lie in Gide's sexuality, but in his tortuous relation to truth.

Truth

Alan Sheridan observes that 'the heritage of Gide's Protestantism was that he hated lies… His cult of sincerity was untypically French, undoubtedly inherited from his Huguenot forebears'.

Gide had loved truth from his early youth. He eventually abandoned the faith of his childhood (a forsaking that was not achieved without painful and dramatic reversals), but he retained until death a passionate need for self-justification.

'Lying' haunted his imagination as a worthy subject for tragedy. He explained to Schlumberger: 'Believe me, nothing can be as dramatic as the destruction of a mind through lying—whether it is self-deception or hypocrisy… If I were still in the habit of praying, I would pray without ceasing: My God, preserve me from lying!' Some of the characters in his fiction were odious to him, but he knew them from inside, and he painted them with such understanding that—to his dismay—many critics interpreted them as projections of himself. Thus Gide said of Edouard, a character in *Les Faux-monnayeurs* often seen as a mouthpiece for the author: 'He is the archetype of the impotent, both as a writer and as a lover… He constantly lies to himself in his *Journal*, like the pastor in *La Symphonie Pastorale*. It is the same problem… What fascinates me more than anything else is this self-deception.'

Once, his friend the philosopher Bernard Groethuysen was talking to him about the psychology of 'the ambiguous person' (*l'être louche*), which he defined as 'a man who never succeeds in transforming lies into his own truth, and who constantly shifts his position'. Gide replied: 'It would be fun to create such a character, but if I were to write it, people would once again say that I was painting my own portrait.'

On the basis of his own observation, Herbart came to this conclusion: 'For Gide, lies are as attractive as the truth.' With more subtlety, the Tiny Lady pinpointed the invisible confusion that enabled Gide to reconcile the two at the end of his life: 'His commitment to sincerity is stronger than ever, but sincerity does not necessarily coincide with truth.'

The queasiness (so hard to describe, yet so intensely felt) which readers as different as Flannery O'Connor and Julien Green experienced when confronted with Gide (in neither case, was it a question of being shocked by his sexual proclivities: Green himself was homosexual, and O'Connor was shockproof) is obviously related to a deeper issue. St Augustine—probably the first modern psychologist—identified it 1,600 years ago: 'People have such a love for truth that when they happen to love something else, they want it to be the truth; and because they do not wish to be proven wrong, they refuse to be shown their mistake. And so, they end up hating the truth for the sake of the object which they came to love instead of the truth.'

Notes on Contributors

John Birmingham's *Leviathan: The Unauthorised Biography of Sydney* has recently come out in paperback.

Geoffrey Blainey is the author of many works of history including *The Tyranny of Distance* and *The Triumph of the Nomads*. His *A Short History of the World* has just been published by Viking.

Edmund Campion's books include *Rockchoppers*. He is a priest, journalist and historian.

John Carroll is the reader in sociology at La Trobe University. His most recent book is *Ego and Soul*.

John Clarke is one of Australia's best known comedians and comic writers. Two series of 'The Games' were shown on ABC television.

Inga Clendinnen's *Tiger's Eye* was published earlier this year. She gave the 1999 Boyer Lectures.

Peter Conrad is a fellow of All Souls, Oxford. He is the author of *The Everyman History of English Literature* and *Modern Times, Modern Places*, a study of twentieth-century culture.

Sophie Cunningham is a publisher at Allen & Unwin.

Robyn Davidson's books include *Tracks* and *Desert Places*.

Stephen Downes is a food critic.

Notes on Contributors

Cameron Forbes is the Washington correspondent of the *Australian*.

Catherine Ford's novel *NYC* was published this year.

Raimond Gaita's books include *Romulus, My Father* and *Towards a Common Humanity*.

Helen Garner's books include *Monkey Grip* and *The First Stone*.

Richard Hall is writing a biography of Gough Whitlam.

Kevin Hart's most recent collection of poetry, *Wicked Heat* is published by Paperbark. He is professor of English and Comparative Literature at Monash University.

Gideon Haigh's *One of a Kind* is published by Text.

Ihab Hassan books include *Radical Innocence: Studies in the Contemporary American Novel, The Postmodern Turn: Essays in Postmodern Theory and Culture* and *Between the Eagle and the Sun: Traces of Japan*.

Jack Hibberd's plays include *A Stretch of the Imagination* and *Dimboola*.

Juliette Hughes is the television critic for *Eureka Street* as well as a singer and a teacher of music.

Linda Jaivin's books include *Eat Me, Rock and Roll Babies From Outer Space* and *Confessions of an S & M Virgin*.

Clive James's books include *Unreliable Memoirs, The Crystal Bucket* and *Brilliant Creatures*.

Margo Kingston is the chief of staff of the *Sydney Morning Herald*'s Canberra bureau and the author of *Off the Rails: the Pauline Hanson Trip*.

Notes on Contributors

Hilary McPhee was one of the founding partners of McPhee Gribble. She subsequently published for Penguin and for Pan Macmillan and was executive chair of the Australia Council. Pan Macmillan will be publishing her book of memoirs next year from which the excerpts that appear in this book are taken.

Kim Mahood's *Craft for a Dry Lake* won the *Age* prize for non-fiction.

David Malouf is the author of *Johnno*, *An Imaginary Life* and *Conversations at Curlow Creek*. His book of short stories, *Dream Stuff*, was published by Chatto and Windus earlier this year.

Robert Manne's political journalism is collected in *The Way We Live Now*.

Adrian Martin writes about film for the *Age*. He has written a study of Sergio Leone's *Once Upon a Time in America*.

Drusilla Modjeska is the author of *Poppy*, *Secrets* and *Stravinsky's Lunch*.

Ruth Park's books include *The Harp in the South* and *Poor Man's Orange*. She is the creator of the *Muddle-Headed Wombat* and her autobiography *Fishing in the Styx* appeared in 1993.

Peter Porter's *Collected Poems* is published by Oxford University Press.

Andrew Riemer taught English for many years at Sydney University. His most recent book is *Sandstone Gothic*.

Guy Rundle is the editor of *Arena* magazine. He has written comedy scripts for Max Gillies, 'Full Frontal' and 'Back Berner'.

Peter Ryan is a former head of Melbourne University Press. His account of his wartime experiences *Fear Drive My Feet* is a classic.

Notes on Contributors

Pierre Ryckmans publishes internationally under the name Simon Leys. He has translated the Analects of Confucius and is the author of *The Death of Napoleon*.

Nicholas Shakespeare is a novelist and the biographer of Bruce Chatwin.

Paul Sheehan is a journalist at the *Sydney Morning Herald* and the author of *Among the Barbarians*.

Craig Sherborne writes for the *Herald Sun*.

Hugh Stretton's books include *Ideas for Australian Cities* and *Morals, Markets and Public Policy*. His *Economics: A New Introduction* was published in 1999.

Christina Thompson is the co-ordinating editor of the *Harvard Review* and a former editor of *Meanjin*.

Jack Waterford is the editor of the *Canberra Times*.

Don Watson is currently writing a book about Paul Keating.

Fay Zwicky's books include *Kaddish and Other Poems* and *Poems 1970-1993*. Her essays are collected in *The Lyre in the Pawnshop*.

Notes on Contributors

The essays by Robyn Davidson, Geoffrey Blainey, Hugh Stretton, John Birmingham, Paul Sheehan, Fay Zwicky, Andrew Riemer, Kim Mahood and Stephen Downes appear for the first time in this anthology.

David Malouf's 'The People's Judgment' appeared in the *Australian*, 1 January 2000.

Peter Ryan's 'The Twitterers' Defeat' was published in *Quadrant*, December 1999.

The pieces comprising Clive James's 'Party Town' were commissioned by the *Independent* and appeared in the *Sunday Age*, 24 October and the *Age* 5 October, 2000.

Don Watson's 'Garibaldi in an Armani Suit' was published as a pamphlet by the History Council of New South Wales.

Margo Kingston's 'Hansonism Then and Now' is adapted from a speech given to the Sydney Institute in October 1999.

Gideon Haigh's 'The Last Barbarian' appeared in the *Eye* 4-17 November 1999.

The components of Jack Waterford's 'Capital Letters' appeared in *Eureka Street* in July, August, September and October 2000.

Cameron Forbes's profiles appeared in the Focus section of the *Australian* on 5 and 12 August 2000.

John Clarke's 'Apology' was broadcast on 'The Games', ABC Television, 3 July 2000.

Raimond Gaita's 'Who Speaks, About What, To Whom, On Whose Behalf, With What Right?' was published in *Australian Book Review*, October 2000.

Robert Manne's 'What Justice O'Loughlin Could Not See' appeared in the *Age*, 2 September 2000.

Notes on Contributors

An earlier version of Guy Rundle's 'A Town Called Hackney Nation' appeared in *Arena* magazine April-May 2000.

Christina Thompson's 'Turton's Land Deeds' was published in *Meanjin* 3, 2000.

The pieces comprising Helen Garner's contribution were published in the *Age* on 12 and 26 July; 9 and 16 August; 20 September; and in *Women's Weekly*, November 2000.

Edmund Campion's 'At the University of Sydney' appeared in *Eureka Street*, November 2000.

Peter Porter's 'John Forbes in Europe' is to appear in a festschrift about John Forbes to be edited by Ken Bolton and published by Wakefield Press.

A version of Richard Hall's 'Reading Sydney: Three Ages, Three Winds' constituted the introduction of *Sydney: An Oxford Anthology* which he edited for Oxford University Press. It is reproduced by permission of the publisher.

Sophie Cunningham's 'Buddhist Bootcamp' appeared in the *Age*, 8 April 2000.

Drusilla Modjeska's 'Dots on the Landscape' was published in the *Australian Review of Books* in March 2000.

Hilary McPhee's 'First Words' is made up of extracts from a work in progress, *Other People's Words* to be published by Pan Macmillan in April 2001.

Craig Sherborne's 'No Ordinary Neighbourhood' appeared in the *Sunday Herald-Sun* in October 2000.

A version of Catherine Ford's 'Surgery' appeared in the *Age*.

A shorter version of John Carroll's 'Let's Reclaim the Game' was published in the *Age*, 1 May 2000.

Notes on Contributors

Jack Hibberd's 'The Kingdom of the Imagination' appeared in the *Australian Review of Books* in December 1999.

Nicholas Shakespeare's 'Reflective Anglers' was published in the *Australian Review of Books* in October 2000.

Inga Clendinnen's 'Penelope Fitzgerald 1916–2000' appeared in the *Australian Review of Books* in September 2000.

The items comprising Ruth Park's 'VP Day' appeared in the *Bulletin*, 21 December 1999–4 January 2000 and *Australian Book Review* in May 2000. They are republished here courtesy of the copyright owner Kemdale Pty Ltd c/- Curtis Brown, (Aust) Pty Ltd, Sydney.

Ihab Hassan's 'How Australian is it?' was published in *Australian Book Review* in September 2000.

Peter Conrad's 'Sydney, Not the Bush' appeared in the ASAL publication edited by Fran de Groen and Ken Stewart, *Australian Writing and the City*.

Juliette Hughes's 'The Uses of Enchantment' was published in *Eureka Street* in September 2000.

Adrian Martin's 'The Offended Critic' appeared in *Australian Quarterly*, Vol.72/No. 2, 2000.

The pieces comprising Kevin Hart's 'Bitter Light' appeared in the *Australian Review of Books* in June and August 2000.

A somewhat shorter and differently edited version of Pierre Ryckmans's 'A Portrait of Proteus' appeared in the *Australian Review of Books* in May and June 2000.

This is the latest in literary critic Peter Craven's bestselling series of annual essay collections which bring together the best non-fiction writing to have appeared in Australia in the last twelve months. The essays range from Helen Garner on Alzheimer's to Clive James on the Olympic ceremonies, from Hugh Stretton on how Paul Keating has diminished our political and economic policies to Nicholas Shakespeare on Robert Hughes and fishing, and John Birmingham on S11. Some of these essays are literary and some of them are stories about politics and the media, but they all crackle with the energy of the best Australian writing. This is a book for everyone who's alive to the best that's thought and said in our society, a book that will make you remember the year that has just been and make you grateful for its reflection in the writer's eye.

Robyn Davidson *A Mother Remembered* • David Malouf *Millennial Meditation* • Peter Ryan *Down with the Republic* • Clive James *Olympic Openings and Closings* • Geoffrey Blainey *Globalisation* • Hugh Stretton *Keating's Tragic Legacy* • Don Watson *Keating and History* • Margo Kingston *Pauline Hanson and the Media* • John Birmingham *The S11 Coverage* • Paul Sheehan *The Death of Political Parties* • Gideon Haigh *Paul Sheehan* • Jack Waterford *Letters from Canberra* • Cameron Forbes *Gore and Bush* • John Clarke *John Howard Apologises* • Raimond Gaita *Who Speaks for the Blacks?* • Robert Manne *The Stolen Generation Case* • Guy Rundle *Hackney* • Edmund Campion *University Catholics* • Christina Thompson *A Lament for the Maoris* • Helen Garner *Mother's Alzheimer's* • Fay Zwicky *Looking for the Light* • Richard Hall *Sydney Voices* • Peter Porter *John Forbes* • Andrew Riemer *Klemperer and Memory* • Hilary McPhee *Travelling with Books* • Kim Mahood *A Dancer's Predicament* • Sophie Cunningham *Buddhist Bootcamp* • Drusilla Modjeska *Eucalypts and Art Shows* • Craig Sherborne *Child Murder in Wagga* • Catherine Ford *Surgeons and Children* • Linda Jaivin *Fengshui* • John Carroll *Docklands Perfidy* • Jack Hibberd *Theatre Be Damned* • Stephen Downes *Food, Glorious Food* • Nicholas Shakespeare *Robert Hughes and Fishing* • Inga Clendinnen *Penelope Fitzgerald* • Ruth Park *VP Day* • Ihab Hassan *Australian Literature* • Peter Conrad *The City versus the Bush* • Juliette Hughes *Harry Potter* • Adrian Martin *Paul Verhoeven* • Kevin Hart *French Fascists* • Pierre Ryckmans *A Glossary for André Gide*

ISBN 1-86395-250-0

9 781863 952507